BIOGRAPHICAL DICTIONARY OF LITERARY INFLUENCES

The Nineteenth Century, 1800–1914

JOHN POWELL, Editor

Derek W. Blakeley, Associate Editor
Tessa Powell, Editorial Assistant

James S. Olson, Advisory Editor

GREENWOOD PRESS
Westport, Connecticut • London

Library of Congress Cataloging-in-Publication Data

Biographical dictionary of literary influences : the nineteenth century, 1800–1914 / John
Powell, editor ; Derek W. Blakeley, associate editor ; Tessa Powell, editorial assistant.
    p. cm.
    Includes bibliographical references and index.
    ISBN 0–313–30422–X (alk. paper)
    1. Celebrities—Books and reading—Europe—History—19th century. 2.
Celebrities—Books and reading—Europe—History—20th century. 3. Celebrities—Books
and reading—America—History—19th century. 4. Celebrities—Books and
reading—America—History—20th century. 5. Civilization, Modern—19th century. 6.
Civilization, Modern—20th century. 7. Intellectuals—Books and
reading—Europe—History—19th century. 8. Intellectuals—Books and
reading—Europe—History—20th century. 9. Intellectuals—Books and
reading—America—History—19th century. 10. Intellectuals—Books and
reading—America—History—20th century. I. Powell, John, 1954– II. Blakeley, Derek W.
III. Powell, Tessa.
    Z1039.C45B56 2001
    028'.9'09034—dc21   99–462057

British Library Cataloguing in Publication Data is available.

Library of Congress Catalog Card Number: 99–462057
ISBN: 0–313–30422–X

First published in 2001

Greenwood Press, 88 Post Road West, Westport, CT 06881
An imprint of Greenwood Publishing Group, Inc.
www.greenwood.com

Printed in the United States of America

The paper used in this book complies with the
Permanent Paper Standard issued by the National
Information Standards Organization (Z39.48–1984).

10 9 8 7 6 5 4 3 2 1

Copyright Acknowledgment

Every reasonable effort has been made to trace the owners of copyright materials in this book, but
in some instances this has proven impossible. The author and publisher will be glad to receive
information leading to more complete acknowledgments in subsequent printings of the book and in
the meantime extend their apologies for any omissions.

For John and Hilda, who saw the world and made a mark

CONTENTS

PREFACE

During the past two decades there has been growing interest in the process of cultural development and, more specifically, in the role of reading as a part of that process. Unlike earlier and largely unsuccessful attempts to systematically define a sociology of knowledge, recent efforts have been episodic, diverse, and idiosyncratic, and thus have followed the humanistic vision of a unique mental development in each person. In keeping with Edmund Burke's dictum, recent writers implicitly have accepted that "circumstance gives to every situation its distinctive characteristic." However true this may be, the evidence suggests that some ideas in print have had more influence, and influence of a different kind, than others. It is also true that identifying certain patterns about the relationship between reading, achievement, and culture will enlarge our understanding regarding the pivotal role of reading in the creation of the social, economic, and political institutions that continue to characterize the Western worldview.

It is our purpose in this work to bring together for the first time research devoted specifically to the reading habits of individual men and women who shaped Western culture in the nineteenth century. The 271 subjects of these inquiries provide a limited sample but one substantial enough to suggest broad, cross-cultural habits and effects that will help us better understand the relationship between reading and culture.

In some cases, contributors have principally gathered materials already published in biographies, memoirs, or monographs. In other cases, scholars have undertaken for the first time significant research about the relationship between cultural development and the achievement of a single individual. From an examination of the combined results, I have made a few observations in the Introduction about why we read, and what that reading eventually means to our culture.

DESIGN

We have asked contributors to conduct their research with two goals in mind: first, to provide a concise summary of literary influences; and second, to provide clear direction for further research. Each entry includes three components:

1. *An introductory section provides basic biographical data*, including educational information and a concise assessment of the contribution of the subject to the development of Western culture.

2. *The body of each article is devoted to an assessment of specific literary works and authors known to have influenced the subject.* The emphasis is factual and specific, though a succinct analysis may be included if the research warrants.

3. *Following the body of each entry, a bibliography includes principal archival collections, standard biographical resources, and published materials relating specifically to the subject's reading.* This section is necessarily uneven from entry to entry, as some figures left excellent sources for reconstructing their reading past, others almost none, and most a modest collection of odd resources that require careful piecing.

The *Biographical Dictionary of Literary Influences: The Nineteenth Century, 1800–1914*, then, is principally a factual rather than interpretive work of reference. Its purpose is not to suggest that successful men and women have only influenced their cultures through the printed exchange of ideas. Indeed, many of the subjects of this study are musicians, painters, educators, politicians, and explorers, many of whom wrote little or nothing; but all were significantly influenced by what they read and, in turn, shaped Western culture in dramatic ways. Nor do we imagine that influence can be measured only in easily demonstrable ways. Each subject in this study owes something to his or her biological heritage, to social conditioning, and to a general cultural environment filled with indistinct traces of a thousand ideas both ancient and modern. It is nevertheless important that we understand as clearly as we can the impact of ideas transmitted in print. By the nineteenth century, the printed word clearly had become the principal means of teaching and learning in the West, even in those areas of cultural expression not primarily conveyed in words.

Biographical Dictionary of Literary Influences is a study in one aspect of the subtle anarchy of intellectual development. It was designed with the assumption that ideas—written and otherwise—are important to culture, but without a preconceived thesis regarding the ultimate role of literature. It is meant to be a practical tool for scholars interested in tracing the actual reading experience of important Western cultural figures. The articles have yielded a number of preliminary implications that will be discussed in the Introduction, but definition of the broader relationship between reading and culture is largely left to the reader.

PRINCIPLES OF SELECTION

We began by identifying the people most responsible for the general cultural development of Europe, Britain and the British empire, and the Americas between 1800 and 1914. To be included, a figure

1. must have influenced Western culture in an important way during this time period;
2. must have exerted some influence beyond the local or regional borders of his or her home region; and
3. must have defined his or her career by substantial achievement during the period.

Choosing the top tier of entries was easy, as no one seriously questions the importance of Darwin, Dickens, or Dostoevsky, or of Goethe, Marx, or Ibsen. Beyond the 50 or so giants, however, there is considerable room for debate as to the actual impact of a figure's work. With this in mind, there has been a conscious attempt to consider the claims of women generally (Elizabeth Fry, Margaret Fuller) and cultural figures from regions marginalized in the nineteenth century (Sienkiewicz, Shevchenko, Sigurdsson).

The list of subjects admittedly is selective. Surveying the 271 entries in the *Biographical Dictionary of Literary Influences*, readers undoubtedly will be chagrined to find that some personal inspiration is not there. Some will argue, for instance, that it is madness to omit Friedrich von Schiller or Charles Baudelaire while including Samuel Smiles and John Greenleaf Whittier. I will not disagree; I will even commiserate and will wish with my critics that there had been room for more entries. In the end, there had to be some sort of balance struck between high and popular culture, between men and women of action and those of contemplation. This is my selection, but I will happily support any movement for supplemental publications.

Adding to the difficulty of selection, the nature of the project inherently suggests its own inadequacy, for it seeks to identify literary influences that were important but that often have not been acknowledged. Edward Bellamy, for instance, failed to earn an alphabetized entry, but the research suggests that he may have been more influential than most people imagine. While the number of entries clearly could be expanded, this sample should be large enough to enable scholars to draw some conclusions and wide enough to cover the acknowledged giants of cultural development who were reading and acting principally between 1800 and 1914.

The number of entries was, for the most part, simply the function of an editorial word limit. There were other considerations, however, that guided selection, the most important being the relationship between reading and certain forms of cultural achievement. Literary and political figures are extensively represented, for instance, because in the nineteenth century they dealt explicitly in the written word, leaving written records that enable scholars to trace and evaluate the course of their development. The relationship between literary influences and some other areas of achievement is more problematic. Many scholars when approached about this project were reluctant to link literature and their nonliterary specialties, however tentatively. As a result, musicians, visual artists, inventors, and businessmen, all of whom influenced culture in dramatic ways, are underrepresented.

Given the space limitations, these omissions were a blessing in disguise. There are enough entries drawn from essentially nonliterary categories, however, to suggest both the relevance of literary influences and the need for further research in any kind of comprehensive treatment of the subject. The French impressionist Claude Monet, for instance, clearly adopted in his painting a written "retinal physiology" drawn from Hippolyte Taine's *De L'Intelligence* (1870). American popular musician Stephen Foster frequently set newspaper poetry to music. The French sculptor Rodin conceived of an intimate relationship between his own cultural achievement and literature. "Dante," he said, "was a literary sculptor" who "spoke in gestures as well as in words."

NATURE OF THE ENTRIES

Readers will immediately notice the considerable variety of content in the various entries. This was dictated by many factors, including the availability of records and the contributors' ability to consult the records that were available. In some cases, there are virtually no records that speak directly to reading (Jenny Lind), whereas in others there is so much information that nothing short of a lifetime of specialized research would likely yield satisfactory results (William Gladstone, Lord Acton). For some figures, significant research on literary influences has already been done (Disraeli, Thoreau, Pater, Melville), whereas for most the subject has been treated in passing, if at all. A number of contributors were already involved in research projects emphasizing literary influences and thus had located relatively obscure materials relating to the subject. In other cases, contributors had specialized knowledge of some aspect of his or her subject's life but necessarily relied on previously published material regarding literary influences.

As a result of these variations, the balance between narrative text and bibliography varies considerably. In every case, however, it has been our goal to include enough information on each figure so that the reader may (1) identify key literary influences, (2) assess the possible impact of such reading, and (3) continue research in the most significant published and archival resources. In each case we have encouraged contributors to identify educational and other early literary influences, the most important specific printed works read, and the key archival and secondary materials relating to literary influences. What the entries sometimes lack in detail (and often this is unavoidable), we hope will be made up for in suggestive context and practical bibliographical guidance toward further research. When an entry alludes to an individual who has his or her own entry, a cross-reference is indicated by **boldface** type.

ACKNOWLEDGMENTS

Success in a project of this scope requires many skills and much expertise. I am grateful to Derek Blakeley for special assistance as subeditor for Britain and Ireland, as well as for technical help in compiling the volume. Eric v. d. Luft was invaluable as subeditor for Germany and for philosophical topics generally. The final compilation, completed under some duress, would have seemed a hopeless task were it not for the skill and good humor of Tessa Powell. Cynthia Harris of Greenwood Press had no small part in making this a pleasurable project. Finally, my best thanks to all contributors, without whose expert knowledge this work would have been impossible, and to the managers of Internet sites such as Victoria List and H-Net, who helped us assemble a team of 135 scholars from 16 countries.

INTRODUCTION

The exact value of reading has been variously estimated across the past five millennia. When writing was a new kind of magic, and reading an arcane spiritual gift, every reading man knew the power of the written word. Today, having achieved high rates of literacy throughout most of the Western world, we are inclined to imagine that reading is not such a difficult practice after all and that if anyone can do it, it must be a common virtue. Following the lead of administrators and technicians, most college instructors are scrambling to replace the old gifts of clear exposition and competent reading with some form of technological learning that invariably steals from the potential power of a student's mastery of the written word.

Technology itself is a neutral factor, with much potential for good. New forms of technology made this study necessary, for without the development of the printing press and easy means of distribution, the nineteenth century would not have witnessed the explosion of books, pamphlets, newspapers, and journals that made the power of ideas such as liberty, nationalism, democracy, beauty, and individualism so prevalent among the figures in this study. Yet because of our familiarity with the written word at the end of the twentieth century, we frequently forget the magnitude of its power in the nineteenth. We often nod in the direction of literary influences, but in reality, we imagine that they are only props to the great natural abilities and experiential factors of a person's life.

It is a central and general purpose of this study to suggest the distinctive role of reading in shaping culture, in an age when the freshness and power of the written word were for the first time brought to the general populations of the West. Many of the observations about reading in the nineteenth century hold true as we enter the twenty-first century, but I would encourage readers to reconstruct a world without satellites and computers, without motion pictures and documentaries, without telephones and electricity, without public libraries or public education. For all the similarities in our worlds, these differences should be borne in mind as we consider the particular role of literary influences in shaping culture.

This work assumes that ideas, especially in their printed forms, have consequences. Difficulty in isolating printed influences, or in assessing their strength relative to other factors, should not keep us from recognizing that the influence is real. In one of a hundred cases that could be cited, we find that Percy Bysshe Shelley's "passion for reforming the world" led him to write with the intent to influence—and influence he did. His principal reviewers in the Tory *Quarterly Review* and Whig *Edinburgh Review* became, according to Kim Wheatley, "paranoid readers; for them there is no moment when there is not something crucial at stake."[1]

The *Biographical Dictionary of Literary Influences* does not propose definitive conclusions regarding the nature, relation, and variety of factors that influence people's activities. The entries contained herein do, however, suggest a number of observations regarding literary influences on cultural development in the nineteenth century, and it is hoped that these will stimulate further research along more specific lines.

1. *There was a canon of essential literary works accepted by Western societies and by most of those who influenced Western culture.* At the head of this canon were the Bible and the works of Shakespeare. This speaks both to the power of the works themselves and to their accessibility. Both had been translated into virtually every Western language and were therefore available to almost anyone who could read. In addition to use for quotation, illustration, and adornment of every sort, however, Shakespeare and the Bible often were used to define cultural figures—sometimes unconsciously—and the size and shape of the "stage" on which they were acting. Thus Matthew Arnold was to George Meredith a "dandy Isaiah," and Macaulay to Arnold the "great apostle of the Philistines."

The Victorian age was defined in substantial measure by the dismantling of institutional Christian orthodoxy, but the Bible itself remained an impressive force even among many who rejected its old uses. Few readers will be surprised to learn that Robert La Follette, progressive politician from the rural, religious heartland of the United States, was a committed reader of the Bible. Not many would have guessed that Georges Sorel, the revolutionary French syndicalist, was a great admirer of the New Testament. And if the ranging influence of so divisive a cultural catechism as the Bible is true, how much easier must it have been for readers to accept, or simply absorb, Shakespeare's gospel assertion that "all the world's a stage" and then to populate it with characters from his playbook. Had the great bard not been so pervasive, George Bernard Shaw would not have wasted his time in despising him.

After the Bible and Shakespeare, Greek and Roman classics were considered most essential to the development of a proper understanding of the world. Homer, Aristotle, Plato, Thucydides, Aeschylus, Julius Caesar, Virgil, Tacitus, and a variety of other Greek and Roman authors were taught in schools and universities and often were found in libraries of the well educated. Ideally, one was expected to read them in the original, but there were numerous translations, and classical characters and motifs were widely spread throughout popular culture. As is true with all literature, these ancient works were capable of multiple interpretations. But in an age of growing liberalism and democracy, and one increasingly characterized by an aggressive imperialism and ethnocentrism, the classic works of Greek and Roman thought were particularly well suited to the European worldview. This view was typically stated by Anglo-Irish scholar J. P. Mahaffy in 1874:

Every thinking man who becomes acquainted with the masterpieces of Greek writing, must see plainly that they stand to us in a far closer relation than the other remains of antiquity. . . . They are the writings of men of like culture with ourselves, who argue with the same logic, who reflect with kindred feelings. They have worked out social and moral problems like ourselves, they have expressed them in such language as we should desire to use. In a word, they are thoroughly modern, more modern than the epochs quite proximate to our own.[2]

The French focused their attention on Latin; the English, on Greek. But both recognized the value of classical language and example. However misguided, this kind of affinity with the Greeks and Romans was generally assumed and assiduously cultivated in the West.

Perhaps just as influential, though less commonly cited until later in the century, were the works of Enlightened thinkers, most notably Locke, Montesquieu, Rousseau, Kant, and Adam Smith, men who gave shape to a genuinely modern way of viewing thought, reason, society, and social and economic relations. Instead of replacing the classics, however, these authors were usually used to augment and interpret them. Throughout most of the nineteenth century, eighteenth-century philosophy and philosophical applications were viewed as the necessary means of applying classical truths.

Medieval and early modern figures appealed less universally than the ancients, though each of the great ones had their followings. Dante's *Divine Comedy* rises highest in the canon from this period, sufficiently biblical to suggest orthodox earnestness yet humane enough to accommodate the uncertainties of the nineteenth century. In an age of poetry, Dante was ubiquitous and admired by cultural figures as diverse as Edward Burne-Jones, Eugène Delacroix, William Gladstone, Giuseppe Mazzini, Auguste Rodin, and Taras Shevchenko.

The final category of canonical writers as suggested by our sample would be the influential contemporaries—Goethe, Dickens, Hegel, Darwin, and Sir Walter Scott. As these studies show, there were many other nineteenth-century figures who exerted profound influences, but none were cited as widely or as prominently as these. This in part reflects the bias for "the Greats" and the natural discounting of the modern. Late in life, Louisa May Alcott expressed this natural tendency, suggesting that she read "no modern fiction. It seems poor stuff when one can have the best of the old writers." As Scott Casper notes in this work, however, "[M]any of those 'old works' [Shakespeare, Dante, Emerson, Carlyle,

Thoreau, Eliot, and Charlotte Brontë] had been 'modern fiction' when she first encountered them (herein, p. xx)" Of the five authors mentioned above as "influential contemporaries," only Darwin had not published an important work by the 1830s. A figure like Marx, so important to the twentieth century, was scarcely read outside of narrow political circles until late in the nineteenth.

Only Scott may appear surprising among these listed authors. It is clear from this research, however, that he was read from Poland to Italy, from the Ukraine and Russia to Britain and the United States. Scott clearly had the advantage of writing early in the century (his *Border Minstrelsy* and the *Lay of the Last Minstrel* were published between 1802 and 1805). He also was a gifted poet and storyteller. More important—and this explains his exaltation in the nineteenth century—he was a pioneer in new genres that helped define his age, including the historical novel and the literature of nationalism. In addition to entertaining readers, he gave them new ways of perceiving their pasts and new ways of conceptualizing their futures.

The nature of Scott's influence was as wide-ranging in the nineteenth century as it is surprising in the twenty-first.[3] Few authors can claim to have fired the imagination of both Leopold von Ranke, the great bore and progenitor of modern historical thought, and Walt Whitman, the free-spirited poet of America. As unlikely as it seems, Scott was instrumental in the most important achievements of both men. Whitman acknowledged that Scott was "active at the roots of *Leaves of Grass*," and Ranke that Scott had first turned him to history.

The relatively small "canon" suggested above obviously can be modified, depending upon the criteria one uses. John Milton, for instance, is widely cited but seems to have been less influential than Dante outside of the Anglo-American world. Byron, Shelley, and Keats were enormously influential but perhaps not so generally read or appreciated in the nineteenth century as, say, Scott or Dickens. Bunyan's *Pilgrim's Progress* was widely read but made relatively little mark beyond a cultural world concerned with a particular kind of Christian nonconformity. The works of Tolstoy and Zola taught powerful lessons but came too late in the period to have a general impact.

The crude measure of counting references and assessing their weight has a number of pitfalls; it is meant to be only suggestive. It is possible that some cultural figures, for reasons not here apparent, failed to earn mention in letters, memoirs, and other records while nevertheless playing important roles in cultural development. It should be remembered, too, that in an age of British diplomatic and economic dominance, and at a time when Britain had its own share of great poets, critics, theologians, and novelists, few Britons read other languages and fewer were inclined to learn. A fair number knew French, but even the well-educated rarely could read German, Italian, or Spanish, and only specialists had any knowledge of eastern European languages. In terms of widespread influence, then, those who wrote in English had, for much of the nineteenth century, a decided advantage in widely spreading their messages.

2. This study also suggests *the importance of early reading experience*. It may be argued that early reading experiences are profoundly important, even when they cannot be remembered or traced to specific events.[4] In many cases, however, it can be shown that early reading experiences left indelible marks on later achievements. The young Robert Browning, unsupervised in his father's library, became intrigued with Nathaniel Wanley's *Wonders of the Little World* (1678), whose macabre treatment of bodily disfigurement, for instance, resurfaces later in Browning's morbid poetic sensibilities. The Polish novelist Henryk Sienkiewicz was educated in the modern "greats" of the nineteenth century— Comte, Mill, Darwin, Herbert Spencer—yet it was his boyhood reading of *Robinson Crusoe* and *Swiss Family Robinson*, along with the works of Scott, Dumas, and popular "Western" pulp novels, that shaped his adult "literary vision" of the Polish-Ukrainian steppes of the seventeenth century. Well before Darwin developed an interest in Parkes's *Chemical Catechism* or White's *Natural History of Selborne*, he had read C. C. Clarke's *Wonders of the World*. Although it is impossible to say which of these books influenced him most, Darwin confessed that it was Clarke who first gave him "a wish to travel in remote countries, which was ultimately fulfilled by the voyage of the *Beagle*."[5] Had it not been for Clarke, Darwin might well have become, like his mentor J. S. Henslow, a scientist who practiced on the Isle of Wight or the Isle of Man.

3. The *Biographical Dictionary of Literary Influences* goes some way toward *clarifying the relationship between reading and experience*. In retrospect, people frequently minimize the influence of reading in the face of personal experience, so it is not surprising that later scholars and biographers would follow their lead. Bismarck, for instance, considered himself a pragmatist, rejecting the views of Voltaire and Hegel as being too idealistic. Having said this, it is clear that his ideas were formed in part in reaction to his reading and that in reaction he sought out the learned works of Spinoza and Schleiermacher in support of conservative views. Delacroix was witness to the revolutionary events of the Parisian revolt of 1830, which led him to paint *La Liberté guidant le peuple* (1831); yet it was an interest in Shakespeare and the theater that led him to portray the subject in the manner that he did. H. Rider Haggard was enormously successful as a novelist of the imperial experience, in part because he lived in South Africa (1875–1881). He may never have gone there, however, had he not read Defoe's *Robinson Crusoe* (1719–1720) as a boy, and he may never have become a best-selling author (*King Solomon's Mines*, 1885) had he not learned a trick or two from Stevenson's *Treasure Island* (1883).

These and other experiences suggest that there is no simple relationship between reading and experience but that reading, in some significant way, has shaped the achievements of virtually all those who have had an impact on Western culture. Even when people claimed to dislike reading, it is clear that those shaping culture could not do without it. The father of scientific management, F. W. Taylor, prided himself on keeping up with technical manuals in three languages. His ability to do so, however, was tied both to extensive travel and to youthful reading of foreign novels, a practice that he later repudiated as frivolous.

4. This study also *demonstrates the wide variety of motivations for reading and the equally wide range of results*. Some of the subjects, for instance, read for specific, practical information. As the American historian William Prescott expressed it, he "read for facts, not for reflections of the author." Others read for inspiration. Whereas Prescott consciously rejected the ideas of others so as to heighten his own, Theodore Roosevelt freely admitted that he had few original thoughts. "What I do," he wrote, "is try to get ideas from men whom I regard as experts along certain lines, and then try to work out those ideas." Jeremy Bentham was so struck by the phrase "the greatest good for the greatest number" in Joseph Priestly's *Essay on the First Principles of Government* that he is said to have cried "Eureka!" upon reading it, convinced that it crystallized the complex maze of philosophical abstraction he was seeking to control.

Many nineteenth-century nationalists were inspired by the work of their own cultural figures. Most were well educated in the Western canon but translated the ideas contained therein in light of their own national experiences. Thus, while Poland suffered under Russian political domination, Henryk Sienkiewicz embraced the historical novels of Julian Ursyn Niemcewicz and Józef Ignacy Kraszewski to produce an epic Polish vision of the east European past. Unlike fellow Ukrainian Nikolay Gogol, Taras Shevchenko chose to write in his native language, drawing for inspiration upon Ukrainian folktales and the work of Polish romantics such as Adam Mickiewicz and Zygmunt Krasiński. Marie Curie, best known for her scientific achievements, had as a youth been active in a clandestine movement of Polish nationalist intellectuals, adopting the positivism of Auguste Comte and Herbert Spencer, "yet stamped in a special Polish manner."

This national association was not formulaic. Almost all "makers" of Western culture were to some degree versed in the canon. In many cases, however, canonical reading simply laid the foundations for idiosyncratic identifications. Giuseppe Garibaldi was essentially unlettered but deeply interested in Italian writers and works associated with radical reform—Dante, Manzoni, Ugo Foscolo, Tasso, Saint-Simon, and Voltaire. Camillo Cavour and Giuseppe Mazzini, who with Garibaldi led the Italian unification movement, were less enthusiastic about Italian literature. Cavour lamented Italy's "excessively literary" tradition and found his greatest inspiration in Adam Smith, Shakespeare, Bulwer-Lytton, and Byron, "the favorite of strong spirits and anyone with a too exquisite sensibility." Mazzini read widely in Italian, French, and German literature and philosophy but once remarked that his true country was England; he proved it in a sense by reading Shakespeare, Dickens, Adam Smith, John Locke, John Milton, and every volume of Sir Walter Scott.

Related to inspiration is the motivation of close association. Although many readers find themselves drawn by conviction or sentiment to seek out certain writers or works, for some there is an affinity that transcends intellectual identification. Frederick Douglass, as an active, black abolitionist, naturally would have taken an interest in *Uncle Tom's Cabin* (1852), on account of both his race and his vocation. One should not make everything of this association of experience, for Harriet Beecher Stowe's novel was a worldwide sensation, read among many social groups in many nations. On the other hand, its message—and hence its place in cultural development—would have been more immediate for Douglas than for the French aristocrats or the English clergymen who read it. In another case of reading by association, the condition of slavery led Toussaint-Louverture to read the work of the ancient slave Epictetus. One wonders, had the novel been written first, whether Epictetus would have played a part at all in Louverture's successful Haitian rebellion. Nor is it an idle question, for the teachings and tone of Epictetus—based upon ethics, the supreme value of the will, and an enlightened stoicism—are considerably different from the sentimentality and social criticism of *Uncle Tom's Cabin*.

Sometimes people read because of perceived, rather than natural, affinity. Unlike modern slaves who would naturally find common cause in the wisdom and experience of others who lived without liberty, modern peoples sometimes sought affinities in the wisdom of another age or culture without actually sharing many things in common. Cavour, as we have seen, largely eschewed the Italian worldview in favor of predominant English and French models. German and English scholars from about 1750 began to identify with the ancient Greek experience, leading to a cultural revolution in which the study of Greek language and literature became synonymous with learning. "The Battle of Marathon," John Stuart Mill declared, "even as an event in English history, is more important than the battle of Hastings."[6] This debatable assertion reflects what Frank Turner has called "the moral variety in Greek culture" that allowed for multiple interpretations and provided an ancient authority for the undermining of Christian asceticism and French classicism. "Things Greek," according to Turner, "thus contributed both to the devising of new myths and to the sustaining of old values in novel guises."[7]

An understudied motive for reading is polemic reinforcement. Rather than reading for new ideas or practically useful information, leaders in Western culture have sometimes—and perhaps often—read to reinforce intuitively held but culturally contested positions. This is essentially a combination of purposes, with the reader seeking information principally in support of firmly held views and from this to gain the leverage of authorities in asserting those views. Thomas Carlyle is said to have read "in" books as often as through them, raising questions about his purposes, particularly in light of his declining "reverence" for books. Gladstone, who held strong and controversial opinions on many subjects, often sought out specialist authorities in support of what most considered to be eccentric religious and Homeric views. These were for Gladstone, however, matters of faith rather than of history, and it is unclear in some cases whether he would ever have been convinced by ordinary evidences. Regarding his belief in a highly unusual theory concerning the evolution of the "colour sense" in the ancient world, Gladstone may have been less convinced by Hugo Magnus's *Die geshichtliche Entwickelung des Farbgensinnes* (1877) than he was glad of "authoritative" support for a cherished article of faith.[8]

Once careful research is carried out, one almost invariably finds that motivations for reading are thick and densely packed, that potential sources of influence are numerous, and that the line from written idea to cultural achievement runs along a very crooked path. The variety of the reading relationships is suggestive of the multiplicity of human motivations and paths of development. Take the single case of French painter Edgar Degas. He received a classical education and studied law for two years—reading in common with many others for a general education that served to inform his view of the society. More specific to the role of creative artist, he shared the theories of critics and authors such as Edmond Duranty and Baudelaire, who "argued that it was the duty of the *avante-garde* artist to reflect the social realities of French society." More specific still to the painter, he "read" art books, such as Goya's *Disasters of War*, a book of etchings that influenced Degas in a way distinct from the actual viewing of Goya's paintings.[9]

5. Finally, the articles in the *Biographical Dictionary of Literary Influences* support the idea that *each reader responds uniquely to the written word and thus in unpredictable ways.* While recognizing that ideas do have consequences, this research demonstrates that idiosyncratic interpretations and distortions of important ideas often had as much influence as the pristine originals. One wonders, for instance, what system of thought Auguste Comte might have developed had he clearly understood the work of Friedrich Hegel, Giambattista Vico, and Montesquieu.

One further example will suffice to illustrate this point. In that great philosophical debate over the veracity of Christian teaching that so engrossed so much of Victorian England, the Christian man of the hour was Henry Longueville Mansel, High Church Anglican, Reader in Moral and Metaphysical Philosophy at Magdalen College, and later Dean of St. Paul's. According to Leslie Stephen, he was "the last English writer who professed to defend Christianity with weapons drawn from wide and genuine philosophical knowledge." Mansel's intent clearly was to produce an irrefutable defense of orthodox Christianity. He was widely praised by churchmen for his success. Yet one of the greatest admirers of his logic was Thomas Henry Huxley, the very man who coined the term *agnostic* to describe his own skeptical attitude toward Christianity. Huxley "begged" the geologist Charles Lyell to read Mansel's Bampton Lectures "as a piece of clear and unanswerable reasoning." Mansel may be said to have failed in his purpose with Huxley, though his reasoning and writing were impeccable. As Huxley said, Mansel was like "the drunken fellow in Hogarth's Contested Election, who is sawing through the signpost of the other party's public-house, forgetting that he is sitting at the outer end of it."[10] Good writing and cogent argument frequently bring change—but not always of the expected kind.

The *Biographical Dictionary of Literary Influences* is neither the beginning nor the end of this enterprise. Many biographers have laid the groundwork in careful examinations of their subjects' lives. These specialized treatments are not always well known outside the discipline of their subjects' work and frequently are not available in local libraries. And one would need a continuous biographical study of influences from the beginnings of written history to the present to establish all the discernible intellectual links involved in the process of cultural change. The *Biographical Dictionary of Literary Influences* nevertheless will identify a number of important links in that train of influence and will serve as the first general guide for researchers, from a variety of disciplines, who seek an introduction to the reading habits and the related intellectual development of the most significant cultural figures in the Western world during the nineteenth century.

NOTES

1. Kim Wheatley, *Shelley and His Readers: Beyond Paranoid Politics* (Columbia: University of Missouri Press, 1999), 38.

2. Cited in Frank M. Turner, *The Greek Heritage in Victorian Britain* (New Haven, CT: Yale University Press, 1981), 10.

3. Scott's influence again may be measured by George Bernard Shaw's assertion that "with the single exception of Homer, there is no eminent writer, not even Sir Walter Scott, whom I can despise so entirely as I despise Shakespeare." *Dramatic Opinions and Essays, with an Apology*, 2 vols. (New York: Brentano's, 1907), 2: 52.

4. In his study of William Gladstone, Colin Matthew assesses the fundamental influence of early reading: "The set books a student reads, if taught properly as texts and not via commentaries, stay with him or her throughout life: they have a peculiar grounding quality which is unequalled by later reading. This was certainly the case with Gladstone's undergraduate studies.... They introduced him, amongst others, to Homer, Plato's *Phaedo*, Aristotle's *Ethics and Rhetoric*, Joseph Butler's *Analogy* and Thucydides' *History*.... Of course, the full significance of these works was not apparent to him at the age of 21, when he took the Schools, but their categories were his instinctive points of reference for the rest of his life." Matthew, *Gladstone, 1809–1874* (Oxford: Clarendon Press, 1986), 20.

5. Charles Darwin, *Charles Darwin: His Life Told in an Autobiographical Chapter and in a Selected Series of His Published Letters* (New York: D. Appleton, 1892), 10.

6. John Stuart Mill, *The Collected Works of John Stuart Mill*, ed. J. M. Robson (Toronto: University of Toronto Press, 1963), 11: 273.

7. Turner, *Greek Heritage in Victorian Britain*, 2–3.

8. Following John Morley's early suggestion that Gladstone started from the "principle of authority," Elizabeth Henry Bellmer suggests that "Magnus had provided the catalytic framework, the principle of authority; Gladstone took it as a given, fitting into it his long-fixed views on the state of Homeric colour vision." Bellmer, "The Statesman and the Ophthalmologist: Gladstone and Magnus on the Evolution of Human Colour Vision, One Small Episode of the Nineteenth-century Darwinian Debate," *Annals of Science*, 56 (1999), 42.

9. Christopher Benfey, *Degas in New Orleans: Encounters in the Creole World of Kate Chopin and George Washington Cable* (New York: Knopf, 1997), 10–11, 58, 158.

10. Bernard Lightman, *The Origins of Agnosticism: Victorian Unbelief and the Limits of Knowledge* (Baltimore: Johns Hopkins University Press, 1987), 7.

A

ACTON, JOHN EMERICH EDWARD DALBERG, LORD (1834–1902).
Lord Acton was born in Naples and died at Tergensee, Bavaria. Acton succeeded
to a baronetcy on the death of his father and was raised in England by his
mother, studying first at Oscott and from 1850 to 1859 at Munich under Johannes Joseph Ignaz von Döllinger (1799–1890). From 1859 to 1865 Acton sat as
a Member of Parliament. He was an active supporter of the liberal Catholic
journal *The Rambler* from 1858 to 1864, when he withdrew in frustration with
Vatican conservative policies. Although opposed to the First Vatican Council's
definition of papal primacy and infallibility, he remained within the Catholic
Church. From 1880 to 1885 he was an adviser to **William Ewart Gladstone**
and a strong supporter of Irish Home Rule. In 1895 he was appointed Regius
Professor of Modern History at Cambridge, where he initiated the *Cambridge
Modern History* series.

Because of the breadth of Acton's reading, it is difficult to ascertain specifically all major influences on his work. He once made a list for Mary Gladstone
of the 100 best books, a majority of which were obscure continental volumes.
Moreover, a reflective individual, his intellectual as well as personal relationships with formative figures in his career were highly nuanced. First among
these was Döllinger, the liberal Catholic historian and theologian, who introduced Acton to the new critical historical methods and the liberal Catholic renaissance of the early nineteenth century. It was Döllinger who turned Acton
from his initial interest in **Thomas Babington Macaulay** (1800–1859) to the
more realist approach of Edmund Burke (1729–1797; from whom he also diverged on many issues as his thought developed). Acton came to oppose Macaulay as a historian of "unsuggestive fixity" who framed the past always in
light of the present and thus denied the implicit value of actual historical events.
As a result, Acton was early attracted to **John Henry Newman**'s (1801–1890)
Development of Christian Doctrine (1845) but, while admiring Newman, came

to interpret the latter's work as he did Macaulay's, was ill at ease with Newman's primarily theoretical stance, and was much more drawn to and shaped by the practical liberal politics of Gladstone.

ARCHIVES

Cambridge, University Library: Principal collection of Actoniana, including notebooks, drafts of major works, and commentaries.
Downside Abbey: Correspondence with the liberal Catholic Richard Simpson.
London, British Library: Acton-Gladstone (William Ewart and the latter's daughter, Mary) correspondence.
Oxford, Bodleian Library: Miscellaneous correspondence.
Shrewsbury, Shropshire Record Office: Miscellaneous correspondence.

PRINTED SOURCES

Altholz, Joseph L. *The Liberal Catholic Movement in England: The "Rambler" and Its Contributors, 1848–1864* (London: Burns and Oates, 1962).
Chadwick, Owen. *Acton and History* (Cambridge: Cambridge University Press, 1998).
Himmelfarb, Gertrude. *Lord Acton: A Study in Conscience and Politics* (Chicago: University of Chicago Press, 1962).
Paul, Herbert (ed., with introductory memoir). *Letters of Lord Acton to Mary, Daughter of the Right Hon. W. E. Gladstone* (London: Allen, 1906).
Tulloch, Hugh. *Acton* (New York: St. Martin's Press, 1988).
Watson, George. *Lord Acton's History of Liberty: A Study of His Library, with an Edited Text of His History of Liberty Notes* (Aldershot: Scolar Press, 1994).

Peter C. Erb

ADAMS, HENRY BROOKS (1838–1918). Henry Brooks Adams was born on Beacon Hill, "under the shadow of the Boston State House," in Massachusetts in 1838. Adams graduated from Harvard University in 1858 and became a writer and historian. He was raised as a member of the Unitarian Universalist faith, a liberal religion to which most of Boston's elite adhered. He was the great-grandson of John Adams, grandson of John Quincy Adams, and son of Charles Francis Adams, enjoying many social and intellectual opportunities. The burden of his family legacy eventually led him to contradict the optimistic views of his contemporaries, however, in favor of a theory of historical declension. Adams is best known for his theories of cultural decline, which were expressed most eloquently in his later works, *Mont-Saint-Michel and Chartres* (1905) and *The Education of Henry Adams* (1915).

Growing up in the Adams household, Henry was immersed in the political world, but it was Harvard Professor **Louis Agassiz**'s lectures on paleontology that ignited his interest in the history of change. Agassiz stressed the effect of cataclysmic events, refuting the evidence of gradual mutation presented by **Charles Darwin** in *The Origin of Species* (1859). Agassiz's theories lay the foundation for Adam's lifelong fascination with the process of permutation.

In 1861, with Agassiz's arguments still fresh in his mind, Adams accompanied his father to London, where he met the most important British historical theorists of the time. In conversations with Sir **Charles Lyell**, a geologist and eminent Darwinian, Adams defended the role of the cataclysm in natural history against Lyell's conception of gradual change. Adams also met **John Stuart Mill** and read his book, *Auguste Comte and Positivism* (1865), an explanation of **Comte**'s philosophy of human history that posits a progression of human thought: theological, metaphysical, and ultimately, positive or natural. Comte's ideas greatly influenced Adams, buttressing his view that history moved in scientifically determined stages. The debates encountered in London posed lifelong philosophical questions for Adams. Had the world and mankind developed gradually, or was change more cataclysmic? Did the process move in stages?

In 1905, attempting to answer those questions, Adams published *Mont-Saint-Michel and Chartres*. Through an architectural and artistic review of the High Middle Ages, Adams examines an epoch that was unified in spirit through the cult of the Virgin and the centralizing effects of the Catholic Church. To Adams, the Middle Ages stood as a paradigm, implying that nineteenth-century society had unraveled to the point of disintegration.

In that vein, Adams produced *The Education of Henry Adams* in 1915. Not entirely autobiographical, *The Education* is a third-person account of the life of a cynical man struggling with his times. In this work, Adams accepts Agassiz's theory of cataclysmic change as more likely, but he also incorporates the ideas of Lyell and Comte, reasoning that the cause of change is less important than the consequence. Pointing to the corruption of twentieth-century politics and society and comparing it to the unity of the High Middle Ages, Adams inverts his mentors' more optimistic view of change into a narrative of decline. Adams regards the machine age as the final cataclysm. Society has been disintegrating since the Middle Ages, and Adams perceives the industrial revolution as the disastrous finishing touch.

Henry Adams was a man at odds with his world. Adams took the ideas of Agassiz, Lyell, and Comte to tell the history of the decline of Western society. Comte's stages of human thought were adopted by Adams, but it was the theological stage that was now highest. So, too, did Adams absorb the varying philosophies of natural history in order to demonstrate that humanity was not evolving upward but was sliding into a precipitous decline. The reader of Henry Adam's works should not be surprised by his gloomy outlook, for Adams was a man in love with order and history in a time of anarchy and change.

ARCHIVES

Henry Adams Papers, Massachusetts Historical Society.
Henry Cabot Lodge Papers, Correspondence, 1866–1884. Reels 1 and 2, Massachusetts Historical Society.

PRINTED SOURCES

Bishop, Ferman. *Henry Adams* (Boston: Twayne Publishers, 1979).
Samuels, Ernest. *Henry Adams: The Major Phase* (Cambridge, Mass.: Belknap Press of Harvard University Press, 1964).

————. *Henry Adams: The Middle Years* (Cambridge, Mass.: Belknap Press of Harvard University Press, 1964).
Simpson, Brooks D. *The Political Education of Henry Adams* (Columbia: University of South Carolina Press, 1996).

Michelle C. Morgan

AGASSIZ, JEAN LOUIS RODOLPHE (1807–1873). Jean Louis Rodolphe Agassiz, Swiss naturalist, was born in Friborg (Switzerland). He attended the Universities of Zürich (1824), Heidelberg (1826), and Munich (1827–1830), where he studied under Lorenz Oken, Karl Friedrick Martius, and Ignaz Döllinger. In 1829 he earned the doctorate in philosophy at Munich, nine months after the publication of *Fishes of Brazil*. In 1830, also at Munich, he earned a doctor of medicine degree and began to work on *Poissons fossiles*.

Education by his minister father in Protestant pietism nourished his mind with an idealistic romanticism that saw in the natural world the manifestation of the power of the Creator—a faith that strongly influenced his scientific conclusions. In *An Essay on Classification* (London, 1859) and in *Structure of Animal Life* (New York, 1866), he accepted Oken's convictions that animals are fetal phases of man and that man—as anatomy demonstrates—is the last term in a series beyond which no material progress is possible, according to the plan that rules the whole animal kingdom. This theory was the natural evolution of the hypotheses that Agassiz elaborated when, from 1835 to 1845, he studied the glacial formations of Switzerland, England, and central Europe, concluding that in the recent past northern Europe was covered with ice. The receding of the ice masses was responsible for modern geological configurations, as could be noticed in such areas as Switzerland. But while naturalists such as **Darwin** and **Lyell** considered glaciations the principal cause of the genetic relationship of flora and fauna and of their geographical distribution, Agassiz rejected any evolutionistic theory and found a metaphysical cause for glaciations.

The Ice Age was the result of the will of the Creator to separate the species of the past from those of the present era; the naturalist distinguished 20 different creations in the history of the earth, each of them characterized by vegetal and animal forms of life without relationships to those preceding or following. Applied to mankind, this conception of natural history led Agassiz to distinguish different types of species of men, marked by different physical and intellectual traits, and provided scientific argumentation for defenders of the slave system.

Agassiz's visit to the United States in 1846 was the turning point of his scientific career. He accepted a Harvard professorship and announced, in 1855, the publication of a monumental study, *Contributions to the Natural History of the United States*, which gathered all of the data collected by the naturalist during his explorations of the American natural environment. Further steps in the explication of his theory of natural history and of his working methods were the foundations of the Museum of Comparative Zoology (1859) and of the Anderson School of Natural History on Penikese Island (1873) and the publication of *Lake Superior: Its Physical Character, Vegetation and Animals, Compared with Those of Other and Similar Regions* (1850) and, together with his wife, *A Journey to Brazil* (1868).

But his burning anti-Darwinist controversy alienated him from the other scientists, and even if his name was synonymous, to the public, with the study of natural history, the scientific value of his efforts rests on his working methods, carried on by students such as **William James**, David Starr Jordan, Alexander Agassiz, Frederick Ward Putnam, and Nathaniel Southgate or scientists such as ichthyologist Carl H. Eigenmann.

ARCHIVES

Institute de Géologie, Université de Neuchâtel (Switzerland).
Agassiz Papers at Houghton Library, Harvard University (Boston).
Agassiz Papers at the Museum of Comparative Zoology, Harvard University (Boston).

PRINTED SOURCES

Lurie, E. *Louis Agassiz: A Life in Science* (Chicago: University of Chicago Press, 1960).
———. *Nature and the American Mind: Louis Agassiz and the Culture of Science* (New York: Science History Publications, 1974).
Marcou, J. *Life, Letters, and Works of Louis Agassiz.* 2 vols. (New York: Macmillan, 1896).
Schweizerische Naturforschende Gesellschaft, *Louis Agassiz, 1807–1873: Vortrage an der Gedenkfeier zum 100. Todestag, gehalten an der 153. Jahresversammlung der Schweizerischen Naturforschenden Gesellschaft*, Lugano, 20 October 1973 (Zurich: Kommision Gebr. Fretz, 1974).

Giuseppe Marchetti

ALBERT, PRINCE (1819–1861). Albert was born the second son to the ruler of a tiny German state, the duchy of Saxe-Coburg-Gotha. Albert had close family ties to the royal courts of Russia, Germany, Spain, England, and Belgium. Young Albert was groomed for the role that he was to play from February 1840 until his death, that of husband to his first cousin, **Queen Victoria**, who had become monarch of Great Britain and its empire in June 1837. Although only in 1857 was Albert formally proclaimed "Prince Consort," by the mid-1840s he had become Britain's constitutional "King without a Crown."

From age 4 until age 18, he and his elder bother were under the charge of an idealistic Coburg tutor, one Herr Florschutz, who imposed on his charges an educational regime devoted less to the Latin and Greek Classics and to mathematics than was the custom in English "public schools" of the day. Instead, the stress was on modern languages, history, the natural sciences, geography, philosophy, music, and art. (Albert did also study Latin.) Although German always remained his first language, he was introduced at an early age to the novels of Sir **Walter Scott** (in English). At the age of 16 he wrote a lengthy essay tracing "through the course of History the progress of German civilization." In many respects Albert became a product both of the German romantic movement as exemplified in the writings of Friedrich Gottlieb Klopstock (1724–1803) and of the German Enlightenment as exemplified in the writings, especially *Faust*, of **Johann Wolfgang von Goethe** (1749–1832).

Albert's education continued with 10 months of study in Brussels (1836–1837), where his tutor was Adolphe Quetelet (1796–1874), a mathematician and astronomer who established the theoretical foundations for the use of statistics in the social sciences; there also Albert read **Charles Lyell**'s *Principles of Geology* in English. He spent the next year and a half (1837–1838) at the new University of Bonn, unusual among German institutions in being open to both Protestant and Roman Catholic students. There Albert came under the influence, among others, of August Wilhelm von Schlegel (1767–1845), professor of art and literary history and famed translator of Shakespeare into German, and of a Professor Fichte, who taught Albert that "through work and effort shall come salvation." A tour of Italy under the guidance of Baron Friedrich Christian von Stockmar (the longtime physician confidant of King Leopold of the Belgians, uncle to both Victoria and Albert) familiarized Albert with ancient and Renaissance art. Albert found Italy to be "an inexhaustible source of knowledge."

Once married to Queen Victoria, Albert prepared himself further for his new role by undertaking regular readings in the laws and the constitution of England with one Mr. Selwyn, a distinguished barrister. Albert and Victoria together read Henry Hallam's *Constitutional History of England*, an already classic early nineteenth-century account of the manner in which England's governmental institutions had evolved and improved through the centuries. The royal couple's frequent visits to the theater deliberately included numerous plays by Shakespeare. Albert cultivated a personal acquaintance with Britain's leading scientists, among them Michael Faraday (1791–1867), the developer of electromagnetic induction, and Adam Sedgwick (1785–1873), the geologist.

Unlike the vast majority of constitutional monarchs, Albert was a born academic. He used his influence—as chairman of a Royal Commission on the Fine Arts (1841), as chancellor of Cambridge University (1847–1861), and as inspirer of both the Great Exhibition of the Works of All Nations (1851) and of London's South Kensington museum complex—to promote in the British Isles the teaching of history, philosophy, natural science, music, and art, both at the secondary school and at the university level. During the 1840s and 1850s he drafted and delivered numerous speeches on such subjects; he also served as president of the British Association for the Advancement of Science. In 1859, he addressed that organization of 2,500 on the theme of the difference between the English and German schools of scientific thought. In preparing his presidential address, Albert privately admitted: "I read thick volumes, write, perspire and tear what I have written into shreds," yet the speech itself proved to be a great success. In the eyes of many of his new countrymen, Albert remained a pedantic foreigner who had failed to learn English customs, yet others acknowledged that he could talk to architects as an architect, to painters as a painter, to sculptors as a sculptor, and to chemists as a chemist.

ARCHIVES

Royal Archives, Windsor Castle. Correspondence, Albert's memoranda, and the surviving transcripts of Queen Victoria's daily journal.

PRINTED SOURCES

Bennett, Daphne. *King without a Crown: Albert, Prince Consort of England, 1818–1861* (Philadelphia, Pa.: Lippincott, 1977).

Grey, Charles. *The Early Years of His Royal Highness the Prince Consort* (London: Harper & Bros., 1867).

Hobhouse, Hermione. *Prince Albert: His Life and Work* (London: Hamish Hamilton, 1983).

Martin, Sir Theodore. *The Life of His Royal Highness the Prince Consort*, 5 vols. (London: Smith Elder, 1875–1881).

Walter L. Arnstein

ALCOTT, LOUISA MAY (1832–1888). Louisa May Alcott, U.S. author, was born in Germantown, Pennsylvania, and raised in Boston and Concord, Massachusetts. Her father Bronson Alcott, a leading Transcendentalist and friend of **Ralph Waldo Emerson**, founded the Fruitlands utopian community (1843–1844). However, because of his inability to provide adequately for his wife and four daughters, Louisa's writing played a vital role in the family's economic sustenance. Her earliest publications appeared in newspapers and magazines in the 1850s; in the early 1860s, she published not only sentimental pieces in the *Atlantic Monthly* but also pseudonymous "blood & thunder" psychological thrillers in weekly story papers. Her best-known and best-selling books, beginning with *Little Women* (1868), were novels about childhood and family life.

Alcott's own experiences, above all, shaped the stories she wrote. In her journal for November 1864, she paraphrased Emerson's "Self-Reliance": "Emerson says 'that what is true for your own private life is true for others,' so I wrote from my own life & experience and hope it may suit some one & at least do no harm" (*Journals*, 133). Alcott's books reflected her girlhood and relationships with her sisters (*Little Women*), her service as a Civil War nurse (*Hospital Sketches*, 1863), and her life as a working woman (*Work: A Story of Experience*, 1873). From an early age, literature influenced her thoughts. Bunyan's *Pilgrim's Progress*, which the March sisters in *Little Women* read and from which Alcott took many of the novel's chapter titles, was a family favorite. Modern writers also figured prominently: **Scott, Goethe, Hawthorne**, Frederika Bremer, and Fanny Burney. But **Dickens** ranked above the rest. Alcott's journals over three decades reveal her and her family reading, rereading, and dramatizing scenes from *Oliver Twist, Dombey and Son, David Copperfield*, and *Bleak House*; in *Little Women*, the sisters form the "Pickwick Club," producing a weekly newspaper, *The Pickwick Portfolio*. Alcott's own aspirations to authorship also reflected her appreciation for other women authors: After reading a biography of **Charlotte Brontë** in June 1857, she wrote, "So full of talent, and after working long, just as success, love and happiness come, she dies. Wonder if I shall ever be famous enough for people to care to read my story and struggles. I can't be a C.B., but I may do a little something yet" (*Journals*, 85). Nearly 30 years later, she wrote, "My favorite authors are Shakespeare, Dante, . . . Emerson, **Carlyle, Thoreau** . . . **Geo. Eliot** and C. Brontë"; she added, "I read no modern fiction. It seems poor stuff when one can have the best of the old writers" (*Selected Letters*, 296). Of course, many of those "old" works had been "modern fiction" when she first encountered them. By the time she wrote these words, she had done more than "a little something." Like Brontë, she had barely paused to enjoy her successes before she died at 55.

ARCHIVES

Alcott Papers, Houghton Library, Harvard University.

PRINTED SOURCES

Myerson, Joel, and Daniel Shealy, eds. *The Journals of Louisa May Alcott* (Boston: Little, Brown, 1989).
———. *The Selected Letters of Louisa May Alcott* (Boston: Little, Brown, 1987). [Letter cited: LMA to Viola Price, Dec. 18, 1885, orig. pub. *Overland Monthly* 91 (Aug. 1933): 106; ms unlocated.]
Saxton, Martha. *Louisa May: A Modern Biography of Louisa May Alcott* (Boston: Houghton Mifflin, 1977).
Stern, Madeleine B. *Louisa May Alcott* (Norman: University of Oklahoma Press, 1950).

Scott E. Casper

ALGER, HORATIO, JR. (1832–1899). Horatio Alger, Jr. was born in Chelsea, Massachusetts, in 1832 and received his earliest education from his Congregational minister father. His more formal education began at the Gates Academy in nearby Marlborough, Massachusetts (where his family then had moved), from 1844 to 1847. He attended Harvard College from 1848 to 1852 and proceeded to Harvard's Divinity School the following year. Lack of funds forced him to leave school, however, and he was not able to continue his studies until 1857, finally gaining his divinity degree in 1860.

Since Alger ordered all his personal papers destroyed upon his death, little is known with certainty about the literary influences from his childhood. From his own entry in his Harvard Class Book, we can gather he was a bookish child who received a traditional classical education of the time (including classical Latin and Greek) but took much more enjoyment in reading on his own. He specifically mentions theology and the adventure stories *The Arabian Nights* and "the wonderful adventures of Jack the Giant Killer." While at Harvard, he came to admire greatly one of his instructors, **Henry Wadsworth Longfellow**. Longfellow's poetic style did not directly influence Alger, as the student had little of his teacher's talent for rhyme or meter; but nonetheless, Longfellow's confident outlook and Unitarian moral sense no doubt left their mark.

While Alger wrote some adult fiction and nonfiction, he is best known as the author of more than 100 juvenile novels, nearly all of which have maddeningly similar plots of the poor boy who overcomes all obstacles to become a successful businessman. This archetypal "Horatio Alger Hero" appeared first in *Ragged Dick* (1867). A young orphaned boy of generally good character (called Ragged Dick, as he wore tattered clothes) learns over the course of the novel the values he needs to succeed in an urbanized, industrialized society: hard work, perseverance, and the rewards of delayed gratification. While these values were necessary for the Alger Hero's success, they did not assure it, for at critical (and convenient) points in the story, an older, successful man comes forward to provide financial aid or a job. The novel closes with the hero achieving his goal, respectability, signified by a new suit of clothes, a clerical job, and a new name—Ragged Dick has become Richard Hunter.

While this subject matter, which for the first time placed children's (or more particularly, boy's) literature in the context of urbanizing, industrializing America, the didactic, moralistic, and stylistic roots of Alger's novels can be traced back to both the adventure stories he loved as a boy and the long-standing tradition for children's literature to serve as moral instruction to youth.

ARCHIVES

Library of Congress, Washington, D.C.
Natick Historical Society.

PRINTED SOURCES

Scharnhorst, Gary. *Horatio Alger, Jr.* (Boston: Twayne, 1980).
Scharnhorst, Gary, with Jack Bales. *The Lost Life of Horatio Alger, Jr.* (Bloomington: Indiana University Press, 1985).
Zuckerman, Michael. "The Nursery Tales of Horatio Alger," *American Quarterly*, 24 (March 1972), pp. 191–209.

Christopher Berkeley

ANDERSEN, HANS CHRISTIAN (1805–1875). Hans Christian Andersen was born in Odense, Denmark. His father, a shoemaker, died when Andersen was 11, and his mother, who could neither read nor write, found work as a washerwoman. Despite this modest background, Andersen showed intellectual and artistic promise. He attended a school for children of parents who could not otherwise afford schooling, and his education included Christian Bible teachings.

Andersen spent much of his time as a youth reading and learned Latin. As a youth, he wrote a play based on a German story and another based on a Danish legend and attempted a career in the theater. The board of directors of the Royal Theater rejected his play but recommended that he be sent to grammar school at public expense for 3 years, so at age 17 he found himself being educated alongside 11-year-olds. In grammar school, he succeeded in the subjects of religion, biblical history, and Danish.

In April 1835, Andersen published *Improvisatoren*, which was translated into German, English, and French and made his name known in Europe. His stated goal in this novel was to describe what he saw in his travels to Italy as **Walter Scott** described Scotland and its people. The novel found a success that no Danish fictional work had yet achieved in Europe. In 1835, Andersen began writing children's tales; in May 1835 his *Tales, Told for Children* was published.

His children's stories were published in three series: *Tales, Told for Children*; *Tales and Stories*; and *New Tales and Stories*. In a 1836 letter, Andersen notes that when his muse visits him, "she tells me strange fairy tales, shows me funny characters from daily life—peers as well as commoners—saying, 'Look at those people . . . depict them and—they shall live!' " (Bredsdorff, 123). While his early tales were occasionally inspired by folklore, his original stories such as "The Little Mermaid" were generally the most popular.

Although his greatest fame rests with his children's stories, which have been translated into more than 100 languages, Andersen wrote novels, travel books, and stage plays throughout his life. In fact, his novel *Only a Fiddler* (1837) became the subject of **Søren Kierkegaard**'s first published work, a criticism of this Andersen novel, in 1838.

His fairy tales present child readers with imaginative plots, classic characters, and images of wonder and adult readers with mature themes such as hypocrisy and romantic disappointment.

Hans Christian Andersen was a voracious, wide-ranging reader throughout his entire life, absorbing everything from classical literature to popular stage plays of his day. To begin with, Andersen's father enjoyed the Bible and often read to Hans Christian Andersen from his favorite books, including Holberg's plays and the *Arabian Nights*. In addition to providing their son with stories read aloud, Andersen's parents took him to comic operas and *singspiele*, recognizing his early interest in the stage.

As a youth, his favorite authors were Shakespeare and Sir Walter Scott. In fact, it was Andersen's reading of Shakespeare tragedies such as *King Lear* and *Macbeth* that inspired him to write his first play, a tragedy in which everyone expires at the end. His insatiable appetite for books also included reading biographies of great men, including, for instance, a life of **Byron**.

Andersen had read Walter Scott's *The Heart of Midlothian* in an 1822 Danish translation. His imitative story "Mad Stine" and his tragedy *Alfsol* were published in a book called *Youthful Attempts* (1822), published as a result of connections made in his attempts to enter the theater. For his nom de plume for this book, Andersen chose "William Christian Walter," flanking his own name with those of his two literary heroes, Shakespeare and Scott.

Because some of his early tales were based on traditional Danish folktales he had heard as a child, we must assume Andersen had a wide variety of stories and folktales told to him, read to him, and which he read himself. Folktales we know he read included *Stories and Pictures from the Folk Life of Switzerland* by Jeremias Gotthelf and Auerbach's *Village Stories from the Black Forest* and

Grandpa's Little Treasure Chest. He also read the stories of **Washington Irving** and **James Fenimore Cooper**.

He read *Faust* and **Edward Bulwer-Lytton**'s *Night and Morning* and *Zanoni* as well as philosophy such as *Letters in Opposition to Materialism* by F. Fabri, of which he noted, "They have enlightened me, but I haven't clearly eradicated every materialistic argument" (*Diaries*, 243). In 1825 alone, at age 20, he eagerly read works by Francisco García Calderón, Ludvig Holberg, Christian Molbech, Friedrich von Schiller, Wilhelm von Schlegel, Tobias Smollett, Ludwig Tieck, and Adam Oehlenschläger.

Andersen liked Adam Oehlenschläger's Romantic play *Aladdin* (1805) and wove it and the Arabian Nights' basic premise of a genie granting three wishes into his early story "The Tinder Box." There are traces of Danish legends and folktales as well as elements of **Grimms**' and Hoffman's tales and Boccaccio's *Decameron* as well as the *Arabian Nights* in Hans Christian Andersen's stories.

Andersen's wide-ranging reading meant that his tales had wide-ranging influences. For example, "The Emperor's New Clothes" was based on a story by Spanish author Prince don Juan Manuel (1282–ca. 1349), which Andersen had read in a German translation.

He soaked up contemporary works by vaudeville poet Paul Duport; Hamburg poet Lars Kruse; various European opera composers; poet **Heinrich Heine**; **Victor Hugo**, whose novel *Notre Dame* Andersen considered a "poetical work" with stirring characters; as well as poet Juan Eugenio Hartzenbusch, of German extraction but of Spanish birth, who was a well-known writer of wonder stories.

He was equally interested in literature of other ages and read classical works, such as Aristophanes's *Birds*.

It is safe to assume that he read all of Shakespeare's works and certainly saw many, if not most, of Shakespeare's plays in performance, including *Cymbeline*, *King Lear*, *Macbeth*, and *The Tempest*. He saw untold numbers of dramatic works performed, from serious historical dramas such as *Mary Tudor* and classical theater such as *Phaedra* to comedies and puppet theater.

Andersen's seemingly native talent was matched with a compelling intellect that found fulfillment not only in writing wonderful tales but in reading and seeing performed the best creative works available to him in his travels and in his homeland.

ARCHIVES

Andersen's diaries and other manuscripts are held by the Royal Library, Copenhagen, and the Danish National Literary Archives.
There is a Hans Christian Andersen museum in Odense.

PRINTED SOURCES

Andersen, Hans Christian. *The Fairy Tale of My Life: An Autobiography* (New York: Paddington Press, 1975). This is a translation of *Mit livs eventyr* (1868 ed.).
Bredsdorff, Elias. *Hans Christian Andersen: The Story of His Life and Work* (London: Souvenir Press, 1975).

Conroy, Patricia L., and Sven H. Rossel (ed. and trans.). *The Diaries of Hans Christian Andersen* (Seattle: University of Washington Press, 1990).
Grønbech, Bø. *Hans Christian Andersen* (Boston: Twayne Publishers, 1980).
Spinks, Reginald. *Hans Christian Andersen and His World* (New York: G. P. Putnam's Sons, 1912).

Ann Shillinglaw

ANTHONY, SUSAN BROWNELL (1820–1906). Susan Brownell Anthony, woman suffrage leader, was born on a farm in Massachusetts in 1820 but spent most of her life in New York State, where her parents moved when she was six. She was the second of eight children born to Daniel and Lucy Read Anthony and was educated in district schools, in a home school established by her father, and later at a Quaker seminary near Philadelphia. A belief in women's equality was central to the Friends' background, and despite the fact that her father had been "married out of meeting" to a Baptist, she received her basic upbringing in Quaker principles and faith. Her parents were both unconventional and remained involved in temperance, abolitionism, and women's rights; both, in fact, attended the Seneca Falls women's rights gathering in 1848.

A turning point for her was an auction at which all her family's belongings—including items brought by her mother into the marriage—were sold to pay debts made by her father in business affairs. Her maternal uncle bid and retrieved some of the family items and kept them in his name for her mother's use. Many biographers believe that this incident illustrates why Susan Anthony campaigned for property and civil rights for women all her life. Also, she is said to have refused marriage offers because she believed her energies should be devoted to women's rights, and she remarked several times publicly that she would be no one's property.

Her greatest contribution is agreed to have been her talents for organizing and behind-the-scenes work. She also worked for a time with her lifelong women's rights compatriot **Elizabeth Cady Stanton** as editor/publisher of a woman suffrage paper called *The Revolution*. She credited Stanton with being the force behind much of the rhetoric used in the women's rights movement. She was also a Quaker child who had read much in the tradition of freethinking and of women's equality. According to one biographer, Anthony was particularly taken by a new view of women's lives as depicted by **Charlotte Brontë** and **Elizabeth Barrett Browning** and their characters Jane Eyre and Aurora Leigh. As nineteenth-century characters who refused the denial of personal identity that marriage traditionally required, they provided Anthony with literary models she regarded above "all others" (Barry, 120).

Anthony also used Mary Wollstonecraft's *A Vindication of the Rights of Women* and lauded her efforts in the eighteenth century to address the question of woman's nature. She understood the importance of documentation to women's history and provided, in the early volumes of the history of women's suffrage, original documentation that future historians of the women's movement would utilize. Her willingness to let the documents tell the story may be one day seen as a greater contribution to the women's suffrage movement than those women who might be classed as theorists and writers of the women's enlightenment movement.

ARCHIVES

Susan B. Anthony Memorial Library, Rochester, New York.
Library of Congress, Washington, D.C.
Schlesinger Library, Radcliffe College, Cambridge, Massachusetts.

PRINTED SOURCES

Anthony, Katharine. *Susan B. Anthony: Her Personal History and Her Era* (New York: Doubleday, 1954).
Barry, Kathleen. *Susan B. Anthony: A Biography of a Singular Feminist* (New York: Ballantine, 1988).
Harper, Ida Husted. *The Life and Work of Susan B. Anthony*, 3 vols. (Indianapolis and Kansas City: The Bowen-Merrill Co., 1898–1908).

Ann Mauger Colbert

ARNOLD, MATTHEW (1822–1888). Matthew Arnold was born in Laleham-on-Thames, England, in 1822. He attended Winchester College (1836–1837), then transferred to Rugby (1837–1840), where his father Thomas Arnold, the noted historian and educational reformer, was headmaster. From 1840 to 1844, he attended Balliol College, Oxford, where he took a disappointing Second Class degree. Although the son of an Anglican clergyman, Arnold was not a devoted religious practitioner. Nevertheless, by his own admission, he was influenced by a number of religious thinkers. He began writing poetry as a youngster, publishing his first volume in 1849. He seems to have lost his facility as a poet by the 1850s; nevertheless, his work ranks with that of **Alfred Tennyson** and **Robert Browning** as the best of the Victorian period. Arnold wrote a number of significant prose treatises on education, culture, literature, and religion and was recognized in his own day as one of the principal spokespersons for the importance of morality in both literature and life. Writings such as *Essays in Criticism, Culture and Anarchy, Literature and Dogma,* and *On the Study of Poetry* are recognized as seminal works in shaping attitudes about the role of literature and the significance of culture in determining the value of a community or nation.

Arnold's classical education influenced his outlook on culture. From Greek and Roman sources he borrowed not only the simple style that he praises so highly in "On Translating Homer" (Super, 1:97–116) but also the attitudes of stoicism, optimism, and activism that he celebrates in this essay and in his famous "Preface" to the 1853 volume of his poems (Super, 1:1–15). These characteristics make for great literature because they promote human happiness and perfection. Although he openly professes to value the Greek rather than the

Roman outlook on life, he exhibited a lifelong fascination with the work of the Roman philosopher and poet Titus Lucretius Carus. As early as 1849 he made a note in his diary to "chew Lucretius" (Yale MS), and there is clear evidence that the title character of his poem *Empedocles on Etna* shares affinities with Lucretius as well as with the real-life Empedocles, a Sicilian writer who flourished five centuries before Christ (Murray, 128). From these writers Arnold gleaned an appreciation of the natural world and a sense of sober realism about human nature that served to counterbalance the optimism prevalent among many of Arnold's contemporaries who believed the world was continually progressing toward a Utopian future. The influence of classical authors is evident throughout Arnold's poems. Arnold liked to use classical sources as a means of commenting on modern problems, as he does in his most anthologized poem, "Dover Beach," where the sweeping vision of Sophocles is contrasted with his modern hero's inability to make sense of the fragmented world around him.

The letters and notebooks preserved in collections in England and America provide clear evidence of the dozens of eighteenth- and nineteenth-century men and women who influenced Arnold's ideas about culture. Scattered throughout these are comments praising the ideas of diverse figures such as **William Wordsworth**, **Ralph Waldo Emerson**, Etienne Privert de Senancour, **George Sand**, **Thomas Carlyle**, **John Henry Newman**, and especially **Johann Wolfgang von Goethe**. The last he acknowledges unequivocally as "the clearest, largest, most helpful thinker of modern times." Arnold owned the 60-volume set of Goethe's works, wrote poems dedicated to Goethe, and repeatedly referred to him as "by far our greatest modern man" (Super, 3:110). Able to see through pretext and cant, and to distinguish the worthwhile in modern life from transitory fads, Goethe was for Arnold the quintessential critic of culture.

No less important was the influence of Wordsworth, a family friend with whom the young Matthew visited. Arnold found the simplicity of Wordsworth's style and his celebration of rural life particularly appealing (Murray, 22–23). In 1879, Arnold edited a selection of Wordsworth's poems and published with them an essay outlining Wordsworth's influence as a poet; in an 1872 letter, he cites Wordsworth as one of four people from whom he had learned "habits, methods, ruling ideas, which are constantly with me" (Whitridge, 65–66).

Near the end of his career, Arnold wrote of the excitement he and his fellow collegians had felt at discovering the works of Emerson, Carlyle, and Newman (Super, 10:165). From Newman, Arnold gained what he described as a healthy skepticism for extremist movements in religion (Yale MS). He considered Emerson a "friend and aider of those who would live in the spirit" (Super, 10:177) whose principal merit lay in his ability to spur others to new levels of creativity and understanding. Arnold was also attracted early in life to the "gravity and severity" of Senancour, who was able to make sense of the fragmentation of modern life (Super, 5:295–303). Quotations from George Sand fill Arnold's early notebooks; later in life he wrote that he found her "the most varied and attractive influence" among modern writers (Super, 10:189)—a role similar to the one he attempted to assume throughout his career.

ARCHIVES

Arnold Papers. Balliol College, Oxford. Personal correspondence, manuscripts of poems and essays, notebooks, and books from Arnold's library.

Arnold Papers. Beinecke Library, Yale University, New Haven, Connecticut. Manuscript letters, diaries, notebooks, and other personal papers. Includes Arnold's letters to friend and fellow poet Arthur Hugh Clough.

PRINTED SOURCES

apRoberts, Ruth. *Arnold and God* (Berkeley: University of California Press, 1983). Discusses the sources of Arnold's ideas about religious issues.

Carroll, Joseph. *The Cultural Theory of Matthew Arnold* (Berkeley: University of California Press, 1982). Delineates the major theorists who influenced Arnold's ideas about culture.

DeLaura, David. *Hebrew and Hellene in Victorian England* (Austin: University of Texas Press, 1969).

Honan, Park. *Matthew Arnold: A Life* (New York: McGraw-Hill, 1981).

Lang, Cecil Y. (ed.). *The Letters of Matthew Arnold*, 6 vols. (Charlottesville: University Press of Virginia, 1996—). Not only the most comprehensive collection of Arnold's correspondence but also the best source for identifying the location of letters, manuscripts, and other documents by and about Arnold.

Machann, Clinton. *The Essential Matthew Arnold* (New York: G. K. Hall & Co., 1993). Contains a chapter annotating nearly 100 books, articles, and notes about sources and influences on Arnold's writing.

Murray, Nicholas. *A Life of Matthew Arnold* (New York: St. Martin's Press, 1996).

Super, R. H. (ed.). *The Complete Prose Works of Matthew Arnold*, 11 vols. (Ann Arbor: University of Michigan Press, 1960–1977).

Tinker, C. B., and J. F. Lowry. *The Poetry of Matthew Arnold: A Commentary* (London: Oxford University Press, 1940). Designed to accompany the authors' edition of Arnold's poetry; contains detailed information on sources for individual poems.

Trilling, Lionel. *Matthew Arnold*, rev. ed. (New York: Columbia University Press, 1958).

Whitridge, Arnold (ed.). *Unpublished Letters of Matthew Arnold* (New Haven, CT: Yale University Press, 1923).

Laurence W. Mazzeno

AUDUBON, JOHN JAMES (1785–1851). John James Audubon, painter naturalist, was born out of wedlock in Santo Domingo to his father's mistress and taken to France at age 4; legally adopted by his father's wife, he was allowed to grow up with little formal education. His foster mother, an ardent Roman Catholic, saw to his baptism as he neared the age of 16, and that seems to have been the extent of his religious life.

Audubon was 40 years old when he began in earnest the painting of American birds that would bring him fame, but he had collected eggs, nests, and other artifacts of natural history and had sketched birds from his earliest youth. He was 45 when he began his first serious writing for publication, and that in English, a language not native to him; he also regretted that he had had no formal instruction in French. Although "I have read but Little," he wrote to Reuben Haines, "I have seen a Great deal—in the woods" (25 Dec. 1825, American Philosophical Society). The puzzles of Audubon's career are: How did one who read so little write so well? Why were the bird paintings of this self-trained artist so prized, both by connoisseurs and by ornithologists?

But for his paintings Audubon would have had no need for the prose he produced. He probably started drawing birds life-size because he lacked the skill to reduce them and still keep perspective, but once he decided to publish that size in the double-elephant folio *Birds of America* he set his work apart from that of all others, including the earlier and scientifically more competent Alexander Wilson. Audubon grew so fond of large formats that he once remarked he would paint a whale life-size if he could find the paper for it. His second important innovation was to picture the birds engaged in representative actions, sited against realistic natural backgrounds, in contrast to other competing bird books that presented birds as static specimens. No doubt these resolutions grew out of what Audubon had seen in the woods, but it is also tempting to speculate that something lingered from the brief instruction he had as a boy in the atelier of **Jacques-Louis David**. The pose of David's forceful equestrian **Napoléon** is suggestive of that of Audubon's best-known painting of the wild turkey cock.

Feeling that he needed a narrative to accompany the pictures, Audubon enlisted William MacGillivray as his literary conscience for the composition of *Ornithological Biography*, and a like function was performed by the Rev. John Bachman for the *Viviparous Quadrupeds*. Overseeing all his published prose were the critical eyes of Lucy Audubon, his schoolteacher wife.

ARCHIVES

Audubon's papers are widely scattered. The largest collections are at the American Philosophical Society, Missouri Historical Society, Princeton University, Harvard University, and the Academy of Natural Sciences of Philadelphia.

PRINTED SOURCES

Corning, Howard (ed.). *Letters of John James Audubon, 1826–1840*, 2 vols. (Boston: Club of Odd Volumes, 1930).

Delatte, Carolyn E.. *Lucy Audubon, a Biography* (Baton Rouge: Louisiana State University Press, 1982).

Dorman, James M. (ed.). *Audubon: A Retrospective* (Lafayette: University of Southwestern Louisiana Press, 1990).

Herrick, Francis Hobart. *Audubon the Naturalist: A History of His Life and Time*, 2 vols. (New York: D. Appleton & Co., 1917).

Lindsey, Alton A. (ed.). *The Bicentennial of John James Audubon* (Bloomington: Indiana University Press, 1985).

Charles Boewe

AUSTEN, JANE (1775–1817). Jane Austen was born in Steventon, Hampshire, in 1775 and educated briefly at the Abbey School, Reading (1785–1786). Austen received no other formal education, although as a girl she read English literature and history in the family's private library under the direction of her father, the Reverend George Austen. Reverend Austen also instructed his daughter in an Anglican faith that, by the end of her life, showed signs of Evangelical sympathies. Austen's major novels may be read as critical studies of women's education: Her young female protagonists, most of whom are readers, all struggle to assert their intelligence in a provincial world that devalues them as thinkers. The Abbey School itself comes under fire in *Emma* (1816), satirized as a place where "girls might be sent to be out of the way and scramble themselves into a little education, without any danger of coming back prodigies."

Austen once called herself, with characteristic irony, "the most unlearned, & uninformed Female who ever dared to be an Authoress" (*Letters*, 306). Her reading may have been desultory, but her novels and correspondence reveal a mind deeply and critically engaged with English literary history, if not with classical or foreign literatures. As an Anglican, Austen was immersed from childhood in the King James Bible and the Book of Common Prayer; the rhythms and cadences of these texts may be felt in her own prose style and narrative technique. Austen's letters refer frequently and familiarly to the Augustan tradition of Samuel Johnson, Samuel Richardson, Henry Fielding, Alexander Pope, George Crabbe, **William Cowper**, and Frances Burney; these, with William Shakespeare, are the canonical writers whose imagery and themes most directly shaped her fiction. Austen's shrewd appraisal of these writers may be deduced from the consistent connections she draws between the literary tastes of her characters and their social and moral values.

Austen's literary tastes, as revealed in her letters, also included contemporary women novelists, whom she read and reread, no matter how mediocre. We know, for example, that she read *Clarentine* (1798), a novel by Burney's sister, Sarah Harriet Burney, no fewer than three times, despite the fact that she remembers "liking it much less on a 2^{d} reading than at the 1st" (*Letters*, 120). Austen's own novels, while deeply influenced by her Augustan precursors, are at least as indebted to this domestic fiction by women who are now largely obscured by Austen herself.

ARCHIVES

Gordon N. Ray Collection, Pierpont Morgan Library, New York. Largest single collection of Austen's correspondence.

PRINTED SOURCES

Doody, M. "Jane Austen's Reading." In J. Grey (ed.), *The Jane Austen Companion* (New York: Macmillan, 1986), 347–363. Documentation of references to specific texts in Austen's letters.

Grundy, I. "Jane Austen and Literary Traditions." In E. Copeland and J. McMaster (eds.),

The Cambridge Companion to Jane Austen (Cambridge: Cambridge University Press, 1997), 189–210. Analysis of Austen's reading in relation to her novel writing.

Le Faye, D. *Jane Austen: A Family Record* (London: British Library, 1989). Extensive use of family papers and correspondence.

———— (ed.). *Jane Austen's Letters*, 3rd ed. (Oxford: Oxford University Press, 1995). All extant letters reprinted and annotated.

                                                                    Brian McCuskey

B

BAGEHOT, WALTER (1826–1877). Walter Bagehot was born in 1826 and spent his adult life in Langport, Somersetshire, England. Baptized in the Church of England, Walter also learned of nonconformity from his father, a lifelong Unitarian. Bagehot's biographer, Norman St. John Stevas, credits this unusual religious pair, as well as Bagehot's own "detached intelligence," with preventing him from becoming a dogmatist (Stevas, *Walter Bagehot*). Bagehot's formal education began with Bristol College in 1839 and continued at University College, London, in 1842. He was called to the bar in 1848 but chose not to practice. Instead, in 1851, he went to Paris, where he observed **Louis-Napoléon's (Napoléon III's)** successful coup. He returned to Langport, where he joined the family bank, a profession that afforded him time to write. In 1855, Bagehot and lifelong friend R. H. Hutton founded the *National Review* and coedited the journal until its demise in 1864. In 1857 he became friendly with James Wilson, founder of *The Economist*, also meeting Wilson's daughter, Eliza, whom he married a year later. Upon Wilson's death in 1860, Bagehot became editor of *The Economist*, a position he held until his death in 1877. Editing the journal by himself, contributing at least two articles a week, Bagehot still found time to write several books on diverse subjects like the English constitution and on London's financial system. A keen observer, Bagehot is hailed as one of the luminaries of the mid-Victorian period.

It is not easy to discern the influences on Walter Bagehot's thinking and writing. There is little doubt that young Walter was influenced by his father, Thomas, and we can point to several teachers, such as Dr. James Cowles Pritchard, a famous ethnologist, or George Long, his university professor of ancient languages, whose knowledge and teaching contributed to Bagehot's own critical mind-set. Bagehot also spent time reading both novels and nonfiction; one of his favorite authors was historical fiction writer Sir **Walter Scott**.

G. M. Young, once called Walter Bagehot the "greatest Victorian" because

he seemed the best his age had to offer. Bagehot himself highlighted the influences of his age in his book on the English constitution, which he considered
the greatest document not written. His literary and historical essays expounded
upon the great English writers, poets, and historians. Having read these men, he
considered them most important to understanding the Britain of his day.

In the end, it is not possible to pinpoint one or two literary, philosophical, or
historical influences on Bagehot. Rather, he is the sum and the extension of
what he read, considered, and observed. For example, Bagehot argued in *Physics
and Politics* that early government was created to make society conform to
certain fixed habits, customs, and rules that would subdue arbitrary personal
caprice. This would seem to be a direct Hobbesian line, but there is no doubt
that Bagehot was also influenced by John Locke and Edmund Burke, the latter
the prototypical conservative and the former, an early liberal. His economic
thought was very much influenced by **David Ricardo**, the early nineteenth-
century economist. In many ways, he is the culmination of the scientific thinker,
but with the benefit of little restriction and greater availability of knowledge.

ARCHIVES

No large collection exists. According to Buchan, "Bagehot was a careless man who did
not bother to keep the letters of his friends or copies of letters which he wrote to them"
(p. 11). See also the National Register of Archives for holding.

PRINTED SOURCES

Barrington, Emilie. *Life of Walter Bagehot* (London: Longmans, Green and Co., 1914).
Buchan, Alistair. *The Spare Chancellor: The Life of Walter Bagehot* (London: Chatto
    and Windus, 1959).
Orel, Harold. *Victorian Literary Critics* (New York: St. Martin's Press, 1984).
Sisson, C. H. *The Case of Walter Bagehot* (London: Faber and Faber, 1972).
Stevas, Norman St. John. *Walter Bagehot* (London: Longman, Green & Co., 1963).
————. (ed.). *The Collected Works of Walter Bagehot*, 8 vols. (Cambridge, Mass.: Har-
    vard University Press, 1965).
Sullivan, Harry. *Walter Bagehot* (Boston: Twayne Publisher/G. K. Hall and Co., 1975).
Young, G. M. "The Greatest Victorian." In *Today and Yesterday: Collected Essays and
    Addresses* (London: R. Hart Davis, 1948).

Phyllis L. Soybel

BAKUNIN, MIKHAIL ALEKSANDROVICH (1814–1876). Mikhail Aleksandrovich Bakunin, anarchist theorist, was born into a noble family with liberal
political inclinations on the estate of Premukhino near Torshok in the Russian
province of Tver. The boy Bakunin was educated under the direction of his
father, a disciple of Jean-Jacques Rousseau (1712–1778). Bakunin's father had
been in Paris during the French Revolution and took a doctorate in philosophy
from the University of Padua. Cousins of Bakunin's mother had taken part in
the 1825 Constitutionalist uprising, regarded by some as the first modern Russian revolution.

When he came of age, Bakunin was sent to Artillery School—favored by the aristocracy—in St. Petersburg. He soon developed an interest in philosophy, and in 1835 he obtained a discharge to study in Moscow. At first, Bakunin was attracted to the work of **Johann Gottlieb Fichte** (1762–1814), whose work he translated for Vissarion Belinsky's magazine *The Telescope*. Soon, however, Bakunin joined the circle centered around Nicholas Stankevich, and his interest shifted to **Georg Hegel** (1770–1831), whose work he later called "the algebra of revolution." Bakunin's Hegelianism was at this time still conservative, and he worked to challenge the left-wing thought of **Aleksandr Ivanovich Herzen** (1812–1870), **Claude Henri de Rouvroy, duc de Saint-Simon** (1760–1825), and **Pierre-Joseph Proudhon** (1809–1865).

Granted permission to travel to Germany in 1840, beginning in 1841 he pursued his philosophical studies in Berlin, Dresden, and Leipzig. Bakunin attended the Berlin salon of **Ivan Turgenev** (1818–1883), heard lectures by **Friedrich Wilhelm Joseph von Schelling** (1775–1854), and was instructed by Professor Werder. In 1842, Bakunin moved to Dresden and through Arnold Ruge became affiliated with the circle of materialistic and left-leaning Young Hegelians, who included **Ludwig Feuerbach** (1804–1872) and **David Friedrich Strauss** (1808–1874). Bakunin began reading Lorenz von Stein's writings on **Charles Fourier** (1772–1837) and became converted to a left-wing Hegelianism.

Moving to Switzerland, he came under the influence of revolutionary communist Wilhelm Weitling, Afterwards, he moved to Paris, where he associated with **Karl Marx** (1818–1883), **George Sand** (1804–1876), Hugues Félicité Robert de Lamennais (1782–1854), and Proudhon, whose influence was particularly profound.

Bakunin's pan-Slavism at this time distanced him from Marx. He took part in the Prague revolt of 1848, the insurrectionist government in Saxony, and the Dresden uprising of 1849, where he was captured, convicted, and sentenced to death. He escaped to Austria, was captured, and sentenced to death again. He was instead deported to Russia, where he was held at the Petropavlosky Fortress and exiled to Siberia, from which he escaped in 1861 to Japan, to the United States, and finally to western Europe. With Herzen, he published *Kolokol* and was in 1872 expelled from the Congress of the *Internationale* in The Hague. He took part in revolts in Lyons (1870) and Bologna (1874) and died in Bern. His work also shows the influence of **Comte** and **Darwin**.

ARCHIVES

Archives Bakounine, Internationaal Instituut voor Sociale Geschiedenis, Amsterdam; published in facsimile by A. Lehning (Leiden: E. J. Brill, 1961–); seven of eight volumes complete to date. Guillaume, J. (ed.) *Oeuvres*, 6 vols. (Paris: Stock, 1895–1914).

PRINTED SOURCES

Caff, E. H. *Michael Bakunin* (London: Macmillan & Co., Ltd., 1937; 2nd ed., 1975; Vintage ed., 1961).

Kelly, A. *Mikhail Bakunin: A Study in the Psychology and Politics of Utopianism* (Oxford: Clarendon Press, 1982). Focuses on the influence of idealist philosophy on Bakunin.

Masters, Anthony. *Bakunin: The Father of Anarchism* (New York: Saturday Review Press/E. P. Dutton, 1974).

Peter S. Fosl

BALZAC, HONORÉ DE (1799–1850). Honoré de Balzac was a native of Tours. Despite his claims to nobility, his father was a middle-class employee of the Military Commissariat. He was educated at Tours' Le Guay school, then at the collège of Vendôme, and later at Paris' Ganser School. He studied law to become a solicitor but abandoned the legal field to write, producing mediocre librettos, tragedies (*Cromwell*), and run-of-the-mill historical novels published under various pseudonyms (Auguste Lepoitevin, Lord R'Hoone, Horace de Saint-Aubin). Engaged in business ventures that put him in debt for the rest of his life, he wrote his first major novel *Le Dernier Chouan ou la Bretagne en 1800* (published in 1829). The first novel published under the name "Honoré de Balzac," *El Verdugo*, came the following year. Thus was inaugurated a long series of novels and novellas (up to four per year) that made Balzac one of the most prolific writers of his time and an internationally recognized artist as early as 1831. The novels published (often as serials) between 1835 and 1840 (*Le Père Goriot*, *Le Colonel Chabert*, *Le Lys dans la vallée*, *Illusions perdues*) are thought to be his finest.

In 1839, upon his election as president of the influential Société des gens de lettres, Balzac began developing the concept of a novelistic cycle featuring recurrent characters and loosely interconnected plots. His drama and *Revue parisienne* encountering little success, he concentrated on fiction, signing a contract in 1841 with the publishing house of Frune, Durocher, Hetzel, and Paulin, who agreed to publish his complete works. Officially titled *La Comédie Humaine*, it should have included 125 volumes, of which only 94 were completed. Constantly trying to replenish his creative energy, he crisscrossed Europe, publishing more major novels between 1846 and 1848 (*La Cousine Bette*, *Le Cousin Pons*, *Splendeur et misère des courtisanes*). He married his longtime paramour, Polish countess Eva Hanska in March 1850 but, in a state of complete exhaustion, returned to Paris to die. One of his last visitors was **Victor Hugo**.

In the foreword to the *Comédie*'s first edition (1842), Balzac clearly delineated his artistic objectives and methodology. Asserting his intention to become "society's secretary" (*Avant-propos*), he intended to establish an inventory of human archetypes not unlike Georges-Louis de Buffon's catalog of animal species. He planned to divide his work in three parts, "Studies in Mores," "Philosophical Studies," and "Analytical Studies," covering areas as diverse as provincial life, country life, or military life. Viewing the Revolution as a catastrophe, he depicted French society of the 1820s to 1840s as a stage for permanent economic litigiousness and continuous political, familial, or psychological antagonism whose only chance for pacification was a return to Royalism and Catholicism. Sometimes categorized as a pre-Realist, he was perhaps closer to **Émile Zola**'s naturalism, while the term "idealism" has also been applied to his highly stylized rendition of reality. His fastidious descriptions and the psychological depth of his characters were said to influence generations of writer nationally (Hugo, **Gustave Flaubert**, Marcel Proust) as well as internationally (**Lev Tolstoy, Henry James**).

ARCHIVES

Archives Nationales, Bibliothèque Nationale de France, Paris.

PRINTED SOURCES

Barbéris, P. *Mythes balzaciens* (Paris: A. Colin, 1972).
Maurois, A. *Prométhée ou la vie de Balzac* (Paris: Hachette, 1965).
McCarthy, M. S. *Balzac and His Reader: A Study of the Creation of Meaning in* La Comédie humaine (Columbia: University of Missouri Press, 1982).
Robb, G. *Balzac: A Life* (New York: Norton, 1994).
Troyat, H. *Balzac* (Paris: Flammarion, 1995).

Laurent Ditmann

BARRÈS, AUGUSTE-MAURICE (1862–1923). Auguste-Maurice Barrès was born in 1862 in the Lorraine village of Charmes-sur-Moselle and educated at the lycée in Nancy from 1877 to 1880; he studied law at the University of Nancy in 1881.

Barrès as a novelist was a forerunner of modernism. He broke with the prevailing conventions of the realist and naturalist schools by emphasizing subjectivism and rejecting bourgeois positivist claims of moral and ideological authority. He was wildly popular in his day and dubbed the "Prince of Youth"; yet today there is not a single one of his novels available in print in English. The other notable aspect of his career, which is played out fully in his written work, was his political activity, which commenced as a leftist supporter of General Boulanger; but as his career advanced, he turned increasingly toward right-wing advocacy of integral nationalism. In current literature, Barrès is often portrayed as a precursor of French fascism.

Barrès's affinity for writing and literature was evident early on. He experienced only moderate success as a student, yet despite the lack of application to his studies he managed to broadly canvas contemporary French literature. Even as a youth he was conversant with the works of **Gustave Flaubert**, Pierre Charles Baudelaire, **Victor Hugo, Hippolyte Taine**, and **Joseph-Ernest Renan**. Outside of books, Barrès's first major intellectual influence was Auguste Burdeau, philosophy professor at the Nancy lycée in 1879 (Sirinelli, 91–92). Barrès was less attached to Burdeau's ideas, which in his novel *Les Deracines* he vehemently rejected, than in the force of his personality. Throughout all of his written work there is a consistent effort to engage philosophical themes.

On arrival in Paris in 1882 he frequented the literary circles of both **Émile Zola** and J. K. Huysmans, yet spurned their respective naturalist and decadent schools on the premise that they were not sufficiently original and were destined for exhaustion. The extreme individualism of Barrès's first trilogy of novels, *Culte de moi* (1888–1901), indicates an attempt to carve out an independent identity against reigning schools of thought. Barrès's obsession with the cultivation of the inner self drew from a mélange of sources including Baudelaire, **Schopenhauer**, **Fichte**, and Hartmann. The one consistent influence was Paul Bourget, critic and novelist, who served the roles of mentor and especial adviser on question of style (Bompaire-Evesque, 224–245).

Barrès's second trilogy, *Le Roman de l'energie nationale* (1897–1902), coincided with his entry into politics and opened up an entire new topography of thematic content. Initially he voiced Proudhonian socialist and federalist ideas, yet with the advent of the Dreyfus Affair, he turned sharply to the Right and adopted an outspoken nationalist plank (Sonn, 59–60). Barrès's blood and soil ideology was pieced together from a broad variety of sources, but he was particularly beholden to the scientific racism prescribed by Sorbonne Professor of Physiology Jules Soury (Sternhell, 251–266). Although Barrès employed the discourse of natural science, his aim was to undermine the materialism and abstract rationalism of the despised Third Republic.

His later writings remain faithful to the nationalist creed, yet they are somewhat moderated by a renewed interest in Catholicism and mystical spirituality. Barrès never accepted the dogma of the Church, but he clearly recognized the need for a transcendent authority. With the outbreak of World War I, Barrès further tempered his attacks on the Republic and was a vigorous propagandist against German aggression. At his death in 1923 Barrès was a respected member of the establishment.

ARCHIVES

Barrès Papers and Correspondence, Département des Manuscrits de la Bibliothèque Nationale, Paris.

PRINTED SOURCES

Barrès, M. *Mes cahiers 1896–1923* (Paris: Plon, 1993). Reprint and abridgement of Barrès's diaries. The original 14-volume edition is available to subscribers of the ARTFL database at http://humanities.uchicago.edu/ARTFL/ARTFL.html
Bompaire-Evesque, C. "Paul Bourget collaborateur de Maurice Barrès," *Revue d'Histoire Littéraire de la France*, 92, 2 (1992): 224–245.
Broche, F. *Maurice Barrès* (Paris: J.C. Lattés, 1987). The most recent and comprehensive biography of Barrès.
Doty, C. *From Cultural Rebellion to Counterrevolution: The Politics of Maurice Barrès* (Athens: Ohio University Press, 1976).
Sirinelli, J. "Littérature et politique: le cas Burdeau-Boutellier," *Revue Historique*, 272 (1984): 91–111.

Sonn, R. "The Early Political Career of Maurice Barrès: Anarchist, Socialist or Proto-fascist?" *Clio*, 21, 1 (1991): 41–60.

Soucy, R. *Fascism in France: The Case of Maurice Barrès* (Berkeley: University of California Press, 1972).

Sternhell, Z. *Maurice Barrès et le Nationalism Français* (Paris: Armand Colin, 1972). Consistently controversial but the most probing examination of Barrès's ideology.

James Millhorn

BARRY, CHARLES (1795–1860). Sir Charles Barry was born in London in 1795 and educated at various private schools until articled to Lambeth surveyors Middleton and Bailey at 15. Largely self-trained as an architect, Barry traveled extensively on the Continent and in the Levant from 1817 until 1820, all the time making extensive architectural sketches. During his return journey he met J.(ohn) L.(ewis) Wolfe (1798–1881), with whom he began a study of Renaissance architecture that was to become a hallmark of his style. Soon after, Barry began a small practice in Holborn. Barry found himself out of step with the more spectacular aspects of the Gothic Revival, believing that this style belonged more to institutions of the past than the present. Turning to Italianate design, and thereby sacrificing many possible ecclesiastical commissions, Barry completed significant buildings such as the Traveller's Club (1830–1832) and the Reform Club (1838–1841). In 1836, he won the prestigious award to build the new Houses of Parliament. Although ornamentally Gothic, Barry's design imposed a classical discipline on the form of the new buildings. From 1841 onwards, until his unexpected death in 1860, Barry spent most of his remaining career supervising construction of the Houses. For his work, the Queen conferred a knighthood in 1852. He is buried in Westminster Abbey.

Tracing the literary influences on Barry, and particularly his architectural designs, is made difficult by a lack of notations about what little reading he seems to have done. He had, according to his son, "little advantage of education" and "carried away from it little except a superficial knowledge of English, a good proficiency in arithmetic, and a remarkably beautiful handwriting" (Barry, 5). He was familiar with Stuart and Revett's *Antiquities of Athens*, as one of his traveling companions in Greece and Turkey included William Kinnard (ca. 1788–1839), who was compiling information for a supplementary volume of this great work. Barry no doubt knew the classical canon, although the archives give us no detailed information about this. During his travels from 1817 until 1820, Barry kept a diary, mostly filled with extensive technical notes about buildings that he saw. These notebooks, however, indicate an early interest in the theater, making specific reference to plays by Molière (Journals, RIBA), but these can hardly be said to have influenced Barry's work. Barry states that he purchased foreign plays and read foreign newspapers, although this was more directed at mastering French and Italian than acquiring information or indulging a love of literature.

Barry thrived on long hours of intense work and during his adult life had few interests beyond architecture. His son claimed that Barry was no great letter writer and that he would often listen to reading without allowing this activity to disrupt his main stream of thought. Barry's papers at the Royal Institute of British Architects offer scant information about his reading habits, and his stylistic ideas seem to have come not from any discernible literary source but from the study of the buildings themselves. His later years were spent absorbed in the difficulties surrounding the construction of the Houses of Parliament, one of the greatest works of the nineteenth century, which in the end left him little time for other activities.

ARCHIVES

Barry Journals and Notebooks 1809–1894, Royal Institute of British Architects. Primary collection of archival sources related to Barry. A wide range of material including office out-letter books, some personal correspondence, diaries, miscellaneous papers, and biographical notes.
Barry Journal 1817–1820, RIBA. Diaries from travels supplemented by sketchbooks. Extracts in Adkins below.
Wolfe, J. L., Notebooks and Sketchbooks, RIBA. Includes a biographical sketch on Barry.

PRINTED SOURCES

Adkins, K. *Personal and Historical Extracts from the Travel Diaries (1817–1820) of Sir Charles Barry* (Privately published, 1986). Useful extracts omitting much technical architectural detail.
Barry, A. *The Life and Works of Sir Charles Barry* (London: John Murray, 1867). Informative and useful but regrettably still the only full-scale biography, a lacuna in the literature that ought to be corrected.
Colvin, H. *A Biographical Dictionary of British Architects, 1600–1840*, 3rd ed. (New Haven, Conn.: Yale University Press, 1995). See entries for Sir Charles Barry, William Kinnard, and J. L. Wolfe.

Stephen G. Hague

BAUER, BRUNO (1809–1882). Bruno Bauer was born in Eisenberg, Thuringia, in 1809. He attended Charlottenburg schools and studied theology at the Friedrich Wilhelm Gymnasium in Berlin until 1828, then philosophy under **Georg Wilhelm Friedrich Hegel**, art history under Heinrich Gustav Hotho, and theology under Philipp Konrad Marheineke, **Friedrich Schleiermacher**, Johann August Wilhelm Neander, and Ernst Wilhelm Hengstenberg at Berlin (1828–1834). He won a royal prize in philosophy with an essay on Immanuel Kant's aesthetics (1829), and was esteemed in the 1830s as a rising conservative theologian. Bauer sided with Hengstenberg against Schleiermacher and was Privatdozent for theology at Berlin (1834–1839), then at Bonn (1839–1842). He ghost-edited the second edition of Hegel's *Philosophie der Religion* for Marheineke. Bauer was a radical theologian, an outspoken atheist, and an underground revolutionary from the late 1830s to 1848. In 1842, he was fired and forbidden to teach. Bauer stood aloof from the 1848 revolutions; and after 1848, he was a conservative political publicist and fierce anti-Semite.

Bauer's orthodox approach to Christianity began to shift rapidly when he read and reviewed **David Friedrich Strauss**'s *Das Leben Jesu* (1835–1836). Even though he attacked Strauss from the Right, as August Tholuck and other conservative theologians who had chosen him to write the review expected, by the early 1840s he was attacking Strauss from the Left. The fact that Strauss had cogently used Hegelian methods to criticize the Bible made a deep impression on Bauer, who then experimented with similar methods to create even more extensive critiques of religion in general, Christianity in particular, and the sociohistorical movements and forces that emerge from them. His own results radicalized him and turned him in just a few years from Hengstenberg's darling boy to persona non grata.

Bauer, the main target of **Karl Marx**'s and **Friedrich Engels**'s satire in *Die heilige Familie* (1845), was the most influential Young Hegelian during the short life of that movement. He and Arnold Ruge together were considered its leaders, Bruno's brother Edgar was its anarchist firebrand, and brother Egbert was one of its publishers. His influence evaporated after the 1848 revolutions and has never recovered. Nevertheless, indirectly, partially through **Nietzsche**, he has had some effect on the way theology, biblical criticism, and religious education are conducted today.

ARCHIVES

International Instituut voor Sociale Geschiedenis, Amsterdam. Correspondence, papers, manuscripts.

PRINTED SOURCES

Barnikol, Ernst. *Bruno Bauer: Studien und Materialien* (Assen: Van Gorcum, 1972).
————. *Das entdeckte Christentum im Vormärz* (Jena: Diederichs, 1927).
Brazill, William J. *The Young Hegelians* (New Haven, Conn.: Yale University Press, 1970).
Briefwechsel zwischen Bruno Bauer und Edgar Bauer während der Jahre 1839–1842 aus Bonn und Berlin (Charlottenburg: Egbert Bauer, 1844).
Hertz-Eichenrode, Dieter. *Der junghegelianer Bruno Bauer im Vormärz* (Berlin: Reuter, 1959).
Kegel, Martin. *Bruno Bauers Übergang von der hegelschen Rechten zum Radikalismus* (Leipzig: Quelle & Meyer, 1908).
Sass, Hans-Martin. "Nachwort." In Bruno Bauer, *Feldzüge der reinen Kritik* (Frankfurt: Suhrkamp, 1968).
Stepelevich, Lawrence S. "Translator's Introduction." In Bruno Bauer, *The Trumpet of the Last Judgement against Hegel the Atheist and Antichrist* (Lewiston, N.Y.: Mellen, 1989).
Toews, John Edward. *Hegelianism: The Path toward Dialectical Humanism, 1805–1841* (Cambridge: Cambridge University Press, 1980).

Eric v. d. Luft

BEARDSLEY, AUBREY VINCENT (1872–1898). Aubrey Vincent Beardsley, son of Vincent Paul and Ellen Pitt Beardsley, was born in Brighton in 1872 and educated at Hamilton Lodge, Brighton (1878–1881) and Brighton Grammar School (1885–1888). Beardsley converted to Roman Catholicism in March 1897. His correspondence cites Richard Challenor's *Garden of the Soul* and Crétineau's *Histoire de la Compagnie de Jésus* as influences just prior to his conversion. In 1897 Beardsley concluded, "If Heine is the great warning, Pascal is the great example to all artists and thinkers. He understood that, to become a Christian, a man of letters must sacrifice his gifts" (Maas *Letters*, 249).

At the age of 10, Beardsley was already earning money by drawing dinner placecards that featured characters taken from **Dickens**'s *Hard Times* (Weintraub, *Beardsley: A Biography*, 22).

While at Brighton Grammar School, Beardsley read widely, encouraged by his housemaster, A. W. King (1855–1922). His favorite playwrights were William Congreve and William Wycherley, and though he preferred drama over other genres, he also read **Carlyle**'s *The French Revolution*, Boccaccio's *Decameron*, Thomas Chatterton's works, as well as **Edgar Allan Poe**'s verses and *Tales of Mystery and Imagination* (Weintraub, *Beardsley: A Biography*, 26). Notable among his school reading were Thomas Hood's "Mary's Ghost," the skating scene from Dickens's *Pickwick Papers*, and **Edward Bulwer-Lytton**'s *Eugene Aram*.

Beardsley did not find British realism wholly convincing—"Realism—so-called—does not seem to flourish on British soil" (Maas, *Letters*, 30)—preferring French naturalism, admiring both **Émile Zola**'s novels and his "reputation of being a good bourgeois with no need to be reticent about his tastes." **Stendhal**'s *Le Rouge et Le Noir* he called "an adorable little book" (Maas, *Letters*, 179), and he records "infinite pleasure" (Maas, *Letters*, 242) in rereading Voltaire's *La Pucelle* and "that Catulle Mendès is a great favourite of mine" (Maas, *Letters*, 197).

Beardsley illustrated **Nathaniel Hawthorne**'s *Classic Tales*, Fanny Burney's *Evelina*, and Henry Mackenzie's *A Man of Feeling*, **Robert Browning**'s *The Pied Piper*, Lucian's *Vera Historia*, Poe's *Tales of Mystery and Imagination*, and in some detail, **Oscar Wilde**'s *Salomé*, Sir Thomas Malory's *Morte d' Arthur*, Ben Jonson's *Volpone*, Alexander Pope's *The Rape of the Lock*, and Aristophanes's *Lysistrata*; so it is fair to assume that he was familiar with these texts.

He also translated the *Carmen CI* of Catullus and Juvenal's *Sixth Satire*, which he did not finish. In 1894 his correspondence records that Browning and George Meredith "mean more than much to me just now" (Maas, *Letters*, 71). Beardsley read contemporary literature as diverse as the novels of Grant Allen (for example, *The British Barbarians*) and John Gray's *Spiritual Poems*, which "fairly delighted" him (Maas, *Letters*, 141).

The Story of Venus and Tannhäuser, which he never finished, owes something to Beardsley's reading of the "three-volume Rabelais" that he ordered his publisher to destroy six weeks before his death (Maas, *Letters*, 432).

ARCHIVES

Beardsley papers, Bodleian Library. Principal correspondence. Other papers can be found at Princeton University Library; Henry E. Huntington Library, San Marino, California; Humanities Research Center, University of Texas at Austin; Reading University Library; British Library; Rosenwald Collection, National Gallery of Art, Washington; Brotherton Collection, Brotherton Library, University of Leeds; William Andrews Clark Memorial Library, University of California; Berg Collection, New York Public Library; University of Cambridge Library.

PRINTED SOURCES

Maas, Henry, J. L. Duncan, and W. G. Good (eds.). *The Letters of Aubrey Beardsley* (London: Cassell and Co., Ltd, 1897) (also Deddington, Oxford: Plantin Publishers 1990—references from this edition).

Reade, Brian. *Aubrey Beardsley* (London: Victoria & Albert Museum large picture book no. 32, 1966).

Walker, R. A. (ed.). *Letters from Aubrey Beardsley to Leonard Smithers* (London: First Edition Club, 1937).

Weintraub, Stanley. *Aubrey Beardsley, Imp of the Perverse* (University Park: Pennsylvania State University Press, 1976).

———. *Beardsley: A Biography* (London: W. H. Allen, 1967).

Caroline Dowson

BEBEL, AUGUST (1840–1913). August Bebel, socialist leader and author of *Unsere Ziele* (1870), *Der Delutsche Bauerukrieg* (1876), *Die Frau und die Sozialismus* (1883), and *Christentum und Sozialismus* (1892), was born in Deutz-Köln in 1840 to a military family; he died in Passugg, Switzerland, in 1913. In 1843, his father died, and the following year his mother married his father's brother, also named August Bebel, who treated the children severely, subjecting them to frequent beatings. The new family settled in Brauweiler, near Köln, where Bebel's stepfather worked as a warden at a juvenile reformatory and where young Bebel began his education at the village school. After his stepfather's death in 1846, the family moved once again, this time to Wetzlar in the Lahn valley. There Bebel entered the Poor Law School. In school Bebel excelled, though he earned the reputation of a moral reprobate for his challenges to religious authority. He was especially fond of mathematics. Bebel seems to have been influenced by the peasant revolts he witnessed around Wetzlar at this time. At home he began reading German history and romantic adventure novels. He also read **Harriet Beecher Stowe**'s *Uncle Tom's Cabin* (1851).

After his mother's death in 1853 and his graduation from school in 1854, Bebel worked as a lathe turner. In his memoir *Aus meinem Leben* (1910–1914), Bebel mentions the influence that a remark of St. Ambrose had on him at this time: "Nature gives all goods to all men in common; for God has created all things so that all men may enjoy them in common. Thus it was Nature that gave the right to common enjoyment, while it was unjust usurpation that originated the rights of property."

Bebel traveled across middle Europe, settling in Leipzig, where he joined a "Worker's Improvement Society" and became acquainted with revolutionary politics.

Bebel became deeply influenced by the work of **Ferdinand Lassalle** (1825–1864), **Karl Marx** (1818–1883), **Friedrich Engels** (1820–1895), and the various left-wing newspapers published at the time. Lassalle's *Manifesto* of 1863 was of particular consequence. Bebel followed closely the work and actions produced by figures such as **Wilhelm Liebknecht** in German left-wing political organizations.

Bebel was elected to the Reichstag, serving from 1867 to 1870, when he was imprisoned on a sentence that would hold him until 1878; after his release he resumed his public political work. Bebel's interest in the issue of women may be rooted in his 1865 attendance in Leipzig at the first German Women's Congress.

ARCHIVES

Internationales Institut für Sozialgeschichte, Amsterdam.

PRINTED SOURCES

Bebel, August. *Ausgewählte Reden und Schriften*, Horst Bartel, Rolf Dlubek, and Heinrich Gemkow (eds.) (Berlin: Dietz Verlag, 1970).
———. *My Life* (Chicago: University of Chicago Press, 1912).
Hirsch, Helmut. *August Bebel—Sein Leben in Dokumenten, Reden und Schriften* (Koln: Kiepenheuer & Witsch, 1968).

Peter S. Fosl

BENTHAM, JEREMY (1748–1832). Jeremy Bentham was the founder of utilitarianism, the ethical philosophy based on the "greatest happiness" or "utility" principle. For utilitarians, the morally good action is the one that promotes "the greatest happiness for the greatest number," with *happiness* defined as a surplus of pleasure over pain. Bentham's means of determining the optimally pleasurable act was his "felicific calculus," an analysis of the quantity of pleasure inherent in any activity. This quintessentially rationalistic system has drawn criticism, not least because of its dependence on our ability to measure and predict emotional reactions. Nevertheless, it remains an influential doctrine to this day, particularly in the Anglo-American world.

In his own times, Bentham was known as a philosophical radical, partly because when he applied his calculus to political and legal institutions in his native Britain, he frequently found them wanting. Like many Enlightenment-inspired thinkers, Bentham sought to sweep away irrational traditions and forms, in favor of a coherent system founded on reason, and he touted his utilitarian doctrine as the ultimate rationalist measuring stick. Although Bentham's influence on the spate of reforms in 1830s and 1840s Britain has been exaggerated by many scholars since, he was prominent in radical circles during his life and exercised a strong influence on **John Stuart Mill**, the son of his protégé **James Mill**.

Bentham's intellectual development was precocious. The son of a lawyer, he began studying Latin at age three and later went on to Queen's College, Oxford, to prepare for a legal career. Although he later decided not to practice law, reform of the legal code and penal system were, for him, a lifetime interest that can perhaps be traced to his legal education. More than anything else, Bentham was a child of the Enlightenment. He shared the enthusiasm for science and deep faith in reason held by many other writers at that time, even studying physics for a time at Oxford in the early 1760s. His enthusiasm for Newton's works prompted him to try to uncover scientific laws in the realm of human behavior.

Bentham combined contemporary ideas of science with those of human psychology to continue the line of argument taken up by Aristotle in the *Nicomachean Ethics*, the classic statement of teleological ethics, aimed at happiness. The crucial years for the development of Bentham's utilitarian philosophy came in the late 1760s. In 1768, Bentham was said to have cried "Eureka!" when he read the words "the greatest good for the greatest number" in the *Essay on the First Principles of Government*, written by the radical English writer Joseph Priestly that same year. Several standard Enlightenment texts added further clarification and intellectual heft to Bentham's nascent philosophy. In 1769 Bentham recalled that Montesquieu, Barrington, Beccaria, and Helvétius influenced his development of the principle of utility. The last two may be regarded as the most influential of the four in the development of Bentham's thought. In *An Essay on Crimes and Punishments* (1764), Cesare Bonesana, Marchese di Beccaria's attempt to create a more rational and socially beneficial penal system foreshadowed many of Bentham's later efforts, as did his emphasis on happiness as the appropriate end of legislation. Likewise, Claude Adrien Helvétius's account of psychology in *Of the Mind* (1758) led Bentham to think of happiness in terms of maximized pleasure and minimized pain and to see these feelings as capable of measurement in human sensory experience (Everett, 46–50).

David Hume also had a pronounced impact on Bentham. Hume had drawn conclusions very similar to Bentham's in his *Treatise of Human Nature* (1739–1740), when he associated virtue with "agreeable" impressions on the mind and vice with "uneasy" ones. Likewise, Hume's critique of Lockean natural rights philosophy certainly influenced Bentham's own characterization of that doctrine as "nonsense upon stilts." Hume's strictures on the limits of reason made less of an impression, however, which again demonstrates the expansive account of reason's powers that lay at the heart of Bentham's philosophy.

ARCHIVES

Bentham Manuscripts, University College, London.

PRINTED SOURCES

Bowring, John (ed.). *The Works of Jeremy Bentham* (1838–1843; reprint, New York: Russell and Russell, 1962).
Everett, C. W. *The Education of Jeremy Bentham* (New York: Columbia University Press, 1931).
Hart, H.L.A. *Essays on Bentham: Studies in Jurisprudence and Political Theory* (London: Oxford University Press, 1982).

Christopher Pepus

BEYLE, MARIE-HENRI. *See* **Stendhal**.

BISMARCK, OTTO VON (1815–1898). Otto von Bismarck left an indelible mark on European politics and society between 1860 and 1890. Not only did Bismarck play a critical role in the restatement of German nationalism and the formation of the new German state during this time, but he also dominated European politics via his diplomatic network of interconnected alliances in central and eastern Europe. In the process, Bismarck epitomized the post–1848 German fusion of conservative realism and the belief in state power and their role as the arbiters of human progress.

Intellectually, Bismarck never deviated from the conservative roots of his Prussian origins. He viewed himself as pragmatic and a realist and was suspicious, even distrustful, of those things that were not rooted in the Prussian soil. In addition, Bismarck strongly identified with the individualistic and self-reliant autocratic spirit that was free of restraints and whose function was to impose the beneficial values of the land upon emerging historical events. For Bismarck, then, the German state that he forged after 1860 best suited these values. But the land was not the only influence that shaped Bismarck's intellectual development. Romanticism and German Protestant thought also proved significant contributors as well.

Like many significant figures of the nineteenth century, Bismarck's attitudes were the product of experiential rather than literary influences. Although he participated in the philosophical transformation of the 1830s and 1840s that criticized the artificiality of German idealism, Bismarck never accepted the new abstract rationalism that emerged from this intellectual tumult. From Bismarck's perspective, philosophic abstractions were unrealistic and thus ran counter to his conservative pragmatism. Reality, he argued, was derived from revelation, not reason, and he utilized the writings of Spinoza and **Friedrich Schleiermacher**, an early nineteenth-century German philosopher and theologian, to affirm this view in his own mind. Still, Bismarck did read the literature of his time despite his professed lack of scholarly intent. He was therefore familiar with the works of Shakespeare, **Goethe**, and **Byron** as well as contemporary writers such as

Nikolaus Lenau, Adelbert von Chamisso, Ludwig Uhland, Freidrich Rückert, Pierre Jean de Béranger, Louis Blanc, and **Heinrich Heine**. Even Voltaire, **Hegel**, and the Young Hegelians were examined with some interest. In the end, however, Bismarck rejected them as too artificial or too idealistic.

Having intellectually refuted rationalism, Bismarck sought to establish his own perception of political reality. To accomplish this, Bismarck combined his sense of Prussian nobleness, his ideas of the Christian state, and his deeply rooted conservative experience. On the one hand, he lionized the uniqueness of the individual as well as the ability of the individual to act heroically and independently to create (reveal) a new and beneficial reality. At the same time, Bismarck argued that all institutions, including the state, were concrete, immutable entities and established by God, not man. Thus the state was an integral part of the divine natural order (reality) and demanded the obedience of all subject to its authority. In this way, Bismarck not only defined his role as the founder of the new German state but also legitimized the organization of his international state system. Contributing to the distillation of these attitudes was the influence of the historian Arnold Heeren, whose *History of the European System and Its Colonies* (1809) attracted the young Bismarck while still a student at the University of Göttingen.

ARCHIVES

Bismarck's Collected Works (Bismarck, Otto, Fürst von, *Die Gesammelte Werke* [Friedrichsruh Edition]), which are held at the University of Missouri at Columbia.

PRINTED SOURCES

Eyck, Erich. *Bismarck, Leben und Werk*, 3 vols. [Bismarck, life and work] (Zürich: E. Rentsch, 1941–1944).
Gall, Lothar. *The White Revolutionary*, trans. by J. A. Underwood (London: Unwin and Allen, 1986).
Pflanze, Otto. *Bismarck and the Development of Germany*, 3 vols. 2d ed. (Princeton: Princeton University Press, 1990).
Robertson, C. Grant. *Bismarck* (London: Constable, 1918).
Taylor, A.J.P. *Bismarck: The Man and Statesman* (New York: Knopf, 1965).

David K. McQuilkin

BJØRNSON, BJØRNSTJERNE (1832–1910). Bjørnstjerne Bjørnson, Norwegian dramatist, novelist, poet, journalist, and theater director was born in Kvikne, in eastern Norway but his family moved to Nesset in Ramsdal when he was five. He was a leading figure in nineteenth-century Norway as a literary creator and promoter of Norwegian national culture. His early writings (to the 1860s) consisted of dramas based on historical sagas (including the highly regarded *Sigurd Slembe*) and novels about contemporary peasant life such as *Synnøve Solbakken*. The latter brought him immediate fame in 1857. Although tinged with romanticism, his dramas tended toward the psychological and his stories toward the realistic. He brought an innovative writing style to his novels which incorporated idiomatic speech and spare prose. He later wrote more realistic and contemporary dramas dealing with middle-class life, such as *The Newly-Weds* (1875), *Bankruptcy* (1875), and *The Editor* (1875) which anticipated **Ibsen**'s social plays. Bjørnson was awarded the Nobel Prize for Literature in 1903. As the son of a Lutheran minister, Bjørnson must have had an early introduction to the Bible. He attended secondary school in Molde where he was known less as a scholar than as a leader and enthusiast for literature, culture, and politics, a pattern he repeated in preparatory school, and then at the University of Norway during his two years there. He read widely during those years, however, especially Norwegian, Scandinavian, and other European literature. In his youth, the strongest influences on his literary and cultural activities were Scandinavian. The Norwegian poet-patriot Henrik Wergeland (1809–1845) died when Bjørnson was a youth. Besides inspiring Bjørnson to become a poet, he offered an example of a publicly committed artist, passionately concerned about national and political freedom. Like Wergeland, Bjørnson developed an interest in the thirteenth-century Icelandic historian, Snorri Sturluson, in particular the *Heimskringla* (*History of the Kings of Norway*) which provided the historical material for many of his early dramas. Adam Oehlenschläger (1789–1850), the Danish poet, provided another example of the publicly engaged poet. Also important during Bjørnson's school years were the folk tales of Jorgen Moe and Peter Christen Asbjørnsen and the fairy tales of **Hans Christian Anderson** which enriched his already strong understanding of peasant life. The tales, in particular, brought new attention to the Norwegian language which had survived among the peasants while being almost obliterated among the rest of the populace by the dominance of Danish as Norway's literary language. Shakespeare, **Goethe**, and Schiller are other influences apparent in Bjørnson's writings. He used Sturluson the same way Shakespeare used the Hollinshed Chronicles in portraying the clash of history and character in his plays. Schiller's dramas, with their emphasis on issues of power, affected Bjørnson's writing as did Goethe's restrained romanticism. At preparatory school he met Henrik Ibsen, the dramatist, Aasmund Vinje, the poet, and Jonas Lie, the novelist. The four of them mutually influenced each other throughout their lives.

ARCHIVES

University Library (Universitetsbiblioteket), Oslo, Bjørnson Papers, Norwegian Division. Has a major collection of Bjørnson's papers with excellent guides.

Wisconsin State Historical Society, Rasmus B. Anderson Papers, Manuscript Division. Contains some Bjørnson correspondence, especially from his trip to the United States in 1880–81.

PRINTED SOURCES

Haugen, Eva Lund and Einar Haugen, eds. *Land of the Free: Bjørnstjerne Bjørnson's American Letters*, 1880–1881. Tr. Eva Lund and Einar Haugen. Northfield, Minn.: Norwegian-American Historical Association, 1978. Letters and excerpts of letters written by Bjørnson on a trip to the United States, with explanatory material.

Larson, Harold. *Bjørnstjerne Bjørnson: A Study in Norwegian Nationalism.* New York: King's Crown Press, 1944. A biographical and critical study analyzing Bjørnson's writings and political activities in terms of his national enthusiasm. Contains a list of archival sources and published materials by and about Bjørnson, including various editions of his collected works, letters, and other publications, most of which are in Norwegian.

Kathryn Wagnild Fuller

BLAKE, WILLIAM (1757–1827). William Blake, English poet, engraver, and painter, was born in the Soho district of London. He was apprenticed to James Basire, engraver to the Society of Antiquaries, and later became a student at the Royal Academy. Blake illustrated much of his own poetry using copperplate engravings and watercolors by a process he called "illuminated" printing.

Blake's readings in others was always highly personal—even idiosyncratic, and cases of direct influence are rare. Perhaps the single most important source of Blake's work is the Bible; the writings of Homer and Virgil he viewed as bellicose and "perverted" by comparison. His writing is replete with references to Old and New Testament literature, and this is true not only in terms of theme but of style. Blake's *Book of Urizen,* for example, reworks Genesis and adopts the structure and verse form of the King James Bible, and the epistles of Paul provided him with support for his antinomianism and his concept of the ideal city.

Blake was acquainted with homiletic writings and the verse hymns of Isaac Watts and John and Charles Wesley and the English theologian Richard Watson. He knew accounts of Gnostic practices through Joseph Priestly's *A History of the Corruptions of Christianity* and other of Priestly's works, and possibly through the work of Pierre Bayle, Isaac de Beausobre, Nathaniel Lardner, Johann Lorenz von Mosheim, and Edward Gibbon. Blake referred in his Creation narratives to Ovid's *Metamorphoses* and to Hesiod's *Theogony,* as well as to Norse myth. The Orphic Hymns and the writings of the Platonists were known to him through Thomas Taylor's translations. He was deeply influenced by Plato and the Gospel of St. John.

Early in his reading life Blake was influenced by the "cult of melancholy" popularized by the graveyard poets Robert Blair, Edward Young, and Thomas Gray, and he read Spenser, Dryden and Goldsmith, Thomas Chatterton, James Macpherson, William Collins, Thompson, Thomas Percy's *Reliques,* and the works of the Parnassians. The dramatic lyrics of Shakespeare, Samuel Rowley, Ben Jonson, John Beaumont and John Fletcher, and the Carolines provided models for Blake's explorations in meter. John Milton was an influence that Blake was to cultivate to the end of his career.

John Locke and Francis Bacon he read in his youth, and he makes reference to Voltaire and Jean-Jacques Rousseau in his writings. He read Burke's *Philosophical Enquiry into . . . the Sublime and Beautiful* and was probably familiar with contributions made to the developing theory of the sublime by John Dennis,

Joseph Addison, Hugh Blair, and the Hebraist Robert Lowth. Blake illustrated the works of Ariosto and *The Divine Comedy* of Dante (which he read in Henry Boyd's translation) and contributed illustrations to Chaucer's *Canterbury Tales*. Among his contemporaries he read **Wordsworth**, illustrated Mary Wollstone-craft's *Original Stories*, and reviled the German poet Friedrich Klopstock. Blake's "The Ghost of Abel" was dedicated to **Byron**, but there seems to be no evidence that he knew the work of **Coleridge**, **Shelley**, or **Keats**.

Blake examined spiritual works like the *Bhagvat-Geeta* (in Wilkin's transla-tion) and browsed in philosophical works by the Cambridge Platonist Henry More, as well as the more obscure writings of the German Paracelsus. He ad-mired and annotated Johaan Kaspar Lavater's *Aphorisms on Man* and knew the work of the mythographers William Stukeley, Jacob Bryant, and Davies and incorporated it into his prophetic works, along with the speculative writings of philosophers and occultists such as Emanuel Swedenborg and Jakob Boehme and the German phrenologist Johann Kaspar Spurzheim.

Other sources for Blake's works are popular ballads, rhyming proverbs, and half-penny street ballads, as well as the chapbook, which typically included stories from British history, confessions of Tyburn criminals, and myths and legends of uncertain origin.

He was familiar with the work of historians and antiquarians like Richard Payne Knight and illustrated, for example, Charles Stedman's *Narrative of a Five Years' expedition against the Revolted Slaves of Surinam* (1796).

Blake's verbal-pictorial art indicates a familiarity with manuscript illumina-tion, the *impresa*, the book of icons, and other illustrated book forms. *The Gates of Paradise* series is aligned with the seventeenth-century emblem book, and it has been suggested that the work of well-known emblamatists including Otto van Veen were available in the engraver's shop where Blake worked and the print shops he haunted as a boy.

ARCHIVES

The British Library, London.
J. Pierpont Morgan Library, New York City.
Rosenwald Collection, Library of Congress, Washington, D.C.

PRINTED SOURCES

Ackroyd, Peter. *Blake: A Biography* (New York: Ballantine, 1995).
Bentley, G. E., Jr. *Blake Records* (Oxford: Oxford University Press 1969). Supplement, 1988.
Erdman, David V. (ed.). *The Notebook of William Blake* (Oxford: Oxford University Press, 1973).
Foster Damon, Samuel. *William Blake: His Philosophy and Symbols* (Houghton Mifflin, 1924; New York: Peter Smith, 1947).
Gleckner, Robert. *The Piper and the Bard: A Study of William Blake* (Detroit, Mich.: Wayne State University Press, 1959).

Lister, Raymond. *William Blake: An Introduction to the Man and His Works* (London: Bell, 1968).

Wilson, Mona. *The Life of William Blake* (London: Nonesuch Press, 1927); 3rd ed., Geoffrey Keynes (ed.) (London: Oxford University Press, 1971).

Susan Reilly

BOLÍVAR, SIMÓN (1783–1830). Simón Bolívar was born in Caracas, Venezuela, in 1783. His education was a mix of formal schooling and private tutors until 1798, followed by study in Spain between 1799 and 1802, apparently at the Academia Real de Bellas Artes de San Fernando in Madrid. Born into the elite of a Catholic, colonial society, Bolívar developed republican sympathies and a tolerant, deistic view of religion. Despite the profession of faith found in his will, there is little evidence of religious influence in his writings. Revered as the "Liberator" of Venezuela, Colombia, Ecuador, Peru, and Bolivia, Bolívar died deeply disappointed that his military successes were not followed by the realization of his political aims. His republicanism, internationalism, and often brutal political realism influenced generations of political activists in Spanish America on both Left and Right who claim his legacy as their own.

Orphaned at an early age, Bolívar was put in the care of a maternal uncle who secured a series of distinguished tutors—including Simón Rodriguez, Francisco de Andujar, and Andrés Bello—and arranged a cadetship in the militia in 1797, where Bolívar learned the practical aspects of military science. In Spain, Bolívar pursued a vigorous course of private study, including mathematics, languages, history, the natural sciences, and the classics. His mentor at this time was the Marqués de Ustáriz (Lecuna and Bierck, 501), a minister of government and author of a work on commerce and maritime affairs. Bolívar's limited formal education was not untypical for his time and social standing, which allowed both leisure and access to the heights of society (Pérez Vila, 54). Less typical was the vigor of his private study. A second trip to Europe (1803–1806) exposed him to **Napoléon**'s empire at firsthand (which repelled him), brought him the friendship of **Alexander von Humboldt**, and reacquainted him with Simón Rodriguez. Rodriguez became perhaps the single most important influence on Bolívar's life at precisely the time he pledged himself to liberate the New World from Spain (Pérez Vila, 69–74).

It is unclear exactly what Bolívar was reading at this time, but he would later claim that his education included "Locke, Condillac, Buffon, D'Alambert, Helvetius, Montesquieu, Mably, Filangieri, Lalande, Rousseau, Voltaire, Rollin, Herthot [probably Vertot], and the classics of antiquity . . . as well as the modern classics of Spain, France, Italy, and not a few of the English" (Lecuna and Bierck, 501). Bolívar's devoted aide-de-camp and biographer noted that under Rodriguez's influence Bolívar also studied Paul Henri Holbach, Hume, Hobbes, and Spinoza, becoming an admirer of the latter two and confirming his sceptical view of religion and human nature (O'Leary, 64). Reading such authors remained important to Bolívar even at the height of his activities. Inventories of his book purchases and library dating from the 1820s reflect a mix of classical, modern, and contemporary authors, of arts and sciences, of the theoretical and the practical (Pérez Vila, 184–200).

From his reading, Bolívar drew lessons for his political actions, leaning heavily on the tradition of classical republicanism. Bolívar's letters are peppered with references to the history of Rome and Greece in discussions of contemporary problems. Montesquieu and Rousseau loom large in the vision of government articulated in the "Angostura Discourse" and the "Message to the Congress of Bolivia," with their emphasis on the role of moral power in politics. Machiavelli lurks in the background as well, though Bolívar does not cite him: Besides a common emphasis on republican virtue, the two share a calculated brutality concerning the use of violence and an instrumental view of religion.

Lacking much formal military training or education, Bolívar, the victorious general, collected and read treatises and accounts of military campaigns, such as Caesar's *Gallic Wars*, Arrien's *Expeditions of Alexander*, Raimund Montecuculi's *Art of War*, the Marquis de Vauban's *Principles of Fortification*, Marshal de Saxe's *Reflections*, and especially, Napoléon's campaigns.

Both his strengths and weaknesses as a political leader were rooted in his reading. His appreciation of history encouraged his self-sacrifice, his dispassionate surveys of the military situation, and his belief that laws rule only when backed by men of virtue and strength. For most of his career Bolívar's Enlightenment sympathies encouraged tolerance and a separation of religion and politics, though he turned to the Church as a buttress of state and society towards the end. He was an aristocratic republican, closer to Montesquieu than to his cherished Rousseau, suspicious of both "tyranny" and "anarchy," and strongly committed to the idea of a balanced, constitutional regime with popular representation tempered by civic virtue. Yet when faced with the clash of particular interests, he seemed unable to draw upon the lessons of Hobbes or Machiavelli, instead proposing elaborate solutions based on an idealized republicanism.

ARCHIVES

El Archivo del Libertador, Casa Natal de Bolívar, Caracas, Venezuela. Correspondence, personal papers, proclamations, orders, and other documents.

PRINTED SOURCES

Arciniegas, Germán. *De San Jacinto a Santa Marta: Juventud y Muerte del Libertador* (Bogotá: Planeta, 1988).

Belaunde, Víctor Andrés. *Bolívar and the Political Thought of the Spanish American Revolution* (Baltimore, Md.: Johns Hopkins University Press, 1938).

Bolívar, Simón. *Cartas del Libertador corregidas conforme a los originales*, 12 vols. (Caracas: vols. 1–11, Lit. y Typ. del Comercio, 1929–1959; vol. 12, Fundación John Boulton, 1959). Standard edition of correspondence.

———. *Escritos del Libertador. Edición de la Sociedad Bolivariana de Venezuela*, 7 vols. (Caracas: Editorial Arte, 1964–1969).

Brading, D. A. *The First America: The Spanish Monarchy, Creole Patriots, and the Liberal State* (Cambridge: Cambridge University Press, 1991). Chapter 27 contains a suggestive discussion of Machiavelli's influence.

Lecuna, Vicente, and Harold A. Bierck, Jr. (eds.). *Selected Writings of Bolívar* (New York: Colonial Press, 1951). Useful selection.

Masur, Gerhard. *Simón Bolívar*, rev. ed. (Albuquerque: University of New Mexico Press, 1969).

O'Leary, Daniel Florencio. *Memorias del General Daniel Florencio O'Leary. Narración*, 3 vols. (Caracas: Imprenta Nacional, 1952). 1888 edition includes 29 volumes of letters and documents.

Parra Perez, Caracciolo. *Bolívar: A Contribution to the Study of His Political Ideas* (Paris: Editions Excelsior, 1930). Dated but useful.

Pérez Vila, Manuel. *La Formación Intelectual del Libertador* (Caracas: Ministerio de Educación, 1971). Indispensable.

Zapata, Ramón. *Libros que Leyó el Libertador Simón Bolívar* (Santafé de Bogotá: Instituto Caro y Cuervo, 1997). Discussion of the books in Bolívar's library and their influence on him.

Robert Chisholm

BOOTH, WILLIAM (1829–1912). William Booth was born on April 10, 1829, in Sneiton, a suburb of Nottingham, England, and apprenticed as a child to a local pawnbroker. In 1852, after working for three years in a London pawnbroker's shop, he became a Methodist minister. Nine years later, Booth, along with his wife Catherine Mumford Booth (1829–1890), deserted Methodism and began their career as independent revivalists. The Booths founded a mission in the Whitechapel district of London in 1865 as a base for their conversion of the "heathen" poor of the Metropolis to Christianity; in 1878, Booth renamed his growing organization the Salvation Army. His emphasis on music, marches, open-air preaching, and public conversions and his militant opposition to drinking, gambling, and sexual immorality bespeak the strong influence that John Wesley and American revivalists such as James Caughey, Charles Finney, and Phoebe Palmer had upon him.

To help spread Christ's message, Booth published two newspapers, the *War Cry* (1879–present) being of greatest significance, and a number of books and articles: *How to Reach the Masses with the Gospel* (1872) and "What Is the Salvation Army" (*Contemporary Review*, August 1882), among others. During the late 1880s, Booth, prodded by William T. Stead of the *Pall Mall Gazette* and Frank Smith, decided that in order to garner increased popularity the Salvation Army had to turn more of its energy in a secular direction. The Salvation Army had long provided aid to the poor through its many food depots, soup kitchens, night shelters, clothing and blanket drives, life insurance policies, labor bureaus, and savings banks. Even so, Booth's *In Darkest England, and the Way Out* (1890) marked a dramatic departure. Drawing upon the ideas of Henry George, Arnold White, Herbert Mills, William Rees, and others, Booth declared that if private donors agreed to contribute £100,000 pounds, the first downpayment on a £1 million total, he would establish a system of city workshops and farm colonies in Britain to elevate the so-called submerged tenth. Those who submitted to strict discipline and moral supervision and proved themselves to be of good character would be assisted to immigrate overseas. Unfortunately, despite his best efforts, Booth was never able to reach the bulk of Britain's urban poor; nor was the Salvation Army any more successful in its attempts to evangelize the British working classes prior to Booth's death on August 20, 1912. The publicity that surrounded his "Darkest England" scheme did, however, serve to make the Salvation Army more acceptable to mainstream British society.

ARCHIVES

International Archives of the Salvation Army (London) British Library: Booth Papers; family letters, 1847–1870s.

PRINTED SOURCES

Bailey, Victor. "In Darkest England and the Way Out: The Salvation Army, Social Reform, and the Labor Movement, 1885–1910," *International Review of Social History* 29 (1984): 133–171.
Begbie, Harold. *The Life of General William Booth*, 2 vols. (New York: Macmillan, 1920). Includes transcripts of many letters.
Coutts, Frederick. *Bread for My Neighbor: The Social Influence of William Booth* (London: Hodder and Stoughton, 1978).
Murdoch, Norman. *Origins of the Salvation Army* (Knoxville: Tennessee University Press, 1994).

Robert F. Haggard

BRAHMS, JOHANNES (1833–1897). Johannes Brahms was born in Hamburg on May 7, 1833. His father, Johann Jakob Brahms, played the double bass in the Alster Orchestra. Upon recognizing his son's musical abilities, Johann Jakob enlisted the services of Friedrich Wilhelm Cossel, a local piano teacher. Within a few years, Cossel convinced his own teacher, Eduard Marxsen, to continue Brahms's instruction. Not only did Marxsen develop Brahms's artistry as a pianist, but he introduced him to the harmonic and compositional techniques of Bach and Beethoven.

Brahms attended two different private schools in Hamburg. His education provided a strong foundation in the major academic subjects as well as foreign languages. By the time that Brahms was 15, it became necessary for him to leave school and secure employment. He earned money by giving private music lessons and playing piano in local taverns. In his biography of Brahms, Peter Latham describes the top of the piano in the tavern "where he had placed, not a sheet of music (he always played by heart), but a volume of poetry by Eichendorff or **Heine** in whose company he strove to forget his surroundings" (Latham, 6). Despite this unfortunate situation, Brahms persevered in his pursuit of knowledge.

Brahms was an avid reader. Being a youth with limited monetary resources, Brahms looked forward to receiving books for special occasions. Throughout his correspondence, he enthusiastically describes his latest literary acquisitions to his family and friends. On August 27, 1854, Brahms tells Clara Schumann: "When I [receive] my next 10 louis d'or, I will again have a hard struggle to stay away from book shops" (Alvins, 60). His diverse library consisted of historical works, travel guides, books on art and architecture, religious texts, poetry, drama, and a broad representation of literary masterpieces. In reference to the extensive library that Brahms amassed throughout his lifetime, Michael Musgrave states: "Brahms's library is not merely a collection of books reflecting special enthusiasms, but a body of writings on many subjects which reflect the need to be thoroughly acquainted with the world of ideas, artistic and otherwise, present as well as past" (Musgrave, 4).

While he was reading, Brahms recorded his favorite quotations and verses in a notebook entitled *Des Jungen Kreislers Schatzkastlein* [Young Kreisler's little treasure chest] (ed. Carl Krebs, Berlin, 1909). *The Life and Opinions of Kater Murr* and *Kreisleriana* by E.T.A. Hoffmann were Brahms's particular favorites. Brahms occasionally signed his manuscripts and correspondence "Johannes Kreisler Jun" (Avins, 13). In his biography Malcolm MacDonald explains Brahms's strong identification with Johannes Kreisler: "Hoffmann's Kreisler, unable to cope with philistine society, always found solace in his Art; this 'Young Kreisler' would do likewise" (MacDonald, 9).

In *Johannes Brahms: His Work and Personality*, Hans Gal suggests that poetry's hold on Brahms's imagination is apparent everywhere in his vocal music. Gals states: "And next to the Scriptures, it was above all **Goethe** who brought to life his most profound emotions and his most characteristic imagination" (Gal, 196). Three of Brahms's major choral works—*Song of the Fates*, *Rinaldo*, and *Alto Rhapsody*—were all based on texts by Johann Wolfgang von Goethe.

The musical compositions of Brahms include over 200 lieder and songs, various works for solo and accompanied chorus, four symphonies, four concertos, 25 chamberworks, orchestral serenades and overtures, and numerous works for piano and organ.

ARCHIVES

Archive of the Gesellschaft der Musik-freunde, Vienna.
Brahms Collection, Kammerhof Museum, Gmunden.

PRINTED SOURCES

Avins, Styra. *Johannes Brahms: Life and Letters*, Josef Eisinger and Styra Avins (trans.) (Oxford and New York: Oxford University Press, 1997).
Brahms, Johannes. *Briefwechsel*, 16 vols. (Berlin: Deutsche Brahms Gesellschaft, 1912–1922; reprint, Hans Schneider: Tutzing, 1974).
Gal, Hans. *Johannes Brahms: His Work and Personality*, Joseph Stein (trans.) (New York: Alfred A. Knopf, 1963).

Jacobson, Bernard. *The Music of Johannes Brahms* (London: Tantivy Press, 1977).

Latham, Peter. *Brahms. The Master Musicians Series* (London: J. M. Dent and Sons, Ltd.; New York: Farrar, Straus and Giroux, Inc., 1966).

MacDonald, Malcolm. *Brahms* (New York: Schirmer Books; London: Prentice-Hall International, 1990).

Musgrave, Michael. "The Cultural World of Brahms." In Robert Pascall (ed.), *Brahms: Biographical, Documentary and Analytical Studies* (Cambridge: Cambridge University Press, 1983), 1–26.

Specht, Richard. *Johannes Brahms*, Eric Blom (trans.) (London and Toronto: J. M. Dent and Sons Ltd.; New York: E. P. Dutton & Co., 1930).

Marianne Wilson

BRIGHT, JOHN (1811–1889). John Bright was born in Greenbank, Rochdale, in 1811 to Jacob Bright, cotton spinner–turned–factory owner, and his second wife. Bright was raised in the small Society of Friends in Rochdale and pursued a Quaker education. He began his studies at the Townhead School in Rochdale at the age of 9 as a day boy. Between ages 10 and 15, he attended boarding school at a series of Friends' institutions including Penketh in Warrington, Ackworth near Pontefract, and Newton-in-Bowland in the secluded Pennines. His formal education included some Latin and French, reading, writing, arithmetic, grammar, and geography. By his own admission, it is then that his education in literature, history, economics, and politics began under his own tutelage, largely through the Rochdale Literary and Philosophical Society, Temperance Society, and Bible Society. He began his study of political economy and statistical analysis working in the family factory, and it was this independent study that directly led to Bright's great contributions in economic reform and political organization, namely, the Anti-Corn Law League's success in repealing protective tariffs and his own election to Parliament later in the century.

Always a lover of literature, Bright was heavily influenced as a young man by John Milton's *Paradise Lost* and later in life by Lewis Morris's poem *The Epic of Hades*. His travel diaries boasted frequent references to **Lord Byron**'s poetry, and his later diaries and letters revealed a penchant for reading Shakespeare to his young second wife, particularly the comedies *The Merchant of Venice* and *Midsummer Night's Dream*. As a politician and manufacturer, Bright found himself distrusted by the Victorian intelligentsia, particularly because of his profound spirituality and humility ingrained in him by the Quakers. Nonetheless, he had social relationships with **George Eliot** and **Alfred Tennyson** and was, in turn, responsible for the literary career of Ebenezer Eliot, whom Bright recruited when campaigning in Sheffield. The Radical and writer soon became known as the "Corn Law rhymer" and emerged as an important poet and propagandist for the free trade movement in the early 1840s, assisting Bright in mixing politics, literature, and public education.

ARCHIVES

Bright Papers, British Library (Add. MS. 43383–43392). Political correspondence and papers of Bright, **Richard Cobden**, **William Gladstone**, among others.

—————, private collection of C. and J. Clark, Somerset. Personal correspondence with
    sister, first wife, relatives, and daughter Helen.

—————, J. B. Smith Papers. Correspondence between Bright and Smith, Manchester
    Central Library concerning Anti-Corn Law League and Manchester electoral pol-
    itics.

PRINTED SOURCES

Briggs, Asa. "John Bright and the Creed of Reform." In *Victorian People: A Reassess-
    ment of Persons and Themes, 1851–1867* (New York: Harper and Row, 1955).

Bright, John. *The Diaries of John Bright,* R.A.J. Walling (ed.) (New York: William
    Morrow and Co., 1930).

—————. *The Public Letters of the Right Honorable John Bright,* H. J. Leech (ed.) (Lon-
    don: Samson Low, Marsten & Co., 1895).

Read, Conrad. *Cobden and Bright, a Victorian Political Partnership* (London: Edward
    Arnold, 1967).

Robbins, Keith. *John Bright* (London: Routledge and Kegan Paul, 1979).

Trevelyan, George Macaulay. *The Life of John Bright* (London: Constable & Co., 1913).

Nancy LoPatin-Lummis

BRONTË, CHARLOTTE (1816–1855). Charlotte Brontë was born in Thornton, Yorkshire, in 1816, the third daughter of Evangelical minister Patrick
Brontë and his wife Maria, whose younger children also included novelists **Emily** and Anne. Brontë was educated at Cowan Bridge for 10 months (August
1824–June 1825), which would serve as a model for Lowood in her first
published novel, *Jane Eyre* (1847), and for 17 months at Roe Head (January
1831–June 1832), but she and her siblings were mostly educated at home by
their father. From February to October 1842, Brontë attended the Pensionnat
Heger in Brussels and briefly taught there, from January 1843 to January 1844.

    Brontë's novels, which include *Shirley* (1849), *Villette* (1853), and *The Pro-
fessor* (written in 1846 but published posthumously in 1857) in addition to *Jane
Eyre*, are noted for their power and passion. Particularly, Brontë's status as one
of the English language's most eminent novelists is due to her depiction of the
role and psychological situations of women in Victorian England. Her heroines,
especially Jane Eyre, Shirley Keeldar, and Lucy Snowe, engage in acts of self-
definition in a society that seeks to constrain them or even render them invisible.

    Brontë's early substantial, and sometimes unconventional, reading matter in-
fluenced her juvenile and adult writing and according to Barker, Fraser, and
Gérin, included Burton's *Arabian Nights*, Aesop's *Fables*, Homer, Virgil, Milton, Samuel Johnson, James Thomson, Goldsmith, Hume, **Scott**, Shakespeare,
Byron, Southey, Wordsworth, and the Bible. Reverend Brontë encouraged his
children to read extensively and would regularly hold "discussions [with his
children] of the week's political events, new poetry, articles in literary magazines, all of which gave the Brontës a sophistication and knowledge of art,
poetry and cultural and political affairs quite beyond any of their neighbours"
(Fraser, 46). As a young adult, Brontë admired the writings of **George Sand**

but disliked **Jane Austen**'s novels because "the Passions are perfectly unknown to her" (letter to William Williams, April 12, 1850, in Fraser, 363).

ARCHIVES

Brontë Papers, Brontë Parsonage Museum, Haworth. This collection is the largest of Brontë manuscripts and memorabilia. Many of Charlotte Brontë's poems and juvenilia are housed at the museum, as well as much of the H. H. Bonnell collection of Brontë manuscripts, books, and drawings, on permanent loan.

PRINTED SOURCES

Barker, J. *The Brontës* (New York: St. Martin's Press, 1995). Most recent biography.
Fraser, R. *The Brontës: Charlotte Brontë and Her Family* (New York: Ballantine, 1988). Cites most of Brontë's literary influences.
Gaskell, E. *The Life of Charlotte Brontë* (London: Smith, Elder, 1857). A contemporary and friend of Brontë's, Gaskell wrote the first biography of the author's life.
Gérin, W. "Byron's Influence on the Brontë's," *Keats-Shelley Memorial Bulletin*, 17 (1966), 1–19.
———. *Charlotte Brontë: The Evolution of Genius* (London: Oxford University Press, 1967). Cites most literary influences.
Mermin, D. *Godiva's Ride: Women of Letters in England, 1830–1880* (Bloomington: Indiana University Press, 1993). Byron's influence.
Thomson, P. *George Sand and the Victorians: Her Influence and Reputation in Nineteenth-Century England* (New York: Columbia University Press, 1977).

SueAnn Schatz

BRONTË, EMILY (1818–1848). Emily Jane Brontë was born at Thornton in 1818 and educated briefly at the Clergy Daughter's School at Cowan Bridge (1824–1832) and Miss Wooler's School at Roe Head, near Dewsbury, Yorkshire (1831–1832). In between these brief stints of formal schooling, Brontë, along with her sisters **Charlotte** and Anne and brother Branwell, was educated at home by her father, the Reverend Patrick Brontë. In keeping with the custom of the time, however, Reverend Brontë spent most of his attentions on Branwell, his only son, while his sister-in-law, Elizabeth Branwell, who had come from the Branwell home in Penzance to help Patrick raise the children after her sister's death, instructed the girls in housekeeping and needlework. The Brontë girls were thus largely self-educated, having free access to their father's library as well as the public and circulating libraries of the neighboring towns (Barker, 147–149; Fraser, 52). One of the most important influences on their later literary efforts were the newspapers and magazines of the day, especially *Blackwood's Magazine* (Barker, 149–150; Fraser, 52; Gordon, 86–88; Sherry, 14). Unlike Charlotte and Anne, Emily wrote few letters and had virtually no social connections outside her siblings and Charlotte's close friends, so her religious beliefs (Chitham, 73) are difficult to ascertain. Though her sister Anne was a serious and pious woman as evidenced in her poetry, Emily's poetry is difficult to pin down in religious terms, and her sister Charlotte was so shocked by the wild characters in Emily's novel *Wuthering Heights* that she spent much of the rest of her life after Emily's death trying to tone down criticism of it (in her introduction to the second edition of Emily's own novel, she wondered if it were "right or advisable to create beings like Heathcliff").

All the Brontë children were to one degree or another influenced by the Romantic writers, especially **Byron** (Chitham, 72–73; Fraser, 50), **Shelley**, **Keats**, and **Wordsworth** (Barker, 145–151). The novelist Sir **Walter Scott** is also credited with having influenced all of them (Barker, 273–275; Sherry, 14), especially Emily, who "probably drew on Scott's *The Bride of Lammermoor* for the plot of *Wuthering Heights*" (Gordon, 88).

ARCHIVES

Outside of *Wuthering Heights*, several "diary papers," and her Belgian essays, few of Emily Brontë's writings survive, but the most important collections of Brontë family manuscripts, juvenilia, letters, and so on, are housed in the Brontë Parsonage Museum, the British Library, the Brotherton Library, the Fitzwilliam Museum, and the Bonnell Collection in Philadelphia. The *Transactions of the Brontë Society* is the primary periodical of Brontë studies.

PRINTED SOURCES

Barker, Juliet. *The Brontës* (London: Weidenfeld and Nicolson, 1994).
Benvenuto, Richard. *Emily Brontë* (Boston: Twayne Publishers, 1982).
Chitham, Edward. *A Life of Emily Brontë* (Oxford: Blackwell Publishers, 1987).
Crandell, Norma. *Emily Brontë: A Psychological Portrait* (Rindge, N.H.: Richard R. Smith Publisher, Inc., 1957; Kraus Reprint Co., 1970).
Davies, Stevie. *Emily Brontë: The Artist as a Free Woman* (Manchester: Carcanet Press, 1983).
Fraser, Rebecca. *The Brontës: Charlotte Brontë and her Family* (New York: Crown Publishers, 1988).
Gordon, Felicia. *A Preface to the Brontës* (London: Longman, 1989).
Lonoff, Sue (ed.). *The Belgian Essays: A Critical Edition* (New Haven, Conn.: Yale University Press, 1996).
Sherry, Norman. *Charlotte and Emily Brontë* (New York: Arco, 1969).
Spark, Muriel. *The Essence of the Brontës: A Compilation with Essays* (London: Peter Owen, 1993).

Sandra Hannaford

BROWNING, ELIZABETH BARRETT (1806–1861). Elizabeth Barrett Browning was born near Durham in 1806 but spent most of her childhood at Hope End in Herefordshire. For several years she shared a tutor with her brother Edward, studying Greek, Latin, French, and some Italian. Her father's library, however, was her main educational resource, as described in the semiautobiographical *Aurora Leigh* (1856). The Barretts were dissenters, and when her often poor health permitted, Elizabeth attended services at nearby Congregationalist chapels. She read the Bible regularly, including the original Hebrew and Greek texts, and composed two verse-dramas on religious subjects, *The Seraphim* (1838) and *A Drama of Exile* (1844). She eloped with **Robert Browning** to Italy in 1846, and while the Risorgimento is the focus of *Casa Guidi Windows* (1851) and much of her later work, Barrett Browning read few Italian authors. *Aurora Leigh* was popular and highly acclaimed, and contemporaries consistently ranked its author among the great poets of the Victorian age. In the twentieth century, interest in Barrett Browning's work steadily faded, although the sequence of love poems *Sonnets from the Portuguese* (1850) remained popular. With the advent of feminist literary criticism in the 1970s, her poetry has gained new admirers and scholarly attention.

Barrett Browning was an uncommonly voracious reader, even in an age when the written word was the dominant form of mass communication. An early essay, "Glimpses into My Own Life and Literary Character" (1820), discusses authors who later influenced her poetry, such as **Lord Byron** and Mary Wollstonecraft. *An Essay on Mind* (1826) was an even more ambitious attempt to codify her vast reading, tracing the development of all learning from ancient Greece onward. At 14, Barrett Browning published a Homeric imitation, *The Battle of Marathon* (1820), but she did not begin serious study of the classics until she met and corresponded with her neighbors Uvedale Price and Hugh Stuart Boyd. Between 1826 and 1834, she read all of the major as well as many minor Greek and Latin authors, later publishing a translation of Aeschylus's *Prometheus Bound* (1833; rev. 1850) and, for the journal *Athenaeum* in 1842, studies and translations of early Greek Christian poetry.

After this period of classical immersion, Barrett Browning turned to more contemporary authors. Confinement brought on by respiratory ailments left ample time for reading "almost all the fiction and poetry published in England" from approximately 1835 to 1845 (Taplin, 94). Barrett Browning once suggested for her epitaph "the greatest novel reader in the world" (Kelley and Hudson, 10:117), and her letters are punctuated with references to **Victor Hugo**, **George Sand**, Frédéric Soulié, and **Stendhal**; she had especially high regard for **Honoré de Balzac**, whom she ranked above **Charles Dickens** as the greatest novelist of the age. Sand was the dedicatee of two sonnets, "To George Sand—A Desire" and "To George Sand—A Recognition" (both 1844). *Aurora Leigh*, a self-described "novel-poem," adopts a number of themes and plot features common to nineteenth-century British and French fiction. The title character was inspired by Madame **de Staël**'s *Corinne* (1807), and others have noted the poem's debt to Eugène Sue's *Mysteries of Paris* (1842) and the English novelists **Charlotte Brontë** and **Elizabeth Gaskell**.

Barrett Browning also read travel narratives that influenced her treatment of Italian culture and politics, including **Mary Shelley**'s *Rambles in Germany and Italy* (1844) and works by Anna Jameson. Like many of her contemporaries, Barrett Browning admired the writings of the eighteenth-century mystic Emanuel Swedenborg as well as contemporary spiritualist literature, such as William

Newnham's *Human Magnetism* (1845) and Henry Spicer's *Sights and Sounds* (1853).

ARCHIVES

Wellesley College Library. Principal correspondence as well as diaries and memorandum books.

PRINTED SOURCES

Byrd, Deborah. "Combating an Alien Tyranny: Elizabeth Barrett Browning's Evolution as Feminist Poet," *Browning Institute Studies*, 15 (1987), 23–41. Examines reading of female novelists and poets.
Cooper, Helen. *Elizabeth Barrett Browning, Woman and Artist* (Chapel Hill: University of North Carolina Press, 1988).
Kaplan, Cora. Introduction to Elizabeth Barrett Browning. *"Aurora Leigh" with Other Poems* (London: Women's Press, 1978). Examines poem's connection to other nineteenth-century texts.
Kelley, Phillip, and Ronald Hudson (eds.). *The Brownings' Correspondence*, 14 vols. to date (Winfield, Kans.: Wedgestone Press, 1984–). This and other published editions of the letters provide a rich insight into Barrett Browning's reading.
Lewis, Linda M. *Elizabeth Barrett Browning's Spiritual Progress: Face to Face with God* (Columbia: University of Missouri Press, 1998). Religious and spiritualist reading.
Mermin, Dorothy. *Elizabeth Barrett Browning: The Origins of a New Poetry* (Chicago: University of Chicago Press, 1989).
Stone, Marjorie. *Elizabeth Barrett Browning*, Women Writers 12 (New York: St. Martin's Press, 1995).
Taplin, Gardner B. *The Life of Elizabeth Barrett Browning* (New Haven, Conn.: Yale University Press, 1957). Best overall survey of Barrett Browning's reading habits, but analysis of her poetry and influence is dated.

Christopher M. Keirstead

BROWNING, ROBERT (1812–1889). Robert Browning was born in Camberwell, a suburb of London, to a Congregational family. Even though Browning spent some time at a boarding school and six months at the University of London, he spent his first 34 years living primarily at home, and he received most of his education by reading his father's large book collection. After he married Elizabeth Barrett in 1846, the couple moved to the Mediterranean. It was not until after the death of his wife in 1861 and his move back to London that Browning received attention for his poetry. As a poet, he is best known for his dramatic monologues, and his wide-ranging reading informed his poems considerably—which often resulted in his poetry being labeled "obscure." Because Browning read so much and because his father's library was combined with several other collections, it is difficult to trace Browning's reading history, but Browning does leave some clues in letters and his poetry (Woolford, 7).

In his poem "Development," published in his last collection of poems, *Aso-*

lando (1889), Browning describes how his father introduced him to Homer at age five. Browning continued that education in the classics by reading Pope's translations as well as the original text. During his childhood, Browning was allowed unsupervised freedom in his father's library, and his choice of reading material indicated a somewhat morbid curiosity; Nathaniel Wanley's *Wonders of the Little World: or, A General History of Man in Six Books* (1678), with its grotesque description of bodily disfigurements, was one example. The macabre and morbid appeared frequently in Browning's later poetry.

In his poetry, Browning frequently combined his interest in art with his interest in human nature, as is evident in such poems as "Fra Lippo Lippi" and "Andrea Del Sarto." His father's library contained Giorgio Vasari's *Lives of the Painters* (1550), which he read for biographical material. Browning also read through most of the 50 volumes of the *Biographie Universelle* (1822), which provided him with a broad range of references. The most important visual and imaginative source, however, was Gerard de Lairesse's *The Art of Painting in All Its Branches* (1707). Lairesse, a painter who was stricken blind, describes the technique of painting and demonstrates how to create pictures in the mind. Browning inscribed his father's copy with the following statement: "I read this book more often and with greater delight when I was a child than any other: and still remember the main of it most gratefully for the good I seem to have got from the prints and wonderful text" (Thomas, 14).

Browning also read a great deal of poetry. Francis Quarles's *Emblems*, which rely on sight and sound, were appealing to Browning, along with Donne's complicated metaphysics. The Romantic poets were also important reading material. At 12, Browning wrote a volume of verse entitled *Incondita*, fashioned in the style of **Byron**, a volume that he destroyed later in his life (Irvine and Honan, 13–14). James Silverthorne, a cousin, with the gift of **Shelley**'s *Miscellaneous Poems*, introduced the 14-year-old Browning to an important poet. The following year, his mother, at his request, bought Shelley's *Posthumous Poems* of 1824 and three volumes of **Keats**'s poetry (Irvine and Honan, 15). His early poetry reflected the influence of Byron, Shelley, and Keats.

Browning's extensive reading is pervasive in his poetry, but two of his longer works in particular demonstrate the importance of books for Browning's art. *The Ring and the Book* (1868–1869) relies upon an unusual textual source. Browning, in June 1860, found an old volume of legal pleadings in the case of a husband, Guido Franceschini, who killed his wife for adultery and her parents for deception; in addition, the volume contained all of the letters and manuscripts concerning Franceschini's execution. The 12 books of the poem explore the different viewpoints of the characters as well as consider the relationship between poetry and truth. Browning's later poem *Parleyings with Certain People of Importance in Their Day* (1887) indicates the diversity of his reading. He imaginatively sets up conversations with seven men of the past: Bernard de Mandeville, a political poet; Daniel Bartoli, a historian; Chistopher Smart, a religious poet; George Bubb Doddington, a politician; Francis Furini, a Florentine painter; Gerard de Lairesse, a painter and writer; and Charles Avision, a composer. In his "parleyings" with the writers in particular, Browning focuses on his response to their texts. Browning, as a poet, was a prodigious reader, and the diversity of his reading forcefully shaped the substance of his poetry.

ARCHIVES

Browning Letters. Harvard University.
Manuscript Collection. British Museum.

PRINTED SOURCES

Hudson, Gertrude Reese. *Robert Browning's Literary Life: From First Work to Masterpiece* (Austin, Tex.: Eakin Press, 1992).
Irvine, William, and Park Honan. *The Book, The Ring, and The Poet: A Biography of Robert Browning* (New York: McGraw-Hill, 1974).
Thomas, Donald. *Robert Browning: A Life within a Life* (New York: Viking Press, 1982).
Woolford, John. "Sources and Resources in Browning's Early Reading." In *Robert Browning: Writers and Their Background* (Athens: Ohio University Press, 1975), 1–46.

Sarah R. Marino

BRUNEL, ISAMBARD KINGDOM (1806–1859). Isambard Kingdom Brunel, one of the most innovative Victorian engineers, was born in Portsea in 1806. Marc Isambard Brunel (1769–1849) primed his son in arithmetic and Euclid's geometry. At school in Hove, Brunel read classics, including his favorite Virgil, and made architectural drawings, a habit Marc called the engineer's alphabet. At Caen and at the Lycée Henri-Quatre in Paris, Brunel polished his French and studied mathematics, but he failed to enter the École Polytechnique. While an apprentice to Parisian instrument maker Louis Breguet, Brunel was exposed to Louis XVIII's extravagant *ancien regime*–inspired public works. Back in England, Brunel learned wood- and ironworking and visited engineering works to further his private aim to be "the first engineer and the example to all future ones" (quoted in Vaughan, 29).

From his time as engineer to the Thames Tunnel (1827), Brunel attracted the attention of the technical press, the newspapers and—ultimately—authors from **Whitman** to **Verne**. Since Brunel left but few traces of his own reading, it has been easy for biographers to emphasize his originality rather than his literary debts. But he did profit significantly from a lifetime's Catholic reading. As a young man he devoured David Hume's classic *History of England*; later, he collected topographical works, including J. D. Forbe's popular *Travels through the Alps of Savoy* (1843); scanning the newspapers rather than the Bible on Sundays signified to friends a worrying devotion to mammon.

His father gave him an entrée to elevated circles that included Lord Spencer, whose Althorp library boasted 35,000 volumes, and Charles Babbage, who lent him books. The membership of the Athenaeum, the Institution of Civil Engineers (ICE), and the Royal Society of London brought Brunel within reach of the professional media including the *Civil Engineer and Architects' Journal* and the ICE's *Minutes of Proceedings*.

The best engineers were, notwithstanding Brunel's parentage, Smilesian self-made men. His gentlemanly "pupils" paid exorbitant premiums solely for the opportunity to prove their usefulness: grounded in classics, they received no additional professional training in engineering theory. Confident in his prodigious abilities to put science to work in practice, Brunel wanted young engineers "thoroughly grounded in the grammar" of mathematics (Brunel to Franconi, in Noble, 240), that they might clearly see mechanical truths and rapidly formulate rational arguments for their decisions. From French authors they could learn abstract science but nothing of value in practical mechanics; practice was best learned in the workshop, supplemented by English books that at least contained nothing that need be unlearned.

In youth a cultured individual, Brunel developed in later life as a patron and a practitioner of the fine arts. Through his wife Mary Horsley and her family, he mixed with musicians, artists, actors, and authors. Brunel's Duke Street house was an "oasis of culture," taste, and education (Vaughan, 58). It was a venue for amateur theatricals and, in its mock-Elizabethan "Shakespeare Room," a space in which Brunel, inspired by Moritz Retzsch's illustrations of dramatic works, could show his enthusiasm for the modern British school of painting and for the canon of English literature. He commissioned Landseer and other established English artists to illustrate scenes from Shakespeare. For his architectural works, Brunel dabbled in styles ranging through Norman, Egyptian, Tudor, classical, Romantic, Italian, and Gothic "revival" to the Louis XV of the GWR's Royal Saloon car and the Loire valley château for his never-built country seat. He drew upon an extensive library of works by Henry Shaw, **Ruskin**, the **Pugins**, the Arundel Society, and others on the grammar of European (especially Parisian) architecture, decoration, and antiquities.

This mingling of science and art gave Brunel's works a rare dramatic flair. He combined an eagerness to learn from—if not to acknowledge—the best writings, practices, and works of others with daring experiment, tremendous tenacity, and as the Napoléon of engineers, a love of extravagance that cost shareholders dearly—but ensured his posthumous reputation.

ARCHIVES

Brunel Collection, Bristol University Library. Principal collection of papers, diaries, correspondence (including Private Letter Books), and working documents.

PRINTED SOURCES

Brunel, Isambard. *The Life of Isambard Kingdom Brunel, Civil Engineer. A Reprint with an Introduction by L.T.C. Rolt* (first published, London: Longmans, 1870; new edition, Newton Abbot: David and Charles, 1971). Victorian life and letters containing fragments on reading experience and influence.

Buchanan, R. A. "Science and Engineering: A Case Study in British Experience in the

Mid-19th Century," *Notes and Records of the Royal Society*, 32 (1978), 215–223. Brunel's education and his advice on reading for student engineers.

Catalogue of the Celebrated Collection of Works of Art of Isambard Kingdom Brunel (London: Christie, Manson & Woods, 1860). Details some of Brunel's most valuable books.

Emmerson, George S. "L.T.C. Rolt and the *Great Eastern Affair* of Brunel versus Scott Russell," *Technology and Culture*, 21 (1980), 553–569. Revises Rolt's inept account of the animosity following Brunel's reading of the *Observer* article.

Faberman, Hilarie, and Philip McEvansoneya. "Isambard Kingdom Brunel's 'Shakespeare Room,' " *Burlington Magazine*, 137 (1995), 108–118.

Noble, Celia Brunel. *The Brunels. Father and Son* (London: Cobden-Sanderson, 1938). Many extensive extracts from private letters, diaries, and reports.

Pugsley, Alfred (ed.). *The Works of Isambard Kingdom Brunel: An Engineering Appreciation* (London: Institution of Civil Engineering, 1976). Chapter by T. M. Charlton on Brunel's theoretical work and readings.

Rolt, L.T.C. *Isambard Kingdom Brunel* (first published, London: Longmans, 1957; Harmondsworth: Penguin, 1970). Standard biography favorably inclined to its subject.

Vaughan, Adrian. *Isambard Kingdom Brunel. Engineering Knight-Errant* (London: John Murray, 1991). An antidote to Rolt with much more on Brunel's day-to-day practices.

Ben Marsden

BULWER-LYTTON, EDWARD (1803–1873).

Edward George Earle Bulwer-Lytton, 1st Baron Lytton of Knebworth, was born in London in 1803 and educated at Rottingdean and Ealing (1812–1821), then at Trinity Hall, Cambridge (1822–1824). At Ealing his studies were directed by High Church of England minister Reverend Charles Wallington. Although the later twentieth century views Bulwer-Lytton as a minor nineteenth-century novelist, his considerable literary industry marks him as an innovator in several genres of Victorian fiction. He can rightly be attributed with the creation of the "silver fork" novel and the "Newgate" crime novel and was a leading exponent of both fictional histories and scientific romances. Prose was not the only medium in which he worked, however. His early work was largely poetry, and he also composed several plays, of which *Money* (1840) was the most successful. Intellectual rigor characterizes all of Bulwer-Lytton's literary activities, and it is this dissemination of knowledge through fiction that sets him apart as a writer of importance and influence, to both the general reading public and other literary figures, in the mid-Victorian period.

Bulwer-Lytton's literary education began at an early age when, as James L. Campbell points out, his mother read him Homer, Thomas Gray, and Oliver Goldsmith (Campbell, 3). The most important influence on his early reading, however, was his maternal grandfather Richard Warburton Lytton, whose library he found a source of real scholarship and which came into the possession of his immediate family on his grandfather's death in 1810. From this library Bulwer-

Lytton read a great deal of German metaphysics, which can be seen to greatly influence his later scientific writings and the semimystical novels *Zanoni* (1842) and *A Strange Story* (1862). His continued enthusiasm for all matters of heroism is also highlighted in his reading of **Southey**'s *Amadis of Gaul* (Escott, 22). The heroism Bulwer-Lytton found in Homer and Southey was to be reproduced in many of his own works of fiction, and his interest in accounts of heroism is paralleled in his many works of historical romance, of which the most obviously influenced by his childhood reading is *King Arthur* (1848).

While there is little specific evidence to suggest that his days at Rottingdean or Ealing were as influential in his literary career, Bulwer-Lytton did at least expand his reading during this time. He became greatly enamored of the Greek dramatists and of Shakespeare and in these texts found his earliest interest in Greece and Italy, which were to become the setting for many of his future works. At this stage in his education and later at Trinity College, the curriculum held little sway over Bulwer-Lytton's reading, and he began instead to read the foremost French writers in translation. Rousseau in particular was to affect his political beliefs and influence his one outstanding novel, *The Coming Race* (1871), which attempts to produce a vision of the future along similar lines to Rousseau's social commentary in his *Confessions*.

Although continuing to be an avid reader throughout his life, these early influences were to remain at the center of Bulwer-Lytton's extensive writing career, and his interest in the classics, Romantics, and metaphysics informs each and every one of his many publications.

ARCHIVES

Blackwood Papers, National Library of Scotland. Principal Collection of Bulwer-Lytton's work and papers.

PRINTED SOURCES

Campbell, J. L. *Edward Bulwer-Lytton* (Boston: Twayne, 1986).

Christensen, A. C. *Edward Bulwer-Lytton: The Fiction of New Regions* (Athens: University of Georgia Press, 1976).

Dahl, C. "Benjamin Disraeli and Edward Bulwer-Lytton." In Lionel Stevenson (ed.), *Victorian Fiction: A Guide to Research* (Cambridge, Mass.: Harvard University Press, 1966), 35–43.

————. "Edward Bulwer-Lytton." In George H. Ford (ed.), *Victorian Fiction: A Second Guide To Research* (New York: Modern Languages Association of America, 1978), 28–33.

Escott, T.H.S. *Edward Bulwer: First Baron Lytton of Knebworth* (London: Routledge, 1910).

Lytton, K. G., Earl of *Bulwer-Lytton* (London: Home and Van Thal, 1948).

Lytton, 2nd Earl of. *The Life, Letters and Literary Remains of Edward Bulwer, Lord Lytton*, 2 vols. (London: Kegan Paul, 1883).

Sadleir, M. *Bulwer: A Panorama: Edward and Rosina, 1803–1836* (London: Constable, 1830).

Zipser, R. A. *Edward Bulwer-Lytton and Germany* (Berne: Herbert Lang, 1974).

Martin Willis

BURCKHARDT, JACOB CHRISTOPH (1818–1897). Jacob Burckhardt, art and cultural historian, was born in Basel, Switzerland, the son of a Protestant pastor. Burckhardt studied theology in his native Basel (1837–1839) before losing his faith and switching over to history. In 1839, he left Basel for the University of Berlin, where he studied under renowned historians Johann Gustav Droysen, **Leopold von Ranke**, and Franz Kugler. After completing his studies, he returned to Basel and edited the conservative newspaper the *Basler Zeitung*. In 1848, he became a lecturer at the University of Basel. Seven years later, he accepted a position at the newly established Zurich Polytechnic University before returning in 1858 to Basel, where he taught for the rest of his life. In 1874, he declined a prestigious chair in history at Berlin, preferring to stay in Basel, where, as he put it, "I can say what I want to."

A rather anomalous figure in the nineteenth century, Burckhardt eschewed the political emphasis of the "Prussian School" of historiography and came to pioneer a novel approach to the past, known as "cultural history" (*Kulturgeschichte*). He rejected the historical optimism and progressivism found in much nineteenth-century thought, advocating instead cultural pessimism, which led him to bemoan many aspects of modernity, including nationalism, socialism, mass culture, and industrialization. This pessimism inclined Burckhardt to see Europe's future in bleak terms; for this reason, he is often hailed as a prophet of the crises that befell Europe between 1914 and 1945.

Burckhardt's first major work, *The Age of Constantine the Great* (1852), examined the late Roman Empire during the ascendancy of Christianity. It was followed in 1855 by *The Cicerone*, an art guide to Italy. In 1860, he published *The Civilization of the Renaissance in Italy*, in which he interpreted the Renaissance as the birthplace of modern individualism. This book almost single-handedly established the field of modern Renaissance studies, and it remains today the basis of his enduring legacy. Posthumously, several of Burckhardt's lectures were published and later translated, including *Reflections on History*, *On History and Historians*, and *Greek Cultural History*.

In assessing influences on Burckhardt, emphasis must be placed on Burckhardt's identity as a pastor's son and aspirant to the ministry. Although his faith was unseated by radical German theologian W.M.L. de Wette (1780–1847), an abiding Augustinian skepticism of human nature colored many of Burckhardt's historical judgments. Like many German youth, Burckhardt avidly read **Goethe** as a young man. His time in Berlin brought him into contact with many important personalities and intellectual trends. While he was impressed with Ranke's scholarly methods, it was the art historian Franz Kugler who made the strongest impression and fostered in Burckhardt an interest in art and culture. Burckhardt also encountered many of **Friedrich Hegel**'s epigoni at Berlin. Rejecting their teleological conception of history, Burckhardt came to maintain that his historical work was neither philosophical nor scientific.

Burckhardt's friendship with **Friedrich Nietzsche**, his younger colleague at Basel, has attracted considerable scholarly interest. While Nietzsche greatly admired his older colleague, Burckhardt distanced himself from Nietzsche later in life. Their correspondence reveals that both men read and esteemed the pessimistic philosopher **Arthur Schopenhauer**.

ARCHIVES

Jacob Burckhardt, *Nachlass*, Basel Staatsarchiv, Basel, Switzerland.

PRINTED SOURCES

Burckhardt, Jacob. *Briefe*, 10 vols., Max Burckhardt (ed.) (Basel: Schwabe & Co., 1949–1994).
———. *Gesammelte Werke*, 10 vols. (Basel: Schwabe & Co., 1970).
Gilbert, Felix. *History: Politics or Culture? Reflections on Ranke and Burckhardt* (Princeton, N.J.: Princeton University Press, 1990).
Hardtwig, Wolfgang. *Geschichtsschreibung zwischen Alteuropa und moderner Welt: Jacob Burckhardt in seiner Zeit* (Göttingen: Vandenhoeck & Ruprecht, 1974).
Kaegi, Werner. *Jacob Burckhardt: Eine Biographie*, 7 vols. (Basel: Schwabe & Co. Verlag, 1947–1982).

Thomas Albert Howard

BURNE-JONES, EDWARD (1833–1898). Edward Burne-Jones was born in Birmingham in 1833 and educated at King Edward's School, where it was noted "he was not strong enough to play games; that he delighted in poetry and especially in Ossian" (*DNB*, 3:340). He matriculated from Exeter College, Oxford, in 1852, intending to take orders in the Church of England. His Welsh parents were members of the Church of England, but their influence on Burne-Jones's aspirations toward the clergy is not well documented. At Oxford, Burne-Jones met a fellow Welshman, **William Morris**, and with him helped to create the *Oxford and Cambridge Magazine*—successor in spirit to the Pre-Raphaelite *Germ*.

Burne-Jones, both singly and with Morris, spread a romanticized version of the Middle Ages and is best known for his depiction of diaphanously clothed androgynes arranged as medieval romance figures: Burne-Jones took his subjects from his reading and was especially fond of **Dante Gabriel Rossetti**'s poetry. Burne-Jones met Rossetti after sending him an adulatory letter in 1856 and soon became a follower (*DNB*, 3:341). Rossetti introduced Burne-Jones to the poetry of Dante Alighieri, Chaucer (especially *The Canterbury Tales*), and Greek mythology. Many of Burne-Jones's most celebrated paintings, including *Pygmalion* and the *Briar Rosepanels*, are decorated with verse on the frames and on scrolls included in the paintings' compositions (Phillips, 287). Burne-Jones and Morris were especially keen on early French medieval texts, such the *Song of Roland*, which shows up in many of Burne-Jones's visual allusions to medieval armor styles and idealized perspective (Colvin, 18).

In addition, Burne-Jones, like the Pre-Raphaelites before him, avidly read the Romantic poets and their successors; Frederic George Stephens, art critic for *Portfolio*, says that Burne-Jones's *Love among the Ruins* "recalls Mr. [Robert] Browning's lines on the same subject" (Stephens, 6). Burne-Jones brought "a sense of aestheticism back into the public eye" (Lago, 45), and his paintings were often the result of many years of work. His legacy is most easily seen in the diversity of media in which he worked: oils, watercolors, stained glass, tapestry, and woodblock printing.

ARCHIVES

Correspondence of Frederick George Stephens, Bodlein Library (MSS. Don. E.78, d. 116–119, e.57–87).

PRINTED SOURCES

Ash, Russell. *Sir Edward Burne-Jones* (New York: Harry N. Abrams, 1993).

Bell, Malcolm. *Sir Edward Burne-Jones: A Record and Review* (New York: AMS Press, 1973).

Colvin, Sidney. "English Painters of the Present Day, III: Edward Burne-Jones," *Portfolio* I (February 1870), 17–22.

Fitzgerald, Penelope. *Edward Burne-Jones* (London: Sutton, 1997).

Fredeman, William E. *Pre-Raphaelitism: A Bibliocritical Study* (Cambridge, Mass. Harvard University Press, 1965).

Lago, Mary, ed. *Burne-Jones Talking, His Conversations 1895–1898: Preserved by His Studio Assistant Thomas Rooke* (London: Books on Demand, n.d.).

Phillips, Claude. "Edward Burne-Jones," *Magazine of Art*, 8 (1885), 286–294.

Stephens, Frederick George. "Mr. Edward Burne-Jones, A.R.A., as a Decorative Artist," *Portfolio*, 20 (November 1889), 214–219.

Wolsey, Thomas Hale. "Burne-Jones, Sir Edward Coley." In Sidney Lee (ed.), *The Dictionary of National Biography from the Earliest Times to 1900*, 23 vols. (London: Smith, Elder, 1901), 3:340–344.

Thomas J. Tobin

BYRON, GEORGE GORDON NOEL (LORD) (1788–1824).

George Gordon, Lord Byron, was born into an aristocratic family in 1788. Byron inherited the title when he was 10 years old upon the death of his grandfather. Unfortunately, the estate had been squandered, and only a government allowance permitted his attendance at Harrow and Trinity College, Cambridge, after his mother had moved to the capital from Aberdeen, where she had retreated after the death of her husband in 1791. Teased for both his withered leg and his Scottish accent, he generally felt isolated while at Harrow; and at both there and at Cambridge, while exhibiting great powers of work when necessary, he generally displayed a lack of discipline and self-indulgence. Although acquiring the traditional, albeit quite limited, classical education of the day, his academic career left primarily a series of romantic attachments (with both men and women) and accumulating debts that ultimately forced his retirement from Cambridge—although he also claimed that the school had nothing left to teach him (Grosskurth, 59). He subsequently came to believe, perhaps in justification of his own failures in school, that "education has more effect in quelling the passions than people are aware of" (Blessington, 179–180).

Despite his lack of success in school—or perhaps in reaction to it—Byron read throughout his life. He was, however, forced to sell his books at public auction before going into foreign exile in 1816 in order to escape his debts, something that plagued him throughout his life. Although his friends purchased some of the volumes, it proved both a humiliating episode and less lucrative than had been hoped (Grosskurth, 266). He, nonetheless, continued his wide reading, having instructed his publisher, John Murray, to send packets of recently published works to him.

His reading, though wide, seems to have been cursory in many cases. Leigh Hunt described his book collection as "poor, and consisted chiefly of new ones. . . . He was anxious to show you that he possessed no Shakespeare and Milton, 'because,' he said, 'he had been accused of borrowing from them!' " (Hunt, 44–45). Indeed, a number of plagiarism charges circulated throughout his career, but Hunt's comment perhaps understates Byron's admiration for Milton, whom he elsewhere described as surpassing any of his own contemporaries and found the first two books of *Paradise Lost* to be "the very finest poetry that has ever been produced in this world." He did believe, however, that Shakespeare "stands absurdly too high and will go down." If his writings had "some flashes of genius," the plots were utterly derivative of other plays (*Selected Letters*, 100).

Instead, he favored history and travel writing, with Gibbon and Benjamin Franklin standing out as particular favorites (Hunt, 44–46). He also had a deep appreciation of Sir **Walter Scott**, whose novels he regularly reread. Amongst his nearer contemporaries, Byron often found little to praise, and some of the authors whom he did have subsequently faded into obscurity such as Samuel Rogers and Tom Moore (Eisler, 309). He had little appreciation for the Lake School, although **Coleridge** was "the best of the trio—but bad is the best. **Southey** should have been a parish-clerk, and **Wordsworth** a man-midwife" (*Letters*, 100–101). Ultimately, he came to believe Alexander Pope set a model in "*Imagination* Passion—& *Invention*" that the Romantics would have been wise to follow (Marchand, 547).

Frequently a harsh critic on his contemporaries, he had little praise for **Keats**, describing his work as "p-ss a bed poetry" and "a sort of mental masturbation" to his own publisher, although he regretted his harshness after Keats's death (Marchand, 346–347). Although **Shelley**'s radicalism and atheism repelled Byron, he valued his friendship and thought highly of his imagination.

The publication of the first canto of *Childe Harold*, a somewhat autobiographical epic poem showing the influence of Spenser in its structure, in 1812 made Byron a major figure after his return to London, meeting with Scott, Sheridan, and others. Scandal continued to encircle his private life, and after the collapse of his brief, troubled marriage to Annabella Milbanke, he left England, this time for good, in 1816.

Eventually Byron settled in Italy and continued to write, working especially on further cantos of *Childe Harold* and his new epic *Don Juan*. After further romantic entanglements, he eventually settled down with the Countess Teresa Guiccioli (herself separated from her husband) outside Pisa, where he also renewed contact with Shelley, Leigh Hunt, and other members of his circle. He was much affected by the death of Shelley and removed his household, including **Mary Shelley**, to Genoa. Influenced by the Italian nationalism of his mistress's relations and also seeking personal glory, Byron became interested in the cause of Greek nationalism. In 1823, he traveled to Greece in pursuit of this cause and endeavored to unite the various factions in the fight against the Turks. The following year, still in Greece, he died of fever, and his body was taken back to England for burial.

ARCHIVES

Lovelace Byron Papers, Bodleian Library, Oxford.
Egerton Collection, British Library, London.
John Murray Archives, London.
Roe-Byron Collection, Newstad Abbey.
Carl H. Pforzheimer Collection of "Shelley and His Circle," New York Public Library.

PRINTED SOURCES

Blessington, Lady. *Lady Blessington's Conversations of Lord Byron*, Ernest J. Lovell, Jr. (ed.) (Princeton, N.J.: Princeton University Press, 1969; originally published 1834).
Byron, Lord. *Byron's Letters and Journals*, Leslie A. Marchand (ed.), 12 vols. (London: John Murray, 1973–1981).
———. *Letters and Journals of Lord Byron, with Notices of His Life*, Tom Moore (ed.), 2 vols. (Paris: Gagliani, 1829).
———. *Lord Byron: The Complete Miscellaneous Prose*, Andrew Nicholson (ed.) (Oxford: Clarendon Press, 1991).
———. *Lord Byron: The Complete Poetical Works*, Jerome J. McGann (ed.), 7 vols. (Oxford: Clarendon Press, 1991).
———. *Selected Letters and Journals*, Leslie A. Marchand (ed.) (Cambridge, Mass.: Belknap Press, 1982). (References in the article are to this edition.)
Eisler, Benita. *Byron. Child of Passion, Fool of Fame* (New York: Alfred A. Knopf, 1999).
Grosskurth, Phyllis. *Byron. The Flawed Angel* (London: Hodder & Stoughton, 1997).
Hunt, Leigh. *Lord Byron and Some of His Contemporaries*, 2nd ed, 2 vols. (London, 1828).
Marchand, Leslie. *Byron: A Biography*, 3 vols. (New York: Alfred A. Knopf, 1957).

Derek Blakeley

C

CALDECOTT, RANDOLPH (1846–1886). Randolph Caldecott, an illustrator of children's books, was born in Chester, England, on March 22, 1846. The son of a hatter and tailor, he attended King Henry VIII's School, where he earned the designation as "head boy." His interest in art began at the age of six when he started drawing nature scenes and carving and molding wildlife figurines. Although the young Caldecott displayed his familiarity with classical literature through illustrations such as those of the Trojan Aeneas, whose countenance was suspiciously like that of his father, his illustrations soon reflected natural rather than classical themes. In 1861, Caldecott began working at a bank at Whitchurch, Shropshire. Six years later he transferred to Manchester and Salford Bank in Manchester. In 1861, he published his first drawing, in the *Illustrated London News*, a sketch of a fire at Queen's Hotel. Thereafter, he regularly contributed illustrations to *Will O' the Wisp* and to *Sphinx*.

After London Society began publishing his drawings in 1870, Caldecott decided to move to London and focus exclusively on contributing illustrations to London periodicals. Henry Blackburn, editor of *London Society* and Caldecott's close friend, was, however, concerned about the artist's persistent ill health and thus encouraged him to illustrate travel books, which would relieve the artist of the constant pressure of meeting deadlines and stimulate him to travel to healthier locales. Caldecott followed his friend's advice and traveled to northern Italy, where he drew *The Hartz Mountains: A Tour of the Toy Country*. Some of the illustrations in this book would later be published in the *London Graphic* and in *Harper's Monthly Magazine*, bringing Caldecott to the attention of an American public in 1873. Thereafter, Caldecott traveled frequently. During his frequent excursions he read such novelists as Oliver Goldsmith, George de Maurier, and **Charlotte Brontë**. Nevertheless, his primary interest continued to be his art; literary works were apparently less influential than a leisurely stroll or the etchings of the eighteenth-century engraver William Hogarth. Caldecott's fame grew following his illustration of **Washington Irving**'s *Old Christmas* (1875) and *Breckenridge Hall* (1877). Impressed with Caldecott's simplicity of style and with his keen sense of humor, Edmund Evans, a well-known London publisher, asked Caldecott in 1877 to succeed William Crane as his illustrator of children's books. It was as an illustrator of the so-called toy books that Caldecott was able to take advantage of his keen sense of humor, subtle use of color, and attention to detail. As an artist, he sought aesthetic simplicity, often explaining "the fewer the lines the less error committed." Caldecott illustrated an average of two books a year, often depicting characters and events from an idealized English countryside. His ability to animate scenes and to incorporate humor into his sketches often endeared him to his readers. Among his more renowned works were *The Diverting History of Jack Gilpen*, *The Great Panjandrum Himself*, *Jack and the Beanstalk*, and *The House That Jack Built*.

Caldecott married Marian Brind on March 18, 1880; they had no children. Troubled by tuberculosis, gastritis, and weakness resulting from the rheumatic fever he suffered as a child, and by his demanding work schedule, Caldecott suffered poor health throughout his life. On February 12, 1886, he died in St. Augustine, Florida, while touring the United States. In 1938, the American Library Association began awarding the Caldecott Award for excellence in the illustration of children's books.

ARCHIVES

Randolph Caldecott Correspondence, Houghton Library, Harvard University, Cambridge, Massachusetts.
Randolph Caldecott Page Proofs and Wood Blocks, de Grummond Collection, University of Southern Mississippi, Hattiesburg, Mississippi.

PRINTED SOURCES

Billington, Elizabeth T. (ed.). *The Randolph Caldecott Treasury* (New York: Frederick Warne, 1978).
Blackburne, Henry. *Randolph Caldecott: A Personal Memoir of His Early Art Career* (London: S. Low, Marson, Searle & Rivington, 1886).
Finlay, Nancy. *Randolph Caldecott, 1846–1886* (Cambridge, Mass.: Houghton, 1986).
Hutchins, Michael. *Yours Pictorially: Illustrated Letters of Randolph Caldecott* (London: Frederick Warne, 1976).
Ray, Gordon N. *The Illustrator and the Book in England from 1790 to 1914* (New York: Pierpont Morgan Library, Oxford University Press, 1976).

David B. Mock

CANOVA, ANTONIO (1757–1822). Antonio Canova, Italian sculptor, painter, draftsman, and architect, was born in Possagno (Treviso) in 1757. His mother, after the untimely death of her husband, entrusted the young Antonio to his grandfather, a stonecutter and mediocre architect. Canova worked as a workshop boy in Venice from an early age, at the same time attending the nude school at the Accademia and copying the molds of the ancient sculptures in the gallery of Filippo Farsetti. The proceeds from his first important sculpture, *Dedalus and Icarus*, allowed him to move to Rome, where he entered the circle of Gavin Hamilton, a group of intellectuals with interests in archeology, painting, and sculpture. In Rome he studied French and English and devoted himself to the study of the Latin and Greek classics. Canova's work is therefore not a mere imitation of ancient patterns but the reinterpretation, even the re-creation, of the spirit of the ancient fables; it reflects, in the style of Hellenistic literature, works of art as examples of emotional suggestion, as human expressions of affections and feelings. In this way, Canova's work contrasted sharply with the absolute imperturbability that Johann Winckelmann saw in the white eyes of ancient statues as well as with the prevalent neoclassicism, characterized by an often indiscriminate imitation of the classics. In a letter (November 26, 1806) addressed to Quatremère de Quincy he wrote: "It takes much more than to steal here and there ancient pieces and to bring them together without discretion, to win fame as an artist. You must sweat day and night on the Greek models, sink yourself in their style, assimilate it in your blood, create your own style having always in mind the beautiful nature, and reading in it the same rules." He considered himself a modern artist working like his ancestors, with the same aims of simplicity and idealism. His own intention was to undress the figure from the excessive ornament in order to reveal its soul.

The theme of death, very common in the neoclassic culture, is one of the constants of Canova's art. He develops it on a double register, civil and elegiac, similarly to what Ugo Foscolo did in his literary work *I Sepolcri*: On the one hand, he celebrates the dead personage as *exemplum virtutis* (monument for Vittorio Alfieri, Firenze, Santa Croce); on the other, he underlines the remembrance of personal affections and virtues. But his name was known especially for his mythological subjects: *Love and Psyche* (1787–1793), *Venus and Adonis* (1789–1794), *Venus italica* (1804–1808) and the *Graces* (1812–1816). In these works, Canova realized the idea of grace theorized by Winckelmann: "what is pleasant according to reason." Few artists have been so highly praised in their lifetime as Canova, acclaimed for his art but also for his exemplary life: His achievements far transcended his modest beginnings, and he intended to devote his life wholly to art. Canova's works inspired the juvenile art of Danish sculptor Bertel Thorvaldsen.

Forgotten during the Romantic period, Canova was rediscovered only in the second half of the twentieth century as the creator of an art form and the connecting figure between the Ancients' world and modern sensitivity, thanks to the studies of H. Honour and M. Praz.

ARCHIVES

Biografia manoscritta di Antonio Canova (1804 ca.), Museo Civico, Bassano del Grappa.
Quaderni di viaggio (1779–1780), Museo Civico, Bassano del Grappa.

PRINTED SOURCES

Antonio Canova. Atti del Conegno di Studi (Venezia, October 6–9, 1992), Venezia, Istituto veneto di Scienze, 1997.

Argan, G. C. *Antonio Canova* (Roma: Bulzoni, 1969).

Cicognara L. *Biografia di Antonio Canova* (Venezia: Missiaglia, 1823).

———. *Storia della scultura* (Prato: Fratelli Giachetti, 1824). The last volume entirely concerns Canova, who cooperated with its writing.

Honour, H. "Canova's Studio Practice," *Burlington Magazine* 114 (1972): 149–159, 214–229.

Licht, F. *Canova* (New York: Abbeville Press, 1983).

Moses, H. *The Works of A. Canova* (1824; London: Chatto & Windus, 1876).

Pavanello, G. *L'opera completa del Canova* (Milano: Rizzoli, 1976).

Stefani, O. *Antonio Canova. La statuaria* (Milano: Electa, 1999).

———. *Canova pittore: tra Eros e Thanatos* (Milano: Electa, 1992).

Zanella, A. *Canova in Rome* (Rome: Palombi Fratelli, 1993).

Maria Tabaglio

CANTOR, GEORG FERDINAND LUDWIG PHILIPP (1845–1918). Georg Cantor, mathematician and one of the founders of set theory, was born in St. Petersburg, Russia, in 1845 to a wealthy merchant family. He died in Halle, Germany, in 1918. Having moved to Germany in 1856, Cantor was educated principally by his father, Georg Woldemar Cantor, though the child attended a number of schools.

After a term at the University of Zurich in 1862, Cantor studied mathematics briefly at Göttingen and then, from 1862 until 1867, at Berlin University, where he came under the influence of Karl Weierstrass (1815–1897), whose lectures attracted students from all over the world and whose work on complex functions was widely influential. Weierstrass lectured in 1863–1864 on real numbers. At Berlin, Cantor was also influenced by Leopold Kronecker (1823–1891) and Ernst Kummer (1810–1893), who supervised Cantor's doctoral thesis of 1867. Kronecker and Kummer may have influenced Cantor's ideas about number theory, though Kronecker would later become one of Cantor's most strident critics.

Cantor took up a professorship at Halle in 1869, becoming full professor in 1879. At the suggestion of Halle mathematician Eduard Heine, Cantor began work on trigonometric series, which led to his developing a foundation for the concept of "real number" theory he developed contemporaneously but independently of Richard Dedekind (1831–1916), with whom he began a correspondence that would last his entire career.

Cantor's work on set theory, infinity, cardinality, and transfinite numbers began properly with his 1874 paper "Ober eine Eigenschaft des Inbegriffes aller reelen algebraischen Zahlen." From 1879 to 1884, Cantor produced the six parts of his comprehensive "Ober unendliche lineare Punktmannichfaltigkeiten." The work exhibits sustained study of the history of mathematics in its criticisms of finitist thinkers from the Greeks through scholastic thinkers to Benedictus Spinoza (1632–1677), Gottfried Freiherr von Leibniz (1646–1716), and Immanuel Kant (1724–1804).

Cantor was also influenced by Plato (428–347 B.C.E.) and by his religious convictions. Although Cantor's work was severely criticized by many, he was supported by Dedekind, Weierstrass, David Hilbert, Bertrand Russell, and Ernst Zermelo.

ARCHIVES

Most of Cantor's original papers were destroyed during World War II. Remaining documents can be found at Archiv der Martin-Luther-Universitat Halle-Wittenberg, including material on his habilitation; University of Göttingen; and Berlin University, including material on his dissertation.

PRINTED SOURCES

Fraenkel, Abraham. "Georg Cantor," *Jahresbericht der Deutschen Mathenzatiker Vereinigung*, 39 (1930), 189–266.
Grattan-Guinness, I. "Towards a Biography of Georg Cantor," *Annals of Science*, 27 (1971), 345–391.
Meschkowski, H. *Georg Cantor: Leben, Werk und Wirkung* (Mannheim: Bibliographisches Institut, 1983). Delineates influences and relates Cantor's work to those of contemporaries and successors.
Purkert, W., and H. J. Ilgauds. *Georg Cantor, 1845–1918* (Basel: Birkhauser, 1987).
Zermelo, Ernst (ed.). *Gesammelte Abhandlungen* (1932; reprint, Hildesheim: Georg Olms, 1962). Contains biography by Abraham A. Fraenkel.

Peter S. Fosl

CARLYLE, THOMAS (1795–1881). Thomas Carlyle was born in Ecclefechan, Scotland, in 1795. His first reading, in a strict Presbyterian home, was the Bible. At Annan Academy and Edinburgh University he read Latin classics, Scottish philosophers, French, and English mathematical and scientific work. Intended for the Scottish ministry, he became the Sage of Chelsea, the century's cant-battling Jeremiah.

He early read Shakespeare (whose plays he was still rereading a year before his death) and Milton; before the mid-1830s he read widely in eighteenth- and nineteenth-century British, French, and German literature and philosophy; he even read "the most unutterable trash of [Gothic?] novels" (*Coll. Letters*, 3:146). Jessop argues (xiii) that he probably absorbed the thought of some writers from the intellectual climate rather than from reading; his letters comment on works that he has not read but of which he has some knowledge (sometimes culled from periodicals, which he read all his life). Often he "read in" books, not through them. With other books he carried on a dialogue still available in the margins of volumes scattered among several archives. He read actively, recreating and even transforming texts, melding the new text into his own thought.

In the 1820s **Goethe** (*Wilhelm Meister*, both parts of *Faust*), Jean Paul (Friedrich Richter), and other German authors showed him the way to spiritual rebirth and a new style, both seen in *Sartor Resartus*. After the 1830s, as he turned more than ever to history and to the "State of England" question, books were research tools, not moral guides. While the difficulty of borrowing books led to his role in founding the London Library in 1840, five years later he claimed, "My reverence for Books does not increase with my years" (*Coll. Letters* 19: 70); during the rest of his life he spoke of "idle" reading in current English fiction and verse. Nevertheless these, like periodicals, were significant, conveying the often distressing voices of the times that remained his constant study.

ARCHIVES

National Library of Scotland, Edinburgh.

Carlyle House, Cheyne Row, London.

University of California at Santa Cruz, Strouse Collection. See Charles S. Fineman and Jerry D. James, *Carlyle: Books & Margins . . . with a transcription of Carlyle's Marginalia in John Stuart Mill's Principles of Political Economy and an Interpretative Essay Thereon* [by Murray Baumgarten] (Santa Cruz, Calif.: Santa Cruz University Library, 1980).

Harvard College Library. "Books on Cromwell and Frederick the Great bequeathed by Carlyle." Catalogue by William Coolidge Lane, 1888.

University of Michigan Library, Dr. Samuel A. Jones Carlyle Collection. Catalogue ed. Mary E. Weed, 1919.

PRINTED SOURCES

Campbell, Ian. "Carlyle's Borrowings from the Theological Library of Edinburgh University," *Bibliotheck*, 5 (1969), 165–168.

Carlyle, Thomas. *Collected Letters of Thomas and Jane Welsh Carlyle* (Durham, N.C.: Duke University Press, 1970–). Vols. 1–27 cover the years 1812 to 1852.

———. *Sartor Resartus*, C. F. Harrold (ed.) (New York: Doubleday, 1937).

———. *Works*, H. D. Traill (ed.), 30 vols. (London: Chapman and Hall, 1896–1899).

Harrison, Frederic. *Carlyle and the London Library* (London: Chapman and Hall, 1906).

Harrold, Charles Frederick. *Carlyle and German Thought: 1819–1834* (New Haven, Conn.: Yale University Press, 1934).

Jessop, Ralph. *Carlyle and Scottish Thought* (Basingstoke, England: Macmillan, 1997).

Kaplan, Fred. *Thomas Carlyle* (Ithaca, N.Y.: Cornell University Press, 1983).

Shine, Hill. *Carlyle's Early Reading, to 1834* (Lexington: University of Kentucky Libraries, 1953).

Vida, Elizabeth M. *Romantic Affinities: German Authors and Carlyle* (Toronto: University of Toronto Press, 1993).

Eileen M. Curran

CARNEGIE, ANDREW (1835–1919). Andrew Carnegie was born in Dunfermline, Scotland, in 1835 to a master weaver and the daughter of a cobbler. Five years of instruction in a one-room schoolhouse there was his only formal education. Carnegie and his family immigrated to the United States in 1848 because of hard times brought on by the rise of the factory system. His subsequent rise from rags to riches remains the stuff of legends in the annals of American capitalism. Carnegie often credited his success to hard work, but an appreciation for the value of cutting-edge technology, rich patrons, and luck were equally responsible for his becoming the dominant steel magnate of the late nineteenth century. Carnegie developed a reputation as an author and social critic from the time he published his first magazine article in 1882. The subjects of his many books and essays ranged from "The Negro in America" to a biography of the inventor James Watt. The success of his writing brought him fame even before his wealth distinguished him from other industrialists of the time. When the founders of United States Steel bought Carnegie's firm in 1901, he became the richest man in the world and the foremost philanthropist of his era.

Carnegie was self-educated. Unable to attend school in America because of a need to help support his family, he constantly patronized the few free lending libraries around his home in Pittsburgh, Pennsylvania. His love of reading stayed with him for his entire life. According to Carnegie's foremost biographer, "He read constantly [and] remembered what he read" (Wall, 887). Carnegie was not against formal education, but his experience and that of his partners in business convinced him that schooling was not a prerequisite to being successful in a democratic nation like the United States.

As a boy, Carnegie most enjoyed writers such as **Thomas Macaulay**, Charles Lamb, the Scottish poet Robert Burns, and the American historian George Bancroft. When he first encountered the writings of **Charles Darwin** and **Herbert Spencer** is uncertain, but the influence of these authors on his worldview was profound. Carnegie's encounter with evolutionary doctrine led him to abandon his Presbyterian upbringing and become a scientific humanist. Carnegie saw evolution as a universal law. It served as his framework for understanding nature, business, society, and politics. His belief in evolution was also responsible for his optimistic outlook on life. "All is well, since all grows better," he liked to say.

After he made his fortune, Carnegie took to sponsoring those scholars and intellectuals whose work he admired most. His relationship with Herbert Spencer is particularly important because of Carnegie's close identification with Social Darwinism. Carnegie sought out Spencer before his first tour of America in 1882. He convinced Spencer to come to Pittsburgh, but once there the author preferred the company of Carnegie's brother Tom. Nevertheless, before departing Spencer publicly called Carnegie one of his "two best American friends." Carnegie, in turn, referred to Spencer as his mentor. The industrialist was not, however, an orthodox Social Darwinist. Carnegie latched on to the general Spencerian notion that mankind would improve over time through social and technological advancement, but unlike Spencer, he championed the principle of egalitarianism and the possibility of individual achievement more than any other ideals. For these reasons, Carnegie's interest in Spencer waned as he became involved in the Progressive movement after the turn of the twentieth century.

Spencer was only one of many writers and intellectuals who benefited from Carnegie's largesse. Carnegie sponsored a U.S. tour by **Matthew Arnold** in 1883 and one by the poet Edwin Arnold in 1891. He kept both **Rudyard Kipling** and Booker T. Washington on private pensions reserved for family members and close friends. When **Lord Acton** wished to sell his library in 1890 in order to pay debts, Carnegie bought it on condition that Acton would keep it for the rest of his life. Carnegie corresponded regularly with **Mark Twain**, who often wrote to ask for money. After his retirement from business in 1901, Carnegie continued to seek out prominent scholars and intellectuals to teach him about the world and to help him decide how to dispense his money. His philanthropy, particularly the building of countless libraries in America and Great Britain, remains the most tangible evidence of how Carnegie's value of reading affected the development of Western culture.

ARCHIVES

Andrew Carnegie Papers, Library of Congress, Washington, D.C. There is a smaller collection of Carnegie materials at the New York Public Library.

PRINTED SOURCES

Carnegie, Andrew. *The Autobiography of Andrew Carnegie* (Boston: Houghton Mifflin, 1920).
Hendrick, Burton J. (ed.). *The Books of Andrew Carnegie* (Garden City, N.Y.: Doubleday, Doran & Company, 1933).
———. *The Life of Andrew Carnegie*, 2 vols. (Garden City, N.Y.: Doubleday, Doran & Company, 1933)
Swetnam, George. *Andrew Carnegie* (Boston: G. K. Hall & Company, 1980). Focuses on Carnegie's writing and speeches.
Wall, Joseph Frazier. *Andrew Carnegie* (New York: Oxford University Press, 1970). The definitive biography.

Jonathan Rees

CARROLL, LEWIS (1832–1898). Lewis Carroll is the pseudonym of English children's author Charles Lutwidge Dodgson, best known for *Alice's Adventures in Wonderland* (1865) and its sequel, *Alice Through the Looking-Glass* (1871). Carroll is also recognized as one of the great amateur photographers of children of the Victorian period. Carroll was born in Daresbury, the third of 10 children and the eldest son of Reverend Charles Dodgson and Frances Jane Lutwidge. He attended preparatory school at Richmond (1844–1845) and Rugby (1846–1849) and attended Christ Church, Oxford, arriving in 1851. He earned a B.A. in 1854 with First Class Honors in Mathematics and Second Class in Classics and an M.A. in 1857. He became a Mathematical Lecturer in 1855, a position he held until 1881, when he resigned the lectureship but retained his studentship, allowing him to remain at Christ Church until his death. Carroll was influenced by the religious beliefs of his father, an archdeacon in the Anglican Church. Ordained as a deacon in 1861, Carroll did not become a priest as was expected of Oxford faculty at the time. He held High Church views; and while he was intensely religious in his personal life, the *Alice* books are remarkably free of religious or social lessons that appeared in most Victorian children's literature. The *Alice* books encouraged entertainment, rather than instruction or morality, for child readers and helped liberate nineteenth-century children's literature from overt didacticism.

As a child, Carroll read nursery rhymes and fairy tales that would provide him with models for characters such as Humpty Dumpty and Tweedledum and Tweedledee in the *Alice* books. Auction catalogs of his personal library and the many references to books and authors in his diary and letters suggest that he read widely in many fields ranging from theology to psychic research. Morton Cohen suggests that next to the Bible and Shakespeare Carroll was most strongly influenced by **Blake**, **Wordsworth**, **Coleridge**, **Dickens**, and **Tennyson**—all of whom wrote on the nature of childhood (106). Carroll's idealization of childhood was influenced by his reading of Romantic poets and formed his concept of the innocence of childhood that permeates his children's books and photographs of children. Carroll frequently attended the theater, where he enjoyed pantomime, plays based of fairy tales intended for children, as well as Shakespeare. One of his uncompleted projects was an edition of Shakespeare for girls, since he felt Thomas Bowdler did not sufficiently expurgate the plays. The *Alice* books are influenced by Carroll's love of theater in that they are structured like plays; they are primarily dialogue and rely on the illustrations to convey description. Despite his admiration for Romantic poets, Carroll parodied them, as he did Wordsworth's "Resolution and Independence" (1807), which appears as "The White Knight's Song" in *Looking-Glass*.

The *Alice* books include frequent comic reworkings of earlier, didactic children's texts. The distorted geography lessons in *Wonderland* are based on William Pinnock's *A Catechism of Geography* (1822), whereas Abraham Chear's *A Looking Glass for Children* (1673) is a source of the looking-glass world of *Looking-Glass*. Moralizing poems are parodied in *Wonderland* so that Isaac Watts's "Against Idleness and Mischief" (1715) becomes "How Doth the Little Crocodile," Jane Taylor's "The Star" (1804) becomes "Twinkle, Twinkle, Little Bat," and **Robert Southey**'s "The Old Man's Comforts, and How He Gained Them" (1799) becomes "You Are Old, Father William." Carroll's nonsense verse, such as "Jabberwocky" in *Wonderland* or *The Hunting of the Snark* (1876), would seem to suggest a knowledge of Edward Lear's limericks, but there is no evidence that Carroll ever read Lear. Catherine Sinclair's *Holiday House* (1839), with its mischievous children as well as its interpolated fairy tale "Uncle David's Nonsensical Story about Giants and Fairies," was a children's novel that Carroll gave in 1861 to Alice Liddell, the girl for whom his wrote *Wonderland*, and influenced the creation of his assertive protagonist. The literary fairy tales of George MacDonald and Charles Kingsley's *The Water-Babies* (1863) are two important fantasy sources that Carroll read and used as models to create his own literary fairy tales. MacDonald and Carroll were friends during the period Carroll wrote the *Alice* books. The MacDonald family read the manuscript of *Wonderland* and encouraged him to expand and publish it.

ARCHIVES

Lewis Carroll Diaries. British Library.

PRINTED SOURCES

Cohen, Morton N. *Lewis Carroll: A Biography* (New York: Knopf, 1995).
Doherty, John. *The Literary Products of the Lewis Carroll—George MacDonald Friendship* (Lewiston, N.Y.: Edwin Mellen Press, 1995).
Knoepflmacher, U. C. "Revisiting Wordsworth: Lewis Carroll's 'The White Knight's Song,' " *Victorian Institute Journal*, 14 (1986), 1–20.
Rackin, Donald. "Corrective Laughter: Carroll's Alice and Popular Children's Literature of the Nineteenth Century," *Journal of Popular Culture*, 1 (1967), 243–255.
Reichertz, Ronald. *The Making of the Alice Books: Lewis Carroll's Use of Earlier Children's Literature* (Montreal: McGill-Queen's University Press, 1997).
Stern, Jeffrey (ed.). *Lewis Carroll's Library* (Charlottesville, Va.: Lewis Carroll Society of North America, distributed by University of Virginia Press, 1981).

Jan Susina

CARVER, GEORGE WASHINGTON (ca. 1864–1943). George Washington Carver was born about 1864 on the Moses Carver Plantation around Diamond, Missouri. His parents had been born slaves. Carver may have been the son of Moses Carver, the slave owner on whose plantation he was born. He named the Bible as his favorite early reading and lifelong influence. Carver became an outstanding scientist, noted teacher, and a humanitarian, though music and art were his first career goals. He changed fields at the urging of one of his college instructors and became the founder of the new field of chemurgy.

Carver was the first African American to be graduated from Iowa State and its first black professor. In 1896, he left the University of Iowa at Booker T. Washington's invitation to join him at Tuskegee Institute. There he organized the Agricultural Department, teaching chemistry and botany and conducting his significant research.

Carver developed over 300 products from peanuts, 100 from sweet potatoes, and numerous others from clay, cotton, soybeans, and other materials. In 1939 Hollywood portrayed his life, emphasizing his humanization of science.

The works of Booker T. Washington greatly influenced Carver, who attempted to be faithful to their self-help message. Carver received many honorary degrees and awards in his life both for his example and for his products, which did much to save the southern economy.

ARCHIVES

University of Iowa, Ames, Iowa. Includes biographical material, newspaper clippings, publications (including his B.S. thesis), bibliographies, lists of awards and honors, correspondence (chiefly with Louis H. Pammel, 1897–1928), interviews and rem-

iniscences of colleagues, television script, and subject files on Tuskegee Institute and Carver Foundation and Museum, Carver National Monument at Diamond Grove, Missouri, and ISU Carver Hall Dedication.
George Washington Carver papers at Tuskegee Institute (S417.c3A2 1975x Microfilm).

PRINTED SOURCES

Holt, Rackham. *George Washington Carver: An American Biography* (Garden City, N.Y.: Doubleday, Doran and Company, 1943).
McMurray, Linda. *George Washington Carver: Scientist and Symbol* (New York: Oxford University Press), 1981. Utilizes Robert P. Muller and Merrill J. Mattes, *The Early Life of George Washington Carver* (November 26, 1957) typescript, [George Washington Carver National Monument archives], 12–18.
Smith, Alvin D. *George Washington Carver: Man of God* (New York: Exposition Press, 1954).

Frank A. Salamone

CASSATT, MARY (1845–1926). Mary Cassatt was born into a wealthy family in Pittsburgh. She spent her childhood in several places, including a country estate where she was educated by a private governess, and in Europe, where she learned French and German before age 12. She attended the Pennsylvania Academy of the Fine Arts in Philadelphia from 1860 to 1862. Cassatt's formal schooling ended here, as she left the United States for Paris in 1865, where she became the private student of Jean-Léon Gérôme. While Gérôme's reputation has since been eclipsed by Cassatt's, it was then a major accomplishment for Cassatt to be accepted by such a renowned master, and she spent several years under his tutelage. Cassatt sketched and copied works in the Louvre and visited an artists' community in Écouen, where she absorbed the style and subject material of genre painters from another teacher, Paul Constant Soyer, who depicted peasant scenes. Cassatt's first painting exhibited in the Paris Salon, *A Mandoline Player* (1868), is in this style. In 1868 Cassatt moved to Villiers-le-Bel to study with Thomas Couture, whose romantic, dramatic work represented a move away from genre painting. Cassatt completed a picture based on **Tennyson**'s poem "Mariana" with Couture, but the picture does not survive. Although Cassatt was a voracious reader of poetry and fiction, no other painting of hers is known to have been inspired by a work of literature (Matthews, 54).

Cassatt returned to America in 1870, where she visited John Sartain, the Philadelphia engraver, and became friendly with his daughter Emily, another artist. Cassatt and Emily Sartain returned to Europe together, and upon the 1877 invitation of **Edgar Degas**, Cassatt became the only American to join the group of Impressionist painters working in Paris. Among the Impressionists, Cassatt named **Édouard Manet** and Gustave Courbet as being influential, and she worked closely with Berthe Morisot, Camille Pissarro, and Degas. She described the moment of her invitation as the point where she "began to live" (Segard, 7–8). In 1879, Cassatt and other Impressionists began to experiment with printmaking in the style of "Impressionist printmakers" Armand Guillauman, Henri

Guérard, Henri Somm, Jean-Louis Forain, and Dr. Paul Gachet. Despite her Old Master and Impressionist influences, Cassatt's signature theme, the mother and child portrait, seems to have been prompted by the birth of nephews and nieces into her family. Late in life, Cassatt remained an active reader; she read Milton but disliked **Henry James** and Edith Wharton. Cassatt became committed to women's suffrage in America, through her prominent feminist friends Theodate Pope and Louisine Havemeyer. She completed a mural depicting "Modern Woman" for the 1893 Columbian Exposition in Chicago and donated or loaned artworks to exhibits benefiting suffragettes.

ARCHIVAL SOURCES

No archival sources known to exist.

PRINTED SOURCES

Matthews, Nancy Mowll. *Mary Cassatt: A Life* (New York: Villard, 1994). Extensive bibliography.
Segard, Achille. *Mary Cassatt* (Paris: Librairie Paul Ollendorff, 1913). In French; only biography based on interviews with Cassatt.
"Selected Bibliography: Mary Cassatt." In National Museum of Women in the Arts Website. Includes profile and extensive bibliographical and curatorial information. Available at http://www.nmwa.org/library/bibs/cassatt.htm

Deborah Banner

CAVOUR, CAMILLO BENSO DI (1810–1861). Camillo Benso di Cavour, Italian politician, statesman, and—along with **Giuseppe Mazzini** and **Giuseppe Garibaldi**—architect of Italy's unification. The English historian George Macaulay Trevelyan called him "the Master Statesman of his century—if not all time (Trevelyan, 23)." Cavour was born in Turin and deeply immersed in Piedmontese, Swiss, and French culture. French and Piedmontese were his first languages. His English biographer, Denis Mack Smith, noted that he "received a defective education . . . and found reading difficult." Proficient in mathematics and mechanics, he was nonetheless deficient in Italian language and literature. A military education of seven years proved to be of little help; for concealing forbidden books, he was sentenced to arrest for 10 days.

He studied the French, English, and Scottish historians, especially Edward Gibbon on religion and **François Guizot**, who imparted the idea that history could be as logical as mathematics and the physical sciences. Cavour's youthful notebooks contain extensive notes on Dean Milman's *History of the Jews* and William Robertson's *History of Charles V*. From David Hume's *History of England*, he made extensive annotations on the English heretic John Wycliffe, King Henry's battle with St. Thomas Becket, and Charles I's reckless disregard of Parliament. He was influenced by the Geneva of Voltaire and Rousseau and read the radical *Westminster Review*. From the British economists, he read Nassau Senior, **David Ricardo**, and **Thomas Malthus**. As Mack Smith recounts, he told an English friend that he learned English by rising at 4:00 A.M. to read Adam Smith and blamed some of Italy's troubles on an excessively literary education. In English literature, he was drawn to Alexander Pope and **Walter Scott**; declared Shakespeare "incomparable," and read everything written by **Bulwer-Lytton**. A favorite writer was **Jeremy Bentham** ("that great inquirer into the secrets of the human heart"), but for Cavour, **Byron** was the greatest poet of the nineteenth century: "the favorite of strong spirits and anyone with a too exquisite sensibility."

In Genoa, Cavour frequented both the salon and bedroom of the Marquise Anne Giustiniani, a French intellectual with republican sentiments. From French literature he admired **Victor Hugo, Honoré de Balzac**, de Musset, Gautier, **Stendahl**, **de Staël**, and **Chateaubriand**. He admired the French sociologist **Auguste Comte** and **Alexis de Tocqueville**. Throughout his life, Cavour remained closer to French than Italian literature. He did admire Nicolo Machiavelli but was indifferent to Dante and Petrarca. Instead, his notebooks carry copious notes from Shakespeare.

ARCHIVES

Soprintendenza Archivistica Regione Piemonte, Archivio di Stato di Torino.
Fondo Famiglia Benso di Cavour, Archivio Centrale dello Stato, Rome.
Miscellanea di Carte Politiche o Riservate, 1848–1861, Archivio Centrale dello Stato, Rome.

PRINTED SOURCES

Hearder, Harry. *Cavour* (London: Longman, 1994).
Mack Smith, Denis. *Cavour* (London: Weidenfeld and Nicolson, 1985).
Pishedda, Carlo. *Camillo Cavour: la famiglia e il patrimonio* (Vercelli, Italy: Società storica vercellese Cuneo, 1997).
Ruggiero, Michele. *Cavour e l'altra Italia* (Milan: Rusconi, 1997).
Trevelyan, George Macaulay. *Garibaldi and the Making of Italy* (London: Longmans, Green and Co., 1911).

Stanislao G. Pugliese

CÉZANNE, PAUL (1839–1906). Paul Cézanne, a painter, was born in Aix-en-Provence and educated at Lycée d'Aix (College Bourbon today, 1852–1858). Later he studied law at the Law Faculty at Aix (1858–1861), while taking art classes at the Municipal School of Drawing. In 1861, he moved to Paris and joined the Atelier Suisse, an informal art school where artists could sketch from the nude.

Cézanne, a serious student at the lycée, was particularly interested in classical literature and later freely quoted from classical authors in his private correspondence. He shared his earliest interest in literature with his childhood friend **Émile Zola**. They read de Musset, **Hugo**, and **Lamartine** together, and Cézanne himself engaged in writing poetry and music.

His painting *The Rape* (1867) reflects not only his enthusiasm for themes of classical literature but also his fascination with the macabre. The latter he shared with Zola, as it is reflected by Zola's depiction of morbid passion in *Thérèse Raquin*. Other echoes of *Thérèse Raquin* also appear in Cézanne's *Preparation for a Funeral* (ca. 1868) in which two figures prepare a corpse for the burial, again recalling lurid and morbid events of Zola's novel.

Another literary influence on Cézanne's painting is **Flaubert**'s novel *The Temptation of St. Anthony* (1857–1858). Cézanne's own *The Temptation of St. Anthony* (ca. 1870) depicts the battle between St. Anthony and the sensuality of female tempters, while the painting *The Feast or The Orgy* (ca. 1870) is also based on a scene from the same novel. Later, however, Cézanne grew increasingly suspicious of "literary spirit" in painting, which led to his final rupture with Zola.

His later work was influenced by his reading of Bergson, in particular Bergson's concept of duration, which privileges a flow of observation over a period of time rather than a single moment of sensory perception preferred by the Impressionists.

ARCHIVES

Bibliothèque Nationale, Paris. Includes correspondence with Zola.
Courtland Institute, London. Correspondence with Émile Bernard.

PRINTED SOURCES

Cézanne, Paul. *Cézanne's Letters*, J. Rewald (ed.) (London: Bruno Cassirer, 1941).
Fry, Roger. *Cézanne, a Study of His Development* (Chicago and London: Chicago University Press, 1989).
Niess, R. J. *Zola, Cézanne and Manet* (Ann Arbor: University of Michigan Press, 1968).
Rewald, John. *Cézanne, a Biography* (London and New York: Thames and Hudson, 1986).
Verdi, Richard. *Cézanne* (London and New York: Thames and Hudson, 1992).
Vollard, Ambroise. *Paul Cézanne* (London: Brentano's Ltd., 1924).

Zsuzsanna Varga

CHAMBERLAIN, HOUSTON STEWART (1855–1927). Houston Stewart Chamberlain was born in Southsea, near Portsmouth, and educated at the Lycée Impérial, Versailles (France), a private school near Portsmouth (1866), and Cheltenham College (1867–1870). From 1870 to 1874 he had a private tutor in France, Otto Kuntze, then a student of theology, who instilled in him the image of an idealized Germany. At the University of Geneva (Natural Sciences, 1879–1884), he earned a Bacheliers ès sciences physiques et naturelles in 1881; his thesis entitled "Recherches sur la sève ascendante," was not finished until 1897 and did not culminate with a degree. He studied botany with Professor Julius von Wiesner at the University of Vienna in 1889–1890. He is well known for his excessive praise of a Germanic race and his idea of its mission to regenerate Western civilization, for his conception of history as a struggle between—good and evil—races, for his pseudoscientific justification of anti-semitism, and for his idea of a Germanic Christianity, aristocratic as well as militant.

Receiving an intermittent education and, except for an interval in the early 1880s, freed from the need to earn his income, from the age of 18 onward Chamberlain read widely all his life, spanning a wide range of topics from biology or natural sciences in general to philosophy, literature, and aesthetics. He acquired an encyclopedic knowledge of French, English, and German literature, historiography, and philosophy, as well as Indian philosophy, and remained proud of being a dilettante. The strongest formative influence undoubtedly came from the music and writings of **Richard Wagner**, whom Chamberlain once called "the sun of his life" (*Lebenswege*, 160). In Wagner's *Collected Works* he found confirmation of his inflated conception of Germanity, of his perception of present times as an era of crisis, and of the idea of a regeneration of civilization through art. In his conception of art he showed himself indebted to Wagner's *Religion und Kunst* as well as to Friedrich Schiller's *Briefe über die ästhetische Erziehung des Menschen* ("Brief an H.S.", 226).

Chamberlain's racial thought was based on many sources including **Charles Darwin**, whose *Origin of Species* he considered a revelation when reading it as a student of natural sciences (*Lebenswege*, 83), though later he strongly repudiated the theory's evolutionary element and the materialistic approach in science; Arthur Joseph de Gobineau's *Essai sur l'inégalité des races humaines*; though Chamberlain did not think of himself as a true anti-semite (*Briefe*, 1: 77); and Paul de Lagarde's *Deutsche Schriften*, one of the books most dear to him (*Wehr und Gegenwehr*, 61f) with its conception of a Germanic christianity and its emphasis on a German(ic) race consciousness.

Chamberlain considered Immanuel Kant, "the true master of my thought" (*Lebenswege*, 161). Kant's criticism of the limits of empiricism (*Erkenntniskritik*) as well as **Goethe**'s universalism, combining literature, philosophy, and science, stayed with him throughout his intellectual life. In his *Tagebuecher*, now in the Chamberlain Nachlass, he kept a record of his readings, sometimes exact to the number of pages.

ARCHIVES

Chamberlain Nachlass, Richard Wagner Gedenkstaette, Bayreuth.

PRINTED SOURCES

Chamberlain, Anna. *Meine Erinnerungen an Houston Stewart Chamberlain* (Munich: Beck, 1923).

Chamberlain, H. S. *Briefe 1882–1924 und Briefwechsel mit Kaiser Wilhelm II*, Paul Pretzsch (ed.), 2 vols. (Munich: Bruckmann, 1928).

———. "Brief an H. S. (Hans Sachs) über die Bestimmung der Wagnerverein," *Bayreuther Blätter* (1910), pp. 225–228.

———. *Die Grundlagen des 19. Jahrhunderts*, 2 vols. (Munich: Bruckmann 1899). Published in English translation, *The Foundations of the Nineteenth Century* (London: Lane 1911).

————. *Lebenswege meines Denkens* (Munich: Bruckmann, 1919).

————. *Wehr und Gegenwehr* (Munich: Bruckmann, 1912).

Field, Geoffrey C. *Evangelist of Race. The Germanic Vision of Houston Stewart Chamberlain* (New York: Columbia University Press, 1981).

Pretzsch, Paul (ed.). *Cosima Wagner und Houston Stewart Chamberlain im Briefwechsel 1888–1908* (Leipzig: Reclam, 1934).

Angela Schwarz

CHATEAUBRIAND, FRANÇOISE-AUGUSTE-RENÉ, VICOMTE DE (1768–1848). François Chateaubriand, an inaugural member of the Romantic movement in literature, was born at St. Malo in Brittany on September 14, 1768. He was raised at his family's medieval château and attended grammar school at Rennes, finishing his education at Dol College. Unsure of the direction to take in life after years of preparation for the priesthood, he joined the army in August 1786. Disillusioned by the aims of a military life, he embarked for America on April 7, 1791, in an attempt to discover the Northwest Passage. This trip would become fodder for much of his work and inspired his idyllic portrayals of nature. After several months in America, he returned to France on January 2, 1792, to fight for King Louis XVI and the Royalist army. Wounded in battle at Thionville, he retired to England for eight years, a period marked by skepticism and disillusionment, as reflected in works such as *Essai historique, politique et moral sur les revolutions anciennes et modernes considerées dans leurs rapports avec la revolution française*, published in 1797. His tone changed after the death of his mother in 1798, and the nineteenth-century Chateaubriand began to emerge.

His contributions to the Western canon included *Le génie du christianisme* (1802), his contention that conceptual reasoning was no longer sufficient in the age of power play and argumentation. Although somewhat exaggerated in tone, Chateaubriand may have single-handedly helped revive an interest in religion since the publication of *Le génie du christianisme* coincided with the resurgence of Roman Catholicism in France. This work attracted **Napoléon**, who appointed him secretary to the Rome embassy in 1802, the beginning of a life in politics for Chateaubriand. However, on March 21, 1804, he resigned from the diplomatic service in order to make a pilgrimage to the Holy Land. His travels became the inspiration for his 1811 work *Itineraire de Paris à Jerusalem et de Jerusalem à Paris, en allant par la Grèce, et revenant par l'Egypte, la Barbarie, et l'Espagne*. After its publication in 1811, Chateaubriand's political career occupied center stage. He became the French ambassador to Berlin, a delegate at the Congress of Verona, and Minister of Foreign Affairs. In 1815, he was honored as a peer of the realm, a title that he relinquished in 1830, unwilling to dedicate himself to Louis Philippe. This event essentially marked the retirement of Chateaubriand, and he dedicated the remainder of his life to his "raison d'être," his *Mémoirs d'outre tombe*, published posthumously in pamphlet form from 1849 to 1859.

Chateaubriand can be credited with facilitating the transition from the classical school to the Romantic style, and it was a characteristic he did not take lightly. Not surprisingly, his influences included George Washington, Napoléon, Pius VII, and Burke, each of whom influenced Chateaubriand's work ethic: "[F]reedom is preserved only by work, because work produces strength . . . the strength of the body is maintained by physical exercise; once labour is lacking, strength disappears" (*Memoires*, 373). This inspired much of Chateaubriand's work, as well as his life. His urge to explore the exotic had led him to America in 1791 and the writing of *Atala*, the "painting of two lovers who walk and talk in solitude; all lies in the picture of the turmoil and love in the midst of the calm of the wilderness" (preface to *Atala*). Keeping in mind that Chateaubriand believed that thoughts made the man, he created Chactas, the Indian protagonist, who was unable to assimilate to the civilized world, and Atala, the white female, who was torn between her desire for Chactas and her desire for home. Yet this was also a tale of brotherhood, a work representing the state of nature and the problems of populating it.

The introspective tone and egotism so expressive of the *mal du siècle*, and found in *Atala*, is also found in *René*. Self-titled, this work is the tale of a man imprisoned in himself; it is the tale of a man on a mission to find true happiness. It is the ultimate tale of ennui, the story of a man so self-absorbed that he ignores his wife and children, as well as the world around him. His mental anguish mirrored his incapacity to deal with the end of the Ancien Regime, and only in nature, or physical exile, could the answers be found. This was a tale in which man's suffering was central to the story line but in which religion and faith remained victorious. Father Souel, the Catholic priest, supported René through his toughest times, an event that perhaps mirrored the French Catholic revival in early nineteenth-century France.

Chateaubriand popularized the notion of the individual with the publication of *René*. His writing was an attempt to justify the events of the two centuries in which he lived. For he was a man caught between two centuries, a turmoil revealed in his writing. He noted, "I have found myself caught between two ages, as in the conflux of two rivers, and I have plunged into their waters, turning regretfully from the old bank upon which I was born, yet swimming hopefully towards the unknown shore at which the new generations are to land" (*Memoires*, xxiv).

ARCHIVES

Widely scattered in private collections and libraries.

PRINTED SOURCES

Chateaubriand, François René. *Correspondence générale*, 5 vols., ed. Louis Thomas (Paris: Champion, 1912–1924).
———. *Le Génie du christianisme* (Paris: Garmier-Flammarion, 1966) 1:58.
———. *Lettres à Madame Récamier* ed. Maurice Levaillant and E. Beau de Loménie (Paris: Flammarion, 1951).

—————. *Memoires d'outre tombe*, vol. I, Alexander Teixeira de Mattos (trans.) (New York: G. P. Putnam's Sons, 1902), xxiv–xxvi, 373.

George, Albert J. "Transition." In *Short Fiction in France: 1800–1850* (Syracuse, N.Y.: Syracuse University Press, 1964), 23–29.

Roulin, J. M. "Chateaubriand: l'exil et la gloire," *French Studies*, 50, 3 (1996), 338–350.

—————. *Chateaubriand, l'exil et la gloire: du roman familial à l'identité littéraire dans l'oeuvre de Chateaubriand* (Paris: Champion, 1994).

Wang, Ban. "Writing, Self, and the Other: Chateaubriand and His *Atala*," *French Forum*, 22, 2 (May 1997), 133–148.

Jennifer Harrison

CHEKHOV, ANTON PAVLOVICH (1860–1904). Anton Chekhov was born in Taganrog, Russia, in 1860 and attended the Taganrog *gimnaziia* from 1869 to 1879. He reunited with his family in Moscow and enrolled at the Medical School of Moscow University in 1879. He wrote the play *That Worthless Fellow Platonov* in 1880–1881; published his first collection of short stories, *The Tales of Melpomene and Motley Tales*, in 1884–1886; and wrote the play *Ivanov* and published *Twilight* and *Innocent Words*, all in 1887. Chekhov was awarded the Pushkin Prize by the Academy of Sciences in 1888. He journeyed to Sakhalin and published *Gloomy People* in 1890, premiered *The Wood Demon* in 1889, and traveled to western Europe in 1891, purchasing an estate near the village of Melikhovo in 1892. After traveling in the Crimea and southern Europe in 1894, he published *The Island of Sakhalin* and visited **Lev Tolstoy** at Yasnaya Polyana, in 1895, then traveled to the Crimea and the Caucasus in 1896, the same year he premiered *The Seagull*. In 1899, Chekhov sold the rights to publish all his works to Adolf Marx, published 10 volumes of his collected works, and premiered *Uncle Vanya*. The following year he was elected, with Tolstoy, as an honorary member of the newly established Section of Belles Lettres of the Academy of Sciences. In 1901 he premiered *The Three Sisters* and married actress Olga Knipper. To protest **Maksim Gorky**'s exclusion, Chekhov resigned membership in the Academy of Sciences in 1902. In 1904, the year *The Cherry Orchard* premiered, he died in Badenweiler, Germany, and was buried in Moscow (Yarmolinsky, 28–30).

In 1886, Dmitry Grigorovich praised Chekhov's talents and predicted a great literary future for him. Chekhov would go on to write Russian prose masterpieces, become in the opinion of D. S. Mirsky one of the three finest letter writers in Russia (Karlinsky, x), and revolutionize modern theater through his four major plays produced by the Moscow Art Theater. Compassion, a freedom from heresies, and an honest appreciation for the value of both human beings and the natural world characterize his worldview.

In his correspondence, Chekhov relied heavily on the Bible, Alexander Griboyedov's *The Misfortune of Being Clever* (1828), the fables of Ivan Krylov (1769–1844), and Shakespeare's plays in early nineteenth-century Russian translations (Karlinsky, x). His early religious training is evident in his short stories as well. Furthermore, Chekhov constantly read **Darwin**, books by travelers and explorers such as Nevelskoy and Przhevalsky, and the works of Russian biological scientists (Karlinsky, 27). In addition, he corresponded with many leading cultural figures such as Pyotr Tchaikovsky, Ivan Bunin, Sergei Diaghilev, Konstantin Balmont, and **Konstantin Stanislavsky**.

ARCHIVES

The State Literary Museum (Moscow), the Saltykov-Shchedrin State Public Museum (St. Petersburg), the Chekhov Literary Museum (Taganrog), the Central State Archive of Literature and Art (Moscow), the Checkhov House Museum in Moscow, and the Central State Archive of the City of Moscow all include material on Chekhov.

PRINTED SOURCES

Chekhov, Anton Pavlovich. *Polnoe sobranie sochinenii i pisem v tridtsati tomakh* (Moscow: Nauka, 1974).

Jackson, Robert Louis (ed.). *Chekhov: A Collection of Critical Essays* (Englewood Cliffs, N.J.: Prentice-Hall, 1967).

Karlinsky, Simon, and Michael Henry Heim. *Anton Chekhov's Life & Thought* (Berkeley: University of California Press, 1973).

Magarshack, David. *Chekhov the Dramatist* (New York: Hill and Wang, 1960).

Matlaw, Ralph E. (ed). *Anton Chekhov's Short Stories* (New York: W. W. Norton & Company, 1979).

Rayfield, Donald. *Anton Chekhov: A Life* (New York: Henry Holt and Company, 1998).

Styan, J. L. *Chekhov in Performance* (London: Cambridge University Press, 1971).

Valency, Maurice Jacques. *The Breaking String: The Plays of Anton Chekhov* (New York: Oxford University Press, 1966).

Yarmolinsky, Avrahm. *The Portable Chekhov* (New York: Penguin Books, 1977).

Winner, Thomas Gustav. *Chekhov and His Prose* (New York: Holt, Rinehart and Winston, 1966).

Doug Stenberg

CHILD, LYDIA MARIA (1802–1880). Lydia Maria (Francis) Child, born the daughter of a baker in Medford, Massachusetts, in 1802, was educated in public town schools, with one year in Miss Swan's Academy (1814–1815). Her parents kept only didactic Christian volumes and nonfiction in their small library, so Child supplemented her studies by reading the college preparatory and Harvard Divinity texts of her older brother, Convers Francis. Child knew—and quoted—the Bible but rejected her father's Calvinism and her brother's Unitarianism to join the Swedenborgians; her *Progress of Religious Ideas* (1855) promoted sympathy for non-Christian religions. Child was a precursor of women's rights activism, according to **Elizabeth Cady Stanton**. She converted prominent people—including William Ellery Channing—to abolitionist views and assisted with the landmark lawsuit involving Meg Sommerset. African Americans, including Harriet Jacobs, honored her as a benefactor, and she fought fearlessly and without compromise for Indian rights. The general public praised her as an endlessly entertaining author of children's literature and an advocate of progressive child rearing, sending her no-nonsense domestic advice manual for the "middling classes" into 35 editions.

Child's earliest extant letter (1817), written to Convers, questioned John Milton's sexism in *Paradise Lost*, and she never ceased writing on behalf of the underprivileged. Child's first novel, *Hobomok* (1824), was inspired by the 1820 poem *Yamoyden*, by James Wallis Eastburn and Robert Sands, and by an 1821 review of it by John Gorham Palfrey. Shakespeare's *Othello* probably also influenced the novel. Child gained free access to the Boston Athenaeum library (1832–1835), a privilege that was apparently revoked when she published— prompted by conversations with her husband, David Lee Child and by his impassioned articles in abolitionist newspapers—*An Appeal in Favor of That Class of Americans Called Africans* (1833). From the Athenaeum Child borrowed Plato, Aristophanes, and Homer, as well as books written in French, German, and English on European history, on travel in the Southern Hemisphere, and on women, mythology, and world religions. She checked out books on and by **Anne-Louise-Germaine** (Necker) **de Staël** and Jeanne-Marie Phlipon Roland and the *Biographe Universelle*, which informed her biographies of the two French women. She used William Alexander's *History of Women* (1779) as the starting point for her *History of the Condition of Women* (1835) (Karcher, 221). With **Margaret Fuller**'s 1839 Conversation group she read Greek mythology. Child wrote so clearly and so compellingly that canonized intellectuals adopted her perspectives. As much as any man, and more than most, Child contributed to Western culture with writings that, while borrowing knowledge from others' texts, derived focus and meaning from her experience as a self-educated woman passionately committed to ending human misery.

ARCHIVES

Borrowing Records. Ms. I. 1827–1834. Boston Athenaeum.
Ellis Gray Loring Collection, Schlesinger Library, Radcliffe College.
Ellis Gray Loring Family Papers (1828–1919), Schlesinger Library, Radcliffe College.

PRINTED SOURCES

Child, Lydia Marie. *The Collected Correspondence of Lydia Maria Child*, Patricia G. Holland and Milton Meltzer (eds.) (Millwood, N.Y.: Kraus Microform, 1979).
Holland, Patricia G., Milton Meltzer, and Francine Krasno (eds.). *The Collected Correspondence of Lydia Maria Child, 1817–1880: Guide and Index to the Microfiche Edition* (Millwood, N.Y.: Kraus Microform, 1980).
Karcher, Carolyn L. *The First Woman in the Republic: A Cultural Biography of Lydia Maria Child* (Durham, N.C.: Duke University Press, 1994).
Meltzer, Milton, and Patricia C. Holland (eds.). Francine Krasno (assoc. ed.). *Lydia Maria Child, Selected Letters, 1817–1880* (Amherst: University of Massachusetts Press, 1982).

Mills, Bruce. *Cultural Reformations: Lydia Maria Child and the Literature of Reform* (Athens: University of Georgia Press, 1994).

Osborne, William S. "Lydia Maria Child." In Lewis Leary (ed.), *Twayne's United States Authors Series* (Boston: Twayne Publishers, 1980).

Robin Meader

CHOPIN, FRÉDÉRIC (1810–1849). Fryderyk Franciszek (Frédéric François) Chopin, a composer, was born in Żelazowa Wola, Prussian-occupied Poland, on March 1, 1810. He died in Paris on October 17, 1849. Educated in Warsaw (at Warsaw Conservatory) where he studied both performance and composition, with lengthy stays in Germany, Vienna, and finally Paris, he knew Polish, French, Latin, German, Italian, and some English and Russian. Born to a Polish mother and her French expatriate husband, Chopin was one of several children. The children were raised in an intensely Polish atmosphere, with Polish as the primary language of the home (and French learned as a second language) and Roman Catholicism as the religion. From an early age, the young Fryderyk was recognized as a child prodigy at the piano, and his first-known composition dates from the age of seven. Chopin was the greatest musical figure of the Romantic era and the foremost Polish composer of the nineteenth century, known for his incorporation of traditional dances and folk songs into the classical repertory of the day. His influence on generations of musicians and composers is well known and continues to the present day.

Unlike many Romantic composers, it is not easy to pinpoint with any precision particular external influences on specific works by Chopin. He was most clearly influenced by Polish folk and national themes. His polonaises were based on a dance form that had originated among the Polish nobility centuries earlier and that continued in popularity through Chopin's day. The rhythms and sounds of the Polish countryside and its folk music were also important, as reflected in composition titles like *Krakowiak* op.14 or in his mazurkas. (The *Krakowiak* is a folk dance from the Kraków region of southern Poland; the mazurka is from the region of Mazuria.) Chopin was one of the many composers, writers, and artists who "discovered" the peasants and their folk culture in an effort to create "authentic" national forms in music, literature, and art.

Chopin also absorbed the basic repertory of the times, which included the works of Handel, Mendelssohn, Mozart, and the operas of Rossini, along with a whole range of forms: from masses to sonatas to fugues. His early literary influences are harder to pin down, but his education in Polish, French, and Latin would have exposed him to basic primers and the Catholic catechism, and his correspondence shows a familiarity with the major popular newspapers in his cities of residence, as well as the popular theater and opera of the day.

Following the failure of the November Uprising against Russian rule in Poland in 1830–1831, and the mass emigration of Polish revolutionaries and intellectuals to France, Chopin rubbed shoulders with many of the leading Polish literary figures of his day. Foremost among them were Adam Mickiewicz (whose work he had known as early as 1826) and Juliusz Słowacki. At parties hosted by expatriate Polish nobles, the Polish exiles—soldiers, poets, musicians, nobles—spoke long into the night about Polish politics and the cause of freedom and listened to poetry and music. Such evenings had a great emotional impact on the intense and deeply patriotic Chopin.

Of course, Chopin's most celebrated literary association was with French writer **George Sand**. His relationship to Sand, about which so much has been written, was variously that of lover, companion, dependent. With Sand, Chopin came into contact with a circle of French writers, such **Honoré de Balzac** and **Victor Hugo**, as well as numerous painters, singers, musicians, and composers ranging from major figures to minor ones. Precisely what influence Sand and her circle had on the Polish composer's work is unclear, for his musical output during his time with the French writer was relatively small. He did not lose his enthusiasm for the Polish cause (which was, at any rate, very fashionable in Paris), nor did he alter his fundamental Catholicism, even though the religion was not favored by the *artistes* of Sand's circle. (Chopin's influence on Sand seems clearer: For example, he appeared as the character "Prince Karol" in her novel *Lucrezia Floriani*.)

Chopin's compositional talent was often at its greatest when he improvised before small audiences, a skill that demands sensitivity to the mood and feelings of the listeners as well as a mastery of standard artistic conventions. One observer wrote: "I heard Chopin improvise at George Sand's house. It is marvelous to hear Chopin compose this way: his inspiration is so immediate and complete that he plays without hesitation. . . . But when it comes to writing it down and recapturing the original thought in all its details, he spends days of nervous strain and almost frightening desperation" (Chopin, *Korespondencja*, 1962, 217). The general artistic and literary atmosphere of Paris certainly had its effect, yet perhaps the more important influence was that of the messianic, Romantic nationalism of the Polish exiles, a nationalism that linked the liberation of Poland to the universal liberation of humanity and vice versa.

ARCHIVES

National Archives, Warsaw.

PRINTED SOURCES.

Atwood, William G. *Fryderyk Chopin: Pianist from Warsaw* (New York: Columbia University Press, 1987).
———. *The Lioness and the Little One: The Liaison of George Sand and Frédéric Chopin* (New York: Columbia University Press, 1980).
Belza, Igor. *Fryderyk F. Chopin* (Warsaw: Instytut Wydawniczy Pax, 1969).
Chopin, Frédéric. *Correspondance de Frédéric Chopin*, 3 vols. (Saint-Herblain: Richard Massey, 1981).
———. *Selected Correspondence of Fryderyk Chopin*, Arthur Hedley (trans.) (London: Heinemann, 1962).

———. *Korespondencja Fryderyka Chopina*, Bronistaw Sydow ed., 2 vols., (Warsaw: Panstwowy Instytut Wydawniczy, 1955).

Cortot, Alfred. *In Search of Chopin* (London: Peter Nevill, 1951).

Eigeldinger, Jean-Jacques. *Chopin: Pianist and Teacher as Seen by His Pupils* (Cambridge: Cambridge University Press, 1986).

Glinski, Matteo. *Chopin the Unknown* (Windsor: Assumption University of Windsor Press, 1963).

Jeżewska, Zofia. *Chopin* (Warsaw: Interpress, 1980).

Mizwa, Stephan P. *Frédéric Chopin, 1810–1849* (New York: Macmillan, 1949).

Rink, John, and Jim Samson (eds.). *Chopin Studies 2* (Cambridge: Cambridge University Press, 1994).

Samson, Jim. *The Music of Chopin* (London: Routledge and Keegan Paul, 1985).

Siepmann, Jeremy. *Chopin: The Reluctant Romantic* (Boston: Northeastern University Press, 1995).

Zamoyski, Adam. *Chopin: A New Biography* (New York: Doubleday and Co., 1980).

John Radzilowski

CHOPIN, KATE (1850–1904). Kate Chopin was born in St. Louis to an Irish father, Thomas O'Flaherty, and a French Creole mother, Eliza Faris, whose family traced their lineage to the 1764 founding of St. Louis. Raised in a devout Catholic family, she was educated at the Academy of the Sacred Heart (1860–1868) but fell away from the Church as an adult. Chopin achieved renown for several collections of short stories, but *The Awakening* (1899), her best-known novel, was published to mixed reviews and sparked moral outrage for its depiction of a married woman with explicit sensual desires who chooses suicide over a life of luxurious dependence upon her husband. A century after its publication, *The Awakening* is celebrated as a classic of American realism and a landmark in women's writing. Chopin is remembered for her early advocacy of female independence in thought, social conduct, and intellectual development. She wrote only sporadically in her final years, perhaps because of the negative response to *The Awakening*.

Chopin was the contemporary of several major American feminists (Charlotte Perkins Gilman, **Susan B. Anthony**) but never joined a social reform or political group and produced her eloquent feminist works independent of a women's "movement" or organization. Her first teacher, her great-grandmother Victoire Verdon Charleville, taught her French at an early age and told her legends of famous St. Louis women who had flouted convention; these stories inform much of Chopin's subsequent subject matter. As a child, she read Sir **Walter Scott** and **Charles Dickens** and popular books by women writers such as Susan Warner, Jane Porter, Margaret Oliphant, and Dina Mulock. Her standard classical education included biblical study, Racine, Moliére, Shakespeare, and the poetry of Spenser, Pope, and Gray. Chopin read **Emerson** later in her life but disagreed with his views on separate gender spheres.

Chopin read contemporary American realist and regionalist authors: She especially admired Sarah Orne Jewett, Mary E. Wilkins Freeman, and **William**

Dean Howells, although she later became disappointed with what she saw as Howell's conventional subject matter and self-censorship. Her most direct influences were French writers **Guy de Maupassant** and Adrien Vely, whose short stories she translated. She respected **Émile Zola** but found his work too didactic, preferring Maupassant's more subtle, minimalist instruction, which she emulates in her own work. Late in her career she encountered the short stories of Norwegian author Alexander Kielland, whose realist treatment of class difference she admired. In her book reviews and literary essays, however, Chopin attempts to stake out an individual position and hold herself apart from particular schools or traditions of writing.

ARCHIVES

Missouri Historical Society, St. Louis, Missouri. Manuscripts, diary, photographs, letters.
Bayou Folk Museum/Kate Chopin House, Cloutierville, Louisiana. Notebooks, photographs, letters.

PRINTED SOURCES

Bonner, Thomas, Jr. *The Kate Chopin Companion* (New York: Greenwood Press, 1988). Includes dictionary of terms and individuals from Chopin's life and work and Chopin's unpublished translations from French.
Seyersted, Per. *Kate Chopin: A Critical Biography* (New York: Octagon Books, 1980).
Toth, Emily. *Kate Chopin* (New York: William Morrow and Company, Inc., 1990). Thorough biography; extensive bibliographical material.

Deborah Banner

CLAUSEWITZ, CARL VON (1780–1831). Carl von Clausewitz was born in Burg, Prussia, a small town outside of Berlin. With the help of his father, Clausewitz was accepted into the 34th Infantry Regiment at the age of 12 and was sent to war immediately against revolutionary France. He attended the Burg town school sporadically during the mid-1790s and eventually enrolled in the recently created Militärische Gesellschaft in Berlin from 1801 to 1804. While Clausewitz was ambivalent about his Lutheran background, his early education was influenced by the flourishing Pietist movement in northern Prussia. Clausewitz's informal education was spent in the library of the local Illuminati chapter, where he consumed the major works of the Enlightenment and read German authors interested in cultivating a German Enlightenment. Clausewitz's favorite authors included C. L. de Secondat Montesquieu, Friedrich von Schiller, **Alexander von Humboldt**, **Johann Gottlieb Fichte**, **Friedrich Hegel**, and Immanuel Kant. Living and studying in Berlin exposed Clausewitz to the growing neoclassical movement and allowed him to attend the lectures of Germany's most notable scholars.

Bred to be a Prussian officer from birth, Clausewitz was nevertheless extremely well read and benefited from living during the turbulent aftermath of Prussia's crushing defeat at the hands of **Napoléon** in 1806. Clausewitz's single greatest influence was the Prussian military reformer Gerhard von Scharnhorst. Scharnhorst founded the Militärärische Gesellschaft that Clausewitz attended as an experiment in military education. Scharnhorst and his colleagues recognized the dramatic changes in warfare inaugurated by the French Revolution and insisted that Prussia's future depended on understanding and taming war's new dynamics. Clausewitz was a devoted student of the new learning and dedicated his life to promoting a greater intellectual understanding of war and pressing for the necessary political and economic reforms to make Prussia a viable practitioner of war.

Despite fighting in three separate military campaigns against Napoléon's armies, Clausewitz was a genuine academic officer who found teaching to be his true calling. Clausewitz was impressed particularly with Niccolo Machiavelli and found Frederick the Great's famous retort to *The Prince* amateurish. Clausewitz valued Machiavelli because Machiavelli, as Scharnhorst instructed, used history to cover the gap between theory and practice. Clausewitz shared Machiavelli's perspective that one should be more concerned with how the world was, not how it ought to be. Even a cursory glance of Clausewitz's seminal work *On War* reveals many similarities between it and Machiavelli's *The Art of War*. Fichte's *Addresses to the German Nation* inspired Clausewitz to consider the power of national sentiment for motivating and unifying an army. Clausewitz, like Scharnhorst and the elder Prussian reformers, recognized that a significant reason for France's success was the expansion of war to include the masses. Despite Clausewitz's impressive education, he understood that war itself provided the only authentic education, and out of all his teachers, Napoléon inspired him above and beyond all others.

ARCHIVES

Berlin. *Geheimes Staatsarchiv Preussischer Kulturbesitz*, Rep. 92 (von Canitz Nr. 4). Contains much of Clausewitz's correspondence.
Staatsbibliothek Prüssischer Kulturbesitz, Clausewitz (2f, 1820). Includes lectures and manuscripts of early writings.

PRINTED SOURCES

Paret, Peter. *Clausewitz and the State: The Man, His Theories, and His Times* (Princeton, N.J.: Princeton University Press, 1985). The premier biography; stresses Clausewitz's intellectual environment and the evolution of his academic maturity.
———. "Education, Politics, and War in the Life of Clausewitz," *Journal of the History of Ideas*, 29, 3 (1968), 394–408.
Weniger, E. "Philosophie und Bildung im Denken von Clausewitz," in W. Hubatsch (ed.), *Schicksalswege deutscher Vergangenheit* (Düsseldorf: Droste Verlâg, 1950). Considers Clausewitz's views on education and his exposure to major philosophers.

Brian Crim

CLEMENS, SAMUEL LANGHORNE. *See* **Mark Twain**.

COBBETT, WILLIAM (1763–1835). William Cobbett was born at Farnham in Surrey in 1763 into an Anglican family and spent his first 21 years working in farming. Most of his education occurred in the evening under his father's tutelage. At some point between 1779 and 1781, Cobbett worked for Reverend James Barclay—who wrote *A Complete and Universal English Dictionary* (1744)—and had access to his library. After enlisting in a line regiment in the 1780s, Cobbett educated himself in English linguistics and literature and spent the rest of his career writing about culture, politics, and agriculture in England and, for a total of 10 years, in America. During his lifetime, he moved from political conservatism to radicalism, a shift reflected in his writing.

A prolific writer and practiced stylist, Cobbett relied on a rich and varied reading selection. In the autobiographical *Life and Adventures of Peter Porcupine* (1801), Cobbett remarks that during his first year of enlistment he read everything available to him (Cobbett, 32–33). While he deplored his haphazardness, it resulted in a broad range of references evident in the *Political Register*, a weekly newspaper published, with a few gaps and changes, between 1802 and 1835, and in his other writings. An earlier reading episode guided Cobbett's satirical tone in his political and cultural writing. In an 1820 essay in the *Political Register*, Cobbett recounts his purchase of Jonathan Swift's *Tale of a Tub* (1707) at age 14 and his delight in reading the satire, which, in his words, caused "a sort of birth of intellect" (*Political Register*, February 19, 1820). Cobbett found Oliver Goldsmith's "The Deserted Village" (1770) a provocative political poem, commenting that he could "repeat by heart" every word of it (*Political Register*, June 23, 1832). In addition to admiring eighteenth-century writers, Cobbett rebelled against them as well: His *Grammar of the English Language* (1818) reflects his distaste for the century's grammarians, stylists, and rhetoricians such as Samuel Johnson, Joseph Addison, and Hugh Blair (Sambrook, 104).

Even though Cobbett had an extensive knowledge of literature, he also disdained its frivolity, valuing historical writing over fictional texts. Cobbett read widely among the economic and political books of the time. Such books as Thomas Paine's *The Decline and Fall of the English System of Finance* (1796), **Thomas Malthus**'s *Essay on the Principle of Population* (1798), and many others aided Cobbett in developing his own eternally iconoclastic stance on the economic state and fate of England. He demonstrates his diverse reading background in all of his publications with his comments on past and contemporary literature.

ARCHIVES

Cobbett Archive, Nuffield College, Oxford. Papers, letters, and manuscripts as well as the unpublished "Memoir of William Cobbett" by J. P. Cobbett.
Correspondence. British Museum.

PRINTED SOURCES

Cobbett, William. *The Life and Adventures of Peter Porcupine.* 1796. Reprinted with Introduction and Notes by G.D.H. Cole. (London: Kennikat Press, 1927).

Sambrook, James. *William Cobbett* (London: Routledge & Kegan Paul, 1973).
Schwizer, Karl W., and John W. Osborne. *Cobbett in His Times* (Savage, Md.: Barnes and Noble Books, 1990).
Spater, George. *William Cobbett: The Poor Man's Friend*, 2 vol. (Cambridge: Cambridge University Press, 1982).

Sarah R. Marino

COBDEN, RICHARD (1804–1865). Richard Cobden was born in Dunford, Sussex, in 1804. Cobden's childhood years were marked by financial misfortune for his family and frequent relocations. Initially, he attended Midhurst School. As the family's financial situation worsened, he was sent to London to be raised from the age of 10 on by his mother's brother-in-law and was then sent to boarding school in the north Yorkshire dales and trained as a warehouse clerk. He pursued his own education upon returning to work at his uncle's business at the age of 15. Born an Anglican, Cobden was a devout observer of the faith, although he strongly believed faith to be a private matter and abhorred displays of religiosity as well as proselytizing. His career in politics—from organizing the Anti-Corn Law League to representing Stockport in Parliament and emerging as a Liberal leader—all reflected the interests of a well-read man of letters.

Cobden's limited schooling left him with a selective knowledge of the classics but a deep love of literature. He read widely and frequently quoted Cervantes, Shakespeare, and Burns. Cobden frequently quoted **Lord Byron** in letters and in his diary during early travels to the Mediterranean. His travels were motivated by the literature he read, and he published serious political and social accounts of his travels in Ireland, America, and Russia. Around the age of 20, Cobden submitted a play to the manager of Covent Garden in the hopes of beginning a literary career. Unsuccessful, he turned to modern history, travel literature, and the works of the British and French Enlightenment *philosophes*. Cobden freely admitted that the greatest influence on his intellectual development came from Adam Smith and his *Wealth of Nations*, which ignited a passion and understanding of political economy. His organization of the Anti-Corn Law League, public speeches against factory reform, trade union organization, and government intervention in business, the negotiation of an Anglo-French free trade treaty, and staunch support for the North in the American Civil War all reflected his reading of Enlightenment literature. His histories, such as *Herald of Peace*, intended to facilitate peaceful resolutions to diplomatic and trade problems of the day. Later in his life, Cobden became interested in phrenology after reading George Combe, the leading British proponent of the theory that man's character was understandable through the shape of his head.

Perhaps Cobden's greatest contribution to cultural development was his outspoken campaign for a national education system as the chief means of creating educated citizens. His pilot project in Lancashire in the early 1850s sought to include all religious faiths and teach a secular curriculum of history, geography, classical literature, and basic political and economic principles—an education not unlike his own.

ARCHIVES

Cobden Papers, West Sussex Record Office, Chichester. Personal and political correspondence and papers.
Cobden Papers, British Library. Political correspondence.
Cobden Papers, J. B. Smith Papers, Manchester Central Library. Correspondence and
papers.

PRINTED SOURCES

Bright, John. *Mr. Cobden and* The Times: *Correspondence between Mr. Cobden, M.P.,
and Mr. Delane, Editor of* The Times (Manchester: A. Ireland and Company,
1867).
Cobden, Richard. *The Political Writings of Mr. Cobden*, John Bright (ed.) (London:
Ridgway, 1867).
————. *Speeches on Questions of Public Policy by Richard Cobden, M.P.*, John Bright
(ed.) (London: Macmillan, 1870).
Edsall, Nicholas. *Richard Cobden: Independent Radical* (Cambridge, Mass.: Harvard
University Press, 1986).
Hinde, Wendy. *Richard Cobden: A Victorian Outsider* (New Haven, Conn.: Yale Uni-
versity Press, 1987).
Morley, John. *The Life of Richard Cobden* (London: Chapman and Hall, 1881).

Nancy LoPatin-Lummis

COLERIDGE, SAMUEL TAYLOR (1772–1834). Samuel Coleridge was born
in 1772 at Ottery St. Mary in Devonshire, where his learned but impecunious
father was vicar and headmaster of the King's School. The youngest of his
father's 13 children, he was bullied by his next senior brother and sought refuge,
as he later told the novelist and philosopher William Godwin, "in early and
immoderate reading, particularly the Arabian nights" (quoted Ashton, 14). Following his father's death, he was educated as a charity boy at Christ's Hospital
School in London (1782–1791) and at Jesus College, Cambridge (1791–1794;
he did not take a degree). At the end of his time at Cambridge, his enthusiasm
for the radical ideals of the French Revolution and rejection of oppressive orthodoxy deflected him from the Church of England to Unitarianism, and for a
time in the later 1790s he acted as a lay preacher; around the turn of the century,
however, his disappointment at what the Revolution had become and the influence of idealist philosophy combined with personal factors to lead him back to
the Church of England after 1802. Uneven though his output is, Coleridge ranks
as one of the greatest English poets. As a literary theorist and critic, he has no
rival in the English tradition. As a cultural mediator, he familiarized English
readers with German philosophy, especially the thinking of Immanuel Kant,
Johann Gottlieb Fichte, and **Friedrich Wilhelm Joseph von Schelling**. In later
life he became influential both personally and through his writings on younger
men such as **William Ewart Gladstone**, F. D. Maurice, and John Sterling in
England and **Ralph Waldo Emerson** and James Marsh in the United States. In

an insightful essay, **John Stuart Mill** shows Coleridge's importance as a thinker to his own time.

From his earliest years Coleridge was, in his own phrase, "a book glutton." Perpetually short of money, he did not accumulate a large personal library, as did his brother-in-law **Robert Southey**. Nevertheless, he is an unusually well-documented reader, since he made copious references to his reading in his letters and notebooks and habitually annotated the books that he read. Much material in all three categories survives and is in great part now available in modern and well-indexed editions. The marginalia especially reveal Coleridge's intense engagement with whatever he was reading and the highly retentive memory of a genuine polymath.

The best short introduction to Coleridge's mature thought is a piece originally written in 1816 as a program for an encyclopedia and printed in its final form as "Essays on the Principles of Method" in *The Friend* (1818; *Works* 4.1: 448–524). Coleridge's early career had been a struggle to escape from the conclusion to which the empiricist tradition of John Locke and David Hartley seemed to lead: that the human mind is merely the observer of a mechanical universe of material particulars that it is powerless to influence or to understand. The writings of Benedict de Spinoza, Richard Hooker, Richard Baxter, Jeremy Taylor, and other seventeenth-century divines and, finally, the German idealists helped him to find in the divine spirit the ground of being that brought the individual human spirit into genuine community with both the natural world and other human spirits in society. True learning is thus not a knowledge of particulars but an understanding of relationships. To think creatively is to exercise the imagination; the "shaping power," replicating in a human mind the divine act of creation; compared to this, the manipulation by the fancy of predefined entities, which is the best the empiricist can hope to do, is both trivial and sterile. In two of his great poems of the late 1790s, "The Rime of the Ancient Mariner" and "Kubla Khan," he had memorably demonstrated the imagination's power to dissolve and reconstitute into haunting poetry a mass of details gleaned from reading books of travel and antiquities, the subject of a famous study by J. L. Lowes.

In his intellectual autobiography, suitably entitled *Biographia Literaria* (1817), Coleridge rejects the writings of René Descartes, Gottfried Leibnitz, Locke, Hartley, and George Berkeley and records his debt to those of Plato, Plotinus, Giordano Bruno, Jakob Behmen, George Fox, and William Law, as well as to Kant, Fichte, and Schelling. Imagination is seen at work in poetry by Shakespeare and **Wordsworth**, even in the sonnets of the minor poet William Lisle Bowles. Such poetic examples are convenient for written exposition, but for Coleridge, imagination is universally valid, equally essential to the scientific research of his friend **Humphry Davy**.

Aids to Reflection (1825) makes a commentary on the First Epistle of Peter by the late seventeenth-century divine Robert Leighton the basis for an exposition of Coleridge's theological views. In his later years, Coleridge read widely in German biblical scholarship, accepting Johann Gottfried Eichhorn's controversial views on the synoptic gospels. His last published work, however, *On the Constitution of Church and State* (1829), deals not with theology but with a burning issue of the day.

ARCHIVES

British Library. Notebooks, letters, books with marginalia.
Victoria University, Toronto. Smaller holdings of same.

PRINTED SOURCES

Ashton, R. *The Life of Samuel Taylor Coleridge* (Oxford: Blackwell, 1998).
Coburn, K. (ed.). *The Collected Works of Samuel Taylor Coleridge* (Princeton, N.J.: Princeton University Press, 1969–); *Biographia Literaria* (2 vols.), part 7; *Marginalia* (4 vols. of 6, to date), part 12.
Coburn, K., and M. Christensen (eds.). *The Notebooks of Samuel Taylor Coleridge*, 4 vols., to date (London: Routledge, 1957–).
Coleman, D. *Coleridge and "The Friend" (1809–1810)* (Oxford: Clarendon, 1988). Influence of Hooker, Burke, Kant, and Rousseau.
Griggs, E. L. (ed.). *The Collected Letters of Samuel Taylor Coleridge*, 6 vols. (Oxford: Clarendon, 1956–1972).
Leavis, F. R. (ed.). *Mill on Bentham and Coleridge* (New York: Harper, 1962).
Lowes, J. L. *The Road to Xanadu* (Boston: Houghton Mifflin, 1927).
McFarland, T. *Coleridge and the Pantheist Tradition* (Oxford: Clarendon, 1969). Good discussion of plagiarism charges.
Wheeler, K. M. *Sources, Processes and Methods in Coleridge's "Biographia Literaria"* (Cambridge: Cambridge University Press, 1980).
Wylie, I. *Young Coleridge and the Philosophers of Nature* (Oxford: Clarendon, 1989). Influence of Newton, Locke, and Hartley.

John D. Baird

COMTE, AUGUSTE (1798–1857). Isidore-Auguste-Marie-François-Xavier Comte, known as Auguste, was born in Montpellier, France, in 1798 into a Catholic Royalist family headed by a conservative civil servant father. Relations with his family were always strained and ambivalent and probably contributed to his nervous breakdown in 1826, suicide attempt in 1827, and eventual insanity. From 1807 to 1814 he attended the lycée in Montpellier, where, at the age of 14, he declared himself a non-Catholic and a republican. In 1814 he enrolled at the École Polytechnique, Paris, excelled in science and mathematics, and absorbed the works of Lazare-Nicolas-Marguerite Carnot, Joseph-Louis Lagrange, and Pierre-Simon de Laplace but was expelled in 1816, a victim of the politics of the Bourbon Restoration.

Continuing studies in both Montpellier and Paris but never earning a degree, the young Comte was impressed by Pierre-Jean-Georges Cabanis; Antoine-Louis-Claude Destutt de Tracy; Jean-Baptiste Say; Constantin-François de Chasseboeuf, Comte de Volney; and the Scottish Enlightenment, especially Adam

Smith and David Hume but also Adam Ferguson, Dugald Stewart, and William Robertson. In 1817 he succeeded Jacques-Nicolas-Augustin Thierry as secretary to **Claude Henri de Rouvroy, Comte de Saint-Simon**, but in 1824 they parted in anger. Unable to secure an instructorship under the regime of Charles X, he began teaching mathematics, mechanics, astronomy, and his own positive philosophy at his home in 1826. These private lectures won him his first followers and evolved into his greatest work, *Cours de philosophie positive*, which appeared in six volumes between 1830 and 1842. After the July Revolution he lectured sporadically at École Polytechnique until 1851, and in later years he lived mostly on subsidies from his disciples.

Comte came to know the works of Félix Vicq d'Azyr, Paul Henri Dietrich d'Holbach, **Jeremy Bentham**, Aristotle, and Francis Bacon chiefly through Saint-Simon, from whom he evolved a tendency to notice "positive" elements in nearly everyone he read, such as René Descartes, Thomas Hobbes, Pierre Bayle, Baruch Spinoza, Denis Diderot, François-Marie Arouet de Voltaire, and Jean-Jacques Rousseau. Comte engaged in a lifelong struggle with Rousseau, admiring his respect for nature but disparaging his reliance on emotion.

Comte's early disciple Gustave d'Eichthal translated German philosophy into French for Comte, who previously had been unfamiliar with it. In the 1820s the works of Johann Gottfried von Herder helped Comte to finalize the intellectual break with Saint-Simon. Comte thought that Immanuel Kant was too theological but respected whatever degree of detached scientific method he found in Kant. Eichthal either misunderstood **Georg Wilhelm Friedrich Hegel** or willfully fed Comte a distortion of Hegel's thought. In any event, Comte believed that Hegelianism and his own thought were closer than they in fact were.

Comte claimed that the major influence on his development was Marie-Jean-Antoine-Nicholas de Caritat, Marquis de Condorcet, who proposed grounding social sciences in mathematics. Comte derived support for this approach from Anne-Robert-Jacques Turgot, Jean Burdin, and **Anne-Louise-Germaine de Staël**. He detected, sometimes inaccurately, tendencies in Giambattista Vico and Charles de Secondat, Baron de Montesquieu, to apply methods of natural science to the humanities and social sciences.

Comte was conversant with various medical theories competing for scientific authority in the early nineteenth century. He agreed with François-Joseph-Victor Broussais that disease was caused by "irritation" and could be cured by violent intervention. He acknowledged Marie-François-Xavier Bichat as a paragon of a scientific investigator but sided with Broussais's attack on Bichat's vitalism. He saw merit in Franz Joseph Gall's research in cerebral localization and, while not embracing phrenology entirely, still took direction from Gall for his reductionist, materials philosophy of mind. **John Stuart Mill**, with whom Comte began a long correspondence in 1841, criticized Comte for preferring phrenology to the emerging science of psychology.

Comte coined the term *sociology* and is generally regarded as the founder of that discipline. Comtean positivism, the doctrine that both philosophy and social theory should be informed at every step by natural science because humanity is ultimately subject to natural law, was in the mid-nineteenth century a force to be reckoned with, influencing Henri Marie Ducrotay de Blainville, Nicolas-Léonard-Sadi Carnot, Lazare Hippolyte Carnot, Jean-Étienne-Dominique Esquirol, **Charles Fourier**, Jean-Baptiste-Joseph Fourier, Émile Littré, **George Eliot**, Edward Bellamy, **Émile Zola**, and **George Bernard Shaw**; but interest in Comte today is mainly historical.

ARCHIVES

Pickering (712; see reference below) lists 16 French repositories of Comte's papers and correspondence, including Archives Nationales, Bibliothèque Nationale, Maison d'Auguste Comte, and École Polytechnique.

PRINTED SOURCES

Arbousse-Bastide, Paul. *Auguste Comte* (Paris: PUF, 1968).

Cresson, André. *Auguste Comte* (Paris: PUF, 1957).

Gouhier, Henri. *La jeunesse d'Auguste Comte*, 3 vols. (Paris: J. Vrin, 1933–1941).

———. *La vie d'Auguste Comte* (Paris: Gallimard, 1931).

Gould, F. J. *The Life Story of Auguste Comte* (Austin, Tex.: American Atheist Press, 1984).

Mill, John Stuart. *Auguste Comte and Positivism* (Ann Arbor: University of Michigan Press, 1965).

———. *The Correspondence of John Stuart Mill and Auguste Comte*, Oscar A. Haac (trans.) (New Brunswick, N.J.: Transaction Publishers, 1994). Contains discussion and comments on a wide variety of French, German, English, and Italian authors and philosophers, including **Carlyle**, John and Sarah Austin, and Alexander Bain.

Pickering, Mary. *Auguste Comte: An Intellectual Biography*, vol. 1 (New York: Cambridge University Press, 1993).

Simpson, George. *Auguste Comte: Sire of Sociology* (New York: Crowell, 1969).

Sokoloff, Boris. *The "Mad" Philosopher: Auguste Comte* (New York: Vantage, 1961).

Standley, Arline Reilein. *Auguste Comte* (Boston: Twayne, 1981).

Eric v. d. Luft

CONRAD, JOSEPH (1857–1924). Joseph Conrad was born Józef Teodor Konrad Korzeniowski in Berdichev, Poland, then a part of the Russian empire and now a part of the Ukraine. His father, Apollo Nałęcz Korzeniowski, was arrested in 1861 for resisting the Russian occupation of Poland, and the family was sent into exile in Vologda in northern Russia. His mother died in 1865, and his father died in 1869. Under the care of his maternal uncle, Tadeusz Bobrowski, he was educated in Cracow, Poland, and traveled to Italy, Switzerland, and France. At the age of 17 he began his career as a sailor, first with the French merchant service, from 1874 to 1878, then with the British merchant service, from 1878 to 1894.

In 1895 Conrad's first novel, *Almayer's Folly*, was published. This novel and other early works such as *The Nigger of the "Narcissus"* (1897) and *Lord Jim* (1900) gave Conrad a reputation as a writer of sea adventures set in exotic locations. Later works such as "Heart of Darkness" (1902) and *Nostromo* (1904) proved him to be a writer more interested in the inner state of the individual rather than external events. His work had a powerful influence on later writers, and he has obtained a reputation as one of the most important psychological novelists in English.

As a child, Conrad was familiar with the work of many classic Polish writers, including Adam Bernard Mickiewicz, whose poem *Konrad Wallenrod* (1828) depicts a protagonist similar to Conrad's own doomed romantics. His father earned a living as a translator of English works, so Conrad became familiar with the works of William Shakespeare, Sir **Walter Scott**, **Charles Dickens**, and **William Makepeace Thackeray**. He also read nonfiction depictions of life at sea and world travel. Works such as **James Fenimore Cooper**'s *The Pilot* (1823) and Frederick Marryat's *Mr. Midshipman Easy* (1836) may have influenced his decision to go to sea.

Conrad continued to read voraciously throughout his adult life. Such literary artists as **Gustave Flaubert**, Marcel Proust, and **Henry James**, who wrote with an eye for detail and a tendency to delve into the psychology of a character, were read by Conrad deliberately as he attempted to write similar works in English. *Madame Bovary* (1857), along with works by **Guy de Maupassant**, led Conrad to emphasize observation and description in his works. Each novel preparation was accompanied by massive readings on the subject; for example, for *Lord Jim*, Conrad read several books about Malay. In keeping with his original intent to write adventure, Conrad familiarized himself with the writings of **Robert Louis Stevenson**, **Henry Rider Haggard**, **Rudyard Kipling**, and Anthony Hope, while late in life he praised the works of **Samuel Taylor Coleridge** and **Edgar Allan Poe**. Perhaps, however, it was the range of his reading, from French poetry to American Gothic, that most influenced such powerful works as "Heart of Darkness."

ARCHIVES

Beinecke Rare Book and Manuscript Library, Yale.
Berg Collection of the New York Public Library.
Indiana University Lilly Library, Indianapolis.
University of Texas Humanities Research Center at Austin.
Scattered over dozens of libraries, mostly in the United States.

PRINTED SOURCES

Karl, Frederick K. and Laurence Davies, eds. *Collected Letters of Joseph Conrad*, 5 vols. (NY: Cambridge University Press, 1983–1996).
Karl, Frederick R. *Joseph Conrad: The Three Lives* (New York: Farrar, Straus, and Giroux, 1979).

Reid, S. W., Chief exec. ed. *Cambridge Edition of the Works of Joseph Conrad*, 30 vols. currently in preparation.
Tutein, David W. *Joseph Conrad's Reading: An Annotated Bibliography* (West Cornwall, Conn.: Locust Hill Press, 1990).

Rose Secrest

COOPER, JAMES FENIMORE (1789–1851). James Fenimore Cooper was born in Burlington, New Jersey, in 1789 and educated at Yale (1803–1805). Of Quaker ancestry, he drew closer to Anglicanism and was confirmed by the Episcopal Church shortly before his death. His religious views were complex— thematic elements and a strong moral tone in his fiction reflect New England's Calvinist heritage in spite of his parodies of Puritan dogmatism. Cooper is in many respects the "father of the American novel." He played a role in the early Republic's search for identity and established through his fiction many of the su bjects, themes, and genres that would become identified with America. The Leatherstocking novels romanticize Native Americans and the frontier while initiating the American mythology of rugged individualism; *The Pilot* was the first serious American novel of the sea; *The Spy*, set in the American Revolution, established the American historical novel. Cooper was the first American to make a successful career as a novelist.

Cooper took up writing when he purportedly threw down an English novel he was reading to his wife and declared he could write a better story. From his reading he was most familiar with the historical romance of Sir **Walter Scott** and the domestic novel of manners typified by **Jane Austen** and other English authors. He later turned for inspiration to the works of such writers as **Honoré de Balzac**, Richard Dana, and Tobias Smollett, as well as to biography and travel narratives, but his landscape remained American. For example, Walter Scott's England and Scotland border country became for Cooper the neutral ground around New York City in *The Spy*.

Cooper's literary tastes can be inferred from the chapter epigraphs he inserted into his novels. He quotes William Shakespeare most often, followed by the English Romantics. Among the novelists, playwrights, and poets Cooper quotes in these epigraphs are **Lord Byron, Percy Shelley**, William Bryant, Philip Massinger, Philip Freneau, Thomas Campbell, Walter Scott, Oliver Goldsmith, Alexander Pope, Samuel Butler, Robert Burns, Thomas Gray, Thomas Parnell, Thomas Moore, Edmund Spenser, **William Wordsworth, William Cowper**, John Milton, John Dryden, **Robert Southey, Samuel Coleridge, Henry Longfellow**, Richard Dana, William Collins, Giles Fletcher, and Thomas Chatterton.

These quotations always signal parallels between a chapter's action and the quoted masterwork. For example, in *The Last of the Mohicans*, Magua's eloquent defense of his quest for vengence is informed by passages from *The Merchant of Venice*; his call for an Indian rebellion follows from an allusion to Milton's Satan; Munro's anguish at the loss of his daughters is preceded by a quotation from *King Lear*, the rugged American terrain is preceded by a descriptive passage from *Childe Harold*, and Natty's adventures are associated with those of the epic heroes in *The Odyssey* and *The Iliad*.

ARCHIVES

American Antiquarian Society, Worcester, Massachusetts. Major collection of correspondence, manuscripts.
Beinecke Rare Book and Manuscript Library. Yale University. Correspondence, manuscripts.

PRINTED SOURCES

Beard, James F. (ed.). *Letters and Journals of James Fenimore Cooper*, 6 vols. (Cambridge, Mass.: Harvard University Press, 1960–1968).
Dekker, George. *James Fenimore Cooper: The American Scott* (New York: Barnes and Noble, 1967).
Franklin, Wayne. *The New World of James Fenimore Cooper* (Chicago: University of Chicago Press, 1982).
Grossman, James. *James Fenimore Cooper* (Stanford, Calif.: Stanford University Press, 1949).
Kelly, William P. *Plotting America's Past: Fenimore Cooper and the Leatherstocking Tales* (Carbondale: Southern Illinois University Press, 1983).
Morrison, Grant. "James Fenimore Cooper and American Republicanism," *Modern Age* (Spring 1992), 214–226.
Oliver, Lawrence J. "Their Foot Shall Slide in Due Time: Cooper's Calvinist Motif," *Nineteenth Century Literature* (March 1988), 433–447.
Philbrick, Thomas. *James Fenimore Cooper and the Development of American Sea Fiction* (Cambridge, Mass.: Harvard University Press, 1961).
Spiller, Robert E. "James Fenimore Cooper." In Leonard Unger (ed.), *American Writers: A Collection of Literary Biographies*, vol. 1 (New York: Simon and Schuster, 1972), 335–357.
Verhoeven, W. M. (ed.). *James Fenimore Cooper: New Historical and Literary Contexts* (Atlanta, Ga.: Rodopi, 1993).

Richard N. Swanson

COWPER, WILLIAM (1731–1800). William Cowper was born in 1731 at Great Berkhamstead, Hertfordshire, where his father, the Rev. John Cowper, was rector. He was educated at Dr. Pitman's school in Market Street and at Westminster School (1742–1748). Raised a conventional eighteenth-century Anglican, in 1764 he had a conversion experience that led him to the Evangelical wing of the Church of England. Several of his hymns published in *Olney Hymns* (1779) have appeared in many later hymnals. The poetry of his later years is informed by Evangelical tenets, although Cowper himself ceased to be a practicing Christian after a complete nervous collapse in 1773. His *Poems* (1782) and his masterpiece *The Task* (1785) quickly became popular with all classes of readers. They were widely read and, later, prescribed for study in schools, until the revival of Donne and the metaphysical poets after World War I changed the accepted canon. The charm of his personal letters has survived all changes of fashion.

The classical education Cowper received at Westminster School was genuinely formative, demonstrated by numerous allusions and references in prose and verse, as well as a lifelong habit of translating from and into Latin and Greek. Horace and Virgil are prominent, but he was most drawn to Homer. During the 1750s, when he was supposed to be reading law, he was in fact reading literature, in particular comparing Alexander Pope's translations of the *Iliad* and the *Odyssey* with the Greek originals, becoming convinced that Pope's couplets misrepresented Homer. He also studied John Milton; an annotated copy of Richard Bentley's edition of *Paradise Lost* gives insight into his manner of reading (Murray and Rushdie). Thirty years later, he translated Homer into Miltonic blank verse (1791). This translation became a standard English version of Homer; it is discussed by **Matthew Arnold** in *On Translating Homer* (1861). His translation of the *Odyssey* represented this poem in Everyman's Library until the middle of the twentieth century.

Among English poets, Milton was the most powerful influence on Cowper's imagination and practice; in *The Task* he showed how Milton's epic manner might be adapted successfully to mundane subject matter while retaining its grandeur when appropriate, a lesson not lost on **William Wordsworth** and **Samuel Taylor Coleridge**, whose poetics required the highest flights of imagination to be sustained by the stuff of everyday life. Pope, whatever his limitations as a translator, ranks second. The poet and essayist Abraham Cowley (1618–1667), a predecessor at Westminster School, soon came to seem old-fashioned but never lost Cowper's affection. Throughout his life, Cowper read extensively in accounts of travels, such as the voyages of George Anson and James Cook. The story of a sailor fallen overboard from Anson's ship inspired his best-known short poem, "The Cast-Away." The most important single book for Cowper, however, was the Bible.

ARCHIVES

The Hannay Collection of William Cowper, Princeton University Library. Letters and poems.
Letters to William Unwin, British Library Additional MSS. 24154-5.

PRINTED SOURCES

Cowper, William. *The Letters and Prose Writings of William Cowper*, J. King and C. Ryskamp (eds.), 5 vols. (Oxford: Clarendon Press, 1979–1986).
———. *The Poems of William Cowper*, J. D. Baird and C. Ryskamp (eds.), 3 vols. (Oxford: Clarendon Press, 1980–1995).
Keynes, G. "The Library of William Cowper," *Transactions of the Cambridge Bibliographical Society*, 3 (1959–1963), 47–69, 167. (See addenda by N. H. Russell on pages 225–231.)
King, J. *William Cowper: A Biography* (Durham, N.C.: Duke University Press, 1986).
Murray, S., and A.S.F. Rushdie. "On the Margins of an Unnoted Annotator of Milton:

William Hayley's Dialogue with Richard Bentley," *Milton Studies*, XXXI (1995), 197–241. Cowper's handwriting misidentified as William Hayley's.

Priestman, M. *Cowper's* Task: *Structure and Influence* (Cambridge: Cambridge University Press, 1983). Discusses sources.

Russell, N. *A Bibliography of William Cowper to 1837* (Oxford: Clarendon Press, 1963).

Ryskamp, C. *William Cowper of the Inner Temple, Esq. A Study of His Life and Works to the Year 1768* (Cambridge: Cambridge University Press, 1959). Chapter on reading.

John D. Baird

CRANE, STEPHEN (1871–1900). Stephen Crane was born in Newark, New Jersey, in 1871 and educated at Claverack College, New York (1888–1890); Lafayette College, Easton, Pennsylvania (1890); and Syracuse University, New York (1891). An impressionistic narrative style, keen sense of irony, and deep psychological character development made Crane one of the most influential of the American writers in the 1890s who were expanding upon the mode of fiction known as realism. His depictions of isolated individuals adrift in a harsh and indifferent universe undermined prevailing notions of reality and prefigured the modernist era in American fiction.

The son of a Methodist minister and a pious mother, Crane and his siblings read aloud from the King James Bible at home as well as in church. Crane eventually rejected much of his Christian upbringing but remained preoccupied with questions of faith, moral conduct, and redemption—the sermons and hymns of his youth echo in the phraseology and imagery of his novels, short stories, and poetry. In Crane's masterwork *The Red Badge of Courage*, the protagonist undergoes a profound change of vision that simulates a religious conversion. At a critical point in this novel, Crane's hero enters a forest "chapel" where a "hymn of twilight" is heard.

Crane was reticent to talk about literature, and a paucity of documentation leads one to suspect that he had at best a spotty familiarity with major works. Nevertheless, Crane's first biographer wrote in 1923 that Crane offered several pronouncements on literary contemporaries while at Lafayette College. Crane purportedly said **Leo Tolstoy** was "the world's greatest writer," **Gustave Flaubert**'s *Salammbô* was "too long," **Henry James**'s *The Reverberator* was "a tedious bore," **Émile Zola** was "tiresome," and **Robert Louis Stevenson**'s work was "insincere" (Beer, 55, 148, 231). Many subsequent biographers reiterated the account, but Crane's remarks are largely unsubstantiated in letters or recorded reminiscences.

While Crane was a reporter for the *New York Tribune* and developing his writing, he met and was influenced by Hamlin Garland, a radical writer and critic who lectured on avant-garde theories of art and literature. Garland's ideas, adopted from Eugene Veron's *Aesthetics*, were about the fundamental relation of personality to representation in art. Garland valued the power of individual impressionism above objective observation as a means to imparting truth.

Inspired by Garland's philosophy, Crane drew upon the personal accounts of Civil War veterans to develop *The Red Badge of Courage*. His impressionistic narrative style and his vivid imagery were also influenced by his readings of Tolstoy and **Rudyard Kipling**. He was especially moved by Kipling's *The Light That Failed* and made similar use of light and color description (particularly evidenced by the wrathful sun-red image in *The Red Badge of Courage*).

Crane typically resented inquiries about his literary influences, preferring to think that his methods were arrived at wholly through intuition and experimentation. When Ford Madox Ford questioned him about his debt to the French realists, pointing out similarities to his approach and **Guy Maupassant**'s, Crane denied ever reading Maupassant but admitted that he knew of Henry James's critical essays on French authors.

In the final years of his short life, Crane settled in England and developed a close friendship with **Joseph Conrad**; the writers highly respected each other's work, and occasional critical advice went both ways.

ARCHIVES

Clifton Waller Barrett Collection, Alderman Library, University of Virginia. Manuscript of *The Red Badge of Courage*, letters.

Stephen Crane Collection, Syracuse University Library. Correspondence including letters to literary agents; important secondary research materials.

Stephen Crane Papers, The Rare Book and Manuscript Library, Columbia University. Letters from prominent literary figures, 74 books from Crane's library, much secondary research material.

PRINTED SOURCES

Beer, T. *Stephen Crane: A Study in American Letters* (New York: Knopf, 1923). Influential but highly impressionistic, thinly documented first biography.

Benfey, C. *The Double Life of Stephen Crane* (London: Andre Deutsch, 1993).

Colvert, J. *Stephen Crane* (New York: Harcourt Brace, 1984).

———. "Stephen Crane." In D. Pizer and E. Harbert (eds.), *American Realists and Naturalists* (Detroit, Mich.: Gale Research Co., 1982), 100–124. Focus is on Crane's literary influences.

Solomon, E. *Stephen Crane in England: A Portrait of the Artist* (Columbus: Ohio State University Press, 1964). Crane's friendship with British authors.

Sorrentino, P., and S. Wertheim. *The Crane Log: A Documentary Life of Stephen Crane, 1871–1900* (New York: Macmillan, 1994). Incorporates material unknown to previous biographers and refutes earlier misrepresentations.

———. (eds.). *The Correspondence of Stephen Crane*, 2 vols. (New York: Columbia University Press, 1988).

Stallman, R. (ed.). *Stephen Crane: A Biography* (New York: George Braziller, 1968).

———. *Stephen Crane: Letters* (New York: New York University Press, 1960).

Richard N. Swanson

CRUIKSHANK, GEORGE (1792–1878). George Cruikshank was born in Bloomsbury in 1792 and briefly attended school at Mortlake and then Edgeware. The youngest son of Isaac Cruikshank, who was an engraver, caricaturist, and artist, Cruikshank had no formal training in drawing. He did, however, assist his father in the studio. Cruikshank contributed considerably to the history of caricature and illustration, first by his political cartoons, then by his illustrations of books.

Even though Cruikshank had little formal education, he did enjoy listening to stories. His nurse, Mary, told him fairy tales (Patten 1:28–29), and in 1798, Mungo Park, after his famous African trip, lodged with the Cruikshanks and told George and his brother Robert travel and adventure tales. Robert read and reread Daniel Defoe's *Robinson Crusoe* (1719), and it is assumed that George Cruikshank read that along with John Bunyan and Miguel de Cervantes (Patten 1:35). Living theater, however, particularly the plays of William Shakespeare, impressed Cruikshank even more (Patten, 1:35). In "My Portrait (1841)," a response to a brief biography published by James Grant in 1841, Cruikshank discusses how he derives his characters by frequently passing a public house patronized by coal-heavers. Once in passing he saw a bust of Shakespeare viewing all of the "jolly coal-heavers." Cruikshank asserted, "The living Shakspeare [*sic*], had he been, indeed, in the presence, would but have seen a common humanity working out its objects" (3). Cruikshank found much of his material in the streets and public places, and he learned how to read character from those living texts. In addition, as a political caricaturist, he read a number of newspapers.

His illustrations of books demonstrate his facility to read quickly for graphic details (Patten, 1:35). Difficult as it is to find precise titles that Cruikshank particularly enjoyed in his adult life, from 1823 on he was dedicated to the illustration of books because of their popularity with the public and the financial remuneration (Jones, 51). His illustrations of the **Grimms'** Fairy Tales (1812–1822) were immensely popular and introduced visual themes that recurred in his later work. He also illustrated a number of classic works, of such novelists as Tobias Smollett, Henry Fielding, Oliver Goldsmith, Cervantes, Lawrence Sterne, and William Scott, among many others.

While Cruikshank had marvelous successes in illustrating the classics, some of his relationships with contemporary authors, notably **Charles Dickens** and William Ainsworth, were slightly more contentious. Cruikshank asserted that Dickens became so enamored of some of Cruikshank's sketches about the life of a thief in 1841 that he derived from that the idea of Oliver Twist's story. Similarly, he argued that Ainsworth had derived the ideas for *Guy Fawkes* and *The Tower of London* (1841) from sketches that Cruikshank had supplied (Patten, 2:132–135). These conflicts reveal the interrelated nature of the partnerships with artist and author in the nineteenth century and illuminate Cruikshank's merging of reading and drawing.

ARCHIVES

George Cruikshank Collection, Princeton University.
George Cruikshank Collection, Victoria and Albert Museum.

PRINTED SOURCES

Cruikshank, George. "My Portrait." In *George Cruikshank's Omnibus, 1841–1842* (London: Bell and Daldy, 1869).

Jones, Michael Wynn. *George Cruikshank: His Life and London* (London: Macmillan, 1978).

Patten, Robert L. *George Cruikshank's Life, Times, and Art*, 2 vols. (New Brunswick, N.J.: Rutgers University Press, 1996).

Sarah R. Marino

CURIE, MARIE SKŁODOWSKA (1867–1934). Marie Curie, née Maria Salomea Skłodowska, was born in Warsaw (Poland, then Russian Empire) as the youngest of five children into a teachers' family. After successful completion of her secondary education at the Russian lycée, she worked as governess and financed her sister Bronislawa's medical studies in Paris. In 1891 she went to Paris for physics studies at the Sorbonne. In 1893, she gained her license in physical sciences; in 1894, her licence in mathematical sciences; and in 1904, her Ph.D. In 1895 she married French physicist Pierre Curie (1859–1906), with whom she had two daughters, Irène and Eve; from this time on she was a French citizen.

When Marie Curie was looking for a subject for her thesis, she came upon A. H. Becquerel's discovery (1896) of a phenomenon in uranium that she later named *radioactivity*. She wanted to find out whether this special property was also to be found in other materials, and almost simultaneously with the discovery by German chemist G. C. Schmidt, she found thorium showing this effect, too. By investigating pitchblende, she furthermore predicted that there must be another still unknown substance, which showed a much higher radioactivity. Together with her husband, who more and more joined her work, she discovered (1898) the new radioactive elements radium and polonium.

Marie Curie was appointed lecturer in physics at the École Normale Supérieure for girls in Sèvres (1900), and after the sudden death of Pierre Curie, she followed him in the professorship of physics at the Sorbonne; she was the first woman to teach at this institution. She supported teaching radioactivity by writing a treatise (1910) on this subject. She developed a method for measuring radioactive emanations and prepared an official standard for the measurement of radioactivity (1910), which was deposited with the International Bureau of Weights and Measures. She founded the Radium Institute, which was linked to both the Paris Faculté des Sciences and the Pasteur Institute, for research on the medical applications of radium. It was opened in 1914 (but it took up its work only after World War I), and she was in charge of the department for basic research. Although the laboratory lacked money and Marie Curie spent most of her time on raising funds, it was to become an international center for radioactive physics and chemistry in the 1920s and 1930s.

Marie Curie was the first woman to win a Nobel Prize—in 1903 she shared the Nobel Prize in Physics with her husband Pierre and A. H. Becquerel for their investigation of radioactivity. Furthermore, she was the first person to receive two Nobel Prizes—in 1911 she won the Nobel Prize in Chemistry for her discovery of radium and polonium and for the isolation of pure radium.

During her youth in Poland, Marie was active in the clandestine movement of young Polish nationalist intellectuals, and her philosophy of life was especially influenced by the positivism of **Auguste Comte** and **Herbert Spencer**, yet stamped in a special Polish manner. Her religion was anticlerical, with a Catholic background. She saw herself as a "positive idealist." This background undoubtedly influenced both her belief in the free availability of scientific results (she was against patenting them) and her 12 years serving on the League of Nation's International Commission on Intellectual Cooperation.

ARCHIVES

Curie Papers, Bibliothèque Nationale, Paris.

PRINTED SOURCES

Curie, Eve. *Madame Curie* (New York: Doubleday, Doran & Co., 1937).
Fölsing, Ulla. *Marie Curie—Wegbereiterin einer neuen Wissenschaft* (München: Piper, 1990).
Giroud, François. *Une Femme Honorable* (Paris: Fayard, 1981).
Ksoll, Peter, and Fritz Vögtle. *Marie Curie in Selbstzeugnissen und Bilddokumenten* (Reinbek bei Hamburg: Rowohlt, 1988).
Quinn, Susan. *Marie Curie. A Life* (New York: Simon & Schuster, 1995).
Reid, Robert. *Marie Curie* (New York: Collins, 1974).
Skłodowska-Curie, Marie. *Selbstbiographie* (Leipzig: B. G. Teubner Verlagsgesellschaft, 1962).

Horst Kant

D

DAGUERRE, LOUIS-JACQUES-MANDÉ (1787–1851). Louis Daguerre was born in Cormeilles-en-Parisis on November 18, 1787. Best known as an inventor of photography, Daguerre won contemporary renown as an artist, stage designer, and impresario of the Diorama. The French Revolution and the Napoleonic Wars (*see* **Napoléon**) disrupted his formal education, but he was ambitious and intelligent and possessed natural artistic ability. Moving to Paris in 1804, Daguerre was first apprenticed to a designer of stage sets, and he later worked with Pierre Prévost (1764–1823), a painter of panoramic cityscapes and scenes celebrated for their lifelike realism. Early fame came from his theater sets, with their illusions and spectacular lighting effects, his paintings, six of which were shown at the Salons beginning in 1814, and his lithographs, including those for Baron Isidore Taylor's *Voyages pittoresques et romantiques en l'ancienne France* (1820–1878). On July 11, 1822, Daguerre opened the Diorama, a commercial establishment for the showing of dramatic topographical images of celebrated buildings such as Chartres Cathedral, picturesque towns and cities, and sublime landscapes like the Valley of Chamonix. Diorama images were animated by light, artfully manipulated so as to simulate temporal change. Meanwhile, Daguerre devoted years searching for a method of permanently fixing the images produced by optical devices like the *camera obscura*, long used by topographers and other artists as a drawing aid, and perhaps as early as 1835, he produced his first daguerreotype. François Arago (1786–1853) announced the discovery before the Académie des Sciences on January 7, 1839, and Daguerre's images, including three admired views of the Boulevard du Temple, were exhibited. The French government purchased his method, making it public on August 19, 1839. Daguerre's *Histoire et description des procédés du daguerréotype et du diorama* appeared in 1839 and was immediately translated into at least seven languages. He died on July 10, 1851, at Bry-sur-Marne, near Paris.

Little is known about Daguerre's education or reading. His publications are technical manuals for the reproduction of images for the Diorama and the making of daguerreotypes, and his letters describe experiments with photography. References to literary or other sources are absent, and regrettably, neither his set designs nor the Diorama images have survived. Consequently, the influences on Daguerre's work and his intentions must be inferred. Invaluable for this task are his surviving lithographs and paintings as well as contemporary reactions in the press to the Diorama and the daguerreotype. Nonetheless, Daguerre's motives for the obsessive experiments that led to his invention of photography remain unknown. They likely grew out of efforts to manipulate light so as to create illusions for the theater and the Diorama in keeping with the romantic and picturesque conventions then in vogue. Equally important was Daguerre's ambition to achieve precise topographical accuracy in his images. Commercial considerations and a thirst for recognition were doubtless also factors. In short, contemporary artistic conventions with popular appeal and a desire for fame and profit more likely shaped Daguerre's career and impelled him to invent a type of photography than did any sort of reading.

The daguerreotypes exhibited by Daguerre consisted of architectural views, street scenes, still lifes, and portraits. Great public enthusiasm greeted these lifelike illusions of reality, and studios promptly opened to make portraits and city views. Expeditions soon set out to rural France and other areas, including the Holy Land, to make images of famous sites and buildings. Meanwhile, a vociferous debate erupted in the press over the nature of photography, with some claiming it was art and others that it was not. Additional contemporary responses were poems, cartoons, and stories, including Eugénie Foa's "The Daguerreotype: Accuser and Avenger" (December 1839). Improvements in photography soon rendered the daguerreotype, with its unique and reversed image, obsolete. Negatives and paper prints replaced it, making possible the work of later masters like Gustave Le Grey, Charles Nègre, Roger Fenton, and Charles Marville.

ARCHIVES

The Gernsheim Collection, Harry Ransom Humanities Research Center, University of Texas at Austin.
International Museum of Photography and Film, George Eastman House, Rochester, New York.

PRINTED SOURCES

Adamson, Keith I. P. "1839—The Year of Daguerre," *History of Photography*, 13 (July–September 1989), 191–202.
Buerger, Janet E. *French Daguerreotypes* (forward by Walter Clark) (Chicago: University of Chicago Press, 1989).
Gasser, Martin. "Between 'From Today, Painting Is Dead' and 'How the Sun Became a Painter': A Close Look at Reactions to Photography in Paris, 1839–1853," *Image*, 33 (Winter 1990–1991), 8–29.
Gernsheim, Helmut, and Alison Gernsheim. *L.J.M. Daguerre. The History of the Diorama and the Daguerreotype* (New York: Dover Publications, 1968).

Stuhlman, Rachel. "Luxury, Novelty, Fidelity: Madame Foa's Daguerreian Tale," *Image*, 40 (1997), 3–61.

Robert W. Brown

D'ANNUNZIO, GABRIELE (1863–1938). Gabriele D'Annunzio, an Italian writer, was born in Pescara in 1863 and died in Gardone Riviera (Brescia) in 1938. He was educated at a secondary school in Prato, near Florence, then studied at the university in Rome, though he never graduated. He admired the works of Algernon Charles Swinburne, **Walter Pater**, Émile Verhaeren, **Richard Wagner**, and **Arthur Schopenauer**. D'Annunzio lived under the banner of worldly pleasure and aestheticism, always searching for new sensations. He learned from the Decadents ideals of elegance and sensitivity and the taste of formal technicality (*Il Piacere*, 1889, translated as *The Child of Pleasure*; *Giovanni Episcopo*, 1892, translated as *Episcopo and Company*; *L'innocente*, 1892, translated as *The Victim*). In the last two novels, one finds lessons from **Tolstoy** and **Dostoevsky**, but reduced to a languid ostentation of morbidity.

D'Annunzio intended to fill a moral emptiness, whose awkwardness he strongly felt, through the myth of the "superman" derived from **Friedrich Nietzsche**; but he replaced the "will of power" theorized by the German philosopher with aesthetic ideals as foundations for an "inimitable life." To this period belong the novels *Il Trionfo della morte* (1894), translated as *The Triumph of Death*; *Le vergini delle rocce* (1896), translated as *The Maidens of the Rocks*; *Il fuoco* (1900), translated as *The Flame*; and the play *La Gioconda* (1899).

The years from 1901 to 1915 saw a new phase in D'Annunzio's literary production and theoretic elaboration. The myth of "superman" was supported now by the myth of the "supernation," whose destiny it is to transform itself into an empire, a doctrine expressed poetically in the masterworks *Laudi del cielo, del mare, della terra e degli eroi* (1903). He moved to France to escape creditors and wrote *Le martyre de Saint-Sébastien*, a miracle-play showing the influences of **Gustave Flaubert** and Anatole France, dedicated to **Maurice Barrès** and presented in Paris in 1911, with the musical accompaniment of Claude Debussy. At the outbreak of World War I, D'Annunzio served in the Italian infantry, navy, and air force and after the war, with a handful of volunteers, occupied Fiume (Rijeka), proclaiming his regency. Removed by the Italian army, he retired in Gardone to a lakeside villa called "Il Vittoriale degli Italiani," where he lived in splendid confinement until his death.

The main character of D'Annunzio's art is the capacity to catch, and the ability to express, the communion of senses and mind with the whole, the charm of a nature made of sensations and atmosphere, the fading away of the self and the appearing of a new, sensual relationship with the outer world. This particular characteristic was highly appreciated by Guillaume Apollinaire, Stefan George, and Hugo von Hofmannsthal. And this is the lesson that D'Annunzio left to the twentieth century, the splendor of an analogic language that works through suggestion and not through communication, as the poetry of Cesare Pavese, of

Robert de Montesquiou, of Henri de Montherlant, of Paul Valéry, of Henri Bordeaux, and in part, of Marcel Proust will show.

ARCHIVES

Il Vittoriale, Gardone Riviera (Brescia). See "Inventario dei manoscritti di Gabriele D'Annunzio al Vittoriale," *Quaderni dannunziani*, n. 36–37, Gardone Riviera, Il Vittoriale degli italiani, 1968. Biblioteca Nazionale, Rome.

PRINTED SOURCES

Alatri, P. *D'Annunzio* (Torino: UTET, 1983).
Antongini, T. *Vita segreta di Gabriele D'Annunzio* (Milano: Mondadori, 1938).
Chiara, P. *D'Annunzio* (Milano: Mondadori, 1978).
Fucilla, J. G., and J. M. Carrière. *D'Annunzio Abroad: A Bibliographical Essay*, 2 vols. (New York: Columbia University Press, 1935–1937).
Marabini Moevs, M. T. *G. D'Annunzio e le estetiche della fine del secolo* (L'Aquila: Japadre, 1976).
Praz, M. *La carne, la morte e il diavolo nella letteratura romantica* (1930; Firenze: Sansoni, 1966).
Tedeschi, T. *D'Annunzio e la musica* (Firenze: La Nuova Italia, 1988).
Valesio, P. *Gabriele D'Annunzio: The Dark Flame* (New Haven, Conn.: Yale University Press, 1992).
Vecchioni, M. *Bibliografia critica di Gabriele D'Annunzio* (Pescara-Roma: Edizioni aternine, 1970).
Winwar, F. *Wingless Victory: A Biography of Gabriele D'Annunzio and Eleonora Duse* (1956; Westport, Conn.: Greenwood Press, 1974).

Giuseppe Marchetti

DARÍO, RUBÉN (1867–1916). Rubén Darío, known as the founder of modernism for Latin America and Spain, was born in Metapa, Nicaragua, to Manuel Darío and Rosa Sarmiento. His family moved to León, where he was subsequently educated. His childhood was marked by prodigious efforts to gain a scholarship for study in Europe through the publication of his poetry. His first published volume of poetry (1879) led to his eventual recitation of *The Book* for Nicaragua's conservative president Joaquín Zavala as part of a scholarship competition. Although he didn't win, his poem had a profound effect on the political leader, who warned against the young poet's hostility toward the religion of his parents. During his lifetime, Darío held several diplomatic posts for the government of Nicaragua; these posts compelled him to travel extensively throughout Latin America and Europe.

Living primarily in Chile and Argentina, then France and Spain, his first visit to Chile in 1886 was marked by racism and indifference. The Southern Cone countries were commonly understood as the cosmopolitan centers of Latin America. As Darío remarked in his autobiography (Darío), his Central American heritage and "the color of his skin" offended the sensibilities of the Chilean bourgeoisie and intellectual community. This experience with racism pushed him to embrace and transform European aesthetics as a means of escaping the conditions of his reception. He is commonly accepted as the first Latin American literary figure to continue the tradition of such key Spanish writers as Garcilaso, Sor Juana de la Cruz, Góngora, and Bécquer.

While in Chile he published his most important and foundational modernist text, *Azul* (1888). This text became the "call to arms" for a loosely united group of writers and artists in Latin America who considered themselves to be in the process of blending European literary and artistic forms with Latin American sensibilities and realities. Although some scholars in the twentieth century decried the modernist vision as largely a colonial and assimilationist aesthetic, which ignored the indigenous and pre-Conquest traditions of Latin America's original inhabitants, Darío's form of modernism derived directly from his rejection of a Spanish tradition of imperialism. Darío's experience with Spanish hegemony, with the imperial ban historically on "imaginative literature," compelled him to search for the conditions of aesthetic experience in his own understanding of Latin American identity and subjectivity. Like other modernists in Europe and Britain, Darío was intent on discovering an aesthetic experience of his own that united European form to his own idiosyncratic, in this case, Latin American, content. This idea of promoting an aesthetic experience from outside of the canonically recognized constituency associated with modernism forced Darío, then, into the role of the founder of the movement.

His work eventually united Latin American and Iberian writers around the idea of "art for art's sake" rather than the former colonial relationship of sovereign to colonized that had dictated prior exchanges. Ultimately, Darío ended up changing the conditions and relationship between colonizer and colonized in ways that were not only transgressive of several imperial edicts but also unimaginable to Spanish readers on the European Continent. For this reason, Darío's artistic vision was both inclusive and recuperative of Europe's artistic and aesthetic traditions. Thus Darío's vision reshaped the relationship between Latin Americans, specifically Central Americans, and their Spanish counterparts. By bringing modernism to Latin America and then exporting it back to Europe, Darío was able to alter the imagination and image of the Latin American intellectual in the minds of their "colonial masters."

In other words, his work fostered an interlocutory relationship previously unknown between writers in the Americas and Europe. In this way, Spain's "Generation of 1898" felt a close link to Darío's modernist vision, even as he set about renovating their poetic language. By targeting the disjunction inherent in European form and Latin American content, Darío looked to discover an artistic form in language that would mimetically express the realities of the Latin American writer. His use of "metrical innovations . . . lucent language" gave to Spain what C. M. Bowra called "a new poetry."

ARCHIVES

Woodbridge, Hensley Charles. *Rubén Darío: A Selective Classified and Annotated Bibliography* (Metuchen, N.J.: Scarecrow Press, 1975).

PRINTED SOURCES

Bowra, C. M. *Inspiration and Poetry* (London: Macmillan, 1955).

Brotherston, Gordon. *Latin American Poetry: Origins and Presence* (Cambridge: Cambridge University Press, 1975).

Darío, Rubén. *La vida de Rubén Darío e Rubén Darío scrita por el mismo* (Managua, Nicaragua: Editorial Nueva, 1990).

Fernández, Teodosio. *Rubén Darío* (Madrid: Ediciones Quorum, 1986).

Fiore, Dolores Ackel. *Rubén Darío in Search of Inspiration: Greco-Roman Mythology in His Stories and Poetry* (New York: Las Americas, 1963).

Florit, Eugenio, and José Olivio Jiménez. *La poesía hispanoamericana desde el modernismo* (Englewood Cliffs, N.J.: Prentice-Hall, 1963).

Torres, Edelberto. *La dramática vida de Rubén Darío* (San José, Costa Rica: Editorial Universitaria Centroamericana, 1966).

Watland, Charles Dunton. "The Literary Education of Rubén Darío: An Examination of the Extent and Nature of His Literary Culture to the Period of Azul (1888)" (Ph.D. diss., University of Minnesota, 1953).

Kitty Millet

DARWIN, CHARLES ROBERT (1809–1882). Charles Darwin was born in Shrewsbury, the son of respected doctor Robert Darwin and grandson of famous physician and philosopher Erasmus Darwin. Charles Darwin began his education at the Shrewsbury School, (1818–1825), went on to Edinburgh University to study medicine at his father's insistence (1825–1827), then entered Cambridge to train as a clergyman (1828–1831). Darwin was christened an Anglican and intended to enter the established priesthood; however, his father was a religious skeptic, as was his mother, and the first school Darwin attended was a Unitarian institution.

Darwin had little interest in his schooling: "Nothing could have been worse for the development of my mind than Dr. Butler's school [in Shrewsbury], as it was strictly classical" (*Autobiography*, 27). At Edinburgh University, Darwin attended medical lectures and did some clinical work, but he seems to have spent much of his time hiking, collecting specimens, shooting birds, and helping his brother with his chemistry experiments. Darwin was interested in doing scientific work, not in studying it. Darwin's father realized that Charles had little interest in a medical education, so, with some misgivings, he arranged to have him enter Cambridge to become a clergyman. The younger Darwin seems to have acquiesced in this choice when he realized that life as a "country clergyman" (*Autobiography*, 57) would provide him with both financial support and the freedom to pursue his interests as a naturalist.

At Cambridge, Darwin discovered a sense of purpose, though not the professed one for his attendance. He began attending lectures, then taking long walks and holding animated discussions with the deeply religious botanist John Stevens Henslow. This connection between religion and science was reinforced by Darwin's reading, at Henslow's insistence, of the religious naturalism of William Paley; his *View of the Evidences of Christianity* (1794) and *Natural Theology* (1802) convinced Darwin that science and religion were wholly compatible (Brown, 6). An awakening sense of religious mission can be seen in Darwin when he wrote: "During my last year at Cambridge I read with care and profound interest **Humboldt**'s *Personal Narrative*. This work and Sir J. Hershel's *Introduction to the Study of Natural Philosophy* stirred up in me a burning zeal to add even the most humble contribution to the noble structure of Natural Science" (*Autobiography*, 67–68). He would certainly achieve that goal.

Henslow also urged Darwin to study geology; accordingly, he read and profited greatly from the arguments in **Charles Lyell**'s *Principles of Geology* (1830–1833) explaining geological change as a natural process continuing over vast periods of time. Henslow also recommended Darwin as naturalist on the voyage of the H.M.S. *Beagle*, which explored the Southern Hemisphere from 1831 to 1836. Here Darwin used his understanding of inexorable geological change to try to understand the formation of coral reefs and atolls—the product of small creatures working tirelessly for centuries. He also observed the minute variations in animals, especially birds, living in differing habitats and regions—the same attention to detail he had put into his collection of insects during his college days. But Darwin was not content to merely observe change and variation; he wished to understand it. This impetus was furthered by his reading a review of **Auguste Comte**'s *Cours de philosophie positive* (1838) and Comte's claim that knowledge passed from theological to scientific understandings (Brown, 15). Darwin set out to remove theology from biology.

In 1838 Darwin read **Thomas Malthus**'s *Essay on the Principle of Population* (1798), which suggested to him that "Natural Selection" explained the divergence of species. Darwin wrestled with this theory for some 20 years before **Alfred Russel Wallace** sent him an essay containing the argument for evolution in 1858. Stung to action, Darwin completed *The Origin of Species* in less than a year; the entire first edition sold out on the day of publication. *The Descent of Man* followed in 1871, linking humans directly to the rest of the animal kingdom and explicitly denying the role of God in explaining life. The personal toll on Darwin was tremendous; so, too, the toll on the relationship between science and religion.

ARCHIVES

The Darwin Papers. University Library. Cambridge, England.

PRINTED SOURCES

Bowler, Peter J. *Evolution: The History of an Idea* (Berkeley: University of California Press, 1984). A comparative discussion of several contributors to evolutionary theory.

Brown, Frank Burch. *The Evolution of Darwin's Religious Views*, NABPR Special Studies Series, no. 10. (Macon, Ga.: Mercer University Press, 1986). A suggestive
analysis of Darwin's religious ambivalence.
Darwin, Charles. *Autobiography*, Nora Barlow (ed.) (London: Collins, 1958).

Charles M. Roll

DAVID, JACQUES-LOUIS (1748–1825). Jacques-Louis David was born in
Paris in 1748 and studied at Picpus (1755–1758), the Collège de Beauvais and
the Collège de Quatre Nations (1758–1764), the Académie de Saint-Luc, the
Académie royale de peinture et de sculpture (1766–1774); and the French Academy in Rome (1774–1780).

David broke with the Rococo of the 1750s and the 1760s and traditional
history painting to become the dominant figure of late eighteenth-century neoclassical painting. His gift for dynamic, revolutionary compositions, expressive
motifs, and tragic situations, seconded by a talent for politics and self-promotion,
made him the most influential European artist of the early nineteenth century.

From an early age, David attended some of the finest schools in France. He
began studying under the history painter Joseph-Marie Vien in 1766. David drew
upon texts for personages, situations, costumes, and décor. In many cases, the
incidents narrated in his painting can be found in classical authors such as
Homer, Herodotus, Xenophon, Plutarch, Apuleius, Virgil, Ovid, and Livy. They
also appear in the seventeenth-century drama of Corneille, Racine, and Moliére,
in the works of various eighteenth-century playwrights such as Voltaire, Alfieri,
and Jean François Marmontel, as well as in eighteenth-century histories such as
Charles Rollin's *Histoire ancienne* (Johnson, 26, 258–260; Crow, 38–45; Brookner, 70). David wrote that he ruined his 1772 entry for the *prix de Rome*, *Diana
and Apollo Piercing the Children of Niobe with Their Arrows*, when he hastily
repainted the wet canvas after rereading the relevant passages from Ovid's *Metamorphoses* (Wildenstein, 6). In his history paintings, he often imagined scenes
without textual sources for expressive and thematic ends. In both *The Oath of
the Horatii* (1785) and *The Lictors Bringing Brutus the Body of his Son* (1789),
he invented the central action of the canvas in order to extol stoicism and the
sacrifice of family sentiment for the sake of male civic virtue. In the late 1780s,
his discussions with the poet André Chénier and others of Denis Diderot's *Discours sur la poésie dramatique* (1758) may have influenced his composition of
The Death of Socrates (1787) (Crow, 93–99). David had close ties to the *Comédie française* (Régis, 167–198). Several of his works dramatized tragic dilemmas and relied on theatrical gesture. Jailed in 1794 for his involvement in
the Reign of Terror, he quoted from Racine's *Phèdre* to protest his innocence
(Wildenstein, 114).

At the French Academy in Rome, David encountered antiquarianism and the
ideas of Johann-Joachim Winckelmann. David's Roman notebooks reveal the
importance of compendia of classical motifs (Winckelmann, Montfaucon, Piranesi, Caylus, Mengs, Hamilton) (Delécluze, 128–132) to his later oeuvre. He

appreciated the expressive power of ancient sculpture at least as much as archaeological exactitude, but he did annotate his Roman drawings and tracings to indicate their sources. His student Miette de Villars speaks of his study of Johann Kaspar Lavater's work on physiognomy (Brookner, 48).

ARCHIVES

Archives nationales de France.
Archives des musées nationaux.
Bibliothèque des musées nationaux.
Bibliothèque de l'École des Beaux-arts.
Bibliothèque nationale de France (Paris).

PRINTED SOURCES

Brookner, Anita. *Jacques-Louis David* (London: Chatto & Windus, 1980).
Crow, Thomas. *Emulation: Making Artists for Revolutionary France* (New Haven, Conn.: Yale University Press, 1995).
Delécluze, E. J. *Louis David, son école et son temps* (1855; Paris: Macula, 1983).
Dowd, David Lloyd. *Pageant-Master of the Republic: Jacques-Louis David and the Revolution* (Lincoln: University of Nebraska, 1948).
Johnson, Dorothy. *Jacques-Louis David: Art in Metamorphosis* (Princeton University Press, 1993).
Régis, Michael (ed.). *David contre David* (Paris: La documentation française, 1993).
Schnapper, Antoine, and Arlette Serullaz (eds.). *Jacques-Louis David, 1748–1825* (Paris: Ministère de la culture, 1989). Includes chronology that updates and supplements Wildenstein.
Verbraeken, René. *Jacques-Louis David jugé par ses contemporains et par la postérité* (L. Laget, 1973).
Wildenstein, Daniel, and Guy Wildenstein. *Documents complémentaries au catalogue de l'oeuvre de Louis David* ([Paris]: Fondation Wildenstein, 1973). Excellent starting point for archival sources.

Aaron J. Segal

DAVY, HUMPHRY (1778–1829). Sir Humphry Davy was born at Penzance, Cornwall, on December 17, 1778. When he was yet a boy, Davy lived with John Tonkin, a local surgeon and apothecary, while attending preparatory school. He was later educated at the Penzance grammar school and then the prestigious Grammar School at Truro in 1793. His remaining education was self-directed. Davy revolutionized the study of chemistry and was a strong advocate for the practical application of his discoveries.

In 1794 Tonkin helped Davy attain an apprenticeship to John Bingham Borlase, a prosperous surgeon and apothecary in Penzance. Davy would have pursued a medical degree at Edinburgh but was introduced to the mysteries of natural science while working in the apothecary's dispensary. At about the same time, Davy read Lavoisier's *Traité elementaire de chimie* and William Nicholson's *Dictionary of Chemistry*. Through a series of chance acquaintances with contemporary natural scientists both resident in and visiting Penzance, including

Gregory Watt, the son of James Watt, Davy cultivated his nascent interests in philosophy and chemistry.

Davies Giddy (later Gilbert), an influential Cornish Member of Parliament, introduced Davy to Dr. Thomas Beddoes, founder of the Pneumatic Institution in Bristol. Davy's inclination toward medicine attracted him to the possible connections between gases and illness, a topic of contemporary debate. In 1798 Davy accepted the position of superintendent of the Pneumatic Institution. At Bristol, Davy made extensive study of nitrous oxide and tested the effects of "laughing gas" on himself and his friends **Robert Southey** and **Samuel Taylor Coleridge**. Davy also began experiments in galvanism and voltaic electricity while at the Pneumatic Institution, while cultivating his talents as a poet through friendships with Southey, Coleridge, and **Wordsworth**. Some of Davy's own poems were published in Southey's *Annual Anthology*.

Davy's scientific publications led to an invitation from Count Rumford to lecture at the Institution for Diffusing Knowledge in London, later the Royal Institution. In July 1801, Davy was made an assistant lecturer there and in November was elected a fellow. Once established in London, Davy continued his experiments in pneumatic chemistry, minerology, and galvanism. His experiments on the chemical properties of Volta's pile electric battery led to the discovery of two new elements, potassium and sodium. He also overturned Lavoisier's claim that all acids contained oxygen by proving that muriatic acid contained an as yet undiscovered element, which Davy called *chlorine*. These major discoveries were made within the more empirical climate of the Royal Institute, whose gentlemen backers sought practical applications for the new philosophical sciences. Davy's natural talents as a raconteur made him a gifted lecturer, and the Royal Institute capitalized on his name and reputation to draw subscribers to his series of public lectures.

Davy's rapid celebrity led to invited lectures abroad and a place among London's high society. In 1812 he resigned from the Royal Institution, was knighted, and married a wealthy widow. He toured Europe from 1813 to 1815, to consult with contemporary scientists, and took with him the young Michael Faraday as his secretary and assistant. Thus began Faraday's scientific apprenticeship. Davy also applied his knowledge to practical and social causes, including agricultural chemistry, the fumigation of London's Newgate prison, and his development of the miner's safety lamp. He later served as president of the Royal Society, from 1820 to 1827.

A stroke in late 1826 left Davy partially paralyzed. He retired to Italy and, though unable to continue his scientific research, wrote *Salmonia; or Days of Fly-Fishing*, a book on angling inspired by Walton's *Compleat Angler*. He died on May 29, 1829, in Geneva.

ARCHIVES

R. I. Davy Manuscripts in the Archives of the Royal Institution, London.

PRINTED SOURCES

Davy, John (ed.). *The Collected Works of Sir Humphry Davy*, 9 vols. (London: Smith and Elder, 1839–1840).

———. *Fragmentary Remains, Literary and Scientific of Sir Humphry Davy, Bart* (London: J. Churchill, 1858).

———. *Memoirs of the Life of Sir Humphry Davy*, 2 vols. (London: Longman, Rees, Orme, Brown, Green, & Longman, 1836).

Golinski, Jan. *Science as Public Culture* (Cambridge: Cambridge University Press, 1992), chapter 7.

Hartley, Sir Harold. *Humphry Davy* (London: Nelson, 1966).

Knight, David. *Humphry Davy: Science and Power* (Cambridge: Cambridge University Press, 1992).

Levere, Trevor. *Affinity and Matter: Elements of Chemical Philosophy 1800–1865* (Oxford: Oxford University Press, 1971), chapter 2.

Paris, John Ayrton. *The Life of Sir Humphry Davy*, 2 vols. (London: Henry Colburn and Richard Bentley, 1831).

Treneer, Anne. *The Mercurial Chemist: A Life of Sir Humphry Davy* (London: Methuen & Co., 1963).

Greg T. Smith

DEÁK, FERENC (1803–1876). Ferenc Deák of Hungary was born at Sojtor in the county of Zala and died in Pest. His primary education was at Köszeg (1808–1811). He attended secondary school first at the Keszthely Premonstratensian Gymnasium (1811–1812), and finished at the Nagykanizsa Piarist Gymnasium (1813–1817). Upon finishing secondary school, Deák began studying at the Royal Law Academy in Györ, graduating in 1821 and passing the bar two years later. Deák was a Roman Catholic, and while he was nonpracticing, Christian teachings influenced his political beliefs.

Deák was an active Hungarian nationalist from a very early age whose political career as a reformer began at age 30 when he was elected junior deputy to the Zala county diet. His prominence grew quickly, as he was a senior deputy within one year. While Deák was recognized as the leader of the liberal opposition from 1840 onward, his most important legacy to Hungary was his work on the Compromise of 1867, insuring the political stability necessary for Hungary to continue internal progress and development.

Throughout his life, Deák's liberal reforms were based largely on four personal beliefs and influences: the teachings of the ancient Hebrews, the Hellenistic tradition, Roman law, and Christianity (Király, 20). Deák had just started his formal schooling when **Napoléon Bonaparte**'s Proclamation to the Hungarian nation was issued in 1809. He would have been well aware of the excitement generated by the Proclamation, for his brother, Antal Deák, fought in the Battle of Györ against Napoléon (Király, 27).

The most important influence on Deák's intellectual development, however, was the poet Mihaly Vörösmarty. Deák's sense of romanticism and patriotism were very similar to Vörösmary's, and he was greatly influenced by the latter. For Vörösmarty, humanity and patriotism were identical, and humanity was best served through love for the nation. Vörösmarty's epic poem "Zolan's Flight" initiated an era of national romanticism in literature that provided a unifying spiritual force that helped eliminate sectional and religious differences among the many Hungarian intellectuals (Barany, 190). Deák and Vörösmarty's deep friendship lasted from 1824 when they first met until Vörösmarty's death. Such was their closeness that Deák saw to the upkeep of Vörösmarty's widow and son after his death in 1855 (Király, 148).

Like most Hungarian nationalist reformers of the era, Deák was also deeply influenced by the work of István Széchenyi. Széchenyi published his first major work, *Credit*, in 1830, and its publication marks the beginning of the Reform Era in Hungary. Although sometimes disagreeing, Széchenyi and Deák corresponded frequently and Széchenyi's influence on Deák is significant (Király, 12, 37).

ARCHIVES

Deák Papers. National Archives. Budapest, Hungary.

PRINTED SOURCES

Barany, George. *A History of Hungary*, Peter Sugar (ed.) (Bloomington: Indiana University Press, 1990).
Deák, Ferenc. *Deák Ferenc Beszédei* [The speeches of Ferenc Deák], Manó Kónyi (ed.), 6 vols. (Budapest: Franklin-Tarsulat, 1903).
Király, Béla. *Ferenc Deák* (Boston: Twayne Publishers, 1975).

Phillip A. Cantrell II

DEGAS, EDGAR (1834–1917). Hilaire Germain Edgar Degas was born in Paris in 1834 and studied from the age of 11 to 18 at the Lycée Louis le Grand, where he received a classical education and became fluent in Latin and Greek. Abandoning two years of law school, he enrolled in the École des Beaux-Arts in 1855, where he copied the works of past masters under the instruction of Louis Lamothe, a pupil of the famous French linearist Jean-Auguste Dominique Ingres. Degas traveled throughout Italy from 1857 to 1860, and his encounters with the artists of the Cal d'arrosti enabled him to free his style from the restraints of his learned classicism. Upon returning to France, Degas concentrated on depicting the contemporary Parisian scene in works that reflected the social milieu in informal compositions, capturing the movements of dancers, the working classes, and common individuals in masterpieces such as *Ballet Rehearsal* (1876) and *The Morning Bath* (1890). Degas participated in seven out of eight Impressionist exhibitions from 1874 to 1886, becoming a proponent and leader of the Impressionist movement, and despite his failing eyesight, prodigiously produced oils and pastels that demonstrated his innovative techniques and principles until the time of his death during World War I.

Literature in France during the era of Degas was experiencing profound changes that deeply influenced the cultural expression of artists. Proponents of a literary movement called *naturalism* espoused that writers should strive to scientifically depict individuals and their surroundings, as they were shaped by the determining forces of their environment, a belief that eventually let to Realism and, later, the Decadence school. Advocates of the Decadence school such as the poets Laforgue and Verlaine sought to capture fleeting moments of material existence in their work, just as Degas caught the incidental movements of individuals in his canvasses and drawings. The novel was also born during this era, as writers such as **Émile Zola**, whose works *Nana* (1880) and *Germinal* (1885) were read by Degas despite the artist's anti-Dreyfusard stance, depicted the realistic social conditions of the lower classes in French society and contrasted them sharply with the lives of the bourgeoisie. Degas also came into contact with the work of Edmond and Jules Goncourt, two brothers who together wrote realistic novels reflecting the relationship of the individual to the world around him. **Gustave Flaubert**'s *Madame Bovary* (1857) and the short stories of **Guy de Maupassant** such as "The Necklace" and "Tallow Ball," with their psychological realism, also served to inspire Degas, who shared the belief of critics such as Edmond Duranty, the theorist of the Impressionist movement, and Baudelaire, who wrote *Le Peintre de la Vie Moderne*, that it was the duty of the avante-garde artist to reflect the social realities of French society. If not for these literary influences, artists such as Degas and his contemporaries would never have been able to break free from the controlling influences of the Salon to experiment with the fugitive effects of light and motion and develop their own highly influential style.

ARCHIVES

Getty Research Institute for the History of Art and Humanities, Special Collections, Los Angeles, California, control no. CJPA86-A702.

PRINTED SOURCES

Boggs, Jean Sutherland. *Portraits by Degas: California Studies in the History of Art*, vol. 2 (Berkeley: University of California Press, 1962).

Boggs, Jean Sutherland, Henri Loyrette, Michael Pantazzi, and Gary Tinterow. *Degas* (New York: Metropolitan Museum of Art, 1988).

Callen, Anthea. *The Spectacular Body: Science, Method and Meaning in the Work of Degas* (London: Yale University Press, 1995).

Huyghe, René (ed.). *Larousse Encyclopedia of Modern Art* (London: Paul Hamlyn, 1965).

Kendall, Richard. *Degas: Beyond Impressionism* (London: National Gallery Publications, 1996).

Kielty, Bernardine. *Masters of Painting: Their Work, Their Lives, Their Times* (New York: Doubleday and Company, Inc., 1964).

McMullen, Roy. *Degas: His Life, Times and Work* (Boston: Houghton Mifflin, 1984).

Pool, Phoebe. *Degas* (London: Spring Books, 1966).

Reff, Theodore. *Degas: The Artist's Mind* (New York: Harper and Row Publishers, 1976).

Smith, Bradley. *France: A History in Art* (London: Weidensfeld and Nicolson, 1984).

Gregory L. Schnurr

DELACROIX, EUGÈNE (1798–1863). Eugène Delacroix, a French painter whose works personified the essence of Romanticism, was born the son of a lawyer at Charenton St. Maurice. He inherited his artistic talent from his mother, and after receiving his education in Paris, he joined the workshop of the painter Jean-Baptiste Guerin. The 1819 death of his father left him penniless, and painting became his sole source of income. At his death in 1863, he left 863 paintings, 1,500 watercolors and pastels, and 6,600 drawings. Although Delacroix painted during the Romantic era, he rejected the label of Romantic painter, preferring to think of himself as a classical painter. His thematic paintings displayed a concern for detail, color, and texture, as well as an interest in animal imagery. His first masterpiece, *Dante and Virgil*, was exhibited at the 1822 Salon in France. This success was followed by *Massacres at Scio* in the 1824 Salon, a piece criticized by many; however, it now hangs in the Louvre.

His acute interest in the events surrounding him was evident in both his artwork and later in his *Journal*. Not only was Delacroix a visual cataloger of historic events, but he was also a historian of the arts. His world travels made him very much aware of other cultures, particularly the six months he spent in Morocco in 1832. He wrote in a letter that "it was among these people that I discovered for myself the beauty of antiquity." Following his visit to Morocco, he revealed how deeply his travels had affected him in his art. These paintings, full of animal imagery, personified the human virtues of constancy and nobility. His focus in these paintings was on the link between man and animal and the contrast between human rationality and animal irrationality. He wrote in *Oeuvres litteraires*, "Learn to draw, and you will carry away with you . . . memories. . . . That simple pencil line . . . reminds you of [things] . . . that the pen cannot translate" (12–13).

The passion for interpreting what "the pen cannot translate" was similar to Delacroix's passion for English, literature, art, and culture, as well as his interest in historical images. Perhaps best known is his image *La Liberté guidant le peuple*, first exhibited at the 1831 Salon. Inspired by popular battle prints and history itself, the events surrounding the July Revolution, Delacroix emphasized the theatrical nature of this revolt, which took place on the streets of Paris rather than on a battlefield. Delacroix himself had been a witness to the tumult in the streets, and he used various elements, such as the barricades in the streets, to function in a more theatrical manner. Since Delacroix admired Shakespeare, perhaps he was remembering Jacque's "Seven Ages" speech in Shakespeare's *As You Like It* (Act 2, Scene 7) in which he says, "All the world's a stage/ And all the men and women merely players." This theatrical spirit, a trademark of Romanticism, is evident in all of Delacroix's works, and this label clung to him despite his repeated attempts to deny his involvement in the Romantic movement. His *Journal*, or diary, mirrored the freedom expressed by Romanticism in its irregularity. Delacroix skipped days, weeks, even years; for example, he wrote readily from 1822 to 1824 but not again until 1847 to his death in 1863. Yet this is not a source in which Delacroix "tells all" but, rather, a repository for his thoughts covering his concern for unity, proportion, and order in his art. The improvisation and spontaneity found in Delacroix's journal mirrored his working methods. He would often alter his original composition, as in the case of *La Liberté*, as he rarely followed a fixed plan.

Not following a fixed plan allowed Delacroix to explore his creative genius. Between 1838 and 1847, he received commissions for the Salon du Roi and the decorations for the Palais Bourbon, as well as the Luxembourg libraries. The theme of civilization, and in particular, antiquity, dominated the artworks for each of these constructions. The Palais Bourbon included the theme of Alexander preserving the poems of Homer, while the decorations in the Luxembourg libraries represented mythological events, such as Dante's Elysian fields. The use of allegorical elements continued in the central ceiling panel of the Apollo Gallery in the Louvre, *Apollo—Slayer of the Serpent Python*, which pictured the victory of the sun god over the serpent, or perhaps the triumph of enlightened thought over prejudice and ignorance. His fame was cemented with the 1855 "Exposition Universelle" in which five paintings by Delacroix were displayed together in a room devoted entirely to his art; however, this was not the last artwork he finished prior to his death. In 1861, he painted his last decorative series, the Chapel of the Holy Angels at the Church of Saint-Sulpice.

Although Delacroix resisted the label of Romanticism, he was in many ways the epitome of the Romantic movement. Known for his attention to detail, vivid colors, and daring steps, the man who began life as a painter out of necessity ended life consumed by his work. As he wrote on January 1, 1861, in his *Journal*, "Painting harasses me and indeed torments me in a thousand ways like the most demanding of mistresses . . . [T]his eternal struggle, instead of beating me down, raises me up" (317). Painting had become his "modus operandi," and merely the number of works to his name explain the effect Western culture had on him—and he on it.

ARCHIVES

No substantial archival sources known to exist.

PRINTED SOURCES

Delacroix, Eugene. *Journal*, William Pach (ed.), 3 vols. (New York: Phaidon Press, 1972).

———. *Oeuvres litteraires*, Elie Faure (ed.), 2 vols. (Paris: G. Crescent, 1923).

Hannoosh, Michele. *Painting and the Journal of Eugene Delacroix* (Princeton, N.J.: Princeton University Press, 1995).

Johnson, L. *The Paintings of Eugene Delacroix: A Critical Catalogue* (Oxford: Oxford University Press, 1981).

Trapp, Frank Anderson. "Introduction." *Delacroix and the Romantic Image: Oriental Themes, Wild Beasts, and the Hunt* (Amherst, Mass.: Mead Art Museum, 1988), 7–31.

Tscherny, Nadia. "An English Source for Delacroix's 'Liberty Leading the People," *Notes in the History of Art*, (2 Spring 1983), 3, 9–13.

Jennifer Harrison

DE QUINCEY, THOMAS (1785–1859). Thomas De Quincey, English critic and essayist, was born in Manchester in 1785 and educated at schools in Bath and Winkfield, at Manchester Grammar School, and at Worcester College, Oxford. Except for *The Logic of Political Economy* (1841) and an unsuccessful Gothic novel entitled *Klosterheim*, his entire literary output consisted of magazine articles in publications such as *Blackwood's Magazine*, Tait's *Edinburgh Magazine*, the *Glasgow Evening Post*, and occasionally, *The Quarterly*. De Quincey's subject matter ranged from criticism and rhetorical analysis to political economy and metaphysics, and he also produced a number of translations, biographical sketches, and works of imaginative prose.

His reading was prodigious, and like other classically trained authors of his time, he received a thorough grounding in Latin and Greek. He read and later wrote on works by Homer and Herodotus, Demosthenes, Thucydides, and Cicero. The "Grecian wits" he grouped around Pericles and Alexander, and these include Themistocles and Pindar; the tragedians Æschylus, Sophocles, and Euripedes; Aristophanes; and the philosophers Anaxagoras, Socrates, Plato, Xenophon, and Aristotle.

Allusions in the *Opium-eater*, De Quincey's autobiographical study of his opium addiction, suggest that he read the prose and sermon literature of Isaac Barrow, John Donne, Thomas Browne, Jeremy Taylor, Milton, South, and Chillingworth, and he so revered their writing that he referred to them as a "*pleiad* of seven golden stars" (Folio *Opium-eater*, 41). He published essays on Pope, **Coleridge**, and Goldsmith and the great English classicist Richard Bentley. Shakespeare, Spenser, James Thompson, William Collins, Thomas Chatterton, James Beattie, Robert Burns, William Penrose, **Robert Southey**, **Wordsworth**, and Coleridge were considered by De Quincey to be among the most highly rated authors writing in English.

De Quincey admired **Cowper** and Johnson and read Anna Barbauld, *The Arabian Nights*, and the fables of Æsop in the Latin verse translations of Phaedrus. He had a high opinion of English drama from all periods. His schoolmaster at Manchester required him to read selections from Steele's *Spectator*, and in his youth he immersed himself in Johnson's *Rambler*, Sir William Jones's *Asiatic Researches*, Joseph Milner's *Church History*, and John Hoole's translations of Tasso. He studied the Greek of the New Testament and read extensively enough in the King James Bible as to have whole passages memorized by heart, and he seems to have read the Dutch theologian Grotius by the age of 15 and while still at grammar school. De Quincey's biographers have reported that he conversed on St. Basil, Thomas Aquinas, and St. John Chrysostom.

In 1809 he arrived at Dove Cottage, Grasmere (the former home of the Wordsworths), with 29 chests full of books, which he placed at the poet's disposal.

De Quincey's theory of "involutes" depended on his reading of Wordsworth's *Prelude*, and he read and in many cases wrote pieces on contemporary authors, including Sir **Walter Scott**; Hannah More; the Lakers (especially Coleridge and Southey); Walter Savage Landor; the writers of the Satanic School (**Byron** and **Shelley**); and **Keats**, Hunt, and Hazlitt from the Cockney School. In his paper on Coleridge, De Quincey asserted that he had read for 30 years in the same track as the older poet and that "few of any age" were likely to follow them in their study of the German metaphysicians, Latin schoolmen, thaumaturgic Platonists, and religious mystics (De Quincey, *Collected Works*, 2:147). His biographic sketches indicate a familiarity with the writings of Kant, Lessing (especially the *Laocoön*), Herder, **Goethe** (*Wilhelm Meister*), Schiller, Spinoza, and Richter. His reading in German extended even to obscure works by Ernst Hartmann and the *Gespensterbruch* of Johann August Apel.

In politics and political economy he read the works of James Mackintosh (*Vindiciae Gallicae*), **Malthus** (*Measure of Value*), Adam Smith, and **Ricardo**'s *Principles of Political Economy*. It has been argued that De Quincey relied heavily on secondary sources in his writings; "The Two Caesars," for example, seems to have been derived in part from Casaubon, Salmasius, and Suetonius, and his biography of Kant draws upon the works of Wasianski, Jachmann, and Borowski. For his writings on French drama De Quincey consulted the work of Montesquieu, and his papers on the Essenes are based on Josephus's *History of the Jews*.

ARCHIVES

National Library of Scotland, Edinburgh.
Berg Collection, New York Public Library.
Worcester College Library, Oxford.

PRINTED SOURCES

De Quincey, Thomas. *The Collected Writings of Thomas De Quincey*, David Masson (ed.) (London: A. C. Black, 1896). Marred by unauthorized rewritings and bowdlerizations. Pickering and Chatto is preparing a 21-volume edition of the works under the general editorship of Grevel Lindop, scheduled for publication by December 2001.

Goldman, Albert Harry. *The Mine and the Mint: Sources for the Writings of Thomas De Quincey* (Carbondale: Southern Illinois State Press, 1965).

———. *The Confessions of an English Opium-eater*. First appeared in *London Magazine*, 1821; extended in collected works, 1856. Copy text (London: The Folio Society, 1948, 1993).

Japp, Alexander H. [see also H. A. Page]. *De Quincey Memorials*, 2 vols. (London: William Heinman, 1891).

Lindop, Grevel. *The Opium Eater: A Life of Thomas De Quincey*, (London: Dent, 1981).

Metcalf, John Calvin. *De Quincey: A Portrait* (Cambridge, Massachusetts: Harvard University Press, 1940).

Page, H. A. [pseudonym of A. H. Japp]. *Life and Writings, with Unpublished Corre-

spondence, 2 vols. (London: J. Hogg, 1877; New York: Scribner, Armstrong, 1877; rev. and enlarg. ed. 1 vol. (London: J. Hogg, 1890).

Susan Reilly

DICKENS, CHARLES JOHN HUFFAM (1812–1870). Charles Dickens was born in Portsmouth in 1812 and spent his childhood in Chatham, where he was educated briefly (1821–1822) at a school run by William Giles, the son of a local Baptist minister. That minister's lengthy and strict sermons gave rise to the specific hatred of Nonconformity and general distrust of organized religion that characterized Dickens's adult life and writing. Dickens was forced to discontinue his education when his family, oppressed by debt, relocated to London. Giles's parting gift to his favorite pupil was a copy of Oliver Goldsmith's periodical *The Bee* (1759), which Dickens "kept for his sake, and its own, a long time afterwards" (Forster, 9). Once his family had recovered financially, and Dickens had quit his menial labor in the now-legendary blacking warehouse, he was sent back to school at Wellington House Academy in London (1824–1827), before beginning the world as an office boy in a Gray's Inn legal firm.

Dickens's childhood reading exerted a tremendous influence on his adult novel writing. In an autobiographical section of *David Copperfield* (1849–1850), Dickens recalls his father's small library at Chatham: "From that blessed little room, Roderick Random, Peregrine Pickle, Humphrey Clinker, Tom Jones, the Vicar of Wakefield, Don Quixote, Gil Blas, and Robinson Crusoe, came out, a glorious host, to keep me company. They kept alive my fancy, and my hope of something beyond that place and time—they, and the *Arabian Nights*, and the *Tales of the Genii*." The melodramatic plots and grotesque characters of Dickens's fiction owe at least as much to these last two books of fantasy and romance as to the eighteenth-century picaresque tradition first described. Dickens's numerous stories and essays of reminiscence contain references to further eighteenth-century authors, particularly Jonathan Swift, Laurence Sterne, Joseph Addison, and Samuel Johnson. Equally, if not more, present in Dickens's fiction, however, are the lurid accounts of shipwrecks, cannibalism, and murder he read as a boy in such sensational periodicals as the *Terrific Register* (1824–1825).

On his eighteenth birthday, Dickens applied for a pass to the British Museum's reading room, where he became an "assiduous attendant" (Forster, 47). Dickens later referred to his time in the reading room as "decidedly the usefullest to himself he had ever passed" (Forster, 48). Some records of his reading there have survived: Oliver Goldsmith's *History of England* (1764), the works of Addison, and most important, William Shakespeare, whose plays exerted a profound influence on Dickens's own life and work. This influence runs much deeper than the frequent literary allusions to be found in Dickens's writing. Shakespeare determined not only Dickens's lifelong fascination with the theater but also, more specifically, his understanding of social and psychological identity as a series of performances. Dickens's characters behave so eccentrically because they intuit that all the world's a stage and that they exist as individuals in this increasingly bureaucratic world only to the extent that they overact.

Dickens's novels also contain frequent and specific allusions to the Old and New Testaments, which he would also have read in his boyhood. Often these allusions simply underscore his satirical portraits of religious hypocrites, but Dickens's novels may also be read collectively as an effort to recover meaning from these texts in a time of religious doubt and anxiety. Christianity, for Dickens, had more to do with social ethics than with spiritual faith; his fiction engages with Scripture in order to revise and apply its moral lessons within a secular context.

Dickens did not seem to pay much attention to the Romantic poets, although he was very familiar with Romantic prose writers, especially Sir **Walter Scott**, William Hazlitt, **Thomas De Quincey**, and Charles Lamb. Among his contemporaries, Dickens most admired **Alfred Tennyson** as a poet and **Thomas Carlyle** as an essayist. Dickens dedicated *Hard Times* (1854) to Carlyle, and his theories inform Dickens's social criticism in other novels as well. As a periodical editor, Dickens also read countless popular essays on science, medicine, psychology, education, penology, architecture, and so on; no doubt that this eclectic reading contributed to the immense scope and starting detail of the Dickensian universe.

ARCHIVES

Pierpont Morgan Library, New York. Largest of the many collections of Dickens's correspondence held by British and American libraries.

PRINTED SOURCES

Ackroyd, P. *Dickens* (New York: HarperCollins, 1990). Most comprehensive biographical use of Dickens's published and unpublished correspondence.
Collins, P. "Dickens's Reading," *Dickensian*, 60 (1964), 136–151. Summary of Dickens's childhood and adult reading, with references to further primary and secondary secondary sources.
Dickens, C. *The Letters of Charles Dickens*, Pilgrim Edition, 7 vols. (Oxford: Clarendon Press, 1965–). Provides references to further archival sources.
Forster, J. *The Life of Charles Dickens*, J.W.T. Ley (ed.) (London: C. Palmer, 1928). Seminal source of information on Dickens's reading tastes and habits.
Gager, V. *Shakespeare and Dickens: The Dynamics of Influence* (Cambridge: Cambridge University Press, 1996). Includes an annotated catalog of Dickens's references to Shakespeare.
Larson, J. *Dickens and the Broken Scripture* (Athens: University of Georgia Press, 1985). Documentation and analysis of biblical allusions in Dickens's fiction.
Oddie, W. *Dickens and Carlyle: The Question of Influence* (London: Centenary Press, 1972). Analysis of Carlyle's influence on Dickens's thought and writing.
Stone, H. *The Night Side of Dickens: Cannibalism, Passion, Necessity* (Columbus: Ohio State University Press, 1994). Detailed analysis of Dickens's childhood periodical reading in relation to his novel writing.

Brian McCuskey

DICKINSON, EMILY ELIZABETH (1830–1886). Emily Dickinson was born at home in Amherst, Massachussetts, in 1830. She attended Amherst Academy

(1840–1847), where she "was an outstanding student," and later Mount Holyoke Female Seminary in South Hadley (1847–1848). At Amherst Academy the instruction was "deeply religious" (Wolff, 77). In fact, "throughout the curriculum at both institutions, religion was held to be the most important study of all" (Wolff, 80).

The Bible was the most influential book in Emily Dickinson's life. In Dickinson's childhood, her father began the day with a Bible reading and prayer. As biographer Cynthia Griffin Wolff points out, Emily "knew every line of the Bible intimately, quoted from it extensively, referred to it many times more often than she referred to any other work" (72). Wolff also notes that as Emily "grew older, the family's own library provided more elegant and sophisticated models of the 'correlative type' [more elegant, that is, than the 'doggerel verse' of the *New England Primer*], such as those found in John Foster's *Miscellaneous Essays*" (73; see also n. 13, 558–559) and "the Dickinson family took several newspapers and all the best journals, and Emily Dickinson, along with her father and brother, read omnivorously" (67). Perhaps strange to today's college student, Dickinson also considered her "Lexicon" a treasured possession (Wolff, 65). Her "Lexicon" was in fact Noah Webster's *American Dictionary* (see Wolff, 91–92 and n. 34, 562, for an interesting discussion of the influence of Webster's devout Trinitarian religious beliefs on his dictionary). It is evident that Dickinson was also influenced by other writers: her poem "We don't cry—Tim and I" shows that she read **Charles Dickens** (Wolff, 179), while Robert F. Fleissner notes the influence of Shakespeare's *Othello* on poems such as "Good Night! Which Put the Candle Out?" (55).

ARCHIVES

Because control of Dickinson's letters and papers was disputed after her death, they eventually ended up principally in two collections: the Houghton Library at Harvard University and the Frost Library at Amherst College. Some of her other papers made their way to Princeton University, Yale University, the Boston Public Library, and the Jones Library at Amherst.

PRINTED SOURCES

Capps, Jack L. *Emily Dickinson's Reading 1836–1886* (Cambridge, Mass.: Harvard University Press, 1966).
Chase, Richard. *Emily Dickinson* (New York: Dell, 1965).
Farr, Judith. *The Passion of Emily Dickinson* (Cambridge, Mass.: Harvard University Press, 1992).
Fleissner, Robert F. "If Dickinson Did Not See a Moor, She at Least Read of *the* Moor," *College Language Association Journal*, 37 (September 1993), 55–63.
Orzeck, Martin, and Robert Weisbuch (eds.). *Dickinson and Audience* (Ann Arbor: University of Michigan Press, 1996).
Petrino, Elizabeth A. *Emily Dickinson and Her Contemporaries: Women's Verse in America, 1820–1885* (Hanover: University Press of New England, 1998).
Sewall, Richard B. "Emily Dickinson's Books and Reading." In Judith Farr (ed.), *Emily*

Dickinson: A Collection of Critical Essays (Upper Saddle River, N.J.: Prentice-Hall, 1996).

———— (ed.). *Emily Dickinson: A Collection of Critical Essays* (Englewood Cliffs, N.J.: Prentice-Hall, 1963).

Wolff, Cynthia Griffin. *Emily Dickinson* (New York: Alfred A. Knopf, 1986).

Sandra Hannaford

DISRAELI, BENJAMIN (1804–1881). Benjamin Disraeli, 1st Earl of Beaconsfield, was born in London in 1804. He was educated at a boarding school in Blackheath and at Higham Hall in Walthamstow (1817–1820). He spent 1820–1821 reading in his father Isaac's 25,000-volume library and was probably influenced by the latter's works on James I and Charles I (Richmond, "Disraeli's Education," 26). He never attended the university. Scholars do not agree as to Disraeli's contribution to Western culture, but there is a growing consensus that it was posthumous. He bequeathed to the Conservative Party a collection of insights and ideas that enabled it, as a party of aristocracy and privilege, to survive in a democratic age.

Although Disraeli studied classics, and was a passable Latin scholar, he never gained a firm grounding in Greek. He was influenced more by the Moderns— whose works were readily available in his father's library and at Higham Hall— than the Ancients. The reading diaries that he kept in 1818 and in the early 1820s contain notations from sixteenth- to eighteenth-century English and European historical works such as Lord Herbert's *Life and Reign of King Henry the Eighth*, Holinshed's *Chronicles of England, Scotland and Ireland*, and Hall's *Chronicle* (Hughenden Papers, Box 11, A/III/E/4; A/III/E/2). This reading laid the foundation for the very extensive knowledge of English history displayed in his later writings (Jupp, 131–151). In 1821, he records in his diary the Machiavellian idea expressed by Bacon in his essay on "Great Place"—that the great man purges the state of corruption and returns it to first principles (Hughenden Papers, Box 11, A/III/E/8). Probably in 1824, he read Madame **de Staël**'s *Germany* and became aware of how the romantic vision might recreate the world in the image of desire, or, as he summarized Kant's teaching in his diary, how it is "understanding which gives laws to exterior nature and not exterior nature to it" (Hughenden Papers, Box 11, A/III/E/1). Between 1827 and 1833, he studied the history and literature of the Jews while writing his novel *Alroy* (1833). In the 1830s, in his speeches and writings, especially *Vindication of the English Constitution in a letter to a noble and learned Lord* (1835) (the very name of which indicates the influence of Burke), Disraeli returned to the "Primitive Toryism" of Bolingbroke's Country Party opposition politics; and in an inversion of Whig representations, Disraeli transformed the Tories into the "National Party"—composed of the gentlemen of England and the laboring population— an image upon which subsequent generations of Conservatives have drawn with advantage.

ARCHIVES

Disraeli Papers, Bodleian Library, known as the Hughenden Papers. Principal political
    correspondence and papers.

PRINTED SOURCES

Blake, R. *Disraeli* (London: Eyre & Spottiswoode, 1966).

Faber, R. *Beaconsfield and Bolingbroke* (London: Faber and Faber, 1961).

Jupp, P. "Disraeli's Interpretation of English History." In C. Richmond and P. Smith
    (eds.), *The Self-Fashioning of Benjamin Disraeli* (Cambridge: Cambridge Uni-
    versity Press, 1999).

Monypenny, W. F., and G. E. Buckle. *The Life of Benjamin Disraeli, Earl of Beacons-
    field*, 6 vols. (London: John Murray, 1910–1920). Publishes Disraeli's classical
    diaries.

Nickerson, C. C. "Disraeli and the Reverend Eli Cogan," *Disraeli Newsletter*, 2, 2 (1977),
    14–17.

O'Kell, R. "The Revolutionary Epick: Tory Democracy or Radical Gallomania?" *Disraeli
    Newsletter*, 2, 1 (1977), 24–39.

Richmond, C. "Benjamin Disraeli: A Psychological Biography, 1804–1832" (M.Litt.
    diss., University of Oxford, 1982). Chapter 2 deals in part with Jewish reading.

———. Richmond, C. "Disraeli's Education." In C. Richmond and P. Smith (eds), *The
    Self-Fashioning of Benjamin Disraeli* (Cambridge: Cambridge University Press,
    1999). Extensive use of reading diaries, 1818–1824.

Smith, P. *Disraeli. A Brief Life* (Cambridge: Cambridge University Press, 1996). Should
    be read in conjunction with Blake.

Charles Richmond

DOSTOEVSKY, FYODOR MIKHAYLOVICH (1821–1881). Fyodor Dostoevsky, a Russian novelist, was born in Moscow to military physician Mikhail
Dostoevsky and Maria Fyodorovna Nechayeva. Fyodor was the couple's second
of seven children and the second son. The household was relatively devout, and
the children received a strong religious education from their parents and nanny.
Dostoevsky's father enforced a rigorous education in Latin as well as in French.

As a child, Dostoevsky was deeply moved by a performance of Friedrich
Schiller's (1759–1805) *The Robbers*. He adored romantic stories and the work
of **Aleksandr Pushkin** (1799–1837). Although he wished to pursue a university
education in literature, in 1837 Fyodor entered the School for Military Engineers
in St. Petersburg, a city he came to love.

Dostoevsky studied engineering for the next six years and acquired a lifelong
interest in architecture. He also became a voracious reader, devouring the work
of Pushkin, Shakespeare, **George Sand**, **Victor Hugo**, **Walter Scott**, **Lord Byron**, **Goethe**, Homer, the progressive Swiss religious author H. D. Zschokke,
Novalis, V. A. Zhukovsky, **Friedrich von Schelling**, and the Bible. Job and
Hamlet would become particularly important to him. He attended many theological lectures and began translating **Honoré de Balzac**'s novel *Eugenie Grandet* (1834); the translation would appear in 1844.

In 1843, Dostoevsky resigned from the military on grounds of ill health and devoted himself fully to writing. His first novel, *Poor Folk* (1846), was inspired by his observations of the poor in St. Petersburg. *Poor Folk* attracted the attention of the famous socialist literary critic Vissarion Belinsky, who promoted his newly discovered "genius" and introduced Dostoevsky to left Hegelianism, the thought of François Fourier, **Nikolay Gogol**, **David Friedrich Strauss**, and **Ludwig A. Feuerbach**.

Upon his separation from the group and Belinsky's death, Dostoevsky entered the less atheistic Beketov group. Following that, he associated himself with the Petrashevsky Circle, which advanced positions along the lines of Belinsky. Petrashevsky's group also maintained the Rousseauian theses that human nature is basically good and that evil is produced through environmental causes. Within the Petrashevsky Circle, Dostoevsky joined the secret subgroup; the Durov Circle, through which Dostoevsky was influenced by the radical Nikolai Speshnyov. The group advocated armed direct action as a means to social change, and whose members planned to join the armed struggle once a revolt broke out.

At 4:00 A.M. on April 23, 1849, Dostoevsky was arrested for his membership in the Petrashevsky Circle. Detained in the Petropavlosky Fortress, he read the periodical *Fatherland Notes*, Shakespeare, two accounts of journeys to the Holy Land, St. Dimitry of Rostov, three volumes of Vladimir I. Dahl's *Tales of the Cossack*, Lugansky, and Sakharov's *Legends of the Russian People*. A short story he composed there ("A Little Hero") bears similarities to *Much Ado about Nothing*.

First sentenced to death and subsequently to prison, Dostoevsky was held in Omskprison near Tobolsk for the next four years, followed by four years in the military. Just before entering prison, Dostoevsky received a copy of the New Testament, which he read avidly. In prison he also read the Qu'ran, the works of **Charles Dickens**, and Immanuel Kant's *Critique of Pure Reason* (1781).

Dostoevsky visited Nikolai Chernshevsky in 1862 and worked clandestinely for the journal *Time*, which in 1861 his brother founded and edited. *Time* opposed the Westernization of Russia, a position at odds with the pro-Western views of Dostoevsky's competitors **Ivan Turgenev** and Nicolai Nekrasov. In *Time* Dostoevsky published *The Insulted and Injured* (1861), which depicted his view of the redemptive effects of suffering. From 1862 to 1863, Dostoevsky traveled in Europe (including Paris, London, Berlin, Dresden, Wiesbaden, Baden-Baden, Köln, Lucerne, Genoa, Milan, Venice, Florence, Vienna, and Geneva).

Dostoevsky's brother Mikhail began a second journal, *Epoch*, in 1864, in which Dostoevsky first published censored portions of *Notes from Underground*. During his four years abroad (1866–1871) with his spouse Anna he read much of the work of Swedenborg. During these travels the couple lived in Geneva, Florence, and Dresden. Dostoevsky found Voltaire's *Candide* consonant with his views on utopianism.

Dostoevsky's character Father Zosima, in the *Brothers*, seems to have been influenced by his reading of St. Tikhon's religious and moral work. Anti-Semitism is evident in his *Diary of a Writer* (1873, 1876–1877). The influence of pro-Slavic politics is indicated in his 1876 article on the Turkish suppression of Slavs in the Balkans. In 1878, Dostoevsky became close to, and was influenced by, V. S. Solovyov, a young docent at Moscow University, whose master's thesis "The Crisis of Western Philosophy" and subsequent *The Philosophical Principles of Integral Knowledge* attracted him through their mysticism. Dostoevsky was also a reader of A. K. Tolstoy, **Heinrich Heine**, and **Aleksandr Herzen**. Many portions of Dostoevsky's work were influenced by daily newspapers.

ARCHIVES

Academy of Sciences, Moscow.
Polnoe sobranie sochinenii F. M. Dostoevskogo, 30 vols. (St. Petersburg/Leningrad: Nauka, 1972–1990).

PRINTED SOURCES

Joseph, Frank. *Dostoevsky*, 5 vols. (Princeton, N.J.: Princeton University Press, 1976, 1983, 1986, 1995). Only four volumes released to date. The most complete and erudite account yet produced.
Mochulsky, Konstantin. *Dostoevsky: His Life and Work*, Michael A. Minihan (trans.) (Paris, 1947; Princeton, N.J.: Princeton University Press, 1967).

Peter S. Fosl

DOUGLASS, FREDERICK (1817–1895). Frederick Douglass, originally named Frederick Augustus Washington Bailey, was born a slave in Tuckahoe, Maryland, in 1817. He received no formal education but began to learn to read and write at the age of 8 under the tutelage of Sophia Auld, the wife of his owner, in Baltimore, Maryland. When his owner, Hugh Auld, brought an end to this illegal activity, Douglass continued his education surreptitiously by enlisting the aid of white playmates and through the use of written materials including the Bible, hymnbooks, and schoolbooks. Douglass received religious education before he was 15 from a series of instructors, including Mr. Hanson, a white evangelist who preached equality, Charles Johnson, a black lay preacher who worked at the African Methodist Episcopal Church, and "Uncle Lawson," a black lay preacher who held Bible study with Douglass. Converting to Christianity at the age of 13, Douglass went on to speak and write in support of the antislavery movement and the struggle for civil rights for blacks and women.

When Douglass was 12, he overheard a schoolboy reading from an anthology of oratory. For 50 cents he purchased *The Columbian Orator* (1797), a collection of famous speeches throughout history, compiled by Caleb Bingham. Douglass read the introduction, which assured him that a great orator had impressive political power, and began to practice the published speeches.

For years afterward, Douglass read accounts in Baltimore newspapers of speeches made in the U.S. Congress by politicians such as John Quincy Adams promoting the abolition of slavery. It was not until 1839, at the age of 22, that he came across a newspaper that was completely antislavery. *The Liberator*, published by **William Lloyd Garrison**, a white abolitionist who began his activism upon being exposed to the cruelties of slave trading, began in 1831. Douglass was impressed with Garrison's biblical arguments against slavery, including a comparison between delivering slaves from bondage with Moses' deliverance of the Israelites from Egypt. Reading *The Liberator* led Douglass to confirm his calling as an activist orator, although he later broke away from the Garrisonians in the belief that churches only acted to preserve slavery.

As Douglass continued to make speeches against slavery, he drew extensively from Theodore Dwight Weld's *American Slavery as It Is* (1839), which detailed the beatings, rapes, and tortures of slaves. In 1853, he wrote his most famous letter in response to **Harriet Beecher Stowe**'s *Uncle Tom's Cabin* (1852). Once the slaves were freed, he argued, they would still have problems becoming educated or trained so as to obtain well-paying jobs. Earlier, Douglass had come away from reading phrenologist George Combe's *The Constitution of Man Considered in Relation to External Objects* (1835) with the sense that oppression ought to be relieved by a sense of personal accomplishment. Freed slaves, he believed, should focus on securing a good education, developing a system of morals, and improving the self.

Douglass had always admired European culture as opposed to African heritage, seeking out books that emphasized Africa's connection with these cultures. Ethnographer James Cowles Prichard wrote two books, *Researches into the Physical History of Mankind* (1813) and *The Natural History of Man* (1845), in which he argued that all human beings have a common origin and that Africans can claim to be descendants of one of the world's oldest civilizations, ancient Egypt. Douglass emerged from his readings as an example of conservative accommodation.

ARCHIVES

Frederick Douglass Papers, Library of Congress, Washington, D.C.

PRINTED SOURCES

Martin, Waldo E., Jr. *The Mind of Frederick Douglass* (Chapel Hill: University of North Carolina Press, 1984).
McFeely, William S. *Frederick Douglass* (New York: W. W. Norton, 1991).

Rose Secrest

DOUWES DEKKER, EDUARD (1820–1887). Eduard Douwes Dekker, known by the pseudonym Multatuli, was born in Amsterdam in 1820 and attended the city's best French and Latin schools. As his writings show, this education gave him a good basic command of the classics. His family was

Baptist, but as an adult, Dekker was profoundly agnostic and rather critical of established religions, even though he often quoted from the Bible.

In the mid-nineteenth century, Multatuli's debut novel and political tirade *Max Havelaar of de Koffieveilingen der Nederlandse Handelmaatschappy* [Max Havelaar or the coffee auctions of the Dutch Trading Company] was a powerful attack on the practice of European colonialism from inside of one of the colonial powers. After its publication in 1860 the brilliant, megalomaniac author published thousands of pages more on a great variety of subjects, both fiction and nonfiction, but it is *Max Havelaar* that has secured his historical reputation. Aside from a rare nineteenth-century European critique of colonialism, the book is also a literary classic.

It is easier to praise Multatuli than to demonstrate the sources of his artistry. The author himself proudly claimed that virtually everything he wrote "resembles nothing" (VW, 3:545). He once wrote, "[M]y style, that's me" (VW, 8: 115, 117), fervently believing that the basis for good writing is a writer's own interpretation of reality, or nature, based on serious study and personal experience.

Personal experience—as a civil servant in the Dutch East Indies—is what triggered the start of Dekker's career as Multatuli, the writer. When in 1856 his superiors failed to back him in the so-called Lebak affair—in which he had rashly intervened with the exploitation of the population by local leaders—Dekker resigned in protest. He wrote *Max Havelaar* as part of a quest for rehabilitation. However, he had been an aspiring writer from his student days.

Personal mission pervaded his work, but Multatuli did have his literary examples. Characteristically, these were as much a personal inspiration for Dekker the individual as literary examples for Multatuli the author. Multatuli's theme of the heroic, idealistic nonconformist can perhaps be traced back to the young Dekker's reverence for the robber stories by Christian Vulpius, in particular *Glorioso* (1800), as well as the works of August Lafontaine, especially *Hermann Lange* (1801). Dekker also was a product of both the Romantic movement and the Enlightenment. He read Jean Jacques Rousseau, for example, *Émile ou l'Éducation* (1762), and Eugène Sue's *Les Mystères de Paris*, with its emphasis on social ills, was one of his favorite books. Together with Hermann Lange, Sue's hero Rodolphe was Dekker's favorite literary character. Throughout his life Dekker also admired Sir **Walter Scott** (*Waverly*, 1814; *Ivanhoe*, 1820; *Kenilworth*, 1821) particularly because of Scott's commitment to historical, anthropological, and psychological accuracy.

Otherwise, Dekker tended to comment on how not to write, often taking popular Dutch authors as examples. Their major problem, he argued, was that they were not original. This brings us back to the signature aspect of Multatuli's work: It was unlike anything else because he was unlike anybody else in his passionate idealism, biting criticism of others, and his excessive self-esteem.

ARCHIVES

Multatuli Museum, Amsterdam.

PRINTED SOURCES

Francken, Eep. *De veelzinnige muze van E. Douwes Dekker* [The multi-faceted muse of E. Douwes Dekker] (Amsterdam: G. A. van Oorschot, 1990).

Keijsper, Chantal (ed.). *K. ter Laan's Multatuli Encyclopedie* [K. ter Laan's Multatuli encyclopedia] (Den Haag: Sdu Uitgeverij, 1995).

Multatuli. *Max Havelaar or the Coffee Auctions of the Dutch Trading Company* (London and New York: Penguin, 1995).

————. *Volledige Werken* [Complete works—VW], 25 vols. (Amsterdam: G. A. van Oorschot, 1950–1995).

Straten, Hans van. *Multatuli: van blanke radja tot bedelman* [Multatuli: from white rajah to beggar] (N.p.: Bas Lubberhuizen, 1995).

Veer, Paul van't. *Het leven van Multatuli* [The life of Multatuli] (Amsterdam: De Arbeiderspers, 1979).

Ruud van Dijk

DREISER, THEODORE (1871–1945). Theodore Dreiser, American novelist, was born in Terre Haute, Indiana, in 1871. The ninth of 10 surviving children, he spent his childhood in a number of small midwestern towns, and for one year he attended the University of Indiana in Bloomington. Soon afterward, he began newspaper work in Chicago, and he spent time in a number of burgeoning American cities, including St. Louis and Pittsburgh. His most productive working years were spent in New York, however. The critical triumph of *Sister Carrie*, his first novel, did not bring immediate commercial success, but from the second decade of the twentieth century, he was viewed as an influential figure in American letters, author of *An American Tragedy*, *The Genius*, and *Jennie Gerhardt*.

Dreiser rejected many of the experiments of literary modernism, but by stretching the conventions of American literature, he established a distinctive voice. His earliest influences included **Honoré de Balzac**, **Thomas Hardy**, **Lev Tolstoy**, and **Charles Dickens**. He read the work of **Charles Darwin** and **Herbert Spencer**, whose ideas on natural selection and fate gave Dreiser's stories of American society a naturalist bent. Although for most of his life he claimed ignorance of many European masters of realism like **Émile Zola**, he immersed himself in the writings of American realists like Harold Fredric, Henry Fuller, Hamlin Garland, and **William Dean Howells**. Dreiser's first publications shared a great affinity with Howells's novels, though Dreiser sought to distance himself from this suggestion as he found his own success.

While his work was concerned with the plight of the individual, his interest in **Karl Marx** forced Dreiser to reconsider the power of the collective. While he read Marx, he was a vocal critic of Soviet communism. He was much more sympathetic to the Left in the United States, however, though his bourgeois views prevented him from gaining membership in the American Communist Party.

Like his contemporaries, Dreiser read **Sigmund Freud**; while he was not wholly convinced by the psychoanalytic method, he saw Freud as a key to many of the thematic concerns explored in his own work. In his lifetime, Dreiser took an active interest in the work of men like Randolph Bourne, Ludwig Lewisohn, H. L. Mencken, John Cowper Powys, and Upton Sinclair. While the older writer enjoyed the adulation of a new generation of writers, he also read and gained inspiration from their enthusiasms. His relationship with Mencken is perhaps most representative: Dreiser could rely on the younger writer for favorable notices and judicious editing, but once Mencken became a more outspoken and independent critical voice, their friendship soured. Still, in his time, Dreiser was unique in allowing himself to be influenced by this younger group of writers, and these relationships helped him both develop as a novelist and extend his literary reputation.

ARCHIVES

Theodore Dreiser Collection, Van Pelt Library, University of Pennsylvania. Principal papers.

PRINTED SOURCES

Dreiser, Theodore. *Letters of Theodore Dreiser*, Robert H. Elias (ed.), 3 vols. (Philadelphia: University of Pennsylvania Press, 1959).
————. *Newspaper Days*, T. D. Nostwich (ed.) (Philadelphia: University of Pennsylvania Press, 1991).
Gogol, Miriam (ed.). *Theodore Dreiser: Beyond Naturalism* (New York: New York University Press, 1995).
Hakutani, Yoshinobu. *Young Dreiser: A Critical Study* (Rutherford, N.J.: Fairleigh Dickinson University Press, 1980).
Lehan, Richard. *Theodore Dreiser: His World and His Novels* (Carbondale: Southern Illinois University Press, 1969).
Lingeman, Richard. *Theodore Dreiser*, 2 vols. (New York: G. P. Putnam's Sons, 1986).
Pizer, Donald. *Theodore Dreiser: A Primary Bibliography and Research Guide* (Boston: G. K. Hall, 1991).
Riggio, Thomas P. (ed.). *American Diaries, 1902–1926* (Philadelphia: University of Pennsylvania Press, 1982).
Takeda, Miyoko. *The Quest for the Reality of Life: Dreiser's Spiritual and Esthetical Pilgrimage* (New York: Peter Lang, 1991).
Zanine, Louis J. *Mechanism and Mysticism: The Influence of Science on the Thought and Work of Theodore Dreiser* (Philadelphia: University of Pennsylvania Press, 1993).

Craig Monk

DU BOIS, WILLIAM EDWARD BURGHARDT (W.E.B.) (1868–1963).
William Du Bois was born in Great Barrington, Massachusetts, in 1868 and educated at Great Barrington High School (1881–1885); Fisk University, Tennessee (1885–1888); Harvard University (1888–1892); and the University of Berlin (1892–1894). Du Bois was reared in the strongly Calvinist and theologically liberal New England Congregationalist faith and when young was also active in the entirely African American Great Barrington American Methodist

Zion Church; by the time he left Fisk, he had adopted his lifelong agnosticism, still retaining a Congregationalist insistence upon high ethical standards. Throughout his adult career Du Bois was a leading radical African American intellectual voice, devoting his career as a prolific academic historian and sociologist, journalist, and writer to publicizing American blacks' disabilities and attempting to win full equality for them. Ultimately, he lost faith in the possibility of achieving his goals, joined the Communist Party, and in 1961, emigrated to Ghana.

In his teens Du Bois read **Thomas Babington Macaulay**'s *History of England*, which greatly influenced his literary style, and at Fisk he discovered the High Tory writings of **Thomas Carlyle**, whose use of rhetoric and invective Du Bois emulated while rejecting his politics (Lewis, 38, 74–75). Entering Harvard, he was much influenced by the philosophers Josiah Royce, George Santayana, and **William James**. Intellectually, Royce's Kantian and Hegelian insistence on the existence of Absolute Truth and the need for the highest morals appealed to Du Bois's idealist temperament. Personally close to James, Du Bois attempted to meld ethical principles with his mentor's insistence on subjecting all beliefs and acts to rigorous scientific scrutiny and justification and his attribution of morality to the real-life advantages ethical conduct conferred. Du Bois may also have been influenced by James's pluralism and opposition to racism and possibly by insights in James's *Principles of Psychology*, which seem to anticipate Du Bois's later concept of African American "double consciousness." He decided to combine James's pragmatism with the research methodology of detailed documentary study instilled in him by the historian Alfred Bushnell Hart by "applying philosophy to an historical interpretation of race relations" (Du Bois, *Reader*, 282), a choice that directed him to the developing discipline of sociology. He undertook a doctorate at the University of Berlin, where his existing skepticism as to the free market economics expounded at Harvard was reinforced by exposure to German teachers who stressed the state's potential economic role. He also felt an affinity with **Goethe** and **Hegel**, both of whom emphasized the role of great men in history and an almost mystical universalism. Throughout his long life, Du Bois's multifarious activities would be influenced by the wide-ranging literary works to which his exceptionally broad education exposed him.

ARCHIVES

W.E.B. Du Bois Papers. University of Massachusetts, Amherst.

PRINTED SOURCES

Du Bois, W.E.B. *The Autobiography: A Soliloquy on Viewing My Life from the Last Decade of Its First Century* (New York: International Publishers Co., 1968).
———. *Reader*, David Levering Lewis (ed.) (New York: Henry Holt, 1995).
———. *Writings* (New York: Library of America, 1986).
Lewis, David Levering. *W.E.B. Du Bois: Biography of a Race 1868–1919* (New York: Henry Holt, 1993).

Moore, Jack B. *W.E.B. Du Bois* (Boston: Twayne, 1981).

Rampersad, Arnold. *The Art and Imagination of W.E.B. Du Bois* (New York: Schocken Books, 1976).

Zamir, Shamoon. *Dark Voices: W.E.B. Du Bois and American Thought, 1888–1903* (Chicago: University of Chicago Press, 1995). Detailed study of early intellectual influences.

Priscilla Roberts

DUCASSE, ISIDORE-LUCIEN. *See* **Lautréamont, Comte de**.

DUMAS, ALEXANDRE (*PÈRE*) (1802–1870). Alexandre Dumas (*père* [French "father"]), French novelist and playwright, was born in Villers-Cotterêts in 1802. Son of a French general of mulatto origin, he was a man of insufficient learning but exceptionally creative and vital. His novels, mostly of historical subjects according to the taste of the time, were a success and helped establish a new genre, the *roman feuilleton*, or serial novel, published serially in the newspapers. Dumas's most famous novels are *The Count of Monte Cristo* (1844–1845), based on a truculent news item, and the most famous trilogy, set in the France of Louis XIII and Louis XIV, *The Three Musketeers* (1844), *Twenty Years after* (1845), and *The Iron Mask* (1848–1850). Other works are set in the eighteenth-century France, including *Balsamo, or Memoirs of a Physician* (1846–1848) on the character of Cagliostro; *The Chevalier de Maison-Rouge* (1847); *Diane* (1846), and *The Queen's Necklace* (1848–1850). Dumas also produced numerous dramas, including *Léo Burckart* (1839), written together with Gerard de Nerval; the romantic *Henri III et sa cour* (1829); *Antony* (1831); and *Edmund Kean, or The Genius and the Libertine* (1836). He also published a *Dictionary of Cuisine* (published posthumously in 1873), the 22 volumes of *My Memories* (1852–1855), and *On Board the "Emma": Adventures with **Garibaldi**'s "Thouand" in Sicily* (1861), written during the Garibaldian expedition that Dumas joined in Sicily.

Clever in perceiving the tastes and the expectations of the reading public, Dumas worked on a large scale, gathering round himself a number of collaborators who did research and organized the material, which was then rewritten in Dumas's own hand. The literary value of Dumas's works is mediocre and the historical exactness sometimes far from accurate, but his plots are so rich in characters and adventures that his novels are still translated and reprinted. Alexandre Dumas was acclaimed as a dramatist, too, but his plays show to the modern reader a lack of psychological depth. Dumas's fame knew only a decade of decline when his son, Alexandre Dumas *fils*, became a successful playwright. But modern times have rediscovered the eclecticism of this man who was interested in history, mythology, swordsmanship, geography, names, and dates. More than 300 films have been made from his novels, plays, and from his life. He died in Puys, near Dieppe, in 1870.

ARCHIVES

Bibliothèque historique de la Ville de Paris.
Bibliothèque publique et universitaire de Geneve.
Bibliothèque National de Paris.
Bibliothèque de Havre.
Bibliothèque de Dieppe (cod. 81—Ivanhoe).
Musee Alexandre Dumas, Viller-Cotterets.
Pierpont Morgan Library, New York.
Huntington Library, Los Angeles.

PRINTED SOURCES

Bell, A. Craig. *Alexandre Dumas: A Biography and Study* (Folcroft, Pa.: Folcroft Library
    Editions, 1979).
Hemmings, F.W.J. *The King of Romance: A Portrait of Alexandre Dumas* (New York:
    Scribner, 1979).
Ross, M. *Alexandre Dumas* (Newton Abbot, Devon: David and Charles, 1981).
Schopp, C. *Alexandre Dumas: Genius of Life* (New York: Franklin Watts, 1988).
Spurr, H. A. *The Life and Writings of Alexandre Dumas* (1929; New York: Haskell
    House Publishers, 1973).
Stowe, R. S. *Alexandre Dumas Père* (Boston: Twayne, 1976).
Zimmerman, D. *Alexandre Dumas le Grand: Biographie* (Paris: Julliard, 1993).

Maria Tabaglio

DUPIN, AMANDINE-AURORE-LUCILE. *See* **Sand, George**.

E

EDDY, MARY BAKER (1821–1910). Mary Baker Eddy, founder of the Church of Christ, Scientist, was born in Bow, New Hampshire, in 1821 on a farm along the Merrimack River. She was the youngest of six children of Mark and Abigail Baker and had three brothers and two sisters. Her childhood was made more pleasant by an indulgent grandmother, a fortunate situation because she is said to have been given to tantrums and unaccountable fevers. Mary Baker married three times—first to a neighbor, George Washington Glover in 1843, second to an itinerant dentist, Dr. Daniel Patterson, and finally to Asa Gilbert Eddy, a traveling sewing-machine salesman. Her early education was interrupted by chronic, perhaps organic, spinal troubles. Despite irregular attendance at schools, she was given a basic education on the Sabbath from the Westminster Catechism. She was tutored by an older brother home from college on vacations, and she began to read and copy the English poets. According to some of her biographers, this fascination with the poets led to an ability to express herself and to a fascination with subjects like life and immortality. She seemed to have been particularly inspired by Lindley Murray's *English Reader*, and in fact, Edwin Franden Dakin, who has written a bitter biography, goes so far as to offer long passages from her writings and show the similarities to various selections. Dakin notes that **Carlyle**, **Ruskin**, and Amiel are among the writers who seem to offer her the greatest inspiration—sometimes nearly verbatim, he suggests.

She has been accused of plagiarism in her thinking, as well. Many credit Phineas Parkhurst Quimby, a healer whom she acknowledges with aiding her miraculous recovery from a back problem, with the original thought and writing concerning what came to be known as "Christian Science." Whatever its origins and despite the contradictory biographical material available, Mrs. Eddy must be credited with the impulse to teach the healing doctrines and with bringing a new approach to religion and the ministry of healing. She herself acknowledges her debt to Quimby, and her official biographer writes that she had spent hours talking with him and editing or "correcting" Quimby's documents (Peel, *Years of Discovery*, 181). As she provided the impetus for broader activity, her efforts were extremely successful, and she remains one of the most important women of the nineteenth century. Her church, with headquarters in Boston, has supported what has become an international communications industry; and her message has been credited with reawakening Christian concern with healing and the human will.

ARCHIVES

Eddy Papers, Church of Christ, Scientist, Trustees. Unavailable for unrestricted use.
Bridwell Library, Southern Methodist University. Open to qualified scholars upon written application.

PRINTED SOURCES

Ahlstrom, Sydney E. "Mary Baker Eddy." In Edward T. James and Janet James (eds.), *Notable American Women* (Cambridge, Mass.: Belknap Press, 1971).
Cather, Willa, and Georgine Milmine. *The Life of Mary Baker G. Eddy and the History of Christian Science* (Lincoln: University of Nebraska, 1993).
Dakin, Edwin Franden. *Mrs Eddy: The Biography of a Virginal Mind* (New York: Charles Scribner's Sons, 1930).
Orcutt, William Dana. *Mary Baker Eddy and Her Books.* (Boston: Christian Science Publishing Society, 1950).
Peel, Robert. *Mary Baker Eddy, The Years of Discovery* (Boston: Christian Science Publishing Society, 1966).
————. *Mary Baker Eddy, The Years of Trial* (New York: Holt, Rinehart and Winston, 1971).
Wilbur, Sibyl. *The Life of Mary Baker Eddy* (Boston: Christian Science Publishing Society, 1923).

Ann Mauger Colbert

EDISON, THOMAS ALVA (1847–1931). Thomas Edison was born in Milan, Ohio, in 1847. He attended one public and two private schools and received tutoring at home from his mother, a devout Presbyterian. Although she made him study the Bible and attend church every Sunday, Edison was a freethinker who disdained organized religion. Edison's free-ranging thought, experimentation, and methodical but nonselective scientific testing led him to envision, develop, and market some of the most important inventions—both practical and topical—of the twentieth century.

From his father's library, Edison and his mother read together books about religion and politics, particularly Edward Gibbon's *Decline and Fall of the Roman Empire* and David Hume's *History of England*. When he read *The Age of Reason* he identified with Thomas Paine, the inventor and independent thinker (Conot, 7, 10; Baldwin, 26; Israel, 8). The idea that the primary source of true knowledge was natural law rather than divine revelation awakened Edison to a skeptical, anticlerical world. Edison also followed the abstemious diet and health recommendations in Luigi Cornaro's *The Temperate Life* (Israel, 10).

Edison learned physical science from R. G. Parker's *A School Compendium of Natural and Experimental Philosophy*—using its instructions to build electrical experiments and to learn **Morse** code—and analytical chemistry experiments from Carl Fresenius's *System of Instruction in Qualitative Chemical Analysis* (Baldwin, 26; Israel, 7, 11). He considered William Shakespeare's plays, particularly *Richard III*, to be his creative inspiration (Israel, 19).

As a young newsboy, he discovered Isaac Newton's *Principia Mathematica* and Thomas Burton's *Anatomy of Melancholy* (Baldwin, 29–30). Pursuing his interest in electricity and telegraphy, Edison read Dionysius Lardner's *Electric Telegraph* and *Handbook of Electricity, Magnetism and Acoustics*, Richard Culley's *Handbook of Practical Telegraphy*, Charles Walker's *Electric Telegraph Manipulation*, Robert Sabine's *History and Practice of the Electric Telegraph*, and Sabine and Latimer Clark's *Electrical Tables and Formulae for the Use of Telegraph Inspectors and Operators* (Baldwin, 42; Israel, 37, 90, 91). Aside from his job as a telegraph operator, Edison experimented with electricity, based particularly on Michael Faraday's three-volume *Experimental Researches in Electricity and Magnetism* (Baldwin, 42). Faraday, along with Paine, was a role model for Edison's working methodology.

Edison resumed his experiments in chemistry in 1873 guided by John Pepper's *Cyclopedia of Science Simplified* and his *Playbook of Metals* in 1874 (Israel, 92). He systematized his chemical experiments influenced by British chemists William Crookes (*Select Methods of Chemical Analysis, Chiefly Inorganic* and his journal *Chemical News*) and Charles Bloxam's *Laboratory Teaching* (Israel, 93). In 1875 Edison discovered Hermann von Helmholtz's writings on thermodynamics, conservation of energy, and perception in the English translation (*Sensations of Tone as a Physiological Basis for the Theory of Music*) of his 1863 pioneering book. Edison incorporated Helmholtz's theories on aesthetic ideas of music and sound, the "science of the beautiful," into his work on the phonograph (Baldwin, 320).

Throughout his life Edison read intensely and widely among a vast array of subjects and authors including two or three daily newspapers and popular magazines in addition to **Victor Hugo, Dickens, Goethe, Hawthorne, Darwin**, and **Longfellow**. Edison believed that the same creative faculty that produced success also stimulated invention. As a result, he read anything that helped the imagination, in addition to scientific works.

ARCHIVES

Edison Papers, Edison National Historic Site, West Orange, New Jersey.

PRINTED SOURCES

Baldwin, N. *Edison: Inventing the Century* (New York: Hyperion, 1995).
Conot, R. *A Streak of Luck* (New York: Seaview Books, 1979).

Israel, P. *Edison, a Life of Invention* (New York: John Wiley & Sons, 1998).
The Papers of Thomas A. Edison, vol. 1– (Baltimore: Johns Hopkins University Press, 1989–).
Runes, Dagobert D. (ed.). *The Diary and Sundry Observations of Thomas Alva Edison* (New York: Greenwood Press, 1968).
Wachhorst, W. *Thomas Alva Edison, an American Myth* (Cambridge, Mass.: MIT Press, 1981).

Susan Hamburger

ELIOT, GEORGE (1819–1880). George Eliot was born Mary Ann Evans at South Farm, Arbury, in 1819 and educated at Miss Lathom's School in Attleborough (1824–1828), Miss Wallington's School at Nuneaton (1828–1832), and Miss Franklins' School in Coventry (1832–1836). Although she was an evangelical member of the Church of England in her youth, Eliot's introduction to freethinkers Charles and Cara Bray and Charles Hennell sparked religious inquiries that ultimately led to her declaring herself an agnostic in 1842. Eliot's early novels set in rural England established her belief in duty as "peremptory and absolute" (Haight, Biography, 464). By the publication of *The Mill on the Floss* (1860), her novels were widely read and admired. Eliot's strong intellectual background shaped the development of the Victorian novel and its preoccupation with social and moral questions.

As a child, Eliot first encountered fiction through the works of Sir **Walter Scott**, whose Waverley novels impressed upon her the importance of historical context. She studied the Bible diligently at Miss Wallington's School and gained her first appreciation of the English authors at Miss Franklins' School (Haight, 13). Quotations from the works of Shakespeare and **Wordsworth** appear most frequently as epigraphs in her works. Eliot's friendship with the Brays encouraged her investigations into Christian belief. She read Charles Bray's *Philosophy of Necessity* and Charles Hennell's *An Inquiry into the Origins of Christianity* with great interest, "considerably shaken by the impression that religion was not a requisite to moral excellence" (*Letters*, 1:45). She thereafter translated *The Essence of Christianity* by **Ludwig Feuerbach** (1841) and Spinoza's *Ethics* (1855). After completing her 1846 translation of *The Life of Jesus, Critically Examined* by **David Strauss**, Eliot read the works of **George Sand** and Rousseau, whom she defended to her friends: "Rousseau's genius has sent that electric thrill through my intellectual and moral frame which has awakened me to new perceptions . . . It is thus with G. Sand. . . . I cannot read six pages of hers without feeling that it is given her to delineate human passion and its results" (*Letters*, 1:277–278). Eliot later read all of **Johann Goethe**, and much Schiller, Lessing, Schlegel, and **Heinrich Heine** (Haight, *Biography*, 174). She also found the positivism of **Auguste Comte** appealing, though she did not become a disciple.

Eliot often read during the composition of her novels. She reread **Jane Austen** while writing *Scenes of Clerical Life* and returned to the tragedies of Sophocles and Aeschylus while writing *Felix Holt* (1866) (Rendell, 55; Haight, *Biography*, 383). Her appreciation of the classics influenced her use of tragedy in the later novels.

ARCHIVES

George Eliot Papers, British Museum.
George Eliot Papers, Beineke Rare Book and Manuscript Library of Yale University.
George Eliot Papers, New York Public Library and the Pforzheimer Library.
George Eliot Papers, Folger Shakespeare Library.
George Eliot Papers, Princeton University Library.

PRINTED SOURCES

Ashton, Rosemary. "Mixed and Erring Humanity: George Eliot, G. H. Lewes, and Goethe," *George Eliot and George Henry Lewes Studies*, 24–25, 2 (September 1993), 93–117.

Baker, William. *The Libraries of George Eliot and George Henry Lewes*, English Literary Studies Monograph Series No. 24 (Victoria, British Columbia: University of Victoria Press, 1981).

Dodd, Valerie A. *George Eliot: An Intellectual Life* (New York: St. Martin's Press, 1990).

Haight, Gordon. *George Eliot: A Biography* (New York: Penguin, 1968).

———. (ed.). *The George Eliot Letters*, 9 vols. (New Haven, Conn.: Yale University Press, 1954–1955, 1978).

Rendell, Vernon. "George Eliot and the Classics," *Notes and Queries*, 192 (December 13 and 27, 1947), 54–66, 564–565; 193 (April 3–June 26, 1948), 148–49, 272–274.

Vitaglione, Daniel. *George Eliot and George Sand* (New York: Peter Lang, 1993).

Nancy Anne Marck

ELLIS, HENRY HAVELOCK (1859–1939). Henry Ellis, a sexologist and social critic, was born in Croydon, Surrey, in 1859. He was educated at Merton College (1868–1871), "The Poplars," Mitcham (1871–1874), and St. Thomas's Hospital (1880–1887). Ellis was a religious boy but fell away from Christianity during his youth after critically reading **Friedrich Strauss**'s *Der alte und der neue Glaube* (1872) and **Ernst Renan**'s *La Vie du Jésus* (1863) (*My Life*, 103). He was employed as a school teacher in outback New South Wales between 1875 and 1879. The virtual solitude Ellis experienced made it possible for him to read widely, although he also spent time in the city, frequenting Sydney Public Library. Books important to his intellectual development in Australia include James Hinton's *Life in Nature* and George Drysdale's anonymous *Elements of Social Science*. After reading these texts, Ellis resolved to devote his life to studying sexuality, resulting in his *Studies in the Psychology of Sex* (1897–1928). To achieve this aim, Ellis returned to London and enrolled as a medical student at St. Thomas's. As a student he became involved with secular political groups. Here he met Olive Schreiner, Edward Carpenter, and other radicals. His involvement with such organizations, as well as his eclectic reading, provided Ellis with the reformative social agenda that was later manifest in his *Studies*.

Ellis is an important figure in the history of sexual medicine. His first book on sex, *Sexual Inversion*, coauthored with John Addington Symonds, argued that homosexuality was a natural manifestation of the sexual instinct and should therefore not be illegal in England. Ellis's argument extended the theses of continental sexological works, including Richard von Krafft-Ebing's *Psychopathia Sexualis* (1886) and Albert Moll's *Die Conträre Sexualempfindung* (1891). Ellis wrote similar studies of other sexual conditions: fetishes, autoeroticism, cross-dressing, and so on. He treated these conditions as different manifestations of the sexual instinct, his theory of which influenced **Sigmund Freud**'s *Three Contributions to the Theory of Sex* (1905). Later sexologists also influenced by Ellis include Margaret Sanger, Norman Haire, Alfred Kinsey and William Masters and Virginia Johnson.

Apart from his contributions to sexology, Ellis was an astute literary critic and social philosopher, being among the few who favorably reviewed **Thomas Hardy**'s *Jude the Obscure* (1895). He was the first Briton to publish on **Friedrich Nietzsche** and an early advocate of Freud (with whom he became a long-time correspondent). Ellis also edited the Mermaid Series of Reformation dramatists and the Contemporary Science Series, which introduced new scientific works by authors such as Moll and Cesare Lombroso to the British public at a low price; additionally, he was an advisory editor of the *Journal of Mental Science*. Ellis's "nonsexual" writings include *The New Spirit* (1890), *The Criminal* (1890), *Man and Woman* (1894), *The Dance of Life* (1923), and *From Marlowe to Shaw* (1950).

ARCHIVES

Havelock Ellis Papers, British Library. The major Ellis collection.
Havelock Ellis Papers, New South Wales State Library, A6904/1–8. Includes six volumes of Ellis's reading notes made between 1875 and 1879.

PRINTED SOURCES

Ellis, Havelock. "Concerning *Jude the Obscure*," *The Savoy* (1896).
———. *My Life* (London: Heinemann, 1939).
———. "Nietzsche," *The Savoy* (1895).
Grosskurth, Phyllis. *Havelock Ellis* (New York: Alfred A. Knopf, 1980).

Ivan Crozier

EMERSON, RALPH WALDO (1803–1882). Ralph Waldo Emerson was born in Boston in 1803, the son and grandson of Harvard-educated Congregationalist clergy. He attended Boston Latin School (1812–1817) and Harvard College (1817–1821) and taught at a girls' school (1821–1825). Emerson attended Harvard Divinity School (1825–1826), preaching his first sermon in 1826. After becoming the ordained minister of Second Church, Boston, in 1829, he resigned his position there in 1832 and toured Europe (1832–1833, 1847–1848, 1872–1873). He began a new career as a lecturer in 1834 and settled in Concord, Massachusetts in 1835. After publishing *Nature* in 1836, he thenceforth earned his living as an independent essayist, poet, and lecturer. He cofounded the Transcendental Club in 1836 and became a close friend of **Henry David Thoreau** (1837–1862). In 1852–1853 he toured the northern United States. He was active in the abolitionist movement (1855–1863), including fund-raising for John Brown. He met **John Muir** in California in 1871. Emerson's philosophy of self-reliance has influenced writers as diverse as **Walt Whitman**, **Emily Dickinson**, **William James**, **Friedrich Nietzsche**, Robert Frost, and Vladimir Nabokov.

Emerson's father had drifted from Congregationalism toward Unitarianism, and Emerson's own ordination was as a Unitarian, but both father and son proved too secular for the ministry. Nevertheless, the same ethical universalism and spiritualism that led him to Unitarianism in his teens and twenties, abetted by William Ellery Channing the Elder and William Henry Furness, also led him to Transcendentalism in his thirties. American Transcendentalism is a version of the idealist epistemology and deontological morality of Immanuel Kant, filtered through the mysticism of **Samuel Taylor Coleridge**. Many of its adherents, including Emerson, were inspired by Eastern religions, especially Hinduism.

Emerson knew the works of **Johann Wolfgang von Goethe**, **Anne-Louise-Germaine de Staël**, Friedrich von Hardenberg ("Novalis"), August and Friedrich Schlegel, **Friedrich Wilhelm Joseph von Schelling**, **Georg Wilhelm Friedrich Hegel**, Jakob Boehme, Emmanuel Swedenborg, **Johann Gottlieb Fichte**, and **Friedrich Schleiermacher**, though mostly either secondhand or in translation. He was steeped in British Romanticism. At Harvard he read Plato, Milton, and Shakespeare; was impressed by Sampson Reed's 1821 "Oration on Genius"; and preferred the poetry of **Lord Byron** to that of **William Wordsworth** but later reversed that opinion. He visited Coleridge, **Thomas Carlyle**, Wordsworth, **Harriet Martineau**, and Walter Savage Landor on his first trip to Europe; Carlyle, Wordsworth, and Martineau on his second; and Carlyle, **John Ruskin**, Friedrich Max Müller, and **William Ewart Gladstone** on his third. His 50-year-long correspondence with Carlyle is a remarkable record of the development and mutual influence of two great thinkers.

ARCHIVES

Papers and correspondence scattered among institutional and individual owners; largest collection at Houghton Library of Harvard University.

PRINTED SOURCES

Allen, Gay Wilson. *Waldo Emerson: A Biography* (New York: Viking, 1981).
Burkholder, Robert E., and Joel Myerson. *Emerson: An Annotated Secondary Bibliography* (Pittsburgh: University of Pittsburgh Press, 1985).
Cameron, Kenneth W. *Ralph Waldo Emerson's Reading* (Raleigh, N.C.: Thistle, 1941).

Harding, Walter. *Emerson's Library* (Charlottesville: University of Virginia Press, 1967).

McAleer, John. *Ralph Waldo Emerson: Days of Encounter* (Boston: Little, Brown, 1984).

Richardson, Richard D. *Emerson: The Mind on Fire* (Berkeley: University of California Press, 1995).

Rusk, Ralph L. *The Life of Ralph Waldo Emerson* (New York: Columbia University Press, 1949).

Snider, Denton J. *A Biography of Ralph Waldo Emerson* (St. Louis, Mo.: Miner, 1921).

Von Frank, Albert J. *An Emerson Chronology* (New York: G. K. Hall, 1994).

Eric v. d. Luft

ENGELS, FRIEDRICH (1820–1895). Friedrich Engels was born in the Rhineland (Barmen) in 1820. He withdrew from high school to serve an apprenticeship in Barmen and Bremen (1838–1841) and performed military service in Berlin, although he exhibited more interest in philosophical studies than all other pursuits. He completed a commercial apprenticeship and training in Manchester, England (1842–1844). Engels collaborated and was cofounder with **Karl Marx** of the movement eventually called *Marxism*. Engels translated Marx's critiques into a more popular idiom, thereby increasing the influence of their movement, and contributed substantially to the concept of historical materialism within social and political thought. Engels devoted himself completely to the practical and theoretical task of promoting Marx's legacy after Marx's death in 1883.

In his youth, Engels became a critic of religion and his family's tendency to associate Protestantism with capitalism. In 1839, he pseudonymously published a short criticism of his family's worldview entitled "Letters from the Wuppertal" (*Works*, Vol. 1). As an advocate of radicalism in many forms, Engles was early influenced by **Friedrich Schleiermacher**, **David Strauss**, **Bruno Bauer**, and **Ludwig Feuerbach**. While in Berlin, Engels became attracted to the works of **Hegel**, especially Hegel's emphasis on the superiority of reason to faith. In Hegel, Engels found inspiration for his rejection of religion and his understanding of human action, institutional change, and the dialectical process of history.

For Engels, Hegel provided a philosophical system based upon the elevation of human reason that provided a "dialectic," or process, for explaining the evolution of human development. Borrowing from Hegel, Engels posited the law of the interpenetration of opposites, which suggested the possibility that objective contradictions were present in reality. Engels suggested this dialectic formed a "labor of the negative," as reality was ascertained only by the successive testing of concepts and premises. Conflicts between ideas are remedied by a dialectical union, which results in a more comprehensive understanding of reality when each concept's fallacies are negated by other theories. Engels also criticized thinkers who (he perceived) had rejected or diminished Hegel's important advancement of reason. In his *Schelling und die Offenbarung* (1842), Engels attacked **Friedrich Schelling**'s failure to assimilate the progression of human reason, accusing Schelling of succumbing to irrationalism. As a Young Hegelian, Engels also encountered the works of early socialist theorists, including Wilhelm Weitling and Arnold Ruge. Engels's first major work, *The Con-dition of the Working Class in England* (1845), a cogent essay on the situation of the proletariat in an industrial society, evinces the influence of early socialist philosophers. Engels suggested the proletariat was a new social force that would transform the world.

The primary literary and philosophical influence upon Engels was Karl Marx. The two men first met and began their long friendship in 1844. Engels would spend the remainder of his life defending Marx's theory of communism, as well as coauthoring many of the primary works of Marx's philosophy, notably *The Holy Family* (1845), *The German Ideology* (1845–1846), and the *Communist Manifesto* (1848). While Engels claimed Marx was a more original and prescient thinker than himself, Engels not only influenced Marx, but he also supplied a more lucid and accessible rearticulation of Marx's own philosophical work. His popular works on political economy, the relationship between historical mate-rialism and the natural sciences, and the Marxist view of history were of great importance. Engels's theory of dialectical materialism received further elabo-ration in his later works, *Anti-Dühring* (1878) and the posthumous *Dialectics of Nature* (1925). After Marx's death, Engels spent the last 12 years of his life editing Marx's unfinished manuscripts, including volumes two and three of *Das Kapital*. While the compatibility between the work of Engels and Marx remains an issue of great concern to scholars, Engels was nevertheless central to the founding of Marxism and the rise of modern revolutionary movements.

ARCHIVES

The Socio-Political State Library, Moscow.
The British Library, London.

PRINTED SOURCES

Carver, Terrell. *Engels: His Life and Thought* (New York: St. Martin's Press, 1990).
Eubanks, Cecil. *Karl Marx and Friedrich Engels: An Analytical Bibliography*, 2nd ed. (New York: Garland, 1984).
Henderson, William Otto. *Life of Friedrich Engels*, 2 vols. (London: Frank Cass and Company, 1976).
Hunt, Richard H. *The Political Ideas of Marx and Engels*, 2 vols. (London: Macmillan, 1974, 1984).
Jones, Gareth Stedman. "Engels and the Genesis of Marxism," *New Left Review*, no. 106 (1977), 79–104.
Marx, Karl, and Frederick Engels. *Collected Works* (New York: International Publishers, 1973–1981).
McLellan, David. *Friedrich Engels* (New York: Viking Press, 1978).

H. Lee Cheek, Jr.

EVANS, MARY ANN. *See* **Eliot, George**.

F

FEUERBACH, LUDWIG ANDREAS (1804–1872). Ludwig Feuerbach, born at Landshut in 1804, studied in Heidelberg and in 1824 went to Berlin under **Georg Wilhelm Friedrich Hegel**'s (1770–1831) tutelage. As a *Privatdocent* in Erlangen he published his *Thoughts on Death and Immortality* (1830), lost his position, and taught privately thereafter. Antitheological and expressly anti-Christian, his best-known work, *The Essence of Christianity* (1841), was translated by novelist **George Eliot** into English in 1854, and his *The Essence of Religion* and *Lectures on the Essence of Religion* (delivered at Heidelberg in 1848) appeared in 1845 and 1851, respectively. Central to his philosophical position is the dissolution of theology into anthropology: God is the projection of human ideals. Widely influential, his thought had particular importance for **Karl Marx**, **Friedrich Nietzsche**, and **Sigmund Freud**.

As a youth Feuerbach was strongly attached to a somewhat simple Christian trust in a beneficent all-knowing Father God and in the Bible as one central source of theological knowledge. Initially turning to a study of Romantic "mystical" writers, Feuerbach was first introduced to Hegel by Karl Daub (1765–1836), his teacher at Heidelberg who linked Hegelianism and Christianity. As a result he went to study with the philosopher himself, and it was Hegel, above all other thinkers, who was a formative influence on Feuerbach's thought, even as the latter separated himself radically from Hegelian principles and found himself loosely linked with writers such as **Bruno Bauer** (1809–1882) and **David Friedrich Strauss** (1808–1874) as a "left-wing" Hegelian. In keeping with his earlier training, he concluded that the Hegelian position was a form of theology and thereby limited and in need of transference into anthropology. Beginning with human consciousness, for example, as does Hegel, Feuerbach finds in its infinity the roots of the human construction of eternity. It may be that Luther's assertion that "one has one's God in the way one thinks of him" played a role in Feuerbach's projection theory. The importance of Luther for his thought is especially clear in *The Essence of Faith according to Luther* (1846). Earlier in his career he directed close attention to a number of philosophers, all of whose importance for his developing thought is evident in his 1833 *Geschichte der neueren Philosophie* (treating Francis Bacon, Thomas Hobbes, Pierre Gassendi, Jacob Boehme, René Descartes, Arnold Geulincx, Nicholas Malebranche, and Baruch Spinoza) as well as in his monographs on Leibnitz's thought in 1837 and on Pierre Bayle (1647–1706) in 1838. All these figures were important for Feuerbach's intellectual formation, not necessarily as direct influences but as foils with and against whom he formulated his positions. Likewise among his contemporaries **Friedrich Schleiermacher**'s (1768–1834) notion of the feeling of absolute dependence at the base of human consciousness was applied by Feuerbach to humanity's relationship to nature.

ARCHIVES

For details on archival collections and an ongoing critical edition, see Werner Schuffenhauer (hrsg.), *Gesammelte Werke* (Berlin: Akadamie-Verlag, 1981–).

PRINTED SOURCES

Harvey, Van A. *Feuerbach and the Interpretation of Religion* (Cambridge: Cambridge University Press, 1995).
Kamenka, Eugene. *The Philosophy of Ludwig Feuerbach* (London: Routledge & Kegan Paul, 1970).
Löwith, Karl. *From Hegel to Nietzsche: The Revolution in Nineteenth Century Thought*, David E. Green (trans.) (Garden City, N.Y.: Doubleday, 1967).
Sass, Hans-Martin. *Ludwig Feuerbach mit Selbstzeugnissen und Bilddokumenten* (Reinbek bei Hamburg: Rowohlt, 1978).
Toews, John Edward. *Hegelianism: The Path toward Dialectical Humanism, 1805–1841* (Cambridge: Cambridge University Press, 1980).
Wartofsky, Marx W. *Feuerbach* (Cambridge: Cambridge University Press, 1977).

Peter C. Erb

FICHTE, JOHANN GOTTLIEB (1762–1814). Johann Fichte, idealist philosopher, was born on May 19, 1762, in Rammenau, Lusatia, near Bischofswerda (20 miles east-northeast of Dresden). The son of a poor weaver and ribbonmaker, Fichte's intellectual powers impressed Baron von Miltitz, who provided for the boy's education, first at the home of a pastor, then at public school in Meissen and the charity Schulpforta, from which he graduated with distinction.

Fichte attended the University of Jena and afterward the Universities of Wittenberg and Leipzig. Strongly affected by his religious education and reading of the Bible, at Jena, Fichte first registered as a student of theology. His interests soon turned to philosophy, where he was initially influenced by Gotthold Ephraim Lessing (1729–1781), whose *Reuttungen* (1754) and *Die Erziehung des Menschengeschlects* (1780) promoted free thinking, tolerance, and a progressive educational system to advance those ideals. Fichte would express a similar vision in his *Reden an die Deutsche Nation* (1808).

Fichte was exposed to the public exchanges between Moses Mendelssohn (1729–1786) and Friedrich Jacobi (1743–1819) concerning Lessing's theological views; Fichte apparently sided with Mendelssohn's determinism. Study of Lessing led Fichte to Benedictus de Spinoza (1632–1677), who laid out in his *Ethica* (1677) a rigorous and compelling, quasi-pantheistic vision of absolute necessity. Fichte also came to admire greatly the work of Jean-Jacques Rousseau (1712–1778).

The most profound influence upon Fichte, however, came through the work of Immanuel Kant (1724–1804), especially Kant's *Kritik der praktischen Vernuft* (1788). In 1792, Fichte traveled to Königsberg, where he listened to Kant lecture. At their first meetings, Kant was decidedly cool to his ardent admirer. Determined to attract Kant's interest and approval, Fichte composed in four weeks that year his *Versuch einer Kritik aller Offenbarung* (1792), which earned him wide acclaim and a professorship at Jena in 1794. Fichte's lectures there show the influence of the ideals of the French Revolution (beginning 1789), and he acquired the reputation of being a Jacobin. Fichte subsequently wrote "Beitrag zur Berichtigung der Urtheile des Publikums über die französische Revolution" (1793–1794). At Jena, Fichte became friends with the poet Johann Christoph Friedrich Schiller (1759–1805) and later with **Johann Wolfgang von Goethe** (1749–1832). Fichte's unshakeable moral absolutism distanced him from the work of those like Friedrich von Schlegel (1772–1829) and other Romantics among whom he briefly circulated after leaving Jena in 1799. Kant's critical philosophy was given a metaphysical turn in Fichte's *Begriff der Wissenschaftslehre* and *Grundlage der gasamten Wissenschaftslehre* (both 1794). Kant's focus on uncompromising duty is interpreted and elaborated in terms of this metaphysic in *Das System der Sittenlehre nach den Principien der Wissenschaftslehre* (1798).

Fichte died of typhus while enmeshed in the national struggle against **Napoléon**.

ARCHIVES

Humbodt Universität, Berlin.

Bavarian Academy of Sciences, Munich; under the care of the editors of *J. G. Fichte Gesamtausbgabe der Bayerischen Akademie der Wissenschaften*: Reinhard Lauth, Hans Jacob, and Hans Gliwitsky. Twenty-nine large quarto volumes have appeared since 1962, in the continuing project that aims to publish Fichte's entire corpus in four definitive critical series: works, manuscripts, correspondence, and transcripts.

PRINTED SOURCES

Fichte, Johann Gottlieb. *Fichte: Early Philosophical Writing*, Daniel Breazeale (ed.) (Ithaca: Cornell University Press, 1988). Contains an informative introduction.

————. *Johann Gottlieb Fichtes nachgelassene Werke*, I. H. Fichte (ed.), 3 vols. (Bonn: Adolph-Marcus, 1834–1835).

————. *Johann Gottlieb Fichtes sämmtliche Werke*, I. H. Fichte (ed.), 8 vols. (Berlin: Veit, 1845–1846).

Fuchs, Erich (ed.). *J. G. Fichte im Gespräch: Berichte der Zeitgenossen*, 2 vols. (Stuttgart-Bad Cannstatt: Frommann-Holzboog, 1978–1980).

Léon, Xavier. *Fichte et son temps*, 3 vols. (Paris: Colin, 1922–1927). The best biography to date.

Martin, Wayne M. *Idealism and Objectivity: Understanding Fichte's Jena Project* (Stanford: Stanford University Press, 1997).

Medicus, Fritz. *Fichtes Leben*, 2nd ed. (Leipzig: Meiner, 1922).

Neuhouser, Frederick. *Fichte's Theory of Subjectivity* (New York: Cambridge University Press, 1990).

Schulz, Walter. *J. G. Fichte: Vernunft und Freiheit* (Pfullingen: Neske, 1962).

Zöller, Günter. *Fichte's Transcendental Philosophy* (New York: Cambridge University Press, 1998).

Peter S. Fosl

FLAUBERT, GUSTAVE (1821–1880). Gustave Flaubert was born to Dr. Achille-Cléophas Flaubert and Justine-Caroline Fleuriot Flaubert at Rouen in 1821. He was educated at the Collège Royal de Rouen (1832–1840). He had an older brother, Achille, who would follow his father into the medical profession as a doctor and a sister, Caroline, who would die in 1846, after the birth of her first child. Named as a Knight in the Legion of Honor in 1866, Flaubert studied law originally in Paris (1841–1842) but did not complete his studies. After the second year of law school, he failed his exams and retired from vocational pursuits altogether, in order to pursue his artistic vision. That artistic vision spanned several decades and included the works of *Madame Bovary* (1857); *Salammbô* (1863); *Sentimental Education* (1870); *The Temptation of St. Anthony* (1874); and the posthumously published *Bouvard et Pecuchet* (1881).

This artistic vision was marked early on by his fundamental belief that there must be an art that would unite in itself the logical precision of science and the subjective intuition of aesthetic experience. Thus he set about to create just such an art; it would be the final unification between object and subject.

Flaubert's aesthetic visions were ultimately tied to his reading of Homer, Rabelais, **Goethe**, and Shakespeare. These writers modeled for Flaubert that same precision in language that he hoped to realize with the publication of *Madame Bovary*. In their works, Flaubert saw competing forces seamlessly united: "they are motionless as cliffs," yet "stormy as the ocean." In other words, these writers' texts bring together the antithetical forces of nature, that is, what Flaubert would understand as the subject and the object, in order to produce a totality of meaning, a unity in thought. This outcome was essentially what Flaubert deemed to be the "highest and most difficult achievement of art." Thus his fascination with the tension between the subject and the object fueled his reading of Homer and Goethe, for example, and enabled him to imagine language as the intersection of wildly disparate powers. Especially, in relation to Homer, Flaubert was already beginning to imagine an aesthetic project in which mimesis was not an imitation of reality but rather expressed the intersection between two divergent forces.

Such a vision regarding language, furthermore, pushed Flaubert to identify with the Romantic writers whom he read voraciously. Flaubert saw both his own work and sentiment as precisely tied to the Romantic generation of 1830 so that his aesthetic project was to his mind a "romantic one." The importance of this conclusion for Flaubert is made even more explicit by his remarks to critic Sainte-Beuve after Sainte-Beuve's review of *Madame Bovary*. Thus in a letter to Sainte-Beuve, Flaubert corrects the critic's published belief that *Madame Bovary* is "a conscious attempt to reproduce reality." In this way, Flaubert's reading of the Romantics brings him to a fundamental rethinking of the nature of mimesis in language.

ARCHIVES

Bibliothèque Nationale de France, Tolbiac Collection.

PRINTED SOURCES

Berg, William J., and Laurey K. Martin. *Gustave Flaubert* (New York: Twayne Publishers, 1997).
Flaubert, Gustave. *Correspondence*, 9 vols. (Paris: Conard, 1926–1933). Supplement 4 vols. (Paris: Conard, 1954).
Madame Bovary. Eleanor Marx Aveling (trans.), updated by Paul de Man (New York: W. W. Norton, 1965).

Kitty Millet

FOSTER, STEPHEN COLLINS (1826–1864). Stephen Foster was born in 1826 in Lawrenceville and raised in Allegheny, near Pittsburgh, Pennsylvania. He received tutoring at home in Latin and Greek and attended Allegheny Academy, Athens Academy in Tioga for the 1839–1841 school sessions, and Jefferson College at Canonsburg from July to August 1841, where he studied French and German. After leaving Canonsburg, Foster returned home and briefly studied mathematics in Pittsburgh before devoting himself to life as America's first professional songwriter. Foster's gift for melody and lyrics left a musical legacy that enjoys worldwide renown more than a century after his death.

Under the tutelage of Moses Warner at Athens Academy, Stephen Foster memorized and recited the slow-paced poems of Oliver Goldsmith and James Thomson, heavily laced with rustic scenes and country incidents. Brisker patterns in Campbell and Scots folksongs and the political balladry of the day promoted swifter stanza-flow when Foster first wrote his own poems (Murray, 28–29).

Chafing at the discipline of school, Foster preferred to ramble among the woods yet performed his recitations perfectly. His older brother Morrison recalled that Foster's earliest textbooks included Lindley Murray's *The English Reader or Pieces in Prose and Verse, Selected from the Best Writers* (1827). While at home, Stephen heard his mother recite from the works of the "best authors."

Characterized as an omnivorous reader, Stephen Foster developed a literary taste molded by Celtic balladry, the poetry of **Alfred Tennyson**, John Milton, and the minor Romantic poet Thomas Moore (Emerson, 42; Gaul, 41). Foster often recited **Edgar Allan Poe**'s poetry and adopted a similar fondness for ululating women's names (Emerson, 167). As a child he met **Charles Dickens** and later avidly read his novels, particularly *Bleak House* (Stephen Foster Sketchbook, University of Pittsburgh). Undoubtedly *Hard Times* and the economic hardship in the country inspired the song "Hard Times Come Again No More." Foster set to music poems published in *Littell's Living Age*, *The Home Journal*, and other literary newspapers of the day that printed excerpts from the British press (Emerson, 142, 167, 246). Influenced by the singer-composer Henry Russell, Foster set to music one of the poems he had heard Russell sing and hoped to supply sentimental songs for Russell and his imitators (Austin, 18). Foster may have been aware also of the songs and poetry of Charles Mackay, William Cullen Bryant, and **James Russell Lowell**.

Foster used his knowledge of the traditional Anglo-Scots-Irish music, popular parlor songs, and blackface minstrelsy to create his own blend of memorable tunes.

ARCHIVES

Stephen Foster Memorial, Center for American Music, University of Pittsburgh, Pennsylvania.

PRINTED SOURCES

Austin, W. W. " 'Susanna,' 'Jeanie,' and 'The Old Folks at Home.' " In *The Songs of Stephen C. Foster from His Time to Ours*, 2nd ed. (Urbana and Chicago: University of Illinois Press, 1987).

Emerson, K. *Doo-dah!: Stephen Foster and the Rise of American Popular Culture* (New York: Simon & Schuster, 1997).

Gaul, H. *The Minstrel of the Alleghenies* (Pittsburgh, Pa.: Friends of Harvey Gaul, Inc., 1952).

Hamm, C. *Yesterdays: Popular Song in America* (New York: W. W. Norton, 1979).

Howard, J. T. *Stephen Foster, America's Troubadour* (New York: Thomas Y. Crowell, 1934).

Morneweck, E. F. *Chronicles of Stephen Foster's Family*, 2 vols. (Pittsburgh, Pa.: University of Pittsburgh Press, 1944).

Murray, E. *Stephen C. Foster at Athens: His First Composition* (Athens, Pa.: Tioga Point Museum, 1941).

Susan Hamburger

FOURIER, CHARLES (1772–1837). Charles Fourier was born in Besançon, France, in 1772 and received his formal education at the Collège de Besançon

(1781–1787); there is some evidence that he may have completed an additional year of schooling in Dijon (1787–1788) before following in his father's footsteps as a cloth merchant. He rejected the pious Catholicism of his family while still in his youth, and denunciations of the Church and theology can be found throughout his writings. Largely self-taught, he began developing his critique of commercial civilization and his theories of human psychology and social organization in the 1790s. Along with **Robert Owen** and **Claude-Henri Saint-Simon**, he gained greater prominence posthumously as one of the "utopian" socialists singled out for criticism by **Karl Marx** and **Friedrich Engels**. Fourier's ideas and writings have had a wide-ranging impact; though most commonly categorized as an early socialist and precursor of Marx, Fourier has also been hailed as a literary stylist and an early proponent of women's equality and sexual freedom.

Because Fourier emphasized the originality of his system, it can be difficult to determine the sources of his ideas. His published works are peppered with quotations from a broad range of sources, mostly French writers of the seventeenth and eighteenth centuries, but ranging from ancient history to contemporary political journalism and religious tracts. Often Fourier quoted from other authors' works simply to denounce them as misguided. More evidence regarding Fourier's sources can be found in the collection of his manuscripts and papers (Fonds Fourier, Archives Nationales [AN]); some of the manuscripts include notes on Fourier's readings, especially references to book reviews and articles in the periodical press.

One thinker whose influence Fourier freely acknowledged was the English physicist Isaac Newton, whose ideas had been widely popularized in France. Presenting his doctrine as the application of Newtonian principles to human psychology and society, Fourier labeled his system the "calculus of passionate attraction." Fourier's admiration for Newton did not extend to all Enlightenment philosophy; though familiar with the works of many Enlightenment philosophers and political economists, Fourier tended to issue sweeping condemnations of all "civilized philosophers" and theologians. He sometimes made an exception for Voltaire, the baron de Montesquieu, and especially Jean-Jacques Rousseau, acknowledging them as "honorable" and "expectant" philosophers whose ideas foreshadowed Fourier's theory (*Oeuvres Complètes*, 3:109–110).

Fourier also identified "expectant philosophers" among his contemporaries; by 1820, Fourier had become aware of the English socialist Owen and was describing the Owenite community of New Lanark as a forerunner of his own plan. Owen's works had been translated into French, but much of Fourier's information was obtained indirectly through book reviews and reports in the press. In 1824 Fourier opened up a correspondence with Owen; as he learned more about Owenism, he lost his enthusiasm for it and condemned its "monastic" moralism (Fonds Fourier, AN). Although he learned of the ideas of fellow social theorist Saint-Simon after his own doctrine was developed, Fourier recognized the Saint-Simonian movement as both a rival and a potential source of support (Beecher, *Fourier*, 409, passim). Fourier's contacts with the Saint-Simonians shaped the ways in which he and his followers presented his doctrine to the public through journals, pamphlets, and public debates.

ARCHIVES

Fonds Fourier et Considérant, Archives Nationales, Paris. Principal archival collection.

PRINTED SOURCES

Barthes, R. *Sade, Fourier, Loyola* (Paris: Editions du Seuil, 1974). Focuses on Fourier's use of language.
Beecher, J. *Charles Fourier: The Visionary and His World* (Berkeley: University of California Press, 1986). The best biography and a good overview of Fourier's doctrine.
Beecher, J., and R. Bienvenu (eds.). *The Utopian Vision of Charles Fourier: Selected Texts on Work, Love, and Passionate Attraction* (Columbia: University of Missouri Press, 1983). Collection of Fourier's writings in English translation.
Fourier, C. *Oeuvres Complètes de Charles Fourier*, 12 vols. (Paris: Editions Anthropos, 1966–1967).
Manuel, F. *The Prophets of Paris* (Cambridge, Mass.: Harvard University Press, 1962).
Riasanovsky, N. *The Teaching of Charles Fourier* (Berkeley: University of California Press, 1969).

Deirdre Weaver

FREUD, SIGMUND (1856–1939). Sigmund Freud was born in Freiberg, Moravia, in 1856, the oldest of seven children in an orthodox Jewish household. After graduating from the Gymnasium, Freud attended the faculty of medicine at Vienna University (1873–1881) and worked briefly with the famed neurologist Jean-Martin Charcot at the Salpêtrière hospital in Paris (1885–1886). After several years spent in private practice and research in Vienna, Freud produced his first significant work, *Studies in Hysteria* (1892), which he cowrote with Josef Breuer. Although Freud saw himself as an assimilated Jew, he was nevertheless profoundly affected by the rampant anti-semitism of fin de siècle Vienna and expressed ambivalence about his Jewish identity in a number of his writings. This issue became particularly salient when he was forced to leave Vienna for England after Austria was invaded by Hitler's Germany in 1938. Freud died in London the following year from cancer of the jaw.

As a neurologist with great professional ambitions, Freud naturally steeped himself in the medical literature of his day, and in his work one may discern the influences of such luminaries as Charcot, Hippolyte Bernheim, J. F. Herbart, Ernst Brücke, and his teacher Theodor Meynert. In his well-known study *Three Essays on the Theory of Sexuality* (1905), Freud also acknowledged his debt to contemporary sexologists like **Havelock Ellis**, Richard Krafft-Ebing, Iwan Bloch, and Magnus Hirschfeld. As the later Freud widened the scope of psychoanalysis to include social, religious, and cultural matters, he tried to incorporate recent developments in sociology and anthropology and acquired a familiarity with prominent works in these fields. In studies like *Group Psychology and the Analysis of the Ego* (1921), for instance, Freud employed the work of crowd psychologist Gustave Le Bon to understand the collective mind. When preparing anthropological works like *Totem and Taboo* (1913), he availed himself of a wider range of relevant contemporary sources, from the works of **Charles Darwin** and the biblical scholar W. Robertson Smith to those of anthropologists like Edward Burnett Tylor and James G. Frazer.

Although he generally saw his work as nothing less than a hard-nosed scientific inquiry into the nature of the unconscious, Freud nevertheless drew widely from literary and philosophical sources for inspiration. Scattered throughout his writings are references to some of the most important thinkers of the Western tradition, from Friedrich Schiller, **Heinrich Heine**, and Shakespeare to Plato, J. J. Bachofen, and Eduard von Hartmann. It is even possible to trace some of Freud's central concepts to particular writers, especially Romantics. For instance, early glimpses into the process of sublimation may be found in **Johann Wolfgang von Goethe**, whereas the concept of the id (*das Es*) has origins in **Friedrich Nietzsche**, and the notion of a death drive is prefigured to some extent in Novalis and Gotthilf Heinrich von Schubert. Freud's greatest cultural passion, however, was classical antiquity, and in addition to his personal collection of ancient artifacts, he also used examples from Greek mythology for some of the basic concepts of psychoanalysis, including the idea of Eros and, most famously, Sophocles's story of Oedipus.

ARCHIVES

Sigmund Freud Collection, Manuscript Division, Library of Congress, Washington, D.C.

PRINTED SOURCES

Freud, Sigmund. *Gesammelte Werke*, 18 vols., (Frankfurt am Main; Fischer Taschenbuch Verlag, 1999).
Gay, Peter. *Freud: A Life for Our Time* (New York: Norton, 1988).
Gilman, Sander. *Freud, Race, and Gender* (Princeton, N. J.: Princeton University Press, 1993).
Strachey, Edward (ed.), in collaboration with Anna Freud. *Standard Edition of the Complete Psychological Works of Sigmund Freud*, 24 vols. (London: Hogarth Press, 1953–1974).

Christopher E. Forth

FROUDE, JAMES ANTHONY (1818–1894). James Froude was born in Devon in 1818 and educated at Westminster (1830–1834) and Oriel College, Oxford (1836–1840). At Oxford, in part due to his elder brother Hurell's influence, Froude fell within the orbit of the Oxford movement, that Catholicizing trend within the Church of England that stressed the Church's antiquity, independence, and ritual. **John Henry Newman**, the leading light of the movement, persuaded Froude to undertake research for a planned book on the lives of the saints. The almost total lack of reliable evidence for the early centuries of Christianity fueled Froude's growing skepticism, precipitating his disengagement from the Oxford movement and, for a while, from the Church of England itself. Developments in science, especially Robert Chambers's *Vestiges of Creation* (1844), caused Froude to question all dogmatic authority, and in 1848 he published his *Nemesis of Faith*. This ringing affirmation of the primacy of reason led to the loss of his Oriel College fellowship and the necessity of earning his livelihood. Froude turned his hand to writing historical sketches for various publications. His success with these pieces, together with an enduring interest in the exploits of the Elizabethan "sea dogs" of his native county, led him to fasten upon history as the most suitable career.

Froude began work on his massive study of sixteenth-century England in the early 1850s, researching a wide array of manuscript sources, including those at the Spanish archives in Simancas. His 12-volume *History of England from the Fall of Cardinal Wolsey to the Spanish Armanda* was published between 1856 and 1869. It is a vividly written, highly patriotic account in which the Protestant Reformation is seen as unlocking the true greatness of the English people. It reflected **Thomas Carlyle**'s influence in its adulation of Henry VIII and other "great men," who were depicted as agents of an unfolding providential plan. Such a ready invoking of Providence in history tended to make Froude's fellow historians uncomfortable. Moreover, the book was sharply criticized by Edward Augustus Freeman and other "Whig" historians for ignoring the dangers to traditional English liberties represented by the rise of "Tudor despotism." In spite of such criticisms, the book's readability and triumphalist tone made it a resounding success throughout the English-speaking world.

Froude's other major literary production was his biography of Carlyle, with whom he had a close and enduring friendship. When Carlyle commissioned him for the project, Froude gave up his planned lives of Charles V and Philip II, as well as his editorship of *Fraser's*. The project proved demanding and vexatious, not least because of a protracted legal dispute with Carlyle's niece over possession of his letters. The four-volume *Life of Carlyle* (1882–1884), though criticized by some of Carlyle's admirer's for its frankness regarding his domestic life, is often considered a literary masterpiece.

Several other books followed, the most notable of which was *Oceana* (1886). Written after Froude had returned from an around-the-world tour, it is a paean to the British Empire, the inception of which he had celebrated in his *History of England*. In 1892, he was named Regius Professor of History at Oxford (ironically in succession to his nemesis E. A. Freeman), a post he held until his death in 1894.

ARCHIVES

Widely scattered out-letters. See, especially, Bodleian Library, Letters to Max Müller, Richard Bentley, George Bentley.

PRINTED SOURCES

Dunn, Waldo Hilary. *James Anthony Froude: A Biography*, 2 vols. (Oxford: Clarendon Press, 1961).

Reynolds, Beatrice. "James Anthony Froude." In Herman Ausubel et al. (eds.), *Some Modern Historians of Britain: Essays in Honor of R. L. Schuyler* (New York: Dryden Press, 1951), 49–65.

Von Arx, Jeffrey Paul. *Progress and Pessimism: Religion, Politics, and History in Late Nineteenth-Century Britain* (Cambridge, Mass.: Harvard University Press, 1985).

Anthony Brundage

FRY, ELIZABETH (1780–1845). Elizabeth Fry was born at Earlham in Norfolk in 1780 to the Quaker family of John and Catherine Gurney. She struggled with the social restrictions of the Society of Friends, longing for society life but also recognizing its frivolity, during her teenage years. After her marriage to Joseph Fry in 1800, she cheerfully reconciled herself to her religion and was called to the ministry at age 29, receiving a great deal of recognition as a speaker and reader. Best known for her prison reform work, Fry also involved herself in a number of philanthropic movements.

During Fry's childhood, her mother, who died in 1782, would read the Scriptures or tell her children Bible stories to educate them. While daily Bible readings were an influence on her that cannot be overemphasized, she struggled with her formal education. In the *Memoir*, Fry writes: "I was considered and called very stupid and obstinate. I certainly did not like learning, nor did I, I believe, attend to my lessons, partly from a delicate state of health that produced languor of mind as well as body; but I think having the name of being stupid really tended to make me so, and discouraged my efforts to learn" (1:21).

The Quaker tradition of oral literature adds another dimension to Elizabeth Fry's reading history. During her teenage years, she heard William Savery speak and was greatly influenced by him and other speakers in the Quaker ministry. In addition, she also, through keeping a journal, read herself. Comments such as "it is most comforting to read it over and see the different workings of my heart and soul" (1:21) recur in her journal entries, and she also mentions that if reading her journals "would conduce to strengthen others in the faith" (1:210), she would be willing to have them read after her death.

Books and reading played an important role in her prison reform and other charities. In 1827, she published *Observations on the Visiting Superintendance and Government of Female Prisoners*, arguing that prisoners should be provided with books of a religious and instructive nature. She and other volunteers would go to the prison and read the Scriptures; along with that, she also established a school for the children of the female prisoners. Another one of her charities focused on the Coast Guard men whom she sought to help in their isolation by establishing libraries for them. Each library contained 52 books that included adventure stories, biography, and religious literature. In devoting her life to her religious beliefs and charitable works, Fry evidently relied upon the spirit of divine books, particularly the Bible, to inspire her.

ARCHIVES

Elizabeth Fry's Journals (44 out of 46). Library of the Society of Friends, London.

PRINTED SOURCES

Fry, Katharine, and Rachel Creswell (eds.). *Memoir of the Life of Elizabeth Fry with Extracts from Her Journals and Letters*, 2 vols. (1847; Montclair, N.J.: Patterson Smith, 1974).
Jackaman, Peter. "Books for Blockade Men: The Concern of Mistress Fry," *Library Review* (Summer 1982), 111–120.
Rose, June. *Elizabeth Fry* (New York: St. Martin's, Press 1981).

Sarah R. Marino

FULLER, MARGARET (1810–1850). (Sarah) Margaret Fuller Ossoli, born in Cambridgeport, Massachusetts, in 1810, began her education at the age of three. Instructed by her father, Timothy, she learned much the same curriculum he had studied at Harvard. Fuller was formally educated at Cambridgeport Private Grammar School (1819–1820), Boston Lyceum for Young Ladies (1821–1822), and Miss Prescott's Young Ladies Seminary at Groton (1824–1825). Her parents practiced Unitarianism, and while she lived with them, Fuller attended services, although she "almost always suffered much in church from a feeling of disunion with the hearers and dissent from the preacher" (Fuller, *Essential*, 10). As a participant in Hedge's (Transcendental) Club, Fuller critiqued **Ralph Waldo Emerson**'s writing as well as that of other Transcendentalists, and as first editor (1840–1842) of the Transcendentalists' journal, *The Dial*, she solicited and brought to light many of these writings. The leader of educational Conversations for Boston women (1842–1844), Fuller inspired the public careers of Caroline Dall and Ednah Cheney. As one of the first American literary critics of stature, author of the first influential American feminist treatise (*Woman in the Nineteenth Century*, 1845), and one of the first foreign correspondents for an American newspaper (1846–1850), Fuller led Americans in claiming an identity within Western culture.

Taught by her father Latin grammar and Greek playwrights in translation, Fuller's letters to him while he served in Congress report that she read the classical Greek and Roman writers. Thus trained, she engaged throughout her life in nearly continuous study and strove to integrate her studies into her life by training other women in critical thinking. Many of Fuller's letters critiqued the classical Greeks as the epitome of Western culture; she once compared the life in Concord among the Transcendentalists with that of "the academic Grove" of Plato (Hudspeth, 3:93). Fuller's feminism was early inspired by **Anne-Louise-Germaine de Staël** and her contemporary Jeanne-Marie Roland, whom Fuller read in her youth with the older **Lydia Child** (Capper, 89, 127). The foremost inspiration for Fuller's Romanticism was **Johann Goethe**, whose works she studied and translated avidly and whose biography she planned to write (Fuller Manuscripts and Works, Houghton Lib.). She also greatly admired English Romantics **William Wordsworth** and **Samuel Coledridge**, as well as **Percy Shelley** and **Lord Byron** (Capper, 86, 91). Fuller's Conversations and literary productions drew on all these interests. In Europe in the last years of her life Fuller befriended Polish poet Adam Mickiewicz and Italian revolutionary **Giuseppe Mazzini** (Blanchard, 246). Her Romantic idealism was refreshed and inspired by these revolutionaries, and her subsequent dispatches for the New York *Tribune* drew on their ideas to excite American public opinion in support of the political upheavals she was witnessing in Europe.

ARCHIVES

Fuller Manuscripts and Works, Houghton Library, Harvard University.
Margaret Fuller Papers, Massachusetts Historical Society.

PRINTED SOURCES

Blanchard, Paula. *Margaret Fuller: From Transcendentalism to Revolution* (1978; Radcliffe Biography Series, Reading: Addison-Wesley, 1987).

Capper, Charles. *Margaret Fuller: An American Romantic Life, the Private Years* (New York: Oxford University Press, 1992).

Chevigny, Bell Gale. *The Woman and the Myth: Margaret Fuller's Life and Writings* (Old Westbury, N.Y.: Feminist Press, 1976; rev. and expanded, Boston: Northeastern University Press, 1994).

Emerson, R. W., W. H. Channing, and J. F. Clarke (eds.). *Memoirs of Margaret Fuller Ossoli, with a Portrait and an Appendix*, 2 vols. (New York: Burt Franklin [Lenox Hill Publ. and Dist. Co.], 1972 reprint). First published in 1852 and 1884.

Fuller, Margaret. *The Essential Margaret Fuller*, Jeffrey Steele (ed. and introduction) (New Brunswick, N.J.: Rutgers University Press, 1992).

Healey [Dall], Caroline W. *Margaret and Her Friends; or, Ten Conversations with Margaret Fuller upon the Mythology of the Greeks and Its Expression in Art* (Boston: Roberts, 1897). First published in 1895.

Higginson, Thomas Wentworth. *Margaret Fuller Ossoli*, American Men of Letters series (Boston: Houghton Mifflin, 1884).

Hudspeth, Robert N. (ed.). *The Letters of Margaret Fuller*, 6 vols. (Ithaca, N.Y.: Cornell University Press, 1983–1994).

Robin Meader

G

GARIBALDI, GIUSEPPE (1807–1882). Giuseppe Garibaldi, an Italian patriot and soldier, was, along with **Camillo Benso di Cavour** and **Giuseppe Mazzini**, responsible for the unification of Italy.

To his enemies, Garibaldi was notoriously and shamefully unlettered, a result of his birth into a humble fishing family. The following anecdote—perhaps apocryphal—is recounted in several biographies. Garibaldi's father hired a tutor for his young son. One day, the teacher happened upon the future condottiere with a book in his lap, dreamily gazing out to sea. The teacher inquired as to what he was doing; the young boy replied that he was "reading." When the keenly observant tutor pointed out that the boy wasn't even looking at the book, Giuseppe candidly replied that it was true. "Then what are you reading?" asked the tutor. "I am reading the sky and the sea," replied the boy. "And what do they tell you?" "I don't know," replied Garibaldi, "but it seems to me that I read there finer things than I could in books made of paper."

Although he admitted in his autobiography that "I was fonder of play than of study," the stereotype of the unlettered and ignorant guerilla is no doubt false. **Dumas (*père*)** recounts that Garibaldi's father was a spendthrift but derived his greatest pleasure from spending money on his son's education. Possession of a captain's certificate demonstrates knowledge of mathematics, geometry, astronomy, geography, and commercial and naval law. Despite his ferocious anticlericalism, Garibaldi knew the Bible. He was fascinated with **Saint-Simon**, utopian socialism, and Saint-Simon's *New Christianity*. He was familiar with nineteenth-century socialist and anarchist literature. Although he recounted in his autobiography that "I earnestly sought out any book or article about Italian freedom," the various versions of his autobiography and his many biographers fail to mention what exactly he read. One can deduce from his speeches and writings that he was familiar with ancient Roman history. Toward the end of his life he tried his hand at writing and managed to finish three novels ("three volumes . . . which history ought to forget about him," Giuseppe Guerzoni remarked tartly) as well as his autobiography. In the preface to his first novel, he specifically mentions **Alessandro Manzoni** and **Victor Hugo** as great writers. A friend commented that Garibaldi had some awareness of literature but that knowledge was "a bit muddled, even odd, and in general undigested and disorganized." The same commentator noted that Garibaldi often wrote poetry and in later life could recite all the *Sepolcri* of Ugo Foscolo, whole passages from Voltaire, episodes from the *Iliad*, Dante's *Divine Comedy*, and Torquato Tasso's *Gerusalemme Liberata*.

ARCHIVES

Archivio Centrale dello Stato, Rome.
Archivio Communale, Genoa.
Archivio Communale, Palermo.
Museo del Risorgimento, Milan.
Museo Storico del Risorgimento, Rome.
Museo Garibaldino, Caprera, La Maddalena, Sardinia, Italy.
Public Records Office, London.
British Museum, London.

PRINTED SOURCES

Campanella, Anthony P. (ed.). *Garibaldi's Memoirs: From His Manuscript, Personal Notes, and Authentic Sources*, assembled and published by Elpis Melena, translated from the German by Erica Sigeri Campanella (Sarasota, Fla.: International Institute of Garibaldian Studies, 1981).
Garibaldi, Giuseppe. *Autobiography of Giuseppe Garibaldi*, translated by A. Werner, with an introduction by A. William Salomone, supplement by Jessie White Mario (New York: H. Fertig, 1971).
————. *Memorie: con una appendice di scritti politici; introduzione e note di Giuseppe Armani* (Milano: Rizzoli, 1982).
Mack Smith, Denis. *Garibaldi: A Great Life in Brief* (New York: Knopf, 1956).
Ridley, Jasper. *Garibaldi* (London: Constable, 1974).
Trevelyan, George Macaulay. *Garibaldi and the Making of Italy* (London: Longmans, Green and Co., 1911).

Stanislao G. Pugliese

GARRISON, WILLIAM LLOYD (1805–1879). William Lloyd Garrison was born in Newburyport, Massachusetts, in 1805 and educated sporadically in primary and grammar schools near his home (1811–1816). He also read sermons and religious tracts, was tutored in Latin and English and American literature by a newspaper coworker, and read suggestions from a prominent townsman. His piously Baptist mother heavily influenced his strong religious beliefs. Garrison's vehement, radical journalistic editorials and lectures for the immediate abolition of slavery, women's rights, and temperance carried him to the forefront of the nineteenth-century reform movement.

While serving an apprenticeship at the Newburyport *Herald*, Garrison read constantly and widely from the works of Shakespeare and the novels and poetry of Alexander Pope, **Lord Byron**, Robert Burns, John Milton, Sir **Walter Scott**, and Mrs. Felicia Hemans. He later quoted extensively from the Bible, Shakespeare (*Hamlet, Macbeth, Romeo and Juliet, Henry V, A Midsummer Night's Dream, Much Ado about Nothing, As You Like It, Othello*), and Pope (*An Essay on Man*) in his letters and publications.

Next to the Bible (Garrison, 229), George Bourne's *The Book and Slavery Irreconcilable* (1816) became the major influence on Garrison's thoughts on emancipation (*Letters*, 1:172, n.10), followed by James Duncan's 1824 book *Treatise on Slavery* (Thomas, 105). He received a full indoctrination in Federalist beliefs, the art of dramaturgy, and championing an unpopular cause against impossible odds by studying the writings of Fisher Ames, Harrison Gray Otis, Benjamin Russell, and Timothy Pickering. Garrison modeled his invective style of writing on *The Letters of Junius* (1821), the pen name of an unidentified—possibly Sir Philip Francis—critic of King George III in the London *Public Advertiser*, 1769–1772 (*Letters*, 1:20, n. 3).

The young politician Caleb Cushing first alerted Garrison to slavery as a serious problem and urged him to read more widely. As editor at a succession of newspapers, Garrison read a variety of exchange newspapers where he discovered the monthly *Genius of Universal Emancipation* published by Benjamin Lundy. This paper focused his attention on the plight of slaves and the righteous cause of emancipation.

In March 1837 Garrison met John Humphrey Noyes, editor of a Vermont newspaper, *The Perfectionist*, and preacher of the theology that man was perfectible. Garrison, admiring Noyes's perfectionist ideas, incorporated this new influence into his life and praised his pamphlet *The Doctrine of Salvation from Sin* in an 1843 *Liberator* review (Merrill, *Against Wind and Tide*, 133–134, 181). But by the end of that year Garrison broke with Noyes over his editorial lambasting abolitionism as subordinate to the great religious reform. Supplementing the Perfectionist tinge on his religious views, Garrison discovered a recently published edition of the religious works of Thomas Paine, heretofore considered a "monster of iniquity" (*Liberator*, November 21, 1845).

Garrison revered the Declaration of Independence with its radical phrases "all men are created equal" and endowed with "certain unalienable rights" but believed the Constitution betrayed both the Declaration and the Bible as a bargain between whites and the devil at the expense of the slaves, particularly regarding the three-fifths clause.

Garrison, the great publicist of the abolition movement, brought the problem of slavery to the nation's attention in his religious and moral crusade.

ARCHIVES

William Lloyd Garrison Papers, Massachusetts Historical Society, Boston.
William Lloyd Garrison Papers, Boston Public Library.

Garrison Family Papers, Houghton Library, Harvard University, Cambridge, Massachusetts.

PRINTED SOURCES

Cain, W. E. (ed.). *William Lloyd Garrison and the Fight against Slavery; Selections from The Liberator* (New York: Bedford Books of St. Martin's Press, 1995).

Chapman, J. J. *William Lloyd Garrison* (Boston: Atlantic Monthly Press, 1921).

Garrison, W. L. *Selections from the Writings and Speeches of William Lloyd Garrison* (Boston: R. F. Wallcut, 1852).

Johnson, O. *William Lloyd Garrison and His Times* (Boston: B. B. Russell & Co., 1880).

Merrill, W. M. *Against Wind and Tide, a Biography of William Lloyd Garrison* (Cambridge, Mass.: Harvard University Press, 1963).

Merrill, W. M., and L. Ruchames (eds.). *The Letters of William Lloyd Garrison*, 6 vols. (Cambridge, Mass.: Belknap Press of Harvard University Press, 1971–1981).

Nye, R. B. *William Lloyd Garrison and the Humanitarian Reformers* (Boston: Little, Brown, 1955).

Stewart, J. B. *William Lloyd Garrison and the Challenge of Emancipation* (Arlington Heights, Ill.: Harlan Davidson, 1992).

Thomas, J. L. *The Liberator, William Lloyd Garrison, a Biography* (Boston: Little, Brown, 1963).

Susan Hamburger

GASKELL, ELIZABETH CLEGHORN (1810–1865). Elizabeth Gaskell, novelist and biographer, was born in London in 1810 but spent her formative years with her aunt in Knutsford, Cheshire. She was educated at Avonbank, an enlightened school, which offered girls instruction in literature, history, French, Italian, and music. In addition to the improving literature of Anna Maria Barbauld, she devoured novels (Sterne, Smollett, Richardson, **Scott**), and poetry (**Byron**, **Coleridge**, **Wordsworth**) in vast quantities. From 1832, she lived in the heart of industrial Manchester where her husband was a Unitarian minister and a friend of James Martineau. The Unitarian simplicity of belief and tolerance appealed to Gaskell's sense of Christian religion as direct, scriptural, and practical. Her novels are an important connecting link between those of **Jane Austen** and **George Eliot**. They are also important cultural documents in terms of the "condition of England" question of the 1840s. Her biography of **Charlotte Brontë** (1857) remains a key example of the genre.

As critics have noted, Gaskell's use of her reading is complex and often fleeting. Her novels carry traces of her religious belief, as well as a vast range of literary references. Wordsworth's "The Old Cumberland Beggar" with its line "we have all of us one human heart" stands with **Carlyle**'s *Past and Present* as a key part of her thinking on class and reconciliation in *Mary Barton* and *North and South* (Easson, 22). Wordworth's *Lucy* poems also appear in *Cousin Phillis* (Spencer, 124), where the description of rural life is buoyed up by references to Virgil's *Georgics*. Overall, the intention is generally to heighten tone or mood, to heighten emotion or control an incident. An admirer of **Tennyson**, both *Cranford* and *Sylvia's Lovers* contain direct references to his works (Shaw, 43). What her characters read is always important, as in the unfinished *Wives and Daughters*, and their varied choices reveal the breadth of Gaskell's knowledge.

ARCHIVES

Brotherton Collection, Brotherton Library, Leeds University.
Gaskell Collection, John Rylands Library, Manchester University.

PRINTED SOURCES

Ashberg, E. "Maria Edgeworth, Fredrika Bremer and Elizabeth Gaskell," *Gaskell Society Journal*, 6 (1992), 73–76.

Chapple, J., and A. Pollard (eds.). *Letters of Mrs Gaskell* (Manchester: Manchester University Press, 1966).

Easson, A. *Elizabeth Gaskell* (London: Routledge, 1979).

Handley, G. "Mrs Gaskell's Reading," *Durham University Journal*, 28 (1967), 131–138.

Jordan, E. "Spectres and Scorpions: Allusions and Confusions in *Mary Barton*," *Literature and History*, 7 (1981), 46–61.

Shaw, M. "Elizabeth Gaskell, Tennyson and the Fatal Return," *Gaskell Society Journal*, 9 (1995), 43–54.

Spencer, J. *Elizabeth Gaskell* (London: Macmillan, 1993).

Unsworth, A. "Elizabeth Gaskell and German Romanticism," *Gaskell Society Journal*, 8 (1994), 1–14.

Wheeler, M. "Mrs Gaskell's Reading," *Notes and Queries*, 222 (1977), 25–30.

Andrew Maunder

GAUGUIN, PAUL (1848–1903). Paul Gauguin was born in Paris, although his early education (1855–1862) took place in Orléans, where he attended a primary school and then the Junior Seminary of the Saint-Mesmin Chapel. After a year (1862–1863) at the Institut Loriol in Paris, Gauguin returned for his final year of formal education as a boarder at an Orléans lycée. Along with **Seurat** and **Van Gogh**, Gauguin is seen as one of the pioneers of modern Western art. His life, which moved from a comfortable existence as a stockbroker to the penury of the self-exiled experimental artist, has been seen as prototypical of that of the modern "tortured" artist. His symbolist painting was clearly much influenced by his artistic surroundings and contemporaries in Paris, Brittany, Provence, and later, Tahiti. His stylistic innovation and spiritual questing might now be countered by readings of his work that attend to their "Orientalist" (after Said, 1995) tendencies.

Schooled in the classics—**Balzac, Dumas, Hugo, Thomas Carlyle, James Fenimore Cooper**—Gauguin had a deep love of literature and incorporated ideas and motifs from these writers (such as the Hugo-inspired self-portrait of 1888, *Les Misérables*) into his work. More contemporary writers who influenced his production included **Flaubert**, Octave Mirbeau, **Renan, Zola, Edgar Allan Poe** (for whom Gauguin had a deep admiration), and most obviously, the Tahitian novels of Pierre Loti. Notes on Gauguin's tastes in both art and writing are plentiful in his journals (Gauguin). While clearly influenced by painters such as **Delacroix**, Camille Pissarro, Van Gogh, Ingres, **Degas**, Corot, **Monet**, and Puvis de Chavannes, much of Gauguin's artistic heritage clearly derives from his studies of Egyptian, Greek, Japanese, and Javanese culture. Works such as Schuré's *Les Grands Initiés*, which claimed that the Tahitians were descended from the Egyptians, and J. A. Moerenhout's *Voyage aux Iles du Grand Océan* clearly influenced Gauguin's conceptions of the Pacific Islands.

ARCHIVES

Bibliothèque Nationale, Paris.
Louvre, Département des Manuscrits.
Getty Centre for the History of Art and the Humanities, Los Angeles.

PRINTED SOURCES

Clement, Russell T. *Paul Gauguin: A Bio-Bibliography* (New York: Greenwood Press, 1991).
Gauguin, Paul. *Avant et Après* [The intimate journals of Paul Gauguin], Van Wyck Brooks (trans.) (London: William Heinemann, 1930).
Jirat-Wasiutynsk, Vojtech. *Paul Gauguin in the Context of Symbolism* (New York: Garland, 1978).
Prather, Martha, and Charles F. Stuckey (eds.). *Gauguin: A Retrospective* (New York: Hugh Lauter Levin, 1987).
Rewald, John. *Gauguin* (London: Hyperion Press, 1949).
Said, Edward. *Orientalism: Western Conceptions of the Orient* (London: Penguin, 1995).
Thomson, Belinda. *Gauguin* (London: Thames and Hudson, 1987).

William Gallois

GILBERT, WILLIAM SCHWENCK (1836–1911), and SULLIVAN, AR-
THUR (1842–1900). In tracing the influences on the comic operas produced by the partnership of William Schwenck Gilbert and Arthur Sullivan, it is worthwhile to remember as well how influential these works proved for later dramatists like Noel Coward and P. G. Wodehouse, aiding in the construction of an image of a glorious Victorian Britain and serving as sources for popular patriotic sentiment, usually in wartime. Neither man could have imagined such a result.

Arthur Sullivan, the son of a penurious clarinetist in the Surrey Theatre, later a bandmaster at Sandhurst, found an early appreciation for his talents, having been selected to join the choir of the Chapel Royal at St. James's Palace. He then received a scholarship to the Royal Academy of Music and moved on to the Leipzig Conservatory at age 16, where he turned his full attention to composing. Upon his return to London, Sullivan took church organist posts in upscale London parishes. His earliest work reflected these experiences. His training as a chorister had coincided with a great revival in English church music, prompted by the new liturgical emphases of the Tractarian movement, of which the choirmaster of the Chapel Royal, Thomas Helmore, was an enthusiastic exponent. Among Sullivan's first efforts were sacred music (*Te Deum*, 1872), oratorios (*The Prodigal Son*, 1869; *The Light of the World*, 1872), and hymns, including "Onward, Christian Soldiers," throughout the 1870s. These efforts alone hardly provided financial support, however, so Sullivan turned to popular opera, collaborating, though not exclusively, with Gilbert from 1871 through the 1890s. Sullivan's scores demonstrated his extensive classical training and his imitative abilities. Schooled in the English tradition, and then among devotees of Mendelssohn and Schubert in Leipzig, Sullivan filled the scores with intricate melodies that echoed his continental influences, with hornpipes, anthems, and waltzes, and with wry parodies of Handel and **Verdi**, among others. Although the operettas proved immensely popular, critics who had welcomed his earlier works accused Sullivan of squandering his talents on unworthy projects. Racked with illness, the composer died in 1900, but his familiar compositions, and a new sense of their sophistication, have survived.

Sullivan's memorable scores, nonetheless, followed W. S. Gilbert's remarkable librettos. And it might be appropriate not to examine what went into those lyrics but what few items Gilbert left out. The son of a naval surgeon who retired young upon an inheritance, Gilbert embraced drama during his public school years. During his early, and brief, stints in the civil service and at the bar, he began to write for *Eun*, one of the many satirical weeklies that appeared in the mid-nineteenth century. His collection of comic verse, *Bab's Ballads*, which appeared in the late 1860s, summed up these efforts and provided both plot and verse inspiration for the patter songs that would explain the qualifications and benefits of, most famously, a modern major general and a pirate king.

Gilbert soon took to writing for the theater, following the usual trend in penning burlesques and melodramas for the London stage. His familiarity with earlier dramatic works, both in England and France, allowed him to concoct parodic versions of the same, the normal requirement for the burlesque. However, as many modern critics and historians have noted, Gilbert also wished to restore the respectability of London theater—his solution was the comic opera taken to new heights of wit and sophistication.

Although his librettos would focus on the doings of pirates, fairies, Japanese potentates, and love-struck lord chancellors, Gilbert drew on many facets of his own life and, valuably for historians, used his work to reflect on developments in late Victorian Britain. For plot and setting he drew on his own familiarity with the armed services, bureaucracy, and the law, creating scenarios dependent on the disposition of wards of court and on naval hierarchy, while also sketching songs of praise for the 1862 Companies Act. His outsized characters and neatly resolved plots resembled, but surpassed, the usual staples of contemporary London theater. Dialogue and lyrics showed Gilbert's awareness of Sheridan's and Congreve's biting wit, as well as his own experience with the weekly papers, while the operettas' use of many variations on a single plot echoed the formula employed in French comedies of a century earlier. Most important, however, Gilbert related his plots, characters, and lyrics to topics of interest and relevance to the late Victorian middle-class audiences who flocked to the Savoy Theatre. Sir Garnett Wolseley, the general who seemed present at all imperial skirmishes of the time, was a recognizable model for the modern major general, as were **Oscar Wilde** and the aesthetics for the poets of patience. In a society that saw a growing electorate, with pressure for the women's vote as well, and a declining aristocracy, Gilbert's "topsy-turvy" world could intrigue, with its questioning of the equation between birth and status and its depiction of educated, independent women, yet also soothe through laughter by taking such attitudes to extremes. Gilbert's intention in providing these situations—revolutionary, reactionary, or simply commercial—remains an issue for historical debate. Where there is agreement is that Gilbert and Sullivan used their educations and talents to produce works that reflected their own experiences and times while retaining a resonance lasting over a century.

ARCHIVES

Gilbert and Sullivan Collection, Pierpont Morgan Library, New York.
Arthur Sullivan Diaries, 22 volumes, 1881–1900, Beinecke Rare Books and Manuscript Library, Yale University, New Haven, Connecticut.
Manuscript scores and letters, British Library Music Library.
Miscellaneous letters, British Library. Add. Mss. 49289–353, 54315, 54999.
Arthur Sullivan Archive, Royal Academy of Music Library.
Letters to Lord Chamberlain's licensee, British Theatre Museum.

PRINTED SOURCES

Allen, Reginald (ed.). *The Life and Work of Sir Arthur Sullivan, Composer for Victorian England* (New York: Pierpont Morgan Library; Boston: David R. Godine, 1975).
Dark, Sidney, and Rowland Grey. *W. S. Gilbert: His Life and Letters* (London: Methuen, 1923).
Dillard, Philip H. *Sir Arthur Sullivan: A Resource Book* (Lanham, Md.: Scarecrow Press, 1996).
Eden, David. *Gilbert and Sullivan: The Creative Conflict* (Rutherford, N.J.: Fairleigh Dickinson University Press, 1986).
Gilbert, W. S., and Arthur Sullivan. *The Complete Annotated Gilbert and Sullivan*, Ian Bradley (ed.) (Oxford: Oxford University Press, 1996).
Hibbert, Christopher. *Gilbert & Sullivan and Their Victorian World* (New York: American Heritage Publishing Co., 1976).
Jacobs, Arthur. *Arthur Sullivan: A Victorian Musician*, 2nd ed. (Portland, Oreg.: Amadeus Press, 1996).
Lawrence, Arthur. *Sir Arthur Sullivan: Life-story, Letters and Reminiscences* (London: James Bowden, 1899).
Pearson, Hesketh. *Gilbert and Sullivan: A Biography* (St. Clair Shores, Mich.: Scholarly Press, 1951).
———. *Gilbert: His Life and Strife* (London: Methuen, 1957).
Stedman, Jane (ed.). *Gilbert before Sullivan* (Chicago: University of Chicago Press, 1967).

Sullivan, Herbert, and Newman Flower. *Sir Arthur Sullivan. His Life, Letters, and Diaries* (New York: George H. Doran Co., 1927).

Andrew Muldoon

GLADSTONE, WILLIAM EWART (1809–1898). William Gladstone was born in Liverpool in 1809 and educated at Eton (1821–1827) and Christ Church, Oxford (1828–1831). Having been trained by his mother Anne as an Evangelical, he gradually moved toward a High Church stance and from the 1850s also saw merit in various Broad Church positions. Although beginning his parliamentary career in 1832 as a Tory, he eventually became the popular embodiment of international Liberalism. He was four times prime minister of the United Kingdom. His political standing enabled him to gain a hearing for his theories on Homer, Christian apologetic, and a host of other issues.

We probably know more about Gladstone's reading than about that of any other figure in human history. He kept a diary in which he noted the books and articles examined each day, and its index runs to over 20,000 titles. The bulk of his personal book collection survives because he donated it as the core of a residential library at Hawarden in North Wales. Many are annotated in Gladstone's own hand. The British Library contains his voluminous correspondence, together with frequently copious notes on his reading. Although his taste was Catholic, his concerns were primarily with the humanities—with classics, history, biography, and literature—and supremely with theology.

Gladstone's "four doctors," he used to say, were Aristotle, Augustine, Dante, and Bishop Butler. Aristotle, whose *Nicomachean Ethics* was the chief item on the Oxford classical curriculum, shaped his analytical rigor as well as his understanding of the world. In the mid-1830s he also absorbed Aristotle's *Politics*. Augustine, many of whose treatises he studied in Latin at the same period, gave him his mature theological foundations. It was also in the 1830s that Gladstone became an enthusiast for Dante, who fused the Aristotelian worldview with Catholic doctrine in a beautiful synthesis. *The Analogy of Religion* (1736) by Bishop Joseph Butler vindicated Gladstone's conviction that providence ruled the world and supplied the germ of the idea that probability is "the guide of life" (Matthew, *Gladstone, 1809–1898*, 625).

In religion Gladstone devoured an immense range of contemporary publications, many of them ephemeral. His spiritual life was nurtured on past devotional writings such as those by Thomas à Kempis and Bishop Lancelot Andrewes. Edward Bouverie Pusey's writings impressed him, and **John Henry Newman**'s sermons as an Anglican profoundly moved him. The most important single theological work for him was *A Treatise on the Church of Christ* (1838) by William Palmer, a robust defense of Anglican claims to apostolicity. **Samuel Taylor Coleridge** encouraged Gladstone's early assertion of the duty of the state to establish the church, the French Liberal Catholic the Abbe de Lammenais reinforced his apologetic stance, and the Munich Catholic theologian Ignaz

Von Döllinger gave him hopes of a rapproachement with other branches of Christendom.

Homer dominated Gladstone's literary interests. The statesman read most of the current secondary literature on the poet, in German as well as in English, down to the 1860s but not beyond. Those who swayed him in the 1850s were those who supplied support for Gladstone's traditional views on the poet, but he was persuaded by such scholars as F. G. Welcker to liberalize his opinions in the following decade. Homer himself gave the statesman an unending source of anecdote and illustration. The influence of Gladstone's schoolfellow Arthur Hallam had formed his general taste. Italian literature, especially by Giacomo Leopardi and **Allessandro Manzoni**, appealed to him. Among near contemporaries in Britain, Sir **Walter Scott** was always his favorite novelist, and from the first publication of *The Idylls of the King* (1859), **Alfred Tennyson** was the equivalent poet.

Of political writers, Edmund Burke probably exercised the strongest enduring influence over Gladstone. **Alexis de Tocqueville** informed his political understanding, Adam Smith gave him the elements of political economy, and legal theorist A. V. Dicey, together with W.E.H. Lecky on the history of Ireland, contributed a great deal to his rationale for Home Rule in 1886. Gladstone's practical politics were formed more by personal influences, especially that of Sir Robert Peel, yet because of his bookishness, his superb speeches were studded with literary allusions.

ARCHIVES

Gladstone Papers, British Library. Includes political correspondence.
Glynne-Gladstone Manuscripts, Flintshire County Record Office. Family papers.

PRINTED SOURCES

Butler, P. *Gladstone: Church, State and Tractarianism: A Study of His Religious Ideas and Attitudes, 1809–1859* (Oxford: Clarendon Press, 1982).

Chadwick, O. "Young Gladstone and Italy," *Journal of Ecclesiastical History*, 30 (1979), 243–259; reprinted in Jagger, P. J. (ed.), *Gladstone, Politics and Religion* (London: Macmillan, 1985), 68–87.

Helmstadter, R. J. "Conscience and Politics: Gladstone's First Book." In B. L. Kinzer (ed.), *The Gladstonian Turn of Mind* (Toronto: University of Toronto Press, 1985), 3–42.

Matthew, H.C.G. *Gladstone, 1809–1898* (Oxford: Clarendon Press, 1997).

———. (ed.). *The Gladstone Diaries with Cabinet Minutes and Prime-Ministerial Correspondence*, 14 vols. (Oxford: Clarendon Press, 1968–1994). Vol. 14 contains index of "Gladstone's Reading."

Powell, J. "Small Marks and Instinctual Responses: A Study in the Uses of Gladstone's Marginalia," *Nineteenth Century Prose*, 19 (Special Issue, 1992), 1–17.

Ramm, A. "Gladstone as Man of Letters," *Nineteenth-Century Prose*, 17 (Winter 1989–1990), 1–46.

Turner, F. M. *The Greek Heritage in Victorian Britain* (New Haven, Conn.: Yale University Press, 1981). Contains analysis of Gladstone's engagement with Homer.

David W. Bebbington

GOETHE, JOHANN WOLFGANG VON (1749–1832). Johann Wolfgang Goethe was born in Frankfurt in 1749 and educated at Leipzig (1765–1768) and Strasbourg, where he obtained his license to practice law in 1770–1771. His appointment to the nobility, by the duke of Wiemar, Karl August, required his permanent residence at Weimar, where he was both a political and literary public figure. However, Goethe's legal and political careers were always secondary occupations; his first passion was devoted to art and aesthetics. Thus his greatest artistic achievements, beginning with *The Sorrows of Young Werther* (1774), were often performed against the backdrop of his legal practice and political duties. The greatest of his literary works is undoubtedly *Faust* (1808; 1831), because it is with *Faust* that Goethe explored the dramatic themes that would mark the German soul indelibly; Faust's "wager with the devil" would go on to haunt German writers, philosophers, and statesmen in ways unimaginable to the Weimar writer. It was a lengthy aesthetic project that he continued to work on throughout his life; in fact, the second part of the novel was only completed during the year before he died. Between the span of these two literary events, then, Goethe wrote numerous texts, ranging from a wide variety of literature to extensive treatises on color and the sciences. The most significant of these texts included: "Iphigenia in Tauris (1787)"; "Egmont" (1788), *Conversation of German Refugees: The Fairy Tale* (1795); *Wilhelm Meister's Apprenticeship* (1796); *Hermann and Dorothea* (1798); *Elective Affinities* (1810); *Theory of Colors* (1810); *Poetry and Truth* (1811); and *Wilhelm Meister's Wanderings* (1827).

The expansiveness of Goethe's literary vision can only be explained by his lifelong preoccupation with the Greco-Roman classical tradition. From the texts of Lucian and Aristotle, Goethe began to interrogate his own artistic endeavors, with a view to creating what he would understand as a thoroughly "German" literary project. Thus Aristotelian aesthetic theory pushed him to imitate with *Faust* what he believed the classical writer Sophocles had done with Oedipus. In other words, Goethe's attempt to create a German "Oedipus" derived extensively from his reading of Aristotle's *Poetics*. With *Faust*, Goethe hoped to develop a character who would trigger the "catharsis" he associated with the Greek trilogy *Oedipus at Kolonus*. Such a catharsis required a protagonist whose "tragic flaw" would lead him ultimately to redemption and justification.

Goethe's focus on classicism brought him to an extremely conflicted relationship with other writers and artists during the eighteenth century. Perhaps this conflict can be best understood through the lens of Goethe's reading of Kant. Kant proposed an interesting counterpoint to the Goethean literary legacy by focusing on the distinctly different properties of the subject and the object.

Like Goethe, Kant was preoccupied with the rethinking of a classical tradition within the context of German arts and letters. Furthermore, while Goethe agreed for the most part with Kant's understanding of the nature of objective knowledge—an understanding largely dependent on Aristotelian perception—Goethe was fascinated by Kant's theory of aesthetic judgment. In that theory, Kant's exploration of sublimity prompts the subject to lose sight of the boundaries between subject and object. Goethe had long explored this same theme of sublimity in his fictional characters' romantic feelings. Thus Goethe saw in Kant's work the contours and outline of his own aesthetic vision. But the Kant with whom Goethe became increasingly familiar was largely shaped through Goethe's correspondence and collaboration with Friedrich Schiller.

As a result, much of what scholars know about Kant's influence on Goethe comes about through an analysis of Goethe and Schiller's correspondence over the development of their collaborative journal *Die Horen*. Although Goethe's letters to Schiller attest to his lifelong interest in Kantian and classical aesthetics, the correspondence also provides a glimpse into how Goethe constructed aesthetic experience.

ARCHIVES

Weimarer Ausgabe. Goethe- und Schiller-Archiv, Weimar, Germany.
Goethe -und Schiller-Archiv. Bestandsverzeichnis, bearbeitet von Karl-Heinz Hahn, Weimar, 1961.
Bestandserschließung in Literaturarchiv. Arbeitsgrundsätze des Goethe- und Schiller-Archivs, hrsg. von Gerhard Schmid, München U.A.O., 1996.
The Speck Collection in the Beinecke Rare Books Library, Yale University.

PRINTED SOURCES

Dieckmann, Liselotte (trans.). *Correspondence between Goethe and Schiller, 1794–1805* (New York: Peter Lang, 1994).
Friedenthal, Richard. *Goethe: His Life and Times* (Cleveland and London: World Publishing Company, 1963).
Springarn, J. E. *Goethe's Literary Essays. A Selection in English* (New York: Frederick Ungar Publishing Company, 1964).

Kitty Millet

GOGOL, NIKOLAI VASILYEVICH (1809–1852).

Nikolai Gogol was born in Sorochintzy, in the Ukraine, in 1809 and educated at the Poltava District School (1819–1821) and at the School of Higher Studies in Nezhin (1821–1828). A playwright and novelist, Gogol was among the most influential figures in the nineteenth-century Russian literary renaissance.

Gogol's earliest influences were Ukrainian folklore, fairy tales, songs, and nativity puppet plays, all of which he was exposed to through his father, a writer of poems and comedic plays. At school he read voraciously and began acting as well as writing poetry and plays. Gogol's letters home reveal his familiarity with classical writers and Russian adaptations thereof, as when Gogol played

Creon in a production of Ozerov's adaptation of *Oedipus*. He was also influenced by Molière and acted in a production of *L'Avare*. The inevitable early influence, which was to be lifelong, was the great **Aleksandr Pushkin**; Gogol copied chapters of *Eugene Onegin* as they came out and decorated them with his own drawings. Gogol became supervisor of the student library and spent his own money to obtain subscriptions to Russian and German periodicals, also buying Friedrich Schiller's works in the original.

After graduating, Gogol moved to St. Petersburg and began his literary career. An early idyll, *Hanz Kuchelgarten*, shows the strong Romantic influence of **Lord Byron**'s *Childe Harold* and **François-René de Chateaubriand**'s *René* and ends with a glorification of Germany and of "the great **Goethe**." The critical failure of this work devastated Gogol and turned him away from poetry. Searching for a prose style, Gogol turned toward his roots in Ukrainian folkloric tales. His model for this planned series of tales was Orest Somov, who wrote *Tales of Hidden Treasures* and other works based on folk legends. Gogol's *Evenings on a Farm Near Dikanka* also reflects the influence of E.T.A. Hoffmann, Ludwig Tieck, and **Washington Irving**.

In 1831, flush with the success of *Evenings on a Farm Near Dikanka*, Gogol met the poets Vasily Zhukovsky and Pushkin. He would later say of Pushkin, "[N]ot a single line was written without my imagining him standing before me."

Gogol was fond of travel, and letters from his voyages reveal his continued voracious reading. Gogol mentions reading Samuel Richardson's *Clarissa Harlowe* on a 1832 trip to Moscow. In 1835, he ended a brief, unsatisfying career as a teacher and worked on his comic masterpiece *The Inspector General*, which was staged in 1836. Traveling and living abroad from 1836 to 1839, he read through Shakespeare's, Molière's, and **Walter Scott**'s works. In his great novel *Dead Souls* (1842), Gogol's narrator mentions "the portraits of Shakespeare, Ariosto, Fielding, Cervantes and Pushkin that hang before him." Homeric influence is also evident in *Dead Souls*, and Gogol's admiration for *The Odyssey* is documented in his essay "On *The Odyssey*." Gogol was also influenced by the axis between Eastern Orthodoxy, Roman Catholic mysticism, and neoplatonist thought, as evidenced by his references, in *Selected Passages from Correspondence with My Friends*, to *The Celestial Hierarchy* and *The Ecclesiastical Hierarchy* by Pseudo-Dionysius.

ARCHIVES

No substantial archival sources known to exist.

PRINTED SOURCES

Frantz, Philip E. (ed.). *Gogol: A Bibliography* (Ann Arbor, Mich.: Ardis, 1989).
Gippius, V. V. *Gogol*, Robert A. Maguire (ed. and trans.) (Ann Arbor, Mich.: Ardis, 1981).
Setchkarev, Vsevolod. *Gogol: His Life and Works* (New York: New York University Press, 1965).

Weiskopf, Mikhail. "The Bird Troika and the Chariot of the Soul: Plato and Gogol." In
    Susanne Fusso and Priscilla Meyer (eds. and trans.), *Essays on Gogol: Logos and
    the Russian Word* (Evanston, Ill.: Northwestern University Press, 1992).

                                                                    Douglas King

GORKY, MAKSIM (1868–1936). Maksim Gorky was born Aleksei Maksi-
movich Peshkov in Nizhni Novgorod (renamed Gorky in 1932). Gorky attended
Kumavino elementary school (1877–1878) as his only formal schooling and
became an influential voice of the Soviet revolution and a founder of socialist
realism in fiction and drama.

   The death of his father when Gorky was only three brought him to live with
his maternal grandparents. His grandfather taught him to read using the Slavonic
psalter and the Old Testament, mainly the Psalms. His grandmother taught the
boy the lives of the saints and other religious folk ballads. Other early literary
experiences included *Robinson Crusoe* and **Andersen**'s fairy tales.

   Apprenticed at age 10 to a shoemaker and then to a draftsman, Gorky ran
away and was hired on a steamboat; the ship's chef befriended Gorky and read
with him: **Walter Scott**'s *Ivanhoe*, Henry Fielding's *Tom Jones*, and **Nikolay
Gogol**'s *Taras Bulba* and *Dead Souls*. Other informal teachers followed. Returning briefly to his draftsman's apprenticeship, Gorky was given books by a
tailor's wife, including **Stendhal**, Greenwood's *A True History of a Little Waif*,
and **Honoré de Balzac**'s *Eugenie Grandet*. An officer's widow exposed the boy
to the poems of Pierre Beranger and to Fyodor Tyutchev, Sergei Aksakov, **Ivan
Turgenev**'s *Notes of a Sportsman*, and **Aleksandr Pushkin**. Gorky was bored
with chivalric romances, such as Prince Meshchersky's *The Mysteries of Petersburg*, and sought on his own richer fare: **Fyodor Dostoyevsky**'s "House of
the Dead," **Lev Tolstoy**'s *Three Deaths*, Edmond de Goncourt's *The Brothers
Zemganno*, works by **Charles Dickens**, **Herbert Spencer**, **Heinrich Heine**,
Paul de Kock, Ponson de Terraile, and **Gustave Flaubert**'s "Temptation of St.
Anthony," "A Simple Heart," and *Madame Bovary*.

   Living in Samara in 1895–1896, Gorky wrote a column for the local newspaper, which carried excerpts from **Friedrich Nietzsche**'s "Thus Spake Zarathustra," said to be his "favorite bedside book." He evinced familiarity with a
tremendous range of writers, including **Edgar Allan Poe**, Shakespeare, **Lord
Byron**, **William Thackeray**, Charles Dickens, Friedrich Schiller, **Johann von
Goethe**, and **Guy de Maupassant**.

   In 1898 Gorky began a correspondence—to evolve into a friendship—with
Anton Chekhov and placed himself under the influence of the acknowledged
master of drama and short fiction. Chekhov introduced Gorky to Tolstoy, who
also gave the younger writer pointed critiques of his work. Later Gorky would
write memoirs of both men in his *Reminiscences* (1919–1922).

   At Chekhov's exhortation, Gorky began writing plays to be performed by the
Moscow Art Theatre under **Konstantin Stanislavsky**. From this partnership

came the first production of Gorky's dramatic masterpiece *The Lower Depths* (1902).

The other predominant strain of influence in Gorky's life and thought was the revolutionary. He was, of course, thoroughly familiar with the works of **Karl Marx** and **Friedrich Engels**, as well as those of his Vladimir Lenin, with whom he had a turbulent and complex friendship.

ARCHIVES

The Gorky Institute of World Literature, Moscow.

PRINTED SOURCES

Barratt, Andrew, and Barry P. Scherr (eds. and trans.). *Selected Letters* (Oxford: Clarendon Press, 1997).
Borras, F. M. *Maxim Gorky the Writer* (Oxford: Clarendon Press, 1967).
Kaun, Alexander. *Maxim Gorky and His Russia* (New York: Benjamin Blom, Inc., 1968).
Levin, Dan. *Stormy Petrel: The Life and Work of Maxim Gorky* (New York: Appleton-Century, 1965).
Weil, Irwin. *Gorky: His Literary Development and Influence on Soviet Intellectual Life* (New York: Random House, 1966).

Douglas King

GRIMM, JACOB LUDWIG CARL (1785–1863), and GRIMM, WILHELM (1786–1859). Jacob and Wilhelm Grimm were born in Hanau. Both studied jurisprudence at the University of Marburg (Wilhelm, 1803–1806; Jacob, 1802, broke off his studies). The Grimm brothers became highly influential by collecting, translating, and editing German medieval literature. They are the founders of German philology.

The Grimm brothers had access to Romantic literature and writers early in their lives, thanks to their father's extensive library (Denecke, 10). They got to know representatives of German Romanticism such as Clemens Brentano and Bettina von Arnim while studying in Marburg. Over the years they built up their personal libraries, which included more than 7,000 books and papers from all fields of knowledge.

Friedrich Karl von Savigny, Jacob's teacher of the history of law, encouraged their literary interests. In Savigny's library, Jacob discovered the inspiring *Sammlung von Minnesingern aus dem schwäbischen Zeitpuncte* (1758–1759), a collection of minnesongs, edited by the Swiss scholars Johann Jacob Bodmer and Johann Jacob Breitinger, a book Jacob kept reading throughout his life (Papp, 161; Jacob Grimm, 20). From this point on, the Grimm brothers began collecting and editing medieval manuscripts. Ludwig Tieck's *Minnelieder aus dem schwäbischen Zeitalter* (1803) became a model for the textual presentation and similar projects: As an editor Tieck strove for the deduction of the literal sense, for the consideration of meter and rhyme and the partition of verses and strophes, and finally for the systematic structure of texts by means of modern punctuation. In later years the Grimm brothers distanced themselves from Tieck's methods.

The efforts of German Romanticism to revalue the Middle Ages and to focus on the cultural heritage of the common people instead of antique literature became influential for the brothers' collecting and editing German legends and fairy tales. The *Kinder- und Hausmärchen* (vol. 1, 1812; vol. 2, 1815) resulted from oral narrations. Also the *Deutsches Wörterbuch* (16 vols., 1852–1960) and the *Deutsche Grammatik* (4 vols., 1819–1837) are inspired by their investigations on national traditions.

ARCHIVES

Brüder Grimm-Museum, Kassel. Biographical manuscripts, first editions, reprints.
Kreismuseum Haldensleben, Haldensleben. Books, photographies, handwritten notes, parts of the literary bequest, parts of Wilhelm's, Jacob's and Herman's library.
Staatsbibliothek Preußischer Kulturbesitz, Berlin. Literary bequest of Jacob Grimm.

PRINTED SOURCES

Denecke, Ludwig and Irmgard Teitge. *Die Bibliothek der Brüder Grimm: Annotiertes Verzeichnis des festgestellten Bestandes* (Stuttgart: Wissenschaftliche Verlagsgesellschaft Stuttgart, 1989).
Gerstner, Hermann. *Brüder Grimm mit Selbstzeugnissen und Bilddokumenten* (Reinbek: Rowohlt, 1994).
———. Gerstner, Hermann. *Die Brüder Grimm* (Gerabronn: Hohenloher Druck- und Verlagshaus, 1972).
Grimm, Jacob. "Selbstbiographie." In *Jacob Grimm/Wilhelm Grimm: Schriften und Reden* (Stuttgart: Reclam, 1985), 15–34.
Grimm, Wilhelm. "Selbstbiographie." In *Jacob Grimm/Wilhelm Grimm: Schriften und Reden* (Stuttgart: Reclam, 1985), 163–186.
Papp, Edgar. "Jacob und Wilhelm Grimm und die Erforschung der mittelalterlichen Literatur." In Wilfried Kürschner and Edgar Papp (eds.), *Jacob und Wilhelm Grimm: Fachwissenschaftliche und fachdidaktische Beiträge zur Werk- und Wirkungsgeschichte* (Cloppenburg: Runge, 1989), 161–182.

Ernst Grabovszki

GUIZOT, FRANÇOIS-PIERRE-GUILLAUME (1787–1874). François Guizot, a native of the southern French town of Nîmes, lost his father to the 1793–1794 Terror. His family then emigrated to Geneva where he received a strict Calvinist upbringing. Having completed his secondary education, he left for Paris in 1805 to work in journalism. Capitalizing on his superb intellectual capacities, he also joined academic circles and, at the early age of 25, received a professorship in modern French history at the Sorbonne. Under the Bourbon Restoration, Guizot, sponsored by Pierre-Paul Royer-Collard, created the Parti des Doctrinaires, a political organization promoting an English-style constitutional monarchy. Noticed by Prime Minister Elie Decazes, he occupied various administrative positions at the Ministry of the Interior and the Ministry of Justice between 1816 and 1820. Considered too moderate by the Ultraroyalists, he lost his position upon the fall of his protector's cabinet. He returned to the Sorbonne but, enraging Ultras with his antiabsolutist pronouncements, was banned from teaching in 1822. The voice of economic liberalism and an active commentator of social affairs, he used his column in *Le Globe* to excoriate reactionary king Charles X. Elected to Parliament in January 1830 with his Parti de la Résistance, he vociferously attacked Prime Minister Jules-Armand de Polignac's conservative policies and was instrumental in the success of the July 1830 revolution. His party became dominant after 1832, Guizot using his power as Minister of Public Education to organize public communal schools in 1833–1837. Elected to the Académie Française in 1836, he was also Minister of Foreign Affairs between 1840 and 1847, forging close ties with Great Britain and thus paving the way for the later Entente Cordiale.

The true ideologue behind Louis-Philippe's government, Guizot favored the expansion of industrial capitalism while granting token political or social liberties to the disenfranchised peasantry and nascent urban proletariat. Criticized from his right by radical Royalists as well as from his left by Republicans, his rule became increasingly authoritarian. In January 1848 he banned all political parties, thus triggering a rebellion that even his resignation would not quell. The rebellion evolved into a full-fledged revolution leading to Louis-Philippe's abdication and the establishment of the short-lived Second Republic. Exiled in Belgium and later in Great Britain, Guizot returned to France in 1849, spending the last years of his life in semi-isolation devoted to the writing of his *Mémoires pour servir à l'histoire de mon temps*.

It was during his 1822 forced retirement that Guizot revised and published his major works (*Histoire de la Révolution d'Angleterre*, *Histoire de la Civilisation en Europe*, *Histoire de la Civilisation en France*, and *Histoire des origines de gouvernement représentatif*). These rigorously critical studies, focusing on the history of ideas rather than on specific individuals or events, described French history as a natural movement toward a perfect constitutional monarchy integrating some of the achievements of the bourgeois phase of the Great Revolution while relying on the electoral privileges of rich landowners, merchants, and industrialists. It was in large part against such ideas that later French historiographic thought evolved, **Alexis de Tocqueville** emphasizing the role of Divine Providence in human affairs and **Jules Michelet** extolling the people's triumph in liberty and republicanism.

ARCHIVES

Archives Nationales, Paris.

PRINTED SOURCES

Coco, M. *François Guizot* (Naples: Guida, 1983).
Johnson, D.W.J. *Guizot: Aspects of French History, 1787–1874* (Toronto: University of Toronto Press, 1963).

O'Connor, M. C. *The Historical Thought of François Guizot* (Washington, D.C.: Catholic University of America Press, 1955).
Rosanvallon, P. *Le Moment Guizot* (Paris: Gallimard, 1985).

Laurent Ditmann

H

HAGGARD, HENRY RIDER (1856–1925). Henry Rider Haggard was born at Bradenham, the Haggard family estate, in Norfolk, England in 1856. Unlike most of his brothers, he did not attend public schools or university. Rather, Haggard's appointment as a government official in South Africa was the most influential experience in shaping his later life as a writer and public servant.

In 1875 at the age of 19 Haggard sailed to Africa. The young man's early impressions of the landscape, learning the Zulu language, and witnessing native rituals would later become romanticized representations in his fiction. Haggard was among the British servants to investigate the Transvaal crisis between the Boers and the Zulus. As the annexation of the Transvaal became official in 1877, the Union Jack was lifted over the region for the first time by Haggard himself. After leaving his administrative position in the colonial government to get married, Haggard turned his interests to ostrich farming in Natal. The Boer rebellion in 1880, however, squelched his farming plans, and he returned to England.

While Haggard achieved literary fame with the adventure novel *King Solomon's Mines* (1885), several less successful books preceded the work. He started his writing career with travel articles, a commentary on the contemporary African situation, and several realistic novels. None, however, met the success of his rugged adventure tale about three male Britons in search of diamonds. Colonial Africa deeply interested the reading public. Diamonds had become a large industry after their discovery on the banks of the Orange River in 1866. Additionally, *King Solomon's Mines* appeared shortly after the Berlin Conference on African Affairs which decided rules for dividing borders within Africa (Cohen, 90).

Haggard's powerful adventures undoubtedly owed something to the strong impression *Robinson Crusoe* made on him as a boy (Ellis, 24), but **Robert Louis Stevenson**'s *Treasure Island* (1883) gave Haggard the concept for *King Solo-*

mon's Mines. One of Haggard's brothers challenged the novelist to write something better than Stevenson's book. Without delay, Haggard began his novel of African adventure, borrowing the idea of a treasure map from *Treasure Island.* He finished it in six weeks, and his publisher, Cassell, distributed many broadsheets that stated: "King Solomon's Mines—The Most Amazing Story Ever Written." The novel became an immediate sensation.

In 1887 Haggard followed the success of *King Solomon's Mines* with *She* and *Allan Quatermain.* In these novels he capitalized on the formula of male adventurers who discover primitive civilizations deep within Africa. The same year Haggard also wrote a realistic novel, *Jess,* which was serialized in *Cornhill* magazine. While this novel's ostrich farm setting comes from Haggard's own experience of trying to farm during the Boer rebellion of 1880, it also shows the influence of Olive Schreiner's *Story of an African Farm* (1884) (Etherington, 27–28).

At the turn of the century English agricultural reform became one of Haggard's passions, and he expressed his ideals for farming in several nonfiction works, including *A Farmer's Year* (1898). He pushed for the government to take an active role in preserving the country's declining agricultural tradition. His official appointment as Dominions Commissioner also took him around the globe surveying numerous British territories. In 1919 Haggard was knighted for his service to the empire. Haggard continued to write for the rest of his life, leaving behind over 50 works of fiction and nonfiction. His early adventure novels have remained the most popular.

ARCHIVES

Haggard's papers are located in the Norfolk Record Office, Norwich. Additional correspondence is located at the Lockwood Memorial Library, University of Buffalo, and the Columbia University Library.

PRINTED SOURCES

Ching-Liang Low, Gail. *White Skins/Black Masks: Representation and Colonialism* (London: Routledge, 1996). Usefully explores Haggard's adventure novels in a historical context.
Cohen, Morton. *Rider Haggard: His Life and Work* (London: Macmillan, 1968).
Ellis, Peter Berresford. *H. Rider Haggard: A Voice from the Infinite* (London: Routledge & Kegan Paul, 1978).
Etherington, Norman. *Rider Haggard* (Boston: Twayne, 1984).
Katz, Wendy R. *Rider Haggard and the Fiction of Empire: A Critical Study of British Imperial Fiction* (Cambridge: Cambridge University Press, 1987).

Albert C. Sears

HAMSUN, KNUT (1859–1952). Knut Hamsun, Norwegian novelist, dramatist, poet, and winner of the Nobel Prize in 1920, was born in Lom in south central Norway as Knud Pederson in 1859. He changed his name several times during his youth and eventually settled on Knut Hamsun. When he was two, his family moved to Harmaroy in Northland, above the Arctic Circle, where he spent his childhood. Hamsun started writing for publication in his teens but did not receive significant literary notice until 1890 with the publication of *Hunger*. This novel, and 10 others that he produced in the next three decades (including *Mysteries* in 1892, *Victoria* in 1898, *Dreamers* in 1904, and *Growth of the Soil* in 1917), had a formative influence on the modern novel. His distinctive approach to the novel, which involved psychological complexity, combinations of humor and pathos, and a lyrical but simple writing style, brought him recognition as an important Western literary figure, a position somewhat tarnished by his support for the Nazis during World War II.

Hamsun was largely self-educated through reading. He had most likely been taught to read by his parents. A letter from his father to his mother, written when his older brothers were young, urged her not to "forget to test the boys in reading" (quoted in Ferguson, 8). There was little to read in the household, however; some psalm books, perhaps a Bible, and a few newspapers. He received some schooling from "traveling schools," which came to remote parts of Norway to offer rural children at least the rudiments of an education. At age 9, Hamsun was forced to leave his family home and work for an uncle in the nearby town. While the uncle was harsh and demanding in the services he expected of the young boy, he also had been the organizer of the town library, which provided Hamsun with considerable reading material, especially on Norwegian literature. After leaving his uncle's home at age 14, he followed a path of itinerant work for the next 11 years that took him through Norway and on two trips to the United States. In various places he was befriended by individuals who supported his literary ambitions and also gave him access to personal libraries in which he expanded his reading to the classics, ancient history, other European literatures, and a wide range of other topics.

The earliest literary influences on Hamsun were Norwegian folktales collected by Peter Christen Asbjørnsen and Jorgen Moe, **Grimms'** fairy tales, and the writings of the most popular Norwegian writer of the time, Bjørnsterne Bjørnson (1832–1910). Bjørnson, one of Norway's most prominent nineteenth-century writers, wrote of rural life and featured peasants prominently in his plays and novels. He also experimented with a shorter, sparer writing style than was the fashion and effectively introduced idiomatic speech in his writings. To Hamsun, he and Kristofer Janson, another Norwegian novelist and playwright and early influence, stood out from other writers in addressing "the larger questions . . . [which] concern human beings" (*Selected Letters*, 1:46). **Henrik Ibsen** also made an impression on the young Hamsun, especially the social criticism expressed in his plays. Hamsun eventually turned away from such direct treatment of social issues toward a more aesthetic approach, but many of his works bear traces of Ibsen. Hamsun also read widely in other European literatures in his youth and by his early twenties gave critical talks and wrote articles about such writers as **Balzac**, **Dostoyevsky**, **Flaubert**, **Nietzsche**, **Whitman**, **Tolstoy**,

Strindberg, Lie, Kielland, **Emerson**, and **Twain**. They represented the Romantic, realist, and naturalist writings trends of the nineteenth century, and Hamsun engaged with them all as he strove to develop a unique style as a writer. In addition to the Norwegian writers, possibly Dostoyevsky, with his emphasis on psychology, had the greatest impact on him. Tolstoy and Emerson, on the other hand, represented the writers whom he disliked for what he considered their simplistic moralism. Of American writers he identified most closely with Mark Twain—in part because of their comparable experience as self-educated writers but also because of the humor and skepticism expressed in his works.

ARCHIVES

National Library, Oslo Division, Norway, has a large collection of Hamsun materials including correspondence; manuscripts, drafts, and fragments of his novels; copies of articles and lectures; and manuscripts about him.

PRINTED SOURCES

Ferguson, Robert. *Enigma: The Life of Knut Hamsun* (New York: Farrar, Straus and Giroux, 1987). Contains descriptions of important archival collections and secondary literature on Hamsun. There is no one preeminent collection, but many Hamsun papers are available in scattered repositories.
Hamsun, Tore. *Knut Hamsun* (Oslo: Gyldendahl Norsk Forlag, 1959). Revised version of Knut Hamsun, *Min Far* (1952). This biography, by Hamsun's oldest son, contains a large amount of material on Hamsun's childhood.
Langfeldt, Gabriel, and Ørnulv Ødegard. *Den rettpsykiatriske erklaering om Knut Hamsun* (Oslo: Gyldendal, 1978). A report on Hamsun by two psychiatrists to determine his fitness to stand trial for his pro-Nazi stance during World War II. Includes material from interviews with him.
Naess, Harald. *Knut Hamsun* (Boston: Twayne Publishers, 1984). Contains critical essays on his writing and a brief biographical sketch.
Naess, Harald, and James McFarlane (eds.). *Selected Letters: Knut Hamsun.* Vol. 1, *1879–1898* (Norwich, England: Norvik Press, 1990).
———. *Selected Letters.* Vol. 2, *1898–1952* (Norwich, England: Norvik Press, 1998).
Skavlan, Einar. *Knut Hamsun*, 2 vols. (Oslo: Gyldendal Norsk Forlag, 1934). Classic biography in Norwegian.

Kathryn Wagnild Fuller

HARDY, THOMAS (1840–1928). Thomas Hardy was born in Higher Bockhampton, near Dorchester, Dorset, and educated at the Dorchester village school (1848–1850), Dorchester British School (1850–1853), and Dorchester Academy (1853–1856), then apprenticed to a Dorchester architect (1856–1860). Hardy was confirmed a member of the Church of England at Stinsford and actively practiced his faith through Bible study and church attendance until about 1864, when his views shifted toward agnosticism: "The erosion of Hardy's religious convictions was . . . a gradual process rather than the consequence of a single moment" (Millgate, 91). Hardy left architecture to pursue literature, but his novels provoked Victorian audiences with their frank treatment of sexuality and their criticism of social mores. His return to poetry, which he considered a higher art, produced seven volumes of verse.

Under his mother's influence, Hardy read widely from childhood. He enjoyed her gifts of a translation of *The Works of Vergil* by John Dryden and *Rasselas* by Samuel Johnson and admired the Romantic poets, particularly **William Wordsworth**, **John Keats**, and **Percy Bysshe Shelley**. Wordsworth's "The Excursion" and "Ode: Intimations of Immortality" and Keats's "Ode to a Nightingale" provided early models for Hardy the poet, but his preference for Shelley shows in his imagery, philosophy, and allusions to Shelley's work. While apprenticed to architect John Hicks, he read the New Testament in Greek and studied the classics, including Homer, Sophocles, and Virgil (Gibson, 14). Hardy's appreciation of the Bible influenced the poetic language and imagery of his novels; he was particularly fond of the stories of Saul and David (Pinion, 273). As a young man in London, Hardy read the work of **John Stuart Mill**, **John Henry Newman**, and a translation of *A General View of Positivism* by **Auguste Comte**. He was a self-proclaimed "born bookworm" who read widely in British literature, as allusions in his work to Shakespeare, Bunyan, and Milton suggest (Pinion, 264–265, 274). Hardy was also well read in contemporary literature, and his scientific view of life was partly shaped by *The Origin of Species* by **Charles Darwin** and the essays of **Matthew Arnold**, **Thomas Carlyle**, and **Walter Pater**. Of Victorian poets, he admired the poetry of **Robert Browning** and **Alfred Tennyson**, especially Browning's "The Statue and the Bust" and Tennyson's *In Memoriam*, and was among the first to recognize the merit of Algernon Charles Swinburne, whose criticisms of Victorian morality Hardy endorsed: "When they met in June 1905, Swinburne could quote with amusement from Scottish newspaper: 'Swinburne planteth, Hardy watereth, and Satan giveth the increase' " (Hardy, 349). Hardy's novels suggest the important influence of **George Eliot**, with whom he shared a love of pastoral settings and characters, religious skepticism, and a belief in the importance of human actions (Pinion, 15–23).

ARCHIVES

Thomas Hardy Papers, Birmingham City Museum and Art Gallery.

PRINTED SOURCES

Gibson, James. *Thomas Hardy: A Literary Life* (New York: St. Martin's Press, 1996).
Hardy, Florence Emily. *The Life of Thomas Hardy, 1840–1928* (London: Macmillan, 1962; New York: St. Martin's Press, 1962).
Millgate, Michael. *Thomas Hardy: A Biography* (New York: Random, 1982).
Page, Norman. *Thomas Hardy: The Writer and His Background* (London: Bell & Hyman, 1980).
Pinion, F. B. *Hardy the Writer: Surveys and Assessments* (New York: St. Martin's Press, 1990).

Nancy Anne Marck

HARRIS, JOEL CHANDLER (1848–1908). Joel Chandler Harris was born to Mary Harris, whose lover abandoned her after their son's birth. Mary Harris moved to Eatonton, Georgia, where Joel attended Hillsborough Academy (1856– 1862). Perhaps because of his illegitimacy, Harris was not religious for most of his life, although his wife was Catholic, and he converted to Catholicism before his death. In 1862, he left school to spend four years as a printer's apprentice to Joseph Addison Turner, a planter with a weekly newspaper. Shy and a loner, Harris sought entertainment listening to the folktales of Turner's slaves, which he reprinted in the *Atlanta Constitution* upon joining its staff in 1876. Harris created "Uncle Remus," a former slave who tells of Brer Rabbit, a trickster figure who outsmarts Brer Fox and Brer Bear, the more powerful animals. While the framing device of the Remus character is criticized for its stereotypical, patronizing depiction of African Americans, the Brer Rabbit stories themselves are parables of resistance, in that the weaker animals best their stronger oppressors. Harris's reputation is controversial: **W.E.B. Du Bois** saw him as a well-meaning but misguided exploiter of African American culture, while other scholars credit him with preserving valuable nineteenth-century folklore, faulting the grotesque illustrations in the Remus books for the popular perception of Remus as a foolish old man. Harris himself believed in African American intellectual inferiority at the same time that he recognized the sophistication of the folklore and worked to preserve it. He popularized the American genre of plantation nostalgia but also recorded a valuable African American oral tradition.

In addition to the folk legends of Turner's slaves, Harris took advantage of his employer's library and read Chaucer, **Dickens**, Sir Thomas Browne, the **Grimms**' fairy tales, *The Arabian Nights*, Shakespeare, Milton, Swift, Addison and Steele, Pope, **Thackeray**, **Emerson**, and **Harriet Beecher Stowe**'s *Uncle Tom's Cabin*. He tried to write poetry in the style of **Poe** but abandoned that pursuit in favor of journalism as a young man. Following the publication of the first Remus collection in 1880, Harris received attention from folklore scholars such as Major J. W. Powell, T. F. Crane, and Joseph Jacobs, who were interested in the origins of the tales, the products of cross-fertilization among African, European, and Native American legend. Harris subsequently spent years researching folklore (one Remus collection, the 1883 *Nights with Uncle Remus*, bears Harris's own scholarly introduction) before giving it up as a serious pursuit and eventually lampooning it in later volumes. Harris was familiar with contemporary fiction and corresponded with George Washington Cable and **Mark Twain**, but stage fright prevented him from making public appearances despite offers from Twain that they tour together.

ARCHIVES

Joel Chandler Harris Collection, Special Collections, Robert W. Woodruff Library, Emory University. Manuscripts and letters.

PRINTED SOURCES

Bickley, R. Bruce, Jr. *Critical Essays on Joel Chandler Harris* (Boston: G.K. Hall and Co., 1981). Contemporary and recent criticism and reviews.

————. *Joel Chandler Harris*, Twayne's United States Author Series 308 (Boston: Twayne Publishers, 1978).

Cousins, Paul M. *Joel Chandler Harris: A Biography* (Baton Rouge: Louisiana State University Press, 1968).

Deborah Banner

HAWTHORNE, NATHANIEL (1804–1864). Nathaniel Hawthorne was born in Salem, Massachusetts, the city in which his ancestors had lived since the seventeenth century. His father died when he was 4 years old, and the family went to live with his mother's brothers. Hawthorne's education in Salem at the school of Joseph Emerson Worcester was interrupted when he injured his leg at the age of 9 and did not fully recover until he was 12, although Worcester sometimes visited him at home. He later attended Samuel H. Archer's school in Salem, then was taught at home by a tutor, Benjamin L. Oliver. From 1821 to 1825, Hawthorne attended Bowdoin College in Brunswick, Maine. He was not a distinguished student, excelling only in composition.

After graduation, Hawthorne was determined to become a writer. His first novel, *Fanshawe* (1828), was printed anonymously at his own expense. After this unremarkable first effort, he went on to produce important stories such as "My Kinsman, Major Molineux" and "Young Goodman Brown" in the 1830s. Hawthorne's best known works, *The Scarlet Letter* (1850) and *The House of Seven Gables* (1851), earned him a lasting reputation as one of the most important writers of allegorical fiction. His work had a powerful influence on symbolic fiction in later American writers.

When Hawthorne was a boy, he read Edmund Spenser's *The Faerie Queen* (1590), James Thomson's *Castle of Indolence* (1748), an allegory against laziness written in Spenserian stanzas, Shakespeare's plays, and John Bunyan's *Pilgrim's Progress* (1678). Later in life he wrote an appreciation of Bunyan, who, Hawthorne claimed, was to be admired for endowing allegorical characters with convincing human traits, much as Hawthorne himself accomplished. As an adolescent, Hawthorne also read *Mysteries of Udolpho* (1794) by Ann Radcliffe, a melodramatic dark Gothic novel complete with a kidnapping and a gloomy castle, and *1001 Arabian Nights*. Hawthorne at one point commented that he liked Sir **Walter Scott**, Henry Fielding's *Tom Jones* (1749) and *Amelia* (1751), a somber work about the evils of society, Jean-Jacques Rousseau's *Heloise* (1761), Matthew Gregory Lewis's romantic works, and other English Gothic romantic literature that he could find in the library. Bowdoin College did not teach literature, except for the Holy Bible, so after college Hawthorne determined to read fiction so he could learn how to write it. He also took time to read nonfiction, such as histories of early New England, one of which was Thomas Hutchinson's three-volume set *History of the Colony and Province of Massachusetts Bay* (1764–1828). Certainly Hawthorne familiarized himself also with the accounts of the Salem witch trials, using a curse mentioned therein as a plot point in *The House of Seven Gables*.

Late in life Hawthorne was found reading Milton, Pope, **Dickens**, and Defoe, while returning to other favorites such as Shakespeare, Cervantes, and Scott and acquainting himself with fellow contemporary American writers. The combination of religious allegory, traditional romance, and regional color afforded Hawthorne a unique place in American literature.

ARCHIVES

Hawthorne-Manning Collection, Essex Institute, Salem, Massachusetts. Letters and documents.
Pierpont Morgan Library, New York City. Almost complete manuscripts.

PRINTED SOURCES

Miller, Edwin Haviland. *Salem Is My Dwelling Place: A Life of Nathaniel Hawthorne* (Iowa City: University of Iowa Press, 1991).
Turner, Arlin. *Nathaniel Hawthorne: A Biography* (New York: Oxford University Press, 1980).

Rose Secrest

HEGEL, GEORG WILHELM FRIEDRICH (1770–1831). Georg Hegel was born in Stuttgart on August 27, 1770. He was early well trained in classical and German literature before entering the Tübingen Stift in 1788, where he developed close friendships with the poet Johann Christian Friedrich Hölderlin (1770–1843) and the philosopher **Friedrich Wilhelm Joseph von Schelling** (1775–1854), both of whom stimulated his continuing study of the Greek and Latin classics, Jean-Jacques Rousseau (1712–1778), Johann Christoph Friedrich Schiller (1759–1805), and **Johann Wolfgang von Goethe** (1749–1832). On Hölderlin's suggestion he began a study of Immanuel Kant (1724–1804) and **Johann Gottlieb Fichte** (1762–1814) in 1794 and in 1801 moved to the University of Jena, where he finished the draft of his *The Phenomenology of Spirit* in 1806. Serving for a short while as a journalist, he undertook a position at Nürnberg as the headmaster of the gymnasium, completing his *The Science of Logic* before moving to Heidelberg as professor of philosophy in 1816. In 1818 he began teaching at the University of Berlin, where he remained until his death of cholera on November 14, 1831. During the Berlin years he published *The Philosophy of Right* (1821). His Berlin lectures on the fine arts, the history of philosophy, the philosophy of religion, and the philosophy of history all appeared posthumously in the 1830s.

A polymath like his contemporary Goethe, Hegel's work was stimulated by close reading in many areas. First among these were the Greek and Latin classics (Hegel had studied Latin under his mother's direction prior to his entrance into primary school), large sections of which he had committed to memory. His classical learning was intensified by the like interests of Hölderlin and Schelling, among others, particularly on aesthetic, moral, and political topics. His appropriation of classical authors, above all, Plato whom he read early and carefully, is perhaps best reflected in his well-known exegesis of Sophocles's *Antigone* in

The Phenomenology of Spirit. As a young theological student he was attracted to Gotthold Ephraim Lessing (1729–1781), Friedrich Heinrich Jacobi (1743–1819), and Moses Mendelssohn (1729–1786), and his first approach to Baruch Spinoza (1632–1677) must certainly have been mediated through the controversy over the Dutch philosopher at the time. While at Tübingen he began his reading of Johann Gottfried Herder (1744–1803), his intensive study of Christian von Wolff (1679–1754), and above all of Kant, with whose thought Hegel's earliest writing demonstrates close engagement. How much of his theological training in his first years at Tübingen was formative is difficult to ascertain. Certainly the most important of his Tübingen teachers was Gottlob Christian Storr (1746–1805). Much more complex is Hegel's relationship to Schelling, whose philosophical system he affirmed and distinguished from that of Fichte in an early work in 1801 but from whom, after 1807, he clearly parted, as he did from central influences on Schelling such as Jacob Boehme (1575–1624). Although atextual and common for its impact on many thinkers of the day, the French Revolution and the role of **Napoléon** served as important stimulations for Hegel's thoughts on freedom. From the publication of the *Phenomenology* in 1806 Hegel continued to be inspired by a great number of his contemporaries. Particularly to be noted in this respect, for example, are his Heidelberg colleagues Heinrich Eberhardt Gottlob Paulus (1751–1861), Karl Daub (1765–1836), and George Friedrich Creuzer (1771–1858).

ARCHIVES

The Hegel-Archiv, formerly at Bonn, is now in Bochum. For details, see the ongoing critical edition of the *Gesammelte Werke*, edited under the direction of Walter Jaeschke (Hamburg: F. Meiner, 1968–).

PRINTED SOURCES

Crites, Stephen. *Dialectic and Gospel in the Development of Hegel's Thinking* (University Park: Pennsylvania State University Press, 1998).
Haering, Theodor Lorenz. *Hegel, sein Wollen und sein Werk; eine chronologische Entwicklungsgeschichte der Gedanken und der Sprache Hegels*, 2 vols. (Leipzig: B. G. Teubner, 1929, 1938).
Harris, H. S. *Hegel's Development*, 2 vols (Oxford: Oxford University Press, 1972, 1983).
Steinhauer, Kurt, and Gitta Hausen. *Hegel Bibliography: Background Material on the International Reception of Hegel within the Context of the History of Philosophy: Hegel Bibliographic: Materialen zur Geschichte der internationalen Hegel-Rezeption und zur Philosophie-Geschichte* (München and New York: K. G. Saur, 1998).
Taylor, Charles. *Hegel* (Cambridge: Cambridge University Press, 1975).
Wiedmann, Franz. *Georg Wilhelm Friedrich Hegel in Sebstzeugnissen und Bilddokumenten* (Reinbeck bei Hamburg: Rowohlt, 1965).

Peter C. Erb

HEINE, HEINRICH (1797–1856). Heinrich Heine was born in Düsseldorf as Harry Heine; he attended the Lyceum (1810–1814), where he became acquainted with French language and culture. Heine studied law in Bonn, Göttingen, and Berlin (1819–1825). From 1831 onward he lived in Paris. Born as a Jew, Heine converted to evangelic confession in 1825 (Christian Johann Heinrich) in order to be able to take up a career as a lawyer.

Early poetical inspirations came from the salon of Rahel Varnhagen in Berlin, where he learned of **Goethe** and became familiar with **Georg Wilhelm Friedrich Hegel**'s philosophy of history. There he also became acquainted with representatives of Jewish thought, including the historical writings of Leopold Zunz. Heine became a member of the "Verein für Cultur und Wissenschaft der Juden" and endeavored to establish a science of Jewish culture, expounded in his *Rabbi von Bacherach* (1840) (Hauschild, 75; Trilse-Finkelstein, 64).

Heine's early works were inspired by German Romanticism. The major figure to lead Heine to Romanticism was Friedrich Schlegel, whose oriental themes and motives remained present even in his late works. The early poems are also influenced by the "Gesellschaftslyrik" of the eighteenth century, Goethe, Johann Gottfried Herder's collection of folk songs, medieval poetry, Francesco Petrarca, and **Lord Byron**.

Heine's concept of history was formed to a great extent by Hegel. As a student Heine attended Hegel's lecture on "Philosophie der Rechtsgeschichte." Hegel's theories regarding the profanation of nature and a world history not determined by divine influences left their mark on the *Harzreise* (1826), on the travel narrations, and on *Ideen. Das Buch Le Grand* (1827). In this work Heine connects individual biography with world history. Heine was attracted by Hegel's subversive political role and observed the development of his thought. In 1842 he carefully read *Philosophie der Geschichte* and considered the Junghegeliander from **Ludwig Feuerbach** to **Karl Marx** to be the most powerful leaders of the social movement. His appreciation for Hegel decreased dramatically as soon as the counterrevolution in France came to the fore and the political situation in Germany became reactionary again. From this point, his view of the perfection of mankind gave way to a deeply felt skepticism.

Heine's profane thought was mostly stimulated by **Claude-Henri Comte de Saint-Simon** and his followers, who considered history to be a succession of class conflicts. His reading of St. Armand Bazard's *Exposition de la Doctrine Saint-Simonienne* strengthened his decision to go to Paris and to widen his knowledge about the socialist movement, which covered a new sexual ethic as well as the human emancipation from a quest for spiritual salvation. Heine's new intellectual background supplied his conception of the artist's role in society: a moral authority who strives for a new social order and peace between the nations. These influences become strikingly apparent in *Deutschland, ein Wintermärchen* (1844) and in *Zur Geschichte der Religion und Philosophie in Deutschland* (1833), which was even characterized as "ein Manifest der Gebote Saint-Simons" (Raddatz, 175).

ARCHIVES

Heinrich-Heine-Institut, Düsseldorf. Manuscripts, letters, notes.
Goethe- und Schiller-Archiv, Nationale Forschungs- und Gedenkstätten der klassischen Literatur, Weimar. Manuscripts.

PRINTED SOURCES

Clasen, Herbert. *Heinrich Heines Romantikkritik. Tradition—Produktion—Rezeption* (Hamburg: Hoffmann & Campe, 1979).
Hauschild, Jan-Christoph, and Michael Werner. *Der Zweck des Lebens ist das Leben selbst. Heinrich Heine: Eine Biographie* (Cologne: Kiepenheuer & Witsch, 1997).
Mende, Fritz. *Heinrich Heine. Chronik seines Lebens und Werkes* (Stuttgart: Kohlhammer, 1981).
Preisendanz, Wolfgang. *Heinrich Heine. Werkstrukturen und Epochenbezüge* (Munich: Fink, 1973).
Raddatz, Fritz J. *Taubenherz und Geierschnabel: Heinrich Heine. Eine Biographie* (Berlin: Beltz Quadriga, 1997).
Robertson, Ritchie. *Heine* (London: Grove Press, 1988).
Sammons, Jeffrey L. *Heinrich Heine: A Modern Biography* (Princeton, N.J.: Princeton University Press, 1976).
Spencer, Hanna. *Heinrich Heine* (Boston: Twayne Publishers, 1982).
Trilse-Finkelstein, Jochanan. *Gelebter Widerspruch: Heinrich Heine Biographie* (Berlin: Aufbau, 1997).

Ernst Grabovszki

HERZEN, ALEKSANDR IVANOVICH (1812–1870). Aleksandr Herzen, literary critic, novelist, social critic, political thinker, and publicist, was born in Moscow in 1812 and educated at Moscow University. He was prominent among intellectual circles in Russia and part of the "Natural School" in literature, which in the 1840s set Russian literature on a path toward realism. After two periods of exile to the provinces imposed by the tsarist government for his political views, Herzen left Russia in 1847 and lived in various parts of Europe until his death in London in 1870. While abroad, he continued to influence political thought and activity in Russia through his journalistic and philosophical writings and work as a publisher of expatriate newspapers and journals.

Herzen left records of his early reading in his memoir *My Past and Thoughts* and the essay "Notes of a Young Man," which are both available in English as *My Past and Thoughts*, translated by Constance Garnett. He began reading widely and unsystematically at around the age of seven, selecting from the diverse literature found in his home. This reading included Russian children's books and popular literature, German sentimental novels and other popular literature (much of it collected by his German mother), and French novels, plays (Beaumarchais's *Marriage of Figaro* was a favorite), and philosophical writings, especially those of the philosophes, which were found in his father's and uncle's libraries of eighteenth-century French books. German romantic novels such as those by August Lafontaine and **Goethe** exerted strong appeal. By adolescence he exhibited considerable enthusiasm for the writings of Friedrich von Schiller. Schiller's romantic heroes, Karl Moor, Wallenstein, and William Tell, who were portrayed as seekers of liberty and self-realization, captured his imagination. Schiller's writings formed the basis for his long-standing idealistic and aesthetic views of the world, according to Martin Malia, who wrote an extensive analysis of literary and political influences on Herzen's socialist thought. The poetry of **Aleksandr Pushkin**, introduced to Herzen by a Russian tutor, reinforced his romanticism and enriched his aesthetic sensibilities.

While at the University of Moscow, Herzen's interest in German Romanticism expanded into an attraction to German philosophical idealism, especially that of **Friedrich Schelling**, which emphasized the importance of nature or the natural along with the spiritual. Later he studied Hegel and adopted the dialectic but interpreted it from the perspective of his beliefs in progress and the potential for societal transformation. Malia suggested that Herzen acquired much of his knowledge of contemporary philosophers from popularized versions but did not pursue the implications of this possibility (Malia, 94).

Practical and political concerns tempered Herzen's youthful idealism. He had a strong political sensibility that derived in large part from his readings about the French Revolution and from the stories he heard and literature he read as a youth about the Decembrist uprising, a failed revolt against the tsar led by military officers that took place in 1825. Much of the secretly distributed literature that grew out of this event, including that of the poet Kondraty Ryleev, reached the Herzen household through relatives and his tutor.

ARCHIVES

Herzen-Herwegh Collection, British Library.

PRINTED SOURCES

Gertsen, A. I. *Sobranie sochinenii v 30 tomakh* [Collected works in thirty volumes] (Moscow: Akademia Nauk SSR, 1954–1966). The definitive text of Herzen's writings, including published works, novels, essays, letters, and other personal writings.

Herzen, Alexander. *My Past and Thoughts: The Memoirs of Alexander Herzen* [translation of *Byloe i dumy* and some essays], Constance Garnett (trans.), rev. Humphrey Higgens, 4 vols. (New York: Knopf, 1968).

Malia, Martin. *Alexander Herzen and the Birth of Russian Socialism, 1812–1855* (Cambridge, Mass.: Harvard University Press, 1961). This is the best-known study, in English, of Herzen's thought. A definitive biography of Herzen has yet to be written.

Partridge, Monica. *Alexander Herzen: Collected Studies*, 2nd ed. (Nottingham, England: Astra Press, 1993). A collection of articles, several of which discuss Herzen's reading and other literary influences. Partridge also wrote a brief biography, *Alexander Herzen, 1812–1870* (Paris: UNESCO, 1984).

Kathryn Wagnild Fuller

HERZL, THEODOR (1860–1904). Theodor Herzl, the founder of modern political Zionism, was born in Budapest, Hungary, in 1860 and educated at a local Jewish school (1866–1870); in Vienna, he eventually obtained a law degree (1878–1884). Although he worked as a journalist in France, Herzl primarily refined his literary and rhetorical style through *Die Welt* (1897–1914), the newspaper he founded. Herzl's articulation of Zionism initally began with his aesthetic vision, a vision developed in large part from his extensive reading of German Enlightenment and Haskalah philosophers, as well as early nationalist ideologies that circulated in the Prussian empire throughout the nineteenth and early twentieth centuries. Thus Herzl's Zionist vision is anticipated in his earlier works, *The Jewish State* (1897), *The New Ghetto* (1897), and *The Old New Land* (ca. 1902).

Captivated by his reading of **Heine**, Herzl initially imagined himself as a dramatist and satirist in the same vein. Heine's influence was especially important for Herzl because Heine personified the image of the successfully assimilated Jew. In other words, Herzl identified with Heine and Heine's role in German culture; moreover, it was Heine's work that suggested a model of Jewish assimilation within German society. Herzl's reading of Heine prompted him, then, to write several Jewish farces during his college years; these college plays underlined Herzl's belief in the need for a radical assimilation of Jewry within the German-speaking countries.

Furthermore, during Herzl's youth, Jewish assimilationist culture did much to promulgate the idea that the Austro-Habsburg empire was becoming a "liberated" society. Herzl's reading of Heine only confirmed this perspective. Thus much of Herzl's earliest reading followed a utopian dream, in which Jews and Gentiles lived without the spectres of anti-Semitism and racism. With Heine as his model, then, Herzl sought initially to produce an aesthetic vision of his life and work that erased the cultural parameters of anti-semitism.

However, as Herzl's utopic vision came into conflict with history, he began to question the possibility of radical assimilation in European countries as the answer for Jewish culture. Thus in 1882, when Herzl read Eugen Dühring's *The Jewish Problem as a Problem of Racial Character and Its Danger to the Existence of Peoples, Morals, and Cultures*, an anti-Semitic tract, he realized the need for Jews to articulate "a Jewish consciousness." In other words, Dühring's text forced Herzl to realize that assimilation was not the answer to Europe's "perceived" Jewish problem.

As notes from Central Zionist Archives show, Herzl's reading focused, then, on a theme advanced by Christian Wilhelm Dohm in his text *Concerning the Amelioration of the Civil Status of the Jews* (1781): the idea of a mythical Jewish kingdom where Jews displayed all the attributes Herzl felt to be missing in contemporary Jewish identity. The old biblical narratives of Jewish kingdoms, and of Jewish kings who were able to "defend the Jewish State in war," offered a historical counterpoint to Jewish stereotypes circulating in Viennese popular and academic cultures. Herzl's renewed interest in a biblical Jewish identity motivated not only Herzl's aesthetic vision, best exemplified in the subsequent production of *The New Ghetto*, but also the beginning of his political articulation of Zionism. Thus Herzl used the biblical narrative to envision both a Jewish State that would return to Jewry the dignity and greatness lost after the Diaspora as well as a political identity that would ensure the safety and security of Jews under the rubric of a nation–state.

ARCHIVES

Central Zionist Archives, Jerusalem.

PRINTED SOURCES

Bein, Alex. *Theodore Herzl, a Biography*, Maurice Samuel (trans.) (Philadelphia: Jewish Publication Society of America, 1940).
Beller, Steven. *Herzl* (London: Weidenfeld & Nicholson, 1991).
Elon, Amos. *Herzl* (New York: Holt, Rinehart and Winston, 1975).
Herzl, Theodor. *Complete Diaries*, Raphael Patai (ed.), Harry Zohn (trans.) (New York: Herzl Press, 1960–1961).
———. *Diaries of Theodor Herzl*, Marvin Lowenthal (ed.) (New York: Dial Press, 1956).
———. *Theodor Herzl's Tagebücher* (Berlin: Jüdischer Verlag, 1922–1923).
Kornberg, Jacques. *Theodor Herzl: From Assimilation to Zionism* (Bloomington: Indiana University Press, 1993).

Kitty Millet

HOLMES, OLIVER WENDELL (1809–1894). Oliver Wendell Holmes was a Boston "Brahmin," a term he invented and best exemplifies. Born in Cambridge, Massachusetts, the son of a Congregational minister, he rejected his father's Calvinism in favor of Unitarianism partly as a result of reading Bunyan's *Pilgrim's Progress* in his father's well-stocked library. Books were an important factor in the making of New England's Brahmin Caste, persons like himself who benefited from the "inheritance of good instincts, a good name, and a bringing up in a library" ("The Pulpit and the Pew," in *Works*, 8:411).

Holmes's earliest education was in a series of private schools, culminating in one year at Phillips Academy, Andover. After Harvard (class of 1829) he had a year of law school, switched career plans, and spent three years at the private Tremont Medical School, followed in the years 1833–1835 by clinical study in the hospitals and lecture rooms of Paris; on his return he was awarded the M.D. by the Harvard Medical School. His professional life thereafter centered on the Harvard Medical School, where he was professor of anatomy from 1847 to 1882 and its dean for six years.

His most important single medical contribution, the essay "The Contagiousness of Puerperal Fever," hardly would have been possible without his understanding of previous literature on the subject, including that in professional journals, which he indexed himself for ready reference. His deep interest in medical literature, both ancient and contemporary, led to his effort to establish the Boston Medical Library and dated back to his student days in Paris, when he made the acquisition of a 1532 copy of the *Aphorisms of Hippocrates* with a preface by Dr. François Rabelais.

Holmes is remembered for his essays, his poems, and to a lesser extent, his three novels. Like Samuel Johnson, whom he greatly admired, he used books by reading *in* them, seldom through them to the end. Even for what appears to be the spontaneous flow of conversation in *The Autocrat of the Breakfast-Table*, we know from the record of his borrowings at the Boston Athenaeum that he checked out Cicero to write about old age and Michaux to write about trees (Tilton, 243–244). "Old Ironsides," the first poem to bring him national attention, was written in response to a note in the Boston *Daily Advertiser*, with the result that his poem has preserved the warship *Constitution* down to our own time. "The Chambered Nautilus," Holmes's own favorite among his poems, was introduced by a reference to Roget's *Bridgewater Treatise* and was written in the awareness that moral exemplars had been drawn from this shellfish by at least four earlier poets, among whom were Alexander Pope and Hartley Coleridge. All three of his novels make psychological capital of "reflex action," the physiological principle enunciated by Marshall Hall, whose *Principles of the Theory and Practice of Medicine* Holmes edited for an American edition.

Late in life Holmes enumerated some of the books he found worth coming back to. They included Boswell's *Life of Johnson*, Robert Burton's *Anatomy of Melancholy*, Cotton Mather's *Magnalia Christi Americana*, Pascal's *Pensées*, and Montaigne's *Essais*. On Montaigne's essay on books he jotted "very delightful."

ARCHIVES

Holmes Papers. Houghton Library, Harvard University.

PRINTED SOURCES

Holmes, Oliver Wendell. *The Works of Oliver Wendell Holmes*, 13 vols. (Boston: Houghton Mifflin, 1892).

Hoyt, Edwin P. *The Improper Bostonian: Dr. Oliver Wendell Holmes* (New York: William Morrow and Co., 1979).

Morse, John T., Jr. (ed.). *Life and Letters of Oliver Wendell Holmes*, 2 vols. (Boston: Houghton Mifflin, 1896).

Small, Miriam Rossiter. *Oliver Wendell Holmes* (New York: Twayne Publishers, 1962).

Tilton, Eleanor M. *Amiable Autocrat: A Biography of Oliver Wendell Holmes* (New York: Henry Schuman, 1947).

Charles Boewe

HOPKINS, GERARD MANLEY (1844–1889). Gerard Manley Hopkins was born in Stratford, England, in 1844 and educated at Higate School (1854–1863) and Balliol College, Oxford (1863–1867). He converted from Anglicanism to Catholicism in 1866, entering the Society of Jesus in 1868. His poetry is vivid, passionate, and innovative in rhyme and the sprung rhythm he created. He captures Victorian particularity, nostalgia for the disappearing wilderness, and the hunger for a God they feared lost. Norman White's *Hopkins: A Literary Biography* provides the most detailed look at his life, although Walter J. Ong's *Hopkins, the Self, and God* offers a fuller character portrait.

Hopkins's poetry and faith were influenced by **John Henry Newman**'s life and works, especially *Apologia Pro Vita Sua* (1858), in which Newman wrote of his own religious exploration. Hopkins was intrigued by Newman's journey and in "Let me be to Thee as the circling bird" (1865) writes of considering "each pleasurable throat" before finding "the authentic cadence." He was also influenced early in his career by Pindar and the Greek Choral ode, as well as by John Milton, evidenced in "Wreck of the *Deutschland*" (1876) (White, 254). He also toyed with the Elizabethan/Jacobean mode after reading *Love's Labor's Lost*, but his *Shakespeare* (ca. 1864) evidences the stylistic influence of **Matthew Arnold**.

One of the greatest influences was Duns Scotus. Intrigued by the creation of the concrete and particular individual out of the divine, Scotus validated Hopkins's theories on the detectible presence of God in individual particularities. This accounts for the combination of particularization, natural imagery, religious themes, and personal experience that typify his poetry in lines like "Glory be to God for dappled things."

That particularization was further reinforced by St. Ignatius Loyola's *Spiritual Exercises* (1548), the cornerstone text for the Jesuits and the annual retreats Hopkins both made and led yearly. The *Exercises* urge one to be aware of specifics in imaging scenes from Christ's life and to use the scenes to enter the presence of God. The poetry Hopkins wrote as a Jesuit, even when he feared he'd been abandoned by God, reflects this influence, resulting in such lines as "God's most deep decree/Bitter would have me taste, my taste was me" (1885). The *Exercises*, combined with Scotus's celebration of individuality, lie at the heart of Hopkins's poetry and faith. His particularly was further reinforced by **John Ruskin**'s writing on art and architecture.

Hopkins read voraciously and critically most of his life and was familiar with Greek, Latin, and French literature as well as James Joyce, **Edgar Allan Poe**, Algernon Charles Swinburne, **George Eliot**, **Christina Rossetti**, Robert Bridges, Coventry Patmore, and the *Autobiography* of St. Therese, whose writings on hell influenced the imagery of his final, despairing sonnets. He was too innovative to simply assume the sounds, thinking, imagery of another, but Newman, Scotus, and St. Ignatius clearly shaped his approach to faith and the means by which he expressed it, capturing the universal in the personal and particular.

ARCHIVES

Hopkins Papers. Bodleian Library, Oxford. Principal manuscripts and documents.

PRINTED SOURCES

Abbott, C. C. (ed.). *The Letters of Gerard Manley Hopkins to Robert Bridges* (London: Oxford University Press, 1935).

Bergonzi, B. *Gerard Manley Hopkins* (New York: Collier Books, 1977).

Cotter, J. F. *Inscape: The Christology and Poetry of Gerard Manley Hopkins* (Pittsburgh: University of Pittsburgh Press, 1972).

Devlin, C. (ed.). *The Sermons and Devotional Writings of Gerard Manley Hopkins* (London: Oxford University Press, 1959).

Gardner, W. H. *Gerard Manley Hopkins 1844–1889: A Study of Poetic Idiosyncrasy in Relation to Poetic Tradition* (London: Martin Secker & Warburg, 1949).

Gardner, W. H., and N. H. MacKenzie (eds.). *The Poems of Gerard Manley Hopkins* (London: Oxford University Press, 1967).

House, H. (ed.). *The Journals and Papers of Gerard Manley Hopkins* (London: Oxford University Press, 1959).

McDermott, J. *A Hopkins Chronology* (New York: St. Martin's Press, 1997).

Ong, W. J. *Hopkins, the Self and God* (Toronto: University of Toronto Press, 1986).

White, N. *Hopkins: A Literary Biography* (Oxford: Clarendon Press, 1992).

Andrea Dixon

HOUSMAN, ALFRED EDWARD (1859–1936). Alfred Housman was born at Fockbury, Worcestershire, in 1859 and died in Cambridge in 1936. He was educated at Bromsgrove School (1870–1877) and St. John's College, Oxford (1877–1881), but because of his attachment to a fellow student, Moses Jackson, who did not reciprocate his affection, he never received his degree.

Housman's religious background was "Church of England and in the High Church party" (Maas, *Letters*, 328), but he recalled that Lemprière's *Classical Dictionary* "attached my affections to paganism" (Maas, *Letters*, 238), although he also said that by the age of 21 he was an atheist.

At St. John's, Housman followed the prescribed reading, which included Plato, Aristotle, Cicero, Herodotus, Tacitus, Locke, Bacon, and Kant. He worked for 10 years between 1882 and 1892 as a clerk in the Patent Office in London, spending his evenings in the British Museum, reading Latin texts.

Housman's correspondence records that "my favourite Greek poet is Aeschylus. No doubt I have been unconsciously influenced by the Greeks and Latins." Moreover, he wrote that "sources of which I am conscious are Shakespeare's songs, the Scottish border ballads and **Heine**" (Maas, *Letters*, 329) in the poems that made up *A Shropshire Lad* (1896).

Housman was professor of Latin at the University of London between 1892 and 1911. He was then appointed Kennedy Professor of Latin at the University of Cambridge, and he remained in Cambridge, at Trinity College, until his death. Housman's edition of the *Astronomica* of Manilius was published in five volumes between 1903 and 1930. However, Housman claimed not to like the poetry of Manilius and that "my interest in him is purely technical" (Maas, *Letters*, 222).

Throughout his life he edited texts such as Lucan, Ovid, Aeschylus, Sophocles, and Euripides, and he published papers on the manuscripts of Ovid, Propertius, Lucilius, and Juvenal. He liked Aristippus because "he was not afraid of words" (*DNB, 1931–1940*, 452).

In the discussions that followed debates at the Literary Society, Housman spoke dismissively of **Tennyson**, suggesting that *In Memoriam* was somewhat formulaic and that "things must come right in the end, because it would be so very unpleasant if they did not" (Chambers, 43). *The Idylls of the King*, according to Housman, in no way captured the spirit of Malory (Chambers, 44). He put forward the idea, considered extraordinary at the time, that **Matthew Arnold** was probably the superior of—or at the least the equal to—Tennyson and **Robert Browning** (Chambers, 44). Housman admitted to "great admiration for some of the poetry which Browning wrote between 1835 and 1869, especially in the period of *Bells and Pomegranates*, but . . . on my own writing he has had no influence at all" (Maas, *Letters*, 329). For **Hardy**, Housman "felt affection and high admiration for some of his novels" (Maas, *Letters*, 329). Similarly, he had the "greatest admiration" for **Keats**, but he said in 1928 that "I should not have thought that my writing had any affinity to his" (Maas, *Letters*, 265). The **Leslie Stephen** Lecture that Housman delivered in 1933, *The Name and Nature of Poetry*, is surprisingly dismissive of much seventeenth- and eighteenth-century poetry.

ARCHIVES

Housman Papers, Rare Book and Manuscript Library, Columbia University.
University of Cambridge, also in Fitzwilliam Museum and King's College, Cambridge, and Trinity College, Cambridge.
Geoffrey Keynes Collection, Department of Rare Books, University of Cambridge Library.
British Library.
Oxford, Bodleian Library.
St. John's College, Oxford, and Merton College, Oxford.
University College Library, London.
National Library of Scotland, Edinburgh.
University College Library.
Dublin, and Trinity College, Dublin.
University of Reading Library.
Yale University Library.
University of Texas Library.

PRINTED SOURCES

Chambers, R. W. *Alfred Edward Housman: 26th March 1859–30th April 1936; Bromsgrove School, 1870–1877* (Bromsgrove: Bromsgrove School, 1936).
Dictionary of National Biography, 1931–1940 (London: Oxford University Press, 1949), 449–453.
Gow, A.S.F. *A. E. Housman, a Sketch, Together with a List of His Writings and Indexes to His Classical Papers* (Cambridge: Cambridge University Press, 1936).

Graves, Richard Perceval. *A. E. Housman. The Scholar Poet* (London: Routledge and Kegan Paul, 1979).

Housman, A. E. *The Name and Nature of Poetry*, The Leslie Stephen Memorial Lecture 1933, (Cambridge: Cambridge University Press, 1933).

Housman, Laurence, *A.E.H. Some Poems, Some Letters and a Personal Memoir by His Brother Laurence Housman* (London: Jonathan Cape, 1937).

Maas, Henry (ed.). *The Letters of A. E. Housman* (London: Rupert Hart-Davis, 1971).

Page, Normal. *A. E. Housman: A Critical Biography* (London: Macmillan, 1983).

Richards, F.T.G. *Housman: 1897–1936* (London: Oxford University Press, 1941).

Ricks, Christopher (ed.). *A. E. Housman: A Collection of Critical Essays* (Englewood Cliffs, N.J.: Prentice-Hall, 1968).

Caroline Dowson

HOWELLS, WILLIAM DEAN (1837–1920). William Dean Howells, U.S. author, critic, and editor, was born in Martinsville, Ohio, in 1837. His formal education consisted of several years of schooling as a boy in Hamilton, Ohio. Lacking higher education but employed from the age of nine in print shops and newspapers, he read voraciously from childhood. He remained a lifelong religious doubter, despite his father's ardent Swedenborgianism. Howells's novels, notably *A Modern Instance* (1882), *The Rise of Silas Lapham* (1885), and *A Hazard of New Fortunes* (1890), are among the foremost examples of American realism. As assistant editor and editor of the *Atlantic Monthly* (1866–1881), Howells also became the chief American champion of realistic fiction through his reviews and his encouragement of such writers as Constance Fenimore Woolson, Sarah Orne Jewett, and H. H. Boyesen (Sedgwick, 113). He continued to espouse the realist credo as a critic and editor at *Harper's Monthly*, *Harper's Weekly*, and *Cosmopolitan* in the 1880s and 1890s.

Among Howells's numerous published autobiographical books and articles, *My Literary Passions* (1895) describes in detail his first half-century of reading—from his earliest passions for Goldsmith and Cervantes to the recent influence of **Tolstoy**, of whom he wrote, "As much as one merely human being can help another I believe that he has helped me; he has not influenced me in aesthetics only, but in ethics, too, so that I can never again see life in the way I saw it before I knew him" (*My Literary Passions* [*MLP*], 183). Howells's early poetry reflected his reading of Pope's pastorals (*MLP*, 40); his immersion in Italian literature as consul to Venice (1861–1865) influenced his volumes about Italy in the post–Civil War years. As he turned from Romanticism toward realism in these years, **Heine**'s work showed him "that the life of literature was from the springs of the best common speech, and that the nearer it could be made to conform, in voice, look, and gait, to graceful, easy, picturesque and humorous talk, the better it was" (*MLP*, 129). Although he read widely in "the English classics," he believed that "contemporary literature," especially novels, had most affected him (*MLP*, 167). His distinction between romances and novels (he propounded the realism of the latter) owed much to **Hawthorne**'s preface to *The House of the Seven Gables* (Lynn, 184). In the 1870s, the decade before his own greatest fiction, he read **Balzac**, **Flaubert**, Bjørnson, **Eliot**, and especially **Turgenev** (Lynn, 222). Reading Tolstoy in the mid-1880s led Howells to appreciate novels of social protest and criticism, as well as to argue in print for commuting the death sentences of the anarchists accused of throwing a bomb in Chicago's Haymarket Square in 1886. Despite Tolstoy's influence, however, Howells's own fiction never adopted the imaginative point of view of America's own growing working class, much of it immigrant. Rather, his working-class and immigrant characters remained minor ones, seen through the eyes of his middle-class protagonists, the realistic characters for whom he has been most celebrated.

ARCHIVES

William Dean Howells Collection (b MS Am 1784), Houghton Library, Harvard University.

PRINTED SOURCES

Howells, William Dean. *My Literary Passions* (New York: Harper & Brothers, 1895).
Lynn, Kenneth S. *William Dean Howells: An American Life* (New York: Harcourt Brace Jovanovich, 1970).
Sedgwick, Ellery. *A History of the Atlantic Monthly 1857–1909: Yankee Humanism at High Tide and Ebb* (Amherst: University of Massachussetts Press, 1994).
Wagenknecht, Edward. *William Dean Howells: The Friendly Eye* (New York: Oxford University Press, 1969). First chapter is "Howells's Life and Reading."

Scott E. Casper

HUGO, VICTOR-MARIE (1802–1885). Victor Hugo was born at Besançon in 1802. His mother was a Royalist and his father was an officer under **Napoléon**. Hugo was never baptized and did not believe in a churchgoing god. He had a sporadic education, but from an early age he was a skilled poet. He edited *The Literary Conservative* (1819) and *The French Muse* (1823–1824). In 1822, he married Adèle Foucher. Hugo became a democrat after 1848 and was elected to the Constitutional Assembly. He spent from 1851 to 1870 in exile, often in Guernsey (Jersey). Hugo was the central figure of the Romantic movement in France, writing 17 novels, 18 volumes of poetry, and 21 plays and producing a variety of paintings, drawings, and other writings. His mistress for over 50 years was Juliette Drouet.

As a child, Hugo saw violence in war-torn Spain and Italy, and he was a lifelong opponent of the death penalty. While in school he translated *The Aeneid*. An early hero of Hugo's was **François-René de Chateaubriand**, and he also admired Lamartine, particularly his *Meditations Poetiques*. Young Hugo also read Rousseau, Voltaire, Diderot, *Faublas*, the *Voyages of Captain Cook*, Virgil, Lucretius, and Horace.

When he was 21, Hugo called for a new fiction that would "give epic scope to the moral and social consciousness of his period" (Brombert, 1). In the 1820s he read *Le Mémorial de Sainte-Hélène*, the record of Napoléon's life in exile, having "already inducted the Emperor into his personal mythology" (Robb, 125). In a careful study, Mary O'Connor looked at the sources of Hugo's early novel *Hans d'Islande* (1823), which include *Histoire de Dannemarc* by Pierre-Henri Mallet, *Voyage en Norvège* by Johan Christian Fabricius, *Les Soirées de Saint-Petersbourg* by Joseph de Maistre, and Diderot's article "Exécuteur." O'Connor also mentions that Hugo "shared the French enthusiasm for Sir **Walter Scott**" (40). However, Hugo also read a number of little-known books, including *Fabricius's Voyage en Norvége to L'Hèritier du Danemark* by P-H. Mallet.

By the 1840s, Hugo had streamlined reading: He opened a book and read random pages. If after three tries he was unengaged, he would "deem it bad" (Robb, 257). Hugo's connection with Voltaire was strengthened during his exile, when he said "remoteness is an excellent thing for the fame, and the sounding voice, of a living man: Voltaire at Ferney, Hugo in Jersey—two solitudes which hold something of the same significance" (qtd. in Maurois, 343). In his 1853 poetic work *Les Châtiments*, Hugo consulted Chateaubriand's dramatic pictures that appeared in *De Buonaparte et des Bourbons* and *Mémoires d'Outre-Tombe*; the Comte de Ségur's *Histoire de Napoléon et de la Grande Armée en 1812*; and Napoléon's memories in the Papiers de Sainte-Hélène (Grant, 174).

Hugo believed in metempsychosis and was apparently influenced in this area by his readings of Alexandre Weill's *Mystères de la création* and **Charles Fourier**'s *Théorie de l'unité universelle*.

In *Les Contemplations* (1856), Hugo invokes Milton and Dante, whom "he considered to be his literary ancestors" (Nash, 18). In "William Shakespeare," a long, critical essay published in 1864, Hugo said the true geniuses were Shakespeare, Homer, Job, Aeschylus, Isaiah, Ezekiel, Lucretius, Juvenal, Tacitus, Saint John, Dante, Rabelais, and Cervantes.

ARCHIVES

Manuscript sources: Bibliothèque nationale: département des manuscrits. N.A.F. (Archives nationales en France; Victor Hugo Collections), 13464, 13466, 13467, 13468, 13471, 13475, 13479: Victor Hugo's private diaries.

PRINTED SOURCES

Brombert, Victor. *Victor Hugo and the Visionary Novel* (Cambridge, Mass.: Harvard University Press, 1984).

Grant, Elliot M. *The Career of Victor Hugo* (Cambridge, Mass.: Harvard University Press, 1946).

Maurios, André. *Olympio: The Life of Victor Hugo*, Gerard Hopkins (trans.) (New York: Harper & Brothers, 1956).

Nash, Suzanne. *Les Contemplations of Victor Hugo* (Princeton, N.J.: Princeton University Press, 1976).

O'Connor, Mary Irene. *A Study of the Sources of* Han d'Islande *and Their Significance in the Literary Development of Victor Hugo* (New York: AMS Press, 1942).

Robb, Graham. *Victor Hugo* (London: W. W. Norton, 1997).

Scott Warnock

HUMBOLDT, FRIEDRICH HEINRICH ALEXANDER VON (1769–1859).

Alexander von Humboldt, the founder of modern physical geography, systematic meteorology, and the geography of plants, was born in Berlin. Alexander and his brother Wilhelm came from a wealthy family, which offered them the opportunity to receive a fine education. Their first tutor was Joachim Heinrich Campe, an educationist and author of children's books. Campe introduced the boys to the works of Jean-Jacques Rousseau (Alexander owned *Gesammelte Kritische Schriften, Erster Band*). In 1787, the brothers began their university studies at Frankfurt-on-the-Oder. After a short stay at the small school, the brothers chose to attend Göttingen University. Before beginning, Humboldt spent a year in Berlin studying factory processes and Greek language and history, including Sophocles and Aeschylus's *Agamemnon, Choephorae, und Eumenides* and *Tragodien ubersetzt von C. de Haas, vol. I*. Upon his arrival at Göttingen, he studied physics and chemistry under the tutelage of G. C. Lichtenberg. In 1789, Alexander's professor, Christian Gottlob Heyne, introduced Alexander to Georg Forster, whose *Delineations of the South Sea Islands* influenced Humboldt's desire to visit tropical lands. In 1797, after a stay in Vienna, he moved to Jena to continue his studies of anatomy and physiology and renewed his friendship with **Goethe** and Schiller.

In June 1799, Humboldt and friend, Aime Bonpland, left Spain for South America. During their journey, the two scientists' research completely altered all previous understanding of the physics, resources, and culture of the region.

Humboldt's literary interests varied from the natural sciences to an interest in classical and contemporary literature. At the time of his death, his library collection exceeded 11,000 books. In addition to works on the natural sciences, Humboldt read the writings of Rousseau and Voltaire. He also read much of Leibniz's work, including *Dritte Folge* and *Nouvelles Lettres*.

Humboldt created a new respect for the study of the earth—through his systematic and relentless work ethic. He offered his genius to foster awareness in the culture that flourished in the "New World," and he was a pioneer for the emancipation of the slaves in Latin America.

ARCHIVES

Berlin-Brandenburgische Akademie der Wissenschaften: Alexander-von-Humboldt-Forschungsstelle; American Philosophical Society, Philadelphia.

PRINTED SOURCES

Borch, Rudolf, *Alexander von Humboldt, Sein Leben in Selbstzeugnissen, Briefen, und Berichten* (Berlin: Verlag des Druckhauses Tempelhof, 1948). A first person accounting—through documents and letters—of the readings that influenced Alexander's thinking.

De Terra, Helmut. *The Life and Times of Alexander von Humboldt*, 1769–1859 (New York: Alfred A. Knopf, 1955).

Stevens, Henry. *The Humboldt Library, a Catalogue of the Library of Alexander von Humboldt* (London: Trafalgar Square, 1967). Listing of the books that Humboldt owned, including annotations or other distinguishing features.

Stoddard, Richard Henry. *The Life, Travels, and Books of Alexander von Humboldt* (New York: Rudd and Carelton, 1859). A comprehensive look at how Alexander's schooling and literary interests influenced his career.

N. Michael Zampetti

HUNT, WILLIAM HOLMAN (1827–1910).

William Hunt was born in London in 1827 and educated in "a private school" (Dictionary of National Biography [*DNB*], 323) until his thirteenth year, when he began working as an apprentice to a surveyor. In 1843 he "left his mercantile employment" (*DNB*, 323) and became a student at the British Museum; in 1844 Hunt was accepted into the Royal Academy schools as a probationer. He was raised an Anglican, but later in life he studied Islamic and Jewish mysticism during his travels to the Holy Land. Hunt is known for faithfully painting according to the original tenets of Pre-Raphaelitism—minute attention to detail and fidelity to nature.

When Hunt met **John Everett Millais** and **Dante Gabriel Rossetti** at the Academy in the late 1840s, the three became the nucleus of the Pre-Raphaelite Brotherhood. Hunt's contributions to their "fist of Immortals" included "the author of the book of Job . . . Homer . . . Chaucer, Leonardo, **Goethe, Keats, Shelley**, King Alfred . . . **Thackeray**, Washington; and **[Robert] Browning**" (Hilton, 34) and show his early interests in religion, philosophy, and contemporary authors—of this last most notably **John Ruskin**'s *Modern Painters* (1846) (Hilton, 38). Hunt's paintings take their subjects from his reading: *Rienzi Vowing to Obtain Justice* (1849), for instance, is taken from **Edward Bulwer-Lytton**'s novel *Rienzi: The Last of the Roman Tribunes* (1848). During the years 1854–1856, 1869–1871, and 1875–1878, Hunt traveled in the Holy Land, reading the Bible and the Koran (W. Hunt, 2:260), which led to paintings such as *The Scapegoat* (1854) and *A Street Scene in Cairo* (1854).

When he was not traveling, Hunt lived in London, meeting the very authors whom he was reading, including **Alfred Tennyson**, who chastised Hunt for painting *The Lady of Shalott* (ca. 1889–1892)—based on Tennyson's "The Lady of Shalott" (1842)—with too much artistic license (W. Hunt, 2:124). Hunt also read Shakespeare; witness *Claudio and Isabella* (1850). He describes encounters—in books and in person—with Robert and **Elizabeth Barrett Browning** (W. Hunt, 2:126), William Makepeace Thackeray (W. Hunt, 2:240), George Meredith (W. Hunt, 2:242), and **Thomas Carlyle** (W. Hunt, 2:130).

ARCHIVES

Correspondence of Frederick George Stephens, Bodleian Library (MSS. Don. e.78, d. 116–119, e. 57–87).

PRINTED SOURCES

Armstrong, Walter. "Hunt, William Holman." In Sidney Lee (ed.), *The Dictionary of National Biography from the Earliest Times to 1900*, Supplement, 3 vols. (London: Smith, Elder, 1901), 1:323–328.
Gissing, A. C. *William Holman Hunt. A Biography* (London: Duckworth, 1936). Reference to reading notebooks and travel journals.
Hilton, Timothy. *The Pre-Raphaelites* (New York: Thames and Hudson, 1970).
Hunt, Diana Holman. *My Grandfather, His Wives and Loves* (New York: Norton, 1969). Use of family diaries and marked books.
Hunt, William Holman. *Pre-Raphaelitism and the Pre-Raphaelite Brotherhood*, 2 vols. (London: Macmillan, 1906).
Rossetti, William Michael. *The P.R.B. Journal 1849–1853, Together with Other Pre-Raphaelite Documents*, and introd. William E. Fredeman (ed.) (Oxford: Clarendon Press, 1975). Extensive collection of letters to and from W.H.H.

Thomas J. Tobin

HUXLEY, THOMAS HENRY (1826–1895). Thomas Huxley was born in Ealing in 1825 and educated first by his father (1832–1835), then apprenticed to his brother-in-law in medicine (1839–1841). He received a scholarship to study at Charing Cross Hospital (1842–1844) and graduated from the College of Surgeons at London University in 1845. This varied and practical education prepared him well for his famous expedition as ship's surgeon aboard the *Rattlesnake* on a voyage of discovery (1846–1850). Huxley is best known as a public defender of the evolutionary views of **Charles Darwin**; his more enduring legacy may be his work in developing and administering an educational system for British science.

As a boy, Thomas Huxley was largely left to pursue his own educational interests. These centered around philosophy and the sciences, but it was the writings of **Thomas Carlyle** that sparked his imagination. On reading Carlyle's translation of **Goethe**'s *Wilhelm Meister*, he was driven to teach himself German and to have "an intense hatred of shams of every sort and kind" (Huxley, 1:9). Both impulses would serve him well throughout his life. At the age of 15, young Huxley began a notebook in German where he comments on his readings and experiments in electricity—here German books on physiology are mixed with **François Guizot**'s monumental *History of Civilization in Europe*. His social conscience quickly developed as a young medical apprentice, treating the sick in the slums of London's East End. This mixed background prepared him to receive a scholarship for his medical degree.

Much of Huxley's scientific training was acquired by hands-on experience. The British Admiralty assigned him as ship's surgeon and scientific observer aboard the HMS *Rattlesnake,* due to sail on a five-year voyage of discovery to the waters off Indonesia and the South Pacific. Here Huxley came into his own, analyzing zoological specimens and speculating upon "the very basis of a philosophical zoology, and of a true conception of the affinities of animals" (Huxley, 1:43). Upon his return to England, Huxley began publishing a series of scientific papers explaining his discoveries, bringing him to the attention of the Royal Society, which elected him a Fellow in 1851. This was the beginning of his long and distinguished teaching career.

Thomas Huxley is best remembered as "Darwin's bulldog," an unflagging public champion of evolutionary biology against the criticisms of the Church. Darwin thought enough of Huxley's judgment to have him review the *Origin of Species* before it went to press. Huxley's reaction to the theory of evolution was as "the flash of light which, to a man who has lost himself on a dark night, suddenly reveals a road. . . . That which we were looking for, and could not find, was a hypothesis respecting the origin of known organic forms" (Huxley, 1:182). Huxley realized "the considerable abuse and misrepresentation" that Darwin's book would receive, and he immediately offered the biologist "an amount of combativeness which (though you have often and justly rebuked it) may stand you in good stead. I am sharpening up my claws and beak in readiness" (Huxley, 1:189). Huxley soon had use for these claws in his famous debate with Bishop Wilberforce at Oxford. The opening shot was fired in a new war between science and religion, between evolution and creation, and Thomas Huxley had dedicated his life to the fight for scientific truth.

ARCHIVES

The Huxley Papers. Imperial College Library, University of London.

PRINTED SOURCES

Desmond, Adrian. *Huxley: The Devil's Disciple,* 2 vols. (London: Michael Joseph, 1994).
Huxley, Leonard. *Life and Letters of Thomas H. Huxley,* 2 vols. (New York: D. Appleton and Co., 1900).
Matthews, Brander (ed.). *Autobiography and Essays by Thomas Henry Huxley* (New York: Gregg Publishing, 1919; New York: Kraus Reprint, 1969).

Charles M. Roll

I

IBSEN, HENRIK (1828–1906). Henrik Ibsen was born in Skien, Norway, in 1828 and apprenticed as a pharmacist's assistant in Grimstad (1843–1849); he failed entrance to the University of Christiania (now Oslo) as a medical student but was granted nominal status and membership to the student society (1850–1851). His plays, characterized by profound psychological insight, cutting exposure of social hypocrisy, and dramatic realism, changed the course of Western drama and set the philosophical tone for the modern era.

Scholarship in nineteenth-century northern Europe was heavily influenced by German Romanticism, and Ibsen learned both German and Latin in his early school years in Skien. His childhood introduction to the Greek and Roman classics influenced his philosophy and aesthetics: He remained committed to the Socratic ideals of truth and personal liberty throughout his career and once declared his calling to be "that of arousing the nation and leading it to think great thoughts" (Ibsen, 102).

Long hours as a pharmacist's apprentice could not suppress young Ibsen's voracious appetite for literature, philosophy, and history. He borrowed books from the Grimstad Reading Society and spent his spare time reading classical texts as well as the works of more contemporary writers such as Friedrich Schiller, Ludvig Holberg, and **Johann Goethe**, knowledge of whom was expected of educated Scandinavians in Ibsen's day. Ibsen's mature letters contain numerous references to Goethe's works: He indicated in 1888 that the new Danish translation of Goethe's *Faust* was the best in existence because neither the Romance languages nor Swedish succeeded in reproducing the "Gothic ring" of the original German (Ibsen, 414).

Ibsen also borrowed books from an Englishwoman who lived in Grimstad, including the works of Danish poet Adam Oehlenscläger, whose historical tragedies would inform Ibsen's saga dramas; the Norwegian poet and dramatist Henrik Wergeland, whose fiery patriotism and Romantic vision inspired Ibsen;

and the philosophy of **Søren Kierkegaard**. Newspapers reported details of the political revolutions across western and central Europe in the late 1840s, and Ibsen found in them new causes advocating individual liberty. Kierkegaard's insistence on personal liberation mirrored Ibsen's growing convictions, and discussions of Kierkegaard were frequent among Ibsen and his companions.

Ancient history was Ibsen's best academic subject, and in his last two years at Grimstad, he wrote *Catiline*, based on a Roman nobleman of the first century B.C. whom he came across in his readings of Cicero, Ovid, and Sallust.

Georg Wilhelm Hegel's philosophy had reached Scandinavia full force by 1850 when Ibsen moved to Christiania to prepare for his university entrance examinations. One advocate of Hegel's theories was the Danish poet and critic John Ludvig Heiberg, whose essays Ibsen said were integral in his development as a dramatic critic. It is likely that Ibsen's Hegelian thinking initially came from his reading of Heiberg while in Christiania. Ibsen adopted elements of Hegel's aesthetic theories and terminology and imitated Hegel's dialectical structuring in many of his plays, particularly in the complex layering of his characters.

Ibsen began his playwriting career within a tradition of late Romanticism, in which historical drama still enjoyed great prestige. Ibsen was struggling with how he might succeed in creating a genuine national drama within this tradition when in 1852 he discovered Hermann Hettner's *Das moderne Drama* while on a study tour of theaters in Germany and Denmark. The monograph was a theoretical study of current dramatic types, but Hettner devoted most of the book to historical tragedy. Hettner maintained, arguing on the basis of William Shakespeare's *Hamlet*, that drama must hold up a mirror to its own age and that it is this which must guide the dramatist in his choice of historical material. Ibsen's articles on the art of the theater show that he embraced Hettner's conviction. In 1855 Ibsen's first significant drama, *Lady Inger of Østeraad*, fulfilled Hettner's qualifications in that it was a historical character tragedy but with a message to the age.

While many scholars cite the influence of Shakespeare in Ibsen's earliest plays, others provide evidence to support that Ibsen probably did not read Shakespeare until after 1852, when he would have been inspired to do so by Hettner's book (Van Laan, "Ibsen and Shakespeare," 290). Hettner drew most heavily from Shakespeare's tragedies in presenting what he considered models of good artistic practice. It is likely that Ibsen, who so desperately wanted to write good drama, would have thus been inspired to develop his familiarity with Shakespeare by reading the available German or Danish translations. Several subsequent plays do suggest that Ibsen was becoming familiar with Shakespeare, and much later in Ibsen's career, his *Hedda Gabler* contained an extended allusion to Shakespeare's *Antony and Cleopatra* that involved parallels in theme, situation, characters, and action.

Some of Ibsen's other literary influences are more readily identifiable in his plays. Ibsen based *The Vikings of Helgeland* on Icelandic family legends and attempted to intensify the historical color by using the Old Norse saga style. In *Brand* Ibsen's strongest literary influence is the Bible, which is the only book he read while writing the play. It is the Old Testament in particular that influences the manner of expression, the allusions, and the main character's concept of God. In *Peer Gynt*, Peer quotes directly from the Bible, Shakespeare, Jean-Baptiste Molière, and Goethe. *A Doll's House*, with its economy of dramatic action and particular technique of exposition, closely resembles the structure of ancient Greek drama. *Ghosts* shows the contemporary influence of **Charles Darwin**'s writings, as Mrs. Alving is confronted with a biological determinism. At the time Ibsen wrote *The Master Builder*, the ideas of **Friedrich Nietzsche** were widely discussed in Scandinavia. Nietzsche's "Übermensch" appealed to the individualist Ibsen, while at the same time the Übermensch morality challenged the humanist and democrat in him. This conflict is embodied in *The Master Builder*.

Throughout his career, Ibsen closely followed with the writing activity of his greatest Norwegian contemporary, Bjørnstjerne Bjørnson, recipient of the 1903 Nobel Prize for Literature. Bjørnson's approach was considered bold and daring compared to Ibsen's. Today Bjørnson is largely forgotten outside Scandinavia, whereas Ibsen is considered one of the greatest dramatists of all time.

ARCHIVES

The Ibsen Centre, University Library, University of Oslo, Norway. Manuscripts, books owned by Ibsen and his family; world's largest collection of Ibsen scholarship.

PRINTED SOURCES

Aarseth, A. "Ibsen's Dramatic Apprenticeship." In *The Cambridge Companion to Ibsen* (New York: Cambridge University Press, 1994), 1–11.
Beyer, E. *Ibsen: The Man and His Work* (New York: Taplinger Publishing, 1978).
Hemmer, B. "Ibsen and Historical Drama." In *The Cambridge Companion to Ibsen* (New York: Cambridge University Press, 1994), 12–27.
Ibsen, H. *The Correspondence of Henrik Ibsen*, M. Morison (ed.) (New York: Haskell House Publishers, 1970).
Koht, H. *The Life of Ibsen* (London: Allen and Unwin, 1934).
Lebowitz, N. *Ibsen and the Great World* (Baton Rouge: Louisiana State University Press, 1990).
Rhodes, N. *Ibsen and the Greeks* (Lewisburg, Pa.: Bucknell University Press, 1995). Classical Greek elements in German and Scandinavian culture and Ibsen's work.
Van Laan, T. "Ibsen and Shakespeare," *Scandinavian Studies* (Summer 1995), 227–305.
———. "Lady Inger as Tragedy." In B. Hemmer (ed.), *Contemporary Approaches to Ibsen* (New York: Oxford University Press, 1994), 25–46.

Richard N. Swanson

IRVING, WASHINGTON (1783–1859). Washington Irving was born in New York City in 1783. He was a student at the seminary of Josiah Henderson, but it seems that "he did not impress any of his teachers as being outstanding"

(Bowden, 13–14). He studied law (1801–1802), first with Brockholst Livingston and then with Josiah Ogden Hoffman. He appears to have been largely self-taught. Bowden says that "his knowledge was immense. He knew French early, he taught himself German, Italian, and Spanish, and there is some indication he may have begun the study of Arabic. He learned the languages, then read the literatures of these languages. He was deeply read in ancient and modern English literature; his knowledge of drama was especially profound" (183). Irving was particularly influenced by his reading of the early Romantics and later by German Romantics such as Tieck, Burger, and Hoffman. Wagenknecht says that "among the older English writers, Shakespeare was necessarily the one Irving knew best" (55), and "he probably quotes from Shakespeare more than from any other author" (56). However, Wagenknecht sees a variety of other literary influences: Chaucer (55); Milton and Bunyan (56); Smollett, Swift, Sterne, and Mrs. Radcliffe (57); and **Scott** and **Byron** (58). Myers notes that Irving's two most popular tales, "Rip Van Winkle" and "The Legend of Sleepy Hollow," were based on "Irving's study, prompted by Scott, in German literature" and that for "Rip Van Winkle" scholars have traced convincingly his readings to the 'Peter Klaus' legend, as fashioned by 'Otmar' (J.C.C. Nachtigal) in a volume of folktales collected by J. G. Busching" (174). Similarly, Myers says that "the 'Legend of Sleepy Hollow' also has a Germanic origin. Irving borrowed the climactic sequence of the headless rider from one of the Rubezahl legends in the *Volksmärchen* collection by J. A. Musaus" (174).

ARCHIVES

The largest collection of Irving's papers is located at the New York Public Library. Other collections are in the Huntington Library, the Carl H. Pforzheimer Library, Yale University Library, the University of Virginia Library, Columbia University Library, Harvard University Library and Historic Hudson Valley.

PRINTED SOURCES

Aderman, Ralph, (ed.). *Critical Essays on Washington Irving* (Boston: G. K. Hall & Co., 1990).
Bowden, Mary Weatherspoon. *Washington Irving* (Boston: Twayne Publishers, 1981).
Myers, Andrew B. "Washington Irving." In *Dictionary of Literary Biography: Antebellum Writers in New York and the South*, vol. 3 (Detroit, Mich.: Gale, 1979).
Wagenknecht, Edward. *Washington Irving: Moderation Displayed* (New York: Oxford University Press, 1962).

Sandra Hannaford

J

JACKSON, ANDREW (1767–1845). Andrew Jackson, seventh president of the United States (1828–1836), was born in Waxhaw, South Carolina, in 1767 and variously attended schools taught by Dr. William Humphries, the Rev. James White Stephenson, and Robert McCulloch in Waxhaw (1775–1781). He later read law with Spruce McKay in Salisbury, North Carolina (1784–1786) and John Stokes (1786–1787) and was admitted to the North Carolina Bar in 1787. Jackson influenced the course of American territorial expansion for much of the nineteenth century, symbolized the rise of the common man, and signaled the growth of Western political power. While president, Jackson increased presidential power through his use of the veto and by his insistence that the president alone, because he was popularly elected, represented the will of the people. Jackson held several public and military positions including public prosecutor in North Carolina (1788), U.S. senator for Tennessee (1797–1798, 1823–1825), major general of the Tennessee militia (1802–1814), major general of the United States Army (1814–1821), and territorial governor of Florida (1821). Although Jackson attended church infrequently, he regularly read the Bible and considered himself a practicing Christian; he joined the Presbyterian Church on July 15, 1838. On June 8, 1845, Jackson died at his home, the Hermitage, in Tennessee.

Andrew Jackson highly valued reading and advised his nephew, Andrew Jackson Donelson, to build a personal library. Unfortunately, however, Jackson's correspondence contains almost no mention of books, personal reading tastes, or influences. Because of Jackson's legal training, much of his early reading was professional and concentrated on standard works like those of William Blackstone and Edward Coke. Throughout Jackson's political career he subscribed to 20 or more newspapers to keep abreast of political news. Jackson, like most Democrats of the time, read the Constitution as a document that accorded only limited power to the national government. This point of view, coupled with his understanding of Emmerich de Vattel's *Law of Nations* (1758), convinced him that John Jay's 1795 Treaty with Great Britain was unconstitutional because the Senate had not fully participated in the negotiations and it violated the law of nations because, according to Jackson, Vattel envisioned the head of state as an administrator who took his cues from the legislature. However, by the time Jackson assumed the presidency, his philosophy had evolved. Although Jackson was ostensibly committed to a narrow interpretation of the Constitution, he expanded the powers of the presidency by proposing legislation, and in doing so he helped create the modern activist presidency. Indeed, Jackson's actions elevated the executive branch to the first among equals in the federal government. But as a proponent of limited government, Jackson's understanding of the Constitution and his personal prejudices against banks led him to reduce the federal government's influence in national finances by vetoing the recharter of the Second Bank of the United States (1832). President Jackson, a former soldier, was fond of the histories of Scottish chieftains because of his self-perceived resemblance to them. In Jackson's opinion, William Wallace was " 'the best model for a young man' " because of his " 'truly undaunted courage, always ready to brave any dangers, for the relief of his country or his friends' " (quoted in Remini, 1:8). Jackson's favorite work was Oliver Goldsmith's *Vicar of Wakefield* (1766). Jackson did not explain his taste for Goldsmith, but it may be that it appealed to him for its sarcastic humor, its underlying theme of proper conduct, or its representation of the chief of state as the champion of the common man (Murray; Dykstal).

ARCHIVES

Jackson Papers, Library of Congress.

PRINTED SOURCES

Curtis, James C. *Andrew Jackson and the Search for Vindication*, Library of American Biography, Oscar Handlin (ed.) (Boston: Little, Brown, 1976). Psychobiographical approach.

Dykstal, Timothy. "The Story of O: Politics and Pleasure in *The Vicar of Wakefield*," *ELH: A Journal of English Literary History*, 62 (1995), 329–346.

Jackson, Andrew. *The Correspondence of Andrew Jackson*, John Spencer Bassett (ed.), 6 vols. (Washington, D.C.: Carnegie Institute of Washington, 1926–1935).

Murray, David Aaron. "From Patrimony to Paternity in *The Vicar of Wakefield*," *Eighteenth–Century Fiction*, 9 (April 1997), 327–336.

Remini, Robert V. *Andrew Jackson*, 3 vols. (New York: Harper & Row, 1977–1984). Comprehensive biography.

Schlesinger, Arthur M., Jr. *The Age of Jackson* (Boston: Little, Brown, 1946).

Smith, Sam B., and Harriet Chappell Owsley et al., (eds). *The Papers of Andrew Jackson*, 5 vols. (Knoxville: University of Tennessee Press, 1980–).

Walker, Arda. "The Educational Training and Views of Andrew Jackson," *East Tennessee Historical Society Publications* 16 (1944), 22–29; 18 (1946), 56–86.

Ward, John William. *Andrew Jackson: Symbol for an Age* (New York: Oxford University

Press, 1953). Social and intellectual study of popular culture using Jackson as the product and "symbol of an age."

Ricardo A. Herrera

JAMES, HENRY (1843–1916). Henry James was born at 2 Washington Place, New York City, in 1843. Like his friend **Robert Louis Stevenson**, James's formal childhood education was erratic: "[T]he home, not the school, played the more important role in the children's development" (Le Clair 41). He attended Harvard University (1862–1863), where he briefly studied law: "[T]he falling of the curtain on Harry's Law School studies followed not long after his attempt, one day, to argue a case with a fellow student, under what seemed to him an awful glare of publicity, although the audience consisted merely of a few other students," and James subsequently spent most of his time in "general reading in the College library" (Le Clair, 360) until his eventual withdrawal from academic life.

Biographer Le Clair notes James's debt to **George Eliot** by saying "what brought him close to the work of George Eliot was a basic resemblance to his own tendencies . . . Even more helpful was the observation that her treatment of the lower classes was far more successful than of the remote upper classes, as in *Felix Holt*; the moral then was to observe with the keenest penetration the people one knew, the class he represented and understood" (383). **George Sand** seems to have influenced James's story "Gabrielle de Bergerac" (Le Clair, 426). Other influences include Mary Elizabeth Braddon (Novick, 129–130); Shakespeare's *Hamlet* (Novick, 235; Kaplan, 23); **Dickens** (Novick, 238; Kaplan, 23, 80); **Irving** and **Thackeray** (Kaplan, 23).

ARCHIVES

The Houghton Library at Harvard University has most of James's manuscripts. Other papers are in the collections of the Century Association in New York City, the Beinecke Library at Yale University, the University of California at Los Angeles, the Library of Congress, Colby College, the British Library, the Huntington Library, the University of Rochester Library, the New York Public Library, the University of Leeds Library, the Buffalo Public Library, the Morgan Library, and the Charles Scribner's Sons archives at Princeton University.

PRINTED SOURCES

Kaplan, Fred. *Henry James: The Imagination of Genius. A Biography* (New York: William Morrow and Company, Inc., 1992).
Kelley, Cornelia Pulsifer. *The Early Development of Henry James* (Urbana: University of Illinois Press, 1965).
Le Clair, Robert C. *Young Henry James: 1843–1870* (New York: AMS Press, 1971).
Novick, Sheldon M. *Henry James: The Young Master* (New York: Random House, 1996).

Seymour, Miranda. *A Ring of Conspirators: Henry James and His Literary Circle, 1895–1915* (London: Hodder & Stoughton, 1988).

Sandra Hannaford

JAMES, WILLIAM (1842–1910). William James was born in New York in 1842 and educated discontinuously from 1852 to 1869 at Bonn, Boulogne, Geneva, London, Paris, and Cambridge, Massachusetts. His father Henry James was a well-known philosopher who profoundly influenced the young William, although scholars have long debated the consequences of his upbringing. James maintained a strong lifelong religious impulse, yet he never articulated a concrete explanation of his beliefs. Although personally noncommittal, his philosophical ideas reveal that he valued "the right to believe at our own risk any hypothesis that is live enough to tempt our will." James was internationally recognized in his day as a philosopher and psychologist, traveling often, meeting with prominent intellectuals, and writing such highly influential works as *Principles of Psychology* (1890), *The Varieties of Religious Experience* (1902), and *Pragmatism, New Name for Some Old Ways of Thinking* (1907). The development and exposition of Pragmatism is his most lasting contribution to the Western intellectual tradition.

Discerning the literary influences on William James is difficult for several reasons. Scholar Gerald E. Meyers indicates that "definitive influences are not easy to determine because James based his thinking on steadfast convictions and tended to take from other thinkers only what harmonized with those convictions" (Myers, xiii). His praise for Henri Bergson's *L' Évolution Créatice* (1907), in which James saw the articulation of the central tenents of Pragmatism, is just one example. However, certain literary influences can be identified.

Although his interests included science, art, and psychology, philosophy was his primary preoccupation, especially as he grew older. From an early age, James was confronted by ostensibly two schools of philosophic writings: the rationalistic, monistic mode of **Georg W. F. Hegel** and the post-Kantians, and the empirical-pluralistic ways of **John Stuart Mill** and the British Empiricists. James leaned toward the Empiricists but rejected their tendency toward associationism, deeming their metaphysics insufficient.

James found his solution in French philosopher Charles Renouvier's *Psychologie rationalle* (1859). He had suffered from severe depression to the point of contemplating suicide largely as a result of this philosophical conflict, but his reading of Renouvier in 1870 provided an explanation of free will that gave him new insight on life and his work. Although Renouvier's conception of free will in particular helped save James (along with his reading of **William Wordsworth** and **Johann Goethe**), the French philosopher's system of thought confirmed many of his own ideas and convinced him that he had something to contribute to his time. The manner in which Renouvier connected fideism, moralism, phenomenalism, pluralism, and theism fascinated James. Even though James would later disagree with certain aspects of his ideas on metaphysics, Renouvier's thought resembled James's more closely than any other intellectual he encountered.

Next to Renouvier, the English philosopher Shadworth Hodgeson probably exercised the strongest influence on James's intellect. He admired Hodgeson's abjuration of unfounded assumptions and focus on conscious experience, although Hodgeson's effort to conflate a deterministic worldview with a sense of moral freedom repelled James. Lifelong friend **Charles S. Peirce**, to whom James credited the creation of Pragmatism, also had a decisive influence on James's philosophy.

Politics also interested James, particularly in the late 1890s when the Spanish American War made a deep impression on him. E. L. Godkin, editor of the *Nation* and the *Evening Post* at the time, was probably the most influential writer in the shaping of James's political thought.

ARCHIVES

William James Papers, The Houghton Library, Harvard University, Cambridge, Massachusetts.

PRINTED SOURCES

Allen, Gay Wilson. *William James: A Biography* (New York: Viking Press, 1967).
James III, Henry (ed.). *The Letters of William James*, 2 vols. (New York: Kraus Reprint Co., 1969).
Kucklick, Bruce. *The Rise of American Philosophy: 1860–1930* (New Haven, Conn.: Yale University Press, 1977).
Myers, Gerald E. *William James: His Life and Thought* (New Haven, Conn.: Yale University Press, 1986). See Chapter 1, "Life and Career," for an overview of literary influences.
Perry, Ralph Barton. *The Thought and Character of William James*, 2 vols. (Boston: Little, Brown, 1935). Still the best in-depth study of James's literary influences; documentation provides specific guidance to letters and manuscripts.
Putnam, Ruth Anna (ed.). *The Cambridge Companion to William James* (Cambridge: Cambridge University Press, 1997). Includes up-to-date bibliography and Thomas Carlson, "James and the Kantian Tradition."

Stephen Levine

JEFFERSON, THOMAS (1743–1826). Thomas Jefferson was born in Albemarle County, Virginia. Upon his father's death in 1757, Jefferson inherited a substantial estate, a small library, and a love of books and reading. In his youth, Jefferson studied Greek, Latin, and French under the tutelage of Rev. William Douglas and Rev. James Maury until he entered the College of William and Mary in 1760 to study law. After two years of college, Jefferson entered an apprenticeship with George Wythe who tutored him in both legal and classical studies. Jefferson was admitted to the Virginia bar in 1767 and was elected to the House of Burgesses in 1769. He served as a member of the Second Continental Congress where he was selected to draft the American Declaration of

Independence. From 1784–1789 Jefferson served as a diplomat in France, which gave him an opportunity to explore the Parisian bookshops on an almost daily basis. In 1800, Jefferson was elected as the third President of the United States, an office he held until, following Washington's example, Jefferson retired after his second term. He returned to his estate at Monticello where he worked to create the University of Virginia which first opened its doors to students in 1825, one year before Jefferson's death.

During his early education, Jefferson kept a journal, or commonplace book, in which he recorded passages of note from his readings. The bulk of the entries are excerpts of poetry from antiquity as well as from Shakespeare, Milton, and Dryden, among others. Jefferson transcribed the passages from the classical works in their original Greek and Latin. Of the few prose works recorded in his commonplace book, Jefferson noted fifty-four passages from Henry Saint-John Bolingbroke's *Philosophical Works*, more than for any other single work (Jefferson, *Jefferson's Literary Commonplace Book*, 24–55). It is probable Jefferson first derived his views on rationality and materialism from the English statesman and enlightened philosopher. In 1821, Jefferson wrote to his grandson, Francis Wayles Eppes, to recommend that he read Bolingbroke, "[his] eloquence is of the highest order. . . . His [philosophy] for those who are not afraid to trust their reason with discussions of right and wrong" (Jefferson, *Family Letters*, 438).

Jefferson's greatest literary influences came from the Enlightenment. His famous phrase from the Declaration of Independence, "that all men are created equal, that they are endowed by their Creator with inalienable Rights, that among these are Life, Liberty, and the pursuit of Happiness," was paraphrased from John Locke's *Second Treatise on Government*. Additionally, Jefferson admired Charles Louis de Secondat Montesquieu's *The Spirit of the Laws*; he helped the French philosopher Antoine Louis Claude Destutt de Tracy publish a critical edition of Montesquieu's work in America that Jefferson himself translated. Tracey's commentary was, in Jefferson's view, "the best elementary book on government which has ever been published" (Jefferson, *Family Letters*, 440). In the only book written by Jefferson, *Notes on the State of Virginia*, penned between 1780 and 1784, he cited Voltaire, the Abbé Raynal, and the naturalist Georges Louis Leclerc, comte de Buffon. Jefferson, in true Enlightenment fashion, was an accomplished amateur scientist, architect, naturalist, and student of medicine; he read widely in these fields as well.

Jefferson read the classics in their original Greek and Latin and he urged others to do so; he viewed the knowledge of classical languages as the mark of a proper education. Moreover, reading in ancient languages was an exercise that tested the abilities of a free people in a new republic. In 1787, Jefferson wrote to his daughter who complained of her difficulties with Latin, "I do not like your saying that you are unable to read the ancient print of your Livy. . . . It is a part of the American character to consider nothing as desperate. . . . Consider therefore conquering your Livy as an exercise in the habit of surmounting difficulties" (Jefferson, *Family Letters*, 35). Jefferson's correspondence with John

Adams included lengthy discussions of the classics, including Plato's *Republic*, which Jefferson read in 1814, a work Jefferson considered unworthy of its reputation (Jefferson, *Crusade*, 110).

Reading, for Jefferson, was a means for improving "morals and faculties" (Jefferson, *Crusade*, 117). The purpose of reading was not to amuse, nor was it to intellectually engage in abstract principles of metaphysics. Instead, the aim of reading and education was "to become a useful and distinguished member of your country" (Jefferson, *Family Letters*, 415). Jefferson was not interested in fiction, although he claimed the works of "Pope, Dryden, Thompson, Shakespeare, and of the French, Molière, Racine, the Corneilles, may be read with pleasure and improvement" (Jefferson, *Crusade*, 154).

Jefferson personally owned one of the largest private libraries in the United States. Following the burning of Washington by the British during the War of 1812, he sold most of the books in his library to the United States government, creating the core of what is now the Library of Congress. He was also instrumental in acquiring new books for the library at the University of Virginia and Jefferson designed the campus so that the library was the central feature of the university. When not engaged in political affairs, or keeping up with his correspondence, Jefferson spent his time reading. For a daily regimen of reading, he once advised: "If you read Law from breakfast four or five hours . . . the morning may be given to Natural philosophy and Astronomy, the afternoon to Rhetoric and Belles lettres and the night to history and ethics" (Jefferson, *Family Letters*, 443). Jefferson spent approximately 11 hours per day reading, at least when not occupied with public matters, on a vast range of subjects that helped him earn the reputation as one of the United States' premier intellectuals.

ARCHIVES

The Library of Congress: the 2,375 titles purchased by Congress, from Jefferson, in 1815 and an additional 134 books from his library.

The University of Virginia: Jefferson's personal and official correspondence and papers. Some of the books selected for the University library, although most were destroyed in an 1895 fire.

PRINTED SOURCES

Boorstin, Daniel J. *The Lost World of Thomas Jefferson* (Chicago: University of Chicago Press, 1993). A new edition of a classic biography.

Jefferson, Thomas. *The Commonplace Book of Thomas Jefferson: A Repertory of his Ideas on Government.* Gilbert Chinard (ed.) (Baltimore: Johns Hopkins University Press, 1926). Jefferson's notes on books of political philosophy.

———. *Crusade against Ignorance: Thomas Jefferson on Education.* Gordon C. Lee (ed.) (New York: Teachers College, Columbia University, 1961).

———. *The Family Letters of Thomas Jefferson.* Edwin Morris Betts and James Adam Beak, Jr. (eds.) (Columbia Mo.: University of Missouri Press, 1966).

———. *Jefferson's Literary Commonplace Book.* Douglas L. Wilson (ed.) (Princeton: Princeton University Press, 1989).

―――. *The Papers of Thomas Jefferson*. Julian P. Boyd, et al. (eds.) 27 vols. (Princeton: Princeton University Press, 1950–). This is the most complete and authoritative primary source.

Sanford, Charles B. *Thomas Jefferson and His Library: A Study of His Literary Interests and of the Religious Attitudes Revealed by Relevant Titles in His Library* (Hamden, Conn.: Archon Books, 1977). A primarily statistical study of the books in Jefferson's library.

Douglas B. Palmer

JEVONS, WILLIAM STANLEY (1835–1882). William Jevons was born in Liverpool in 1835 and educated at University College, London (1851–1853, 1859–1862). A Unitarian, he grew up in an intellectual and progressive environment, his father Thomas being an iron merchant. His father's firm went bankrupt after the railway boom crisis of 1847. Jevons studied natural sciences and especially chemistry, mathematics, and logic but did not finish his education. He became an assayer at the Australian Mint in 1854 and remained there until his return to England in 1859, when he resumed his education. Jevons taught at Owen's College, Manchester; Queen's College, Liverpool; and University College, London. He drowned near Hastings in 1882.

He formulated his basic ideas on economics and logic in the early 1860s: his switch from a labor theory of value to a marginal utility theory of value, his theory of capital and the rate of interest, and the "substitution of similars" as a general principle of knowledge acquisition. His most important works include *A Serious Fall in the Value of Gold* (1863), *The Coal Question* (1865), *The Theory of Political Economy* (1871), and *The Principles of Science* (1874). Jevons is generally seen as an interdisciplinary scholar who touched numerous fields of inquiry and developed many interesting insights but who was not always very careful regarding the development of the details. He was not only a pioneer in mathematical economic theory and philosophy of science but also one of the first economists to apply statistics to the social sciences.

The chemistry classes of Thomas Graham and Alexander Williamson influenced Jevons's intellectual development thoroughly, as atomic theory remained an important "metaphysical background" for his scientific inquiries (Könekamp, 13–15). Even more important are De Morgan's mathematics classes: Jevons attended his lower junior, higher junior, and lower senior classes in 1851–1853 and the lower senior and higher senior classes in 1859–1861. He derived from these classes not only the idea that mathematics has a logical foundation but also his general vision on science as expressed in both *The Theory* and *The Principles*. He corresponded with George Boole on logic in 1863–1864. Jevons's economic thought emerged in the context of the railway and land policy debates in Australia. An important influence was Morris Pell's 1856 paper "On the Application of Certain Principles of Political Economy to the Question of Railways," which appeared in *Sydney Magazine of Science and Art* in 1857. Jevons's reading of Richard Whately's *Introductory Lectures on Political Economy*

(1831) and Dionysius Lardner's *Railway Economy* (1850) should be mentioned as well (although the influence of the latter is generally overestimated). John Woolley's lecture on "The Selfish Theory of Morals" in 1856 supplied Jevons's reflections on "selfishness" with more analytical rigor. His construction of representative agents in economic theory was borrowed from Richard Jennings's *Natural Elements of Political Economy* (1855). His concern for the sanitary circumstances of the poor was probably derived from **Charles Dickens**'s work (*Barnaby Rudge* was Jevons's favorite novel). In the preface to the second edition of his *Theory*, Jevons wrote that his system was "more or less consciously" derived from "certain passages of **Bentham**, Senior, Jennings and other authors." Jevons used mechanical analogies and referred to Siméon-Dennis Poisson's *Traité de Méchanique* (second edition, 1833) in this context. Other references in *The Theory* include Alexander Bain's *The Emotions and the Will* (1859) and William Edward Hearn's *Plutology* (1864). He was influenced by Bentham and Paley's utilitarianism and criticized **John Stuart Mill**'s "inconsistent" writings on this topic. Jevons was an adherent of **Charles Darwin**'s and **Herbert Spencer**'s evolutionary theory.

ARCHIVES

Jevons Archives, John Rylands Library, University of Manchester.
Seton-Jevons Papers, Seton Hall University, New Jersey.

PRINTED SOURCES

Black, R.D.C. "Jevons, Bentham and De Morgan," *Economica*, 39, 153 (1972), 119–134.
———. (ed.). *Papers and Correspondence of William Stanley Jevons*, 7 vols. (London and Basingstoke: Macmillan, 1972–1981).
Grattan-Guinness, I. "The Correspondence between George Boole and Stanley Jevons, 1863–1864," *History and Philosophy of Logic*, 12 (1991), 15–35.
Könekamp, R. "Biographical Introduction." In R.D.C. Black and R. Könekamp (eds.), *Papers and Correspondence of William Stanley Jevons*, Volume I. (London and Basingstoke: Macmillan, 1972), 1–52.
Peart, S. *The Economics of William Stanley Jevons* (London: Routledge, 1996).
Schabas, M. *A World Ruled by Number. William Stanley Jevons and the Rise of Mathematical Economics* (Princeton, N.J.: Princeton University Press, 1990).
White, M. V. "Jevons in Australia: A Reassessment," *Economic Record*, 58, 160 (1982), 32–45.
———. "The Moment of Richard Jennings: The Production of Jevons's Marginalist Economic Agent." In P. Mirowski (ed.), *Natural Images in Economic Thought* (Cambridge: Cambridge University Press, 1994), 197–230.

Bert Mosselmans

K

KEATS, JOHN (1795–1821). John Keats, English Romantic poet, was born in London, the eldest child of Thomas and Frances Keats, owners of a livery stable. Although both of his parents died before he was 15, he attended the well-regarded school of John Clarke and established a lasting friendship with his schoolmaster's son, Charles Cowden Clarke, who would establish his own career as an author and critic. After the death of his grandmother, Keats was removed from school and apprenticed as an apothecary; in 1816, he passed the necessary examinations to practice this trade. In the same year, he had his first poem published, and he turned to a career in poetry rather than medicine.

Under the elder Clarke's tutelage, Keats was schooled in the great English authors. He read everything available in the school library from schoolboy thrillers and Defoe's *Robinson Crusoe* to the works of classical Greece and Rome and the great English poets (Motion, 37). Both as a student and later, Keats could be stirred in his own writing upon reading other poets' work. His first known poem was in imitation of Spenser, and "On the First Looking into Chapman's Homer" was hastily written after a long night reading George Chapman's translation of Homer, which Keats found quite superior to Alexander Pope's (Ward, 74–77). Several years later, he returned to this practice, with "On Sitting-Down to Read *King Lear* Once Again," suggesting not only the impact of the drama on his thinking but how often he had returned to it.

Historical works, in particular, attracted the interest of Keats, providing role models for the young orphan. Both as a student and in his later poetry, Keats particularly admired those who had helped develop individual freedom, a list that included King Alfred, William Tell, Robert Burns, and the English republicans of the seventeenth century (Ward, 18; Cook, xxiii). Although this interest was sparked by reading Gilbert Burnet's *History of His Own Time*, describing the establishment of civil and religious liberty in the seventeenth century, ultimately John Milton provided the young student's keenest examplar, with his "combination of active republicanism with great poetic achievement" (Motion, 38; also see Cook, xix). Keats looked not only to Milton's life for guidance but also to his poetry; shortly before his death, Keats was studying "Paradise Lost" as a stylistic example for his planned "Hyperion" (*DNB*, 1173).

Clearly Keats's interest in the development of liberty and the fate of the common man arose from his own modest beginnings and the fact that he had to make his own way in life without either family connections or wealth. A radical political perspective was a natural outgrowth, and while still serving his apprenticeship, Keats came to admire Leigh Hunt, a radical editor and author imprisoned for libelling the Prince Regent in his newspaper *The Examiner* in 1812. When Cowden Clarke traveled into London in 1815 to visit Hunt on his release from prison, Keats passed his friend a sonnet he had written for the occasion: verses that both marked his respect for the politically liberal poet and Keats's own desire to make a career in poetry rather than medicine. Later Keats would enter Hunt's circle in London, share his political views, and through him come to know **Byron**, **Shelley**, and the remainder of the Romantic circle.

William Hazlitt, a member of this circle, influenced Keats as another examplar of a multifaceted poet, in this case blending poetry with liberal philosophy. Keats particularly found Hazlitt's writings on "poetic identity"—or the relationship between a poet's inner thoughts and the world at large—influencing his own views on the role of literature in the world and his own ambitions (Motion, 125).

Keats reserved his greatest admiration, however, for William Shakespeare. He regularly reread Shakespeare's works after first being introduced to him, suggesting to a friend that "indeed I shall I think never read any other Book much. . . . I am very near Agreeing with Hazlitt that Shakespeare is enough for us" (May 11, 1817, in Cook, 357). Throughout writing *Endymion*, Keats's study was adorned with Shakespeare's portrait, and taking a break from the composition, he visited Stratford-upon-Avon with a friend. He found Shakespeare's birthplace and the memorials there somewhat disappointing, but his admiration for the Bard's poetic achievements was undimmed (Ward, 131–132).

Keats died in 1821 after a prolonged illness. In the fall of 1820 he had sailed to Italy in an unsuccessful effort to recoup his health. He was buried in the Protestant cemetery in Rome, where Percy Bysshe Shelley also lay. Keats's will stipulated that his "Chest of Books" was to be divided among his friends, which his brother subsequently fulfilled (Forman, 230–231).

ARCHIVES

British Library.
Houghton Library, Harvard University.
Camden Public Libraries, Keats House.

PRINTED SOURCES

Coate, Stephen. *John Keats: A Life* (London: Hodder and Stoughton, 1995).
Cook, Elizabeth. "Introduction." *John Keats*, The Oxford Authors series (Oxford: Oxford University Press, 1990).

Dictionary of National Biography (London: Oxford University Press, 1921), 10:1164–1176.

Keat, John. *John Keats: Complete Poems*, Jack Stillinger (ed.) (Cambridge, Mass.: Harvard University Press, 1978).

———. *The Keats Circle: Letters and Papers 1816–1878*, Hyder E. Rollin (ed.), 2 vols. (Cambridge, Mass.: Harvard University Press, 1948).

———. *The Letters and Poems of John Keats*, John Gilmer Speed (ed.), 3 vols. (New York: Dodd, Meade and Co., 1883).

———. *Letters of John Keats*, Robert Gittings (ed.), 2nd ed. (Oxford: Oxford University Press, 1975).

———. *The Letters of John Keats 1814–21*, Hyder E. Rollins (ed.), 2 vols. (Cambridge, Mass.: Harvard University Press, 1958).

———. *The Poetical Works and Other Writings of John Keats*, H. Buxton Forman (ed., Notes and Appendices by Forman), 8 vols. (New York: Charles Scribner's Sons, 1939).

Motion, Andrew. *Keats* (New York: Farrar, Straus and Giroux, 1997).

Spurgeon, Caroline F. E. *Keats's Shakespeare* (Oxford: Oxford University Press, 1928). Describes the seven-volume collection of Shakespeare's works that Keats owned.

Ward, Aileen. *John Keats: The Making of a Poet*, rev. ed. (1963; New York: Farrar, Straus and Giroux, 1986).

Derek Blakeley

KIERKEGAARD, SØREN AABYE (1813–1855). Søren Kierkegaard, Danish writer, was born in Copenhagen in 1813 and educated at the University of Copenhagen (1830–1840) and at Berlin (1841–1842).

Kierkegaard has been subject to much psychological speculation—and rightfully so since so much of his work is autobiographical in content. Kierkegaard wrote that the chief influence upon him was his "strict Christian upbringing" (*Journals*, 299). His father, who thought he had been cursed by God, passed his own melancholy on to his son. Kierkegaard later had a broken relationship with Regine Olson that exacerbated his feelings of loneliness. He wrote, "It is essentially owing to her, to my melancholy and to my money that I became an author" (*Journals*, 748, 235).

Kierkegaard's most notable biographer, Walter Lowrie, writes that Johann Georg Hamann was "the only author by whom S.K. was profoundly influenced" (Lowrie, 164). While a student, Kierkegaard had been exposed to the writings of Hamann. Hamann's attacks upon rationalism were foundational to the polemic later employed by Kierkegaard against the Church of Denmark. While it is perhaps true that Hamann is the person who most influenced Kierkegaard's work, the latter's own testimony, remembrances of family and friends, and the tracings of his commentators point to a number of others who exerted significant literary influence upon him.

It was Hamann who sparked Kierkegaard's interest in Socrates. Kierkegaard admired Socrates for his commitment to the methodology of indirect communication. This led to Kierkegaard's master's thesis "On the Concept of Irony with Particular Reference to Socrates." His admiration for Socratic epistemology may be what induced Kierkegaard's friend, Hans Brochner, to claim that Plato was Kierkegaard's model, that "he shaped his art after him" (Brochner, 36). However, Kierkegaard differed greatly from Plato in that Plato believed that the purpose of indirect communication was to recollect the truth already within the individual, whereas Kierkegaard viewed truth as so completely apart from man that only God could bring it to him. Kierkegaard's use of maieutic methodology was instead a way to free individuals from the cultural hegemony of formal Lutheranism and to restore individual existential virtue.

Kierkegaard believed that the infusion of Hegelian thought into Christianity had so corrupted the Church that it could no longer be called Christianity. **Georg Wilhelm Friedrich Hegel** had sought an objective and scientific metaphysics that Kierkegaard believed to be incompatible with biblical faith. Thus, it is not surprising that much of Kierkegaard's writing is given to polemic against the system of Hegel. Hegel was the philosopher whom Kierkegaard loved to hate. However, Kierkegaard seems to have been influenced almost as much by those with competing ideas as by those with whom he allied himself—and Hegel was no exception to this phenomenon.

Kierkegaard's attempt to restore the Church to New Testament purity was not only anti-Hegelian but opposed to all forms of rationalistic theology. His rejection of rationalism and his emphasis upon faith and subjective apprehension explain his attention to the work of Gotthold Ephraim Lessing. Kierkegaard indicates that Lessing was important in the preparation of his own *Philosophical Fragments* and *Concluding Unscientific Postscript*. He had become aware of Lessing's essay "On the Proof of the Spirit and of Power" while reading **David Friedrich Strauss**'s *The Christian Faith*. In addressing the dilemma of Lessing's ditch, Kierkegaard notes that since Christian dogma cannot be validated through historical considerations, a "leap" of faith is necessary. Kierkegaard claimed that the sum of his entire corpus had this single theme: faith.

Consistent with his commitment to a biblical faith is Kierkegaard's extensive use of biblical texts throughout his work. In *Repetition*, his pseudonym Constantine Constantius claims great love for the book of Job, and in *Stages upon Life's Way*, Quidam writes, "The Bible is always on my table and is the book I read most." This is most certainly true of Kierkegaard as well as his pseudonyms.

In addition to Hamann, Socrates, Hegel, Lessing, and the authors of the Bible, we can add a plethora of other writers to whom some level of tacit influence could be attributed. In a letter to C.K.F. Molbech, Hans Brochner notes the influence of Friedrich Heinrich Jacobi, Friedrich von Schlegel, Immanuel Kant, and the Greeks. At another time he recollects that in their conversations Kierkegaard often spoke of **Ludwig Feuerbach**. Kierkegaard derived his use of pseudonyms from the method of **Friedrich Schleiermacher**, and his exploration of multivocalization was inspired by the operas of Wolfgang Amadeus Mozart. Additionally, within his books and journals, he quotes and interacts with such authors as Johann Arndt, François de Salignac de La Mothe Fénelon, Franz von

Baader, Karl Rosenkranz, Karl Daub, Adolph Trendelenburg, Baruch Spinoza, Martin Luther, René Descartes, Gottfried Wilhelm Leibniz, Pierre Bayle, Plotinus, **Johann Gottlieb Fichte**, J. H. Fichte, Ludwig Tieck, E.T.A. Hoffman, Philipp Marheineke, and many others.

At the time of his death, Kierkegaard's library contained 2,748 volumes. His niece Henrietta Lund writes that his reading habits were "desultory" (Lund, 59). This is consistent with what we know from other sources. When he applied for admission to the university, his teacher's recommendation indicated that he had broad interests and that he tended to become involved in too many areas to develope expertise in any. Kierkegaard writes that it took him 10 years to gain his degree due to his preference for an indefinite course of study. No doubt, it was his diverse interests and "desultory" reading habits that resulted in his ability to produce a literary corpus of such enduring value. His philosophical sophistication was enabled through his vast reading in philosophy and theology, and his literary artistry was enhanced through his broad reading of the Romantics.

ARCHIVES

Kierkegaard Papers, Kierkegaard Library of St. Olaf College. Northfield, Minnesota.
Kierkegaard Papers, Kierkegaard-Malantschuk Library Collection of McGill University. Montreal, Canada.
Kierkegaard Papers, Royal Library of Copenhagen.

PRINTED SOURCES

Brochner, Hans. "Recollections." In T. H. Croxall (trans.), *Glimpses and Impressions of Kierkegaard* (Digswell Place: James Nisbet and Co. Ltd., 1959).
Dru, Alexander (ed. and trans.). *The Journals of Søren Kierkegaard* (London: Oxford University Press, 1951).
Kierkegaard, Søren. *Johannes Climacus or De omnibus Dubitandum Est, and A Sermon*, T. H. Croxall (trans.) (London: Adam and Charles Black, 1958). Also an assessment by Croxall. A volume of the Library of Modern Religious Thought, Henry Chadwick, general editor.
Lapointe, François H. (comp.). *Søren Kierkegaard and His Critics; An International Bibliography of Criticism* (Westport, Conn.: Greenwood Press, 1980).
Lowrie, Walter. *Kierkegaard* (London: Oxford University Press, 1938).
Lund, Henrietta. "Recollections from Home." In T. H. Croxall (trans.), *Glimpses and Impressions of Kierkegaard* (Digswell Place: James Nisbet and Co. Ltd., 1959).
Malantschuk, Gregor. *Kierkegaard's Thought*, Howard V. Hong and Edna H. Hong (eds. and trans.) (Princeton, N.J.: Princeton University Press, 1971).
Minear, Paul S., and Paul S. Morimoto (eds.). *Kierkegaard and the Bible. An Index* (Princeton, N.J.: Book Agency Theological Seminar, 1953).
Stucki, Pierre-Andre. *Le Christianisme et l'Histoire D'Apres Kierkegaard* (Basel: Verlag fur Recht und Gesellschaft, 1963).

Kevin Stilley

KIPLING, RUDYARD (1865–1936). Rudyard Kipling, author, was born in Bombay in 1865, the son of John Lockwood Kipling, a sculptor and member of the Victorian Arts and Craft movement, and Alice Macdonald, the daughter of a Methodist minister. The couple departed for India shortly after their wedding, where John Kipling became the principal of a school of art, and their eldest son, Joseph Rudyard, was born shortly after their arrival.

Kipling returned to England at the age of 6 to begin his education, living for the next five years with a retired naval officer and his wife in Southsea with whom his parents had contracted the care of Kipling and his sister. At age 12, Kipling began attending the new United Services College at Westward Ho, Cornwall, which was run by a friend of his parents, Cormell Price, who was a member of the Morris circle. More secular in its tone than most of its colleagues, the United Services College was, in the tradition of Haileybury, intended to be an inexpensive training ground for boys preparing to enter the military or the imperial civil service. Here he received a typical Victorian education in the classics, an appreciation of which remained within him throughout his life (Carrington, 373). His experiences as a schoolboy also provided the setting for his later work, *Stalky & Co.*, which, if anything, gave a too-realistic account of life in a Victorian boarding school for some contemporary critics (Carrington, 22).

Even though he attended a school intended for those preparing to enter the military, Kipling was always meant for a literary career and benefited from the skilled teaching of Price. Through his father's contacts, furthermore, Kipling even as a schoolboy was in touch with literary and artistic circles in London, as well as his scattered Macdonald cousins, often going down to the capital or to Paris to visit exhibitions. Even in Southsea, Kipling had read widely, especially the great novelists—Defoe, Fielding, **Dickens**, **Thackeray**—as well as both American and English poets of the nineteenth century. He certainly admired **Mark Twain** and was influenced by the thoughts of **Carlyle**, **Ruskin**, and **Emerson**. At Westward Ho!, Price gave him free reign over his library, where he was introduced to a wide variety of authors from Hakluyt to Dryden to **Rossetti** (Carrington, 27–28). His family unable to afford to send him on to Oxford, Kipling returned to India in 1882 and, at the age of 17, became assistant editor of the *Civil and Military Gazette* in Lahore.

Kipling relished his return to India, working both in the production of the *Civil and Military Gazette* and later as a reporter and acquiring the knowledge and experiences of India that would be reproduced in many of his later stories. He stayed in the position for the next four years, although he continued to study literature with his mother and sister in his available hours. His collection of imitative poems, *Echoes*, published in 1884, both reflected the scale of his reading and, along with his articles for Indian papers, began to attract notice in India. Kipling's experiences in India provided many of the subjects for his stories and poems, but his wide reading provided a stockpile of imagery and language that he adapted and utilized for his own purpose (Carrington, 79–80). He continued to work and write in India until he returned to London in 1889, having been a success with his early publications *Plain Tales from the Hills*, *Soldiers Three*, and *Wee Willie Winkie*. Even after his return, he traveled widely throughout the empire as he became its foremost literary advocate.

Throughout he continued to read widely, although critics frequently did not recognize others' influences in his work. On one occasion, he was asked by a fellow dinner guest if he "ever read much" (Weygandt, 1). Even those who found influences in his work scarcely agree on where they came from as they witnessed the influence of everyone from Bret Harte to Swinburne. Even if others were less prescient, Kipling recognized his literary debts to others from the beginning, as evidenced by his 1884 publication of *Echoes*, many of the pieces of which were parodies or heavily derivative poems. Subsequently, influences from Old English to Modern American literature have been identified, which certainly suggests his wide reading. The interest in the Romantic movement of the Pre-Raphaelite circle of his parents was passed to Kipling, with **Keats** and **Coleridge** being the most venerated of the poets; and he had obviously read the Victorian canon, his work containing numerous references to Ruskin, Dickens, and Thackeray. At the same time, he admired the comic novels of Surtees, which are referred to throughout *Stalky*, as well as the mysteries of Wilkie Collins. Kipling's aptitude for children's literature also demonstrated the continuing influence of Lewis Carroll's works, which Kipling had read since childhood (Weygandt, chap. 4). But his reading always remained wide and varied. On one occasion, he wrote, "I haven't been doing much outside reading of late. Beaumont and Fletcher mostly, and some Dekker and Evelyn's Tree-book [*Sylva*] and John Milton" (Carrington, 372).

Although Kipling had his own unique voice and style, he was clearly influenced by a wide variety of other works, from both the past and the present, which he continued to read throughout his life. The imperialism of men such as **Cecil Rhodes** also was present in his writings, especially when he became the foremost literary proponent of the British Empire in the 1890s. Throughout his life he also corresponded with both political and imperial figures as well as with other contemporary authors such as **Henry Rider Haggard** and became an established and well-regarded figure in British literary circles. Throughout, he maintained his reading habits. Upon reading *Eminent Victorians* in the 1920s, he thought Lytton Strachey's work "downright wicked in its heart." Although he refused nomination as Poet Laureate and, on three occasions, the honor of having the Order of Merit bestowed on him by the queen, he was awarded the 1907 Nobel Prize for Literature.

ARCHIVES

Sussex University Library. Correspondence, papers, and literary manuscripts.
British Library. Literary manuscripts.
Houghton Library, Harvard University. Correspondence and papers.
Library of Congress, Manuscript Division. Correspondence, papers, and manuscripts.

PRINTED SOURCES

Birkenhead, Lord. *Rudyard Kipling* (London: Weidenfeld & Nicolson, 1978).
Carrington, C. E. *The Life of Rudyard Kipling* (Garden City, N.Y.: Doubleday and Co., 1955).

Kipling, Rudyard. *"Something of Myself" and Oher Autobiographical Writings*, Thomas Pinney (ed.) (Cambridge: Cambridge University Press, 1990).

Page, N. *A Kipling Companion* (London: Macmillan, 1984).

Seymour-Smith, Martin. *Rudyard Kipling* (New York: St. Martin's Press, 1989). Incorporates a psychoanalytical examination of Kipling's life and sexuality.

Steart, J. McG. *Rudyard Kipling: A Bibliographical Catalogue* (London: Oxford University Press, 1959).

Weygandt, Ann M. *Kipling's Reading and Its Influence on His Poetry* (Philadelphia: University of Pennsylvania Press, 1939).

Wilson, Angus. *The Strange Ride of Rudyard Kipling: His Life and Works* (London: Secker & Warburg, 1977).

Derek Blakeley

KLIMT, GUSTAV (1862–1918). Gustav Klimt, born in Vienna in 1862, attended Kunstgewerbeschule. In 1897 he left Wiener Künstlerhaus to form the Secession, to create new art for all classes and reform cultural policy. His art resonated with lyricism and mysticism that evoked moods and linked the artistic trends of two centuries.

The title of the Secession's journal, *Ver Sacrum*, is probably from Ludwig Uhland's poem of the same name: "You are the seed of a new world. / That is the sacred springtime that the God wills" (Nebehay, *Ver Sacrum*, 23). The Secession sought to embrace all the arts and to express "creative impulse," a term coined by the Viennese art historian Alois Riegl. Riegl's evolutionary art history aimed to abolish the boundaries between categories, create "harmonism," and encourage the study of ornament (Hofmann, 39–41). One aspect of harmonism extended to the relativization of beauty, which Klimt practiced through stylization. Classical culture played an important role for the Secession. Klimt's poster for the first exhibition used Greek myth to depict Secession's struggle against an older force, and other themes of Greek mythology permeated Klimt's work (Whitford, 53). In *Ver Sacrum* Hermann Bahr urged artists to create a truly Viennese style of total works of art. This view was opposed by Adolf Loos, who in *Ver Sacrum* called for material provision to people before immersing them in art and in *Ornament and Crime* (1908) condemned decorative stylization and advocated mass production (Hofmann, 9–12).

Klimt's *Beethoven frieze* of 1902 illustrated Friedrich Schiller's "Ode to Joy." Leopold Schefer's poetry also appeared in a drawing for the frieze. The inscription in *Nuda Veritas* of 1899 is also from Schiller: "If you cannot please everyone with your actions and your art, you should satisfy a few. To please many is dangerous." The text, along with the mirror that the female figure holds out, bids spectators to examine themselves (Dean, 52). The rebellious tone might also derive from artistic individualism. Klimt had been immersed in Cesare Lombroso's *Genie und Irrsinn* (Fischer, 24).

Klimt's University pictures (*Medicine*, *Philosophy*, and *Jurisprudence*) criticized rational culture and declared the superiority of art for revealing human vulnerability. **Friedrich Nietzsche**'s critique of modern civilization and the declaration of the birth of a new tragic culture underlined such ideas. *Jurisprudence* include "the eternal recurrence," formulated by Nietzsche in *Thus Spoke Zarathustra*. Hugo von Hofmannsthal, who contributed to *Ver Sacrum*, in 1893 declared that art can "force open sunken, overgrown trapdoors of the soul," the repressed dimensions. In Klimt's *Music II*, as in Nietzsche's *The Birth of Tragedy*, music leads to the cosmos and the world of buried instincts (Frodl, 60).

Klimt's use of polyvalent symbolism recalls **Sigmund Freud**'s exposition in *The Interpretation of Dreams*, that dreams resist definitive explanation (Hofmann, 23–26). The abstraction in Klimt's work is perhaps influenced by **John Ruskin**'s "innocent eye." Bahr likewise demanded art that was dissociated from objects and was about shapes and colors (Hofmann, 37). Ambiguity was often represented in contemporary literature as the blurring of boundaries between the theater and the real, as in Arthur Schnitzler's "Der grüne Kakadu," Robert Musil's "Das verzauberte Haus," or Rainer Maria Rilke's "Todes-Erfahrung": [T]he world is full of parts for us to act [. . .] But, as you went, a segment of reality / flashed in upon our stage" (Hofmann, 22, 37). This was explored at the Garden Theater of the 1908 exhibition, presided by Klimt. Also depicted were visions from *The Birth of Tragedy* (Hofmann, 22).

ARCHIVES

Historisches Museum der Stadt Wien, Vienna.
Bildarchiv der Österreichischen Nationalbibliothek, Vienna.
Kunsthistorisches Museum, Bibliothek, Vienna.

PRINTED SOURCES

Bäumer, Angelica. *Gustav Klimt: Women*, Ewald Oswers (trans.). (London: Weidenfeld and Nicolson, 1986).
Breicha, Otto. *Gustav Klimt: Die goldene Pforte* (Salzburg: Verlag Galerie Welz, 1978).
Dean, Catherine. *Klimt* (London: Phaidon Press, 1996).
Fischer, Wolfgang G. *Gustav Klint & Emilie Flöge: An Artist and His Muse* (London: Lund Humphries, 1992).
Fliedl, Gottfried. *Gustav Klimt 1862–1918: The World in Female Form* (Cologne: Taschen, 1997).
Frodl, Gerbert. *Klimt*. Alexandra Campbell (trans.) (London: Barrie & Jenkins, 1992).
Hofmann, Werner. *Gustav Klimt*, Inge Goodwin (trans.) (London: Studio Vista, 1971).
Nebehay, Christian M. *Gustav Klimt. Dokumentation* (Vienna: Galerie Christian M. Nebehay, 1969).
———. *Gustav Klimt: Sein Leben nach zeitgenössischen Berichten and Quellen* (Munich: Deutscher Taschenbuch Verlag, 1976).
———. *Ver Sacrum 1898–1903*, Geoffrey Watkins (trans.) (New York: Rizzoli, 1977).
Partsch, Susanna. *Gustav Klimt: Painter of Women* (Munich: Prestel, 1994).
Pirchan, Emil. *Gustav Klimt* (Vienna: Bergland, 1956).
Stooss, Toni, and Christoph Doswald (eds.). *Gustav Klimt* (Stuttgart: Verlag Gerd Hatje, 1992).

Strobl, Alice. *Gustav Klimt. Zeichnungen 1878–1918*, 4 vols. (Salzburg: Verlag Galerie Welz, 1982–1989).

Vergo, Peter. *Art in Vienna 1898–1918: Klimt, Kokoschka, Schiele and Their Contemporaries* (London: Phaidon Press, 1993).

Whitford, Frank. *Gustav Klimt* (London: Collins & Brown, 1993).

Hazel Hahn

KOSSUTH, LAJOS (1802–1894). Lajos Kossuth of Hungary was born in 1802 at Monok in the county of Zemplén and died in exile in Turin, Italy, in 1894. Kossuth first attended school in Ujhély before graduating from a Lutheran high school in Eperjes, where he was the class valedictorian. He received a degree in law from Sárospatak College in 1820, having completed the program in one year. Sárospatak was a Calvinist school, and classes were taught in Hungarian, unusual among colleges at the time. Despite the Calvinism of Sárospatak, Kossuth's father was relatively indifferent to religious education, and Kossuth himself rejected the Bible as a source of authority (Deak, 11–13). Throughout his life, religion had very little influence on Kossuth's attitudes and beliefs.

Regarded by many as the father of modern Hungary, Kossuth first came to national prominence as a deputy at the National Reform Diet of 1832. Kossuth made his name as an advocate of the press, publishing a series of parliamentary reports designed to educate the populace about political events in Hungary. Persisting even when the government banned his publications, Kossuth was jailed for several years. Upon his release, Kossuth began editing a revolutionary newspaper in 1839, the *Pesti Hírlap*. In 1847, as a member of the Reform Party, Kossuth represented the county of Pest at a national diet. When the revolutions of 1848 swept across Europe, it was Kossuth who played the principal role in petitioning the emperor to appoint the first Hungarian cabinet, ratifying a series of new laws drafted primarily by Kossuth.

Despite his great role in Hungarian history, Kossuth's nationalism was not exceptional for an educated Magyar nobleman of the nineteenth century. The origins of the Kossuth family are the subject of debate, but by the time of Lajos's birth, his family was thoroughly Magyar, and Lajos's legal education in Hungarian could only have heightened his sense of nationality. Kossuth was a student of history early in his life, and his admiration for the antiabsolutism of the French Revolution is obvious from his early attempts at writing history himself.

Kossuth abandoned his efforts at history when Hungarian political activity increased in 1825. Inspired in part by the Polish Uprising of 1830–1831, Kossuth became involved in a liberal-minded, intellectual reading club where he likely encountered, if not before then, the writings of two important German historians, Johann Gottfried Herder and Ernst Moritz Arndt. Herder argued that language was the preservative of a people's culture and predicted that Magyar would eventually disappear, overwhelmed by the Slavic languages and culture. His writings inspired Hungarian nationalists to advocate the spreading of Magyar culture by law. Ernst Moritz Arndt warned the Hungarian nationalists that for a nation–state to exist it must have access to the sea, and its inhabitants must speak the same language. Kossuth took Arndt's warning to heart (Deak, 44).

Kossuth also came under the influence and guidance of several Hungarian poets in the decade of the 1830s. While serving as an "absentees' deputy" at the National Reform Diet from 1832 to 1836, Kossuth encountered the guidance of the poet Ferenc Kölcsey, who in his "Second Song of Zrinyi" predicted the death of the Hungarian nation, an argument echoed by the poet Michael Vörösmarty in his "Summons." Other Hungarian poets who gained a nationalist following in the 1830s include Joseph Bajza and Alexander Petöfi (Janos, 38).

ARCHIVES

No substantial archival sources known to exist.

PRINTED SOURCES

Deak, Istvan. *The Lawful Revolution: Louis Kossuth and the Hungarians, 1848–1849* (New York: Columbia University Press, 1979).
Deme, Laszlo. *The Radical Left in the Hungarian Revolution of 1848* (New York: Columbia University Press, 1976).
———. "Writers and Essayists and the Rise of Magyar Nationalism in the 1820's and 1830's," *Slavic Review*, 43, 4 (1984), 624–640.
Janos, Andrew C. *The Politics of Backwardness in Hungary, 1825–1945* (Princeton, N.J.: Princeton University Press, 1982).

Phillip A. Cantrell II

KROPOTKIN, PYOTR ALEKSEYEVICH (1842–1921). Pyotr Kropotkin was born in Moscow in 1842, heir to the Grand Princes of Smolensk. His father, a career military officer, followed Russian aristocratic tradition in having his sons tutored at home. Among the tutors he hired were Poulain, an unreconstructed French Bonapartist; Nikolai Pavlovich Smirnov, a young Muscovite who became Kropotkin's close friend and literary mentor; and Nikolai Mikhailovich Pavlov, a medical student. Smirnov showed Kropotkin secret copies of suppressed writings of **Aleksander Pushkin**, Mikhail Yurievich Lermontov, **Nikolai Gogol**, and the executed Decembrist poet Kondratii Fëdorovich Ryleev and introduced him to the works of Nikolai Alekseevich Nekrasov and **Alexandre Dumas (*père*)**. At the age of 15, Kropotkin discovered that the diaries of his mother, dead since he was 3, contained handwritten passages from Ryleev and such Romantics as **Alphonse-Marie-Louis de Prat de Lamartine** and **George Gordon Noel, Lord Byron**. That his mother should have indulged in forbidden literature impressed him and reinforced his own literary sensibilities.

In 1850 Tsar Nicholas I personally selected Kropotkin for the Corps of Pages, the elite military school in St. Petersburg, which he entered in 1857. His favorite teacher, Vladimir Klassovsky, introduced him to the ideas of Nikolai Shelgunov on the oppressed proletariat, and he read **Alexandr Ivanovich Herzen** on the sly. He was graduated at the top of his class in 1861 and immediately became *page de chambre* to Tsar Alexander II. His gentle nature, profound sense of *noblesse oblige*, desire to lead a useful life, and increasing disgust with the excesses of the Tsarist regime led him to request assignment in Siberia, where, from 1862 to 1867, he distinguished himself as a geologist and geographer. While there, the reformist governor of Transbaikal, Boleslav Kukel, introduced him to the exiled poet Mikhail L. Mikhailov, who advised Kropotkin to read **Pierre-Joseph Proudhon**.

In 1867 he moved with his brother Alexander to St. Petersburg and worked in geography. Reading **Lev Nikolayvich Tolstoy**'s *War and Peace* confirmed his utter loss of faith in the state. Ever more revolutionary, he refused the prestigious Secretariat of the Russian Geographical Society in 1871. The following year he traveled to Switzerland, attended the meeting of the Jura Federation, and met James Guillaume, Benoit Malon, and Adhémar Schwitzguébel but not **Mikhail Aleksandrovich Bakunin**. This trip marked his decisive conversion to anarchism. Upon returning to Russia, he joined the anarchist circle of Nikolai Vasilievich Chaikovski. He was imprisoned in 1874, escaped in 1876, and did not return to Russia until 1917. The Bolsheviks tolerated him because of his revolutionary credentials, despite his anti-statism.

Kropotkin's anarchist-communism owed much to Thomas More, William Godwin, and **Charles Fourier** but not much to individualistic anarchists such as **Max Stirner**. His revolutionary career included interaction with Élisée Reclus, François Dumartheray, Andrea Costa, Paul Brousse, and Enrico Malatesta, all of whom he met in the 1870s. In 1880, a paper by zoologist Karl Kessler modified his views on evolution and symbiosis. Although not a complete pacifist himself (he supported the Allies in World War I), the pacifism of Tolstoy always informed his thought.

ARCHIVES

Cahm (350–351) and Miller (314–319) (see Sources) list a total of 5 Russian, 16 European, and 3 American repositories of Kropotkin's papers, correspondence, and police files, including Gosudarstvennaia Biblioteka imeni Lenina and Tsentral'nyi Gosudarstvennyi Arkhiv, Moscow; International Instituut voor Sociale Geschiedenis, Amsterdam; the British Museum; Institut Français d'Histoire Sociale, Paris; and Stanford University.

PRINTED SOURCES

Cahm, Caroline. *Kropotkin and the Rise of Revolutionary Anarchism, 1872–1886* (Cambridge: Cambridge University Press, 1989).

Cole, George D. H. *Socialist Thought: Marxism and Anarchism, 1850–90* (London: Macmillan, 1954).

Fleming, Marie. *The Anarchist Way to Socialism* (Totowa, N.J.: Rowman & Littlefield, 1979).

Hulse, J. W. *Revolutionists in London* (Oxford: Clarendon Press, 1970).

Kropotkin, Pëtr Alekseevich. *Memoirs of a Revolutionist* [Zapiski revoliutsionera] (Boston: Houghton Mifflin, 1899). First American edition. Autobiography.

Miller, Martin A. *Kropotkin* (Chicago: University of Chicago Press, 1976).

Osofsky, Stephen. *Peter Kropotkin* (Boston: Twayne, 1979).

Pirumova, Natal'ia Mikhailovna. *Pëtr Alekseevich Kropotkin* (Moscow: Nauka, 1972).

Woodcock, George, and Ivan Avakumović *Peter Kropotkin: From Prince to Rebel* (Montreal: Black Rose, 1990).

Eric v. d. Luft

L

LA FOLLETTE, ROBERT MARION (1855–1925). Robert La Follette was born in 1855 in Primrose, Wisconsin, where he attended a mix of private and public schools. Resentful of being forced to attend the Baptist church of his stepfather and mindful of his late father's agnosticism, La Follette shunned religious affiliation as an adult. He excelled at oratory at the University of Wisconsin at Madison, gaining membership into the Athena Literary Society. La Follette developed his oratory skills with dialect readings and a hair-raising rendition of **Edgar Allan Poe**'s *The Raven*. His character analysis of *Othello*'s Iago won first prize at the prestigious Interstate Oratorical Contest in 1879. The following year, La Follette combined reading law with a formal legal education at Madison. The people of Wisconsin flocked to hear La Follette's lengthy, dramatic speeches and repeatedly elected him to public office. He served in the House of Representatives (1885–1889), as governor (1901–1906), and as U.S. senator (1906–1925). In 1909, he founded *La Follette's Weekly Magazine*, currently published monthly as *The Progressive*. A key leader of progressive reforms, La Follette championed the rights of the people against business monopolies and corrupt politicians.

Before entering politics, La Follette seriously considered a career on the stage. In his private life he delighted family and friends with readings from Herminie Templeton Kavanagh's *Darbie Gill and the Good People*, and with other literary amusements. Although he rarely allowed for any levity while on the stump, the dramatic inflections and larger-than-life gestures he incorporated into his readings at home served him well as he spoke for hours at endless county fairs, at Chautauquas, and on the campaign trail.

La Follette's greatest literary influences were the Bible and Shakespeare. His in-depth examination of "*Hamlet*, The World's Greatest Tragedy," was an often requested lecture throughout his entire career. Despite his distaste for organized religion, La Follette was an avid reader of the Bible (one of his notebooks is made up entirely of biblical quotations). He advised his son that the Bible and Shakespeare are the two best things in all of literature: "There is no better way to saturate yourself in them than by committing the noble passages [to memory]. They will enrich your mind and inspire your life and color your expression. Soak yourself full on the Bible & Shakespeare" (La Follette Family Papers, Library of Congress). In short, in the Bible, La Follette found the inspiration for his uncompromising quest to set the newly industrialized and urbanized America on the path of righteousness, and in the drama and power of Shakespeare, he found the tools with which to convincingly convey that vision.

ARCHIVES

La Follette Family Papers, Library of Congress. Principal political and personal correspondence and papers.
La Follette Papers, State Historical Society of Wisconsin. Documents political reform movement in Wisconsin from 1879 to 1910.

PRINTED SOURCES

Burgchardt, Carl R. *Robert M. La Follette, Sr.: The Voice of Conscience* (New York: Greenwood Press, 1992). This rhetorical biography includes La Follette's literary criticisms of a variety of Shakespeare's plays.
La Follette, Belle Case, and Fola La Follette. *Robert M. La Follette*, 2 vols. (New York: Macmillan Company, 1953).
La Follette, Robert. *Autobiography* (Madison, Wis.: Robert M. La Follette Company, 1911; 1913; reprint, Madison: University of Wisconsin Press, 1960).
Unger, Nancy C. *Fighting Bob La Follette: The Righteous Reformer* (Chapel Hill: University of North Carolina Press, 2000).

Nancy C. Unger

LAMARTINE, ALPHONSE-MARIE-LOUIS DE PRAT DE (1790–1869).

Alphonse Lamartine, during a long career, published poetry and essays; earned praise as a diplomat, serving in Italy with note; and spent nearly 20 years as a politician working to better the lives of fellow Frenchmen. He served as the foreign minister and was a major political power in the short life of the Second Republic. When he died, the Second Empire was on the verge of collapse, and Lamartine's own star was rapidly being eclipsed by younger, more radical talents both in literature and in politics.

Lamartine's early life centered around his family's estates. He was educated at the Jesuit college at Belley. While there, he read **Chateaubriand**'s *Génie de christianisme*, an essay that showcased the connection between Christianity and liberty and gave "literary and intellectual stimulus to the French Catholic revival" (Fortescue, 14). *Génie* profoundly influenced the young Lamartine. In addition, he began to write poetry. When he left Belley, there was little he could do; family leanings prevented him from going into the government or the military; and early amorous adventures clearly showed that a church career was not a possibility. With little to do, Lamartine began to read. He gravitated toward the classics and contemporary literature, reading nothing of the medieval or early modern period. His biographer, William Fortescue, wrote that the French Romantics, the poet Ossian, writer Chateaubriand, and the philosopher Rousseau were particularly significant (16). Indeed, Lamartine's early poetry was soundly in the French Romantic tradition.

Chateaubriand, the writer, exerted an influence on the young Lamartine's politics but more so on his poetry. As the first French Romantic writer, he set the tone for the Romantics who would follow. In addition, Lamartine read recent French and British literature, thereby gaining knowledge of authors such as **Blake** and **Coleridge** and their emphasis on emotion and nature. His strongly felt emotions connected with various amorous relationships inspired groups of poems in the 1820s.

Rousseau, as Lamartine's biographer wrote, influenced an entire generation of French radicals. Rousseau saw self-analysis and self-revelation as essential. Rousseau portrayed and defended love as a physical passion "inspired by a divinely implanted human intinct." In addition, one can see within French Romanticism and within Lamartine's writings an "alienation from and disillusion with society, belief in God's presence in nature, and striving for mystical union between man and God" (Fortescue, 16).

Rousseau provided the beginnings of Lamartine's awareness of the problems of the French working class. In 1831, following the fall of the Bourbon government in France, Lamartine began to write on the humanitarian causes with which he would later be connected. In short, he discovered the "social question," particularly the problems of urban poverty, and gradually became associated with political radicalism. Again, it can be strongly argued that this also came of his reading Rousseau. By 1843, he broke with his family's traditional support of the monarchy and announced he was joining the left-wing opposition. In 1848, Lamartine became foreign minister in the new Second Republic government, but he was quickly eclipsed by **Napoléon III**. By 1851, Lamartine was again in private life. He died in 1869 largely ignored.

Best known as a poet, Lamartine was also a social critic, diplomat, and radical. His reputation suffered because of his perceived failure as a government minister. It would take several years after his death for many to go back and read his poetry and other writings.

ARCHIVES

Bibliothèque Nationale, Paris. See also published volumes of correspondence below.

PRINTED SOURCES

Cabeen, D. C., gen. ed. *A Critical Bibliography of French Literature*, Vol. 5, *The Nineteenth Century in Two Parts*, Part I (Syracuse, N.Y.: Syracuse University Press, 1994).
Fortescue, William. *Alphonse de Lamartine: A Political Biography* (New York: St. Martin's Press, 1983).

Ireson, J. C. *Lamartine: A Re-evaluation* (Hull, England: University of Hull Press, 1969)

Lamartine, Alphonse de. *Autour de la correspondance de Lamartine*, Christine Croisille and Marie-Renee Morin (eds.) (Claremont-Ferrand: Universite Blaise Pascal, 1991).

————. *Correspondance Alphonse de Lamartine-Aymon de Virieu*, 2 vols. (Paris: Presses universitaires de France, 1987).

————. *Correspondance de Lamartine avec Charles Dupin et documents epistolaires*, Marie-Renee Morin (ed.) (Paris: Nizet, 1995).

————. *Correspondance generale de 1830 a 1848*, 25 vols. Maurice Levaillant (ed.) (Paris: E. Dros, 1943–).

Lombard, Charles H. *Lamartine* (New York: Twayne Publishers, 1973).

Phyllis L. Soybel

LANG, ANDREW (1844–1912). Andrew Lang was born in Selkirk, Selkirkshire, in 1844 and died in Banchory, Aberdeenshire, in 1912. He was educated at Selkirk Grammar School (1852–1854), the Edinburgh Academy (1854–1861), the University of St. Andrews (1861–1864), the University of Glasgow (1864–1865), and Balliol College, Oxford (1865–1868). In 1868 he was elected a fellow of Merton College, Oxford. In 1875 he married and moved to London to work as a journalist and man of letters.

As a child, Lang read Dasent's *Popular Tales from the Norse* (*DNB 1912–1921*, 320). At the Edinburgh Academy he discovered **Dickens**, **Dumas**, and **Thackeray**. Lang's reading at St. Andrews included Cornelius Agrippa, the Alchemistical Philosophers, **William Morris**, **Robert Browning**, Spenser, the novels of **Bulwer-Lytton**, and *The Mabinogion*—a collection of Welsh folktales he would have seen in Lady Charlotte Guest's translation (3 vols., 1838–1849). In a copy of Cornelius Agrippa he wrote, "Hoc opus diligenter perlexi, et dico ut amplissimo verbi senso Bosh vel Rot vel Bolly sit" [I have read through this work carefully and I say that in the fullest sense of the word it is Bosh or Rot or Bolly]. At Balliol, college library records confirm that Lang read Swinburne and **Matthew Arnold**, designating the latter's *The Scholar Gypsy* "our [Oxford's] *Lycidas*" (Green; *Biography*, 21), and records at Merton show that while there he read John Dennis's *Etruria* (Green; *Biography*, 69).

As an undergraduate, Lang experimented with translations of Villon, Ronsard, Alfred de Musset, Gautier, and Gérard de Nerval. After moving to London, he translated, with S. H. Butcher, Homer's *Odyssey* (1879) and, with Walter Leaf and Ernest Myers, the *Iliad* (1883), and he wrote three studies on Homer between 1893 and 1910. He also published translations of the works of Theocritus, Bion, and Moschus (1880) and, of the *Homeric Hymns* (1899). He collaborated with **Henry Rider Haggard** on a novel, *The World's Desire* (1890), and it is clear that he read much of Haggard's work.

Lang edited a number of the works of **Scott**, including *Lyrics and Ballads* and *The Lady of the Lake*, as well as the Gadshill editions of Dickens. In *Adventures among Books* (1905), Lang recalled how **Edgar Allan Poe**'s *Tales of Mystery and Imagination* remained in his memory.

He found Fielding humorous; he said that the "genius of Tolstoi, Tourgueneff and **Dostoevsky** there is no denying" ("Realism and Romance," 683–93) but found **Zola** "devoid of wit and humour" (Green, 164). Concluding that Victorian novels were not great literature, he experimented with fiction that directly parodied popular novels such as Hugh Conway's *Dark Days* (1884, under the pseudonym F. J. Fargus).

Among other contemporary figures, however, he applauded **Pater** for his economy of expression, but he disliked Morris and **Rossetti** for their use of archaism, which he felt was inappropriate for the age. He praised the Swinburne who wrote *Atalanta in Calydon* as "a new and original poet" (*Adventures among Books*, 32) but wrote of the "disappointment and trouble" that resulted from Swinburne's poems designed to shock the reading public (*Letters on Literature*, 21). Lang also had an antipathy toward lyrical poetry because he felt that it could not perform a didactic social role. Though he was familiar with **Hardy**'s work, he was not impressed by it.

Frazer's *The Golden Bough* (1890) was dismissed by Lang on the grounds that Frazer had been too sweeping in his use of sources and had omitted those that did not accord with his ideas. Similarly, he was out of sympathy with Max Müller.

Lang also published literary criticism that included work on Shakespeare and Bacon, as well as **Coleridge**. He stated that, in his opinion, the "Ancient Mariner" gave birth to English poetry (Lang, ed., ***Samuel Taylor Coleridge: Selections from the Poets***, London: 1898, xl). In his volume on **Wordsworth**, Lang was of the opinion that "his poetry is independent of his theory" (Lang, ed., *William Wordsworth: Selections from the Poets*, 1897, xi). Lang was widely read in Shakespeare's work but expressed a dislike for the plays as theatrical spectacles.

Lang is probably best known for his colored fairy books and for editing the first English version of ***Grimms' Household Tales*** (1884). He also contributed the introduction to the English edition of Perrault's *Contes Populaires* (1888). There is evidence to suggest that Lang was reading Cox's *The Mythology of the Aryan Nations*, the fairy tales of Madame d'Aulnoy, and Scottish and Scandinavian folktales, such as *The Kalevala*—the Finnish national epic poem—as a background to his work on the fairy tale.

ARCHIVES

Lang papers, Lockwood Library, State University of New York at Buffalo.
Houghton Library, Harvard University.
Honnold Library, Claremont, California.
Darlington Collection, University of Indiana Library.
Dundee Reference Library.
Ashley MS, British Library.
National Library of Scotland, Edinburgh.
University of St. Andrews Library.
Bodleian Library, Oxford.

Fitzwilliam Museum, Cambridge.
National Library of Wales, Aberystwyth.
University of Reading Library.
Fowler autograph album, Clifton College Library, Bristol.
Norfolk Record Office, Norwich.
University of Glasgow Library.

PRINTED SOURCES

Dictionary of National Biography: Twentieth Century 1912–1921 (London: Oxford University Press, 1927), pp. 319–323.
Green, Roger Lancelyn. *Andrew Lang: A Critical Biography* (Leicester, England: Ward, 1946).
———. "Andrew Lang: Critic and Dickensian," *The Dickensian* 41 (1944), 10–14.
Lang, Andrew. *Letters on Literature* (London: Longmans and Co., 1889).
———. "Realism and Romance," *Contemporary Review* 52 (November 1887), 683–693.
———, ed. *Samuel Taylor Coleridge*, Selections from the Poets series (London: Longmans, Green and Co., 1898).
———, ed. *William Wordsworth*, Selections from the Poets series (London: Longmans, Green and Co., 1897).
Langstaff, Eleanor de Selms. *Andrew Lang* (Boston: Twayne Publishers, 1978).

Caroline Dowson

LASSALLE, FERDINAND (1825–1864). Ferdinand Lassalle was born in Breslau, Germany, in 1825. His parents were Jewish; and Lassalle, on occasion, agonized about his Jewish heritage. He was determined to make a significant contribution to society as an educated leader. He is most often cited as the "father" of German socialism. Lassalle pursued his education at the University of Breslau (1842–1844) and the University of Berlin (1844–1846). Besides reading the writings of Jean-Jacques Rousseau, **Lord Byron**, **Heinrich Heine**, and **Johann Gottlieb Fichte** during his studies at the University of Breslau, he also discovered the philosophy of **Hegel**. In a 40-page letter written to his father, while he was at the University of Breslau, Lassalle eagerly outlined his own conception of the dialectic. From that moment on, all of his major writings definitely show the influence of Hegel's philosophy: Lassalle remained true to that philosophy throughout his life.

Lassalle penned several works, which have been published in numerous sources, including his first major philosophical treatise, *Heraclitus the Obscure, Philosopher of Ephesus* (1857). Lassalle was determined to show how Heraclitus's concept of world reason was connected to Hegel's concept of the Absolute. He wrote that Heraclitus was to pronounce a truly speculative idea, which was surrender to the universal. Lassalle asserted that this was in keeping with Hegel's concept of the Absolute. Heraclitus, Lassalle wrote, was the first to recognize the dialectical concept of opposites. Lassalle considered his work on Heraclitus to be both philosophical and philological. He did, however, emphasize his concept of the state as a positive force for culture and justice by explaining how Heraclitus, in his conflict with the masses of Ephesus, represented the knowledgeable, that is, knowing the true importance of the universal will. It becomes apparent, in *Heraclitus*, that Lassalle believed the Hegelian concept of the state to be the ultimate force in the dialectic.

Lassalle's commitment to Hegelianism is also recognized in the one drama (in five acts) he wrote, *Franz von Sickingen* (1858). The drama is based on the Peasants War in Germany, and Sickingen and Ulrich von Hutten represent the spirit of revolution. However, because they failed to observe Hegelian dialectics, they perished as heroes trying to redeem themselves. "The work is full of long monologues, Lassallean bombast and Hegelian argument" (Footman, 106). It does demonstrate that even in writing a drama the author remained true to his faith in Hegel.

Lassalle's second major treatise, *The System of Acquired Rights* (1861), is a two-volume work on law. Here again, the influence of Hegel is apparent. Lassalle believed law expressed the national consciousness right. Since the national consciousness is always in a state of flux, no age is bound to the limitation of another. Thus, he concludes that retroactive law can be justified and cites the French Revolution as an example. In the second volume Lassalle discusses the differences between historical and dogmatic treatment of jurisprudence, particularly in its application to the concept of inheritance. Lassalle maintained that inheritance of property was directly related to a society's concept of life after death, using Roman law and German law as the basis for his conclusions. He explains this not in social science methodology but rather attributes the differences in terms of the Volksgeist. Thus, Hegelian philosophy becomes a part of his treatise on law.

In both the major academic treatises, it is evident that Lassalle rejected determinism in Hegelian dialectics, which **Karl Marx** affirmed. It is the spirit of the people ultimately expressed through the state that determines what laws are applicable in a given time period, without obligation to the past. Lassalle believed that man could direct historical consciousness toward specific goals. The most important goal, Lassalle believed, was the rejection of bondage of any kind.

It is Lassalle's writings on socialism that propelled him into prominence and historical importance. His published letters, pamphlets, and speeches show his reaffirmation that only the state can accomplish the lofty goals of socialism. The state, in Hegelian terms (*Staatsrecht*), represented the will of the people, and only through this will can workers achieve economic freedom. Hegelianism, the foundation of his earlier major works, remains the basic concept upon which Lassalle constructs his social theories.

While he had great respect for Karl Marx, the two parted company because of Lassalle's belief that through the mechanism of universal suffrage human liberty could be achieved. Furthermore, Lassalle believed the time (1860s) was ready for socialism to become a reality through the state via universal suffrage. Marx totally disagreed and also criticized Lassalle's acceptance of the concept of the iron law of wages. Ultimately, Marx broke off all relations with Lassalle.

The revolutions of 1848 were the demarcation point for Lassalle. He believed that the fourth class (proletariat) emerged from those revolts, especially in France, and was prepared to lead to the freedom of the human race because its interest was the interest of all of humanity. In his final work, *Herr Bastiat-Schulze von Delitzsch, the Economic Julian, or Capital and Labor* (1864), Lassalle analyzed property and property rights through the eyes of a Marxist. However, he sank to vulgarity and brutishness in his attacks on the Manchester School. To the Lassalleans of the future, and the German Social Democrat Party in particular, the bases of their claim to Lassalle as the founder of the German Social Democrat Party are found primarily in his speeches and pamphlets. It was in those writings that Lassalle developed the concept of a peaceful socialist evolution with definitive humanitarian goals. That alone qualifies Ferdinand Lassalle as one of the great contributors to the development of Western culture.

ARCHIVES

University of Berlin and Berlin Public Library.
Munich Public Library.

PRINTED SOURCES
Note: All of Lassalle's works have been published. The best place to begin for the researcher is Bernstein's edition.
Footman, David. *Ferdinand Lassalle Romantic Revolutionary* (New Haven, Conn.: Yale University Press, 1947).
Lassalle, Ferdinand. *Ferdinand Lassalle, Gesammelte Reden und Schriften*, Edward Bernstein (ed.), 12 vols. (Berlin: Deutsche Verlags, 1920).
———. *Franz von Sickingen*, Daniel De Leon (trans.) (New York: New York Labor News Company, 1910).
———. *Nachgelassene Briefe und Schriften*, 6 vols. (Berlin: Springer, 1921, 1967).
———. *Die Philosophie Herakleitos des Ephesus*, 2 vols. (Berlin: F. Duncker, 1858).
Oncken, Hermann. *Lassalle* (Stuttgart: F. Frommanns Verlag, 1904).

Gene Mueller

LAUTRÉAMONT, COMTE DE (1846–1870). Isidore-Lucien Ducasse, the real name of the French poet who published under the pseudonym Comte de Lautréamont, was born in Montevideo, Uruguay, where his father was a member of the French consulate. His mother died when he was an infant, and his father sent him back to France for schooling. Ducasse spent most of his short adult life in Paris. Best known for his prose poem *Les Chants de Maldoror*, he lived in obscurity and found influence only after his work was rediscovered and lauded by Andre Breton's surrealist group more than five decades after his death.

Very little biographical information exists for Ducasse, and outside of references made in a few surviving letters, evidence of his reading experiences was pieced together by critics who catalogued his references and speculated on his influences. Ducasse's controversial style was such that he frequently employed fragments from the works of others, so his poems allow for an authoritative interpretation of these influences that goes beyond simple speculation. What is known of his adolescent reading suggests that he was preoccupied with poetry, scientific works, and travel literature. Accordingly, *Chants* is a sweeping, imaginative, and dark work, filled with suggestions that Ducasse was fond of a range of texts from the poetry of **Edgar Allan Poe** to **Mary Shelley**'s *Frankenstein*. The wandering motif is clearly reminiscent of Dante, whose work, other than that of the Marquis de Sade, lends the most to the atmosphere of the poem. Ducasse's preoccupation with destiny in *Chants* is suggestive of Charles Baudelaire, **Johann Wolfgang Goethe**, and William Shakespeare. Ducasse seems to have been most familiar with the work of Baudelaire, although his attitude toward the older writer is ambivalent at best. Ducasse is also known for *Poésies*, two short pieces in which the author renounces the work of some of the most important writers in Western literature. He names Baudelaire, **Lord Byron**, **Victor Hugo**, **Alphonse de Lamartine**, and Alfred de Musset as his principal targets, though he touches upon many others, including **Alexandre Dumas** (*père*), Théophile Gautier, and Etienne de Sénancour. In a reversal from the stand taken in *Chants*, Ducasse complained that dark brooding is a waste of the writer's talents. He attempted to improve existing works, rewriting passages from the texts of Jean de la Bruyère, Blaise Pascal, and the Marquis de Vauvenargues to alter their meanings. This later work hints at the true breadth of Ducasse's reading, and recent critics have speculated on whether or not one can read the influence of Ducasse's contemporaries, like the social philosopher **Pierre-Joseph Proudhon**, in his last writings. What is certain, however, is that his sweeping knowledge and irreverent treatment of literary tradition anticipated the stand of the avant-garde writers of the twentieth century who would champion Ducasse's work.

ARCHIVES

No substantial archival sources known to exist.

PRINTED SOURCES

Bachelard, Gaston. *Lautréamont* (Dallas, Tex.: Dallas Institute Publications, 1986).
Bonnet, Marguerite. "Lautréamont et Michelet," *Revue d'Histoire Littéraire de la France*, 64, 4 (October–December 1964), pp 605–622.
de Jonge, Alex. *Nightmare Culture: Lautréamont and Les Chants de Maldoror* (London: Secker and Warburg, 1973).
Fowlie, Wallace. *Lautréamont* (New York: Twayne Publishers, 1973).
Juin, Hubert (ed.). *Œuvres Complètes—Les Chants de Maldoror, Lettres, Poésies I et II* (Paris: Gallimard, 1973).
Peyrouzet, Edouard. *Vie de Lautréamont* (Paris: Grasset, 1970).
Pickering, Robert. *Lautréamont-Ducasse: Image, Theme, and Self-Identity* (Glasgow, Scotland: University of Glasgow French and German Publications, 1990).

Winkelman, Klaus. *Lautréamont Impersonator: A Study in Poetic Autobiography* (New Orleans, La.: Tulane University, 1967).

Winspur, Steven. "Lautréamont and the Question of the Intertext," *Romantic Review*, 76, 2 (March 1985), 192–201.

Zweig, Paul. *Lautréamont: The Violent Narcissus* (Port Washington, N.Y.: Kennikat Press, 1972).

Craig Monk

LIEBKNECHT, WILHELM (1826–1900). Wilhelm Liebknecht was born in Giessen, Hesse-Darmstadt, in 1826 and christened in the Evangelical Church; he graduated from Gymnasium in Giessen (1843), and attended university in Giessen (1843–1845), Berlin (1845–1846), and Marburg (1846–1847), studying theology and philosophy. Liebknecht played an active role in the 1848 revolutions, twice participating in military actions in Baden and only narrowing escaping execution by loyal government troops. After a brief exile in Geneva (1849–1850), Liebknecht went to London. There he met **Karl Marx**, with whom he developed a close working relationship and friendship. In 1862 Liebknecht returned to Prussia, where he attempted unsuccessfully to organize a workers' movement. Consistent criticism of **Otto von Bismarck**'s conservative-nationalist policies led in 1865 to Liebknecht's expulsion from Prussia and relocation to Saxony. In 1869 Liebknecht helped found the Social Democratic Workers' Party (SDAP), and in 1875 he was a driving force behind the Gotha compromise establishing the Socialist Workers' Party of Germany (SAP); both were important forerunners of the Social Democratic Party of Germany (SPD), which was founded in 1891 and stressed internationalism and working for socialism by legal means. During this time, Liebknecht was first elected to the Reichstag (federal parliament); with one interruption he served in that legislative body until his death. During the 1880s, with social democracy outlawed in Germany, Liebknecht labored to keep the party intact and remained committed to peaceful, patient tactics, but always with an ill-defined, long-term goal of revolutionary change. He continued after 1891 to edit the party daily, *Vorwärts*, and sit in the Reichstag, but he lost influence as the SPD adopted gradual change and reformism as official policy. Liebknecht's lasting influence is as a party organizer and architect of compromise in the formative decades (1860s to 1880s) of Germany's social democratic movement. He was also the father of socialist revolutionary Karl Liebknecht.

University was a formative time for Liebknecht, particularly his brief period in Berlin (1845–1846) when he read extensively. In Berlin, he was influenced by the materialism of **Ludwig Feuerbach**'s *On Philosophy and Christianity* and *The Essence of Christianity*. **David Friedrich Strauss**'s *The Life of Jesus Critically Examined*, and his even more skeptical *The Christian Doctrine*, pushed Liebknecht toward a rejection of religion. From **Henri de Saint-Simon**'s *The New Christianity* and other writings, Liebknecht formulated a theory of class struggle and the demand for ownership of goods in common, and he came to believe that a brotherhood of man must accompany the scientific organization of society. **Friedrich Engels**'s *Condition of the Working Class in England* laid bare with scientific precision the excesses of industrial capitalism (Dominick, 17). Already by 1846 Liebknecht referred to himself as a "conscious socialist" (Liebknecht, "Aus der Jugendzeit," 35).

Marx's ideas, first encountered in 1848 and more carefully analyzed during the London years, proved especially influential, especially the *Communist Manifesto* (1848) and those concepts later published in *Capital* (1867). Specifically, Liebknecht drew heavily on Marx's theories concerning economic exploitation, revolutionary tactics, and the need for the collective ownership of the means of production. But Liebknecht deviated from Marx's rigid class orientation, rejected the concept of a dictatorship of the proletariat, and proposed a peaceful transition from capitalism to socialism. Although throughout his career Liebknecht consistently defended many of Marx's ideas, these tactical differences caused continual friction between the two men.

ARCHIVES

Liebknecht Papers, International Institute for Social History, Amsterdam. Principal political correspondence and papers.

PRINTED SOURCES

Dominick, R. *Wilhelm Liebknecht and the Founding of the German Social Democratic Party* (Chapel Hill: University of North Carolina Press, 1982). The standard biography.
Eckart, G. (ed.). *Wilhelm Liebknecht's Briefwechsel mit Karl Marx und Friedrich Engels.* Vol. 1, *1862–1878* (The Hague: Mouton, 1963). Demonstrates exchange of ideas.
Eisner, K. *Wilhelm Liebknecht: Sein Leben und Wirken,* 2nd ed. (Berlin: Vorwärts, 1906). Romantic depiction by a socialist contemporary.
Liebknecht, W. "Aus der Jugendzeit," *Neue Welt Kalendar für 1900* (Berlin: Neue Welt Verlag, 1899). Personal recollections on youth and university years.
———. *Reden* (Berlin: Neuer Deutscher Verlag, 1925).
———. *Robert Blum und seine Zeit* (Nuremberg: Wörlein, 1888). Biography of the 1848 revolutionary that reveals much about Liebknecht's own political ideas and development.
———. *Speeches of Wilhelm Liebknecht* (New York: International Publishers, 1928).
Pelz, W. (ed.). *Wilhelm Liebknecht and German Social Democracy: A Documentary History* (Westport, Conn.: Greenwood Press, 1994). English-language compilation of important writings and speeches.

Thomas Saylor

LINCOLN, ABRAHAM (1809–1865). Abraham Lincoln, sixteenth president of the United States, was born on February 12, 1809, in Hardin County, Kentucky. Tragically, he died from an assassin's bullet on April 15, 1865, in Washington, D.C. He grew up in Indiana and Illinois, where the aggregate of his formal education amounted to less than one year. An avid reader, he memorized passages from the King James Bible, *Aesop's Fables*, *Pilgrim's Progress*, and Shakespeare's plays. One of his favorite books was Parson Weems's *Life of Washington*, a didactic account of the revolutionary hero. Although despised by critics, Lincoln became a revolutionary American because of his ability to express complicated ideas and concepts in understandable terms.

Lincoln considered himself a proverbial self-made man who began his life among the annals of the poor. He left home at age 22 and educated himself while working on a farm, splitting rails for fences, and keeping store at New Salem, Illinois. He served as a militia captain in the Black Hawk War, spent eight years in the Illinois legislature, and rode the circuit of courts. After marriage to Mary Todd in 1842, he became a father to four boys, only one of whom lived to maturity. Following his election to the House of Representatives in 1846, he denounced the Mexican War and supported antislavery measures. He served for one term and returned to his law career in Springfield, Illinois. Then, the new Republican Party in Illinois nominated him in 1858 to challenge Democrat Stephen Douglas for a Senate seat, and the national party selected him in 1860 for president of the United States. He won the election that year and was reelected in 1864.

During this period of national crisis, Lincoln resorted to the figurative language of metaphor, allegory, and myth. "A house divided against itself cannot stand," he proclaimed on June 16, 1858, at Springfield, Illinois. Referencing a familiar quotation from the Gospels, he added: "I believe this government cannot endure, permanently half slave and half free. . . . It will become all one thing, or all the other." In a subsequent series of debates, he warned of a conspiracy among corrupted politicians for nationalizing slavery. Even though he lost that Senate election, Lincoln emerged as an uncompromising voice in opposition to the extension of slavery into the national territories. On February 27, 1860, he delivered the Cooper Union address in New York, wherein he argued that Republicans were the conservatives on constitutional questions about expanding slavery. "Let us have faith that right makes might," he mused, "and in faith, let us, to the end, dare to do our duty as we understand it." His perorations were published in newspapers, pamphlets, broadsides, and books, constituting the first literary works of his canon. Moreover, contemporary biographers such as **William Dean Howells** made "honest Abe" the embodiment of republican manhood and virtue.

Even if the Civil War seemed irrepressible, Lincoln as president struck a conciliatory tone through his rhetoric. Although the states of the lower South seceded in rebellion, his inaugural on March 4, 1861, poetically invoked "the mystic chords of memory," which promised to "swell the chorus of the Union, when again touched, as surely they will be, by the better angels of our nature." While coming to terms with the struggle for the Union on July 4, 1861, he called the Civil War "a people's contest." A republican society, he opined, elevated the condition of all humans by removing unjust barriers and endeavoring "to afford all, an unfettered start, and a fair chance, in the race of life." A critical element in his political philosophy, then, was the concept of free labor, which secured the virtues of small-scale capitalism, social mobility, and individual dignity.

Ironically, Lincoln's most symbolic statement on political philosophy, the Emancipation Proclamation, may have been his least poetic one. On September 22, 1862, he promised through an executive order to continue to press for compensated emancipation within the border states and for the colonization of African Americans. However, "all persons held as slaves" within any state or part of a state in rebellion after January 1, 1863, would be "then, thenceforward, and forever free." Although slavery remained legal in the United States until the Fifteenth Amendment to the Constitution in 1865, nothing but the goal of freedom would justify the enormous sacrifices from the war.

After a Union victory over the Confederacy at Gettysburg, Lincoln authored a memorable statement about the transformation of the nation. Delivered on November 19, 1863, his address contained musical cadences and dialectical metaphysics. The romanticism about the glory of battle at the dawn of the war gave way to millennialism, a belief in the divine guidance of the American people toward a new world order. He began with an account of the events of the past that led to the momentous occasion, and he concluded with an expansive pledge "to be here dedicated to the great task remaining before us." Recalling the casualties of the war, he noted that "they gave the last full measure of devotion." By juxtaposing death to life, he resolved that "these dead shall not have died in vain; that this nation, under God, shall have a new birth of freedom; and that government of the people, by the people, and for the people shall not perish from the Earth." In fact, he used the term "nation" five times in the address, denoting the Union as a living entity.

Lincoln voiced a deeply held sense of brooding over the mysterious ways of Providence, though. Addressing a Bible-reading public during his second inaugural on March 4, 1865, he invoked the doctrine of grace when he, in effect, extended an apology for slavery. If the Civil War represented a punishment to atone for the sins of the nation's forefathers, then "every drop of blood drawn with the lash shall be paid by another drawn with the sword." However, he concluded with a call for redemption, promising "malice toward none, with charity for all" and summoning the nation to fight the war to the last battle. Such an end, he predicted, may achieve "a just and lasting peace among ourselves and with all nations." Indeed, he shifted responsibility for the protracted struggle and its outcomes from himself to the indeterminable forces of history.

Paradoxically, this self-made man sensed that his own life was bounded to the history of the nation. He blended the assumptions of enlightenment with the language of mysticism, constructing a political discourse both progressive and tragic.

ARCHIVES

Abraham Lincoln Papers, Library of Congress, Washington D.C.
Herndon-Weik Collection, Library of Congress, Washington D.C.

PRINTED SOURCES

Basler, Roy P. Marion Delores Pratt, and Lloyd A. Dunlap (eds.). *The Collected Works of Abraham Lincoln*, 8 vols. (New Brunswick, N.J.: Rutgers University Press, 1953).
Donald, David. *Lincoln* (New York: Simon and Schuster, 1995).
McPherson, James. *Abraham Lincoln and the Second American Revolution* (New York: Oxford University Press, 1991).
Neely, Mark A. *The Abraham Lincoln Encyclopedia* (New York: McGraw-Hill, 1982).
Oates, Stephen B. *With Malice toward None: The Life of Abraham Lincoln* (New York: Harper and Row, 1977).
Paludan, Phillip S. *The Presidency of Abraham Lincoln* (Lawrence: University Press of Kansas, 1994).
Peterson, Merrill D. *Lincoln in American Memory* (New York: Oxford University Press, 1994).
Wills, Gary. *Lincoln at Gettysburg: The Words That Remade America* (New York: Simon and Schuster, 1992).

Brad Lookingbill

LIND, JOHANNA MARIA (JENNY) (1820–1887). Jenny Lind, also known as the "Swedish Nightingale," was born in Stockholm, Sweden, the illegitimate daughter of a carpenter and a music teacher. It was at the age of 9 that her operatic talent was discovered by the Royal Opera House in Stockholm, where she was invited to attend, gratis, in September 1830 as the youngest entrant to the theater school. Her literary influences as a child are not apparent, but due to the type of operas she sang at such a young age, an intelligent mind can be inferred. By the age of 17, she had received critical acclaim for her performance in the leading role of Agatha in the opera *Der Freischutz*.

By 1840, Her talent was well known not only in Sweden but also in Denmark, where she befriended the writer **Hans Christian Andersen**. She became the basis for several of his tales, such as "The Angel," "The Emperor's Nightingale," and even, it was rumored, "The Ugly Duckling," written after she rejected a marriage proposal from him and purportedly handed him a mirror, saying, "[N]ot me, with my potato nose!" Her relationship with Andersen, however, opened up a whole new world for Jenny Lind. Virtually unknown outside Scandinavia, Jenny met Hans Meyerbeer of Berlin, who cast her as the lead in his new opera *Camp in Silesia*. On her debut night in Prussia, December 7, 1844, Jenny transposed the aria from the original key of "G" to "F," and the audience gave her a standing ovation, the first ever given to a performer in Germany.

Her performance in Germany cemented her reputation. She debuted in London on May 4, 1845, and by this time the "Jenny Lind craze" in Europe had begun.

Her name had become analogous with the nightingale, "the most celebrated of all warblers." Somehow she had been able to convince her public that a woman could be a performer and still retain her virtue. Considering her desire to retain her virtue, it is interesting that she so willingly accepted the offer of her next benefactor. In October 1849, Phineas T. Barnum, American entrepreneur and museum owner, and notorious collector of all things unusual, offered to bring Jenny Lind to America. Although he had never heard her sing, he certainly knew the impact of her voice on European culture. Despite attempts to dissuade Lind from accepting Barnum's offer, she accepted because of the substantial financial sum he could provide, enough to allow her to continue the charity work for which she had become known in Europe. As an added bonus, Barnum's offer would allow her to free her voice from the continual strain of operatic performances and give medley concerts. Her contract included 150 concerts from September 1850 to May 1852, but after 95 concerts, Lind bought her end of the contract and managed her own concerts. News of her arrival spread due to Barnum's careful networking, and "Lindomania," which had already spread throughout Europe, soon conquered America.

Her "art" coincided with the height of the Romantic movement; her singing was the natural immanence of her soul. She brought a renewed interest in music to America, resulting in the construction of new concert halls. She challenged negative stereotypes in her desire to provide quality performances, and she was a champion for women in her quest to seek respect for women artists. Her arrival in America seemed to have an almost messianic quality, especially since 1850 was a particularly trying year, with slavery as the pivotal issue. Much was made of Lind's arrival in the newspapers, and the September 2, 1850, issue of the *New York Daily Tribune* noted: "God has sent JENNY LIND. . . . [W]ith her benevolence of soul . . . [she] is the woman who could move the world . . . and leave upon her age that which could never be erased" (Gallagher, 207–208). The texts of her songs, such as "Jenny Lind's Greeting to America," were published, and the poet **Henry Wadsworth Longfellow** wrote, "Her power is in her presence which is magnetic and takes the audience captive before she opens her lips. She sings like the morning star: clear, liquid, heavenly sounds."

Her acclaim continued even after her 1852 marriage to fellow musician Otto Goldschmidt, and when the couple returned to Europe, Jenny continued her contributions to charitable causes, although singing very little in public. When Jenny Lind left Europe in 1850, she had departed a lonely woman, well known only in Europe, but she returned a married woman with an international reputation. At her death from a stroke in 1887, the flags in both Britain and Sweden were lowered to half-mast, in honor of the "Swedish nightingale" who so epitomized the talents of Western culture.

ARCHIVES

No substantial archival sources known to exist.

PRINTED SOURCES

Block, Adrienne Fried. "Two Virtuoso Performers in Boston: Jenny Lind and Camilla Urso." In Josephine Wright, (ed.), *New Perspectives on Music: Essays in Honor of Eileen Southern* (Warren, Mich.: Harmonie Park, 1992).

Gallagher, Lowell. "Jenny Lind and the Voice of America." In Corrine E. Blackmer and Patricia J. Smith (eds.), *En travesti: Women, Gender, Subversion, Opera* (New York: Columbia University Press, 1995).

Holland, Henry Scott. *Memoir of Jenny Lind-Goldschmidt: Her Early Art-Life and Dramatic Career, 1820–1851*, 2 vols. (London: John Murray Publishing Company, 1891).

New York Daily Tribune, September 2, 1850.

Schultz, Gladys D. *Jenny Lind: The Swedish Nightingale* (Philadelphia: Lippincott Publishing Company, 1962).

Ware, W. Porter. *P. T. Barnum Presents Jenny Lind: The American Tour of the Swedish Nightingale* (Baton Rouge: Louisiana State University Press, 1980).

Jennifer Harrison

LIVINGSTONE, DAVID (1813–1873). David Livingstone, African missionary and explorer, was born in Blantyre, Scotland, and educated at Anderson's College, Glasgow (1836–1838), and at the London Missionary Society's training college at Chipping Ongar near London, (1838–1840), where he received his medical degree and was ordained to the ministry.

Livingstone's father Neil, a staunch Calvinist member of the Church of Scotland, exercised strict religious discipline over his family and tried to limit David's reading to the Bible and theological works. In fact, Livingstone records that he was once thrashed for refusing to read **Wilberforce**'s *Practical Christianity*. However, even at an early age, young Livingstone was fascinated by the study of natural history, poring over William Patrick's *The Indigenous Plants of Lanarkshire* and *Culpeper's Herbal*. It was only after reading Thomas Dick's *The Philosophy of a Future State* that Livingstone was able to reconcile his scientific studies with Christian belief. Around this same time his father left the established Church for the less predestinarian Independent Congregation at Hamilton.

Livingstone records attending lectures by Dr. Ralph Wardlaw, principal of Congregational College and prominent abolitionist, and reading his book on infant baptism. However, he credits the source of his missionary aspirations to a pamphlet on the need for medical missionaries to China by Dr. Karl Gutzlaff, author of *Three Journeys along the Coast of China*. As a result of the Opium Wars with China, Livingstone turned his attention to Africa. While still a theological student in London, Livingstone was present at the Exeter Hall meeting on June 1, 1840, when Thomas Fowell Buxton launched the Niger expedition to bring "Commerce and Christianity" to Africa in place of the slave trade. Livingstone went to Africa with the same battle cry but met with little success in his quest to find a water route through central Africa to facilitate commerce. Livingstone left the London Missionary Society after his triumphal homecoming in 1857 but returned to Africa as a geographer under the patronage of the British government and the Royal Geographic Society. Livingstone died in Africa in 1872 feeling his life was a failure, but his legend, mediated through Horace Waller's edition of *Livingstone's Last Journals*, shaped late Victorian colonial policy toward Africa.

ARCHIVES

Wilson Collection and the David Livingstone Documentation Project. National Library of Scotland, Edinburgh. Calendar of all Livingstone materials throughout the world.

Livingstone Memorial, Blantyre, Scotland. Miscellaneous journals, diaries, and notebooks.

Livingstone Museum, Lusaka, Zambia. Chiefly unpublished correspondence.

PRINTED SOURCES

Blaikie, William G. *The Personal Life of David Livingstone* (New York: Fleming H. Revell, [1895]).

Jeal, Tim. *Livingstone* (New York: Putnam's, 1973).

Livingstone, David. *The Last Journals of David Livingstone in Central Africa*, Horace Waller (ed.), 2 vols. (1874; Westport, CT: Greenwood Press, 1970).

————. *Missionary Travels and Researches in South Africa* (London: John Murray, 1857).

Livingstone, David and Charles Livingstone. *Narrative of an Expedition to the Zambesi and Its Tributaries* (London: John Murray, 1865).

Mary Angela Schwer

LONDON, JACK (JOHN GRIFFITH CHANEY) (1876–1916).

Jack London was born John Griffith Chaney in San Francisco, California, in 1876 and raised by his mother and stepfather after his father deserted the family. He left school at the age of 14 to escape poverty and seek adventure, living at various times as a sailor and a hobo. During this time he educated himself at public libraries, where he developed a philosophy combining socialism and white supremacy. At the age of 19 he completed a four-year high school program at Oakland High School in one year. He then went on to attend the University of California at Berkeley but left school after one year to seek his fortune in the Alaskan gold rush of 1897.

Returning to California after a year, he turned to writing to earn a living. His first novel *The Son of the Wolf* (1900) won a wide audience. His vivid, realistic depictions of Alaska in *Call of the Wild* (1903) and *White Fang* (1906) remain his best-known works. Other important works include the sea adventure *The Sea Wolf* (1904), the depiction of a future dictatorship in *The Iron Heel* (1907), and the autobiographical novel *Martin Eden* (1909). Although London's reputation declined when more sophisticated American writers appeared in the 1920s, his work strongly influenced later depictions of life in the wilderness and stories dealing with social, political, and economic issues.

London read early on the rags-to-riches novels of **Horatio Alger** and later claimed that he had lived the story. Attracted to history and adventure novels about exotic voyages, such as Captain Cook's *Voyages* and Paul du Chaillu's *Travels*, London also read *Moby Dick* (1851) over and over and read classics such as *Madame Bovary* (1857) and *Anna Karenina* (1858). **Washington Irving, Robert Louis Stevenson, Rudyard Kipling, Joseph Conrad**, and other romantic literature were also favorites. London read Ouida, the pseudonym of Maria Louise Ramé, author of *A Dog of Flanders* (1872), the sea adventures of W. W. Jacobs, and **Thomas Hardy**. Naturalistic writers such as **Émile Zola**, the founder of naturalistic writing who emphasized scientific determinism in his fiction, and Frank Norris, a writer of proletariat novels, were also read by London.

London supplemented his fiction reading with extensive poring over of materialistic philosophers such as Francis Bacon, John Locke, and Immanuel Kant, some of whom were known for advocating personal freedom coupled with personal responsibility. Works by Sigmund Freud, and especially Carl Jung's *Psychology of the Unconscious* (1916), were read eagerly by London, who encountered Adam Smith's *The Wealth of Nations* (1776) and **Charles Darwin**'s *On the Origin of Species* (1859) in his autodidactic quest. An exposure to **Karl Marx** and **Friedrich Engel**'s *The Communist Manifesto* (1848) was tempered by an encounter with **Herbert Spencer**'s writings. London later claimed that Spencer's "Philosophy of Style" taught him how to write in an acceptable manner, while Spencer's *First Principles* (1882) was largely responsible for London's personal philosophy. In this work, Spencer applied the theory of evolution to human society. He claimed that progress was necessary and humans were perfectible but that only the fittest survive.

London, with a proletariat background and a sympathy toward socialism, revealed in his writings a tendency toward believing in the natural supremacy of certain superior individuals in life-threatening situations. His appeal, therefore, to an American capitalistic society was practically inevitable.

ARCHIVES

Jack London Papers, Henry E. Huntington Library, San Marino, California.

PRINTED SOURCES

Hedrick, Joan D. *Solitary Comrade: Jack London and His Work* (Chapel Hill: University of North Carolina Press, 1982).
Kershaw, Alex, *Jack London: A Life* (N.Y.: St. Martin's Press, 1998).
Kingman, Russ. *Jack London: A Definitive Chronology* (Middletown, Calif.: Rejl, 1992).
———. *A Pictorial Life of Jack London* (Middletown, Calif.: Rejl, 1992).

Rose Secrest

LONGFELLOW, HENRY WADSWORTH (1807–1882). Henry Wadsworth Longfellow, poet, editor, and translator, was born in Portland, Maine District, in 1807 and educated at Bowdoin College (1822–1825). He was raised a Unitarian and remained committed to the liberal Christian faith throughout his life. Avoiding his father's plans for a career in law, he became the first professor of modern languages at Bowdoin in 1829 and then, in 1834, was appointed the Smith Professor of Modern Languages at Harvard, a position he held for 18 years. He was cherished as an American icon in the United States and Europe, his birthday was celebrated as a national holiday, and after his death, a bust of him was placed in the Poet's Corner of Westminster Abbey. Longfellow's main contribution to Western culture lay in his success at familiarizing that very concept, both through his own best-selling poetry and his translations and editorial work.

Although the faculty positions he held were both in modern languages, Longfellow received, in his early years, a solid training in the classics, which provided the basis for his enduring love of European literature. His literary interests extended from "Sicily to Norway," in the words of his friend and fellow Dante Club member, the art historian Charles Eliot Norton. These vast interests were facilitated both by repeated "research" trips throughout Europe and by an impressive skill with languages. Longfellow shared in the contemporary passion for Dante, working for years on a translation of the *Divine Comedy* and returning to the Italian poet for solace throughout his life. In addition to Dante, the greatest influences on his work were British and German. Sir **Walter Scott**, whom he first read as a young boy, introduced him to balladry and romantic historic themes—to which he would return in his own work—while among his contemporaries **Dickens** and **Tennyson**, both of whom he knew personally, were his favorites. The Germans, especially Novalis, Schiller, **Goethe**, and Jean-Paul Richter—to whom he devoted an entire chapter in the early *Hyperion* (1839)— provided an important Romantic influence, particularly on Longfellow's conception of the relation between language and national character.

The genius of Longfellow's corpus lay in forging a cultural bridge between the Old and New Worlds. Hoping to share his love for European literature with his American audiences, he edited an anthology of *The Poets and Poetry of Europe* (1845), which included translations of nearly 400 poets in 10 different languages with critical introductory essays on the literature of each language. Yet like the student in his *Tales of a Wayside Inn* (1863) "to whom all tongues and lands were known, and yet a lover of his own," Longfellow strove to include American literature in the tradition of Western culture. He was influenced by the older American writers **Washington Irving**—on whose *Sketch-Book* he modeled his own *Outre-Mer* (1833–1834)—and William Cullen Bryant. Admiring of **Emerson** and his Bowdoin classmate **Hawthorne**, like those men he sought to carve out a place for letters in the new Republic in such early periodical articles as "The Literary Spirit of Our Country" (1825) and "The Defense of Poetry" (1832). While he experimented with many traditional poetic styles, emulating Chaucer, Scott, and Cervantes at times, he often used them to explore distinctively New World themes, as in his controversial *Poems on Slavery* (1842), or the wildly popular French-American romance *Evangeline* (1847), the native American epic *The Song of Hiawatha* (1855), and *The Courtship of Miles Standish* (1858). He addressed *Hiawatha* to those readers "who love a nation's legends, love the ballads of a people," and it was this love, for the literature of all Western nations and peoples, that he sought to instill in his readers.

ARCHIVES

Longfellow Papers, Houghton Library, Harvard University. Correspondence, journals, manuscripts.

PRINTED SOURCES

Cameron, Kenneth Walter. *Longfellow's Reading in Libraries* (Hartford, Conn.: Transcendental Books, 1973).
Goggio, Emilio. "Italian Influences on Longfellow's Works," *Romantic Review*, 25 (July 1925), 208–222.
Hilen, Andrew. *Longfellow and Scandinavia: A Study of the Poet's Relationship with the Northern Languages and Literatures* (New Haven, Conn.: Yale University Press, 1947).
Wagenknecht, Edward. *Henry Wadsworth Longfellow: Portrait of an American Humanist* (New York: Oxford University Press, 1966).

Leslie Butler

LOWELL, JAMES RUSSELL (1819–1891). James Russell Lowell, poet and critic, was born in 1819 in Cambridge, Massachusetts, the son of a Unitarian minister. Like his ancestors, he attended Harvard College (1834–1838), where he studied Latin, Greek, German, and Italian, in addition to philosophy and mathematics. He received a law degree from Harvard in 1841, but his heart was in writing, and he pursued this calling through numerous volumes of poems, collections of critical essays, and editorial ventures. Throughout his life, as a Harvard professor, a foreign diplomat, and a political and cultural critic, Lowell provided a model for the public role of the man of letters, insisting on the importance of "liberal culture" and celebrating the virtues of reading.

Perhaps more revered than read in his own day, and all but ignored in the twentieth century, Lowell's poetry was strongly influenced by, and often derivative of, Shakespeare, Milton, **Keats**, **Wordsworth**, and **Tennyson**. Along with these British writers, Dante provided a major influence as one of Lowell's favorite poets, whom he praised for writing poetry in "the common speech of Florence, in which men bargained and scolded and made love." This use of the vernacular, a trait he admired in Robert Burns as well, surfaced in his most enduring work *The Biglow Papers* (1848). A political satire in the tradition of Cervantes, Molière, and Swift, this work laid out Lowell's opposition to the Mexican War in a folksy Yankee dialect.

Lowell's reputation stands as much on his criticism as his poetry. His Platonic and Romantic view of criticism—that the critic was "set apart in a kind of priesthood" as the "appointed guardian of the ideal in art and life"—insisted that literary standards were universal and immutable. In this light, he singled out Homer, Dante, Shakespeare, Cervantes, and **Goethe** as "the five indispensable authors" whose writings comprised the "gospels in the lay bible of the race," which could "never be displaced." Yet he also followed Goethe's distinction between "productive" versus "destructive" criticism. The "object of all criticism," he wrote in the posthumously published "Criticism and Culture" (1894), "is not to criticize, but to understand," and he refused to allow the critical spirit to interfere with a liberal and open-minded enjoyment of literature.

A voracious reader, Lowell's letters are filled with details of his intensive study of canonical authors from the Greeks to medieval French poets to his peers. He professed himself "one of the last (I fear) of the great readers" and did much through his public utterances to elevate reading into a worthy, if unremunerated, vocation. He shared with **Matthew Arnold** a faith in the edifying powers of what he called "liberal culture," praising local free libraries for providing "a common door of access to the best books by which education may be continued, broadened, and made fruitful." Worried that science and the fragmentation of intellectual life were destroying this ideal, he urged his readers to prepare for their specific duties in life but not to forget "to take [their] 'constitutional' among the classics."

ARCHIVES

Lowell Papers, Houghton Library, Harvard University. Extensive correspondence, manuscripts.

PRINTED SOURCES

Bertholdi, Dennis. "James Russell Lowell." In *Dictionary of Literary Biography*, vol. 64, *American Literary Critics and Scholars, 1850–1880* (Detroit, Mich.: Gale Research Co., 1988).

Duberman, Martin. *James Russell Lowell* (Boston: Houghton Mifflin, 1966).

Howard, Leon. *Victorian Knight-Errant: A Study of the Early Literary Career of James Russell Lowell* (Berkeley: University of California Press, 1952).

Lowell, James Russell. *Letters of James Russell Lowell*, Charles Eliot Norton (ed.), 2 vols. (New York: Harper, 1894).

Leslie Butler

LUXEMBURG, ROSA (1871–1919). Rosa Luxemburg (Róża Luksemburg), a political thinker and activist, was born in Zamość, Russian-occupied Poland (today, Poland). Luxemburg was educated in Warsaw (high school) and at the University of Zurich, where she studied mathematics, natural science, and political economy. Born into a middle-class, assimilated, nonreligious Jewish family, Luxemburg grew up speaking Polish and German in the home but also learned Russian in school at an early age. She later learned French and had a passing knowledge of English, Yiddish, Italian, and Latin. Luxemburg, also known by such nicknames as "Red Rosa" and "Bloody Rosa," was the best-known and best-remembered activist and leader of the internationalist wing of the European communist movement, which stressed liberation of the working masses over and above national independence for any particular nation (as opposed to Vladimir Lenin, who emphasized "revolution within one country" or national self-determination). Luxemburg was the author of several treatises on political economics, and in spite of, or perhaps because of, her early and violent death, she became a radical heroine to later generations of leftists in the West, especially those seeking an alternative to the Soviet pattern of communism.

The most important books in Luxemburg's intellectual development were undoubtedly those of **Karl Marx** and **Friedrich Engels**—especially Marx's *Das Kapital*, a work she cited hundreds of times in her own writing. Although not as slavish to her devotion to Marx as many later communist writers, Luxemburg's view of economics (and hence politics) drew heavily on Marx's mechanistic, even mathematical view of history, something that her education with its strong emphasis on math and science only reinforced. Luxemburg advanced Marx's theories in several areas. For example, she explained imperialism as a result of capitalism's expansion into traditional, precapitalist economies whose natural and human resources helped fuel the capitalist economies of the exploiting powers. In addition to Marx, Luxemburg read almost all of the major works on economics that had been published in the previous century, including those of Adam Smith, **Thomas Malthus**, and **James Mill**, as well as those of her socialist contemporaries throughout Europe. She is known to have read, at one time or another, most of the major socialist periodicals published in Polish, German, and French.

In addition to reading works of political economy, Luxemburg was not insensitive to poetry and literature, although they took a second seat to socialist thought. Foremost among her favorite poets was Adam Mickiewicz, the great bard of Polish literature, who provided her a storehouse of quotations (Nettl, 1: 53; Ettinger, 25). Although Mickiewicz was a proponent of Polish national liberation, his idea that the liberation of Poland was synonymous with the liberation of all humanity must have appealed to Luxemburg. In addition, Luxemburg is known to have read the works of Friedrich von Schiller and other thinkers of the German Enlightenment (Bronner, 4), was acquainted with the poetry **Johann Wolfgang von Goethe** (89), and read Dante's *Divine Comedy* (Ettinger, 137).

ARCHIVES

There is no single Rosa Luxemburg archive. Most of her extant, voluminous correspondence has been published in Polish, German, and/or English.

PRINTED SOURCES

Basso, Lelio. *Rosa Luxemburg: A Reappraisal* (London: Andre Deutsch, 1975).
Dunayevskaya, Raya. *Rosa Luxemburg, Women's Liberation, and Marx's Philosophy of Revolution* (Atlantic Highlands, N.J.: Humanities Press, 1981).

Frölich, Paul. *Rosa Luxemburg: Her Life and Work* (New York: Howard Fertig, 1969).

Geras, Norman. *The Legacy of Rosa Luxemburg* (London: NLB, 1976).

Luxemburg, Rosa. *Comrade and Lover: Rosa Luxemburg's Letters to Leo Jogiches*, Elżbieta Ettinger (ed.) (Cambridge, Mass.: MIT Press, 1979).

———. *The Letters of Rosa Luxemburg*, Stephen Eric Bronner (ed.) (Boulder, Colo.: Westview Press, 1978).

Nettl, J. P. *Rosa Luxemburg*, 2 vols. (Oxford: Oxford University Press, 1966).

Tych, Feliks. *Róża Luksemburg: Listy do Leona Jogiches-Tyszki* [Rosa Luxemburg: Letters to Leon Jogiches-Tyszka], 3 vols. (Warsaw: Książka i Wiedza, 1968–1971).

Waters, Mary-Alice (ed.), *Rosa Luxemburg Speaks* (New York: Pathfinder Press, 1970).

John Radzilowski

LYELL, CHARLES (1797–1875). Sir Charles Lyell was born in Kinnordy, Scotland, in 1797 and raised in England. He read classics at Oxford, in preparation for a career in law, which he gave up to pursue his great interest in geology. One of the foremost scientific minds of Victorian England, Lyell advocated for uniformitarian geology, which held that geologic changes occurred gradually over a vast time from causes that could be seen in operation in the present. A Unitarian, Lyell's worldview was fundamentally deist, a stumbling block as he grappled with the implications of **Darwin**'s theory of evolution.

Growing up in a comfortable home with a well-endowed library, Lyell had early exposure to science and literature. He preserved his feeling for poetry throughout his life, often introducing quotations from Milton into his geological writing. In 1817, he read Robert Bakewell's *Introduction to Geology*, which emphasized the antiquity of the earth and gave Lyell his first awareness of geology as a science (Wilson, *Revolution*, 42). At Oxford, William Buckland's lectures on mineralogy engaged him "heart and soul" (Wilson, *Revolution*, 44). Although he dutifully continued his studies of law, he moved steadily toward a career in geology.

Lyell found further encouragement for geological investigation in William Conybeare and William Phillips's 1822 text *Outlines of the Geology of England and Wales*, based on extensive geological experience and written in a style he called "perfection" (Wilson, *Revolution*, 107). During the 1820s, while a fellow and officer of the Geological Society, he made his own geological explorations throughout the British Isles and on the Continent, meeting the major scientists and learning more about their work. In 1827, he published a positive review of George Poulett Scrope's *On the Geology and Extinct Volcanoes of Central France*. The response to his article convinced him that he could earn money by his writing. In the same year, he first read Jean-Baptiste Lamarck's *Philosophie zoologique*, a book that "delighted him more than any novel" he has ever read" (Wilson, *Revolution*, 161), even as he rejected its ideas about transmutation of species.

Lyell made his reputation with the publication from 1830 to 1833 of his three-volume *Principles of Geology*, which he would revise through 12 editions. Generally supportive of the ideas of the Scottish geologist James Hutton, and providing massive evidence from his own wide observations, Lyell argued carefully that former changes in the earth's surface could be explained by reference to causes presently in action. Although his views offered a direct challenge to the dominant catastrophist theorists, his diplomatic and dispassionate style won him a wide audience. Among those profoundly influenced by the *Principles* was Charles Darwin, who carried the first volume with him on the *Beagle*.

Lyell wrote *Elements of Geology* (1838) as a popular text illustrative of his new theory, incorporating findings from two works not then published, Darwin's *Journal of Researches* and Roderick Murchison's *Silurian System* (Wilson, *Revolution*, 507). Pleased with the publishing success of *Principles* and *Elements*, in the 1840s he undertook the extensive tours of North America that would establish his authority on American geology and society. His expertise attracted the notice of British government officials and of **Prince Albert**. Lyell was knighted at Balmoral in 1848.

At the peak of his influence, Lyell was jolted by his reading of **Alfred Russel Wallace**'s 1855 paper "On the Law which has regulated the Introduction of New Species." (Wilson, *Journals*, xli). In response, he began his own journals on the problem of species, analyzing and commenting upon dozens of contemporary sources on geology and biology (Wilson, *Journals*). At the same time, Lyell's frequent conversations with Darwin began to prepare him for the powerful evolutionary argument of the *Origin of Species*. Although Lyell was deeply disturbed by what he perceived as a degradation of man in the descent theory of Darwin and Wallace, he continued to act as a mentor to them and encouraged them to publish their ideas.

The geological foundation established by Lyell had provided inspiration to Darwin and Wallace. Their views, in turn, stimulated Lyell to reconsider his firmly held beliefs about man and creation. The degree of his intellectual struggle is evident in *The Antiquity of Man* (1863), in which Lyell expressed his adherence to Darwinian theory while still trying to differentiate man's place in nature and retaining Lamarckian perspectives of progressive development. In the 10th edition of *Principles* (1866), Lyell declared his alliance with the Darwinians, but on the understanding that evolution had occurred according to a "preconceived plan." In his partial acceptance of natural selection, Lyell used the theory as a description of the mode of God's creativity, not as a denial of it (Bartholomew, 294).

Lyell's separation of geological speculation from biblical teaching and his extended view of geologic time and of the forces at work across the ages remain his chief intellectual contributions, even as his uniformitarianism has been modified (*BJHS* [1976]). Through his fieldwork, publications, and professional leadership, Lyell significantly advanced the place of science in Victorian society.

ARCHIVES

Kinnordy House, Scotland. Travel letters and journals; Lyell's scientific notebooks.
University of Edinburgh Library. More than 2,000 letters sent to Lyell, mostly from scientists.

PRINTED SOURCES

Bartholomew, Michael. "Lyell and Evolution: An Account of Lyell's Response to the Prospect of an Evolutionary Ancestry for Man," *British Journal for the History of Science*, 6 (1973), 261–303.

Gould, Stephen Jay. *Time's Arrow, Time's Cycle: Myth and Metaphor in the Discovery of Geologic Time* (Cambridge, Mass.: Harvard University Press, 1987).

Lyell, Charles. *The Geological Evidences of the Antiquity of Man, with Remarks on the Theories of the Origin of Species by Variation* (London: John Murray, 1863).

———. *Principles of Geology: Being an Attempt to Explain the Former Changes of the Earth's Surface, by Reference to Causes Now in Operation*, 3 vols. (London: John Murray, 1830–1833 and subsequent editions).

Lyell, Katherine Murray. *Life, Letters and Journals of Sir Charles Lyell, Bt.*, 2 vols. (London: John Murray, 1881).

"Lyell Centenary Issue," *British Journal for the History of Science*, 9 (July 1976), 90–242.

Wilson, Leonard G. *Charles Lyell, the Years to 1841: The Revolution in Geology* (New Haven, Conn.: Yale University Press, 1970).

———. *Lyell in America: Transatlantic Geology, 1841–1853* (Baltimore: Johns Hopkins University Press, 1998).

———. *Sir Charles Lyell's Scientific Journals on the Species Question* (New Haven, Conn.: Yale University Press, 1970).

Susan H. Farnsworth

M

MACAULAY, THOMAS BABINGTON (1800–1859). Thomas Macaulay spent his youth in the Evangelical (Church of England) environment of Clapham, had a distinguished career at Cambridge (B.A., 1822), won fame for contributions to the *Edinburgh Review*, and was first elected to Parliament in 1830. In 1834 he left for an administrative post in India. Returning in 1838, he continued to write essays, publish poetry, and serve in Parliament. But it was with his *History of England* (vols. 1–2, 1848; vols. 3–4, 1855) that Macaulay secured his reputation for giving memorable expression to the great assumptions of his times. In his *History*, he explained how England entered the modern age without crossing a bloodied threshold of revolution. His thesis was simple—"It is because we had a preserving revolution in the seventeenth century that we have not had a destroying revolution in the nineteenth"—but he told this story with a crafted, lucid style that made British history appear to be an inspired tale of providential design.

Known as one of the age's best-read men, Macaulay had his reading habits further stimulated by a private tragedy. In 1835, Macaulay, who never married, lost one sister to scarlet fever and another to marriage. "That I have not utterly sunk under this blow," Macaulay wrote, "I owe chiefly to literature" (*Letters*, 3:129). The reading that saved Macaulay's life and mind was almost all classical (see *Letters*, 3:158–160, 199–202). That he did not turn to the century's most popular consolatory text—the Bible—is one example of Macaulay's ability to defy his reputation as a representative figure. Macaulay's documented reading experiences show that he lacked sympathy for contemporaries who earned enduring admiration. In the writings of **Samuel Taylor Coleridge**, Macaulay saw an intoxicated "cloud of gibberish" (*Letters*, 3:221; Beatty, 340); in the *Prelude* (1850) of **William Wordsworth**, he saw "the old raptures about mountains and cataracts; the old flimsy philosophy about the effect of scenery on the mind; the old, crazy, mystical metaphysics; the endless wilderness of dull, flat, prosaic twaddle" (Beatty, 334); and in 1857, he gave a great growl about the "morbific virus" of "Carlylism, Ruskinism, Browningism" (*Letters*, 6:206) (see **Carlyle**, **Ruskin**, and **Robert Browning**).

Pinney's edition of the *Letters* is the indispensable published source for the study of Macaulay's reading. This work will get its needed supplement when Macaulay's journal (1838–1859) is published. Along with closer attention to the decline of Macaulay's reputation in the 1870s and after, the mapping of Macaulay's reading will contribute to our understanding of the literary values that can distinguish early, mid-, and late-Victorian sensibilities.

ARCHIVES

Macaulay Papers, Trinity College, Cambridge. The journal, a commonplace book, some poetry, and the largest holding of correspondence. For other papers, see David C. Sutton, *Location Register of English Literary Manuscripts and Letters: Eighteenth and Nineteenth Centuries*, 2 vols. (London: British Library, 1995).

PRINTED SOURCES

Beatty, Richmond Croom. *Lord Macaulay: Victorian Liberal* (Norman: University of Oklahoma Press, 1938). Not a distinguished or balanced work, but it quotes the journal liberally.

Clive, John. *Macaulay: The Shaping of the Historian* (Cambridge: Harvard University Press, 1973).

Clive, John, and Thomas Pinney. "Thomas Babington Macaulay." In David J. DeLaura (ed.), *Victorian Prose: A Guide to Research* (New York: MLA, 1973).

Davies, Hugh Sykes. "Macaulay's Marginalia to Lucretius." In R. C. Trevelyan (trans.), *De rerum natura* (Cambridge: Cambridge University Press, 1937).

Edwards, Owen Dudley. *Macaulay* (New York: St. Martin's Press, 1988).

Hamilton, James. "Marginalia of Lord Macaulay," *Macmillan*'s, 7 (April 1863), 489–491.

Hunt, Christopher John. *Catalogue of the Library at Wallington Hall* (Newcastle upon Tyne, England: University of Newcastle upon Tyne, 1968).

Macaulay, Thomas Babington. *The Letters of Thomas Babington Macaulay*, Thomas Pinney (ed.), 6 vols. (Cambridge: Cambridge University Press, 1974–1981).

Millgate, Jane. *Macaulay* (London: Routledge, 1973).

Munby, A.N.L. *Macaulay's Library* (Glasgow, Scotland: Jackson, 1966).

——— (ed.). "Macaulay." In *Sale Catalogues of Libraries of Eminent Persons*, vol. 1. (London: Mansell and Sotheby Parke-Bernet, 1971).

Naufftus, William F. "Thomas Babington Macaulay." In William B. Thesing (ed.), *Victorian Prose Writers before 1867*, vol. 55 of *Dictionary of Literary Biography*, Detroit, Mich.: Bruccoli Clark Layman, 1987).

Trevelyan, George Otto, *The Life and Letters of Lord Macaulay*, 2 vols., New ed. (London: Longmans, 1880).

———. *The Marginal Notes of Lord Macaulay* (London: Longmans, 1907).

Williams, Stanley T. "Macaulay's Reading and Literary Criticism," *Philological Quarterly*, 3 (1924), 119–131.

William R. McKelvy

MAISTRE, JOSEPH DE (1753–1821). Count Joseph de Maistre was born in Chambéry, the capital of Savoy, then part of the Kingdom of Piedmont-Sardinia. Educated by the Jesuits and in the local *collège*, Maistre earned his law degrees from the University of Turin. Like his father, he served in the Senate of Savoy (equivalent to a French *parlement*) and was named a senator in 1788. Following the French invasion of Savoy in 1792, Maistre fled Chambéry and served as a Piedmontese diplomat in Lausanne (1793–1797) and St. Petersburg (1803–1817). His subsequent legal career included service as Regent (head of the court system) in Sardinia (1800–1803) and as Regent of Piedmont-Sardinia (1818–1821). A major theorist of the Counter-Enlightenment, Maistre's writings stimulated such thinkers as **Saint-Simon, Auguste Comte**, and Charles Maurras and inspired generations of French royalists and ultramontane Catholics.

Despite his legal career and the inheritance of a substantial legal library from his maternal grandfather, Maistre's notebooks suggest that he was always much more interested in humanistic subjects such as philosophy, theology, politics, and history. In addition to his native French and the Greek and Latin he acquired as part of an excellent classical education, Maistre read English, Italian, Spanish, Portuguese, and German (with difficulty). His notebooks and works testify that he was very well read in the Hebrew and Christian Scriptures, the Church Fathers, Greek and Latin classical authors, Renaissance and seventeen-century authors, and all the major figures of the European Enlightenment.

Maistre's first major work, *Les Considérations sur la France* (1797), which offered a providential interpretation of the French Revolution, established his reputation as a defender of throne and altar. Maistre read Burke, and he shared Burke's emotional reaction against the violence, "immorality," and "atheism" of the Revolution. Maistre's works echoed Burkean themes, including reverence for established institutions, distrust of innovation, and defense of prejudice, aristocracy, and an established church. Maistre differed from Burke primarily in his providentialism and in his adamant defense of traditional Roman Catholicism and papal authority.

Maistre's later works reveal a gradual shift in emphasis from politics to fundamental philosophical and theological issues. His *Essai sur le principe générateur des constitutions politiques* (written in 1807 and published in 1814) generalized the political principles on which he had based his *Considérations sur la France*. *Du Pape* (1817) argued forcefully for infallible papal authority as a prerequisite for political stability in Europe. *Les Soirées de Saint-Pétersbourg* (published shortly after Maistre's death in 1821), explored a host of philosophical and theological issues in witty dialogue form, while an appendix, an "elucidation on sacrifices," developed Maistre's ideas about the role of suffering and violence. Finally, an *Examen de la philosophie de Bacon* (published in 1826) located the origins of the scientism and atheism of the Enlightenment in the works of the English writer.

Maistre has been sharply criticized for the extremism of his views and in particular for his reflections on the social role of the executioner, on war, and on bloodshed. Maistre's speculations were certainly original; rejecting what he castigated as naive Enlightenment forms of rationality, he sought to comprehend the irrational and violent dimensions of social and political life. He should be regarded as an innovative theorist of violence rather than as its advocate.

ARCHIVES

Archives Maistre, Archives départmentales de Savoie, 2J1 through 2J91, and 76F1 through 76F10. Manuscripts, journals, and correspondence.

PRINTED SOURCES

Bradley, Owen Powell. "Logics of Violence: The Social and Political Thought of Joseph de Maistre" (Ph.D. diss., Cornell University, 1992).

Darcel, Jean-Louis. "Les bibliothèques de Joseph de Maistre," *Revue des études maistriennes*, no. 9 (1985), 5–118.

Dermenghem, Emile. *Joseph de Maistre mystique: ses rapports avec le martinisme, l'illuminisme et la franc-maçonnerie, l'influence du doctrines mystiques et occultes sur sa pensée religieuse* (Paris: La Colombe, 1946).

Garrard, Graeme. "Maistre, Judge of Jean-Jacques: An Examination of the Relationship between Jean-Jacques Rousseau, and the French Enlightenment" (D. Phil. thesis, Oxford University, 1995).

Holdsworth, Frederick. *Joseph de Maistre et Angleterre* (Paris: Campion, 1935).

Lebrun, Richard A. *Joseph de Maistre: An Intellectual Militant* (Kingston and Montreal: Queen's University Press, 1988). Based on the Maistre archives.

———. "Les Lectures de Joseph de Maistre d'après les registres inédits," *Revue des études maistriennes*, no. 9 (1985), 126–194.

Maistre, Henri de. *Joseph de Maistre* (Paris: Perrin, 1990). By a direct descendant who had access to the family archives; see "Archives."

Pranchère, Jean-Yves. "L'Autorité contre les Lumières: la philosophie de Joseph de Maistre" (doctoral thesis, Université de Rouen, 1992). First-rate study.

Richard A. Lebrun

MALTHUS, THOMAS ROBERT (1766–1834). Thomas Malthus was born in Surrey in 1766 and tutored by Richard Graves at his Claverton academy near Bath, by Gilbert Wakefield at the Warrington Dissenting Academy, and by William Frend at Jesus College, Cambridge (1784–1788). Following graduation he was ordained in the Church of England. His *Essay on the Principle of Population* (1798) brought him early fame and, in some quarters, vilification. In it he argued that the chances for human perfectibility or even continuous economic progress were negated by a human tendency to overpopulation. From 1805 until his death Malthus taught political economy at the East India College, Haileybury.

Typically for his time, Malthus's preparation for university study involved an extensive reading of the Ancients. Surviving letters between his tutor (Graves) and his father, and between father and son, indicate that the young Malthus read a variety of Latin and Greek poets, orators, and historians. His personal library, much of it now housed at Jesus College, includes editions of Caesar, Cicero, Horace, Terence, Tertullian, Herodotus, and Thucydides, among others. Classical authors are quoted with some frequency in the population essay.

In college or shortly thereafter, Malthus must have read William Paley's *Principles of Moral and Political Philosophy* (1785), as did generations of Cambridge undergraduates up to the 1840s. He refers to Paley in the 1798 *Essay* as well as in an earlier, unpublished work entitled "The Crisis." It is clear to us today how completely a Paleyite utilitarianism permeates Malthus's social and economic thought. He also appears to have read John Locke's *Elements of Natural Philosophy* (1750) while at Cambridge. His lectures and reading in college are known to have included William Duncan's *Elements of Logick* (1748), as well as Isaac Newton's *Philosophiae Naturalis Principia Mathematica* (1726). Malthus appealed several times in his *Essay* to the authority of Newton in matters of methodology. His extracurricular reading at Cambridge included the earliest installment of Edward Gibbon's *Decline and Fall of the Roman Empire*, which he commended highly to his father.

Malthus claimed, in the preface to the second edition of his *Essay* (1803), that the only authors from whom he had derived his population theory had been Hume, Wallace, Smith, and Price. The works referred to were David Hume's essay "Of the Populousness of Ancient Nations" (1752), Robert Wallace's *Various Prospects of Mankind, Nature, and Providence* (1761), Adam Smith's *The Wealth of Nations* (1776), and Richard Price's *Observations of Reversionary Payments* (1771). But what is also clear in the 1798 *Essay* is the closeness with which Malthus had read the writings of William Godwin, the rhetorical target of his *Essay*, particularly the *Enquiry Concerning Political Justice* (1793) and the essay "Of Avarice and Profusion" in *The Enquirer* (1797). Malthus did not oppose every tenet of Godwin's political philosophy and was, in fact, influenced by it in some important ways.

ARCHIVES

Bonar, J., "Life of Thomas Malthus," typescript, Rare Book Room, Library of the University of Illinois at Urbana-Champaign.

Jesus College, Cambridge. Malthus library; catalog of holdings published as *The Malthus Library Catalogue: The Personal Collection of Thomas Robert Malthus at Jesus College, Cambridge* (New York: Pergamon Press, 1983).

Kanto Gakuen Collection of Malthus Manuscripts, Kanto Gakuen University, Japan.

PRINTED SOURCES

Hollander, S. "On Malthus's Physiocratic References," *History of Political Economy*, 24, 2 (Summer 1992), pp. 369–380.

James, P. *Population Malthus: His Life and Times* (London: Routledge & Kegan Paul, 1979).

Malthus, T. R. *T. R. Malthus: The Unpublished Papers in the Collection of Kanto Gakuen*

University, vol. 1, J. Pullen and T. H. Perry (eds.) (Cambridge: Cambridge University Press, 1997).

Geoffrey Gilbert

MANET, ÉDOUARD (1832–1883). Édouard Manet was born in Paris in 1832, the firstborn son of Auguste Manet, a successful, upper-class civil servant who expected his eldest son to continue the family tradition of law and public service. At 7, Édouard was sent to a local elementary school and, at 12, to the Collège Rollin for his secondary schooling, where he was exposed to a demanding curriculum in mathematics, science, and languages, both ancient and modern, including the classics of French literature. His education was intended to prepare him for the law, but he was a mediocre scholar with no interest in studies or law. He was, however, fascinated by art; he had read Diderot's *Salons* while at the Collège Rollin. His father refused to allow him to pursue art, and so he chose the navy and, in 1848, set sail on board the *Havre et Guadeloupe*, bound for Brazil. A year later, he returned home, having learned that he was not cut out for a naval career but was destined to be an artist. His father yielded, and he enrolled in the studio of Thomas Couture, a leading academician, from whom he learned the established rules for success in the annual Salons, rules that he spent the rest of his career subverting, thereby establishing himself as one of the leaders of the French avant-garde and as one of the principal creators of modernism in art.

Manet's career was marked by significant relationships with writers and intellectuals, many of whose portraits he painted during his career. *La Musique aux Tuileries* (1862) provides a set of portraits of literary friends, the art critics and journalists Zacharie Astruc and Aurélien Scholl, and the poet Charles Baudelaire. Baudelaire's influence was the most significant. Manet's daily companion in the early 1860s, his art criticism, especially his concept of the heroic in modern life, influenced Manet's work, as in *Buveur d'absinthe* (1858–1859), possibly inspired by Baudelaire's poems *Le Vin des chiffonniers*, and *La chanteuse des rues* (1862). Theirs was a relationship based on similar artistic sensibilities; with Baudelaire Manet could discuss the details of his work—the appearance of the Black maid and cat in *Olympia* (1863) being the most famous instance.

Widely attacked in the press for his modernist painting, Manet found in **Émile Zola** a staunch ally to defend his work. Zola wrote the most significant early appreciations of Manet's art, including the brochure for the *Olympia* exhibit. Manet read Zola's novels with enthusiasm, and Zola dedicated to Manet *Madeleine Férat* (1868), a novel whose love scenes, Manet said, "could deflower a virgin" if she merely read them (Brombert, 196). Zola's influence is evident in Manet's *Nana* (1877), a portrait of the titular heroine of Zola's novel and the first of a series of portraits and paintings of Parisian café life inspired by Zola's naturalism. In 1873 Manet met Stéphane Mallarmé and found a defender with an aesthetic sensibility more attuned to his own than Zola's and with whom he formed an intimate friendship. As with Baudelaire, Manet and Mallarmé shared a common artistic vision; they collaborated on a set of translations and illustrations for **Edgar Allan Poe**'s "The Raven" and "Annabel Lee," and while Mallarmé's criticism introduced Manet's art to English audiences, he introduced Manet to English writers, notably Charles Algernon Swinburne, George Moore, and Arthur O'Shaughnessy, whose works he would read and translate to Manet in visits to his studio.

Manet's correspondence reveals an artist who purchased books frequently, read widely among his contemporaries, and praised and recommended volumes to his friends. Charles Blanc's *Histoire des peintres de toutes les écoles*, a copy of which Manet kept in his studio, was "a virtual Bible" (Brombert, 194). Théodore Duret, the art critic who dedicated his *Critique d'avant-garde* to Manet, was a close friend and artistic executor of his will. Manet's friendships with writers and his wide reading suggest the profound impact of their work and ideas on his art.

ARCHIVES

Bibliothèque d'art et d'archéologie, Paris.
Bibliothèque Nationale, Paris.
Bibliothèque de Louvre, Paris.
Musée Stéphane Mallarmé, Paris.
Pierpont Morgan Library, New York.

PRINTED SOURCES

Brombert, Beth Archer. *Édouard Manet: Rebel in a Frock Coat* (Boston: Little, Brown, 1996).
Cachin, Françoise, et. al. *Manet* (Paris and New York: Éditions de la Réunion des musées nationaux, 1983). Published collection of Manet's letters to Zola.
Manet, Édouard. *Manet by himself: Correspondence & Conversation*, Juliet Wilson-Bareau (ed.) (Boston: Little, Brown, 1991).

Mark Reger

MANNING, HENRY EDWARD (1808–1892). Henry Manning was born at Copped Hall, Totteridge, in 1808. He studied at Harrow and Balliol College, Oxford (1827–1830), spent a short time in the Colonial Office, and in 1832 decided to enter the Church of England priesthood. He was installed as the Rector of Lavington and Graffham in Sussex in 1833 and in 1837 began a close correspondence with **William Ewart Gladstone** (1809–1898). An energetic priest of High Church positions and attached to the Oxford movement, Manning was appointed Archdeacon of Chichester in December 1840, wrote extensively on ecclesiastical issues of the day, and played an important role in the National Society for the Education of the Poor. In the turmoil resulting from the Gorham decision (requiring that a clergyman be installed, even though his bishop considered his theology of baptism heretical), Manning resigned his charge and on April 6, 1851, was received into the Roman Catholic Church. In 1865 Manning was appointed archbishop of Westminster and quickly became the preeminent supporter of ultramontane Catholicism in England and of the declaration of papal infallibility at the First Vatican Council. In 1874–1875 he was embroiled in a public debate with Gladstone over the political implications of the infallibility decree, although he worked closely with him on Irish Education and Irish Home Rule. Manning was made a cardinal in 1875.

At midlife Manning described the major influences on his development in a letter to a friend (Bodleian MS Eng. Lett. c. 659, 160–161), pointing to the significance of both High and Low Church Anglican writers. Of these the most important were the standard authors of interest to the Old High Church tradition, above all Joseph Butler's (1692–1752) *The Analogy of Religion* (1736), Richard Hooker's (1554–1600) *Of the Laws of Ecclesiastical Polity* (1593 ff.), and the seventeenth century divines, particularly Jeremy Taylor (1613–1667), through to Herbert Thorndike (1598–1672). Manning makes special mention of Charles Leslie (1650–1722), and he was almost certainly influenced as well by the work of another nonjuror, Thomas Ken (1637–1711), whose works Manning's uncle and mentor, John Anderdon, had edited. Although early associated with Evangelical causes, by 1835 he was distributing the *Tracts for the Times* (London, 1833–1840). His association with the Tractarians, however, was mediated by the firmly Establishment policies of the young Gladstone as reflected in the latter's *The State in Its Relations to the Church* (4th ed., 1841) and his *Church Principles* (1842). Like many other High and Broad Church Anglicans, Manning was also strongly affected by **Samuel Taylor Coleridge** (1772–1834) and, in the 1840s, by the liberal German Roman Catholic Johann Adam Möhler's *Unity in the Church* (1825; Manning annotated a French translation) and the German Romantic Catholic convert Friedrich Schlegel's *Philosophy of History* (1829). In the 1850s Manning insisted that the work of Thomas Aquinas was influential on his eventual decision to enter the Roman Catholic Church, and there are Thomistic citations in Manning's later Anglican work.

ARCHIVES

Pitts Theology Library, Emory University, Atlanta, Georgia. Manning's personal library; Anglican and Catholic sermons; draft manuscripts of published works; annotated Vatican I schemas from Vatican; miscellaneous correspondence.

Université Catholique de l'Ouest, Angers, France. Misc correspondence and manuscripts from the Catholic period.

Bodleian Library, Oxford. Principal Anglican correspondence, 1822–1850. Westminster Archives, London. Archepiscopal correspondence.

PRINTED SOURCES

McClelland, V. Alan. *Cardinal Manning: His Public Life and Influence 1865–1892* (London: Oxford University Press, 1962).

Newsome, David. *The Parting of Friends: The Wilberforces and Henry Manning* (Grand Rapids Mich.: Eerdmans, 1993; first published, London: John Murray, 1966).

Pereiro, James. *Cardinal Manning: An Intellectual Biography* (Oxford: Oxford University Press, 1998).

Purcell, Edmund S. *Life of Cardinal Manning, Archbishop of Westminster*, 2 vols. (London: Macmillan and Co., 1895).

Peter C. Erb

MANTEGAZZA, PAOLO (1831–1910). Paolo Mantegazza, scientist, physician, explorer, anthropologist, senator, and popular literary writer, was born in Monza, Italy, in 1831 and educated in Milan (1846–1848), Pisa (1848–1849), and Pavia, where he graduated in medicine in 1854. Increasingly active in the Italian scientific and cultural life after four years in Argentina (inventor of the "globulimetro" to count red corpuscles, author of new theories of craniology, practitioner of artificial insemination, pioneer in the study of the effects of coca), he founded the Italian Society of Anthropology and Ethnology (Florence, 1870)—of which **Darwin** would become honorary member—and was endowed with the first chair of anthropology. He traveled to Lapland and to India between 1879 and 1882 and continued to teach and lecture until some months before his death at San Terenzo, close to La Spezia.

Mantegazza's writings—over 100 works, most of which were long-lasting best-sellers and in some cases indicted by the Vatican for their alleged immorality—depict a multifaceted human nature, in line with a conception of anthropology as a global discipline, encompassing the entirety of psychic, physical, and social manifestations of mankind in all its ethnic varieties. Mantegazza's uniqueness, as his disciple Paolo Riccardi observed, was not simply due to the vastness of his scientific knowledge but also to his superb imagination and artistic vein. Herder's philosophy and the ecstatic voluptuousness of **Goethe**'s *Faust* in his youthful readings were indeed as pivotal to his formation as his later debt to Linnaeus, Antoine de Jussieu, Alexander von Humboldt, and Alcide D'Orbigny for the natural method in descriptions and classifications. An enthusiastic adherent to evolutionary theories, Mantegazza corresponded with Charles Darwin on issues of sexual selection, pangenesis, and physiognomy, dedicated to him *Fisionomia e mimica*, and was in his turn repeatedly quoted in such volumes as *The Descent of Man*. By extolling the abundance of details and the "sublime disorder" of Darwin's architecture over the static symmetry of Cuvier's catalog of nature (*Commemorazione*, 22), Mantegazza reveals his excitement for the richness and the transformation of life, merging his love for the true with the pursuit of aesthetic pleasure. Similarly, his discussion of "physiology" in many of his treatises (*Fisiologia del piacere, Fisiologia dell'amore, Fisiologia del dolore*) evokes not only medical but above all literary antecedents like **Honoré de Balzac**'s *Physiologie du mariage* and Anthelme B. Savarin's *Physiologie du goût*. Significant intersections can also be traced with the works of other European anthropologists (as Paul Broca, Armand De Quatrefages, John Lubbock, Anders Retzius) postulating a comprehensive notion of culture. Similarities often stretch beyond the restricted scientific domain, as in the case of Mantegazza's *L'arte di essere felici* and Lubbock's *The Pleasure of Life*, both drawing from Epicurus the premises of an enjoyable existence. As a science fiction writer (*L'anno 3000*), Mantegazza revives the utopian and technological worlds of **Jules Verne**, while the hyperbolic sentimentalism of his exotic novel *Un giorno a Madera*, as well as the style and imagery of his novelistic and essayistic prose as a whole, partake of, and often anticipate, a decadent taste that triumphs in Italy with **Gabriele D'Annunzio**. Dismissed by avant-garde Italian intellectuals for the rhetorical and hedonistic excesses of his works, which supposedly overshadow his positivist rigor, Mantegazza, in fact, can be fully appreciated for his modern spirit when interpreted as a passionate and eclectic "scientist–artist" who conceives interdisciplinarity as an exchange and integration of natural and speculative sciences in view of the supreme and unique aim of human happiness.

ARCHIVES

Biblioteca Comunale di La Spezia. Volumes from author's personal library.
Fondo Mantegazza, Museo Nazionale di Antropologia e Etnologia, Florence, Italy. Papers, correspondence, and author's volumes.
Biblioteca Civica di Monza. Manuscripts and microfilms of Mantegazza's 60 volumes of unpublished personal journals.

PRINTED SOURCES

DeGubernatis, A. *Dizionario biografico degli scrittori contemporanei* (Firenze: Le-Monnier, 1879).
Ehrenfreund, E. *Bibliografia degli scritti di Paolo Mantegazza* (Firenze: Stab. Grafico Commerciale, 1926).
Frati, M. E. *Le carte e la biblioteca di Paolo Mantegazza* (Milano: Giunta Regionale Toscana & Editrice Bibliografica, 1991).
Landucci, G. *L'occhio e la mente* (Firenze: Olschki, 1987).
Mantegazza, P. *Commemorazione di Carlo Darwin* (Firenze: Arte della Stampa, 1882).
Misano, G. "Paolo Mantegazza: Mito e realtà del 'senatore erotico.' " In *"Trivialliteratur?" Letteratura di massa e di consumo* (Trieste: Lint, 1979).
Reynaudi, C. *Paolo Mantegazza* (Milano: Treves, 1893).
Riccardi, P. *Saggio di un catalogo bibliografico antropologico italiano* (Modena: Vincenzi, 1883).

Nicoletta Pireddu

MANZONI, ALESSANDRO (1785–1873). Alessandro Manzoni is often termed the "pen" of Italian unification. His *I Promessi Sposi* [The betrothed] is the significant novel of the Risorgimento movement. So valued was its author's place in the unification movement that **Verdi** wrote his *Requiem* for the first anniversary of Manzoni's death.

Manzoni was born on his father's estate near Lake Como, Italy, in 1785. His father, Don Pietro Manzoni, was a pious political conservative. Despite his father's wealth, Manzoni's childhood was not happy. He was sent to school at five, away from home. His mother, Giulia, treated him coldly, failing to visit him at school. She left the family two years after Manzoni entered boarding school, moving to Paris with a liberal from Milan, Carlo Imbonati.

Manzoni went to Paris in 1805, joining his mother. In 1808 he entered into a happy marriage with Henriette Blondel. Blondel was a Swiss Protestant, but any tensions in their marriage concerning religion were overcome when both became practicing Catholics. For Manzoni that required his leaving his anti-Catholic ideals of the French Revolution.

He more than compensated for an anti-Catholic poem, *Il Trionfo della Liberta*, written in 1801, by composing a series of religious poems after his return to Milan in 1810. His study of Italian history led to his writing several historical plays, most notably *Il Conte di Carmagnola*. In 1821 he began to write his masterpiece, based on Italian history. He finished *I Promessi Sposi* in 1827. However, he completely revised the book for the Tuscan definitive edition in 1840. Although the labor required for his revision marked the virtual end of his creative career, Manzoni has continued to be honored in Italian literature.

Manzoni's influences are many. No one, however, seems to have directly influenced his masterpiece. His maternal grandfather, Cesare Beccaria, the penologist, was a major influence on his thinking, as were the thinkers of the French Revolutionary period. In fact, he interrupted finishing *I Promessi Sposi* in order to write an ode on **Napoléon**'s death.

Some writers have alleged that Sir **Walter Scott** influenced Manzoni. Certainly, Manzoni admired Scott, and Scott demonstrated that a historical novel could be a literary success. However, the plot of *I Promessi Sposi* is not found in Scott's works prior to its publication. Moreover, Manzoni's characters speak idiomatic Italian, whereas Scott's characters speak archaic English.

Manzoni further influenced the Risorgimento movement through becoming a convert to the Tuscan school in the Italian-language issue. He became convinced that the Tuscan idiom should form the standard for a common Italian language. Therefore, he rewrote his masterpiece in that idiom, thereby closing the gap between the spoken and written official language.

ARCHIVES

Manzoni's archives are in the Sala Manzoni of the Biblioteca Nazionale Braidense in the Bresa Museum in Milan. The donations of Pietro Bambilla in 1885 are the nucleus of the collection.

PRINTED SOURCES

Barricelli, Gian Piero. *Alessandro Manzoni* (Boston: Twayne, 1976).
Covito, Carmen. "In Search of the Italian Language: Integrated Italian," *World Literature Today*, 71, 2 (Spring 1997), 309–312.
de Lucca, Robert. "Revealed Truth and Acquired Knowledge: Considerations on Manzoni and Gadda," *MLN*, 111, 1 (January 1996), 58–73.

Frank A. Salamone

MARSHALL, JOHN (1755–1835). John Marshall, fourth Chief Justice of the U.S. Supreme Court (1801–1835), was born in Prince William County, Virginia, in 1755 and studied law under George Wythe at the College of William and Mary, Phi Beta Kappa (1780). Under Marshall's leadership, the federal judiciary established its de facto independence from the executive and legislative branches by its power of judicial review in *Marbury v. Madison* (1802). Through its rulings as the binding interpretations of the Constitution, the Marshall Court's decisions bolstered the power of the federal government and contributed signally to the development of American constitutionalism and federalism. Other major decisions were *Fletcher v. Peck* (1810), *Trustees of Dartmouth College v. Woodward* (1819), *McCulloch v. Maryland* (1819), and *Gibbons v. Ogden* (1824). Marshall also distinguished himself as an officer of the Continental Army (1776–1781), diplomat (1797–1798), historian, and secretary of state (1800). Although a nominal Episcopalian, John Marshall was a deist who doubted the divinity of Christ until late in his life. After a long and distinguished public career, Marshall died on July 6, 1835, in Philadelphia.

Marshall's reading in poetry, moral philosophy, history, the common law, and political theory, combined with his experience in the American Revolution, developed in him a decided preference for empirical reasoning and practical knowledge and a decided distrust of abstract legal theory. In turn, these factors were the basis for Marshall's nationalist philosophy of constitutional governance. Marshall, a Federalist, was in favor of a strong central government capable of promoting the national interest. Alexander Pope's *Essay on Man* (1733–1734) had a profound impact on the young Marshall and contributed to his belief that common sense could form the basis for private and public morality, and the two could coincide and advance society's interests. The convergence between public and private interests is similar to Marshall's understanding of the Constitution's legitimacy as having been established through the sovereign will of the people, not of the states. It was through Pope that Marshall was introduced to the theory of a mixed government composed of competing interests that would check and balance one another, thereby preserving liberty. While an adolescent, Marshall read the histories of Horace and Livy. Their philosophy that history was a pedagogical tool by which to teach about life and their underlying patriotism and praise for the Roman Republic reinforced Marshall's rational and practical side and planted the seeds for his later nationalism. Marshall's practical and empirical development was reinforced by William Blackstone's *Commentaries on the Laws of England* (1765–1769). Blackstone systematized English common law and presented it as a coherent whole premised upon deduction and the principles of experience and common sense. This growth continued with Marshall's reading of Emmerich de Vattel's *Law of Nations* (1758), which influenced his thinking on international law, and David Hume's *Treatise of Human Nature* (1739), wherein Hume stressed the importance of experience as a legitimizing factor in law and the protection of property as the basis of an orderly and just society. Importantly, Montesquieu's *Spirit of the Laws* (1748) helped

Marshall refine his thinking and laid much of the intellectual groundwork for his future activities as Chief Justice. Montesquieu's exposition on the separation of powers further contributed to what Marshall had gleaned from Pope on mixed government. Furthermore, Montesquieu formally introduced Marshall to the theory of an independent judiciary.

ARCHIVES

John Marshall Papers, College of William and Mary. Principal correspondence and papers.

PRINTED SOURCES

Baker, Leonard. *John Marshall: A Life in Law* (New York: Macmillan, 1974).

Beveridge, Albert J, *The Life of John Marshall*, 4 vols. (Boston: Houghton Mifflin, 1916–1919). First full-scale biography. Noted for research and narrative.

Hobson, Charles F. "The Great Chief Justice: John Marshall and the Rule of Law." In Wilson Carey McWilliams and Lance Banning (eds.), *American Political Thought* (Lawrence: University Press of Kansas, 1996). Development of a "constitutional nationalist."

Marshall, John. *An Autobiographical Sketch of John Marshall*, John S. Adams (ed.) (Ann Arbor: University of Michigan Press for the William L. Clements Library, 1937). Some attention given to early reading.

———. *The Papers of John Marshall*, Herbert A. Johnson et al. (eds.), 8+ vols. (Chapel Hill: University of North Carolina Press for the Institute of Early American History and Culture, 1974–).

Rhodes, Irwin S. *The Papers of John Marshall: A Descriptive Calendar*, 2 vols. (Norman: University of Oklahoma Press, 1969). Guide to various holdings.

Smith, Jean Edward. *John Marshall: Definer of a Nation*, a Marian Ward Book (New York: Henry Holt, 1996). Comprehensive and analytical with attention to intellectual development.

Smith, William Raymond. *History as Argument: Three Patriot Historians of the American Revolution* (The Hague: Mouton, 1966). Marshall's ideology through his history.

Swindler, William F. *The Constitution and John Marshall*, Warren E. Burger (intro.) (New York: Dodd, Mead, 1978). Review of some of the more important Marshall Court decisions.

Ricardo A. Herrera

MARTINEAU, HARRIET (1802–1876). Harriet Martineau was born in Norwich in 1802 to Unitarian parents and educated by her older siblings until she attended a local Unitarian school (1813–1815). She was then taught for two years by private masters before attending a boarding school in Bristow (1818–1819). Martineau's importance lies in her success as a popular educator and in her advocacy of women's issues. She was a controversial contributor to a large variety of debates through her promotion of political economy, abolition, universal education, and mesmerism and through her rejection of Christianity and promotion of positivism, particularly her translation of **Comte**. She is also noteworthy as a writer of fiction and British history.

Since Martineau requested that her correspondents destroy her letters and therefore few remain, her *Autobiography* is the richest source for understanding her own personal history. As a child, Martineau focused on Christian writings, including the New Testament, biblical commentaries, Milton (especially *Paradise Lost*), and *Pilgrim's Progress*. She also enjoyed Shakespeare and translating Tacitus. At Bristol, Martineau was influenced by Lant Carpenter and introduced to Locke's *Essay Concerning Human Understanding*, work by Joseph Priestley and Dugald Stewart, and Hartley's *Observations on Man*, which she wrote became "the most important book in the world to me, except the Bible" (*Autobiography*, 1:104) and from which she claimed to have attained a desire for self-discipline and devotion to duty. The Necessarianism she adopted during this period provided an impetus for Martineau's educational writings since it argued that an individual could, through education, come more happily into line with natural universal laws.

Illustrations of Political Economy was Martineau's first successful work. In it she promulgates ideas found in Adam Smith's *The Wealth of Nations*; **Thomas Robert Malthus**'s *An Essay on the Principle of Population*; and **James Mill**'s *Elements of Political Economy*. Significantly, however, Martineau was inspired to write on political economy by another female populariser of the subject, Jane Marcet. When she read Marcet's *Conversations*, Martineau reminisces, "groups of personages rose up from the pages" (*Autobiography*, 1:139).

Martineau enhanced her writing style by studying persuasive techniques in Hugh Blair's *Lectures on Rhetoric and Belles Lettres* (*Autobiography*, 1:102). She also read Maria Edgeworth's "The Parent's Assistant" in preparation for her own didactic fiction (*Letters to Fanny Wedgewood*, 36). Walter Scott and **Jane Austen** were both influential in writing *Deerbrook*. Among the poets, Schiller was her "idol" (*Selected Letters*, 92), and she admired **Wordsworth** as "an educator of infinite value" (*Selected Letters*, 110). The eclecticism of Martineau's reading is perhaps most striking since it is reflected in the variety of her own work. Writing to W. J. Fox at the beginning of her career, she notes, "I try to make variety—Belsham's Epistles & Richardson's novels,—metaphysics and romances,—Priestley & Wollstonecraft!" (*Selected Letters*, 24).

ARCHIVES

University of Birmingham Library. Largest collection of Martineau papers. Available on microfilm with a good index: "Women, Emancipation and Literature: The Papers of Harriet Martineau, 1802–1876" (Marlborough, England: Adam Matthew Publications, 1991). Reels 13–14 contain *Autobiography* manuscript.

Manchester College Library, Oxford. Letters to James Martineau, Helen Martineau, and Philip Carpenter.

PRINTED SOURCES

Arbuckle, Elizabeth Sanders (ed.). *Harriet Martineau's Letters to Fanny Wedgewood* (Stanford, Calif.: Stanford University Press, 1983).

Martineau, Harriet. *Autobiography*, vols. 1–3 (London: Smith, Elder, & Co., 1877).

————. *Selected Letters*, Valerie Sanders (ed.) (Oxford: Clarendon Press, 1990).

Peterson, Linda H. "Harriet Martineau: Masculine Discourse, Female Sage." In Thais E. Morgan (ed.), *Victorian Sages and Cultural Discourse* (New Brunswick, N.J.: Rutgers University Press, 1990), 171–186.

Pichanik, Valerie. *Harriet Martineau: The Woman and Her Work, 1802–76* (Ann Arbor: University of Michigan Press, 1980).

Thomas, Gillian. *Harriet Martineau* (Boston: Twayne Publishers, 1985).

Thomson, Dorothy Lampen. *Adam Smith's Daughters* (New York: Exposition Press, 1973).

Webb, R. K. *Harriet Martineau: A Radical Victorian* (London: Heinemann, 1960).

Hilda Hollis

MARX, KARL HEINRICH (1818–1883). Karl Marx was born in Trier, Rhineland, in 1818, graduated from Friedrich Wilhelm Gymnasium in Trier (1835); studied law at Bonn (1835–1836) and philosophy at Berlin (1836–1841); received a doctorate at Jena (1841); edited *Rheinische Zeitung* in Köln (1842–1843); met **Friedrich Engels** (1842); fled to Paris upon suppression of *Rheinische Zeitung* and there coedited *Deutsch-französische Jahrbücher* with Arnold Ruge (1843–1844); fled to Brussels when Prussia tried to extradite him from Paris (1845); cofounded the Kommunistische Korrespondenz Komitee with Engels (1846); cowrote *Manifest der kommunistischen Partei* with Engels (1847–1848); edited *Neue rheinische Zeitung* in Köln, (1848–1849); was exiled from Prussia (1849); lived in London after 1850 with financial support from Engels; occasionally wrote political columns for the *New York Tribune*; cofounded the International Working Men's Association (IWMA) ("The First International") (1864); published the first volume of *Das Kapital* (1867); disbanded the IWMA after a long internal fight against anarchist **Mikhail Aleksandrovich Bakunin** (1872); and continued writing the second and third volumes of *Das Kapital*, which Engels completed and published after Marx's death. As the originator of modern socialism, Marx will always be important both philosophically and historically. Marxism retains its vitality as political and economic theory despite the practical failures of Leninism, Stalinism, Maoism, and other revisions.

Marx read constantly and possessed encyclopedic knowledge of economics, philosophy, history, and literature. After 1857 he frequented the Round Reading Room of the British Museum, primarily to research *Das Kapital*. Yet his ideological direction had already gelled before he settled in London, and his main literary influences his life long were those he acquired in his twenties: **Georg Wilhelm Friedrich Hegel** and the Young Hegelians, especially and symbiotically Engels. It is often difficult to know where Marx ends and Engels begins. For example, to attribute "dialectical materialism" to Marx is false. Georgi Valentinovich Plekhanov coined the term in 1891. Engels, calling it "historical materialism," began to develop that ontology in *Anti-Dühring* (1878) and inserted it into *Das Kapital* after Marx's death. Marx was not a thoroughgoing materialist like Engels, Vladimir Ilich Lenin, or **Ludwig Andreas Feuerbach**. Rather, his materialism was tempered by, for example, the objective idealism and cultural sensitivity of Giambattista Vico.

Marx's first mentor was **Bruno Bauer**. Even though Bauer is important for scholars trying to understand Marx, interest in Marx has not generated much interest in Bauer. Marx admired how Bauer superseded **David Friedrich Strauss** in applying Hegelian critique to the Gospels but was soon disillusioned by Bauer's overextension of the principle of critique into speculative conclusions about world history that reduced absolute spirit to an abstract theological concept of human self-consciousness opposed to a spiritless human "mass." Similarly, Marx believed that **Max Stirner** had pushed Hegelianism too far by turning it into an egoism. Marx and Engels attacked "St. Bruno" in *Die heilige Familie* and "St. Max" in *Die deutsche Ideologie* with satire that shows the influence of Miguel de Cervantes Saavedra, Jonathan Swift, and Voltaire.

Engels was the only influence on Marx with whom he generally agreed. Next to Engels, Marx probably felt closest ideologically to Feuerbach. The thrust of his 11 "Theses on Feuerbach" is to distinguish theoretical from practical philosophy, not to attack Feuerbach.

The foremost source of Marx's socialist thought is Hegel. Although early socialists such as **Charles Fourier**, François Émile Babeuf, **Robert Owen**, and **Claude-Henri de Rouvroy**, **Comte de Saint-Simon** indeed influenced Marx, albeit negatively because of their prevalent utopianism, and although Hegel was no socialist, it was from Hegel that Marx took the very structure and logic of his system. Among the Young Hegelians, only Marx understood Hegelian dialectic well enough to use it fluently and "demystify it" (as he said) or "turn it right side up" (as Engels said) so that it would serve as the engine for such historical, philosophical, economic, and political analyses as Hegel himself never imagined.

Young Marx was influenced mostly by philosophers, but after moving to England, economists were the mainstay of his intellectual life. His doctoral dissertation was on Democritus and Epicurus, but the philosophies of Aristotle, John Locke, Jean-Jacques Rousseau, and Immanuel Kant impressed him more profoundly. Among the economists whose ideas Marx considered were **David Ricardo**, **Thomas Robert Malthus**, Adam Smith, John Ramsay McCulloch, August von Haxthausen, Jean Baptiste Say, and Jean Charles Léonard Simonde de Sismondi. Although François Quesnay was a founder of the modern science of political economy, Marx seems to have paid relatively little attention to the physiocrats. An economic treatise whose effect on Marx is often overlooked is *Die naturgemässe Volkswirthschaft gegenüber dem Monopoliengeiste und dem Communismus* by Karl Arnd (1845).

Among historians, Marx preferred Tacitus and **Louis-Adolphe Thiers**, who exemplified for him a liberal bourgeois interpretation of the French Revolution. He took interest in the politics of Thomas Jefferson, **Ferdinand Lassalle**, and Maximilien de Béthune, Duc de Sully; and in the journalism of **Pierre-Joseph Proudhon** and **William Cobbett**.

ARCHIVES

Gosudarstvennaia Obshchestvenno-Politicheskaia Biblioteka, Moscow. Papers.
International Instituut voor Sociale Geschiedenis, Amsterdam. Papers, personal and financial documents, correspondence, manuscripts.

PRINTED SOURCES

Cornu, Auguste. *Karl Marx et Friedrich Engels: leur vie et leur oeuvre* (Paris: PUF, 1955–1970).

Hook, Sidney. *From Hegel to Marx: Studies in the Intellectual Development of Karl Marx* (New York: Reynal & Hitchcock, 1936).

Institut für Marxismus-Leninismus beim Zentralkomitee der Sozialistischen Einheitspartei Deutschlands. *Ex Libris Karl Marx und Friedrich Engels* (Berlin: Dietz, 1967).

Koigen, David. *Zur Vorgeschichte des modernen philosophischen Socialismus in Deutschland: Zur Geschichte der Philosophie und Socialphilosophie des Junghegelianismus* (Bern: Scheitlin, 1901).

Marx, Karl, and Friedrich Engels. [autobiographical materials in] *Historisch-kritische Gesamtausgabe* ("MEGA-1"), 12 vols. (Moscow and Frankfurt: Marx-Engels Institut, 1927–1935); Werke ("MEW"), 41 vols. (Berlin: Dietz, 1957–1968); *Gesamtausgabe* ("MEGA-2"), 142 vols: (Berlin: Dietz, 1974–); or *Collected Works* ("MECW"), 50 vols. (Moscow: Progress; London: Lawrence & Wishart; New York: International, 1975–).

McLellan, David. *The Young Hegelians and Karl Marx* (New York: Praeger, 1969).

Rosen, Zvi. *Bruno Bauer and Karl Marx: The Influence of Bruno Bauer on Marx's Thought* (The Hague: Nijhoff, 1977).

Tagliacozzo, Giorgio (ed.). *Vico and Marx: Affinities and Contrasts* (Atlantic Highlands, N.J.: Humanities, 1983).

Eric v. d. Luft

MATISSE, HENRI (1869–1954). Henri-Émile Benoît Matisse was born at Le Cateau-Cambrésis, France, in 1869 and attended the lycée in Saint Quentin from the age of 10, where he undertook classical studies. Abandoning further education in law at the University in Paris, he attended the École Quentin de la Louis under Professor Croisé for hour-long art classes in the early mornings of 1889. In 1891 Matisse moved to Paris to study under Adolphe William Bouguereau at the Académie Julian but soon accepted an invitation to practice informally under Professor Gustave Moreau of the École des Beaux-Arts. At age 26, Matisse became an associate member of the Société National des Beaux-Arts and studied the works of his contemporary Impressionist painters such as **Cézanne**, whom he greatly admired. He had his first one-man show in June of 1904 and astounded viewers when he and his fellow painters, who were later to be labeled *Fauves* or "wild beasts" by the critic Louis Vauxcelles, exhibited their revolutionary and anti-Impressionist works at the Salon d'Automne in 1905. Matisse's early masterpieces include *The Green Stripe* (1905), *Luxe, calm et volupté* (1905), and *The Joy of Life* (1906) in which his purity of color and freedom of emotional expression are clearly evident. Matisse's later works such as *The Dance* (1909) and his many book illustrations were to become increasingly simplified and antinaturalistic, and his designs for the Chapel of the Rosary of the Dominican Nuns in Vence, which he completed shortly before his death, remain one of the few great masterpieces of twentieth-century religious art.

Matisse was greatly influenced by the literature of his era. As a law clerk in Saint Quentin, he regularly copied out of the *Fables* of Jean de La Fontaine, with their Aesop-like tales of ethics and morality, on the back of legal foolscap paper. Previous to the turn of the century, Matisse read the French divisionist painter Paul Signac's landmark writings on art entitled *From **Delacroix** to Neo-Impressionism*, which were published in the avante-garde magazine *La Revue Blanche*. Signac, along with fellow artist **Georges Seurat**, developed the pointillist technique and Neo-Impressionist doctrine that inspired Matisse to utilize pure palettes and experimental brush techniques in his early works. Novels by the French liberal author André Gide such as *L'Immoraliste* (1902) were also read by Matisse in midlife, and the artist was encouraged through Gide's literature to seek out his own nature and sense of morality, even if it be at odds with contemporary ethical concepts. Matisse's incomparable spirituality and high level of ethics remained intact throughout his life, as did his creativity and experimentation. The philosopher Henri Bergson in his books *Time and Free Will* (1889) and *Creative Evolution* (1907) espoused that human consciousness exists on two levels, the first of these being the deeper, intuitive self, which Bergson felt was the seat of creative learning and free will. Matisse applied Bergson's concepts to his own art, and in his *Notes of a Painter* (1908), he instructed that the painting should emerge out of deep, unconscious feeling.

ARCHIVES

Getty Research Institute for the History of Art and the Humanities, Special Collection.

PRINTED SOURCES

Barr, Alfred H. *Matisse: His Art and His Public* (New York: Museum of Modern Art, 1966).
Flam, Jack (ed.). *Matisse on Art: Documents of Twentieth-Century Art* (Berkeley: University of California Press, 1995).
Fry, Roger. *Henri Matisse* (London: Zwemmer, 1935).
Gowing, Lawrence. *Matisse* (New York: W. W. Norton, 1985).
Howard, Richard (trans.). *Bonnard/Matisse: Letters between Friends* (New York: Harry N. Abrams, 1992).
Morgan, Genevieve (ed.). *Matisse: The Artist Speaks* (San Francisco: Collins Publishers, 1996).
Raboff, Ernest. *Henri Matisse—Art for Children* (New York: J. P. Lippincott, 1988).
Spurling, Hilary. *The Unknown Matisse: A Life of Henri Matisse: The Early Years, 1869–1908* (New York: Knopf, 1998).
UCLA Art Council. *Henri Matisse* (Berkeley: University of California Press, 1966).

Gregory L. Schnurr

MAUPASSANT, (HENRI-RENÉ-ALBERT) GUY DE (1850–1893). Guy de Maupassant was born near Dieppe, Normandy, in 1850 and educated at the lycées Yvetot and Rouen (1863–1868); he studied law sporadically in Paris (1870–1872).

Maupassant was a master of the short story and also an acclaimed novelist and journalist. He is most often grouped with the realist and naturalist writers, but Maupassant rejected any such affiliation and was beholden to no school. Success at the outset of his career allowed him an independence that few authors of his generation enjoyed. He took full advantage of this freedom to explore a remarkable range of social and thematic material. Maupassant's best stories are distinguished not only by their elegance, tautness, and economy of composition but also by their bitter irony and cynicism. His pessimism was directly attributable to the breakup of the Maupassant family (Steegmuller, 72, 163). Maupassant's mother, Laure, took the exceptional step of formally separating from her husband and taking full command of the children's education. The Church was not a comfort, and Maupassant remained a profound sceptic. There are no happy families or marriages in the fiction of Maupassant.

Maupassant's mother was broadly cultivated and early on introduced him to literature and literary circles. His first formal introduction to writing was through the poet Louis Bouilhet, while he was a student at Rouen. Bouilhet excited an interest in poetry and initiated Maupassant's apprenticeship in the craft of writing. However, the overwhelming influence in shaping his ideas as a writer was **Gustave Flaubert**, who was close friends with both Bouilhet and Maupassant's mother. Following the Franco-Prussian War, Maupassant moved to Paris to work in the Naval Ministry and to pursue a law degree. Sunday afternoons were given over to visits with Flaubert's literary circle, which included such luminaries as **Taine**, **Zola**, **Henry James**, and **Ivan Turgenev**. Flaubert from 1872 on agreed to accept the role of mentor, provided that Maupassant remain selflessly devoted to the craft of writing (Flaubert 2:243–244). Flaubert's notion of art was austere and strongly emphasized discipline and technique. The clarity and precision of Maupassant's writing indicate he learned his lessons well. Throughout his career, Maupassant generously acknowledged the debt he owed to Flaubert.

In the mid-1870s Maupassant also frequented the circle of naturalist writers led by Zola (Artinian, 88–131). Although not an explicit advocate of naturalism, he benefited from their camaraderie and shared with the other naturalists a strong interest in the seamier haunts of Paris. His first notable success as a short-story writer, "Boule-de-suif," was part of joint volume published with other naturalist writers in 1880. In the same year, Maupassant was crushed by the death of Flaubert. On the other hand, freed from strict tutelage to the master allowed Maupassant to pursue an independent path. Flaubert's elevated aesthetic was a limitation for the younger man, and in any case, Maupassant's motives for writing were more mercenary than the master's. Moreover, in complete contrast to Flaubert, Maupassant wrote with great speed and fluidity and was not one to worry the details.

Maupassant was acutely aware of the success of the short-story writer Alphonse Daudet. Although he did not attempt to emulate Daudet's style, he worked to keep his name before the public by publishing in broadly circulated papers such as *Le Gaulois* and *Gil Blas*. The latter in particular was notorious for its raciness and the manner in which it continually tested the limits of the liberalized press law of 1882. Maupassant took full advantage of *Gil Blas* in order to indulge his taste for the scurrilous. Another notable feature of Maupassant's writing was his affinity for the fantastic and perverse as represented in such stories as *La Horla*. Like many short-story writers of the period, he was a close reader of **Poe** but was also interested in the contemporary study of psychoses. He frequented Jean-Martin Charcot's famous public lectures and demonstrations on hysteria and also visited the hypnotist Hippolyte Bernheim's clinic at Nancy (Forestier, 2:1614).

Along with his failing health, the former furious pace of his writing declined after 1888. In the later stages of his life, Maupassant traveled in aristocratic social circles, and with the encouragement of Taine and Paul Bourget, he attempted to portray the upper social strata (Steegmuller, 287–297). The upshot were two unremarkable novels, *Fort Comme le Mort* and *Notre Coeur*, in which Maupassant abandoned his strength in depicting action in favor of psychological analysis. Maupassant desperately attempted to recoup his powers in the last years of his life, but the progressive paralysis owing to syphilis was unremitting. He was confined to a sanitarium in 1892 and died the year after.

ARCHIVES

Maupassant Papers and Correspondence, Département des Manuscrits de la Bibliothèque Nationale.

PRINTED SOURCES

Artinian, R. *Maupassant Criticism: A Centennial Bibliography 1880–1979* (Jefferson, N.C.: McFarland, 1982). This work is a carryover from the noted Maupassant scholar and critic Artine Artinian. Arranged chronologically, it is a vital source for information on Maupassant.

Flaubert, Gustave. *The Letters of Gustave Flaubert 1830–1880*, Francis Steegmuller (ed.), 2 vols. (Cambridge, Mass.: Belknap Press, 1980, 1982).

Forestier, Louis (ed.). *Contes et Nouvelles*, 2 vols. (Paris: Bibliothèque de la Pléiade, 1974, 1979). An essential source in which the editor, Forestier, has rigorously examined the background for each of the stories and novels.

Leclerc, Yvan (ed.). *Gustave Flaubert–Guy de Maupassant: Correspondance* (Paris: Flammarion, 1993). This heavily annotated edition is a rich source for the relations between the two men.

Maupassant, Guy de. *Chroniques*, Hubert Juin (ed.), 3 vols. (Paris: Union générale d'éditions, 1993). An extensive collection of Maupassant's journalism from which he derived many stories.

———. *Correspondance*, Jacques Suffel (ed.), 3 vols. (Geneva: Édito-Service, 1973). The most comprehensive collection of Maupassant's correspondence, yet the editing and annotation are sparse.

———. *Correspondance Inédite de Guy de Maupassant*, Artine Artinian (ed.). (Paris:

Éditions Dominique Wapler, 1951). Letters usefully arranged according to recipient.

Steegmuller, F. *Maupassant: A Lion in the Path* (New York: Grosset & Dunlap, 1949). A solid biography that relies heavily on Maupassant's correspondence and includes many direct quotes. However, the work is beginning to show its age, and Maupassant is due for a comprehensive biographical treatment.

Vial, A. *Guy de Maupassant et l'Art du Roman* (Paris: Librairie Nizet, 1951). An unrivaled exploration of Maupassant's literary milieu.

James Millhorn

MAZZINI, GIUSEPPE (1805–1872). Giuseppe Mazzini was an Italian nationalist who, along with **Giuseppe Garibaldi** and **Camillo Benso di Cavour**, was responsible for the unification of Italy. Mazzini was also responsible for promulgating a humane and cosmopolitan nationalism throughout nineteenth-century Europe. Mazzini was born in Genoa, at that time part of the Napoleonic Empire, and completed a degree in law. He was well versed in the classics, especially Homer and Tacitus, and literary criticism was his first love. Between the age of 23 and 25, he published 20 literary articles on a range of topics, until the journals were suppressed by the government. Giovanni Boccaccio, Giacomo Leopardi, and Voltaire were banned by the Piedmontese government, but Mazzini was undoubtedly familiar with them. His true country, he once remarked, was England. Like many of his age, he read Shakespeare (*Hamlet* was his favorite play), **Charles Dickens**, and Adam Smith's *Wealth of Nations*. In philosophy, he read John Locke and in jurisprudence, Sir William Blackstone. According to the historian and biographer Mack Smith, Mazzini's extant notebooks reveal a passion for **Walter Scott** (he read every volume) and copies of poems by John Milton, Alexander Pope, and **Shelley**. Mazzini was drawn to Romantic literature in response to the neoclassical canon of his early youth. In particular, he read **Wordsworth**, Burns, **Byron**, **Carlyle**, and **John Stuart Mill**. In Italian literature, he admired Dante and Ugo Foscolo because they seemed to presage a united Italian republic. Mazzini also read the Neapolitan counter-Enlightenment philosopher Giambattista Vico, whose *Scienza Nuova* was published in definitive edition in 1744 and established a new science of human societies. From France, he admired the Marquis de Condorcet and Jean-Jacques Rousseau, and an obituary notice mentioned that his knowledge of French literature was "extensive and minute." The Germans **Johann Wolfgang von Goethe** and Johann Gottfried Herder influenced his ideas on nationalism and culture. He was familiar with the ideas of Kant and **Hegel** and a bitter opponent of **Karl Marx**. From the United States he read **Ralph Waldo Emerson** and **Harriet Beecher Stowe**'s *Uncle Tom's Cabin*. In religion, he upheld the New Testament but also looked into the Talmud, the Koran, and the Mahabharata.

ARCHIVES

Archivio Centrale dello Stato, Rome.
Associazione Mazziniana, Milan.

Centro di Studi Mazziniani, Naples.
Domus Mazziniano, Pisa.
Istituto Mazziniano, Genoa.
Istituto per la Storia del Risorgimento, Rome.

PRINTED SOURCES

Ambrosoli, Luigi. *Giuseppe Mazzini: una vita per l'unità d'Italia* (Manduria, Italy: La-
    caita, 1993).
Griffith, Gwilym Oswal. *Mazzini: Prophet of Modern Europe* (New York: H. Fertig,
    1970). Reprint of the 1932 edition.
Mack Smith, Denis. *Mazzini* (New Haven, Conn.: Yale University Press, 1994).
R. Commissione per l'edizione nazionale degli scritti di Giuseppe Mazzini (ed.) *Scritti
    editi e inediti di Giuseppe Mazzini*, 103 vols. (Imola, Italy: Galeati, 1907–1973).
Salvemini, Gaetano. *Mazzini*, I. M. Rawson (trans.) (Stanford, Calif.: Stanford University
    Press, 1957).
Sarti, Roland. *Mazzini: A Life for the Religion of Politics* (Westport, Conn.: Praeger,
    1997).
Scioscioli, Massimo. *Giuseppe Mazzini: i principi e la politica* (Naples: La Guida, 1995).
Silone, Ignazio (ed.). *The Living Thoughts of Mazzini* (New York: Longmans, Green &
    Co., 1939).

Stanislao G. Pugliese

MELVILLE, HERMAN (1819–1891). Herman Melville, an American author,
was born in New York City in 1819. He was educated at the New York Male
High School (1824–1829), Columbia Grammar School (1829–1830), Albany
(New York) Academy (1830–1831), Albany Classical School (1835), Albany
Academy (1836–1837), and Lansingburgh (New York) Academy (1838); was
baptized in the South Dutch Reformed Church; and authored *Moby-Dick*, novels,
poems, essays, reviews, and criticisms.

   Due to the inconsistent nature of his formal schooling, Melville relied upon
private and public libraries to supplement his reading. As a youth, the animated
stories of **James Fenimore Cooper** strongly influenced his quest for adventure
and helped him to develop an inquisitive mind. Once his formal schooling
ended, Melville's poverty and youthful restlessness led him on the first of two
sea voyages. He would use observations from both trips to write many of his
novels. Following his first journey, scholars suggest that Melville's desire to
return to the high seas was heightened after reading Richard Henry Dana's *Two
Years before the Mast* (1840) and Jeremiah N. Reynolds's *Mocha Dick; or, The
White Whale of the Pacific* (1840) in addition to travel narratives and oceanic
studies. Melville would later recommend Dana's book through characters in his
own novels. During his second adventure aboard the whale ship *Acushnet*, Melville became interested in tales about one sailing ship sunk by a whale attack.
On the voyage, Melville borrowed and read an account of this story, Owen
Chase's *Narrative of the Most Extraordinary and Distressing Shipwreck of the
Whale-Ship Essex, of Nantucket; Which Was Attacked and Finally Destroyed by*

a Large Spermaceti-Whale, in the Pacific Ocean; with and Account of the Unparalleled Sufferings of the Captain and Crew (1821), which he would eventually buy and annotate when writing *Moby-Dick*.

When he returned from his second voyage in 1844, Melville began his professional writing career. Again, relying on travel narratives and marine studies, he published several novels about thrilling adventures on the open seas. In addition to nautical tales, Melville also penned a philosophical novel, *Mardi* (1849), after reading works by François Rabelais, Sir Thomas Browne, and Esaias Tegner as well as Charles Barnard's *A Narrative of the Sufferings and Adventures of Capt. Charles H. Barnard* (1829). After writing several novels, Melville acquired, and read for the first time, classical works by Milton and Shakespeare in 1849. Both writers had a profound impact upon his future novels including *Moby-Dick*. While writing *Moby-Dick*, Melville read and wrote notes in the works of both authors. In his copy of Milton's *Paradise Regained*, Melville annotated several passages within the marginalia on pages 132–133 of Book IV, for lines 197 and 220–221. For line 197—"Though sons of God both angels are and men"—Melville wrote in pencil: "Put into Satan's mouth, but spoken with / John Milton's tongue;—it conveys a strong controversial meaning" (Hayford and Horth, "Shakespeare Volume," 958). For lines 220–221—"the childhood shows the man, / As morning shows the day"—Melville noted: "True, if all fair dawnings were followed by high noons / & blazoned sunsets. But as many a merry morn / preceeds a dull & rainy day; so, often, unpromising / mornings have glorious middays & eves. / The greatest, grandest things are unpredicted" (Hayford and Horth, "Shakespeare Volume," 958). Around the same time, Melville bought the multivolume *The Dramatic Works of William Shakespeare*. Scholars note that words or passages from *King Lear*, *Hamlet*, and *Romeo and Juliet* appear in several Melville novels and short stories. On both sides of the last blank leaf (pages [523] and [524]) for Volume VII, Melville wrote extensive notes in pencil. Scholars cannot ascertain whether the notes were written at the same time or in intervals. Some passages in the notes can be referenced to his later writings including *Moby-Dick*, *White-Jacket*, short stories, essays, and letters. While writing *Moby-Dick*, Melville also acquired his own copy of *Chase's Narrative* and attached an extensive memoranda highlighting his trip aboard the *Acushnet*, his knowledge of the *Essex* story, and a postscript detailing the final fate of the *Essex* crew.

Throughout his career, Melville became a voracious reader and amassed a large library of both classical and modern works. Other works and authors thus had a profound impact on Melville. In addition to Milton and Shakespeare, Melville also read and was influenced by his good friend **Nathaniel Hawthorne**, American essayist **Ralph Waldo Emerson**, British authors **Samuel Taylor Coleridge**, Charles Lamb, **Charles Dickens**, and **Thomas Carlyle**, German author **Johann Wolfgang von Goethe**, as well as classical works from Plato and Chaucer. Likewise, scholars also note that philosophical and religious motifs found in several novels can be attributed to Edmund Burke's *A Philosophical*

Inquiry into the Origin of Our Ideas of the Sublime and Beautiful (1806) as well as the Bible.

ARCHIVES

Herman Melville Papers, Houghton Library, Manuscript Department, Harvard University, Cambridge, Massachusetts. Principal correspondence, travel journals, literary manuscripts, publishers' agreements and accounts, and other papers.

Gaansevoort-Lansing Collection, New York Public Library. Family correspondence.

PRINTED SOURCES

Bercaw, Mary K. *Melville's Sources* (Evanston, Ill.: Northwestern University Press, 1987). A checklist of all the sources scholars have suggested Melville used in his works.

Cowen, Walker (ed.). *Melville's Marginalia*, 2 vols. (New York: Garland, 1987). A complete transcription of Melville's marginalia; Cowen's reliability is questioned by the editors of *The Writings of Herman Melville*.

Dillingham, William B. *Melville & His Circle: The Last Years* (Athens: University of Georgia Press, 1996).

Garner, Stanton. *The Civil War World of Herman Melville* (Lawrence: University Press of Kansas, 1993).

Hayford, Harrison, and Lynn Horth. "Melville's Memoranda in Chase's *Narrative of the Essex*." In Harrison Hayford, Hershel Parker, and G. Thomas Tanselle (eds.), *The Writings of Herman Melville*. Vol. 6, *Moby-Dick; or, The Whale* (Evanston and Chicago, Ill.: Northwestern University Press and The Newberry Library, 1988).

————. Hayford, Harrison, and Lynn Horth. "Melville's Notes (1849–51) in a Shakespeare Volume." In Harrison Hayford, Hershel Parker, and G. Thomas Tanselle (eds.), *The Writings of Herman Melville*. Vol. 6, *Moby-Dick; or, The Whale* (Evanston and Chicago, Ill.: Northwestern University Press and The Newberry Library, 1988).

Melville, Herman. *Journals*, Howard C. Horsford and Lynn Horth (eds.) (Evanston and Chicago, Ill.: Northwestern University Press and The Newberry Library, 1989). Complete edition of Melville's journals.

————. *The Letters of Herman Melville*, Merrell R. Davis and William H. Gilman (eds.) (New Haven, Conn.: Yale University Press, 1960).

Robertson-Lorant, Laurie. *Melville: A Biography* (New York: Clarkson Potter, Publishers, 1996).

Sealts, Merton M., Jr. *Melville's Reading*, rev. ed. (Columbia: University of South Carolina, 1988). A checklist of books owned and borrowed by Herman Melville.

Robert J. Zalimas, Jr.

MICHELET, JULES (1798–1874). Jules Michelet was born in Paris in 1798, the only child of a poor printer. Raised in an atheist family, he was nevertheless christened at the age of 17 when he was a student at the College Charlemagne (1808–1819). The greatest French Romantic historian won his popularity through a monumental *Histoire de France* celebrating the nation in its collective identity. He described the French Revolution enthusiastically and first interpreted the Renaissance as a reaction against medieval obscurantism.

His formative year as a disciple of Abel-François Villemain were more concerned with rhetoric and literature. Aged 20, he received his doctorate at the Sorbonne with two short theses on Plutarch and John Locke. Under the influence of Victor Cousin, he read the Scottish philosophers and planned a translation of Thomas Reid. From 1821, his reading lists (Bib. Hist., Paris) reflected his growing interest in the philosophy of history. Michelet translated *Scienza Nuova*, the masterpiece of his "sole master" Giambattista Vico in 1827, and he delved into Vico's idea of primitive symbolism with his *Origines du Droit Français* (1837), a book drawing extensively from **Jacob Grimm**'s *Deutsche Rechtaltertümer*. He ended his career as a translator with a selection from Luther in 1835. Following his appointment as professor of history at the École Normale, Michelet published a *Histoire de Rome* (1830) introducing the teaching of Barthold-Georg Niebuhr. He also gathered his lectures on French history for a book entitled *Introduction à l'Histoire Universelle* (1831) in which, after Augustin Thierry and **François Guizot**, he placed France at the forefront of civilization. "Michelet abandoned any sense of the historian as a straight-forward chronicler of events. He became a maker of meanings" (Crossley, 186).

The elaboration of his *Histoire de France*, in which he created a mythic Joan of Arc after Friedrich von Schiller's *Jungfrau von Orleans*, was interrupted by the publication of *Les Jésuites* (1844) written with Edgar Quinet and *Le Peuple* (1846), an essay praising the patriotic sense of the lower classes. These were followed by a seven-volume *Histoire de la Révolution* (1852–1853), whose sources he found mainly in the Archives Nationales. He resumed working on the *Histoire de France* in 1855 with a volume on the Renaissance, and the whole project was eventually completed in 1869. After 1858, he published a series of books on womanhood inspired by his second wife, and he wrote *La Bible de l'Humanité* (1864) in response to **Ernest Renan**'s *Vie de Jésus-Christ*. A last series of books on natural history, including *L'Oiseau* (1856) or *La Montagne* (1868), vulgarized the works of **Charles Darwin** and **Charles Lyell**. He left voluminous notebooks and a journal so that Rousseau should not remain "the only man who was known."

ARCHIVES

Michelet Papers, Bibliothèque Historique de la Ville de Paris. Manuscripts and principal correspondence.

PRINTED SOURCES

Crossley, C. *French Historians and Romanticism* (London: Routledge, 1993).
Fauquet, E. *Michelet ou la Gloire du Professeur d'Histoire* (Paris: Cerf, 1990). Extensive use of Michelet's reading lists.
Viallaneix, P. *Michelet: Les Travaux et les Jours* (Paris: Gallimard, 1998).

Thierry Vourdon

MILL, JAMES (1773–1836). James Mill, born at Northwater Bridge, Forfar-shire, Scotland, was the son of a shoemaker. He attended parish school, Montrose Academy, and Edinburgh University (1790–1793) and became a licensed Presbyterian preacher in 1798. After working as an itinerant preacher and tutor from 1798 to 1802, he became a journalist in London in 1802 and married in 1805. His first son, **John Stuart Mill**, was born in 1806 and named for James's patron. James devoted himself to John's education, developing him into a child prodigy and later serving both as icon and foil in the development of John's philosophy. James Mill was a politician, colonial administrator, and writer of great influence in Britain, America, and India, whose contributions to utilitarian philosophy and progressive government had wide influence, both in popularizing utilitarian thinking and in contributing to its development.

Mill befriended utilitarian philosopher **Jeremy Bentham** in 1808, with whom he led the "philosophical radicals," who sought a justification for law and government in promoting the greatest sum of happiness among the citizenry. Bentham's ideas influenced Mill's articles on government, education, and law for supplements to the *Encyclopædia Britannica*, printed as a volume of *Essays* in 1823. They were also integral to Mill's more polemical articles on politics and economics for various reviews, culminating in his writings for the *London Review*, later the *London and Westminster*, edited by John Stuart Mill.

Mill's *The History of British India* (1817), in the Scottish Enlightenment style of philosophical history typical of David Hume, Adam Smith, and John Millar, the first comprehensive study of the British conquest, was unrelentingly critical of the colonial administration, particularly the use of local laws under the theories of Sir William Jones. Mill's view of Indian government, based not on tradition, religion, and culture but on utilitarianism, democracy, and Ricardian economics, was his guide as a lower official and after 1830, Examiner, of the East India Company, effectively giving him control of British policy in India for four years.

Mill's *Elements of Political Economy* (1821) essentially the first textbook in that field, was based mainly on the work of **David Ricardo** and **Thomas Malthus** but also betrays the influence of Bentham, which is strongest in *Analysis of the Phenomenon of the Human Mind* (1829), a development of analytical psychology as a basis for utilitarianism.

ARCHIVES

London Library NRA 20043 London L coll. Commonplace Books (5 vols).
London University, British Library of Political and Economic Science. Miscellaneous correspondence and papers.
Bentham Papers, London University, University College Manuscripts Room. Letters to Jeremy Bentham, 1814–1827.
Brougham Papers, London University, University College Manuscripts Room. Letters to Lord Brougham, 1811–1836.
MSS 34611–15, British Library, Manuscript Collections. Letters to Macvey Napier, 1814–1831.

MSS 35144–53, British Library, Manuscript Collections. Correspondence with Francis Place, 1814–1831.

Add 7510, Cambridge University Library, Department of Manuscripts and University Archives. Correspondence with David Ricardo, 1810–1823.

NRA 22241 SDUK, London University, University College Manuscripts Room. Letters to Society for Diffusion of Useful Knowledge, 1827–1835.

Acc 4796, NRA 29136 Stuart-Forbes, National Library of Scotland, Department of Manuscripts. Letters to Sir John Stuart.

PRINTED SOURCES

Bain, Alexander. *James Mill: A Biography* (London: Longmans, Green, and Co., 1882; reprint, New York: A. M. Kelley, 1967).

Fenn, Robert A. *James Mill's Political Thought* (New York: Garland Press, 1987).

Forbes, Duncan. "James Mill and India," *Cambridge Journal* (October 1951), 19–33.

Haakonsen, Knud. "James Mill and Scottish Moral Philosophy," *Political Studies*, 33 (1985), 628–636.

Hamburger, Joseph. *James Mill and the Art of Revolution* (New Haven, Conn.: Yale University Press, 1963).

Mazlish, Bruce. *James and John Stuart Mill* (London: Hutchinson, 1975).

Mill, James. *Analysis of the Phenomena of the Human Mind* (London: Baldwin and Cradock, 1829).

———. *The Collected Works of James Mill* (London: Routledge/Thoemmes Press, 1992).

———. *Elements of Political Economy*, 3rd ed. (London: Baldwin, Cradock, and Joy, 1826; reprint, New York: A. M. Kelley, 1965).

———. *Essays on Government, Jurisprudence, Liberty of the Press, and Law of Nations* (London: J. Innes, 1823; reprint, New York: Augustus M. Kelley, 1986).

———. *A Fragment on Mackintosh; Being Strictures on Some Passages in the Dissertation by Sir James Mackintosh*, Prefixed to the Encyclopaedia Britannica (London: Baldwin and Cradock, 1835).

———. *The History of British India*, 2nd ed. (London: Baldwin, Cradock, and Joy, 1820; reprint, New York: Chelsea House, 1968).

Mill, John Stuart. *Autobiography*, 2nd ed. (London: Longmans, Green, Reader, and Dyer, 1872).

Thomas, William. *Philosophical Radicals* (Oxford: Clarendon Press, 1979).

Stephen, Leslie. *The English Utilitarians* (London: Duckworth and Co., 1900).

Steve Sheppard

MILL, JOHN STUART (1806–1873). John Stuart Mill was born in London in 1806 and educated until the age of 13 by his father, **James Mill**—author, government official, and follower of **Jeremy Bentham**. John Stuart Mill had no religious instruction or affiliation, excepting his education in the rational doctrines of his father and Bentham. John Stuart is best known for his social and political philosophy; his essay *On Liberty* (1859) is justly considered the foremost analysis of personal and political freedom.

Under the stern guidance of his father, John Stuart Mill began to learn Greek and mathematics at the tender age of 3, soon reading *Aesop's Fables* and passing through the classics to the *Dialogues* of Plato at age 7 (Stillinger, 38). When 8 years old, Mill began an extensive education in the Latin classics and subsequently taught these to his siblings. His "light" reading consisted of historical texts, particularly of the ancient world, accompanied by warnings from his father as to the "Tory prejudices" of a particular author (Stillinger, 42). At age 11 he composed, on his own initiative, a history of Roman government. His formal education concluded with a year studying logic, followed by a year reading political economy at the age of 13. After studying under his father, John Stuart Mill then studied law, read economics with **David Ricardo**, and completed his studies with Bentham's treatise on legislation, "the inculcation & diffusion of which could be made the principal outward aim of a life" (Stillinger, 76). By the age of 15, Mill had a more broad and rigorous education than that of a typical university graduate.

It was not only Mill's education that informed his thought. His family had close connections with Jeremy Bentham, even living on his estate for 3 years; at age 14 Mill spent a year in France as a guest of Bentham's brother, where he learned French and was introduced to several French scientists and thinkers. Back in England, Mill's father headed a group of "radicals" arguing for political and electoral reform. Mill even followed his father's lead into government service, joining the East India Company as a clerk at the age of 17 and rising to be in charge of the Company's relations with the Indian states from 1836 to 1858. In 1865 John Stuart Mill became a member of Parliament, supporting causes such as Irish land reform and the franchise for women. Mill's philosophy was not a mere academic exercise; it both informed and was informed by his political experience.

In 1826, at age 20, John Stuart Mill experienced a mental "crisis" when he realized that the sterile rationality of his father and Jeremy Bentham did not provide him a purpose in life. For some 3 years he suffered from a chronic depression, relieved only by reading poetry—particularly that of **William Wordsworth**—and an emerging friendship with Harriet Taylor, who would later become his wife. This crisis forced Mill to reexamine the purpose of his life and to "give its proper place among the prime necessities of human well being, to the internal culture of the individual" (Stillinger, 123). With a new sense of purpose, Mill went on to formulate a vision of liberalism aimed at the development of each individual through education, "making the race infinitely better worth belonging to" (*On Liberty*, 59). It is his ideal that has come to characterize modern liberalism.

Mill's emphasis on individual development can be traced through his several influential works; his *System of Logic* (1843) was a textbook in how to think clearly: the basis of all human progress. His later, political texts (*Representative Government* in 1861) applied that model of clear thinking to an analysis of government and politics: the conditions needed for social progress. Finally, his analysis of ethical theory (*Utilitarianism* in 1863) allows—indeed requires—an understanding of human character: the basis of all moral progress. For John

Stuart Mill was, above all else, an educator, inculcating society with his truth that "a State which dwarfs its men, in order that they may be more docile instruments in its hands even for beneficial purposes—will find that with small men no great thing can really be accomplished" (*On Liberty*, 106). It is this caution that remains John Stuart Mill's greatest contribution to Western culture.

ARCHIVES

Mill, John Stuart. *Collected Works of John Stuart Mill*, John M. Robson (ed.), 33 vols. (Toronto: University of Toronto Press, 1963–1991). A massive undertaking, this series prints all known archival material.

PRINTED SOURCES

Berlin, Isaiah. "Two Concepts of Liberty." In *Four Essays on Liberty* (Oxford: Oxford University Press, 1969), chapter 4. A classic study of the meaning of freedom in Mill's liberalism.

Kahan, Alan S. *Aristocratic Liberalism: The Social and Political Thought of Jacob Burckhardt, John Stuart Mill, and Alexis de Tocqueville* (New York: Oxford University Press, 1992). An excellent comparative account of the varieties of European liberalism.

Laine, Michael. *Bibliography of Works on John Stuart Mill* (Toronto: University of Toronto Press, 1982).

Mill, John Stuart. *The Early Draft of John Stuart Mill's Autobiography*, Jack Stillinger (ed.) (Urbana: University of Illinois Press, 1961).

———. *On Liberty. A Norton Critical Edition* (New York: W. W. Norton and Co., 1975). Contains an excellent assortment of essays and commentary.

Semmel, Bernard. *John Stuart Mill and the Pursuit of Virtue* (New Haven, Conn.: Yale University Press, 1984).

Charles M. Roll

MILLAIS, JOHN EVERETT (1829–1896). Sir John Everett Millais was born in Southampton, England, in 1829 but spent the first 8 years of his life in St. Helier, on the Isle of Jersey, the ancestral home of his father, John William Millais. Although enrolled briefly in the local grammar school, Millais was educated at home by his mother, Emily Mary Evamy Millais, with an emphasis on literature and history. Both parents were well educated, artistically inclined, and accomplished musicians. When his preternatural drawing ability was recognized in 1836, Millais was given lessons with Mr. Bissel, the local drawing master, who recommended that he be sent to London. Rather than merely sending Millais away to school, the whole Millais family moved to London in 1838. Millais was still too young for admittance to the Schools of the Royal Academy (RA), so his mother continued to instruct him at home and took him on daily excursions to the British Museum and National Gallery. In 1839, he began attending the School of Art (known as Sass Academy, after its founder Henry Sass), the youngest student ever accepted there. Millais's acceptance to the Royal Academy Schools came in 1840. Millais had not yet reached his eleventh year of age; his course of study at the RA would continue for 6 years. Millais was, and still is, the youngest person ever admitted to the Royal Academy of Art. He became the preeminent painter and illustrator of his day—daring, traditional, innovative, and conventional in his subjects and depictions, sometimes all at the same time. His skill was astounding, comprising both precision of detail and humanity of spirit; clarity, immediacy, and dramatic impact were his hallmark (Fleming, *Biography*, 25). Honors and recognition followed him throughout his life, culminating in his election to the presidency of the Royal Academy in 1896. His 50-year career was a popular and financial success from beginning to end.

Millais was disinclined toward formal study, and his mother by all accounts was an excellent teacher who taught her son the joy of literature and history, which combined with his own instinctual fascination with the natural world and with people. Under his mother's tutelage, he read widely: the Bible, classical mythology, world history, British history and legend, heraldry, English literature, including Shakespeare, along with foreign literature in translation (Fleming, *Biography*, 8; Millais 1:3). Also, once having arrived in London, his reading was complemented visually by his regular visits to the British Museum and the National Gallery. Added to that were the resources of the Library of the Royal Academy. Millais was a tireless researcher; the details particularly for his historical, literary, and biblical paintings demanded it. The subjects of his early works reflect his breadth of reading, including *The Battle of Bannockburn* (1839), *The Benjamites Seizing Their Brides* (1840), *Cupid Crowned with Flowers* (1841), *Baptism of Guthren the Dane* (1845), and *Pizarro Seizing the Inca of Peru* (1846). The subject of this last work was inspired jointly by the reading of John Luffman's *Elements of Universal History and Chronology* and his discovery of a Henry Briggs engraving depicting Pizarro's duplicity (Fleming, *Biography*, 24). The course of study at the Royal Academy demanded immersion in classical tradition as well as study of the masters and drawing from life, all of which would have required substantial research of artworks, literary texts, and archeological documents. Even after he had graduated from the Royal Academy, his mother continued to read aloud to him from novels and histories as he painted in his studio.

Ideas for Millais seem to have been the results of a combination of influences, seldom coming simply and directly from his reading. His literary painting *Cymon and Iphigenia* is a scene from the first story of the fifth day of Boccaccio's *Decameron*, by way of a similar painting by Sir Joshua Reynolds. The Reynolds work led Millais back to the original literary text from which he then selected his own scene for interpretation. Millais was also resolutely independent and would often resist reading particular texts if they were pressed upon him. For example, he resolutely refused to read the first volume of **John Ruskin**'s *Modern Painters*, which foreshadowed the principles of Pre-Raphaelitism (*DNB*, 1040). And he was a long time coming to the poetry of **John Keats**, but when he did (after tireless urging by **William Holman Hunt**), he proved to be a perceptive and receptive reader; from his understanding of Keat's obscure reference in "Isabella, or the Pot of Basil" came his first Pre-Raphaelite painting, *Lorenzo and Isabella* (1849). Plus, his insistence on accuracy in the minutest detail led him to consult Camillo Bonnard's *Costumi dei Secoli XIII, XIV, e XV* to ensure that his figures were dressed appropriately (Fleming, Biography, 35, 48–49). Ultimately, the goal of Pre-Raphaelitism was to take high art higher, to represent all the old scenes from Holy Writ, all the great themes of history, all the dreams of the poets from Homer to Keats, and all the thought and passion of modern life, with a truth and force that had never been achieved before (Monkhouse, 52).

In the 1860s, reading also became part of his artistic commissions when, in addition to his painting, he began illustrating (most notably for **Tennyson, Thackeray,** and **Trollope**). Sympathy with the text and an ability to read between the lines were integral to successful book illustration, and Millais was highly successful.

Millais was not a great reader of books for pleasure; there was little time for that. The daily newspapers and the weeklies *Punch, The World,* and the *Illustrated London News* comprised most of his personal reading. But he did admire good writing and liked travel books, novels (Braddon, **Dickens,** Thackeray, and Trollope were his favorites), and poetry, especially the poems of Keats and Tennyson (*DNB,* 1045; Millais, 2:228–242, 249–250, 268–270, 382–386).

ARCHIVES

The majority of materials relating to John Everett Millais are held at the Pierpont Morgan Library in New York City. Millais was a prolific correspondent, although he professed to dislike letter writing (Millais, 2:242); other Millais-related materials are scattered among the collections of the following libraries: Bodleian Library, British Library, British Newspaper Library, University of British Columbia Library, Chicago Art Institute Library, Fitzwilliam Museum Department of Manuscripts, Guildhall Library (London), Harvard University's Houghton Library, Huntington Library, Library of Congress Manuscript Division, New York Public Library, Princeton University Library, Royal Academy of Arts Library, John Rylands University Library of Manchester, Victoria and Albert Museum Library, and Yale University's Beinecke Rare Book Room and Manuscript Library.

PRINTED SOURCES

Baldry, A. Lys. *Millais* (London: T. C. & E. C. Jack, n.d.).
Bayliss, Sir Wyke. *Five Great Victorian Painters of the Victorian Era: Leighton, Millais, Burne-Jones, Watts, Holman Hunt* (London: Sampson Low, Marston, 1902).
Burne-Jones, Georgianna. *Memorials of Edward Burne-Jones* (London: Macmillan, 1901).
C. M. "Sir John Everett Millais" In Sidney Lee (ed.), *Dictionary of National Biography,* vol. 22, Supplement, (New York: Macmillan, 1909), 1039–1046.
Fleming, G. H. *John Everett Millais: A Biography* (London: Constable, 1998).
———. *That Ne'er Shall Meet Again: Rossetti, Millais, Hunt* (London: Joseph, 1971).
Frith, William. *My Autobiography and Reminiscences* (London: Bentley, 1887).

Hunt, William Holman. *Pre-Raphaelitism and the Pre-Raphaelite Brotherhood* (London: Macmillan, 1905).

Leslie, George Dunlop. *The Inner Life of the Royal Academy* (London: Murray, 1914).

Marsh, Jan (ed.). *The Pre-Raphaelites: Their Lives in Letters and Diaries* (London: Collins & Brown, 1996).

Millais, John Guille. *The Life and Letters of Sir John Everett Millais*, 2 vols. (London: Methuen, 1899).

Monkhouse, Cosmo. *British Contemporary Artists* (New York: Charles Scribner's Sons, 1899).

Rossetti, William Michael. *Pre-Raphaelite Diaries and Letters* (London: Hurst & Blackett, 1900).

———. *Some Reminiscences* (London: Brown Langham, 1906).

Scott, William Bell. *Autobiographical Notes* (London: Osgood, 1892).

Elizabeth Dominique Lloyd-Kimbrel

MOMMSEN, THEODOR (1817–1903). Theodor Christian Matthias Mommsen was born in Garding, Schleswig (Germany), in 1817. He studied jurisprudence at the University of Kiel (1838–1843), where he became acquainted with Roman law; from 1848 to 1849 he was professor of civil law, then, in 1852, became professor of Roman law in Leipzig. He spent from 1854–1858 in Breslau and from 1858 to 1873 was professor of ancient history in Berlin. Mommsen and his brother Tycho were educated by their father Jens Mommsen, whose instruction was conducive to their linguistic talent and their propensity for poetry (Wickert, 1:26). Mommsen was taught methods of classical philology by his father until he entered school in 1834.

Mommsen supplied the fundamentals of modern and systematic epigraphy with his lifelong project *Corpus Inscriptionum Latinarum*, a collection of Latin inscriptions. He was the first to codify Roman law, in his *Römisches Staatsrecht* (3 vols., 1871–1888), and this created a new understanding of the Roman political system. Mommsen received the Nobel Prize for Literature in 1902 for his *Römische Geschichte* (3 vols., 1854–1855).

His extensive reading ranged from classical writers such as Shakespeare, Molière, and Cervantes to contemporary poets such as **Goethe**, Friedrich Schiller, and **Heinrich Heine**. In his late years, Mommsen often quoted Goethe and Shakespeare. His reading of Schiller and Heine inspired his first poetic efforts (*Liederbuch dreier Freunde* [1843], cowritten with Theodor Storm and Tycho Mommsen). Schiller's narration *Verbrecher aus verlorener Ehre* contributed to his biographical methodology (Wickert, 1:117). His way of writing history, characterized by a synchronous and ethnographic treatment of his subject, was influenced by Tacitus.

Mommsen had been interested in Roman private law since his early years. In his dissertation, he construed a Latin inscription indicating the extension of the domain of historiography into epigraphy by drawing upon nonliterary sources. Through his teacher Otto Jahn, Mommsen learned the value of inscriptions.

Friedrich Karl von Savigny, one of the founders of the historical school of jurisprudence, suggested to Mommsen the idea of the close relationship between law and history; then Mommsen linked juristic research to methods of historical criticism of sources. Through Savigny's works, Mommsen came to the conclusion that Roman civil law—regarded historically—has to inform contemporary political action (Wickert, 1:170).

Methodologically Mommsen's *Römische Geschichte* was highly influenced by the historian Barthold Georg Niebuhr, a founder of modern historiography based on a rigorous criticism of sources.

ARCHIVES

Österreichische Nationalbibliothek, Vienna. Diaries, autobiographical manuscripts.
Yale University Library, New Haven, Connecticut. Correspondence.
New York Public Library. Correspondence.
Stanford University Library, Stanford, California. Correspondence.
Temple University Library, Philadelphia. Correspondence.
Stadtarchiv und Wissenschaftliche Stadtbibliothek, Bonn. Correspondence.
Freies Deutsches Hochstift, Frankfurt am Main. Correspondence.
Universitätsbibliothek Leipzig. Correspondence.

PRINTED SOURCES

Wickert, Lothar. *Theodor Mommsen: Eine Biographie*, 4 vols. (Frankfurt am Main: Klostermann, 1959–1980).
———. *Theodor Mommsen—Otto Jahn: Briefwechsel 1842–1868* (Frankfurt am Main: Klostermann, 1962).

Ernst Grabovszki

MONET, CLAUDE (1840–1926). Claude Monet, born in Paris in 1840, entered Charles Gleyre's studio in 1862. As the most representative and prolific member of Impressionists, he revitalized artistic vision by rendering the vital aspects of nature and urban scenes through open-air realism and the use of bright colors. Impressionism provided the foundation for all subsequent innovations that would completely transform the aesthetics accepted since the Renaissance.

Monet sought to base art entirely on his instinctive response to impressions, sensations of light before the mind schematized them into objects and concepts. He recommended to students *The Elements of Drawing* by **John Ruskin**, who advised that "[e]verything that you can see in the world around you, presents itself to your eyes as an arrangement of different colours variously shaded. . . . The whole technical power of painting depends on our recovery of . . . the innocence of the eye." Monet adopted **Hippolyte Taine**'s retinal physiology in *De L'Intelligence* (1870), which differentiated sensation and perception. Émile Littré likewise defined "impression" in his famous *Dictionnaire* as the "effect which exterior objects make upon the sense organs" (Stuckey, 112). Monet advised painters to "try to forget what objects you have before you" and to paint the patches of colors and shapes, the "naive impression of the scene before you" (Perry, 120). Underscoring such premises, Jules Laforgue wrote in 1883, "The

Impressionist eye is . . . the most advanced eye in human evolution" (Laforgue, 192).

Monet and the naturalist writer **Émile Zola** exerted mutual influence. Impressionism and literary realism developed simultaneously. Zola's implication in *L'Oeuvre* of 1886 that Impressionists had not achieved a masterpiece or a synthesis distressed Monet and fellow Impressionists (Loevgren, 41). Monet's exploration of the serial method might indicate an influence from Zola, who synthesized his work into the Rouguon-Macquart series (Champa, 129).

Monet was acutely aware of literary trends. He knew a sizable portion of the 74 writers featured in Jules Huret's survey on literary evolution in *L'Écho de Paris* in 1891 (Alphant, 503). His work in Norway in 1895 followed an immersion in the dramas of **Henrik Ibsen, August Strindberg**, and **Bjørn Bjørnson** that created a great vogue among French intellectuals in the 1890s (Alphant, 533).

The serial method was inspired by Japanese woodcut art and also by the symbolist views of his friend Stéphane Mallarmé, who believed that real objects can only approximately be described, not defined. Monet embraced visionary dimensions and expressed an altered vision of reality that was both enduring and constantly in motion. This view paralleled the vitalist philosophy of Henri Bergson, to be published in *L'Evolution créatrice* (Sagner-Düchting, 30). Fluid mobility also characterized the literature of Paul Verlaine and Marcel Proust and the music of Claude Debussy and Maurice Ravel. Monet also loved books on botany and often consulted *Flore des serres et des jardins de l'Europe* (Joyes, 89).

ARCHIVES

Musée Claude Monet de Giverny, for Monet's library.
Archives du musée du Louvre, for registers of copyists.
Archives du musée Marmottan, Paris.
Archives municipales de Giverny.

PRINTED SOURCES

Alphant, Marianne. *Claude Monet, une vie dans le paysage* (Paris: Hazan, 1993).
Champa, Kermit Swiler. *"Masterpiece" Studies: Manet, Zola, Van Gogh, & Monet* (University Park: Pennsylvania State University Press, 1994).
Geffroy, Gustave. *Claude Monet: sa vie, son temps, son oeuvre*, 2 vols. (Paris: G. Cres, 1924).
Joyes, Claire. *Claude Monet: Life at Giverny* (New York: Vendome Press, 1985).
Laforgue, Jules. *Selected Writings of Jules Laforgue*, William Jay Smith (ed. and trans.) (New York: Grove Press, 1956).
Loevgren, Sven. *The Genesis of Modernism: Seurat, Gauguin, Van Gogh, and French Symbolism in the 1880s* (Bloomington: Indiana University Press, 1971).
Perry, Lilla Cabot. "Reminiscences of Claude Monet from 1889 to 1909," *American Magazine of Art*, 18, 3 (March 1927), 119–125.
Pissarro, Joachim. *Monet and the Mediterranean* (New York: Rizzoli, 1997).

Sagner-Düchting, Karin. *Monet at Giverny* (New York: Prestel, 1994).

Spate, Virginia. *Claude Monet, Life and Work* (New York: Rizzoli, 1992).

Stuckey, Charles F. "Monet's Art and the Act of Vision." In John Rewald and Frances Weitzenhoffer (eds.), *Aspects of Monet: A Symposium on the Artist's Life and Times* (New York: Harry N. Abrams, 1981).

Tucker, Paul Hayes. *Claude Monet: Life and Art* (New Haven, Conn.: Yale University Press, 1995).

Wildenstein, Daniel. *Claude Monet: biographie et catalogue raisonné*, 3 vols. (Lausanne and Paris: La Bibliothèque des arts, 1974–1991).

Hazel Hahn

MOODY, DWIGHT LYMAN (1837–1899). Dwight Moody, American evangelist, was born at Northfield, Massachusetts, in 1837. Moody's formal education was limited, and he never took ordination in any denomination. However, he was prominent in the organization and provision of education for others, through development of the Moody Bible Institute, Mt. Hermon school for boys, and the Northfield Seminary for girls.

At age 17, he left home, taking a job in his uncle's shoe store. In 1862, he married Emma C. Revell. Moody's first religious affiliation was as a Unitarian, but later he joined a Congregational Church. Moving to Chicago in 1856, Moody joined the Plymouth Church and began practicing evangelism, working to fill the pews he rented. Moody entered the ministry in 1860, independent of any church's financial support. Afterwards, in 1863, he organized a nondenominational church, became president of Chicago's YMCA in 1866, and toured widely in Great Britain, from 1873 to 1875, with singer Ira Sankey. Moody left Great Britain in 1875 and subsequently embarked on evangelistic tours in America (Weigle 103–104).

Interest in the education of others was a concern in addition to preaching. In 1879 he founded Northfield Seminary for girls and in 1881 Mt. Hermon for boys. In 1887, while continuing to tour and preach, he founded the Chicago Bible Institute, later renamed the Moody Bible Institute. Then, in 1894, he founded the Bible Institute Colportage Society, an effort to provide devotional reading materials cheaply to wide audiences (Weigle, 104).

Moody's informal education and reading were influenced by membership in the Boston YMCA. Here his dues entitled him to attend lectures by Boston's leading orators and intellectuals, as well as opening a library to him (Pollock, 9). Biographers have noted that Moody's method of sermon preparation included three books. They were the Bible, Cruden's *Concordance*, and the *Topical Textbook*, which arranged Bible topics for use by teachers. Moody's reading habits varied, but he appeared to lean toward devotional works (Moody). Since most of the educational programs he instituted were centered around the English Bible, it is reasonable that Moody's own reading in the texts and commentaries of his day were English-oriented rather than critical volumes. He remained committed to biblical integrity in spite of growing biblical criticism from German theological schools. Moody's writings are all biblically based, so familiarity with the English Bible is key to understanding his writing.

ARCHIVES

Moody Papers, Moody Bible Institute, Chicago.
Moody Papers, Northfield School, Northfield, Massachusetts.

PRINTED SOURCES

Findlay, James, Jr. *Dwight L. Moody: American Evangelist, 1837–1899* (Chicago: University of Chicago Press, 1969).
Moody, W. R. *The Life of Dwight L. Moody* (New York: Fleming C. Revell, 1900). Describes reading habits but does not mention specific titles.
Pollock, John C. *Moody* (New York: Macmillan, 1963). Contains a brief bibliographic essay that helps in evaluation of works about Moody.
Smith, Wilbur M. *An Annotated Bibliography of D. L. Moody* (Chicago: Moody Press, 1948).
Weigle, Luther Allen. "Dwight Lyman Moody," in *Dictionary of American Biography*, vol. 7, (New York: Charles Scribner's Sons, 1934), 103–106.

Christopher Beckham

MORRIS, WILLIAM (1834–1896). William Morris was born in Walthamstow, a suburb of London, in 1834 and educated at Marlborough College (1848–1851) and Exeter College, Oxford (1853–1856). Following graduation, he worked briefly for the Gothic Revival architect G. B. Street. In 1857, Morris studied painting with **Dante Gabriel Rossetti** and established an art studio of his own in London. Disgusted by the mass production of shoddy goods and inspired by the writings of **John Ruskin**, he founded Morris, Marshall, Faulkner, and Company in 1861, an enterprise dedicated to the design and production of fine textiles, tapestries, furniture, wallpapers, murals, and stained glass, and sponsored a Society for the Protection of Ancient Buildings in 1877. In 1891 Morris revived the typographical arts in Britain by founding the Kelmscott Press, a company that specialized in ornamental borders, initials, and typefaces.

Morris also wrote a large number of prose romances and poems. Many of his early writings—*The Defense of Guenevere* (1858) and *The Earthly Paradise* (1868–1870), for instance—were strongly influenced by Thomas Malory and Jean Froissart. His translation of the *Volsunga Saga* (1870) and publication of the *Story of Sigurd the Volsung and the Fall of the Niblungs* (1876) grew out of his love for works like *Beowulf* that reflected Britain's Anglo-Saxon heritage. The stories Morris wrote during the 1880s and 1890s, such as *A Tale of the House of the Wolfings* (1889), *The Wood beyond the World* (1894), and *The Water of the Wondrous Isles* (1897), reveal a concern for personal fulfillment, societal regeneration, freedom, and justice that cannot be separated from his growing interest in social reform during this period. During the 13 years preceding his death on October 9, 1896, Morris edited a socialist newspaper, *Com-*

monweal, delivered hundreds of speeches, and composed dozens of pamphlets and books espousing socialism. Although familiar with the writings of Henry George, Henry Hyndman, **George Bernard Shaw**, and Sidney Webb, Morris adopted a more communistic brand of socialism than many of his contemporaries. In his most famous work, *News from Nowhere; or, An Epoch of Rest* (1890), which was written in response to the urban, mechanized, and nationalized utopia of Edward Bellamy's *Looking Backward* (1888) and drew strength from his reading of both **Karl Marx** and Sir Thomas More, Morris presents his vision of Britain in the twenty-first century as an idyllic, pastoral, commune-based society.

ARCHIVES

British Library. The largest collection of Morris's writings.
Bodleian Library, Oxford University.
The Victoria and Albert Museum, London.
The William Morris Gallery, Walthamstow, England.

PRINTED SOURCES

Harvey, Charles, and Jon Press. *Art, Enterprise, and Ethics: The Life and Works of William Morris* (London: Frank Cass, 1996).
Morris, William. *The Collected Letters of William Morris*, Norman Kelvin (ed.), 4 vols. (Princeton, N.J.: Princeton University Press, 1984–1996). Volumes include all 2,487 of Morris's extant letters.
Stansky, Peter. *Redesigning the World: William Morris, the 1880s, and the Arts and Crafts* (Princeton, N.J.: Princeton University Press, 1985).
Thompson, E. P. *William Morris: Romantic to Revolutionary* (New York: Pantheon Books, 1977).
Thompson, Paul. *The Work of William Morris* (New York: Viking Press, 1967).

Robert F. Haggard

MORSE, SAMUEL FINLEY BREESE (1791–1872). Samuel Morse was born in Charlestown, Massachusetts, in 1791 and educated at Phillips Academy; he graduated from Yale in 1810. He studied with celebrated painter Benjamin West (1811–1815). He was founder and first president of the National Academy of Design from 1826 to 1845 and again from 1861 to 1862. Morse is considered one of the finest portrait painters in America of the Romantic style. He was among the first in the United States to use the daguerreotype photographic process as early as September 1839 (Morse, 2:31). Morse developed the electromagnetic and chemical recording telegraph and a code consisting of combinations of dots and dashes. To finance his telegraphic and photographic experiments, in 1840 Morse opened in New York City what was perhaps the first school of photography in America (Morse, 2:143). Morse was associated with New York University from 1832 until he retired in 1871.

At Yale, Morse replaced the Calvinist theology of his father with a new evangelical advocacy of human agency and secular activism. Painting, for Morse, was a tool for moral instruction: "Using the brush for the designs of Providence, he viewed his art—and his entire professional life—as an instrument of God" (Staiti, 7). Washington Allston was Morse's friend and master. Morse's acquaintances included **Louis-Jacques-Mandé Daguerre**, Mathew Brady, **S. T. Coleridge**, **Washington Irving**, Samuel Rogers, Charles Lamb, and his roommate in London, painter Charles R. Leslie. Morse claimed a painter needed to read "the old poets" (Morse, 1:101–102). Aside from religious beliefs, Morse "identified himself with [his friend **James Fenimore**] **Cooper**'s beliefs and envied his unguarded exuberance" (Kloss, 130). Morse read American and British newspapers regularly; he helped start the New York *Journal of Commerce*, one of America's first business newspapers. Morse had likely made a Hercules/American equation as he continued his support of American efforts against Great Britain; the political implications of Morse's huge painting *Dying Hercules* (1812) "probably followed Ovid's version of the events leading to the death of Hercules (*Metamorphoses*, Book IX)" (Kloss, 26). Sections of the *Iliad* and the writings by Apollodorus of Carystus probably were used as the basis for Morse's painting *The Judgment of Jupiter* (1815) (Kloss, 31–32). Morse's painting *The House of Representatives* (begun in 1821) "was decisively influenced by François-Marius Granet's *Choir of the Capuchin Church in Rome*, painted in Rome in 1815," and probably his father's report on Indian tribe conditions east of the Mississippi River (Kloss, 70). One 1826 commission, *Una and the Dwarf*, was a subject drawn from Edmund Spenser's *Faerie Queene* (1590) (Kloss, 106). John Scarlett Davis's painting in 1831 inspired the 1831–1833 painting *Gallery of the Louvre* (Kloss, 127–128). It is not clear how Morse applied discoveries by Arago, **Davy**, and Sturgeon in electromagnetism to his development of the telegraph.

ARCHIVES

Collection, 1838–1984 for Morse, Samuel Finley Breese, 1791–1892. New York University Archives.

Samuel Finley Breese Morse papers, 1817–1950. Special Collections Department, Robert W. Woodruff Library, Emory University, Atlanta, Georgia [control no. GAER97-A28].

Letters, articles, pamphlets, photographs, clippings, paintings related to his first wife, his strong Calvinist faith, progress information on his paintings.

PRINTED SOURCES

Kloss, William. *Samuel F. B. Morse* (New York: Harry N. Abrams, 1988). A study of Morse's art in a biographical context. Contains an excellent annotated chronology of Morse's achievements paralleled to national and world events on pages 152–154.

Mabee, Carleton. *The American Leonardo: A Life of Samuel F. B. Morse* (New York: Alfred A. Knopf, 1943). A comprehensive review of Morse's life.

Morse, Edward Lind (ed.). *Samuel F. B. Morse: His Letters and Journals*, 2 vols. (Boston: Houghton Mifflin, 1914).

Prime, Samuel Ireneus. *The Life of Samuel F. B. Morse* (New York: D. Appleton and Company, 1875; reprint, New York: Arno Press, 1974). The official biography of Morse.

Staiti, Paul J. *Samuel F. B. Morse* (Cambridge: Cambridge University Press, 1989). Examines the ideological and intellectual basis of Morse's art. Excellent selected bibliography, 290–292.

Peter Mayeux

MUIR, JOHN (1838–1914). John Muir was born in Dunbar, Scotland, in 1838. Migrating with his family to the United States in 1849, he was self-educated until attending the University of Wisconsin (1861–1863), though he never graduated. His father, Daniel Muir, was a preaching elder of the Disciples of Christ who provided his son with a fundamentalist Christian upbringing to which Muir had reacted by the end of his teenage years. Deeply spiritual, Muir's later religious beliefs went beyond the confines of orthodox Christianity to embrace the transcendental movement and which anticipated the development of a Christian environmental theology. Muir was an inventor and industrial innovator in his youth who later became a leading advocate for nature conservation. Founder of the Sierra Club and a prolific author, Muir conveyed appreciation of the value of wilderness conservation to a popular audience and also anticipated the development of ecology.

An avid reader from an early age, Muir read Shakespeare, the Romantic poets, especially Thomas Campbell, and Milton, memorizing whole passages of *Paradise Lost* and speaking them aloud and applying them to the Wisconsin landscape, learning, as Campbell had written, to "muse on Nature with a poet's eye!" (Turner, 61). Muir was also strongly influenced early by the writings of explorers Mungo Park, and **Alexander von Humboldt** and Aimé Bonpland, whose travel narratives of South and Central America not only helped inspire Muir's travels through the United States and Cuba in 1867 but, along with the writings of **Darwin** and Hooker, also accompanied Muir in his later travels in Africa and South America (1911–1912) in his study of tree distribution (Hall and Mark). In Yosemite in 1870 "he might of an evening be found under the lamp, beside his cozy fireplace, reading the writings of Alexander von Humboldt, Sir **Charles Lyell**, John Tyndall, Charles Darwin and the latest botanical works on trees" (Badè, 1:240). Among Muir's first purchases for his library after marriage was Humboldt's *Cosmos* in five volumes. Social influences on Muir included **Dickens** and Henry George, although the influence of Humboldt on Muir was critical as it provided a basis for the unified scientific and religious understanding of nature that underlies much of Muir's writing and activism.

ARCHIVES

John Muir Papers, Holt-Atherton Center for Western Studies, University of the Pacific, Stockton, California.

Limbaugh, R. H. and K. E. Lewis (eds.). *The Guide and Index to the Microform Edition of the John Muir Papers 1858–1957* (Stockton, Calif.: University of the Pacific, 1986).

PRINTED SOURCES

Austin, R. C. *A Christian Perspective on John Muir* (Atlanta, Ga.: John Knox Press, 1987).

Badè, W. F. *The Life and Letters of John Muir*, 2 vols. (Boston: Houghton, 1924).

Hall, C. M., and S. Mark. "The Botanist's Last Journey: John Muir in South America and Southern Africa, 1911–12." In *John Muir in Historical Perspective: Conference Proceedings* (Stockton, Calif.: University of the Pacific, 1986).

Miller, S. M. (ed.). *John Muir: Life and Work* (Albuquerque: University of New Mexico Press, 1993).

Turner, F. *Rediscovering America: John Muir in His Time and Ours* (New York: Viking, 1985).

Wolfe, L. M. (ed.). *John of the Mountains: The Unpublished Journals of John Muir* (Boston: Houghton, 1938).

C. Michael Hall

MULTATULI. *See* **Douwes Dekker, Eduard**.

N

NAPOLÉON BONAPARTE (1769–1821). Napoléon Bonaparte was in many ways the first truly great historical figure of the nineteenth century. His export of the ideals of the French Revolution throughout Europe between 1796 and 1806 resulted in the destruction of the last remaining vestiges of the ancien régime and the fictional Holy Roman Empire. In turn, he paved the way for the evolution of new political concepts that contributed to the development of the modern national state after 1815.

Napoléon was an individual of considerable learning and literary skill, who had a strong grasp of detail in everything he did and a clear perception of himself as someone of superior leadership. Yet with few exceptions, there is silence in the relevant sources regarding literary influences that shaped Napoléon's intellectual outlook. Nonetheless, a close reading of the literature provides some sense of the broad outlines of these influences. For example, it is noted that during his years at the École Militaire in Brienne (1779–1784), the young Napoléon studied ancient and modern languages, literature, history, and geography as well as the military sciences, with the latter three being his most proficient subjects. As a young artillery sublieutenant prior to the outbreak of the French Revolution (1785–1789), Napoléon intently read the works of the great humanist philosophes of the French Enlightenment including Voltaire, Rousseau, Racine, and Corneille. In particular, Rousseau's *Social Contract* and his attack on Christianity attracted the attention of the young Napoléon. Finally, Napoléon's perceptions of personal grandeur were reinforced by his identification with the noble heroes Plutarch created in his *Discourse upon Universal History.*

Perceiving himself as a man of history, Napoléon avidly studied the military campaigns of the great generals of the past as models for his own military activities. The primary focus was upon those he identified as the "Captains of Antiquity" and included Alexander of Macedonia, Hannibal, and Julius Caesar. However, Napoléon did not ignore the more contemporary successors to these ancient conquerors, as the exploits of Gustavus Adolphus of Sweden, Turenne and Louis XIV of France, and Frederick II of Prussia also influenced Napoléon's grand imperial designs. Not only did they collectively inspire Napoléon with their dramatic and bold accomplishments; they permitted Napoléon to place himself in the pantheon of universal heroes that they represented.

ARCHIVES

Widely scattered, including Bibliothèque nationale, Paris; Quai d'orsay, Paris; Bodleian Library, Oxford; British Library, London; Sterling Library, Yale University.

PRINTED SOURCES

Lefebre, Georges. *Napoléon* (Paris: PUF, 1935). English-language translation, 1990, Columbia University Press.

Masson, Frederic. *Napoleon et sa Famille*, 13 vols. (Paris: Ollendorf, 1897–1919).

Napoléon I. (Bonaparte). *Correspondance de Napoléon*, 32 vols. (Paris: Imprimérie Impérial, 1858–1869).

―――. *Vie de Napoléon par lui-même, d'après les texts, letters, proclamation, écrits* (Paris: Gallimand, 1930).

―――. *The Mind of Napoléon: A Selection of his own Written and Spoken Words*, Herold, J. Christopher (ed. and trans.) (New York: Columbia University Press, 1955).

―――. *Napoléon on the Art of War*, Luvaas, Jay (ed. and trans.) (New York: Free Press, 1999).

Schom, Alan. *Napoléon* (New York: Harper, 1997).

David K. McQuilkin

NAPOLÉON III, CHARLES LOUIS-NAPOLÉON BONAPARTE (1808–1873).

Napoleon III, second and last emperor of the French, was the son of **Napoléon** I's brother Louis and of Hortense de Beauharnais, daughter of the Empress Josephine. After a patchy education with private tutors, with whom he read modern authors such as Shakespeare, **Shelley**, and **Goethe** as well as Homer, Virgil, and Tacitus, he briefly attended the Augsburg gymnasium (1821–1823) and later a military college in Switzerland. After the deaths of Napoléon I and his heir ("Napoléon II"), he inherited the seemingly hopeless Bonapartist cause. Abortive attempts to seize power in 1836 and 1840 led to life imprisonment from which he escaped. His landslide election in December 1848 as the first (and last) president of the Second Republic was followed by a military coup in December 1851 and his assumption of the throne as Napoléon III in 1852. He had dictatorial power to put his ideas into practice.

He was inspired by the acts and pronouncements of his uncle, which he formulated into a Bonapartist program of great importance for France and Europe. In exile and prison (his "university") he studied and wrote, producing two major works that summed up his aims. *Des Idées napoléoniennes* (1839) was inspired by the political ruminations of Napoléon I in exile, widely circulated as the *Mémorial de Saint-Hélène* (1823). *Des Idées* advocated charismatic government combining authority and democracy, as under Napoléon I: "[I]t is the nature of democracy to personify itself in one man." It also heralded a new Europe based on the "nationality principle"—broadly, self-determination. He had no marked religious belief but made the Catholic Church a subordinate political ally. In *L'Extinction du paupérisme* (1844) he urged the elimination of poverty through state action, especially collective agricultural projects. He was influenced by the ideas of state-led socialism propounded by the workers' newspaper *L'Atelier*, to which he subscribed, and by Louis Blanc (whom Louis-Napoléon read and met), and the visions of great modernizing public works projects formulated by **Saint-Simon** and his disciples. Hence, his later nickname, "Saint-Simon on horseback." Once in power he did undertake economic policies ambitious for the time, including the development of credit institutions and above all the wholesale modernization of Paris. But he was also acquainted with the free-trade liberalism of Adam Smith, Jean-Baptiste Say, and the former Saint-Simonian Michel Chevalier, who helped to negotiate an epoch-making commercial treaty with Britain in 1860. He gave France one of its most important periods of free trade and economic growth. He also made tortuous efforts to reorder Europe according to a "nationality principle," which brought about the unification of Italy and indirectly that of Germany—at the cost of France's defeat and his own overthrow in 1870.

ARCHIVES

His correspondence is widely scattered. See, however, at the Bibliothèque Nationale, "Lettres de Napoléon III . . . Mme Cornu," n.a.fr. 1066-7.

PRINTED SOURCES

Bluche, Frédéric. *Le Bonapartisme: Aux origines de la droite autoritaire, 1800–1850* (Paris: Nouvelles Editions Latines, 1980).
Boon, H. N. *Rêve et réalité dans l'oeuvre économique et sociale de Napoléon III* (The Hague: M. Nijhoff, 1936).
Dansette, Adrien. *Louis-Napoléon à la conquête du pouvoir* (Paris: Hachette, 1961).
Simpson, F. A. *The Rise of Louis Napoléon* (London: J. Murray, 1909).

Robert Tombs

NEWMAN, JOHN HENRY (1801–1890). John Henry Newman was born in London in 1801 and educated at a private school at Ealing (1808–1816) and at Trinity College, Oxford (1817–1820), becoming a fellow of Oriel College in 1822. Converted to evangelicalism in youth, he passed through a brief liberal phase to a High Church position, being a founder of the Oxford or Tractarian movement from 1833. Doubts about Anglicanism led to his conversion to Roman Catholicism in 1845. He became a priest, superior of the Birmingham Oratory from 1849. He was raised to the cardinalate in 1879.

Newman was the greatest religious figure of Victorian England, the glory and the problematic of two churches. It is difficult, however, to categorize his greatness, for he nearly always wrote for an occasion, and many of the occasions were controversial. He was the greatest controversialist of an age of controversies. A profound Christian thinker rather than a systematic theologian or philosopher, he nonetheless made important contributions to theology and philosophy, particularly with regard to the rationale for religious belief. He was also important as a preacher, an educator and a contributor to literature: a minor poet and a major prose writer.

Newman was a reader of the Bible from childhood and received a thorough classical education, especially valuing Cicero for style (Ker, 24). He himself mentioned the major works that influenced him in his autobiography, *Apologia pro vita sua*, closely followed by his numerous biographers, and his reading can also be traced through his *Letters and Diaries*, largely drawn from the archives of the Birmingham Oratory. Two facts must be borne in mind when assessing literary influences: All thought that came from reading had to pass through the intensely refractive prism of his mind, and personal influences affected him more strongly than literary ones.

Thus, the book to which he owed his religious conversion, Thomas Scott's *The Force of Truth*, was associated in his mind with the teacher who gave it to him, Walter Mayers. Another book read in this evangelical period had an opposite effect on him: Joseph Milner's *History of the Church of Christ* drew him to the ancient Fathers of the Church, and his later reading of the entire Library of the Fathers was to shape his High Anglican theology. He read Gibbon solely for style (Ker, 11). The Romantic writers, particularly Sir **Walter Scott**, were outside the curriculum but very congenial (*Letters*, 1:72).

Senior colleagues at Oriel led Newman to works that shaped his High Anglican position. Edward Hawkins loaned him John Bird Sumner's *Apostolical Preaching*, which was decisive against his earlier evangelicalism (Ker, 22). John Keble's *Christian Year* reinforced his growing sacramentalism (Ker, 31). The work that was fundamental to his philosophy was an eighteenth-century classic, Joseph Butler's *Analogy of Religion*, which taught him the argument from analogy and the rule of probability as the guide to life (*Apologia*, 23).

Newman's loss of faith in Anglicanism was essentially the working of his own mind, but two Roman Catholic works had some influence. An article by Nicholas Wiseman on the "Anglican Claim" in the *Dublin Review* of April 1838 struck the first blow against his theory of the Anglican *via media* (*Apologia*, 111–113). A priest, Charles Russell, sent him a volume of St. Alfonso Liguori's sermons to remove some of his apprehensions about Rome (Ker, 254).

After Newman's conversion, it is only necessary to note the writings that did *not* influence him: the scholastic tradition, which he could not assimilate.

ARCHIVES

Newman Archive, Birmingham Oratory. Originals or copies of all known papers.

PRINTED SOURCES

Ker, Ian. *John Henry Newman: A Biography* (Oxford: Clarendon Press, 1988). Best of many biographies; entirely favorable.

Newman, John Henry. *Apologia pro vita sua: Being a history of his religious opinions*, Martin J. Svaglic (ed.) (Oxford: Clarendon Press, 1967). A variorum edition; first published in 1864.

————. *The Letters and Diaries of John Henry Newman*, Charles Stephen Dessain et al. (eds.) (Oxford: Clarendon Press, 1961–). Not yet complete. Vols. 1–2 especially useful.

Josef L. Altholz

NIETZSCHE, FRIEDRICH (1844–1900). Friedrich Nietzsche was born at Röcken, in Prussian Saxony, in 1844. He was educated at Schula Pforta (1858–1864), at the University of Bonn (1864–1865), and at Leipzig University, where he studied classical philology (1865–1869). He was appointed to a professorship at the University of Basel in 1869. Nietzsche was originally sent to school to follow in the ecclesiastical tradition of his family. His father, Karl Ludwig, was a Lutheran pastor, his grandfather was superintendent, and his great-grandfather was an archdeacon of the Lutheran Church. His mother, Franziska, was also the daughter of a Lutheran pastor. Nietzsche's own rebellion from this destiny came fairly early; by 1865, he had abandoned theology as his course of study. He showed considerable force of character in resisting family pressure. No doubt the resistance allowed him to feel the weight of the cultural strictures that he would be so fond of exposing in his adult work. Nietzsche's reputation is built upon his role as "cultural physician"; hence, many of the influences on him are ones of which he is ultimately critical. He considered European culture sick, and he set for himself, and those who followed him, an enormous moral and cultural reform project that he called the "reevaluation of all values."

Nietzsche was influenced by poets, artists, and musicians as much as by philosophers and philologists. The influence of **Robert Schumann, Frédéric Chopin,** and **Richard Wagner** is integrated into both his intellectual and artistic life. In his school days he was much moved by the poetry of Friedrich Hölderlin, on whom he wrote an essay in 1861. Nietzsche, who was a pianist and composer, also wrote poetry. Among German writers, he admired the lyric poet **Heinrich Heine**, to whom he compares himself as a stylist. An underappreciated influence is **Johann Wolfgang von Goethe**, whom Nietzsche's friend Otto Benndorf mentions as a primary intellectual influence (Gilman, 17). Nietzsche often constructed "genetic" links with Goethe, noting that he entered Leipzig 100 years to the day after Goethe (Krell, 40), and speculating about Goethe's acquaintance with his paternal grandmother, who grew up at Weimar (Kofman, 40), and tracing a familial relationship to Goethe (Krell, 16). Nietzsche's mature work refers to Goethe primarily as an intellectual who wanted philosophy to serve life.

In school, Nietzsche was especially fond of Aeschylus, Sophocles, and the poet Anacreon. He wrote a scholarly essay in Latin on Theognis of Megara's poetry in 1864. He worked on Theognis for the next few years, and this culminated in a scholarly essay published in *Rheinisches Museum*. His work on the Greek poet explicated the moral notions "good" and "bad," which Theognis associated with "aristocratic" and "plebeian." (Gilman, 15) These are notions to which Nietzsche again refers in the first essay of *The Genealogy of Morals*, where he explains the origins of a master morality. Another important figure of his Leipzig years was Diogenes Laërtius, on whom he wrote a prize-winning essay in 1867. In this period he read and worked on Democritus. It was the breadth of Democritus's thought that Nietzsche admired. He speaks of the philosopher as one who tried to work systematically through everything knowable. It is Heraclitus who is the hero of Nietzsche's later work. The unpublished essay "Philosophy in the Tragic Age of the Greeks" is a homage to that thinker. Nietzsche was influenced by reading Immanuel Kant and **Arthur Schopenhauer**. In 1865, quite by chance, he discovered Schopenhauer's *World as Will and Representation* in a Leipzig bookstore and was much moved by it. Friedrich Albert Lange wrote his influential *History of Materialism and Critique of Its Present Significance*, which Nietzsche read in 1866. Lange extended critiques of metaphysics and idealism to materialist theories that in his understanding also fall prey to Kant's skepticism. These three figures are at the focus of Nietzsche's philosophical maturity.

He first heard Wagner in 1860 during a public lecture. Although he engaged with him intellectually all his life, Nietzsche's aversion to Wagner's anti-Semitism and nationalism forced a breach fairly early on. They saw each other for the last time in 1876. The *Untimely Meditations* of 1873 already address **David Strauss**, Schopenhauer, and Wagner in the form of major critiques. As a mature thinker, additional works that influenced him negatively were British-style historians of morality, which he found tediously psychological and mechanical—for example, Paul Rée's *The Origin of Moral Sensibilities* (1877) and Wagner, Charles Baudelaire, and **Eugène Delacroix**, whom he considered decadents. By his own report, Nietzsche not only read Blaise Pascal but loved him. He admired the philosophes but especially Voltaire, whom he describes as part of a "progress *toward myself*" (*Ecce Homo*, 89).

Nietzsche read **Fyodor Dostoevsky** in the autumn of 1886 in a French translation. This reading was too late to have a significant influence on his mature work, but Dostoevsky was an author with whom he felt a great affinity.

ARCHIVES

Nietzsche Archive in the Goethe-Schiller Archiv, Weimar.

PRINTED SOURCES

Gilman, Sander L. *Conversations with Nietzsche: A Life in the Words of His Contemporaries* (Oxford: Oxford University Press, 1987).

Hayman, Ronald. *Nietzsche: A Critical Life* (Middlesex, England: Penguin, 1982).

Janz, Curt Paul. *Friedrich Nietzsche Biographie*, 3 vols. (Munich: Deutscher Taschenbuch Verlag, 1981).

Kofman, Sara. "A Fantastic Genealogy: Nietzsche's Family Romance." In Peter J. Burgard (ed.), *Nietzsche and the Feminine* (Charlottesville: University of Virginia, 1994).

Krell, David Farrell, and Donald L. Bates. *The Good European: Nietzsche's Work Sites in Word and Image* (Chicago: University of Chicago Press, 1997).

Nietzsche, Friedrich. *Ecce Homo*, R. J. Hollingdale (trans.) (Middlesex, England: Penguin, 1992).

Kathleen J. Wininger

NIGHTINGALE, FLORENCE (1820–1910).

Florence Nightingale was born in Florence, Italy, in 1820. Educated by her father in classics, modern languages, history, and philosophy, her travels included a European tour (1837–1839), a visit to Rome (1847–1848), a tour of Egypt and Greece (1849–1850), and an apprenticeship as a nurse for three months in Kaiserswerth, Germany.

Nightingale's mother's family was Unitarian, with a strong history of interest in reform. However, Nightingale grew up in the Church of England and at the age of 17 believed that she received a specific calling from God. The struggle of her early adulthood was to find a suitable way to express her vocation through public service. She considered entering an Anglican or Roman Catholic religious order but could not accept orthodox rigidity of doctrine.

While searching for a way to use her considerable talents, Nightingale pondered Eastern religions, reading her friend Christian von Bunsen's *The Place of Egypt in Ancient History* and the Gnostic classic *Hermetica*. She read and translated the work of several medieval Christian mystics, intending to create an anthology called *Notes from Devotional Authors of the Middle Ages*, which exists in manuscript but was never published. Impressed by **Harriet Martineau**'s *Eastern Life: Past and Present* (1848), Nightingale initiated a correspondence with her while also taking consolation from the orthodox *Memoir of the Rev. Henry Martyn* (1819).

Nightingale went on to become Superintendent of Nurses in British Army hospitals during the Crimean War (1854–1856). Upon her return to England, she wrote a handbook of hospital administration and a handbook for nurses. The Nightingale Training School for Nursing was founded in 1860, and Nightingale is credited with revolutionizing both nursing practice and public perception of the profession. Less well known but even more influential was her pioneering use of the statistical methods of L.A.J. Quetelet to influence public health policy and her recommendations to the Indian colonial government on public health matters.

ARCHIVES

Florence Nightingale Manuscript Collection. British Library, London. More than 8,000 letters.

Wellcome Institute for Medical History, London.

Florence Nightingale Museum Resource Center, London. Collection of artifacts, letters, published works, and Nightingale's personal library.

PRINTED SOURCES

Bishop, W. J., and Sue Goldie. *A Bio-Bibliography of Florence Nightingale* (London: Dawsons, 1962).

Bullough, Vern, Bonnie Bullough, and Marietta P. Stanton (eds.). *Florence Nightingale and Her Era: A Collection of New Scholarship* (New York: Garland, 1990).

Calabria, Michael E. (ed.). *Florence Nightingale in Egypt and Greece: Her Diary and "Vision"* (Albany: State University of New York, 1997).

Calabria, Michael E., and Janet A. Macrae (eds.). *"Suggestions for Thought" by Florence Nightingale: Selections and Commentaries* (Philadelphia: University of Pennsylvania Press, 1994).

Cook, Sir Edward. *The Life of Florence Nightingale*, 2 vols. (London: Macmillan, 1913). Includes excerpts from still unpublished letters.

Goldie, Sue M. (ed.). *"I have done my duty": Florence Nightingale in the Crimean War, 1854–56* (Manchester: Manchester University Press, 1987).

Goldie, Sue M., and W. J. Bishop (eds.). *A Calendar of the Letters of Florence Nightingale* (Oxford: Oxford Microform Publications for the Wellcome Institute for the History of Medicine, 1983). Microfiche guide arranges Nightingale's letters chronologically and summarizes them. The "Introduction" lists major institutional archives of letters.

Keele, Mary (ed.). *Florence Nightingale in Rome: Letters Written by Florence Nightingale in Rome in the Winter of 1847–48* (Philadelphia: American Philosophical Society, 1980).

Nightingale, Florence. *Ever Yours, Florence Nightingale*, Martha Vicinus and Bea Nergaard (eds.) (Cambridge, Mass.: Harvard University Press, 1990).

Showalter, Elaine. "Florence Nightingale's Feminist Complaint: Women, Religion, and Suggestions for Thought," *Signs*, 6 (1981), 395–412. Sources of Nightingale's theological ideas.

Woodham-Smith, Cecil. *Florence Nightingale: 1829–1910* (New York: McGraw-Hill, 1951).

Mary Angela Schwer

NOBEL, ALFRED BERNHARD (1833–1896). Alfred Nobel was born in Stockholm in 1833. His father, Immanuel Nobel, was an inventor and entrepreneur who repeatedly went bankrupt. Nobel attended school only during 1841–1842 in Stockholm; after his family had moved to St. Petersburg, he and his elder brothers Robert and Ludwig were educated by private teachers. He received some chemical education in the laboratory of N. N. Zinin in St. Petersburg but did not take any graduate education. During 1850–1852, Nobel undertook an education trip through Europe and the United States, where he stayed with chemist Th. J. Pelouze in Paris.

Nobel is the inventor of nitroglycerin (1862), a powerful explosive. His development of a special percussion detonator, called a "blasting cap" or "Nobel lighter," led to his invention of dynamite (1867). Later inventions made in connection with dynamite—besides a lot of smaller improvements—were the so-called blasting gelatin (1875) and ballistite (1887). Between 1865 and 1873, Nobel founded a worldwide industrial empire of nitroglycerin and dynamite plants and became wealthy. From 1873 to 1891, he resided mainly in Paris, later on in San Remo, and in Björkborn after 1895.

Nobel was an inventor, an industrialist, and an administrator in one person, and he was a successful entrepreneur in early industrial capitalism. His interest in explosives resulted from the military inventions of his father (who produced land mines during the Crimean War), but he was basically a pacifist. He felt deep moral conflicts knowing that his explosives could also be used for military purposes—his aim was to use them only for peaceful work, like road and tunnel construction or mining. In later years, however, when he saw that especially military use of his products guaranteed an international market, he became convinced that only an unthinkable destructive weapon could deter mankind from waging wars and came to support arms development as a deterrent.

Nobel's pacifist attitude was influenced in his youth by his favorite writers **Lord Byron** and **Percy Bysshe Shelley**; in later years—though to some extent in conflict with her views—he was influenced by his friend **Bertha von Suttner**. Furthermore, he read with special interest the philosophical and scientific works of Plato, Aristotle, Descartes, Newton, Voltaire, and **Darwin**. John Locke especially influenced his reflections on the methodology of science. Nobel did not reflect on these studies in writings, apart from a few unpublished attempts at poetry and drama and some comments in his private notebook. To some extent their influence was felt in his idea of setting up international prizes in the fields of physics, chemistry, physiology or medicine, literature, and peace (the first Nobel Prizes were awarded in 1901).

ARCHIVES

Nobel Foundation Stockholm. Nobel Files in the Swedish Riksarkiv.

PRINTED SOURCES

Bergengren, Erik. *Alfred Nobel—The Man and His Work* (Edinburgh: Nelson, 1962).
Fant, Kenne. *Alfred Bernhard Nobel, a Biography* (New York: Arcade, 1993).
Frängsmyr, Tore. *Alfred Nobel* (Stockholm: Swedish Institute, 1996).
Kant, Horst. *Alfred Nobel* [Biographien hervorragender Naturwissenschaftler, Techniker und Mediziner Bd. 63] (Leipzig: BSB B. G. Teubner, 1983).
The Nobel Foundation (ed.). *Nobel. The Man and His Prizes*, 3rd rev. ed. (New York: American Elsevier Publishing Company, 1972).
Sohlmann, Ragnar. *The Legacy of Alfred Nobel—The Story behind the Nobel Prizes* (London: Bodley Head, 1983).

Horst Kant

O

O'CONNELL, DANIEL (1775–1847). Daniel O'Connell, the "Liberator," was born in Co. Kerry, Ireland, in 1775. He came from one of the few Catholic landowning families in a country dominated by Protestant landlords and was brought up by his childless uncle, "Hunting-Cap" O'Connell. O'Connell studied at St. Omer and Douai in France (1791–1793) but had to leave because of the increasing violence of the French Revolution. He also witnessed the idealism of the early revolution, and both aspects influenced his later political views, especially those on nonviolence and self-determination. After studying law in London (1794–1796), O'Connell was admitted to the Bar in Dublin in 1798 and became one of the most famous barristers in Ireland.

The campaigns for Catholic Emancipation (which would permit Catholics to sit in Parliament) and Repeal (abolish the Act of Union between Britain and Ireland [1800], giving the latter its own Parliament) were the abiding concerns of O'Connell's political career. He founded a mass movement, the Catholic Association (1823), and was elected to Parliament in 1828. The government introduced the Catholic Emancipation Act of 1829 largely because of his efforts. Repeal, however, was not achieved during his lifetime. Nevertheless, he pursued a number of other reforming causes and was elected Lord Mayor of Dublin in 1841. O'Connell left a legacy of nonviolence, and the methods he used in the Catholic Association influenced later working-class movements.

O'Connell was heir to the traditions of Gaelic Ireland and Enlightenment Europe. The Gaelic influence sprang from a rich oral culture and was instinctive to O'Connell, who frequently cited his country's history and sang its ballads. Fluent in the Irish language, his attitude toward it has been a subject of controversy. The influence of eighteenth-century writers such as Voltaire and Rousseau and of contemporaries like Godwin, Adam Smith, **Bentham**, and **Malthus** is more apparent. Democracy, self-determination, liberalism, utilitarianism, and laissez-faire were all concepts O'Connell was not only familiar with but advocated. However, he was not always in agreement with what he read. For example, he did not believe that Malthus's theory on population should be applied to Ireland. Likewise, while he read Bentham for holiday reading, he disagreed with him about the implementation of the Irish and English Poor Laws (1834 and 1838) (Lee, 73–74). Therefore, native cultural and external literary influences played a large part in shaping O'Connell's outlook, and his blend of the two was unique and particularly suited to his goals.

ARCHIVES

O'Connell Papers, National University of Ireland.
O'Connell MS, University College Dublin Archives.

PRINTED SOURCES

Lee, J. J. "The Social and Economic Ideas of O'Connell." In K. B. Nolan and M. O'Connell (eds.), *Portrait of a Radical* (Dublin: Appletree Press, 1984), 70–86.
Mac Donagh, O. *The Life of Daniel O'Connell 1775–1847* (London: Weidenfeld and Nicolson, 1991).
Murphy, J. A. "O'Connell and the Gaelic World." In K. B. Nolan and M. O'Connell (eds.), *Portrait of a Radical* (Dublin: Appletree Press, 1984), 32–53.
O'Connell, M. (ed.). *The Correspondence of Daniel O'Connell*, 2 vols. (Dublin: Irish University Press, and Blackwater Press, 1973–1980).

Cliona Murphy

OWEN, ROBERT (1771–1858). Robert Owen, socialist and reformer, was born in Newtonn, Montgomeryshire, North Wales, in 1771, the sixth child in a family of seven. He had the barest of educations but writes in his autobiography of loving to read from the libraries of educated men of the town. Among the reading he mentions as important were Daniel Defoe, *Robinson Crusoe*; John Bunyan, *Pilgrim's Progress*; and John Milton, *Paradise Lost*. When a child, he believed every word of the writings he read—even the fictions—to be true. He also wrote of his interest in the circumnavigator voyages, as well as Charles Rollins's *Ancient History*. Of later particular interest were religious discussions and theologies, and he writes that three sermons he wrote were, he later discovered, so much like those of Sterne that he destroyed them so that he would not be considered a plagiarist (Owen *Life*, 5).

His education was of the basic grammar-school three-Rs variety; nevertheless, he is credited with being the first British writer to grasp the importance of the industrial revolution and the first manufacturer to experiment with reforms to improve the lives of workers in the factories. Of particular concern to him was the formation of character in the children of the working class, and he insisted that teachers adopt no scolding, no punishment, and unceasing kindness in tone, look, and action. His efforts at educational reform were somewhat successful, although criticized widely, but his business enterprises were very successful. Later, his fortune financed a utopian experiment at New Harmony, Indiana, one that brought a community of reformers and intellectuals to that small frontier village. One study he published in 1817 on the Shakers asserts that after a comparatively short time, correct manners and industry could provide removal from the fear of want and "abundance without money and without price for all." As he notes, the first step was to form a superior and mental character; a second, to create wealth/abundance for all; and third, to unite the two by "basing society on its true principle." His writings and his experiments with reform at New Lanark, later New Harmony, place him as a seminal socialist philosopher and reformer activist.

ARCHIVES

Cooperative Union Library, Manchester.
National Library of Wales, Aberystwyth.
Glasgow University Archives and Records Centre.
London University Library.

PRINTED SOURCES

Jones, Lloyd. *The Life, Times, and Labours of Robert Owen*, 2 vols. (London: Swan Sonnenschein, 1890).
Owen, Robert. *The Life of Robert Owen by Himself* (New York: Alfred A. Knopf, 1920).
————. *A New View of Society and Report to the County of Lanark* (Baltimore: Penguin, 1970).
Pitzer, Donald E. *Robert Owen's American Legacy: Proceedings of the Robert Owen Bicentennial Conference* (Indianapolis: Indiana Historical Society, 1972).

Ann Mauger Colbert

P

PARKMAN, FRANCIS (1823–1893). Francis Parkman, historian, was born into elite Boston society, the son of a Unitarian minister. He attended Harvard College (1840–1844), where, as a sophomore, he decided on his life's work— to write a multivolume history of the French and English struggle for possession of the New World. Plagued throughout his life with a variety of illnesses that left him able to work for only short periods each day, he nonetheless worshipped the active life and, in his youth, took strenuous trips to the many historic sites he would later vividly describe. As a historian, Parkman ingeniously combined the talents of the archivist and the novelist, employing dramatic narrative devices, intensive character development, and authentic dialogue to make his version of the past come to life.

Parkman received a firm classical grounding in his youth. He credited early work translating Homer and Virgil into idiomatic English and memorizing verse from Milton and Shakespeare with developing his use of language and influencing his literary style. His favorite authors both as a young boy and as an adult included Sir **Walter Scott**, **James Fenimore Cooper**, and the Romantic poets **Byron** and **Wordsworth**. In his early years at Harvard, he received training and encouragement in the use of primary documents from the recently appointed professor of modern history, Jared Sparks. Another American historian he read very closely was George Bancroft, who provided a lasting influence on Parkman's work.

Though library records show that Parkman read many histories and biographies, the strongest influence on his work clearly came from novels. He conceived of the historical craft as an essentially literary undertaking, as an elemental branch of letters, and wrote his histories as a series of dramatic events shaped by the actions of heroic individuals. Parkman particularly emulated Scott's and Cooper's vivid depictions of natural scenery, meticulously reinventing the physical environment of the New World from detailed notebooks he kept on his own visits. In an important review of Cooper for the *North American Review* in 1852, he praised the American novelist's skill at historical verisimilitude in words that could have described his own writing. Cooper's characters, he wrote, were fully embodied "portraitures"; his scenery exhaled "the odors of the pine-woods and the freshness of the mountain-wind." The *Leatherstocking Tales* also inspired Parkman's lifelong interest in Native American history. He shared, however, none of Cooper's romantic views of Indians as noble savages, holding instead social Darwinian (see **Darwin**) theories of the superiority of Protestant England over its Catholic French and savage Indian rivals. The influence of historic fiction on Parkman's works is perhaps easiest to detect in their enduring readability. While few nineteenth-century historians have continued to find readers, Parkman's tales of the *Oregon Trail* and of *Montcalm and Wolfe* are still enjoyed today.

ARCHIVES

Parkman Papers, Massachusetts Historical Society.

PRINTED SOURCES

Jacobs, Wilbur R. *Francis Parkman, Historian as Hero: The Formative Years* (Austin: University of Texas Press, 1991).
Levin, David. *History as Romantic Art: Bancroft, Motley, Prescott, and Parkman* (Stanford, Calif.: Stanford University Press, 1959).
Pease, Otis A. *Parkman's History: The Historian as Literary Artist* (New Haven, Conn.: Yale University Press, 1953).
Vitzthum, Richard C. *The American Compromise: Theme and Method in the Histories of Bancroft, Parkman, and Adams* (Norman: University of Oklahoma Press, 1974).

Leslie Butler

PARNELL, CHARLES STEWART (1846–1891). Charles Parnell was born in Avondale, Co. Wicklow, Ireland, in 1846. While family members were Protestant landlords, their political outlook was not typical of that class. His mother, Delia, was the daughter of Admiral Stewart of the U.S. Navy, a veteran of the Anglo-American War (1812), and his father, John, was a man of "generous liberal political temperament" (Bew, 5). Educated at private schools in England, by tutors at home, and finally at a cramming academy in Chipping Norton in Oxfordshire, Parnell went to university at Magdalene College, Cambridge (1866–1869). He did not graduate; indeed, he left after being involved in a drunken episode. Elected to Westminster in 1875, he wielded the Irish members of Parliament into a slick party machine. They obstructed the business of the House by speaking for hours on various topics with the intent of drawing attention to the cause of Irish Home Rule. Between 1879 and 1882 Parnell united revolutionaries (the Fenians), constitutionalists (the Irish Parliamentary Party), and the Land League into what was known as the New Departure. Along with **Daniel O'Connell** he was without doubt one of the most powerful men in nineteenth-century Ireland. After Parnell was cited as a corespondent in a divorce hearing in December 1889, his career was ruined, his party was split into two hostile factions, and Ireland was left divided for generations to come.

As a student, Parnell enjoyed math, science, and mineralogy; however, the only area he excelled in was cricket. One biographer writes of "the man's groping intelligence" (Lyons, 367). Another, "He was ignorant of public affairs and he read no books" (O'Brien, 85). If this is true, how did he form his opinions? According to Lyons, "he learnt as he went along" (Lyons, 30). Certainly, his family must have influenced his outlook. His two sisters Fanny and Anna (founders of the Ladies Land League) and a brother, John, were also interested in politics. Likewise, his stubborn personality, drive for power, experiences of anti-Irishness, and his belief that the Union with England was unjust equipped him to lead his party and, some believed, his country. While it is the consensus of most of Parnell's biographers that he was not well read, his enigmatic personality, extraordinary career, and final dilemma left a lasting impression on literary influences that followed. James Joyce in *Portrait of an Artist as a Young Man* and **William Yeats** in his poems "Parnell's Funeral" and "Come round me Parnellites" convey the bitterness and heartbreak of what became known as the Parnell tragedy.

ARCHIVES

There is not a "Parnell Collection" however, various Parnell papers can be found in various collections in the National Library of Ireland.

PRINTED SOURCES

Bew, P. *C. S. Parnell* (Dublin: Gill and Macmillan, 1980).

Connolly, S. J. (ed.). *The Oxford Companion to Irish History* (Oxford: Oxford University Press, 1998).

Finneran, R. J. (ed.). *W. B. Yeats: The Poems* (New York: Macmillan, 1983).

Foster, R. F. *Charles Stewart Parnell: The Man and His Family* (Atlantic Highlands, N. J.: Humanities Press, 1976).

Joyce, J. *Portrait of the Artist as a Young Man* (New York: Ben Heubsch, 1916).

Lyons, F.S.L. *Charles Stewart Parnell* (Suffolk: Fontana, 1978).

Martin, G. "Parnell at Cambridge," *Irish Historical Studies*, 19, 73 (March 1974), 72–82.

O'Brien, R. B. *The Life of Charles Stewart Parnell*, vols. 1–2 (London: Smith, Elder and Co., 1899).

Cliona Murphy

PATER, WALTER (1839–1894). Walter Horatio Pater was born in Stepney, a commercial community in southeast London, in 1839, the third child of Maria Hill Pater and Richard Glode Pater, a surgeon. His father died when he was two years and five months; his mother, when he was fourteen; death became a recurring motif in his works. He attended King's School, Canterbury, as a day boy (1853–1858) and graduated from Queen's College, Oxford, in 1862 with a B.A. He was a Classical Fellow at Brasenose College, Oxford, from his election in 1864 until his death. In such works as *Studies in the History of the Renaissance* (1873) and *Appreciations, with an Essay on Style* (1889), Pater lifted criticism to the status of fine art; in *Greek Studies*, a collection of essays written between 1876 and 1894, and *Plato and Platonism* (1893), he fashioned a new Hellenism that blends pagan and Christian values; and in his fictional portraits, such as *Marius the Epicurean* (1885) and "Sebastian van Storck" (1886), he helped create the stage in Western culture when psychology replaced philosophy as the pivot upon which interpretation of human behavior turns.

From boyhood to his second year in college, Pater became well read in ecclesiastical writers, from Richard Hooker to Arthur P. Stanley, and nineteenth-century British poets and novelists, from **Wordsworth** and **Scott** to **Arnold** and **George Eliot**. He also was reading the prose writings of **Carlyle**, **Newman**, **John Stuart Mill**, **Ruskin**, and **Darwin** and was later able to place himself as a distinctive voice in relation to all of these writers. The philosophical depth characteristic of Pater's works throughout his career originated in personal reading, at the Queen's College Library (1860–1863), in all the philosophers of the Western tradition, the impetus for which was his loss of religious faith and desire for self-culture.

Although Pater seemed to his contemporaries to enunciate in his first book, *The Renaissance*, a new aesthetic and humanistic philosophy, there is hardly an idea in the book that had not been stated by another author in a book that Pater is known to have borrowed from a library or to which he alludes in the text. For example, when Pater states in the Conclusion to *The Renaissance*, "Every one of those impressions [to which experience has already been reduced] is the impression of the individual in his isolation, each mind keeping as a solitary prisoner its own dream of a world" (209), he is echoing the description of David Hume's solipsism given by **Johann Gottlieb Fichte** in *Die Bestimmung des Menschen*, which he had borrowed from the Queen's College Library on November 14, 1860 (Inman, *1858–1873*, 14–17). My two books on Pater's library borrowings and literary references are replete with such parallels. However, Pater was never a disciple to any writer. For example, even though he wrote a major essay on Winckelmann, with whom he shared homoerotic tendencies, he measured Winckelmann's significance and found him to be "infinitely less than Goethe" (*Renaissance*, 200). Pater synthesized, personalized, and sometimes transformed ideas of other authors, creating in each of his writings a unique intertextual matrix.

After publishing his first book, in 1873, Pater read extensively in fiction, history, and criticism by French writers and in anthropology, archaeology, mythology, history, and art history by German and English writers. Some of the authors upon whom he drew most heavily were specialists, such as Johannes Adolf Overbeck, whom he names in only two fleeting references, in "Hippolytus Veiled" and "The Marbles of Aegina," but whose *Geschichte der Griechischen*

Plastik was crucial to his essay "The Beginnings of Greek Sculpture" (Inman, *1874–1877*, 413–430), and Comte Franz de Champagny, to whom he makes no reference but whose *Les Antonins—Ans de J. C., 69–180* was more instrumental than any other book (although there were others) in forming his knowledge of and attitude toward the age of Marcus Aurelius, which he describes in *Marius the Epicurean* (Inman, *1874–1877*, 451–453).

ARCHIVES

Faculty Borrowers' Register and Undergraduate Borrowers' Register, 1860–1870, Queen's College Library.

Entry Books, 1864–1877, Bodleian Library.

Librarian's Books and Books of Periodicals Taken Out, 1867–1894, Taylor Institution Library (held in the Bodleian Archives).

Library Books Taken Out, 1864–1894, and *Undergraduate Register*, 1873–1888, Brasenose College Library. All of these libraries are in Oxford, England.

PRINTED SOURCES

Chew, Samuel C., Jr. "Pater's Quotations," *Nation*, 99 (October 1914), 404–405.

Evans, Lawrence. *Letters of Walter Pater* (Oxford: Clarendon Press, 1970).

Hill, Donald L. "Critical and Explanatory Notes." In his edition of Walter Pater's *The Renaissance: Studies in Art and Poetry: The 1893 [4th ed.] Text* (Berkeley: University of California Press, 1980), 277–463.

Inman, Billie Andrew. *Walter Pater and His Reading, 1874–1877, with a Bibliography of His Library Borrowings, 1878–1894* (New York: Garland, 1990).

———. *Walter Pater's Reading: A Bibliography of His Library Borrowings and Literary References, 1858–1873* (New York: Garland, 1981).

Law, Helen H. "Pater's Use of Greek Quotations," *Modern Language Notes*, 58 (December, 1943), 575–585.

Levey, Michael. *The Case of Walter Pater* (London: Thames and Hudson, 1978).

Pater, Walter. *Studies in the History of the Renaissance* (London: Macmillan, 1873).

Rosenberg, Barbara (ed.), with Richard Pearson. "Walter Horatio Pater, 1839–1894." In Barbara Rosenberg (ed.), *Index of English Literary Manuscripts*. Vol. 4, *1800–1900, Part 3: Landor-Patmore* (London: Mansell, 1993), pp. 749–802.

Young, Helen Hawthorne. *The Writings of Walter Pater: A Reflection of British Philosophical Opinion from 1860 to 1890.* A Bryn Mawr dissertation [printed], 1933.

Billie Andrew Inman

PAVLOV, IVAN PETROVICH (1849–1936). Ivan Pavlov was born in the central Russian town of Ryazan, about 200 kilometers southeast of Moscow. The eldest son of a priest, he began his formal education at the age of 11 at the Ryazan Ecclesiastical High School. He went on to attend the Ryazan Ecclesiastical Seminary but abandoned theological studies in 1870 to study chemistry and physiology at the University of St. Petersburg. Pavlov earned a medical degree from the Imperial Medical Academy in St. Petersburg, graduating in 1879 and completing his dissertation in 1883.

From 1884 to 1886 he studied in Germany under the direction of the cardiovascular physiologist Carl Ludwig in Leipzig and the gastrointestinal physiologist Rudolf Heidenhain in Breslau. Influenced by their work, Pavlov investigated the physiology of the circulatory system from 1888 to 1890 and the secretory activity of the digestive system from 1890 to 1900.

He won the Nobel Prize for his study of the digestive system in 1904. A famous experiment, in which a dog salivated when it heard a bell, the sound of which had previously been associated with the presence of food, led Pavlov to develop the concept of conditional response, popularly known as conditioned reflex. Pavlov investigated this phenomenon for the rest of his career, eventually applying it to complex mental states in human beings.

By 1930, Pavlov attempted to explain psychosis as a conditional response to harmful stimuli. This hypothesis led Russian psychiatrists to treat patients with quiet, nonstimulating environments. At this time, Pavlov also suggested that human language could be described as a series of conditional responses to words. Although recent discoveries in the electrical and chemical activity of the brain have shown that some of Pavlov's explanations were too limited, he remains an important pioneer in the scientific study of behavior.

Pavlov was an avid reader from an early age and was encouraged by his father to read any worthwhile book more than once. As a child he received a volume of fables by Ivan Krylov, which he owned for the rest of his life. He was also familiar with the literary works of William Shakespeare and **Aleksandr Pushkin**.

During the 1860s Pavlov read the works of politically liberal critics and journalists such as Vissarion Belinsky, Nikolai Chernyshevsky, Nikolai Dobrolyubov, **Aleksandr Herzen**, and Dmitry Pisarev. He was particularly influenced by Pisarev, through whom he first encountered the ideas of **Charles Darwin**.

Pavlov's interest in science was stimulated by reading the works of George Henry Lewes and Ivan Michailovich Sechenov. In particular, Sechenov's book *Reflexes of the Brain* (1866) inspired Pavlov's quest to explain mental activities in physiological terms. He was also influenced by the writings of materialist philosophers such as Jacob Moleschott and Karl Vogt, both of whom believed that thought could be explained strictly as a physical activity of the brain.

ARCHIVES

No substantial archival sources known to exist.

PRINTED SOURCES

Babkin, Boris Petrovich. *Pavlov: A Biography* (Chicago: University of Chicago Press, 1949).
Gray, Jeffrey A. *Ivan Pavlov* (New York: Viking Press, 1980).

Rose Secrest

PEABODY, ELIZABETH PALMER (1804–1894). Elizabeth Peabody, born in Billerica, Massachusetts, in 1804, was raised in Cambridgeport and Salem.

She was educated privately and in her mother's boarding school for girls; her father taught her Latin, and she eventually acquired 10 languages. The family rejected Calvinism in favor of a liberal Unitarian rationalism that Peabody also embraced, regarding Unitarian minister William Ellery Channing as a mentor throughout her life. Peabody was friend, correspondent, mentor, and champion of many European Romantics and of the New Englanders identified with the American Renaissance. Her Foreign Bookshop and library in Boston (1840–1850)—the first of its kind—housed **Margaret Fuller**'s *Conversations* (1839–1841) and served as gathering place for most of the Transcendentalists. One of the first woman publishers in America, she published *The Dial* from 1842 to 1843. She also copied and published (1836, 1837, 1874) conversations that Amos Bronson Alcott held with students of his Temple School; published **Henry David Thoreau**'s "Resistance to Civil Government," in *Aesthetic Papers* (May 1849); helped Channing publish his sermons; and encouraged **Nathaniel Hawthorne** to publish. In 1860, she founded the American kindergarten movement (Ronda, 34ff), and by the end of her life, she had published over 60 texts about kindergarten (Baylor, 175ff).

A voracious, eclectic reader, Peabody donated nearly a thousand volumes to the Concord Free Public Library (1878). The library's records, those of the Boston Athenaeum for 1832 and 1833, and her letters reveal her lively engagement with Western knowledge, starting with then-standard Greek and Latin texts and ranging across the humanities. She read and commented on, among other authors, Europeans **Johann Goethe**, **Jules Michelet**, Friedrich Schiller, and Algernon Swinburne and on Americans Channing, **Ralph Emerson**, and Fuller. Peabody's own history and grammar textbooks, and her essays on art, education, psychology, religion, and science, contributed to the often impassioned dialogue of her day about education and intellect, as did her "historical reading parties" (1830s), precursors of Fuller's Conversations. The time Peabody spent in Amos Bronson Alcott's Temple School convinced her to eschew authoritarianism in the classroom, while confirming her convictions about the innate enlightenment of children gleaned from **William Wordsworth** and the Transcendentalists. The most powerful influences on her progressive ideas about education came from Europe: Johann Pestalozzi's ideas informed her early thinking. Later she widely propagated in America the theories of Friedrich Froebel about the kindergarten (Baylor; Ronda). Peabody wrote, translated, and published prolifically, synthesizing new and old ideas into curricula for a new generation of Americans to help them experience, as she wrote to Wordsworth, a "more interior revolution" of their lives (Neussendorfer, 184).

ARCHIVES

Peabody, Elizabeth Palmer. Papers, 1843–ca.1894. American Antiquarian Society, Manuscripts Department, 185 Salisbury Street, Worcester, MA 01609–1634. Journal of Fuller's Conversations, ca. 1840, summarizing their discussions of the readings.

PRINTED SOURCES

Baylor, Ruth M. *Elizabeth Palmer Peabody: Kindergarten Pioneer* (Philadelphia: University of Pennsylvania Press, 1965).

Baym, Nina. *American Women Writers and the Work of History, 1790–1860* (New Brunswick, N.J.: Rutgers University Press, 1995).

———. "The Ann Sisters: Elizabeth Peabody's Millenial Historicism," *American Literary History*, 3, 1 (Spring 1991), 27–45.

Neussendorfer, Margaret. "Elizabeth Palmer Peabody to William Wordsworth: Eight Letters, 1825–1845," *Studies in the American Renaissance* (1984), 181–211.

Peabody, Elizabeth Palmer. *Letters of Elizabeth Palmer Peabody, American Renaissance Woman*, Bruce A. Ronda (ed.) (Middletown, Conn.: Wesleyan University Press, 1984).

Stern, Madeleine B. "Elizabeth Peabody's Foreign Library (1840)," *American Transcendental Quarterly: A Journal of New England Writers*, 20 (Supplement) (1973), 5–12.

Tharp, Louise Hall. *The Peabody Sisters of Salem* (Boston: Little, Brown, 1950).

Wilson, Leslie Perrin. "A Bibliography of Books Presented to the Concord Free Public Library by Elizabeth Palmer Peabody" (unpublished thesis, 1982).

Robin Meader

PEIRCE, CHARLES SANDERS (1839–1914). Charles Peirce was born in Cambridge, Massachusetts, in 1839 and educated at Harvard from 1855 to 1863. He deviated from his Unitarian upbringing to join the Episcopalian Church, though he was never dogmatic in his beliefs. Considered by some scholars to be the most original thinker and greatest philosopher in American history, Peirce was a polymath whose intellectual interests ranged from astronomy to algebra to metaphysics, although his most well-known contributions were to philosophy and particularly the evolution of the uniquely American philosophy, Pragmatism. His father Benjamin Peirce, perhaps the foremost mathematician of the time, supervised young Charles's rigorous education and instilled in him an interest in science. Peirce nonetheless thought independently and creatively throughout his life, although his genius was and remains largely unrecognized.

A precocious young student, Peirce had by the age of 12 studied Richard Whately's *Elements of Logic* (1826), a work that instilled in him a lifelong "passion" for logic. It is from Whately, as well as other nominalists such as William of Ockham, Thomas Hobbes, Gottfried Leibniz, and George Berkeley, that Pierce derived his ideas on thoughts as signs. Prior to his college years, it also likely that Peirce was familiar with the writings of eighteenth-century Edinburgh judge Lord Kames and Scottish philosopher Thomas Reid. Peirce identified Reid as the thinker from whom his own "critical common-sensism" was derived. Reid's work probably served as a gateway to Peirce's study of Immanuel Kant and contributed to his rejection of David Hume's skepticism and René Descartes's doubt.

At Harvard, Peirce studied Friedrich Schiller's *Asthetische Briefe* (1795) intensely. Maintaining that "logic needs the help of aesthetics," Schiller's aesthetics served as a precursor to his categories. Peirce proceeded to study Kant and was especially influenced by *Kritik der reinen Vernunft* (ca. 1780–1781), a work he nearly memorized. His study of Kant led him to study further formal logic. Peirce also studied the philosophies of **Hegel** and Baruch Spinoza at this time.

Peirce's influences are not all found in the field of philosophy. His concept of the sign, for example, was based upon Shakespeare's use of language. However, from about 1867 on, logic was Peirce's foremost preoccupation. In the late 1860s, he acknowledged the influence of George Boole, the founder of modern logic, upon whose works *The Mathematical Analysis of Logic* (1847) and *An Investigation of the Laws of Thought* (1854) Peirce built. He also studied intensively men of the British tradition in philosophy from the thirteenth to the late nineteenth century (Roger Bacon, Duns Scotus, Ockham, Francis Bacon, Thomas Hobbes, John Locke, Sir William Hamilton, William Whewell, Augustus De Morgan, **John Stuart Mill**), along with Aristotle, Leibniz, and Kant, for their contributions to logic. It was particularly the writings of Aristotle, Duns Scotus, and Leibniz that he revered. As Peirce states, "They are the only writers known to me who are in the same rank as I."

ARCHIVES

Charles Sanders Peirce Papers. The Houghton Library, Harvard University.

PRINTED SOURCES

Brent, Joseph. *Charles Sanders Peirce: A Life* (Bloomington: Indiana University Press, 1993). See endnotes for guide to manuscripts, letters, and the like.

Buchler, Justus. *Charles Peirce's Empiricism* (New York: Octagon Books, 1966).

Ketner, Kenneth Laine, and Christian J. W. Kloesel (eds.). *Peirce, Semeiotic, and Pragmatism: Essays by Max H. Fisch*, (Bloomington: Indiana University Press, 1986).

Kucklick, Bruce. *The Rise of American Philosophy: 1860–1930* (New Haven, Conn.: Yale University Press, 1977).

Murphey, Murray G. *The Development of Peirce's Philosophy* (Indianapolis: Hackett Publishing Company, 1993).

Peirce, Charles. *Collected Papers of Charles Sanders Peirce*, vols. I–VI, Charles Harshorne and Paul Weiss (eds.) (Cambridge, Mass.: Harvard University Press, 1931–1935).

———. *Collected Papers of Charles Sanders Peirce*, vols. VII–VIII, A. Burks (ed.) (Cambridge, Mass.: Harvard University Press, 1958).

———. "Shakespearean Pronunciation," *North American Review*, 98 (April 1864), 342–369.

The Writings of Charles S. Peirce: A Chronological Edition (Bloomington: Indiana University Press, 1982–).

. *Stephen Levine*

POE, EDGAR ALLAN (1809–1849).

Edgar Allan Poe was born in Boston, Massachusetts, in 1809, the second child of David Poe, Jr., an American actor, and Elizabeth (Arnold), an English actress. At the death of his mother about a month before his third birthday, Poe became the ward of John Allan, a tobacco merchant in Richmond, Virginia. He attended boarding school in Chelsea and Stoke Newington, while the Allans lived in England (1815–1820); private schools in Richmond, Virginia; the University of Virginia (1826–1827) where he studied ancient and modern languages; and the U.S. Military Academy at West Point (1830–1831), though without taking a degree. He is famous for his poetry. In 1845, *The Raven* was an instantaneous success in his own country as well as abroad. His fiction, particularly the tales of horror and the tales of ratiocination, earned him the title of originator of the modern detective story. His criticism of contemporary British and American literature, some of it acidly outspoken, involved him in several literary feuds.

As Poe became increasingly haunted by the idea of plagiarism, especially after a critic had accused him of "metrical imitation" (*Letters*, 1:246) of **Alfred Tennyson**, his letters contain little direct reference to literary influences on his art and thought. However, he drew heavily on his literary ancestors and did not refrain from appropriating material from them. European Romanticism and the tradition of the Gothic novel were his most important sources. For instance, in his early short story "Metzengerstein," he imitated the prose of Ludwig Tieck and E.T.A. Hoffmann. As a young man he emulated **Byron**, both in his art and in the image of himself as poet. Later he came to regard **Keats**, **Shelley**, **Coleridge**, Tennyson, and others of their blend as "the sole poets" (*Letters*, 1:257–258). He was molded by the Romantic poets' theory of art, especially that of Samuel Taylor Coleridge as laid down in his *Biographia Literaria* and that of August Wilhelm Schlegel in his *Lectures on Dramatic Art and Literature*, into a form of his own in which poetry is to touch the soul with a conception of sublime beauty so that man regains an idea of the paradise he has lost. From early on, Poe read widely, becoming well versed in classical and English poetry, European and English fiction and literary theory, and an emerging contemporary American literature. His knowledge extended to philosophy and to science, mainly astronomy, notably the theories of Kepler, Newton, and Laplace, whose nebular hypothesis formed the starting point of his *Eureka*.

ARCHIVES

Ellis and Allan Papers, Library of Congress; Boston Public Library.
Valentine Museum (Richmond).
Henry E. Huntington Library (San Marino, Calif.).
Indiana University Library.
Harvard University Library.
Library of the University of Virginia.

PRINTED SOURCES

Meyers, Jeffrey. *Edgar Allan Poe. His Life and Legacy* (London: John Murray, 1992).
Poe, Edgar Allan. *Collected Writings of Edgar Allan Poe*, Burton Ralph Pollin (ed.), 4 vols. (New York: Gordian Press, 1981–1986).

————. *The Complete Works of Edgar Allan Poe*, James Albert Harrison (ed.), 17 vols. (New York: Thomas Crowell, 1902).

————. *The Letters of Edgar Allan Poe*, John Ward Ostrom (ed.), 2 vols. (New York: Gordian Press, 1966, rev. ed.).

Silverman, Kenneth. *Edgar A. Poe: Mournful and Never-ending Remembrance* (London: Weidenfeld & Nicolson, 1992).

Angela Schwarz

PRESCOTT, WILLIAM HICKLING (1796–1859).

PRESCOTT, WILLIAM HICKLING (1796–1859). William Prescott, American historian of the Spanish Conquest and Imperial Spain, was born into a patrician New England family in Salem, Massachusetts, in 1796 and educated at Harvard College, Phi Beta Kappa (1811–1814). Prescott's *History of the Reign of Ferdinand and Isabella the Catholic* (1837), *The Conquest of Mexico* (1843), *The Conquest of Peru* (1847), *Phillip the Second* (1849), and "The Life of Charles the Fifth after His Abdication" (1856) helped establish the professional reputation of American historical writing and contributed to its development through his extensive research in manuscripts and other primary sources. Prescott was a Romantic historian whose work stressed grand themes about the progress of mankind toward a golden age of liberty. He was one of the first American historians to earn broad European acclaim and is still considered one of the finest historians of Latin America. Although Prescott attended Episcopal services as a young man, he later established and maintained an affiliation with the Unitarian Church. Unitarianism appealed to Prescott's belief in the importance of actions over creeds and in the existence of a benevolent deity. Several learned societies, including the Royal Academy of History, Madrid (1839), the French Institute, Academy of Moral Sciences (1845), and the Royal Society of Berlin (1845) inducted Prescott. William H. Prescott died in Boston of an apoplectic stroke on January 29, 1859.

Prescott's historical and literary training resulted from a rigorous self-directed program of reading and analysis. He counseled himself to *"Read for facts*; not for [the] *reflections"* of the author in order to develop his own abilities (*Papers*, 35). He appreciated the histories of Enlightenment rationalist historians like Edward Gibbon and William Robertson, who stressed the operation of natural law in the universe and had applied scientific methodology stressing cause and effect in history. Although Prescott admired "their attention to environment, culture, government, and races" and their hostility toward superstition, irrationality, and acts of extremism, he did not hold to their overly mechanistic view of the universe; Prescott believed that the actions of a benevolent deity determined the course of history (Darnell, 41). The histories of Italy and Italian literature by Swiss historian Jean Charles Sismondi and those of French historian Gabriel Bonnot de Mably dealing with France and historical method impressed Prescott through their use of controlling moral points for thematic unity. George Bancroft's *History of the United States* (1834–1874), with its nationalist tone emphasizing America's divinely ordained mission to advance human freedom, impressed Prescott for its romantic and nationalist themes. Prescott, like Bancroft, believed that the Anglo-Saxon race, particularly its American branch, was the result of centuries of humanity's historical progress toward liberty, and he implicitly measured and judged the subjects of his studies against the yardstick of American civilization.

ARCHIVES

William H. Prescott Papers, Massachusetts Historical Society. Principal correspondence and papers.
William H. Prescott Papers, Houghton Library, Harvard University.

PRINTED SOURCES

Darnell, Donald G. *William Hickling Prescott*, Twayne's United States Authors Series, no. 251, Sylvia E. Bowman (ed.) (Boston: Twayne, 1975). Development as a writer.
Gardiner, C. Harvey. *William Hickling Prescott: A Biography* (Austin: University of Texas Press, 1969). Definitive biography. Chapters 4 and 5 are especially valuable.
Prescott, William Hickling. *History of the Conquest of Mexico*, 3 vols. (New York: Harper & Bros., 1843).
————. *History of the Conquest of Peru*, 2 vols. (New York: Harper & Bros., 1847).
————. *History of the Reign of Ferdinand and Isabella the Catholic*, 3 vols. (Boston: American Stationer's, 1837).
————. *History of the Reign of Phillip the Second, King of Spain*, 3 vols. (Boston: Phillips, Sampson, 1855–1858).
————. *The Literary Memoranda of William Hickling Prescott*, C. Harvey Gardiner (ed.), 2 vols. (Norman: University of Oklahoma Press, 1961). Details of reading and analysis.
————. *The Papers of William Hickling Prescott*, C. Harvey Gardiner (ed.) (Urbana: University of Illinois Press, 1964).

Ricardo A. Herrera

PROUDHON, PIERRE-JOSEPH (1809–1865). Proudhon was the founder of anarchism, which aims at the elimination of both capitalism and the state. Although some earlier writers had enunciated many principles we would consider anarchistic, Proudhon was the first to apply the term to his own thought. While he greatly influenced anarchists after his time, his own brand of that philosophy was much more pacific than that of such later anarchists as **Mikhail Bakunin** and **Pyotr Kropotkin**. Proudhon is best known for his book *What is Property?* (1840), where he wrote that "property is theft"—an oft-misunderstood phrase, since Proudhon objected not to property per se but rather to ownership of property by those who do not actually perform labor on it. Proudhon sought instead a system of independent producer cooperatives, controlled by laborers and farmers themselves, with loose and voluntary ties to other such organizations; in his system, there would thus be no need for a centralized state at all. Although his views were later rejected by the Marxist-dominated Socialist Internationals, Proudhon remains influential among critics of capitalism and centralized governmental power, particularly in France.

Born to a French peasant family, Proudhon's education came as a result of a series of scholarships and also from his years working in a printshop. It was in his capacity as a printer that he met **Charles Fourier**, whose plan for socioeconomic cooperatives called *phalanstères* (phalanxes) helped develop Proudhon's ideas on communities of producers. Proudhon also drew from more conventional sources: Despite his belief in an evil creator of the universe, he once admitted the influence of the Old Testament on his thought, which may help explain both the moral fervor of his writings and his conservative attitudes on women and sexuality. Moreover, like his onetime admirer and longtime rival **Karl Marx**, Proudhon derived inspiration from **Hegel**, even creating his own dialectic in which property and communism find their synthesis in anarchy.

Ironically, orthodox political economy also played a role in the building of Proudhon's anarchism. Adam Smith's writings led him to search for rules of economic relationships, and Proudhon's idea that property belongs to the laborer can be seen as the actualization of radical potentialities of **David Ricardo**'s "labor theory of value." The general tenor of Proudhon's thought, however, might best be traced to the philosophes of the Enlightenment. His debt to Rousseau's attack on private property is obvious, and his introduction to radicalism came through his reading of anticlerical Enlightenment texts, and before he became more pessimistic in his final years, his description of anarchistic society showed a persistent faith in the capacity of reason and reciprocity to eliminate the need for force in social relations.

ARCHIVES

Proudhon Papers, Besançon Municipal Library, Besançon, France.

PRINTED SOURCES

Cole, G.D.H. "Proudhon." In *Socialist Thought: Volume I, The Forerunners, 1789–1850* (London: St. Martin's Press, 1962).
Dolléans, Edouard. *Proudhon* (Paris: Gallinard, 1948).
Proudhon, Pierre-Joseph. *Oeuvres complètes de P. J. Proudhon* (Paris: M. Rivière, 1867–1870).
———. *What is Property?* Donald R. Kelley and Bonnie G. Smith (trans.) (Cambridge: Cambridge University Press, 1994).
Woodcock, George. *Pierre-Joseph Proudhon, a Biography* (London: Macmillan, 1956).

Christopher Pepus

PUGIN, AUGUSTUS WELBY NORTHMORE (1812–1852).

Augustus Pugin was born on March 1, 1812, in London, the son of Augustus Charles Pugin. Pugin was educated at Christ's Hospital, but it was his father's skill in draftsmanship that played the leading role in Pugin's early development. Pugin mastered French early in life but disliked Latin, commenting that "Latin was much too dry a study for me" (Pugin, "Notes"), presaging the low esteem in which he held all things classical. In 1827 he began designing stage machinery for the theater and from 1829 became increasingly interested in architectural design; by the mid-1830s, and his first collaboration with **Charles Barry**, his architectural career had begun in earnest. In 1835, Pugin converted to Catholicism, which evinced in him an absolute belief that Gothic architecture was the true and moral architecture for England. He went on to design church and domestic architecture, but his most famous work was on the Houses of Parliament with Barry. He published four important treatises on Gothic architecture, including *Contrasts* (1836) and *True Principles of Pointed or Christian Architecture* (1841). At his death, contemporaries regarded him as the foremost advocate of the Gothic style in Britain.

Pugin grew up surrounded by books, and from an early age, "tales of chivalry and romance delighted him" (Ferrey, 35), although just what these tales were is not clear. While Pugin has often been portrayed as a leading figure of the Victorian Gothic revival, recent scholarship has emphasized the influence of the Romantics on his thought. His "sensibilities had been formed by Wordsworth's generation" (Hill, 21), and through family friend Charles James Matthews he may have met **Byron, Coleridge**, Charles Lamb, and Leigh Hunt.

Pugin's involvement in the theater offers early evidence of literary interest and his "Notes for an Uncompleted Autobiography" provide a steady commentary about plays in London from 1822 onward. The theater allowed Pugin ample opportunity to indulge his fascination with the Middle Ages by designing scenery for **Walter Scott**'s *Kenilworth*, **Victor Hugo**'s *Hernani*, and Shakespeare's *King Henry VIII*. This last may have been particularly meaningful to Pugin as its subject material was central to the issue of Catholicism in England. He gave up involvement in the theater in 1833 but continued to admire the medieval images to be found in Scott and others, and his prose style later displayed something of a dramatic character.

After 1835, Pugin's Catholicism influenced all of his work. His first major publication on architecture, *Contrasts*, compares the sterile modernity represented by nineteenth-century Britain with the cohesive social unit and beautiful architecture that was the fifteenth-century Catholic English town. In *Contrasts* Pugin drew primarily upon historical works for inspiration (Stanton, "Sources"), but his fictitious Middle Ages differed somewhat from Scott's or Hugo's (Belcher, "Pugin Writing," 109). Still, it is likely that Pugin's medievalism reflected Scott, although lightened by his own cherished belief that "Catholic England was merry England."

References to other literary works are few, although Pugin called *Vanity Fair* "the most profound awful book I ever read—better than all the moral sermons put together . . . it is wonderful" (HLRO, 304). While it is possible to draw broad conclusions about Pugin's literary antecedents, he remained interested in a visual art, collecting mostly works on architecture and design. His reading, indeed his education, was sporadic and unfocused, even though he wrote a great deal and offered strident opinions on the superiority of Gothic architecture.

ARCHIVES

Pugin, A.W.N., "Notes for an Uncompleted Autobiography," 1812–1831, Victoria & Albert Museum, 886.MM.13. Excellent source for Pugin and the theater.
Pugin-Hardman Correspondence, House of Lords Record Office, Historical Collection 304. Cited as HLRO, 304.

PRINTED SOURCES

Atterbury, P. "Pugin Writing." In P. Atterbury and C. Wainwright (eds.), *Pugin: A Gothic Passion* (London: Yale University Press, 1994).
———— (ed.). *A.W.N. Pugin: Master of Gothic Revival* (New Haven, Conn.: Yale University Press, 1995).
Atterbury, P., and C. Wainwright (eds.). *Pugin: A Gothic Passion* (London: Yale University Press, 1994).
Belcher, M. *A.W.N. Pugin: An Annotated Critical Bibliography* (New York: Mansell Publishing, 1987).
Ferrey, B. *Recollections of A.W.N. Pugin and His Father Augustus Pugin* (London: The Solar Press, 1978). First published in 1861, with an introduction by C. and J. Wainwright.
Hill, R. " 'To Stones a Moral Life:' How Pugin Transformed the Gothic Revival," *Times Literary Supplement* (September 18, 1998), 21–22.
Stanton, P. *Pugin* (London: Thames & Hudson, 1971).
————. "Sources of Pugin's Contrasts." In J. Summerson (ed.), *Concerning Architecture* (London: Penguin Press, 1968).
Wedgewood, A. *Catalogue of the Architectural Drawings in the Victoria & Albert Museum: A.W.N. Pugin and the Pugin Family* (London: Victoria & Albert Museum, 1985).
————. *Catalogue of the RIBA Drawings Collection: The Pugin Family* (London: RIBA, 1977).
Two invaluable transcriptions of Pugin's diaries, notes, and correspondence in the Victoria & Albert and RIBA collections.

Stephen G. Hague

PUSHKIN, ALEKSANDR (1799–1837). Aleksandr Sergeevich Pushkin was born in Moscow in 1799 and educated at the Imperial Lyceum at Tsarskoe Selo (1812–1817). Considered the father of Russian literature, Pushkin was extremely prolific during his short life. His literary legacy includes some 700 lyric poems, over a dozen narrative poems, a novel in verse, as well as a variety of plays, short stories, novellas, fairy tales, critical essays, and some 800 letters. Scholars also credit him with having created the modern Russian literary language.

A voracious reader, Pushkin amassed over 1,500 books, of which two-thirds were foreign titles (Pushkin, *Pushkin on Literature*, 485). Throughout his life, Pushkin read widely and broadly, absorbing, assimilating, and parodying foreign influences in order to create an original, national Russian literature (Blagoy, 14–

15). His childhood reading included eighteenth-century Russian and French classics, and his earliest verses show the clear, crisp elegance of classicism. Exiled from the capital cities from 1820 to 1826, Pushkin lived for a time in exotic southern Russia, where he read **Byron** and fell under the spell of Romanticism. In letters from that period, Pushkin explained that Byron's Eastern poems influenced the form and style of his own narrative poems *A Prisoner of the Caucasus* (1820–1821) and *The Fountain of Bakhchisarai* (1822) (Pushkin, *Polnoe*, 13: 159–160). The historical drama in blank verse *Boris Godunov* (1825) marked the beginning of Pushkin's shift toward the realism of Shakespeare and the historical spirit of **Walter Scott**. Pushkin writes of his preference for Shakespeare over Byron in a letter to his brother in early 1825 (Pushkin, *Polnoe*, 13: 142); in later letters he admits Shakespeare's influence on the content, style, and structure of *Boris Godunov* (Pushkin, *Polnoe*, 13:406–408; 14:46–48). Beginning in 1826, Walter Scott's name appears regularly in Pushkin's letters and on the lists of authors that he wants to read. Scott's influence can be seen most directly in Pushkin's historical project *The History of Pugachev* (1833) and its fictional counterpart "A Captain's Daughter" (1833–1836).

Pushkin originally planned to create his novel in verse *Eugene Onegin* (1823–1831, published in full, 1833) in the style of Byron's *Don Juan* (Pushkin, *Polnoe*, 13:73) but later claimed that comparisons between the two were unfounded (Pushkin, *Polnoe*, 13:155). However, the influence of Byron's *Don Juan* can be felt, for example, in the way in which the author-narrator steps into the text and befriends the hero. Despite the influences, *Eugene Onegin* is a uniquely Russian work, written in the vernacular and highlighting Pushkin's remarkable ability to capture in minute detail the social and historical settings of Russian society from 1819 to 1825. Pushkin considered this to be his best work (Pushkin, *Polnoe*, 13:155).

ARCHIVES

Russian Academy of Sciences Institute of Russian Literature (Pushkin House) in St. Petersburg.
Russian State Archive of Literature and Art (RGALI) in Moscow.

PRINTED SOURCES

Annenkov, P. V. *Materialy dlia biografti Pushkina* (St. Petersburg, 1855; Moscow; Sovremennik, 1984).
Bayley, John. *Pushkin: A Comparative Commentary* (Cambridge: Cambridge University Press, 1971). Contains an excellent bibliography.
Blagoy, Dmitry. "With the Steps of a Giant: Pushkin and the Development of World Literature." In Alex Miller (trans.), *The Sacred Lyre* (Moscow: Raduga, 1982), 13–114.
Pushkin, A. S. *Polnoe sobranie sochinenii* [Complete collected works], 17 vols. (Leningrad: Akademiia nauk, 1937–1959).

————. *Pushkin on Literature*. Tatiana Wolff (ed. and trans.) (London: Methuen, 1971). Includes a catalog of the foreign books in Pushkin's personal library.

Wolff, T. A. "Shakespeare's Influence on Pushkin's Dramatic Work," *Shakespeare Survey*, 5 (1952), 93–105.

Erika Haber

R

RANKE, LEOPOLD VON (1795–1886). Leopold von Ranke was born in Wiehe, Thuringia, in 1795. He studied theology and philology at Donndorf, Pforta, and Leipzig and became professor of history at the University of Berlin in 1825 on the strength of his first book, *Geschichten der romanischen und germanischen Völker von 1494 bis 1535* (1824); he remained there until his retirement in 1871. In 1841 Ranke was appointed Royal Historiographer to the king of Prussia. Because he was the first writer of history to gather evidence and employ scholarly rigor rather than just tell stories and record tradition, he is generally acknowledged as the first professional scientific historian. Despite frequent criticisms, many of which were first voiced by his student **Jacob Burckhardt**, that he was overly conservative, even reactionary, that he was obsessed with the upper classes, and that he held too narrow a view of what properly constitutes history, his position remains secure as the founder of modern historiography.

An amazingly ambitious and prolific writer on a wide variety of historical topics, he was influenced by a correspondingly wide variety of authors, both scholarly and literary, but late in life he declared that what had first turned him toward history were the novels of Sir **Walter Scott**. At Pforta especially, he was encouraged to read freely and copiously. He easily developed this habit and became an avid lifelong bibliophile, amassing both for pleasure and as a research collection the thousands of rare books and manuscripts that his student Wesley Bennett encouraged John and Caroline Reid to buy intact from his son Otto and donate to Syracuse University in 1887.

He had first intended to enter the Lutheran priesthood and was always fascinated by the life and writings of Martin Luther. Influenced by Johann Gottfried von Herder and **Friedrich Wilhelm Joseph von Schelling**, he sought a religious understanding of history in terms of a God of action, not a God of rationalistic theology. Yet he agreed with **Georg Wilhelm Friedrich Hegel** that the real is rational. Accordingly, he always tried to make logical sense of the sequence of events, rather than just report or comment. His critical, judgmental, rather than literary, method of writing history derived from Barthold Georg Niebuhr but was uniquely his own.

ARCHIVES

Ranke Collection, Arents Research Library, Syracuse University. Correspondence, papers, notes, memorabilia, photographs, personal library, and so on.

PRINTED SOURCES

Berg, Günter. *Leopold von Ranke als akademischer Lehrer* (Göttingen: Vandenhoeck & Ruprecht, 1968).
Guglia, Eugen. *Leopold von Rankes Leben und Werke* (Leipzig: Grunow, 1893).
Helbling, Hanno. *Leopold von Ranke und der historische Stil* (Zurich: Weiss, 1953).
Iggers, Georg G., and James M. Powell (eds.). *Leopold von Ranke and the Shaping of Historical Discipline* (Syracuse, N.Y.: Syracuse University Press, 1990).
Krieger, Leonard. *Ranke: The Meaning of History* (Chicago: University of Chicago Press, 1977).
The Manchester Guardian. Obituary. May 25, 1886.
Metz, Karl Heinz. *Grundformen historiographischen Denkens* (Munich: Fink, 1979).
Mommsen, Wolfgang J. (ed.). *Leopold von Ranke und die moderne Geschichtswissenschaft* (Stuttgart: Klett-Cotta, 1988).
Von Laue, Theodore H.. *Leopold Ranke: The Formative Years* (Princeton, N.J.: Princeton University Press, 1950).

Eric v. d. Luft

RENAN, JOSEPH-ERNEST (1823–1892). Joseph-Ernest Renan was born in Tréguier, France, in 1823. He was educated at three Catholic seminaries in Paris (1841–1845) and at the Sorbonne (1849–1851), his doctoral thesis entitled *Averroès et l'Averroïsme*. He was a candidate for the priesthood but left after a religious crisis and became a skeptic. Renan was a writer, philosopher, historian of religion, and French orientalist. Renan was elected to the chair of Hebrew at the Collège de France but was suspended for his opening lecture in which he referred to Jesus as "an incomparable man," which upset the religious establishment. Renan associated with the likes of C. A. Sainte-Beuve, **Gustave Flaubert**, the Goncourt brothers, and **Hippolyte Taine**.

Renan read widely in Pascal, Malebranche, Herder, Locke, Leibniz, Descartes, Kant, and the Scottish philosopher Thomas Reid. Plato, Marcus Aurelius, and the Celtic saints were as much contemporaries of Renan, as was Pasteur and his friend Berthelot. Renan took his ideas on synthesis, the philosophical method known as eclecticism, and the historical concept of humanity's three ages from Victor Cousin (Chadbourne, *Ernest Renan*, 41–42). Renan learned much as a historian from the fusion of poetic beauty and erudition in the work of **Jules Michelet** and Bishop Bossuet. August Thierry, the medieval historian, was a literary mentor of Renan's (14).

As an orientalist, Renan was inspired by Eugène Burnouf, the great pioneer of Sanskrit studies in France, to whom Renan dedicated *L' Avenir de la science*. Renan was also influenced by Claude Fauriel, a pioneer in the study of comparative literature, a method that Renan used to great advantage in his *Life of Jesus*. In contradistinction to **Strauss**, Renan emphasized the concrete historical reality of Jesus. Renan approved naturally of the higher criticism in general while, simultaneously, distancing himself from the radical theories of the mythologues.

Renan's magnum opus, the seven-volume *Histoire des origines du christianisme* (1863–1881) and its five-volume supplement *Histoire du peuple d'Israël* (1887–1892), synthesize Judeo-Christian and Roman history and remain a first-rate blending of scholarship and art.

ARCHIVES

Henry Ludwell Moore Collection (1869–1958), Butler Library, Columbia University, New York City. Correspondence, MMS of writings and notebooks.

PRINTED SOURCES

Chadbourne, R. M. *Ernest Renan* (New York: Twayne, 1968).
————. *Ernest Renan as an Essayist* (Ithaca, N.Y.: Cornell University Press, 1967).
Dussaud R. *L'Oeuvre scientifique d'Ernest Renan* (Paris: P. Geuthner, 1951).
Espinasse, F. *The Life of Ernest Renan* (London: W. Scott, Ltd., 1897).
Girard, H., and M. Moncel. *Bibliographie des oeuvres d'Ernest Renan* (Paris: Les Presses Universitaires de France, 1923).
Pommier, J. *La Pensée religieuse de Renan* (Paris: Rieder, 1925).
————. *Renan, d'après des documents inèdits* (Paris: Perrin, 1923).
Psicharis, H. *Renan d'après lui-même* (Paris: Plon, 1937).
Waardenburg, J. *Classical Approaches to the Study of Religion*, vol. 2 (New York: Walther de Gruyter, 1999). Good bibliography on Renan.
Wardman, H. W. *Ernest Renan: A Critical Biography* (London: Athlone Press, 1964).

Richard Penaskovic

RENOIR, PIERRE-AUGUSTE (1841–1919). Pierre-Auguste Renoir was born in Limoges in 1841, the son of a tailor and a seamstress, the second youngest of the couple's five surviving children. About 1844, the family moved to Paris, settling in a working-class neighborhood near the Tuileries Palace. At 7, Renoir began to attend a school run by Christian Brothers, and at 15, his formal schooling ended when he was apprenticed as a porcelain painter. By 1858, new industrial techniques marked the demise of most hand-painted porcelain concerns, and Renoir found himself and his craft undermined by technological change, an event of profound significance for him. Throughout his life he rejected the aesthetic based on standardized mass production and the subsequent decline in craftsmanship and artistry. Renoir turned to a career in art, entering the atelier of Charles Gleyre in the École des Beaux-Arts, where he met fellow students **Claude Monet**, Alfred Sisley, and Frederic Bazille. Monet soon introduced two other painters to the group, Camille Pissaro and **Paul Cézanne**, thus forming the nucleus of the Impressionists. With his companions, Renoir transformed modern painting in subject, style, and technique as well as pioneering new social roles and financial relationships for artists with dealers, patrons—both individual and institutional, and the new class of bourgeois art consumers.

During the 1860s and 1870s, Renoir's artistic experimentation in color, optics, light, form, and the representation of modern life grew out of daily interchange with his fellow Impressionists with whom he painted, shared studios, and challenged the glossy, faux classicism of Academy painting. He also mixed with leading avant-garde artists and writers, notably **Édouard Manet**, Joris-Karl Huysmans, **Gustave Flaubert**, **Émile Zola**, Alphonse Daudet, and Stéphane Mallarmé, and took part in the famous, late-afternoon café causeries where Manet and others held forth on art, nature, realism, science, and modernism. The many Parisian newspapers were a lively, influential source of intellectual exchange with a growing interest in the world of art, devoting long articles to reviews of the annual Salons, and Renoir read them regularly. He had what **Richard Wagner** told him was a weakness of French artists—reading "the art critics too much" (White, 120).

In the early 1880s, Renoir's artistic crisis turned him toward a more classical style influenced by Ingres, Watteau, Fragonard, and Boucher. Except for his portraits, he turned from the representations of modern life to paintings of women in domestic scenes and female nudes. Here he was also influenced by his close friend Stéphane Mallarmé, whose poetry rejected realism and emphasized the ideal and pure in art, and by Huysmans's antinaturalist novel *A Rebours* (1884), with its emphasis on creating a world of art and sensation apart from the modern world of science, progress, and mechanization. Renoir summed up his new ideas on art in notes for the Society of Irregularists, a movement he tried to initiate based on the idea that art, like nature, should be irregular "with no motif in architecture or ornament being repeated exactly" (White, 146). Resistance to standardization is also the theme of his preface to the French translation of Cennino Cennini's renaissance art manual *Il Libro delle'Arte*. Although Cennini's work simply describes the medieval craftsman's shop and techniques, Renoir reads it as a message against mechanization, blaming the "machine and the division of labour" for transforming "the workman simply into a mechanical hack" and killing "the joy of work." At the same time, he acknowledges that even if modern artists collaborated using medieval modes of production, "nothing could be done" . . . if they had no ideal grounded in religious feeling that had once inspired artists and sustained art. Scientific rationalism was unfit for the task (Renoir, 389–390).

Renoir had read widely in the French classics, but his passion was Rabelais. "The ideal," he claimed, "would be to read only one book during one's whole life. The Jews do it by sticking to the Bible, and the Arabs to the Koran. For myself, give me Rabelais any day" (Renoir, 87). He had told Gleyre that he painted because it amused him. Octave Mirbeau said, "Renoir is perhaps the only painter who never produced a sad painting" (cited in White, 255). Whether producing the "realistic" fetes and dancing figures of his early career or the "ideal" female nudes and bathers of his later, Renoir the artist had a deep affinity for the Rabelaisian world of energy, delight, sensuality, and gaiety of mind. Ultimately, he was not a realist like his mentor Manet, but, like Rabelais, he created his own artistic world, a kind of earthly paradise and mythic reality, full of sensual pleasure and beauty and quite unlike the nineteenth century in which he lived.

ARCHIVES

Collection Durand-Ruel, Paris.

PRINTED SOURCES

Godfroy, Caroline Durand-Ruel. *Correspondence de Renoir et Durand-Ruel*, 2 vols. (Lausanne: Bibliothèque des arts, 1995).
Renoir, Jean. *Renoir, My Father* (London: William Collins Sons & Co. Ltd., 1962).
Venturi, Lionello. *Les Archives de l'Impressionisime: Lettres de Renoir, Monet, Pissarro, Sisley et Autres. Memoires de Paul Durand-Ruel. Documents*, 2 vols. (Paris and New York: Durand-Ruel, 1939).
White, Barbara Ehrlich. *Renoir: His Life, Art, and Letters* (New York: Harry N. Abrams, Inc., 1984).

Mark Reger

RHODES, CECIL JOHN (1853–1902). Cecil Rhodes was born in Bishop's Stortford, Hertfordshire, in 1853, the fifth son of the local vicar. Rhodes, following an elder brother, was sent to South Africa at the age of 17 in an effort to restore his failing health with the notion of subsequently returning to England to attend university. Upon arriving in South Africa, he worked on his brother's cotton plantation in Natal for a time but eventually fell lure to the promise of wealth and success and moved north to the newly discovered diamond fields. With his brother he began working in the mines around Kimberley, gradually accumulating shares in the large De Beers mines. Later he led the amalgamation of the diverse claim owners into the De Beers Mining Company Limited, allowing the miners to more easily regulate production—and price. He would continue to dominate the company and the process of further consolidation over the next decade before moving into South African politics.

Throughout this period, Rhodes still pursued his goal of an Oxford degree—although he cared less about the education than the contacts and respectability it would provide, and which would subsequently assist his other enterprises (Rotberg, 82). Before leaving for South Africa in 1870, he had attended the local grammar school in Bishop's Stortford, "much more of a slave than any ... native" "in a state of slavery for nine mortal years of his life, and it was compulsory slavery too." Although "never a bookworm," according to one contemporary, he studied hard and found some reward in his studies, especially history and geography (Rotberg, 31). Nonetheless, he took many of his books with him to South Africa and, in 1871, carried several with him on an eight-month trip north from Kimberley to the goldfields of the Transvaal. He carried with him several volumes of the classics—his favorite being Aristotle, Marcus Aurelius's *Meditations*, and Gibbon's *Decline and Fall of the Roman Empire* (Thomas, 81). Alas, he lost his treasured copy of Plutarch's *Lives* during the journey (Rotberg, 53).

Throughout his first years in South Africa, he maintained his intention to return to England and enroll in Oxford. This had long been his intention, although not strictly because of his academic interests. As he told one acquaintance, "Have you ever thought how it is that Oxford men figure so largely in all departments of public life? The Oxford system in its most finished form looks very unpractical, yet, wherever you turn your eye—except in science—an Oxford man is at the top of the tree" (Thomas, 88). Rhodes hoped to climb that tree himself in South Africa, as well as acquaint himself with those who did so in Britain.

In 1873, he therefore returned to England to visit his mother, who died soon after his arrival home, mend his own health, and take up studies at Oxford, where he matriculated with Ariel College. When he went up to Oxford, he clearly savored the experience, though apparently spending more time socializing, including becoming master of the Drag Hunt in 1876, than in attending lectures, and soon passed the initial examinations on the classics, "Responsions," in his first year. He continued to read widely and is also thought to have been influenced by **Ruskin**'s belief in public service, which was spreading through Oxford at this time (Lockhart, 62–63). Certainly his imperial beliefs were re-certified during his years at Oxford during the premiership of **Benjamin Disraeli**. After a further tenure in South Africa, Rhodes returned to Oxford again in 1876 to complete his studies, taking a "pass" degree B.A.—clearly his sole academic ambition—and an M.A. in 1881 (Rotberg, 84–91).

One important influence that Rhodes encountered during the 1870s was that of William Winwood Reade, a British Darwinian (see **Darwin**) who published *The Martyrdom of Man* in 1872. Reade traced the history of mankind from ancient days in a pseudoscientific manner, and his interpretation of the development of the human race helped undergird Rhodes's imperialist views and his clear belief in the superiority of British civilization and the desirability of "bringing the whole uncivilized world under British rule" (Rotberg, 100).

Some of these influences—as well as the membership in the secrecy of the Freemasons, if not their beliefs—are present in his "Confession of Faith," written in 1877 at the age of 23. In this he ponders, "Why should we not form a secret society with but one object, the furtherance of the British Empire and the bringing of the whole uncivilised world under British rule, for the recovery of the United States, for making the Anglo-Saxon race but one Empire?" This manifesto, the core of Rhodes's subsequent will, indicates the tenor of his imperial faith and demonstrates the influence of Reade and other imperialist and racialist thinkers. Eventually Rhodes would replace the idea of a secret society based on the Masons or the Jesuits with his famous scholarship program, which brought promising colonial subjects to Oxford, where they could develop their own place in Anglo-Saxon culture and revitalize the bonds of the empire.

Rhodes returned to Africa after taking his degree and continued his successful business dealings while at the same time venturing into colonial politics, eventually rising to the premiership of Cape Colony. At the same time, he expanded the empire northward into central Africa ("Rhodesia") through the efforts of the British South Africa Company, which was dominated by Rhodes, who possessed trade concessions for those lands. Forced out of the premiership after the failure of the Jameson Raid in 1895, Rhodes remained an important figure in South Africa and an influential imperial leader until his death in 1902.

ARCHIVES

Rhodes Archive, the Library of Rhodes House, Oxford.
Milner Papers, Bodleian Library, Oxford.
Papers of N. M. Rothschild and Sons, City of London.
National Archives of Zimbabwe, containing the papers of the British South Africa Company and the correspondence of many of Rhodes's associates.
South African National Archives.
South African Library in Cape Town. Contains many collections of Rhode's associates.

PRINTED SOURCES

Flint, John. *Cecil Rhodes* (Boston: Little, Brown, 1974).
Jourdain, Philip. *Cecil Rhodes: His Private Life by his Private Secretary* (London: John Lane, 1911).
Lockhart, J. G., and Hon. C. M. Woodhouse. *Rhodes* (London: Hodder and Stoughton, 1966).
Roberts, Brian. *Cecil Rodes, Flawed Colossus* (New York: W. W. Norton, 1987).
Rotberg, Robert I. *The Founder: Cecil Rhodes and the Pursuit of Power* (New York: Oxford University Press, 1988).
Thomas, Anthony. *Rhodes. The Race for Africa* (New York: St. Martin's Press, 1996).
Thomson, Daphne W. *Cecil John Rhodes: Bibliography* (Cape Town: University of Cape Town, 1947).

Derek Blakeley

RICARDO, DAVID (1772–1823). David Ricardo was born in London, England, in 1772 to a Jewish Spanish-Dutch stock trader. He was privately tutored, joining his father's office in 1786. He converted to Unitarianism and married a Quaker in 1793, leading to family estrangement. A self-made success in the London markets, he retired a wealthy man in 1815. In 1819 he became a Member of Parliament, influencing economic legislation until his death in 1823. Ricardo, the last "classical economist," systematized the ideas of Adam Smith and **Thomas Malthus** and reflected the legislative ideals of **Jeremy Bentham** and

James Mill, providing a basis for later, abstract economic analysis and laissez-faire economic policy.

In 1799, Ricardo read Adam Smith's *Wealth of Nations*, which launched his study of economics. His letters to the *Morning Chronicle* on Smithian lines in 1809, arguing that the Bank of England's loans must respond to general economic conditions, prefigured his first book in 1810, which spurred parliamentary reform of the Bank.

Ricardo became friends with Bentham and Mill, whose utilitarian philosophical radicalism supported Ricardo's arguments against rents as a monopoly and against wage increases as causing price increases, ideas pronounced in Ricardo's influential pamphlets on monetary policy between 1815 and 1820. Smith, Malthus, and James Anderson influenced Ricardo's *Principles of Political Economy and Taxation* (1817), which analyzed the distribution of goods among the "three classes of the community"—landlords, workers, and owners of capital—an approach that would later influence **Karl Marx**, although the work was a sustained defense of laissez-faire economics.

ARCHIVES

Add. 7510, Cambridge University Library, Department of Manuscripts and University Archives. Correspondence and papers.

B19 NRA 34805 Sraffa, Cambridge University: Trinity College Library, Miscellaneous. Correspondence, 1813–1822.

Guide, vol 1. 1984 SR1124, London University: British Library of Political and Economic Science, 1819–1843. Papers related to Ricardo's estate.

Ex inf David Weatherall Jan. 1977, University of Illinois Library, Chicago. Miscellaneous Papers.

Add. MS. 34545, British Library, Manuscript Collections. Letters to J. R. McCulloch, 1816–1823.

Guide, vol 1. 1984 MS Angl 11, London University: University College Manuscripts Room. Letters to Hutches Trower, 1813–1823.

PRINTED SOURCES

Blaug, Mark. *Ricardian Economics: A Historical Study* (New Haven, Conn.: Yale University Press, 1958).

Franklin, Burt. *David Ricardo and Ricardian Theory, a Bibliographical Checklist* (New York: Burt Franklin, 1949).

McCulloch, John Ramsay. *Treatises and Essays on Money, Exchange, Interest, the Letting of Land, Absenteeism, the History of Commerce, Manufactures, Etc. with Accounts of the Lives and Writings of Quesnay, Adam Smith, and Ricardo*, 2nd ed. (Edinburgh: A. and C. Black, 1859).

Milgate, Murray. *Ricardian Politics* (Princeton, N.J.: Princeton University Press, 1991).

Ricardo, David. *The Works and Correspondence of David Ricardo*, Piero Sraffa and M. H. Dobb (eds.) (Cambridge: Cambridge University Press, 1951).

Shoup, Carl Sumner. *Ricardo on Taxation* (New York: Columbia University Press, 1960).

Stigler, George J. "Sraffa's Ricardo." in George J. Stigler (ed.), *Essays in the History of Economics* (Chicago: University of Chicago Press, 1965), 302–325.

Temin, Peter. "Two Views of the British Industrial Revolution," *Journal of Economic History*, 57 (1997), 63–82.

de Vivo, G. "David Ricardo." In John Eatwell, Murray Milgate, and Peter Newman (eds.), *The New Palgrave: A Dictionary of Economics*, vol. 4 (London: Macmillan Press, 1987), 183–198.

Steve Sheppard

RODIN, FRANÇOIS-AUGUSTE-RENÉ (1840–1917). François Rodin was born in Paris in 1840 and educated at the École Spéciale de Dessin et de Mathématiques (1854–1857). Rodin's formal education actually ceased after 1857. His remaining years as an art student were marked by three failed attempts in 1857, 1858, and 1859 to be admitted to the prestigious École des Beaux-Arts. Admission to the École was considered the most critical first step to success as a painter, architect, or sculptor in nineteenth-century France, and three rejections for admission would have been widely viewed as a sign that Rodin had virtually no chance to become a sculptor of consequence and repute. Despite his multiple rejections from the École des Beaux-Arts, Rodin continued his artistic education by taking sculpting courses at the Musée d'Histoire Naturelle (Paris, France) under the direction of Antoine-Louis Barye, the well-known animal sculptor. He also supplemented his education with human anatomy courses at the École de Médecine and with a position as an assistant to the decorative sculptor Albert Carrier-Belleuse.

Rodin's repeated failure may have been a blessing in disguise: Rodin's unorthodox artistic education allowed him the freedom to develop and refine his unique sculptural style, which certainly would have been stifled by the rigid and conservative academic training that the École provided its students in the 1850s and 1860s. He produced a body of work that was distinguished by a degree of expressiveness and naturalism never before seen in French sculpture, and he has become one of the best-known artists of Western civilization. In essence, Rodin ushered in a style of sculpture that portrayed the human body as full of emotional intensity, raw sexuality, and highly expressive movement, all of which shocked and fascinated the fin de siècle French public.

Rodin's most ambitious work, *The Gates of Hell*, exemplifies not only the dynamic and expressive qualities typical of Rodin's work but also the greatest literary influence on him. A set of doors commissioned in 1880 for the Musée des Arts Décoratifs (Paris, France), *The Gates of Hell* is loosely based on Dante's *Inferno* and depicts male and female figures writhing with physical and mental anguish as the central figure in the upper register (commonly referred to as "The Thinker") calmly reflects upon the fate of humanity. Rodin, though, did not simply look to Dante's writing as the literary source for the subject of his portal commission. The way in which Dante handled words had convinced Rodin that he had found a kindred (artistic) spirit. In a series of interviews conducted between 1888 and 1889, Rodin stated: "[Dante was] a literary sculptor. He speaks in gestures as well as in words; is precise and comprehensive not only in sentiment and idea, but in the movement of the body" (Barlett, 223). For Rodin, Dante's literary work exhibited a visual quality that inspired his own artistic productions. Rodin asserted in this same series of interviews that he only had ever read the "Rivarol" translation of the *Inferno* and always carried it in his pocket (Bartlett, 223). Rodin's admiration for Dante's work was not unusual among nineteenth-century French artists and writers. For instance, the Romantic painter **Eugène Delacroix** (1798–1863), the Second Empire sculptor Jean-Baptiste Carpeaux (1827–1875), the poet Charles Baudelaire (1821–1867), and the novelist and poet **Victor Hugo** (1802–1885) all created works inspired by Dante's writings. Indeed, Hugo's writings were critical to Rodin's earliest development of his own artistic program and philosophy and should be considered the second major literary influence on Rodin. Hugo's writings were widely viewed as a modern literature that heroized ordinary, marginal men and women, and in fact, Rodin represented in his first major work an ordinary, slightly disfigured individual (e.g., *Man with the Broken Nose*, 1863), an extremely rare subject in Western sculpture.

ARCHIVES

Archives du Musée Rodin, Paris, France. Correspondence and papers.

PRINTED SOURCES

Bartlett, Truman H. "Auguste Rodin, Sculptor," *American Architect and Building News*, 25 (January–June 1889), 223.
Butler, Ruth. *Rodin: The Shape of Genius* (New Haven, Conn.: Yale University Press, 1993).
Cladel, Judith. "La Jeunesse de Rodin," *Revue universelle*, 61 (April–June 1935), 320.
Shalon Parker

ROOSEVELT, THEODORE (1858–1919). Theodore Roosevelt, twenty-sixth president of the United States, was born in 1858 into an affluent New York family of Dutch descent. A sickly child who read widely to occupy his time, Roosevelt graduated from Harvard College in 1880. Later in life, after overcoming his physical afflictions, he became a political man of action who translated lofty ideas into concrete governmental policy.

The man who most influenced Roosevelt's early thinking was Henry Cabot Lodge of Massachusetts. Lodge and Roosevelt became lifelong friends during the Mugwump revolt of the 1884 presidential election, when both men remained loyal Republicans and faced the animosity of their colleagues. The author of several histories, including *The Life and Letters of George Cabot* (1878), *Alexander Hamilton* (1882), and *Daniel Webster* (1883), Lodge was a conservative whose writings explained and defended the Federalist ideology. Roosevelt's later support for an active federal government showed the mark of Lodge's ideas. The two men eventually wrote a children's book together, *Hero Tales from American History* (1895). Their political beliefs matched perfectly.

Beyond Lodge's philosophy of a strong central government, Roosevelt became interested in projecting American power abroad. In Brooks Adams, he found an author whose ideas complemented his thinking. Adams's most important works, *The Law of Civilization and Decay: An Essay on History* (1896) and *America's Economic Supremacy* (1900), theorized that world power followed the geographical center of money exchange. Roosevelt reviewed both books and accepted many of their ideas. Adams stressed the significance of the Far East in determining world power and asserted that London was declining as the world's center of capitalism. This center of power, according to Adams, must move westward, to the United States, or eastward, to Germany or even Russia. In his first annual message to Congress as president, Roosevelt gave voice to Adam's writing. In that address, he pointed to the significance of the Pacific, and particularly China, and argued for a balance of power, or equilibrium, to maintain American influence. His later headstrong demands for a canal in Central America were fueled by his desire to exercise American influence more readily in the Pacific. Brooks Adam's theories thus were translated directly into American policy.

Roosevelt recognized early the importance of a powerful navy in cultivating American influence abroad. In 1882, he published *The Naval War of 1812*, a study of American military strategy that stressed coastal defense, which became a required text on every U.S. Navy vessel. His belief in coastal defense was overturned in 1890 after reading Alfred Thayer Mahan's *The Influence of Sea Power upon History*. Mahan stressed the need for an expansionist navy that could control the world's sea lanes. As assistant secretary of the navy in 1898, Roosevelt pushed for the production of oceangoing battleships to enlarge the American blue water fleet as rapidly as possible. As president, with the assistance of his secretary of state, John Hay, Roosevelt acted on the ideas of Mahan and Adams to create an American military presence in the Pacific.

"I have come to the conclusion," Theodore Roosevelt wrote in 1900, "that I have mighty little originality of my own. What I do is try to get ideas from men whom I regard as experts along certain lines, and then try to work out those ideas" (Harbaugh, xvii). With that confession, Roosevelt explained how influential other thinker's work had been on him. Roosevelt may not have been an entirely original thinker, but he was one of the most active presidents the United States has ever had.

ARCHIVES

Theodore Roosevelt Collection, Harvard College Library, Cambridge, Massachusetts.
Theodore Roosevelt Papers, Library of Congress, Washington, D.C.

PRINTED SOURCES

Beale, Howard K. *Theodore Roosevelt and the Rise of America to World Power* (Baltimore and London: Johns Hopkins University Press, 1956).
DiNunzio, Mario R. (ed.). "Introduction" to *Theodore Roosevelt: An American Mind* (New York: St. Martin's Press, 1994).

Harbaugh, William H. (ed.). "Introduction" to *The Writings of Theodore Roosevelt* (Indianapolis and New York: Bobbs-Merrill, 1967).

Morris, Edmund. *The Rise of Theodore Roosevelt* (New York: Coward, McCann & Geoghegan, 1979).

Michelle C. Morgan

ROSSETTI, CHRISTINA GEORGINA (1830–1894).

Christina Rossetti was born in London in 1830 and educated by her father Gabriele in Greek, Italian, and classical literature (Marsh, 37–44). Her mother was a staunchly evangelical Anglican; the family drifted in the 1840s toward Tractarianist thinking. Christina wrote about questions of faith until her death (*DNB*, 17:283). Her early verses are noted for their Pre-Raphaelite decorative detail, whereas her later poems turn increasingly to the themes of childhood, faith, and death (Fredeman, 176). Throughout her life, Christina frequently reread the Bible and Alban Butler's *The Lives of the Saints* (1760), as indicated in *Time Flies* (1885).

Rossetti was raised in a poetical family, and her first attempts at writing poetry were influenced by the work of Charles Robert Maturin, whose sensationalist novels *The Wild Irish Boy* (1818) and *Melmoth the Wanderer* (1820) introduced the theme of doomed love to her writing (Marsh, 44). Felicia Hemans's and George Herbert's poetry, anthologized in *The Sacred Harp* (1844), also influenced Christina to begin writing on religious subjects (Bod. Lib. 1362). Her poem *On the Convent Threshold* (1858) is a thinly disguised retelling of Alexander Pope's *Eloisa to Abelard*, wherein she combines the two themes, saying that she "cannot bear to be silent on . . . christianity" (W. Rossetti [April 4, 1862]).

In 1859, Christina read Emma Shepherd's *An Outstretched Hand to the Fallen* (1857), which inspired her to volunteer at the Saint Mary Magdalene Penitentiary at Highgate Prison, "supervising young prostitutes who wished to relinquish a life of shame" (Marsh, 218–219). From this work came Rossetti's masterpiece "Goblin Market" (1862), which also had roots in the fairy tale *Sagen und Märchen* and Thomas Keightley's *Fairy Mythology* (1860) (Marsh, 229–230).

"[T]he wonderful poet Jean Ingelow's *Poems* (1863) opened to Rossetti the genre of children's verses, which led, eventually, to *Sing-Song* (1872)" (Marsh, 303). In her later years, she read—as proofreader—the works of her brother **Dante Gabriel [Rossetti]**, as well as editions of **Percy Shelley** and **Lord Byron** being prepared by her brother William (Marsh, 378). She also notes using Charlotte Young's article in *Macmillan*'s (July 1869, 233–234) as a reading list for subjects for her own children's verses (Marsh, 378).

ARCHIVES

Correspondence of Frederick George Stephens, Bodleian Library (MSS.Don.e.78, d. 116–119, e. 57–87).

PRINTED SOURCES

Fredeman, William E. *Pre-Raphaelitism: A Bibliocritical Study* (Cambridge: Harvard University Press, 1965).

Garnett, Richard. "Christina Georgina Rossetti." In Sidney Lee (ed.), *Dictionary of National Biography from the Earliest Times to 1900*, 23 vols. (London: Smith, Elder, 1901), 17:283–284.

Marsh, Jan. *Christina Rossetti: A Writer's Life* (New York: Viking, 1994).

Rossetti, Christina. *The Collected Letters of Christina Rossetti*, Antony Harrison (ed.), 2 vols. (Richmond: University Press of Virginia, 1995).

———. *Time Flies: A Reading Diary* (London: Society for the Propagation of Christian Knowledge, 1885).

Rossetti, William Michael (ed.). *The Family Letters of Christina Georgina Rossetti, with Some Supplementary Letters and Appendices* (London: Brown, Langham, 1908).

Thomas J. Tobin

ROSSETTI, DANTE GABRIEL (1828–1882). Dante Rossetti was born in London in 1828 and educated at Mr. Paul's School (1836–1837), King's College School (1837–1842), Cary's Academy of Art (1842–1846), and the Royal Academy (1846–1848). He was christened in the Anglican Church of All Souls, Langham Place, London, but "was never confirmed, professed no religious faith, and practiced no regular religious observances" (Rossetti, *Dante*, 214). By 1847, he had started writing poetry in earnest, torn between poetry and art as creative outlets. In 1848, he became a founding member of the Pre-Raphaelite Brotherhood, a circle of aspiring artists and poets including **John Everett Millais** and **William Holman Hunt**. Rossetti was responsible for the Brotherhood's publication of its own journal, *The Germ*, which featured many of his early poems. The writing of Rossetti's major poetic work, the sonnet sequence *The House of Life* (1862–1871), is paralleled by the production of several of his most memorable paintings, *Beata Beatrix* (1864), *The Beloved* (1865–1866), *Found* (1854), and *Proserpine* (1868). His *Poems* were published privately in 1869. Rossetti's poems and paintings reflect his early involvement with the Pre-Raphaelite Brotherhood, which shaped late nineteenth-century British attitudes toward art and literature.

Rossetti's father Gabriele, a Dante scholar exiled from Italy, and his mother Frances, a former governess, supervised his childhood reading, which included the Bible, the plays of William Shakespeare, **Johann Goethe**'s *Faust*, *The Arabian Nights*, the novels of **Charles Dickens**, and the poetry of **Walter Scott** and **Lord Byron**. Rossetti pursued his interest in poetry by reading **Poe**, **Shelley**, **Coleridge**, **Blake**, **Keats**, **Robert Browning**, and **Tennyson**. His brother William recalled that *Hamlet* and *Ivanhoe* were early favorites (Rossetti, *Dante*, 58–59). By 1845, his favorite poets were Keats and Poe, the latter of whom he described as a "deep well of delight" (qtd. in Cooper, 16). However, Rossetti soon discovered Tennyson and Browning, describing Tennyson's *The Princess* as "the finest poem since Shakespeare, superior even to Sordello" (Rossetti, *Preraphaelite*, 236). In 1871, Rossetti's career as artist and poet suffered permanent damage from Robert Buchanan's critique of "The Fleshly School of Poetry" in the *Contemporary Review*. His patronage declined after this point, and he suffered mentally from the belief that many agreed with Buchanan's censure of his sensual imagery. By 1872, scathed by Buchanan's attack, Rossetti repudiated his former admiration of Tennyson and Browning, both of whom had expressed private criticisms of his poetry. Instead, he identified with the unappreciated Romantic poets who had also been scorned in London. Rossetti helped complete Gilchrist's *Life of Blake* and Buxton Forman's edition of *Keats's Letters*, rereading and commenting on the poems. He also wrote sonnets in honor of his favorite poets Blake, Coleridge, Keats, and Chatterton (Doughty, 612–613).

ARCHIVES

Dante Gabriel Rossetti Papers, the British Library.
Library of the Victoria and Albert Museum.
Library of Congress.

PRINTED SOURCES

Boos, Florence S. *The Poetry of Dante G. Rossetti: A Critical and Source Study* (The Hague: Mouton, 1976).
Cooper, Robert M. *Lost on Both Sides: Dante Gabriel Rossetti: Critic and Poet* (Athens: Ohio University Press, 1970).
Doughty, Oswald. *Dante Gabriel Rossetti: A Victorian Romantic* (New Haven, Conn.: Yale University Press, 1949).
Rossetti, William Michael. *Dante Gabriel Rossetti, Letters and Memoir* (London: Ellis, 1895).
———. *Preraphaelite Diaries and Letters* (London: Hurst & Blackett, 1900).
Turner, A. M. "Rossetti's Reading and His Critical Opinions," *PMLA*, 42 (June 1927), 465–491.

Nancy Anne Marck

ROTHSCHILD, LIONEL NATHAN DE, 1st BARON (1808–1879). Lionel Rothschild, baron of the Austrian Empire and British banker, was born in London in 1808 and educated at a Jewish boarding school in Peckham, where he was sent at age seven. When he left is unclear, but his education was finished in Germany a decade later. It is known that he attended Göttingen, accompanied by his private tutor, but his brothers spent time at more than one German university, and Lionel probably did as well.

In May 1827 **Goethe** noted meeting Lionel, his brother Anthony, and the tutor in Weimar. That the young travelers ever read the famous author, however, is unlikely. Their father, Nathan, the founder of the Rothschild bank in England, had only one recorded brush with a book; he originally subscribed to the first edition of **Audubon**'s magnificently illustrated work on the birds of North

America but reversed himself in horror when he was asked to pay five guineas for it. Nathan's main reason for sending his sons abroad was probably to acquaint them with Europe and their European relatives and to at least introduce them to the family banking operations on the Continent. So far as his father was concerned, Lionel's real education started in 1828, when he began a two-year apprenticeship at the London bank, under Nathan's watchful eye. This was followed by a five-year stint at the Paris bank with his equally demanding Uncle James, and in 1835 Lionel went on to Madrid to take charge of the family operations there. His time in Spain was cut short by Nathan's death the following year, and in 1836, at the age of 28, Lionel returned to England to take his father's place as senior partner of N. M. Rothschild & Sons.

Fortunately, his mother, born Hannah Barent Cohen, was a woman of great courage and strength of character. She was also a first-rate businesswoman. Nathan, who in general had no very high opinion of women, had instructed from his deathbed that his wife was "to co-operate with my sons on all important occasions and to have a vote upon all consultations." And they were not to embark "in any transaction of importance without having previously demanded her motherly advice." The late 1830s were a turbulent time in the financial world, and it was as well that there was a steadying hand on the tiller.

Hannah, however, had more than business sense. She was an Englishwoman who, with great success, encouraged her sons to acquire the attitudes and recreations of upper-class Englishmen. She was also a woman of considerable taste, in houses, pictures, and antiques. These tastes, too, she passed on to her children. Hannah also read books, particularly the novels of the family's close friend **Disraeli**, and she discussed them with her daughter-in-law, the Baroness Lionel—but not with her son.

Groomed by Nathan to succeed him, and taking on the awful responsibility in his twenties, Lionel may have felt that he had little need for books, much less the time to read them. It was not that he didn't read. A large part of his day was spent reading letters, combining reports on, among other things, business, politics, and sport; letters from the Rothschild banks in Frankfurt, Vienna, Naples, and Paris; from Bleichroder in Berlin and August Belmont in New York. An equally large part of his work time was spent writing letters. The rest was taken up with visiting, mostly high government officials. In the evenings there were political dinners and political parties. Disraeli had a standing invitation to Lionel's great town house in Piccadilly. Lords Russell, Lansdowne, Clarendon, and Granville, of the Whig grandees, were also among his guests, as was **Gladstone** and J. T. Delane of *The Times*. Lionel's table was famous for its food and even more for its wines. (Chateau Lafitte and Chateau Mouton were already family properties.) But most of all, Lionel's entertainments were valued for the information given and received. Lionel was almost certainly the best-informed man in Britain. As a great banker he needed to be, and there were few people of importance who did not yearn to know what he knew.

Lionel put his assets to excellent use. Under his leadership, N. M. Rothschild reached the pinnacle of its power and influence. He was widely believed, though wrongly, to have not only Disraeli but *The Times* in his pocket. There is no doubt that he gave Disraeli the greatest coup of his career, the purchase of the Suez Canal shares in 1875. And finally, after an 11-year struggle with the House of Commons, but with the electors of the City of London unswerving in their loyalty, Lionel broke the bar against Jews in Parliament—on his own terms, with his hat on his head and his right hand on the Old Testament.

Lionel de Rothschild was a man of great taste and great learning. But his learning was not from books. His letters and the society he kept were his books.

ARCHIVES

The Rothschild Archive in London contains both business and family papers.

PRINTED SOURCES

Davis, Richard. *The English Rothschilds* (London: Collins; Chapel Hill: University of North Carolina Press, 1983). Contains the most recent biography, based on the most extensive use to date of the Rothschild Archive.

Rothschild, Victor, third Lord. *The Shadow of a Great Man* (London: privately printed, 1982). A contribution on Nathan's career.

———. *"You Have it, Madam"* (London: privately printed, 1980). Original research treating Lionel and the purchase of the Suez Canal shares.

Richard W. Davis

RUSKIN, JOHN (1819–1900). John Ruskin was born in London in 1819 and educated at Christ Church, Oxford (1836–1842). Although Ruskin had little formal training, he became Victorian Britain's most significant art and architectural critic as he helped to establish the credibility of painters such as J.M.W Turner, the Pre-Raphaelites, and architectural trends such as the Gothic Revival. Ruskin's impact went beyond painting, sculpture, literature, and architecture as his ideas about society and economics made an essential contribution to the development of British social thought. Yet Ruskin's ideas encompassed more than the social criticism characteristic of the nineteenth century. With his capacity to write originally about a vast range of subjects, Ruskin raised many new questions about the organization of knowledge, the relationship between the production and consumption of art and social practices, and the dangers associated with scientific discourse. While Ruskin's efforts to reconceptualize and reorganize knowledge around social reforms were not successful, he did challenge many cultural shibboleths—many of which would not be effectively called into question until the closing decades of the twentieth century. The diversity of Ruskin's ideas can be gleaned from the unusual group of figures (**William Morris**, **Tolstoy**, Proust, Gandhi, and Clement Attlee) who claimed that Ruskin had a significant impact on their intellectual development. Therefore, while the combination of Ruskin's Victorian agenda and originality makes his writings less accessible today, the issues he addressed remain central for modern societies.

Even before Ruskin published his autobiography *Praeterita*, many features of his intellectual development were well known to many Victorians. With the publication of *Praeterita*, Ruskin's "education" became one of the most famous instances of Victorian cultural history. Margaret and John James Ruskin educated their son with a daily Scripture lesson, which they later supplemented with literature. In addition to evangelical Christianity, the major intellectual influences on the young Ruskin were Samuel Johnson, **Wordsworth**, **Byron**, **Scott**, Milton, and Shakespeare. No less formative were the family trips across England and on the Continent: Ruskin gained a broad visual sensitivity to art and the natural world. The growth of Ruskin's thought was further promoted by studying the landscapes of Samuel Prout and later those of J.M.W. Turner. While these early influences outweighed what Ruskin learned at Oxford, the university was important because it proved to be his only direct experience with institutional education. The publication of the first volume of *Modern Painters* (the first volume was signed "by a Graduate of Oxford") in 1843 began a career that would last nearly 50 years and often bear the stamp of the autodidact; students of Ruskin's thought have considered much of his writing about art, architecture, and society to be essentially autobiographical, as each work reflects his experience of a particular place and/or time. Therefore, even though the earlier influences are the most significant, Ruskin clearly learned an enormous amount from figures he knew (**Carlyle**, Helps, Max Muller, Charles Eliot Norton, Henry Acland, George McDonald, and others), those historical figures whom he studied as an adult (Carpaccio, Titian, Tintoretto, Plato, Aristotle, and Xenophon), and the places he came to revere (Switzerland, Venice, and the Lake District).

ARCHIVES

The Ruskin Galleries, Bembridge (the Isle of Wight). An enormous body of letters, notebooks, and personal effects.

The Bodleian Library, University of Oxford. "Transcripts" from material left out by Cook and Wedderburn from The Library Edition, *The Works of John Ruskin*.

The Beinecke Library, Yale University. A large collection of letters, notebooks, and other personal effects.

The Pierpoint Morgan Library (New York, New York). A good collection of Ruskin's letters and other materials, including sermon summaries.

The Ruskin Museum (Coniston, United Kingdom). A number of Ruskin's drawings and other memorabilia.

PRINTED SOURCES

Bradley, John Lewis, and Ian Ousby (eds.). *The Correspondence of John Ruskin and Charles Eliot Norton* (Cambridge: Cambridge University Press, 1987).

Burd, Van Akin (ed.). *Christmas Story. John Ruskin's Venetian Letters of 1876–1877* (Newark: University of Delaware Press, 1990).

———. *The Ruskin Family Letters. The Correspondence of John James Ruskin, His*

Wife, and Their Son John, 1801–1843 (Ithaca, N.Y.: Cornell University Press, 1973).

Cate, George Allen (ed.). *The Correspondence of Thomas Carlyle and John Ruskin* (Stanford: Stanford University Press, 1982).

Hilton, Tom. *John Ruskin. The Early Years* (New Haven, Conn.: Yale University Press, 1985).

Hunt, John Dixon. *The Wider Sea. A Life of John Ruskin* (New York: Viking Press, 1982).

Lutyens, Mary (ed.). *The Millais and the Ruskins* (New York: John Murray, 1968).

———. *The Ruskins and the Grays* (New York: John Murray, 1972).

———. *Young Mrs. Ruskin in Venice* (New York: John Murray, 1965).

Ruskin, John. *The Brantwood Diary of John Ruskin: Together with Selected Related Letters and Sketches of Persons Mentioned* (New Haven, Conn.: Yale University Press, 1971).

———. *The Diaries of John Ruskin*, Joan Evans and John Howard Whitehouse (eds.), 3 vols. (Oxford: Clarendon Press, 1956–1959).

———. *Letters of John Ruskin to Lord and Lady Mount-Temple*, John L. Bradley (ed.) (Columbus: Ohio State University Press, 1964).

———. *My Dearest Dora: Letters to Dora Livesy, Her Family and Friends, 1860–1900, from John Ruskin*, Olive Wilson (ed.) (Kendal, Cumbria: Frank Peters, 1984).

———. *Ruskin in Italy. Letters to His Parents 1845*, Harold. L. Shapire (ed.) (Oxford: Clarendon Press, 1972).

———. *Ruskin's Letters from Venice, 1851–1852*, John Lewis Bradley (ed.) (New Haven, Conn.: Yale University Press, 1955).

———. *The Works of John Ruskin*, The Library Edition, E. T. Cook and Alexander Wedderburn (eds.), 39 vols. (London: George Allen, 1903–1912).

Stephen Keck

S

SAINT-SIMON, CLAUDE-HENRI DE ROUVROY, COMTE DE (1760–1825). Saint-Simon was born in Berny, France, in 1760 and received his early education from private tutors at his family's homes in Berny and Paris. Later in life he studied physics and mathematics in Paris at the École Polytechnique (1798–1801) and physiology at the École de Medicine (1801–1802). His early immersion in Enlightenment culture led him away from his family's traditional Catholicism; at 13 he refused to take his first Communion, and as an adult he promoted first a secular "Religion of Newton" and later a "New Christianity" aimed above all at social reform. Although his writings attracted little serious attention during his lifetime, Saint-Simon came to be recognized as one of the founders of socialism and social science, and his ideas had a profound impact on many intellectuals, including **Auguste Comte**, **Heinrich Heine**, **Karl Marx**, and **Friedrich Engels**.

The major writers of the French Enlightenment influenced Saint-Simon from his youth onward, both through published works and personal contacts. While still in his teens, he met Jean-Jacques Rousseau and other eminent figures in the Parisian Salons; the mathematician and philosopher Jean d'Alembert served briefly as his tutor, undoubtedly encouraging his interest in scientific knowledge and its application to society. In an 1807 letter, Saint-Simon credited d'Alembert with turning his mind into "such a tight metaphysical net that not a single important fact could slip through it" (quoted by Taylor, 13). Like the French encyclopedists whom he admired, Saint-Simon was also inspired by the works of English intellectuals, most notably Isaac Newton.

Saint-Simon was deeply affected by his travels outside of France, particularly the two months he spent in America in 1781 while serving in the army. In his *Lettres à un Américain* (1817), he credited his enthusiasm for American society with his decision "to work for the improvement of civilisation" (Taylor, 162). His travels in Germany (1802–1803) reinforced his confidence in science and industry as keys to human progress, an attitude based on his reading of the works of the Marquis de Condorcet, whose influence he acknowledged in his 1804 *Extrait sur l'organisation sociale* (Taylor, 83–85). Presenting his doctrine as an application of Condorcet's thought, Saint-Simon outlined his view of an ideal society governed by scientists, artists, and representatives of industry; the psychological theories of the Abbé de Condillac and the Ideologues also shaped Saint-Simon's science of society. In devising his theory of "industrial liberty," Saint-Simon drew upon the ideas of many earlier French liberals, most importantly the economist Jean-Baptiste Say. Saint-Simon's technocratic vision of a peaceful, productive, "industrial" society was to become a dominant theme throughout his subsequent writings. His emphasis on industry and social science was developed further by Comte, who served as Saint-Simon's assistant and collaborator before breaking away to become the founder of positivism, whereas the Saint-Simonian movement that blossomed after his death drew its primary inspiration from his final writings outlining a "New Christianity."

ARCHIVES

Saint-Simon Papers, Bibliothèque Nationale, Paris. Principal archival collection.
Fonds Enfantin, Bibliothèque de l'Arsenal, Paris. Papers of the Saint-Simonian movement.

PRINTED SOURCES

Dondo, M. *The French Faust, Henri de Saint-Simon* (New York: Philosophical Library, 1955).
Manuel, F. *The New World of Henri Saint-Simon* (Cambridge, Mass.: Harvard University Press, 1956). Combines biography with an overview of the doctrine.
Saint-Simon, C. *Henri Saint-Simon (1760–1825): Selected Writings on Science, Industry and Social Organisation*, K. Taylor (ed.) (New York: Holmes and Meier, 1975).
———. *Oeuvres de Claude-Henri Saint-Simon* (Paris: Editions Anthropos, 1966). The most comprehensive collection of Saint-Simon's published works.
Walch, J. *Bibliographie de Saint-Simonisme* (Paris: Vrin, 1967).

Deirdre Weaver

SAND, GEORGE (1804–1876). George Sand (Amandine-Aurore-Lucile Dupin) was born an illegitimate child in Paris in 1804. Her grandmother became her legal guardian, and George Sand lived with her at her estate in Nohant. She spent two and a half years in a convent in Paris, returning to Nohant at age 17 to care for her dying grandmother. She felt that her studies had been too pedantic since she had not been encouraged to express her creativity, and the studies of subjects such as Latin or botany held no interest for her. At the age of 17, she discovered the works of John Locke, **Chateaubriand**, and Rousseau, but it was Rousseau who influenced her the most with his combination of reason and sentiment. She read the works of philosophers such as Bossuet and Montaigne, as well as the works of Dante and Jean de La Bruyère, and in their words she was able to discover herself. Although the evidence is unclear exactly which works by these authors was most influential, it is likely that Sand read much of their published works, for it was the disagreement between these works that cemented Sand's own convictions. As she later wrote in *Historie de ma vie*, "What pleasure for an awkward and obstinate pupil finally to happen to open her eyes fully and see no clouds before her."

The various images of George Sand, as socialist, feminist, or idealist, or of George Sand the woman, or George Sand the man, describe the personna, formerly known as Aurore Dupin. Sand has been described as the "first liberated woman" due to her male attire, a feat augmented by her choice of a pen name. "George Sand" came from an abbreviated form of the last name of her lover, Jules Sandeau, and the Greek word for "farmer." She often referred to herself in the masculine form, and she cultivated relationships with the major artists of the day. She was friends with **Chopin**, Liszt, and **Delacroix**, and no doubt all parties influenced each other. Yet she was just as comfortable raising her children at her country estate of Nohant. She was ahead of her time in her concern for the forgotten class, the working poor, and she campaigned for the education of women. After reading Montaigne's tirades on the moral inferiority of women in his *Essais*, she argued, "This ineptitude and frivolity that you throw up to us is the result of the bad education to which you have condemned us . . . Improve our lot, . . . and you will see very well that our souls emerged equal from the hands of the Creator" (*Histoire de ma vie, Book IV*). Furthermore, Sand argued that marriage was hell for women due to the demands placed upon them by men. This may have been partly due to her own mistake of a marriage to Casimir Dudevant, for the two shared very few common interests. After nine years of marriage and two children, Sand left her husband in 1831 to live in Paris with writer Jules Sandeau, with whom she collaborated on her first novel, *Rose et Blanche*. Sand's writing was her mark of emancipation, and her masculine attire and "nom de plume" allowed her to transcend spaces not normally reserved for women. After her relationship with Sandeau soured, she published her first novel, *Indiana*, using the pseudonym "George Sand" in May 1832.

The literary influences of Rousseau and Chateaubriand were evident in works such as *Indiana*, *Valentine*, and *Lélia*, the latter of which expressed the "mal du siècle" of the Romantic era. Even before the publication of *Indiana*, Sand had attracted quite a lot of attention, and once she became a more prolific writer, her influence was felt internationally. In Poland and in Italy, she was seen as a champion of freedom, and in Germany, *Lélia* became the model for other similar novels. Her influence was felt in the United States, in England, and in Russia. She wrote during an era deeply concerned with propriety, yet she became a symbol of the emancipated female at a time when the concept of women's rights was only beginning to enter the nineteenth-century mind-set. Due to her association with important political figures, she became involved in French politics and in the 1848 Revolution. She collaborated with **Alexis de Tocqueville** and **Lamartine** and edited the *Bulletin de la République*. However, when the socialist revolt failed, she withdrew to Nohant to work on her autobiography,

Histoire de ma vie, and keep up with her humanitarian efforts by supporting political prisoners.

Her 1,600-page autobiography *Histoire de ma vie* is the tale of a woman making her way into a man's world; however, Sand seemed to be more concerned with explaining her life rather than recounting events. She refused to follow Rousseau's confessorial lead in his *Confessions*; in fact, her autobiography was not completely factual since she omitted some details and embellished others. She not only described her realization of the effect she had on Western culture, as in the case of authors **Flaubert** or **Balzac**; she also described the effect the various nineteenth-century cultural icons had on her, as in the case of her mentor, Pierre Leroux, author of *De l'humanité*. She argued that a comprehension of history is vital, for the end does justify the means (*Histoire*, 65). She wrote during a period of industrialization, represented by the cycle of prosperity and recession in France and in every industrial society. Sand's own life vacillated between prosperity and recession. She wrote 70 novels, numerous short stories, essays, book reviews, and political pamphlets and approximately 40,000 letters; yet because of her propensity to throw lavish parties, her financial situation was often in arrears. Yet this woman who was referred to by her contemporaries as a "great man" never gave up hope that "one day the world will understand me, and if this day never comes, no matter, I will have opened the way for other women" (*Histoire de ma vie*).

ARCHIVES

Musée de la Vie romantique, Paris.
Maison de George Sand, Nohant.
Centre international George Sand et le romantisme.

PRINTED SOURCES

Blount, Paul. *George Sand and the Victorian World* (Athens: University of Georgia Press, 1979).
Christensen, Peter. "Self in Autobiographical Writing." In Natalie Datlof, Jeanne Fuchs, and David Powell (eds.), *The World of George Sand* (New York: Greenwood Press, 1991).
Dickenson, Donna. *George Sand: A Brave Man—The Most Womanly Woman* (New York: Berg Publishers, 1988).
Jurgrau, Thelma. "Introduction." In Natalie Datlof, Jeanne Fuchs, and David Powell (eds.), *The World of George Sand* (New York: Greenwood Press, 1991).
Richards, Sylvie L. "Finding Her Own Voice: George Sand's Autobiography," *Women's Studies*, 22, 2 (1993), 137–144.
Sand, George. *Histoire de ma vie*, Thelma Jurgrau (ed.) (Albany: State University Press of New York, 1991).

Jennifer Harrison

SAN MARTÍN, JOSÉ DE (1778–1850). José San Martín was born in Yapeyú on Argentina's military frontier, where his father served in the colonial government. His education began in Buenos Aires (1783–1784) and continued from

1785 or 1787 to 1789 at Madrid's Seminario de los Nobles, an academy founded to educate sons of the nobility and the officer corps. As a matter of course, San Martín was instructed in the Catholic faith. Honored as Liberator of Chile and Protector of Peru, San Martín's military leadership, organizational genius, and strategic vision were instrumental in achieving the independence of Argentina, Chile, and Peru, while his withdrawal from public life at the height of his career showed an admirable refusal to turn military success into personal power.

San Martín's formal schooling, though brief, exposed him to the liberal arts, as well as the mathematical and applied sciences of concern to a future officer. After entering the Murcia Regiment in 1789, his education became a matter of practical instruction and personal study. For 22 years San Martín served with distinction in the Spanish Army before returning to Buenos Aires and devoting a further 12 years to the struggle against Spanish rule. During this military career he accumulated a personal library of considerable breadth, and his range of knowledge was noted by many contemporaries. Donations of his books were made to found the National Library of Peru, as well as libraries in Mendoza (Argentina) and Chile shortly before San Martín went into exile in France.

Despite San Martín's familiarity with Plutarch and other ancient writers, an inventory of his pre-exile library lists only a few classical works, including *The Iliad*, Sallust's *Histories*, Cicero's *Letters*, and Livy's *Discourses*. A large part of the library was made up of biographies, histories, memoirs, and travelogues concerning the European Great Powers, especially the French Revolution and **Napoléon**'s campaigns, from which he appears to have drawn military and political lessons. The exploration, conquest, and history of the Americas was another significant element, although then-common works disparaging the New World were not included. The largest share of the collection was devoted to works of a practical and scientific nature: agriculture, commerce, engineering, law, manufacturing, military science, the natural sciences, and political economy, as well as atlases and maps. Philosophical and religious works constituted a further small part. The authors found include Barruel, Bossuet, Dumarsais, Gaètano Filangieri, Frederick the Great, Pierre Gassendi, Herrera, **Alexander von Humboldt**, Mirabeau, Montecuccoli, Montesquieu, Necker, Pluche, Rosier, the Maréchal de Saxe, and the various contributors to the *Encyclopèdie*, among others. This emphasis on history, geography, science, and the practical arts suggests an orientation to the concrete, but the collection also contained a varied collection of literature, both classic and contemporary.

San Martín's reading was lightened by the works of Voltaire, *The Letters of Abelard and Heloise*, Rousseau's *Émile*, Barthélemy's *Voyages de Jeune Anacharsis en Grèce*, Calderón de la Barca's comedies, satires by Quevedo and La Bruyère, Tasso's *Jerusalem Delivered*, and several volumes of poetry, as well as Charles Pinot Duclos's gossipy but acute chronicles of French politics and high society at the height of the ancien régime. Furthermore, San Martín possessed a small body of writings by women notable for their expression of ideas and attitudes marking not only the Enlightenment but the rise of Romanticism, including Madame de Lafayette, the Marquise de Tencin, the Marquise de Lambert, and **Madame de Staël** (Martinez, 542–543). In exile, San Martín's library consisted mainly of travelogues and historical works, accompanied by a smattering of literature, classics, and the practical arts.

Largely self-educated, San Martín seems an exemplar of the Spanish Enlightenment, with a concern for the practical application of Reason, leavened by classical virtue and a hint of Romanticism. San Martín himself illustrated the virtues of all three traditions in his self-discipline and sobriety, his interest in the spread and application of knowledge, and his selfless devotion to the cause of a new nation without personal ambition or avarice.

ARCHIVES

Archivo del Museo Mitre, Buenos Aires.
Archivo del Instituto Nacional Sanmartiniano, Buenos Aires.
Archivo Historico de Mendoza, Mendoza.

PRINTED SOURCES

Espíndola, Adolfo S. *El Libertador y el Libro* (Buenos Aires: Año del Libertador General San Martín, 1950). San Martín's libraries and reading habits prior to triumph in Peru and in exile. Lists surviving copies of his books in Argentine libraries.

García-Godoy, Christián. *San Martín y Unánue en la Liberación del Perú* (Buenos Aires: Academia Nacional de la Historia, 1983). Links economic policies in Peru under San Martín to the ideas of Jean-Baptiste Say.

Lappas, Alcibiades. *San Martín y su Ideario Liberal* (Buenos Aires: Simbolo, 1982). San Martín's liberalism and putative links with freemasonry.

Levene, Ricardo. *El Genio Político de San Martín*, 2nd ed. (Buenos Aires: Depalma, 1970). San Martín's formation and political legacy.

Martinez, Beatriz. "Los temas preferidos de San Martín a traves del examen de su biblioteca," *Cuadernos Hispanoamericanos*, 369 (March 1981), 533–550. Analysis of San Martín's pre-exile library.

Mitre, Bartolomé. *Historia de San Martín y de la Emancipación Sudamericano*, 4 vols. 2nd ed. (Buenos Aires: F. Lajouane, 1890). Superseded in certain respects, it remains the classic biography.

Otero, José Pacífico. *Historia del Libertador don José de San Martín*, 4 vols. (Buenos Aires: Cabaut, 1932). Important supplement to Mitre.

Piccirilli, Ricardo. *San Martín y la Política de los Pueblos* (Buenos Aires: Gure, 1957). Relates San Martín's political actions to ideas of the day.

San Martín, Jose de. *Documentos para la Historia del Libertador General San Martín*, 19 vols. as of 1999 (Buenos Aires: Ministerio de Educacion de la Nacion, Instituto Nacional Sanmartiniano, 1953). Intended as the definitive collection of San Martín's papers.

———— *The San Martín Papers*, Chritián García-Godoy (ed.) (Washington, D.C.: Full Life/Vida Plena, 1988). Only English collection of San Martín's papers. Contains inventory of books offered to National Library of Peru.

Robert Chisholm

SCHELLING, FRIEDRICH WILHELM JOSEPH VON (1775–1854).

Friedrich Schelling was born in Leonberg, Württemberg, the son of a Lutheran pastor. He entered the theological seminary at Tübingen in 1790. He was recognized as an intellectual child prodigy and published philosophical works while still a teenager. A protégé of **Johann Gottlieb Fichte**, he became a professor of philosophy at Jena in 1798. Schelling was active in the Jena-Weimar circle of **Johann Wolfgang von Goethe**, August Wilhelm von Schlegel and his wife Caroline, Friedrich Schlegel, Ludwig Tieck, Friedrich von Hardenberg ("Novalis"), and Johann Christoph Friedrich von Schiller. An advocate of the medical system of John Brown, he left Jena after scandal about the death of his betrothed, Caroline's daughter, and his subsequent affair with Caroline. He taught, in order, at Würzburg (1803–1806), Munich and Stuttgart (1806–1820), Erlangen (1820–1827), Munich (1827–1841), and Berlin (1841–1846), developing at least four distinct philosophies: subjective idealism, nature philosophy, identity philosophy (all before he left Jena), and positive philosophy (in his Berlin period). **Samuel Taylor Coleridge** brought his ideas to England, where they had extensive influence on British Romanticism, especially **William Wordsworth**. Paul Tillich's theology owes much to Schelling. Josiah Royce called him the "Prince of the Romanticists."

At Tübingen, Schelling and schoolmates **Georg Wilhelm Friedrich Hegel** and Friedrich Hölderlin were close friends, sharing enthusiasm for the French Revolution. The three together composed a manifesto, *Das älteste Systemprogramm des deutschen Idealismus*, transcribed around 1797 in Hegel's hand. Schelling procured a teaching post for Hegel at Jena, where they coedited *Kritisches Journal der Philosophie* (1801–1803). Schelling took Fichte's subjective idealism in a mystical direction, whereas Hegel reworked it into a dialectical logic. They were still friends when Schelling left for Würzburg, but not after Hegel published *Phänomenologie des Geistes* (1807). Schelling revised his theories so often that Hegel accused him of carrying out his philosophical education in public. Schelling never forgave him for that or for claiming that the Schellingian absolute was so undifferentiated that it seemed like "the night in which all cows are black."

All modern philosophy springs from René Descartes, primarily his problematic concepts of ego, human consciousness, and subjectivity. Schelling filtered Descartes through Augustine's psychology, Giordano Bruno's vitalism, Immanuel Kant's critical philosophy, Jakob Böhme's Protestant mysticism, Franz Xaver von Baader's Catholic mysticism, Baruch Spinoza's metaphysics, Johann Joaquim Winckelmann's art criticism, the Schlegels' oriental scholarship, and the post-Kantian controversies of Gottlob Ernst Schulze, Solomon Maimon, and Karl Leonhard Reinhold.

ARCHIVES

Schelling's gigantic legacy of letters, notes, diaries, manuscript fragments, and lecture drafts is scattered in repositories throughout Germany, for example, the Berlin-Brandenburgische Akademie der Wissenschaften, the Cotta-Archiv, Stuttgart, and the Schiller Museum, Marbach. Allied bombs destroyed a rich collection in Munich in 1944. The Kommission für die Herausgabe der Schriften von Schelling at the Bayerische Akademie der Wissenschaften (whose 80-volume critical edition should be complete by the mid-twenty-first century) and the Schelling-Forschungsstelle at the University of Bremen actively seek Schellingiana.

PRINTED SOURCES

Beach, Edward Allen. *The Potencies of God(s): Schelling's Philosophy of Mythology* (Albany: State University of New York Press, 1994).

Brown, Robert F. *The Later Philosophy of Schelling: The Influence of Boehme on the Works of 1809–1815* (Lewisburg, Pa.: Bucknell University Press, 1977).

Dann, Sigrid. *"Lieber Freund, ich komme weit her schon an diesem frühen Morgen": Caroline Schlegel-Schelling in ihren Briefen* (Darmstadt: Luchterhand, 1981).

di Giovanni, George, and H. S. Harris. *Between Kant and Hegel: Texts in the Development of Post-Kantian Idealism* (Albany: State University of New York Press, 1985).

Fischer, Kuno. *Schellings Leben, Werke, und Lehre* (Heidelberg: Winter, 1899).

Jaspers, Karl. *Schelling: Grösse und Verhängnis* (Munich: Piper, 1955).

Sandkühler, Hans Jörg. *Friedrich Wilhelm Joseph Schelling* (Stuttgart: Metzler, 1970).

——— (ed.). *F.W.J. Schelling* (Stuttgart: Metzler, 1998).

Eric v. d. Luft

SCHLEIERMACHER, FRIEDRICH (1768–1834). Friedrich Daniel Ernst Schleiermacher, German theologian, is considered the "father of modern Protestantism." He was born of Reformed parents who converted to Moravian pietism. Schleiermacher's first religious influence came from his home life and in the Moravian educational centers in Barby and Niesky, Saxony. Finding this form of piety too narrow, in 1787 he entered the University of Halle, where he experienced a religious crisis, which he later overcame. He was ordained as a minister in 1794 and accepted his first appointment in Berlin. In 1804, Schleiermacher took a position at the University of Halle, but after the defeat of Prussia by France in 1806, he returned to Berlin as a preacher. In 1810, he was enlisted to help found the University of Berlin, where he later served as rector and dean of the theological faculty. He remained in Berlin until his death in 1834.

In 1799, Schleiermacher published his first book, *On Religion: Speeches to Its Cultured Despisers*. In this work, which shows the influence of Kant, Spinoza, and his early pietism, Schleiermacher sought to persuade intellectuals influenced by the Enlightenment of the perennial importance of religion. He interpreted religion neither as dogma nor, following Kant, as morality. Rather, he believed that the essence of religion resided in "intuition and feeling," in a basic human "sense and taste of the infinite." Other important later works include *Brief Outline of the Study of Theology* (1811) and his summa *The Christian Faith* (1821–1822; revised edition, 1830–1831). The former sought to provide theology with a credible, scientific basis in the context of the modern university; the latter, based on his lectures in dogmatics, represents Schleiermacher's most systematic attempt to define the nature of Protestant Christianity.

The sources of Schleiermacher's thought are complex, but three main strands of influence are identifiable: his pietist heritage; the philosophies of Plato, Aristotle, Spinoza, and Kant, which he read as a student at Halle; and the spirit of German Romanticism, which he encountered in Berlin, especially through his friendship with Friedrich Schlegel and through reading **Friedrich Schelling**. Schleiermacher combined these influences in creative ways with the abiding goal of making Christian faith speak to modern consciousness and vice versa. His legacy dominated nineteenth-century German and European Protestantism, and it still pervades liberal religious circles today. In the twentieth century, Schleiermacher came under heavy attack from neo-orthodox theologians, especially Karl Barth, who criticized Schleiermacher for basing theology excessively on subjective and experiential criteria (i.e., feeling and intuition). Yet neo-orthodox theologians rarely disputed Schleiermacher's brilliance and influence. Karl Barth put it best when he noted that "the first place in a history of the theology of the most recent times belongs and will always belong to Schleiermacher, and he has no rival" (Barth, 306).

ARCHIVES

Berlin-Brandenburgische Akademie der Wissenschaften.

PRINTED SOURCES

Barth, Karl. "Friedrich Schleiermacher." In *Protestant Thought: From Rousseau to Ritschl* (London: SCM Press, 1959).
Fischer, Hermann, et al. (eds.). *Schleiermacher Archiv*, 19 vols. (Berlin and New York: de Gruyter, 1984–)Gerrish, B. A. *A Prince of the Church: Schleiermacher and the Beginnings of Modern Theology* (London: SCM Press, 1984).
Redeker, Martin. *Schleiermacher: His Life and Thought*, John Wallhauser (trans.) (Philadelphia, Pa.: Fortress Press, 1973).
Schleiermacher, Friedrich. *Kritische Gesamtausgabe*, Hans-Joachim Birkner (ed.) (Berlin: de Gruyter, 1984).

Thomas Albert Howard

SCHOPENHAUER, ARTHUR (1788–1860). Arthur Schopenhauer was born in Danzig (now Gdansk, Poland) in 1788 to a family headed by a wealthy, partly Dutch businessman. Schopenhauer's father may have imbued him with an antipathy for absolutist governments and an admiration for Voltaire. Schopenhauer's mother, Johanna, was a novelist and introduced him to a number of important literary figures, among them **Johann Wolfgang von Goethe**. The boy's formal education began with two years of study in France under the charge of a friend of his father. Afterwards Schopenhauer accompanied his parents on a prolonged tour of France, England (where he attended school for a few months), Switzerland, and Austria. After his father's apparent suicide in Hamburg in 1805, adolescent Schopenhauer received private tutoring in the classics and then entered the University of Göttingen as a medical student, studying physics, chemistry, and botany.

At Göttingen, Schopenhauer first encountered the work of Plato and Immanuel Kant, both of whom would influence him profoundly. In 1811, Schopenhauer left Göttingen for Germany's philosophical center, Berlin, where he attended lectures by **Johann Gottlieb Fichte** and **Friedrich Schleiermacher**, both of whom he found uninteresting. Schopenhauer's doctoral dissertation, "Uber die vierfache wurzel des Satzes vom zureichenden Grunde" (1813), shows intense reading of Kant's critical philosophy.

From 1814 to 1816, Schopenhauer resided in Dresden, where he produced a short book on color entitled *Uber das Sehn und die Farben* (1816), after a text by Goethe of the same name. Through the orientalist Friedrich Majer, Schopenhauer was introduced to Hinduism and Buddhism.

During this period, Schopenhauer immersed himself in writing his magnum opus *Die Welt als Wille und Vorstellung* (1818; second enlarged edition, 1844). The text presents elaborations of Kant's critical philosophy and grounds both the world and the self in a metaphysical "will," a notion that would later inform the work of **Friedrich Nietzsche** and **Sigmund Freud**. It is in this theory of the "will" that Schopenhauer believed himself to have realized a correction of Plato's theory of ideas as well as insight into the true nature of Christianity.

In *Die Welt* Schopenhauer's interest in Indian and Asian thought is apparent. Indeed, Schopenhauer wrote in the Preface to the first edition of *Die Welt* that

> Kant's philosophy is therefore the only one with which a thorough acquaintance is positively assumed in what is to be here discussed. But if in addition to this the reader has dwelt for a while in the school of the divine Plato, he will be the better prepared to hear me and the more susceptible to what I say. But if he has shared in the benefits of the *Vedas*, access to which, opened to us by the *Upanishads*, is in my view the greatest advantage which this still young century has to show over previous centuries . . . then he is best of all prepared to hear what I have to say to him.

Schopenhauer embraced Kantian prohibitions on acquiring knowledge of what lies beyond experience (delineated in Kant's *Kritik der reinen Vernuft*, 1781), but he pressed the manner in which Kant's *Kritik der Urteilskraft* (1790) described the positive possibilities for consciousness to gain a special grasp of the metaphysical through beauty and sublimity. His theories would later strongly influence **Richard Wagner** and important figures in the Romantic movement. The text shows familiarity with many classical authors and is deeply critical of rationalist work, most notably that of Alexander Gottlieb Baumgarten, Leibniz, and Descartes, whose presumptions about reason's abilities and whose theory of the self and its relation to the world he attacked.

Die Welt was not highly regarded but received sufficient attention to secure Schopenhauer a post as lecturer at the University of Berlin, where he presented himself as a propaedeutic to the corruption of Kant exhibited in **Hegel**, Fichte, and **Schelling**. Failing to displace his targets, Schopenhauer retired to Frankfurt am Main, where he continued to publish and develop his theories. It was there that he immersed himself in the study of Buddhism, the Hindu Vedas, and

Upanishads, as well as the work of mystical European authors such as Johannes Meister Eckhart and Jakob Böhme. Schopenhauer also studied many figures prominent in the Renaissance and the Enlightenment such as Petrarch and Rousseau. Schopenhauer became a great admirer of David Hume's *Dialogues concerning Natural Religion* (1779), apparently for its powerful arguments against acquiring metaphysical knowledge of God. Before his death, Schopenhauer had planned to make a German translation of the Scotsman's text, as well as an English translation of Kant's *Critique of Pure Reason*, though neither materialized.

ARCHIVES

Schopenhauer-Archiv, University of Frankfurt. Includes papers, manuscripts, letters, and books from his personal library.

PRINTED SOURCES

Gardiner, Patrick. *Schopenhauer* (Harmondsworth, England, 1963). A comprehensive account.
Hamlyn, D. W. *Schopenhauer* (London: Routledge & Kegan Paul, 1980).
Schopenhauer, Arthur. *Schopenhauer: Der handschriftliche Nachlass*, A. Hubscher (ed.), 5 vols. (Frankfurt am Main: Waldemar Kramer, 1966–1975; E.F.J. Payne (trans.), *Manuscript Remains*, 4 vols. (Oxford, New York, and Hamburg: Berg, 1988–1990).
———. *Schopenhauers sammtliche Werke*, A. Hubscher (ed.), 7 vols. (Wiesbaden: Brockhaus, 1946–1950).

Peter S. Fosl

SCHUMANN, ROBERT ALEXANDER (1810–1856). Robert Schumann was

born in Zwickau, Saxony, in 1810. His father, August Schumann, was an established publisher and editor. Schumann began his formal education in a local private school in 1816. His first piano lessons were with J. G. Kuntzsch. Beginning in 1820, Schumann attended the Zwickau Lyceum for eight years. After passing his final examinations in March of 1828, he matriculated at the University of Leipzig. His mother, Joanna Christiana (née Schnabel), and his guardian, Gottlob Rudel, encouraged Robert to pursue the study of law. However, Robert had no interest in his course work and continued to compose and play the piano. In the spring of 1830, he convinced his mother that he should discontinue his studies at the University of Leipzig and begin studying piano and composition in preparation for a career in music. Shortly thereafter, Schumann commenced piano studies with Friedrich Wieck and theory lessons with C. T. Weinlig. His final year of formal instruction was in thorough bass with Heinrich Dorn, conductor at the Leipzig theater.

August Schumann's career as a self-made publisher and editor had a considerable influence on Robert. Robert had access to thousands of literary masterpieces in August's collection. He devoured the great classics as well as the passionate writings of the Romantic period. In his essay "Schumann and Shakespeare" in *Mendelssohn and Schumann: Essays on Their Music and Its Context*,

Jon W. Finson discusses some of the compositions that were inspired by Shakespearean works. Finson states: "Shakespeare's plays ultimately provided little material for Schumann's published works; but Schumann did undertake some composition based on the dramas at each important juncture of his life" (Finson, 125).

While a student at the lyceum, Robert organized his own literary society. According to Robert Haven Schauffler in his biography *Forestan: The Life and Work of Robert Schumann*, the members would read a portion of prose or verse, then discuss and analyze the work and its author. Schumann felt that "it is the duty of every cultured man to know the literature of his country" (Schauffler, 14).

One of the greatest literary influences on the music and writings of Robert Schumann was the German Romantic novelist Jean Paul Richter (1763–1825). Schumann once wrote about Jean Paul: "He often brought me near to madness; but the rainbow of peace . . . always floats softly above all tears, and the heart is wonderfully lifted and mildly transfigured" (Schauffler, 20).

Many scholars have written about the connection between Jean Paul's writings and Schumann's literary and musical works. While it is known that Schumann spent a great deal of time reading Jean Paul during his adolescence, Leon Botstein's essay in *Schumann and His World* states: "Throughout the late 1840's and 1850's Schumann noted his persistent rereading of Jean Paul" (Botstein, 7).

One of the Jean Paulian literary techniques that Schumann adapted was the use of fictional characters to communicate the conflicting sides of his personality. Two of these characters—Forestan and Eusebius—appeared for the first time in his 1831 critique of **Frédéric Chopin**'s *La ci darem la mano, varié pour le pianoforte*, Opus 2.

Robert Schumann founded and edited the *Neu Zeitschrift für Musik* from 1834 to 1844. Published twice weekly beginning on April 3, 1834, the paper reported on cultural events and presented reviews about musical compositions and performers.

Throughout his career, Robert Schumann composed in many musical genres. His works include over 200 songs, various works for solo piano, vocal and instrumental chamber music, choral music, orchestral overtures, four symphonies, seven concertos, and one opera, *Genoveva* (1847–1848).

ARCHIVES

Robert Schumann-Haus in Zwickau. Account books, correspondence books, diaries.

PRINTED SOURCES

Botstein, Leon. *History, Rhetoric, and the Self: Robert Schumann and Music Making in German-Speaking Europe, 1800–1860. Schumann and His World*, R. Larry Todd (ed.) (Princeton, N.J.: Princeton University Press, 1994), 3–46.

Finson, Jon W. *Schumann and Shakespeare; Mendelssohn and Schumann: Essays on Their Music and Its Context*, Jon W. Finson and R. Larry Todd (eds.) (Durham, N.C.: Duke University Press, 1984), 125–136.

Schauffler, Robert Haven. *Florestan: The Life and Work of Robert Schumann* (New York: Dover, 1945).

Schumann, Robert. *Jugendbriefe* (Leipzig: Breitkopf und Härtel, 1886).

———. *Robert Schumann's Briefe*, F. Gustav Jansen (ed.) (Leipzig: Breitkopf und Härtel, 1904).

Von Wasielewski, Joseph Wilhelm. *Life of Robert Schumann.*, A. L. Alger (ed., with a new introduction by Leon Plantinga) (Detroit: Information Coordinators, 1975).

Walker, Alan (ed.). *Robert Schumann: The Man and His Music* (London: Barrie & Jenkins Ltd., 1972).

Marianne Wilson

SCOTT, WALTER (1771–1832). Sir Walter Scott was born in Edinburgh in 1771, the ninth child (although five died in infancy) of Walter Scott, an Edinburgh lawyer, and his wife, Anne Rutherford. As a child, Scott had a distant and often unhappy relationship with his parents, especially his father, and as an adult often took positions, political or otherwise, quite the opposite of his father's. Nevertheless, from an early age, Scott was influenced by the romantic Jacobitism present in his family—many legends of which were told to him by his grandparents while he stayed with them in the Scottish countryside as a child rehabilitating a lame leg. Certainly, Scott became imbued with a profound feeling with regard to the importance of family and history at a young age. He continued his interest in history as he attended the High School in Edinburgh under a series of tutors. As a student he became well read in both the Greek and Roman classics, although this interest waned during his attendance at Edinburgh University. In their place, he learned Italian, Spanish, French, and German and read widely in each, especially Romantic literature. Throughout this period, reading remained his favorite activity, and he once complained to an uncle, "You cannot think how ignorant those boys are; I am much happier here reading my book" (quoted in Sutherland, 19).

Illness eventually forced him to leave the university, and in 1786 he was apprenticed in his father's office as a Writer to the Signet, preparing legal documents. Within two years, Scott began attending law classes and was called to the bar in 1792 and began his own legal practice. Increasingly, he also took an active part in the Edinburgh cultural community and began his own literary and antiquarian activities. In 1797, he married Charlotte Mary Carpenter, the daughter of a French refugee whose family had settled in England (although she was possibly the illegitimate daughter of an English noble acquainted with the family).

Although Scott's legal practice remained both active and profitable, he increasingly turned to literary pursuits, including the composition of ballads and translating some of **Goethe**'s works into English. These efforts translating Goethe would have a profound influence on him, and elements of *Götz von Berlichingen* and other works would resurface in Scott's own historical novels.

In 1799, Scott was named Sheriff-Depute of Kelkirkshire. This position, largely a sinecure, enabled him to spend much time writing and perfecting the historical novel, although he continued his legal career for a time. Scott's first major literary composition was *Minstrelsy*, a multivolume collection of traditional Scottish ballads that had survived the years. Both Scott's profound influence in Scottish history and the influence of the early Romantic era are evident in this, as well as many of his historical novels. Certainly the publication of *The Lay of the Last Minstrel* (1805) established him as a major literary figure in Scotland and England. Throughout these years, Scott also wrote on a variety of subjects, political and literary, for the *Edinburgh Review* and researched and compiled the *Life and Works of John Dryden* and a similar volume on Jonathan Swift. The latter projects demonstrate the importance of politics, especially Tory politics, to Scott during the tumultuous years of the early nineteenth century and his desire to raise the profile of this poetic tradition alongside that of Milton, Shakespeare, and Spenser. Initially, Scott proposed these works as only two in a series of volumes providing "a complete edition of British Poets ancient and modern," a vast, if unfulfilled, ambition, although one demonstrating the scope of Scott's literary interests and knowledge (Sutherland, 128). Throughout his life, Scott was deeply impressed by the theater, especially the works of Shakespeare, although his own dramatic efforts were less successful than his novels and poetry.

Scott is best remembered as the creator of the historical novel, and thus his influence is enormous. In a very real sense, every historical novelist owes a great debt to Scott's series of novels placed in Scottish history. The publication of the first of these books, *Waverley* (1814), cemented Scott's position as one of the dominant literary figures of his day. Although this work was published anonymously, the author's identity was, in practice, well known, and the book was quickly followed by eight more over the next five years, drawing upon both Scott's historical knowledge of the past and his personal feel for it, in part arising from the Jacobite tales he had been told as a child. *Ivanhoe*, Scott's most profitable work, represented something of a departure from the Waverley series, as it went back to the medieval past and, less distinctly Scottish, appealed more to an English audience.

In 1820, Scott was granted a baronetcy and continued to enjoy a high appreciation in both Scottish and English literary circles, especially among the Romantics. From 1812, effectively retired from practicing law, he primarily lived on his estate at Abbotsford in the Scottish border country. This tranquility was, however, upset when, after 1825, his tangled contracts and loans with his publishers collapsed, in the midst of Scott's work on an ambitious *Life of Napoléon*, and he was left deeply in debt. His final literary efforts, therefore, were largely aimed at, and successful in, retiring his obligations.

ARCHIVES

National Library of Scotland, Edinburgh. Contains letters, journals, and handwritten copies of his books.

PRINTED SOURCES

Clark, Arthur Melville. *Sir Walter Scott: The Formative Years* (Edinburgh and London: Blackwood, 1969).

Cockshut, A.O.J. *The Achievement of Walter Scott* (London: Collins, 1969).

Humphrey, Richard. *Walter Scott, Waverley* (Cambridge: Cambridge University Press, 1993). Deals with the origins of The Forty-Five and previous literary accounts.

Keith, Christina. *The Author of Waverley: A Study in the Personality of Sir Walter Scott* (London: Hale, 1964).

Kerr, James. *Fiction against History: Scott as Storyteller* (Cambridge: Cambridge University Press, 1989).

Lockhart, J. G. *Memoirs of the Life of Sir Walter Scott*, 7 vols. (Philadelphia: Carey, Lea, & Blanchard, 1837–1838).

Macintosh, William. *Scott and Goethe: German Influence on the Writings of Sir Walter Scott* (Port Washington, N.Y.: Kennikat Press [1970]).

Millgate, Jane. *Walter Scott: The Making of the Novelist* (Toronto: University of Toronto Press, 1984).

Rubenstein, Jill. *Sir Walter Scott: A Reference Guide* (Boston: G. K. Hall, 1978).

Scott, Walter. *Familiar Letters of Sir Walter Scott*, David Douglas (ed.) (Boston: Houghton Mifflin, 1893).

————. *The Journal of Sir Walter Scott*, W.E.K. Anderson (ed.) (Oxford: Clarendon Press, 1972).

————. *The Letters of Sir Walter Scott*, H.J.C. Grierson et al. (eds.) (London: Constable & Co., 1932–1937).

————. *The Private Letter-books of Sir Walter Scott: Selections from the Abbotsford Manuscripts, with a Letter to the Reader from Hugh Walpole*, Wilfred Partington (ed.) (London: Hodder and Stoughton, 1930).

Sutherland, John. *The Life of Walter Scott: A Critical Biography* (Oxford, United Kingdom, and Cambridge, Mass.: Blackwell Publishers, 1995).

Frank A. Salamone

SEURAT, GEORGES PIERRE (1859–1891). Georges Seurat was born in Paris in 1859 and received his artistic education at a local École Municipale de Sculpture et de Dessin (1874–1877) and the École des Beaux-Arts (1877–1879) until being called to military service in 1879. The son of a deeply religious father, his acknowledged legacy is the marriage of scientific theory and aesthetic beauty in his pointillist art. The precise character of this ambiguous conjunction of the aesthetic and the scientific has generated considerable debate in the interpretation of his painting, and much of this debate has focused on the relative influence of writers and painters on Seurat's production.

His artistic heritage drew as much from Poussin and Ingres, not to say Raphael and Michelangelo, as it did from French Impressionists and his Post-Impressionist contemporaries. Similarly his considerable library, described as a proto-"Musée Imaginaire," ranged from naturalists and symbolists—Huysmans, **Zola**, Mallarmé—who were concerned, as Seurat was, with the possibility of representing the modern world, to works on the theory of art (Russell, 24). Of especial interest to Seurat's critics were his use of Charles Blanc's, Charles Henry's, Michel Chevreul's and Ogden Rood's work on the scientific analysis of line, form, and color. Writing against the canonical legacy of Rewald, Homer, and Russell, Smith offers a challenging counter to the thesis that Seurat was chiefly motivated by his leftist politics and quest after scientific art, arguing that an idealist reading of his work is more appropriate. This aesthetic reading of the influences apparent in Seurat's painting moves from an analysis of the painter to the political possibilities expressed in his work.

ARCHIVES

De Hauke archives, incorporating Félix Fénéon's archives concerning Seurat.
Bibliothèque d'Art et Archéologie (Fondation Jacques Doucet), Paris.

PRINTED SOURCES

Homer, William Innes. *Seurat and the Science of Painting* (New York: Hacker Art Books, 1985).
Loevgren, Sven. *The Genesis of Modernism: Seurat, Van Gogh and French Symbolism in the 1880s* (Bloomington: Indiana University Press, 1971). Essential work on the literary symbolist influences on Seurat's art.
Rewald, John. *Seurat* (New York: Harry N. Abrams, 1990).
Russell, John. *Seurat* (London: Thames and Hudson, 1989).
Schapiro, Meyer. *Modern Art: The Nineteenth and Twentieth Centuries* (New York: G. Braziller, 1978).
Smith, Paul. *Seurat and the Avant-Garde* (New Haven, Conn.: Yale University Press, 1997).

William Gallois

SHAW, GEORGE BERNARD (1856–1950). George Bernard Shaw was born in Dublin in 1856 and was largely self-educated, although he did attend both Protestant and Catholic day schools. From his mother and George John Vandeleur Lee, a Dublin music teacher, Shaw learned to love music. This love influenced him in one of his professions, as a music critic. Shaw's literary education, which was to influence his thought, consisted of the Bible, Shakespeare, **Dickens**, Bunyan, **Blake**, **Byron**, and **Shelley**. From the Irish playwright Dion Boucicault, Shaw first gained a love for the theater. Shaw's greatest contribution is his revitalization of English drama with his plays of "ideas," realistic dramas that engage social and political issues.

At the age of 20, Shaw joined his mother in London, and it was there during the 1880s that Shaw developed his intellectual, philosophical, and political outlook through his voracious reading and his participation in various literary and intellectual societies, including the Zetetical Society, a debating group, the Shelley Society, the **Browning** Society, and the New Shakespeare Society. The effect of hearing the American economist Henry George speak on the land question in 1882 was Shaw's immediate conversion to socialist causes. This led him to join the Fabian Society, which included members such as **Havelock Ellis**,

Ramsay MacDonald, and later Sidney and Beatrice Webb and **H. G. Wells**. The Society believed that they could effect socialist changes by writing pamphlets and giving speeches, activities Shaw engaged in. Another strain of influence upon Shaw occurred as a result of his meeting with William Archer, an art and drama critic, who observed Shaw reading *Das Kapital* and **Wagner**'s *Tristan und Isolde* in the British Museum. Archer was influential in introducing Shaw to the art and drama scene and in pushing Shaw to become an art and drama critic himself. Shaw's artistic outlook was most strongly influenced by **John Ruskin** and **William Morris**, and like them, he championed the Pre-Raphaelite artists and defended the Impressionists, including **James McNeill Whistler**. As a theater critic, Shaw became the great defender of the new realistic drama, exemplified by the most influential dramatist on Shaw's own playwriting, the Norwegian playwright **Henrik Ibsen**. Because of Shaw's vast output, much remains to be done in editing his correspondence. Probably the most fruitful direction for the study of his plays is in their performance.

ARCHIVES

Shaw Archive, British Library. Manuscripts and correspondence.
University of Texas. Play drafts, Shaw's own letters.
British Library of Political and Economic Science (London School of Economics). Business records and letters to Sidney and Beatrice Webb.
National Library of Ireland. Manuscripts of four of his novels and the fragment of an uncompleted novel.
New York Public Library (Berg Collection). Manuscripts, letters, printed materials.
University of North Carolina at Chapel Hill (Henderson Collection). Manuscripts, letters.
Cornell University (Burgunder Collection). Manuscripts, letters, rehearsal copies, leaflets, and pamphlets.
Houghton Library at Harvard University. Manuscripts, letters.
Bucknell University Library (Butler Collection). Manuscripts, letters.
California State University at Fullerton (Strong Collection). Manuscripts, letters.
Yale University. Manuscripts, letters.
Mugar Memorial Library at Boston University. Manuscripts, letters.
Brown University (Albert Collection). Manuscripts, letters.
Fabian Society Archive. Nuffield College Library, Oxford University.

PRINTED SOURCES

Britain, Ian. "Transplanted Doll's House: Ibsenism, Feminism and Socialism in Late-Victorian and Edwardian England." In Ian Britain (ed.), *Transformations in Modern European Drama* (Atlantic Highlands, N.J.: Humanities, 1983), 14–54.
Ganz, Arthur. "The Playwright as Perfect Wagnerite: Motifs from the Music Dramas in the Theatre of Bernard Shaw," *Comparative Drama*, 13 (1979), 187–209.
Harrison, James. "Destiny or Descent? Responses to Darwin," *Mosaic: A Journal for the Interdisciplinary Study of Literature*, 14, 1 (Winter 1981), 109–124.
Holroyd, Michael. *Bernard Shaw*, 4 vols. (New York: Random House, 1988–1992).
Lawrence, Dan H. *Bernard Shaw: A Bibliography*, 2 vols. (London: Oxford University Press, 1982). This bibliography is the starting point for Shaw research and in-

cludes "[a]n index to eighty-five major Shaw manuscripts and their archival locations" (Weintraub, 6).

Muir, Kenneth. "Shaw and Shakespeare." In Eduard Kolb and Jorg Hasler (eds.), *Festschrift Rudolf Stamm zu seinem sechzigsten Geburtstag* (Bern: Francke, 1969), 13–22.

———. "Shaw and the Fabian Society," *The Aligarh Journal of English Studies*, 14, (October 1989), 142–152.

Quinn, Martin. "Shaw and Dickens: A Special Issue," *Shaw Review*, 20, 3 (1977).

Weintraub, Stanley. *Bernard Shaw: A Guide to Research* (University Park: Pennsylvania State University Press, 1992).

Wisenthal, J. L. (ed.). "Introduction," to *Shaw and Ibsen: Bernard Shaw's The Quintessence of Ibsenism and Related Writings* (Toronto: University of Toronto Press, 1979), 3–73.

John Greenfield

SHELLEY, MARY WOLLSTONECRAFT (1797–1851). Mary Wollstonecraft Godwin Shelley was born in London in 1797, the only child of radical authors William Godwin and Mary Wollstonecraft, who died 10 days after giving birth to her second daughter. Shelley was educated at home, receiving an exemplary education because her father granted her full access to his extensive library. Additionally, Godwin entertained some of the leading thinkers of the day, including **Samuel Taylor Coleridge**; **William Wordsworth**, **Humphry Davy**, and William Hazlitt, allowing Shelley at a young age to listen to philosophical conversations. Godwin and Wollstonecraft were dissenters. Although Godwin was an atheist, Shelley, like her mother, believed in a God but rejected traditional organized religion. Her first novel *Frankenstein* remains Shelley's most popular work, although she wrote five other novels, a novella, and numerous short stories and essays. The novel's enduring appeal lies in its addressing of various themes, including scientific hubris, parental responsibility, women's roles, education, behaviorial influences, revenge, and the psychology of evil, as well as being a critique of her husband **Percy Bysshe Shelley**'s Romanticism. Shelley was a prolific reader, but her parent's writings were probably the most significant of all she read. Specifically, Godwin's *Enquiry Concerning Political Justice* and Wollstonecraft's *A Vindication of the Rights of Women* influenced Shelley's thinking regarding politics (she was a staunch anti-monarchist) and women's rights (although not overtly feminist, most of Shelley's writings concern themselves in some way with women's oppression).

Shelley's literary influences were widespread, including classical, British, and European texts. Her journal reading list contains over 550 items, many read two or three times. Besides Godwin and Wollstonecraft, those writers affecting Shelley most were Rousseau, **Goethe**, Milton, and Shelley. These influences, among others, have been the topic of an almost inexhaustible collection of articles and books.

ARCHIVES

Shelley manuscripts, journals, and letters. Lord Abinger Collection, Bodleian Library, Oxford University.

Shelley manuscripts, Carl H. and Lily Pforzheimer Foundation, New York Public Library.

PRINTED SOURCES

Burwick, R. "Goethe's *Werther* and Mary Shelley's *Frankenstein*," *The Wordsworth Circle*, 24 (Winter 1993), 47–52.

Cantor, P. A. *Creature and Creator: Myth-making and English Romanticism* (New York: Cambridge University Press, 1984). Influence of Rousseau.

Crouch, L. "Davy's *A Discourse, Introductory to a Course of Lectures on Chemistry*: A Possible Scientific Source of *Frankenstein*," *Keats-Shelley Journal*, 27 (1978), 35–44. Influence of Humphry Davy.

Hatlen, B. "Milton, Mary Shelley, and Patriarchy," *Bucknell Review*, 26 (1983), 19–47.

Hill-Miller, K. *"My Hideous Progeny:" Mary Shelley, William Godwin, and the Father-Daughter Relationship* (Newark, N.J.: Delaware, 1995).

Mellor, A. K. *Mary Shelley: Her Life, Her Fiction, Her Monsters* (New York: Routledge, 1989). Biography through a critical reading of Shelley's fiction, including an extensive analysis of Godwin's and Wollstonecraft's influence.

O'Rourke, J. " 'Nothing More Unnatural:' Mary Shelley's Revision of Rousseau," *ELH*, 56 (Fall 1989), 543–569.

de Palacio, J. *Mary Shelley dans son oeuvre* (Paris: Klincksieck, 1969). Influence of Rousseau, Dante, Machiavelli.

Richardson, A. "From *Emile* to *Frankenstein*: The Education of Monsters," *European Romantic Review*, 1 (Winter 1991), 147–162. Influence of Rousseau.

Schopf, S. W. " 'Of What a Strange Nature Is Knowledge!': Hartleian Psychology and the Creature's Arrested Moral Sense in Mary Shelley's *Frankenstein*," *Romanticism Past and Present*, 5 (1981), 33–52. Influence of David Hartley's model of psychological development.

Shelley, Mary Wollstonecraft. *The Journals of Mary Shelley 1814–1884*, P. Feldman and D. Scott-Kilvert (eds.) (Baltimore: Johns Hopkins University Press, 1987).

———. *The Letters of Mary Wollstonecraft Shelley*, B. Bennett (ed.), 3 vols. (Baltimore: Johns Hopkins University Press, 1980, 1983, 1988).

Sunstein, E. W. *Mary Shelley: Romance and Reality* (Boston: Little, Brown, 1989). Biography.

SueAnn Schatz

SHELLEY, PERCY BYSSHE (1792–1822). Percy Bysshe Shelley, English Romantic poet, was born on August 4, 1792, of Timothy (subsequently Sir Timothy, Bt.) and Elizabeth Shelley. He attended typical schools of the day— Sion House, Eton, Oxford University—and received an education in the classics, although at all three schools he pursued his own interests in addition to the standard curriculum. In particular he discovered an interest in science—especially experimental chemistry and electricity—and was fortunate to have tutors at Sion House and Eton who provided guidance in these areas. Aside from his tutors, his early scientific interests were fed by reading the writings of Erasmus

Darwin and other scientific writers of the day. After his expulsion from Oxford in 1811 for publishing—and distributing to Anglican bishops and the heads of Oxford colleges—"The Necessity of Atheism," his interest in experimental science waned, but scientific concepts continued to imbue many of his subsequent works, as in *Prometheus Unbound*, especially through a steady belief in science's ability to better human life (King-Hele, 156).

As a schoolboy and at Oxford, Shelley read widely and with gusto—including as he walked or ate. Popular Gothic romances constituted one of his first interests and shaped the two novels he published while still at Eton—*Zastrozzi* and *St. Irvyne; or, The Rosicrucian*—neither of which broke new ground. He continued to read in the classics, especially Plato, but was most influenced by the rationalist writers of the eighteenth century. Locke and Hume initially held sway, but at Oxford he discovered the writings of William Godwin—his future father-in-law—especially *Political Justice*. He began a correspondence with Godwin, although he rebelled against the elder writer's advice to constrict his efforts to the literary and polemical effort for reform rather than the practical. Shelley briefly attempted to lead a reform movement in Ireland and always believed that poetry should be an instrument for reform and not just argument. This early enthusiasm for reform and the lasting influences of Godwin's rationalist thought are evident in Shelley's early poem "Queen Mab" (1813) as well as the "The Revolt of Islam" (1818) (King-Hele, 18–20).

Although differing widely from his political views, Shelley sought out the more conservative Romantic poet **Robert Southey** in 1811—and hoped to meet **William Wordsworth** and **Samuel Coleridge** at the same time. Although Shelley's vision of nature would remain more scientific than these early Romantic poets, he borrowed some of their imagery and adopted some of the stylistic innovations of Southey and Wordsworth (King-Hele, 43, 63). Ultimately, however, Shelley was disappointed by the innate conservatism of Wordsworth and the older generation of Romantics, perceiving them as increasingly simply poetically gifted supporters of the status quo, rather than seeking to better society according to his model of the poet-activist. This distance became evident with the publication of "Peter Bell the Third" (1819), a direct response to Wordsworth's "Peter Bell" (1819), which finds a correlation between Wordsworth's perceived "dullness" and his conservatism, while making topical political references (O'Neill, 106–107).

Subsequently he read and befriended other Romantic poets—particularly **Byron**, **Keats**, and Leigh Hunt—although he was, at times, at odds with each either personally or artistically. Ultimately Shelley utilized techniques from his wide reading in adopting styles or making allusions to a panoply of poets, both contemporary and historic, while turning these adaptations to his own purpose and voice.

Although from an established family, Shelley's personal life and financial situation were tumultuous. After his expulsion from Oxford and his impulsive first marriage to Harriet Westbrook, Shelley's father curtailed his allowance. His departure with **Mary Wollstonecraft Godwin [Shelley]** in 1814 led to a further estrangement with both families, and only the death of his grandfather recouped Shelley's financial position as his father was forced to negotiate the entailment of the estate with his son. A personal reconciliation did not accompany the financial arrangement, however. The marriage to Mary persisted, and increasingly after 1816 the couple lived abroad in the company of Byron, Leigh Hunt, and other members of the Romantic circle. These happy arrangements came to a sudden end in 1822 when Shelley drowned in a sailing accident off the coast of Italy. Shelley's body washed ashore several days later and was identified, in part, by the volumes of Sophocles and Keats still present in his pockets: volumes that might represent the influences, both ancient and modern, that had contributed to his literary accomplishments. His body was subsequently cremated and interred in the Protestant cemetary in Rome.

ARCHIVES

A collection of manuscripts and working notebooks are held at the Bodleian Library. Also at the Bodleian is the Abinger collection of manuscripts relating to P. B. Shelley and Mary Shelley, including her journal. A microfilm copy of this collection is also available at the Duke University Library, Durham, North Carolina.
Carl H. Pforzheimer Collection of "Shelley and His Circle," New York Public Library. Keats-Shelley Memorial Room, Rome.

PRINTED SOURCES

Barrell, Joseph. *Shelley and the Thought of His Time: A Study in the History of Ideas* (1947; New Haven, Conn.: Yale University Press, 1967).
Blunden, Edmund. *Shelley: A Life Story* (London: Collins, 1946).
Cameron K. N., and D. H. Reiman (eds.). *Shelley and His Circle*, 6 vols. (New York: Carl H. Pforzheimer Library, 1961).
Dowden, E. *The Life of Percy Bysshe Shelley*, 2 vols. (London: Routledge, 1951).
Hogg, Thomas Jefferson. *The Life of Percy Bysshe Shelley* (London: E. Maxson, 1868).
Johnson, R. Brimley, ed. *Shelley-Leigh Hunt: How Friendship Made History* (London: Ingpen & Grant, 1928).
King-Hele, Desmond. *Shelley: The Man and the Poet*, (New York: Thomas Yoselof, 1960).
O'Neill, Michael. *Percy Bysshe Shelley: A Literary Life* (New York: Macmillan, 1989).
Robinson, Charles E. *Shelley and Byron: The Snake and Eagle Wreathed in Fight* (Baltimore and London: Johns Hopkins University Press, 1976).
Scrivener, Michael. *Radical Shelley: The Philosophical Anarchism and Utopian Thought of Percy Bysshe Shelley* (Princeton, N.J.: Princeton University Press, 1982).
Shelley, Percy Bysshe. *The Complete Poetical Works of Percy Bysshe Shelley*, Neville Rogers (ed.) (Oxford: Oxford University Press, 1975).
———. *The Letters of Percy Bysshe Shelley*, F. L. Jones (ed.), 2 vol. (Oxford: Oxford University Press, 1964).
———. *Shelley's Prose: or, The Trumpet of Prophesy*, David Lee Clark (ed.) (Albuquerque: University of New Mexico Press, 1966).

Derek Blakeley

SHEVCHENKO, TARAS (1814–1861). Taras Hryhorovych Shevchenko, writer and painter, was born in Moryntsi, the Russian-occupied Ukraine, in 1814 and died in St. Petersburg, Russia, in 1861. Shevchenko received his basic education from local Orthodox priests and cantors. Orphaned at the age of 12, he was thereafter under the charge of various feudal masters until his emancipation. He showed an early talent for drawing (which was not encouraged by some of his teachers). He received artistic training from a variety of sources and was also exposed to literature from his teachers and the masters he served prior to his emancipation in 1838. At that time, a Russian artist helped purchase his freedom and sent him to university. Shevchenko is considered the father of modern Ukrainian literature, a poet who almost single-handedly created a Ukrainian literary language, woven together from a variety of peasant dialects. Unlike his contemporary **Nikolai Gogol**, Shevchenko opted to work as a Ukrainian writer, rather than write in Russian, a language he knew well, along with Polish and Church Slavonic.

The earliest literary influences on Shevchenko were religious. His father, a rare example of a literate peasant, read to him from the *Mineon* (Lives of Saints). His early education also included readings from an antiquated primer, a breviary, and the Book of Psalms. By the age of 12, Shevchenko had committed large portions of the Book of Psalms to memory, and he even stood in for the local *diak* (cantor) at funeral vigils of local peasants. Other early influences included the Orthodox Slavonic liturgical tradition and Ukrainian folk songs and tales, including stories of Kozak (Cossack) heroes. Following sojourns in Wilno and Warsaw in the service of his masters, Shevchenko took art courses in St. Petersburg, where he also read John Gillis, *History of Ancient Greece*; Abbé Barthélemy, *The Journey of Anacharsis*; Plutarch, *Lives*; Dante, *Inferno*; and other Western authors such as Shakespeare, **Byron**, Richardson, James Macpherson, Defoe, **Dickens**, **Walter Scott**, **Hugo**, Rousseau, **Chateaubriand**, Sue, Schiller, **Goethe**, Körner, **Heine**, and **Washington Irving** (Andrusyshen, xiv). In addition, he read most of the Russian classics, was especially fond of **Pushkin**, and attended courses in history, literature, zoology, physics, and French at the St. Petersburg Academy of Arts.

One key influence on Shevchenko's writing was the work of the Polish Romantics, especially Adam Mickiewicz and Zygmunt Krasiński. As the most important Ukrainian Romantic writer, Shevchenko owed more to these authors than to the Western Romantics. Like his Polish counterparts, he drew on both religious and national imagery to speak for a people that had lost its independence and was searching for a national identity. In poems like "Psalms of David," Shevchenko drew on his early training, creating in the style of the Psalms, but used pointedly national themes, combining the religious and the national, much as Mickiewicz and Juliusz Słowacki did for the Poles. In the *Kobzar* and *Haydamaki*, Shevchenko's best-known epic poems, he drew heavily on Ukrainian folk forms, imitating and amplifying the style of traditional bards and creating a new Ukrainian literary language in the process.

ARCHIVES

Central State Archives, Kiev.

PRINTED SOURCES

Andrusyshen, C. H., and Watson Kirkconnell (eds. and trans.). *The Poetical Works of Taras Shevchenko: The Kobzar* (Toronto: University of Toronto Press, 1964).

————. *The Ukrainian Poets, 1189–1962* (Toronto: University of Toronto Press, 1962.)

Antokhii, M., D. H. Struk, and D. Zelska-Darewych. "Taras Shevchenko." In *Encyclopedia of Ukraine* (Toronto: University of Toronto Press, 1984).

Cyzevśkyj, Dymytro. *A History of Ukrainian Literature (from the Eleventh to the End of the Nineteenth Century)*, Dolly Ferguson et al. (trans.) (Littleton, Colo.: Ukrainian Academic Press, 1975).

Luckyj, George S. N. *Shevchenko and His Critics, 1861–1980* (Toronto: University of Toronto Press, 1980).

Manning, Clarence A. (ed. and trans.). *Taras Shevchenko, the Poet of Ukraine: Selected Poems* (Jersey City, N.J.: Ukrainian National Association, 1945).

Shevchenko, Taras. *Selected Works: Poetry and Prose* (Moscow: Progress Publishers, n.d. [ca. 1961]).

Subtelny, Orest. *Ukraine: A History*, 2nd ed. (Toronto: University of Toronto Press, 1994).

John Radzilowski

SIDGWICK, HENRY (1838–1900). Henry Sidgwick was born at Skipton, Yorkshire, England, in 1838. He was educated at Blackheath between 1849 and 1852 and at Rugby between 1852 and 1855. Sidgwick went to Trinity College, Cambridge, where he was 33rd Wrangler and Senior Classic in 1859 and became a fellow of his college. He was baptized into the Church of England but resigned his Trinity fellowship in 1869 when he found he could no longer accept the doctrinal requirements of the Thirty-Nine Articles. Sidgwick's parents were the Rev. William Sidgwick, the headmaster of Skipton Grammar School, and Mary Crofts. Sidgwick was connected to two great nineteenth-century families through marriage. His sister married the Rev. Edward White Benson, who became the archbishop of Canterbury. He married Eleanor Maitland Balfour, the sister of Arthur J. Balfour. Sidgwick's central contribution to Western culture was his effort to reconstruct religious and social thought to meet the requirements of scientific methods. His most enduring legacies were, as Knightbridge Professor of Moral Philosophy, the creation of the modern university at Cambridge and, with his wife, the foundation of Newnham College.

Sidgwick wrote *The Method of Ethics* (1874), *The Principles of Political Economy* (1883), *The Outline of the History of Ethics* (1886), *The Elements of Politics* (1891), and *Practical Ethics* (1898). Sidgwick, as many others of his generation, was deeply influenced by **John Stuart Mill**, who became the starting point of his studies in ethics and political economy. But Sidgwick found Mill's agnosticism unsettling and his philosophy unsatisfactory. Sidgwick also found **Renan**'s *Etudes d'Histoire Religieuse* especially affective. Most important,

Sidgwick was the creature of the Mathematical and Classical Triposes. Though detached from continental methods of analysis, Cambridge mathematics, as Sidgwick recognized, was an elastic system that promoted methodological speculation and spawned a generation of British physicists and philosophers. Although its austerity separated it from Oxford's more generous system, classical philology at Cambridge was central to Sidgwick's intellectual development. In the midst of his spiritual crisis Sidgwick went to Dresden to study Hebrew and Arabic in order to penetrate "more deeply into the mind of the Hebrews and the Semitic stock" from which Christianity sprang. The renewal of his literary studies brought him tremendous emotional relief. Much of Sidgwick's work was devoted to a reconciliation of utilitarianism and intuitionism. Some felt that Sidgwick preferred to balance two opinions rather than to accept either. His abilities were primarily critical. Sidgwick was acute and subtle, cautious and tentative. His writings may have been austere, but he was personally attractive, compelling, and affectionate. Consequently, the influences on him, and he on others, were personal, informal, and tacit and were transmitted through the Apostles and the Grote Society at Cambridge, through the Ad Eundem Club, that interuniversity society devoted to liberal reform, and through the Synthetic Society.

ARCHIVES

The Henry Sidgwick MSS in Trinity College, Cambridge, and especially his Autobiographical Fragment, dictated between August 13 and August 15, 1900 (Add. Ms. 96), his Journal (Add. Ms. c. 97/25/ff. 1–163), his letters to his mother (Add. Ms. c. 99), and his letters to his sister (Add. Ms. c. 100).

PRINTED SOURCES

Schneewind, J. B. *Sidgwick's Ethics and Victorian Moral Philosophy* (Oxford: Clarendon Press, 1977).
Schultz, Bart (ed.). *Essays on Henry Sidgwick* (Cambridge: Cambridge University Press, 1992). Especially Stefan Collini's essay "The Ordinary Experience of Everyday Life: Sidgwick's Politics and the Method of Reflective Analysis" (333–367).
Sidgwick, Arthur, and Eleanor Sidgwick. *Henry Sidgwick: A Memoir* (London: Macmillan, 1905).

William C. Lubenow

SIENKIEWICZ, HENRYK (1846–1916). Henryk Adam Alexander Pius Sienkiewicz was born in Wola Okrzejska, Russian-occupied Poland (today Poland), in 1846. He was educated in Warsaw (high school) and at the University of Warsaw, where he pursued studies in law, medicine, and finally history and literature (completed course work but never took final exams). Aside from Polish and Russian, Sienkiewicz also seems to have had some ability with German, French, Latin, and English. Sienkiewicz was a Roman Catholic from a minor

Polish gentry family. Although best known outside of Poland from his novel *Quo Vadis*? Sienkiewicz won the Nobel Prize in 1905 for his trilogy of historical novels set in seventeenth-century Poland—*Ogniem i mieczem* [With Fire and Sword], *Potop* [The Deluge], and *Pan Wolodyjowski* (translated variously under the titles Pan Michael and Fire in the Steppe). Other notable works were *Krzyżacy* [The Teutonic Knights] and numerous short stories. Sienkiewicz's work has had a tremendous impact on Poles in the realms of both politics and literature. Read by virtually every Polish student—in Poland and abroad—his trilogy became the great epic prose work of Polish literature. Outside of Poland, Sienkiewicz was recognized as the foremost Polish writer of his day, and his work was widely read in both western Europe and the United States (both places where he took lengthy sojourns).

Sienkiewicz's education exposed him to the great European thinkers, and he was especially enamored of Positivism, which enjoyed great popularity in Poland following the defeat of the January Uprising of 1863–1864 against Russian rule. He read **Auguste Comte**, **John Stuart Mill**, **Charles Darwin**, **Herbert Spencer**, and Ludwig Büchner, among others. Yet his favorite books seem to have been novels. As a boy he read "*Robinson Crusoe* and *Swiss Family Robinson* and even dreamed of settling on an uninhabited island" (Giergielewicz, 22). He also read the works of Sir **Walter Scott** and **Alexandre Dumas** *(père)*. He also seems to have read popular "Western" pulp novels of the day. These books, along with his extensive journeys through the interior of the United States (which included meeting with a band of Lakota), colored Sienkiewicz's literary vision of what the Polish-Ukrainian steppes of the seventeenth century were like. His short stories on immigrant life ("For Bread" and "The Lighthouse Keeper") demonstrate a familiarity with immigrant letters that often appeared in Polish newspapers, as well as his own experiences traveling to the United States and among early Polish-American communities.

Among Polish writers he read Adam Mickiewicz (1798–1855), including works such as *Pan Tadeusz*, and Juliusz Słowacki (1809–1849). Of yet greater importance were Julian Ursyn Niemiewicz (1757–1841) and Józef Ignacy Kraszewski (1812–1887), who popularized and developed the genre of the historical novel in Poland. Among his contemporaries Sienkiewicz read the novels of Aleksander Głowacki (Bolesław Prus) (1847–1912), although they provided little discernible influence on the novelist's work. Books on Polish history were certainly high on Sienkiewicz's reading list, notably the work of the late medieval chronicler Jan Długosz (1415–1480), which appeared in a number of nineteenth-century editions. At the same time, Polish history writing was developing quickly in both Warsaw and Kraków, and Sienkiewicz had access to works from both schools. Finally, the novel for which he is best known in the West—*Quo Vadis*?—demonstrates Sienkiewicz's reading of the Bible and, most notably, popular lives of saints and Church history, which were common fare for Catholic Poles of all ages in Sienkiewicz's day.

ARCHIVES

National Archives, Warsaw.

PRINTED SOURCES

Giergielewicz, Mieczysław. *Henryk Sienkiewicz* (New York: Twayne, 1968).
Günther, Władysław. *Sienkiewiczywy* [Living Sienkiewicz] (London: Gryf Printers, Ltd., 1967).
Kiernicki, Edward (ed.). *H. Sienkiewicz Listy do Mścisława Godlewskiego (1878–1904)* [H. Sienkiewicz's letters to Mścisław Godlewski, 1878–1904] (Wrocław: Ossolineum, 1956).
Krzyżanowski, Jerzy R. "Henryk Sienkiewicz," *Contemporary Authors*, 134 (1991), 440–446.
Krzyżanowski, Julian. *Pokłosie Sienkiewiczowski* [Gleanings of Sienkiewicz] (Warsaw: Panstwowy Instytut Wydawniczny, 1973).
Sienkiewicz, Henryk. *Dzieła* [Works], Julian Krzyżanowski (ed.), 60 vols. (Warsaw: Pantswowy Instytut Wydawniczny, 1947–1955).
———. *Portrait of America: Letters*, Charles Morely (trans.) (New York: Columbia University Press, 1958).
Wandycz, Piotr. "Historiography of the Countries of Eastern Europe: Poland," *American Historical Review*, 97, 4 (October 1992), 1011–1025.
Zabski, Tadeusz. *Poglądy Estetyczno-Literackie Henryka Sienkiewicza* [The aesthetic-literary opinions of Henryk Sienkiewicz] (Wrocław: Ossolineum, 1979).

                                                                    John Radzilowski

SIGURÐSSON, JÓN (1811–1879). Jón Sigurðsson was the undisputed leader of the Icelandic nationalist movement of the nineteenth century. Born on June 17, 1811, to a Lutheran minister in northwestern Iceland, Jón Sigurðsson completed a university entrance exam in 1829. Four years later, he sailed to Denmark to study at the University of Copenhagen. There, he emerged as a leading member of the Icelandic student community, which served at the time as an important intellectual link between the external world and the students' home country. In 1841, he published the first issue of his *Ný félagsrit*, a periodical that was to become a major organ for the Icelandic nationalist cause in the next decades. In 1845, during the first session of the Icelandic Parliament as an elected body, Sigurðsson established himself as the most influential parliamentary politician in Iceland, a role that he was to play until the early 1870s.

Sigurðsson was, from the beginning, a spokesman for a liberal nationalist theory, striving for Iceland's autonomy from Denmark as well as for the development of individual liberty in Iceland. His views were shaped by the political atmosphere in Denmark in the second quarter of the nineteenth century, where demands for personal liberties and democratic rights dominated the political scene. Sigurðsson was not influenced by any particular intellectual authority, and he makes few specific references to other authors in his writings, but it is known that he owned books by **David Ricardo**, Jean-Baptiste Say, and German economist Karl H. Rau. In general, his views reflect opinions very similar to those of other European liberals of his time, emphasizing economic liberty, improved popular education, and democratic principles in the public sphere. In spite of Sigurðsson's uncompromising nationalism, the Danish government looked frequently to him to represent Icelanders in negotiations on Icelandic affairs; the government selected him, for example, as one of five members representing Iceland in the Danish constitutive assembly of 1848–1849.

From the time Sigurðsson moved to Copenhagen to enter university, he returned to Iceland only for taking part in sessions of Parliament, which met every second summer. Thus, the Danish capital was the base for his political work and professional career. Besides his political activities, he distinguished himself as a scholar of Icelandic philology and as a meticulous but productive editor of medieval and early modern Icelandic texts and documents. Although he did not complete any university degree, he was respected in his field, working for different academic institutions and learned societies in Copenhagen.

Since his death on December 7, 1879, Jón Sigurðsson has reached almost saintly status in Icelandic historical literature. He is revered for his role as a leader of the Icelandic struggle for independence and for his part in defining the political arguments of Icelandic nationalism. It is clear, however, that Sigurðsson's political liberalism was often ignored by the more conservative members of the Icelandic Parliament, although they generally accepted his role in leading negotiations with the Danish government for more autonomy for Iceland.

ARCHIVES

The Icelandic National Archives, Reykjavík. Einkaskjöl [Private Papers]: E.10.1-E.10.15. Jón Sigurðsson's political and private correspondence.
The Icelandic National Library, Reykjavík. The Manuscript Collection. The JS collection. A collection of Jón Sigurðsson's manuscripts.

PRINTED SOURCES

Hálfdanarson, Guðmundur. "Þjóðhetjan Jón Sigurðsson," *Andvari*, n.s., 39, 122 (1997), 40–62. A recent attempt to evaluate Sigurðsson's political philosophy.
Ólason, Páll Eggert. *Jón Sigurðsson*, 5 vols. (Reykjavík: Hið íslenzka Þjóðvinafélag, 1929–1933). The best biography of Sigurðsson. It is extremely detailed, albeit not particularly critical.
Sigurðsson, Jón. *Af blöðum Jóns forseta* (Reykjavík: Almenna bókafélagið, 1994). A selection of Sigurðsson's articles from his periodical *Ný félagsrit*.
———. *Blaðagreinar*, 2 vols. (Reykjavík: Menningarsjóður and þjóðvinafélagið, 1961–1962). A selection from Sigurðsson's newspaper articles, originally published in Iceland, Denmark, and Norway.
———. *Bréf Jóns Sigurðssonar: nýtt safn* (Reykjavík: Menningarsjóður, 1933). A volume of Sigurðsson's letters.
———. *Hugvekja til Íslendinga: úrval úr ritum og ræðum Jóns Sigurðssonar til loka þjóðfundar* (Reykjavík: Mál og menning, 1951). A selection of Sigurðsson's articles from his periodical *Ný félagsrit*.
———. *Minningarrit aldarafmælis Jóns Sigurðssonar: 1811–1911* (Reykjavík: Hið íslenska bókmenntafélag, 1911). A selection of Jón Sigurðsson's letters.

Sveinsson, Hallgrímur. *The National Hero of Iceland, Jón Sigurdsson: A Concise Biography* (Hrafnseyri: Vestfirska forlagid, 1996). The only biography of Sigurdsson in English translation.

Gudmundur Hálfdanarson

SMILES, SAMUEL (1812–1904). Samuel Smiles was born in Haddington, Scotland, on December 23, 1812, and studied to be a doctor at Edinburgh University between 1829 and 1832. It was not to be in the field of medicine but as a writer that he was to make his mark. While editor of the *Leeds Times* (1838–1842) he actively sought the repeal of the Corn Laws, advocated education reform, fought for the construction of more public libraries, and opposed the extremism displayed by many of the leaders of the Chartist movement. During this period, his political beliefs were most influenced by **Jeremy Bentham**, **John Stuart Mill**, Edwin Chadwick, and **Richard Cobden**. After leaving journalism, Smiles's employment as a secretary with the Leeds and Thirsk Railroad inspired the composition of a series of works that made him one of the most popular authors of his day. *Self-Help* (1859), which grew out of a series of lectures that Smiles delivered on education and economic mobility to members of the Leeds working class, had sold a quarter of a million copies and been translated into dozens of languages by the turn of the century. With *Self-Help* and its companion volumes—*Character* (1871), *Thrift* (1875), and *Duty* (1880)—Smiles preached a gospel of industry, morality, self-denial, and perseverance by drawing examples from the lives of his Victorian contemporaries. Drawing heavily upon both his Calvinist roots and the writings of **Thomas Carlyle** and William and Robert Chambers, Smiles hoped to encourage the British working classes to improve themselves, both morally and economically. Enamored as he was by those, like George Stephenson, the developer of the railroad locomotive, who had, by their enterprise, innovations, or technical expertise, brought Britain to the pinnacle of industrial greatness during the nineteenth century, it is not surprising that many of his other popular works instructed workers in the art of self-improvement through the *Lives of the Engineers* (1861; five-volume expanded edition, 1874), *Industrial Biography* (1863), the *Lives of Boulton and Watt* (1865), and *Men of Invention and Industry* (1884). While admitting that neither thrift nor character always brought wealth and fame and realizing that the state sometimes had to step in to ameliorate the worst excesses of modern industrial society, Smiles continued to proclaim his philosophy of personal betterment and individual responsibility until his death on April 16, 1904.

ARCHIVES

West Yorkshire Record Office (Leeds). Collection includes roughly 1,000 letters, mostly from 1860 to 1904, Smiles's account book, his book-sale ledger, and other family papers.
The Fitzwilliam Museum (Cambridge).

The National Library of Scotland (Edinburgh).
West Sussex Record Office (Chichester): Cobden Papers.

PRINTED SOURCES

Briggs, Asa. "Samuel Smiles and the Gospel of Work." In *Victorian People*, rev. ed. (Chicago: Chicago University Press, 1972).
Jarvis, Adrian. *Samuel Smiles and the Construction of Victorian Values* (Thrupp, Stroud, Gloucestershire: Sutton, 1997).
Smiles, Aileen. *Samuel Smiles and His Surroundings* (London: R. Hale, 1956).
Smiles, Samuel. *The Autobiography of Samuel Smiles* (New York: E. P. Dutton, 1905).
Travers, Timothy. *Samuel Smiles and the Victorian Work Ethic* (New York: Garland, 1987).

Robert F. Haggard

SOREL, GEORGES (1847–1922). Georges Sorel remains something of a puzzle. He is best known as a supporter of revolutionary syndicalism, which aims at the destruction of capitalism and the state by means of the general strike, yet late in his life he embraced views associated with the extreme Right in his native France. In his most famous work, *Reflexions sur la Violence* (*Reflections on Violence*) (1908), Sorel offered a vigorous theoretical defense of the general strike. Sorel found modern life to be riddled with moral degeneration, which he blamed largely on the complacency of the bourgeoisie. His solution, therefore, was the overthrow of bourgeois society by a heroic proletariat. For Sorel, it mattered little whether the general strike ever took place or not: It was for him a "social myth" that inspired a renewal of ardor among workers. Sorel's career has therefore had the greatest influence on anarchists and anarchosyndicalists who, like him, reject conventional political methods. His emphasis on the purifying nature of struggle has inspired some fascists, most notably Mussolini, and while Sorel's role as a progenitor of fascism has often been overstated, his works contain something for nearly every critic of middle-class conventionality, left or right.

An engineer who turned to writing in his late thirties, Sorel resented what he saw as the stultifying bourgeois education he had received; in 1907 he wrote, "I read books, not so much to learn as to efface from my memory the ideas which had been thrust upon it" (*Reflections*, 3). Yet Sorel found inspiration in many of the most traditional texts, particularly ancient Greek literature and the Bible. In *The Trial of Socrates* (1889), he showed his admiration for the heroic values contained in Homer and the Tragedians and offered a foretaste of his later argument that myth was a uniquely powerful social force. The New Testament likewise drew his admiration, because of the moral intensity and uncompromising struggle of the early Christian Church.

The writings of **Proudhon** and **Marx** assisted Sorel's move to the Left in the 1890s and focused his attention on the impact of capitalism on society. Sorel drew on the former's moralistic attacks on capitalism and the latter's arguments for the centrality of class struggle. Sorel's acceptance of syndicalism in the early years of the twentieth century was partly due to Giambattista Vico's *New Science* (1725). Vico's emphasis on an initial, mythic age of society helped Sorel conceive of the general strike as overarching myth, just as his concept of "artificial nature" fortified Sorel's rejection of positivism. Henri Bergson's impact on Sorel, though significant, has frequently been overstated. Sorel did use Bergson's ideas of intuition and the élan vital to reinforce his concept of myth, but his ideas on the point were already well developed before he studied Bergson (Jennings, 139–142). In short, Sorel drew widely from sources that undermined the ideas of progress, positivism, and liberalism so prominent in the nineteenth century and so aggressively attacked (not least by him) in the twentieth.

ARCHIVES

Bibliothèque Nationale, Paris.

PRINTED SOURCES

Jennings, J. R. *Georges Sorel* (New York: St. Martin's Press, 1985).
Roth, Jack J. *The Cult of Violence: Sorel and the Sorelians* (Berkeley: University of California Press, 1980).
Sorel, Georges. *Illusions of Progress*, John and Charlotte Stanley (trans.) (1908, Berkeley: University of California Press, 1969).
———. *Reflexions sur la Violence*, T. E. Hulme (trans.) (1908; reprint, AMS Press, New York, 1975).

Christopher Pepus

SOUTHEY, ROBERT (1774–1843). Robert Southey, English Romantic poet, historian, critic and later, Poet Laureate, contributed well over 100 articles to the conservative *Quarterly Review* between 1809 and 1839 and wrote biographies in one form or another throughout his long career. At an early age he read the chronicle plays of Shakespeare and was a lifelong admirer of Spenser. Before he entered school, he knew the works of Milton, Pope, Sidney, Beaumont and Fletcher, Chatterton, and Chaucer and read widely in Scripture as a child. The *Spectator* and the *Bristol Journal* were subscribed to in the home, where he read the Jewish historian Josephus, Tasso in Hoole's translation, Ariosto's *Orlando Furioso*, and Mickle's translation of Camoëns's *Lusiad*, as well as *The Arabian Nights*, Malory's *King Arthur*, and the medieval songs, ballads, and metrical romances contained in Percy's *Reliques*. The popular poets of the day—Collins, **Cowper**, Mason, Warton, and Akenside—served as models for much of his juvenile poetry.

At Westminster School, which he entered in 1788, he was given access to the library in Dean's Yard and read Picart's *Religious Ceremonies*, which set him off on an investigation of world mythologies. Latin and Greek were the chief subjects of the curriculum, though the study and composition of English verse were encouraged. Homer, Virgil, Ovid, Tacitus, and Greek and Roman mythology and history were among the authors and subjects Southey studied at this time. Outside the curriculum he read the "obvious books of the age" (Storey, 9), including **Goethe**'s *Werther*, Voltaire, Rousseau, and Gibbon. He read enough of Burke to produce an essay attacking *Reflections on the Revolution in France*.

Southey studied for the clergy and later prepared for the law. In addition to the usual books, he read Glover's *Leonidas* and Mackenzie's sentimental novel *The Man of Feeling* and wrote that while at Oxford he carried the Stoic philosopher Epictetus in his pocket until he had him by heart. At Balliol College, Southey was writing odes in imitation of Gray. He relied on Bysshe's *Art of Poetry* for the rudiments of verse composition and was influenced by Thomas Warton's pioneering *History of English Poetry*. During this time he read *Tristram Shandy* and Watson's *Chemical Essays* and wrote verse that was imitative of Shenstone, the hymn writers Watts and Wesley, and "Della Crusca" (Robert Merry).

The ideals in Godwin's *Political Justice* were the basis for the projected "Pantisocracy," a utopian community that he planned with **Coleridge**. The two poets were admirers of the sonnets of William Bowles and copied out their favorites to share with their friends. Southey was a voracious reader—so much so that the scope of his reading can only be outlined here—and there is no reason to suppose that he was not well acquainted with the writers of the day. The literary scene in the last decade of the eighteenth century was notable for the absence of any single dominating author or groups of authors, but the works of Burns and the Gothic novels of Radcliffe and Lewis stand out. Travel books like those by Bligh and Young and works on the picturesque by Gilpin were popular. The first 20 years of the eighteenth century saw novels by **Austen** and **Scott**, essays in prose by Lamb, Hazlitt, and **De Quincey**, and the poetry of **Keats**, **Byron**, and **Shelley**. **William Blake**, whose poems were issued almost unnoticed during the 1790s, was later acclaimed as a lyrical poet by Southey.

Southey was the English authority on Portuguese and Spanish history and translated works by Vasco Lobiera and Francisco de Moraes. He prepared essays on the life and works of Thomas More, **Malthus**, and Cromwell and wrote biographical accounts that included the works of his lesser-known contemporaries Thornton, Colman, Lloyd, and Churchill. The famous epithet that describes him as "Epic Renegade" is from the dedication to Byron's *Don Juan*.

ARCHIVES

University of Waterloo Library, Ontario.
British Library.
Bodleian Library.
Victoria University Library, Toronto.

PRINTED SOURCES

Bernhardt-Kabisch, Ernest. *Robert Southey* (Boston: Twayne, 1977).
Curry, Kenneth. *Southey* (London and Boston: Routledge and Kegan Paul, 1975).

Dowden, Edward. *Robert Southey* (London: Macmillan, 1879).

Haller, William. *The Early Life of Robert Southey* (New York: Columbia University Press, 1917).

Simmons, Jack. *Southey* (London: Collins, 1945; New Haven, Conn.: Yale University Press, 1948).

Storey, Mark. *Robert Southey: A Life* (Oxford and New York: Oxford University Press, 1997).

Susan Reilly

SPENCER, HERBERT (1820–1903). Herbert Spencer was born in Derby, England, in 1820 and educated privately, first under his uncle William (1827–1830) and subsequently by his uncle Thomas (1830–1836). His formal schooling provided him a firm grounding in mathematics—particularly geometry—and a distaste for the traditional subjects of Latin and Greek. Of especial import were religious and political discussions within the Spencer family; his immediate family debated the political implications of their dissenting, Methodist heritage, while his uncle Thomas was an evangelical Anglican who proselytized on the evils of drink, as well as the Poor and Corn Laws. Herbert Spencer's major contributions to Western culture are twofold: He attempted to justify his radical liberalism—approaching libertarianism—on a scientific philosophy of moral individualism. In the process, he popularized an exhaustive theory of social development commonly termed "Social Darwinism."

The foremost point to note about the literary influences on Herbert Spencer's thought is his disinclination to acknowledge them; indeed, as a philosopher he reveled in the claim, "My ignorance of ancient philosophical writers was absolute" (Duncan, 418). Instead, he relied on lectures and conversations for much of his material. This dates back to his early days when his father—a member of the Derby Philosophical Society—regularly brought young Herbert to scientific lectures and demonstrations of chemistry, mesmerism, and phrenology. From this basis, Herbert Spencer acquired his taste for the wide range of Victorian "science" as the basis of philosophical truths. His scientific interests included the collection of fossils and plant specimens and experiments with electricity in the vain hope of becoming a successful inventor—all while applying his mathematical skills as a surveyor and railway engineer. The few philosophers mentioned in Spencer's published works served as foils for his own ideas.

The greatest influences on the philosophy of Herbert Spencer came from his personal contacts with other thinkers, often in the form of conversations that are difficult to document. Spencer took long walks with **Thomas Henry Huxley**, discussing the implications of evolutionary biology for understanding human society. These men had a long and close friendship until Huxley published an essay disagreeing with Spencer's views. Spencer corresponded with **John Stuart Mill** for several years, discussing politics and social issues in light of their effects on personal liberty. He even contacted **Charles Darwin** on publication of *The Origin of Species*, though Spencer thought the Darwinian view of biological evolution too limiting. These contacts, among many others, ensured that Spencer's philosophical work, the 10 volumes of *The Synthetic Philosophy*, explained his understanding of social evolution in exhaustive detail. And the spread of his thought—translated into 14 languages by the time of his death—ensured the worldwide knowledge of his view of social evolution, even by those who disagreed with his conclusions.

ARCHIVES

The Athenaeum Collection of Herbert Spencer's Papers. Senate House Library, University of London.

The Huxley Papers, vol. 7. Imperial College Library, University of London.

Spencer, Herbert, and John Stuart Mill. Correspondence. Northwestern University Library.

PRINTED SOURCES

Duncan, David. *The Life and Letters of Herbert Spencer* (London: Methuen and Co., 1908).

Perrin, Robert G. *Herbert Spencer: A Primary and Secondary Bibliography*, 2 vols. (New York: Garland Publishing, 1993).

Spencer, Herbert. *An Autobiography*, 2 vols. (London: Williams and Norgate; New York: D. Appleton and Co., 1904).

Charles M. Roll

SPURGEON, CHARLES HADDON (1834–1892). Charles Spurgeon was born in Kelvedon, Essex, England, in 1834 and spent his formative years under the care of his grandparents in nearby Stambourne. His grandfather James was an Independent minister for more than 50 years. Though well versed in theology, he was largely self-taught and had no formal education beyond 16, when he first began to preach. He became pastor of Waterbeach Baptist Chapel, Cambridge, at 17 and of New Park Street Baptist Chapel, London, 3 years later. He was the most popular preacher of his day, drawing congregations of 5,000 and upward every Sunday for nearly 40 years, most famously to the Metropolitan Tabernacle in south London, built for him in 1859. Printed versions of his sermons sold in their thousands every week and were syndicated in major U.S. newspapers. Total sales of his writing have exceeded a hundred million. He founded a (still-flourishing) pastors' training college and several charitable concerns including an orphanage.

From his earliest days, he loved books: He described as "a gold mine" a room in his grandparents' house containing the library of a seventeenth-century rector of Stambourne, a convinced Puritan. Here he discovered Foxe's *Acts and Monuments*—which may have helped shape his views on Catholicism and ritualism—and Bunyan's *Pilgrim's Progress* and *Grace Abounding*, which he absorbed thoroughly. While young he also "read and devoured" Allcine's *Alarm to the Unconverted* and Baxter's *Call to the Unconverted*, both of which aided his spiritual development and conversion. Another early influence was Watts, whose hymns his grandmother encouraged him to learn. His knowledge of the Bible was unsurpassed: He chiefly used the King James but was familiar with the Revised Version.

He claimed to preach "a Calvinist creed and a Puritan morality" and was steeped in works of the Reformation and seventeenth century. He much admired Luther but confessed to being more a follower of Calvin (and—characteristically—"much more a follower of Jesus than of either of them!"). He read Knox and prized Beza's sermons on the Song of Solomon. Among the Puritans he loved were Charnock, Owen, Manton, Gurnall, Gill, Brooks, Henry, and Bunyan: Dickson on the Psalms "drops fatness," he wrote; Sibbes "scatters pearls and diamonds with both hands"; Ferguson of Ayrshire is "a grand, gracious, savoury divine." He liked Rutherford's *Letters*, and republished Watson's *Body of Divinity*. He avidly collected Puritan books, and nearly one-tenth of the 12,000 volumes in his library were printed before 1700. A contemporary book that greatly affected him was John Angell James's *The Anxious Enquirer*.

Spurgeon valued books less as literature than "for the good they may do men's souls"; he thought it more honorable to have composed Watts's *Psalms* than Milton's *Paradise Lost*, to write a small evangelistic booklet than "all the works of Homer." He respected "the genius of Pope, Dryden, and Burns" but preferred "the simple lines of **Cowper**." He admired Doddridge's *Rise and Progress of Religion in the Soul* for "the conversions it has produced." He enjoyed history; dabbled in many other subjects; thought Sir **Walter Scott** "the greatest mind God ever created"; and enjoyed **Tennyson**; but his library contained few non-religious books or works representing theological positions that challenged his own.

ARCHIVES

The Spurgeon Collection, Campus of William Jewell College, Liberty, Missouri.
The Heritage Room, Spurgeon's College, South Norwood Hill, London.

PRINTED SOURCES

Bebbington, David W. "Spurgeon and the Common Man," *Baptist Review of Theology*, 5, 1 (Spring 1995), 63–75.
Kruppa, Patricia Stallings. *Charles Haddon Spurgeon: A Preacher's Progress* (New York: Garland, 1982).
Spurgeon, C. H. *Autobiography*, 2 vol: (1834–1859 & 1860–1892) (Edinburgh and Carlisle, Pa.: Banner of Truth, 1962).

Andrew Bradstock

STAËL, ANNE-LOUISE-GERMAINE DE (1766–1817). Anne Staël, or Madame de Staël as she became known, was born and educated in Paris by her mother, Suzanne Necker, whose Salon acquainted her with the major problems of Enlightenment.

De Staël was, with René Vicomte de Chateaubriand, a leading figure in paving

the way for French Romanticism. Her beginnings of a theory of the novel contributed to the recognition of the novel as a serious literary genre in the nineteenth century. De Staël played a key role in French literature and thought from
Enlightenment to Romanticism. In addition, her novels—*Delphine* (1802) and
Corinne (1807)—inspired women's emancipation in nineteenth-century Europe.

Her early works, such as *Lettres sur les ouvrages et le caractère de Jean-
Jacques Rousseau* (1788), were influenced by Jean-Jacques Rousseau. Like her
mother, de Staël welcomed outstanding European intellectuals in her Salon at
Coppet, Switzerland, where she had to emigrate after the French Revolution
because of her political opposition to **Napoléon** I. Her correspondence with
Europe's most important personages includes approximately 10,000 letters
(Bosse, 818).

During her travels to Germany in 1803–1804 and 1807, she met key figures
of German classical literature such as Friedrich Schiller, **Johann Wolfgang von
Goethe**, **Johann Gottlieb Fichte**, and Christoph Martin Wieland, laying the
foundations of French Romanticism. Also, her second novel *Corinne ou l'Italie*
(1807) was inspired by her travels through Germany. August Wilhelm Schlegel,
who de Staël met in Vienna in 1807, became the teacher of her children and
her personal adviser at Coppet (Bosse, 804). Schlegel took care of the publication of *De l'Allemagne* (1814) in German, after the French edition had been
confiscated and pulped before publication by Napoléon I in 1810.

In her writings, she was committed to the ideas of Enlightenment (the idea
of perfection that she received from, among others, Charles Perrault, Voltaire,
and the Marquis de Condorcet).

ARCHIVES

Bibliothèque publique et universitaire, Geneva. Correspondence.
Fondation pour l'Histoire des Suisses à l'Etranger, Château de Penthes, Pregny-
    Chambésy. Correspondence, manuscripts.

PRINTED SOURCES

Balayé, Simone. *Les carnets de Madame de Staël: Contribution à la genèse des ses
    oeuvres* (Geneva: Droz, 1971).
———. *Madame de Staël: Lumières et liberté* (Paris: Klincksieck, 1979).
Bosse, Monika. "Madame de Staël und der deutsche Geist." In Monika Bosse (ed.),
    Madame de Staël, Über Deutschland: Vollständige Ausgabe (Frankfurt am Main:
    Insel, 1985), 801–857.
Diesbach, Ghislain de. *Madame de Staël* (Paris: Perrin, 1983).
Herold, Christopher. *Madame de Staël: Mistress to an Age* (Indianapolis, Ind.: Bobbs-
    Merrill, 1958).
Le Groupe de Coppet: Actes et documents du deuxième Colloque de Coppet, July 10–
    13, 1974, Société des Etudes Staëliennes under the direction of S. Balayé and
    J. D. Candaux (ed.) (Geneva: Champion, 1977).
Pange, Comtesse Jean de. *August Wilhelm Schlegel und Frau von Staël: Eine schicksal-
    hafte Begegnung* (Hamburg: Goverts, 1940).

Staël, Madame de. *Correspondance générale*, Béatrice Jasanski (ed.) (Paris: Hachette, 1983).

Ernst Grabovszki

STANISLAVSKY, KONSTANTIN (1863–1938). Konstantin Stanislavsky was born Konstantin Serqeevich Alekseev in 1863 in Moscow into a wealthy family. Early education was at home under a series of different tutors for subjects such as gymnastics, dance, music, and French. A governess ("Papusha") was most influential in introducing young Konstantin to creative play, tableaux, and skits. In 1875, as mandated by law, Stanislavsky was sent to the local grammar school, and in 1878 he transferred to the Lazarev Institute for Oriental Languages, from which he graduated in 1881. Stanislavsky became the most influential actor, director, and teacher of acting of the late nineteenth and twentieth century.

Stanislavsky's father built amateur theaters on the family estate, and at age 14 the boy began acting in plays there. At the same time, he steeped himself in the Bolshoi ballet and in opera, appearing in extracts from **Verdi**'s *Aida* and making plans for how he would play Mephistopheles in Gounod's *Faust*. However, vocal problems prohibited his pursuing a career in opera. In 1885 Stanislavsky was accepted to the Moscow Theatre School but dropped out within three weeks, as always discouraged by rote and imitative learning.

Meanwhile, Stanislavsky continued his search for excellence in acting technique. The Mali Theatre, featuring a psychological-realistic acting style, was, as he put it, his "university." Contemporary writers **Alexsandr Pushkin** and **Nikolai Gogol** were involved in the Mali, and Stanislavsky certainly read their works along with the autobiography of the company's leading actor, Mikhail Shchepkin, *Memoirs of a Serf-Actor*. Stanislavsky's heavily annotated copy of this work demonstrates his fascination with this early model of an actor's striving for authenticity in performance. Stanislavsky also attended touring productions, reading the plays in advance, including Jean Racine, Pierre Corneille, and Molière in the original.

Stanislavsky continued performing in the Alekseiev Circle, the family-and-friends troupe performing at Red Gates, the family theater. He took the stage name "Stanislavsky" to conceal from his family that he was also performing in bawdy, improvised, vaudevillian productions with less savory acquaintances.

In 1888 Stanislavsky, in partnership with the director Alexander Fedotov, launched The Society of Art and Literature. From his contact with Fedotov and other intelligentsia, Stanislavsky came to see the ethical-political dimensions of theater. Influential in this regard was polemicist and critic Vissarion Belinski, whose philosophy on the relationship of artist to audience and society gave justification to Stanislavsky's passionate drive to perform. **Tolstoy**'s 1898 *What Is Art* also greatly influenced Stanislavsky's views on the moral dimension of art.

As Stanislavsky worked to put into writing the System of acting he had evolved, he felt the need to place his work in context of what had gone before;

in 1914 he read voraciously including Luigi Riccoboni's *Pensées Sur La Declamation* (1738), Francesco Riccoboni's *Histoire Du Theatre Italien* (1740) and *L'art Du Theatre* (1750), Remond de Saint-Albin's *Le Comedien* (1747), Denis Diderot's notes on Sticcotti's *Garrick Ou Les Acteurs Anglais* (1769), Ludwig Tieck's *Dramaturgische Blatter (1825–1852), Lettres D'Adrienne Lecouvreur* (1892), Fournelle's *Curiosites Theatrales* (1859), Coquelin's *L'Art Du Comedien* (1894), and Bram Stoker's *Personal Reminiscences of Henry Irving* (1906).

ARCHIVES

The Konstantin Stanislavsky Archives, Moscow.

PRINTED SOURCES

Benedetti, Jean. *Stanislavski* (New York: Routledge, 1988).
Magarshack, David. *Stanislavsky: A Life* (New York: Greenwood Press, 1975).
Stanislavsky, Konstantin. *My Life in Art*, J. J. Robbins (trans.) (New York: Theatre Arts Books, 1952).

Douglas King

STANTON, ELIZABETH CADY (1815–1902). Elizabeth Cady Stanton, initiator of the American women's suffrage movement, was born and educated in Johnstown, New York (1826–1830), and at Emma Willard's Troy Female Seminary, Troy (1830–1833).

Stanton was the most prominent nineteenth-century woman's rights leader and feminist pioneer in the United States. Her childhood in her lawyer father's house was spent receiving a somewhat "masculine" education that also included Greek studies. Her first important contribution to feminist issues, the Declaration of Sentiments (1848, Seneca Falls, New York) demanded rights for women in the spirit of the classic Enlightenment natural rights doctrine. As her *History of Woman Suffrage* describes, the document itself was closely modeled on the American Declaration of Independence (1776). The additional twist of extending natural rights to women was reliant on Sarah Grimké's previous attempt (*Letters on Equality*, 1845) of applying the classic liberal natural rights principles to women. Stanton's other most important contribution to nineteenth-century feminism included the writing of her *Woman's Bible* (1895), in which she analyzes the derogatory references made to women in the Bible and reinterprets them in the light of other passages and reason. Her revision of the Bible demonstrates the radical uses to which the natural rights doctrine could be put, as she uses these natural rights to repudiate the validity of biblical ethics. Her argument about an androgynous Godhead echoes **Margaret Fuller**'s similar ideas in *Woman in the Nineteenth Century* (1845).

ARCHIVES

Elizabeth Cady Stanton Papers, Library of Congress, Washington, D.C. Principal correspondence, 0319L.

———. Vassar College Library, Poughkeepsie, New York. Papers 1796–1921: ca.2cu.ft.
———. Henry Huntington Library, San Marino, California.
———. New York Public Library.

PRINTED SOURCES

Donovan, Josephine. *Feminist Theory: The Intellectual Traditions of American Feminism*
    (New York: Continuum, 1992).
Gordon, A. D. (ed.). *The Selected Papers of Elizabeth Cady Stanton and Susan B. An-
    thony* (New Brunswick, N. J., and London: Rutgers University Press, 1997).
Holland, P. G. and A. D. Gordon (eds.). *Papers of E. C. Stanton and S. B. Anthony*
    (Wilmington, Del.: Scholarly Resources, 1991). Microfilm.
Lutz, Alma. *Created Equal: A Biography of E. C. Stanton 1815–1902* (New York: John
    Day Company, 1940).
Stanton, E. C. *Eighty Years and More 1815–1897* (New York: European, 1898).
Stanton, E. C., and S. B. Anthony. *History of Woman Suffrage*, vols. 1–3 (Rochester,
    N.Y.: C. Mann, 1881–1887).
Stanton, T., and H. S. Blatch. *E. C. Stanton as Revealed in Her Letters, Diary and
    Reminiscences*, 2 vols. (New York and London: Harper and Brothers, 1922).

Zsuzsanna Varga

STENDHAL (1783–1842). Stendhal, pseudonym of Marie-Henri Beyle, was
born in the Alpine town of Grenoble. Reared by an emblematically bourgeois
father and a hated Catholic tutor, he enrolled at Grenoble's École Normale and
in 1799 left for Paris to study at the newly created École Polytechnique. In 1800
he was commissioned in the Army of Italy, where he served for two years.
Despite war's horrors, he became enamored with Italian culture, recording his
impressions in his *Journal* (published between 1888 and 1935). In 1806, unable
to find his niche in Paris' literary circles, he joined the Army Commissariat for
the duration of several campaigns and later served in various administrative
capacities.

Upon **Napoléon**'s fall, the anticlerical, antimonarchist Stendhal interrupted
his bureaucratic career. He settled in Milan to publish essays on music (*Vies de
Haydn, Mozart et de Métastase*, 1814) and painting (*Histoire de la peinture en
Italie*, 1817). *Rome, Naples et Florence*, the first book to appear under his nom
de plume, appeared in 1817. His liberalism aroused Austrian suspicions, forcing
him to return to Paris where he was tepidly recognized by Romantic writers.
Working for *La Revue de Deux Mondes*, he wrote on love (*De l'amour*, 1822)
and Shakespeare, then little respected in France. In 1827, assisted by Prosper
Mérimée, he published his first novel, *Armance*, a tale of unrequited love mir-
roring his Italian affairs. In 1830 came his magnum opus *Le Rouge et le Noir*,
which went practically unnoticed. Receiving consular assignments in Italy, he
published *La Chartreuse de Parme* in 1839 while working on *Lucien Leuwen*
(published in 1855) and various autobiographical materials published posthumously (*Souvenirs d'égotisme* in 1893 and *Vie de Henri Brulard* in 1890). Stendhal applied his concept of "*égotisme*" (or "*beylisme*," a highly idiosyncratic

carpe diem in which art serves as the way to perfect contentment) to his last writings, precursors of the "travelogue" (*Les Mémoires d'un touriste* [1838] and *Chroniques Italiennes* [1855]). He died in Paris, leaving his novel *Lamiel* unfinished.

Astride two centuries and two countries, Stendhal paid equal homage to Etienne de Condillac's enlightened sensualism, Pierre-Jean Cabanis's materialism, and François de Volney's historiographic thought. Superficially associated with Romanticism (whose lyricism he despised), he was, as his heroes, a fierce individualist. Purporting to write in a way reminiscent of the Civil Code, he was concerned with stylistic neutrality, psychological truth, and the celebration of individual will and happiness. An advocate of cosmopolitism, he was rediscovered and celebrated by realist novelists of the 1880s and 1890s.

ARCHIVES

Archives Nationales, Bibliothèque Nationale de France, Paris.
Archives Municipales, Grenoble.

PRINTED SOURCES

Alter, R. *A Lion for Love: A Critical Biography of Stendhal* (New York: Basic Books, 1979).
Crouzet, M. *Stendhal, ou, Monsieur Moi-Même* (Paris: Flammarion, 1990).
Petrey, S. *Realism and Revolution: Balzac, Stendhal, Zola, and the Performances of History* (Ithaca, N.Y.: Cornell University Press, 1988).
Tillett, M. G. *Stendhal: The Background to the Novels* (London: Oxford University Press, 1971).

Laurent Ditmann

STEPHEN, LESLIE (1832–1904). Leslie Stephen was born in Kensington Gore, London, in 1832, the fourth child of James Stephen and Jane Venn, descendants of Reformers, the Clapham sect, Evangelicals, and the antislavery movement. He was educated at Guest's School, Brighton (1840–1842); Eton College (1842–1846); King's College, London (1848–1850); and Trinity Hall, Cambridge (1850–1854). Brought up an Anglican, he was ordained a deacon in 1855 and a priest in 1859. He resigned his Trinity Hall tutorship in 1862 because of religious doubts and left Cambridge in 1867 to marry, resigning holy orders in 1875. He was a self-proclaimed agnostic.

Stephen is recognized for his contribution to late nineteenth-century letters and thinking in several fields: as founding editor of and major contributor to the *Dictionary of National Biography*; for his other biographical studies and theoretical essays on biography; for his groundbreaking studies of eighteenth- and nineteenth-century writers and thinkers; for his journalism, philosophical, and ethical writings; and for his mountaineering achievements and associated, often philosophical, writings. He was the father of Virginia Woolf and Vanessa Bell and especially influential in Virginia's education, thought, and writing.

Leslie Stephen's education was in the classics, though he also studied French and German and, later, at Cambridge, mathematics. He was interested in university politics and the reform of the system and later in Liberal Party parliamentary politics, though he never considered a political career. He read English poetry and could easily memorize even the longest poem. Increasingly, it was eighteenth-century literature that pleased him. He was attracted by **James and John Stuart Mill**'s utilitarianism, on which he later wrote extensively. He read Hobbes, **Comte**, Kant, Berkeley, Locke, and Hume. His interest in ethics and the moral sciences, philosophy, history, and political economy eventually led to his decision to abandon the Church and his Cambridge career. He moved to London and took up journalism, sometimes writing as many as four articles a week, and yet he still found time for private study, reading **Hegel**, Spinoza, **Renan**, and **Strauss**. For a while he was caught up in the ideas and politics of the American Civil War, on which he also wrote, having made the first of several visits to the United States. He understood the American scene and found perhaps his closest lifetime friends there: Charles Eliot Norton, **Oliver Wendell Holmes**, and **James Russell Lowell**. In England, editorial work increasingly occupied his time, first with magazines, *Fraser's* and the *Cornhill*, and, by 1882, the *Dictionary of National Biography (DNB)*. He wrote extensively on the ethical and metaphysical issues of the day. He knew James Knowles, W. J. Clifford, **Thomas Huxley**, William Tyndall, **Henry Sidgwick**, Frederic Harrison, and George Croom Robertson. He was interested in their philosophical ideas, and in many cases, he later wrote biographical pieces on them. For the *DNB* articles he wrote, Stephen reread many of his old literary favorites, Swift, Johnson, Pope, **George Eliot**, **Walter Scott**. In the end the *DNB* all but killed him, exhausting him physically and mentally and forcing him into early semiretirement by 1890. But the new freedom gave him time to read and to reflect on his life in letters and on the art of biography in particular. He could devote time to his children's education, particularly the girls, tutored at home by their parents. But his final years were sad. He was by now a widower for a second time. There was the death of his stepdaughter, the mental instability of Virginia, and finally his own ill health. Throughout, he never lost the urge to read and to write. When he entered hospital for surgery on the cancer of the stomach that killed him, he took the novels of **Jane Austen**, and shortly before he died, he was planning another of his *English Men of Letters* series on her. Frederic Maitland's record of a list of books he asked for from the London Library in his final days is an appropriate comment on Leslie Stephen's sustained interests.

It began with the names of Reville, **Martineau**, Brunetiere, Flint, Vauvenargues, Vansal, Sabatier, **Chateaubriand**, **Sorel**, **Pater**, Ostrogorski, W. Watson, and **Dostoevsky**. Some of the biblical critics are there and **Émile Zola**. Then when other books failed, he fell back on the old, old story. Need I name it? He told his nurse that his enjoyment of books had begun and would end with Boswell's *Life of Johnson*.

ARCHIVES

Autograph manuscripts of articles and books: British Library, Macmillan Archive; Cambridge University Library; Trinity Hall, Cambridge, significant holdings of autograph manuscripts; Duke University, North Carolina, Perkins Library, autograph manuscripts of 19 articles and corrected proofs; Harvard University, Houghton Library; New York Public Library.

Correspondence: British Library, Macmillan Archive; Cambridge University Library; Duke University, North Carolina, Perkins Library.

Publishing and family correspondence; Harvard University, Houghton Library; University of Leeds, Brotherton Library; Pierpont Morgan Library, New York; New York Public Library; Bodleian Library, Oxford.

Significant correspondence, relating to the *DNB*: National Library of Scotland, Edinburgh; Harry Ransom Humanities Research Center, University of Texas at Austin; Yale University, Beinecke Library.

Publishing archives: John Murray Ltd, London, Smith, Elder archives; University of Reading, Longman archives; National Library of Scotland, Edinburgh, *Cornhill* payment books.

Other archival materials: Cambridge University Library, Maitland papers contain material from the first biography of Stephen; Trinity Hall, Cambridge, contemporary documents on his college life; Washington State University, Pullman, Washington, Stephen's Library, including many annotated items.

PRINTED SOURCES

Annan, Noel. *Leslie Stephen: His Thought and Character in Relation to His Time* (London: MacGibbon & Key, 1951).

———. *Leslie Stephen: The Godless Victorian* (London: Weidenfeld & Nicolson, 1984).

Fenwick, Gillian. *Leslie Stephen's Life in Letters: A Bibliographical Study* (Aldershot: Scolar Press, 1993).

Maitland, Frederic William. *The Life and Letters of Leslie Stephen* (London: Duckworth & Co., 1906).

Stephen, Leslie. *Selected Letters of Leslie Stephen*, John W. Bicknell (ed.); 2 vols. (London: Macmillan, 1996).

Gillian Fenwick

STEVENSON, ROBERT LOUIS (1850–1894).

Robert Louis Stevenson was born in Edinburgh, Scotland, in 1850. Afflicted by illness for much of his childhood, Stevenson attended a number of schools before he enrolled at the University of Edinburgh (1867–1872) at the age of 16. His father wished him to train as an engineer (like himself), but he switched courses to study law. Despite a reputation for truancy (McLynn, 38–39), Stevenson passed the preliminary examination for the Scottish Bar in 1872 and spent three months as a law clerk later that year.

Biographer Frank McLynn says of Stevenson that "unkind critics have sometimes suggested that the adult RLS was not a particularly well-read man, but the range and breadth of his undergraduate reading compels astonishment. He worked his way through **Carlyle**, **Ruskin**, **Browning** and **Tennyson**, reread *Pilgrim's Progress* and the New Testament, especially his favourite Gospel according to St. Matthew, devoured Penn's aphorisms, Montaigne's essays, **Wordsworth**'s poetry, **Herbert Spencer**'s multifarious output and Mitford's *Tales of Old Japan*" (41). He goes on to say that "it is impossible to read Stevenson without becoming aware of his workship of Shakespeare: he made an early start with *Macbeth*, which his mother read to him in the nursery (taking care to omit the porter's speech), then into early adulthood he conceived a love for *As You Like It* which never died, *Hamlet* was another influence, and *Lear*, where 'Kent's speech over the dying Lear had a great effect on my mind' " (41; see also Bevan, 100; Daiches, 18). When Stevenson came to write *Treasure Island*, "major influences include **Washington Irving**'s *Tales of a Traveller*, Defoe's *Robinson Crusoe*, Captain Johnson's *History of Notorious Pirates*, Kingsley's *At Last* (from which he got the name of the Dead Man's Chest), **Poe**'s short story 'The Gold Bug' and **Fenimore Cooper**'s *The Sea Lions*" (McLynn, 199). Biographer Ian Bell says that "his literary diet does not tell us so very much about the writer he was to become but the voracity is revealing, that and the mixture of headlong narrative tempered with the pointed moralities of essayists. His fiction would reveal the depth of his training" (69).

ARCHIVES

Robert Louis Stevenson's papers are included in a number of library collections: the Stevenson House at Monterey, California; the Beinecke Library at Yale University; the Silverado Museum in Saint Helena, California; the Pierpont Morgan Library in New York; the Widener Library at Harvard University; the Edinburgh Public Library; and the Huntington Library in San Marino, California.

PRINTED SOURCES

Bell, Ian. *Robert Louis Stevenson: Dreams of Exile* (Edinburgh: Mainstream Publishing, 1992).
Bevan, Bryan. *Robert Louis Stevenson: Poet and Teller of Tales* (London: Rubicon Press, 1993).
Daiches, David. *Robert Louis Stevenson and His World* (London: Thames and Hudson, 1973).
Dark, Sidney. *Robert Louis Stevenson* (New York: Haskell House Publishers Ltd., 1971).
McLynn, Frank. *Robert Louis Stevenson: A Biography* (London: Hutchinson, 1993).
Noble, Andrew (ed.). *Robert Louis Stevenson* (London: Vision Press Limited, 1983).

Sandra Hannaford

STIRNER, MAX (1806–1856). Max Stirner was born as Johann Kaspar Schmidt in Bayreuth, Germany, in 1806. He studied philosophy under Georg Andreas Gabler at the Imhof Gymnasium (1819–1826), philosophy under **Georg Wilhelm Friedrich Hegel**, and theology under Philipp Konrad Marheineke, **Friedrich Schleiermacher**, and Johann August Wilhelm Neander at Berlin

(1826–1828); then philosophy under Christian Kapp at Erlangen (1828–1829) and Karl Ludwig Michelet at Berlin (1832–1833). He lived thereafter in Berlin, teaching at various secondary schools, notably Madame Gropius's school for girls. His radical individualist polemic *Der Einzige und sein Eigentum* (1844–1845), scorned by his own Young Hegelian circle, remained almost unread until anarchists such as James L. Walker, John Henry Mackay, Benjamin R. Tucker, and Steven T. Byington rediscovered it in the last two decades of the nineteenth century, especially after they became familiar with Eduard von Hartmann's 1869 criticism of it. Its second German edition appeared in 1882, and Tucker published Byington's English translation in 1907. It has been a mainstay of Western anarchist thought ever since.

Stirner admired **Johann Wolfgang von Goethe**, thought enough of Adam Smith and Jean-Baptiste Say to prepare standard German translations of their major works, and enough of **Pierre-Joseph Proudhon** to make his influence obvious throughout *Der Einzige und sein Eigentum*. Yet his greatest ideological and literary influences were his personal acquaintances, especially Hegelians. **Ludwig Feuerbach** was his fellow student at Erlangen. In the 1830s he became a lifelong friend of **Bruno Bauer** and in 1841 a prominent member of *Die Freien*, the notorious fraternity of Left Hegelians who met at Hippels Weinstube, a rowdy bar in Berlin. Among these "Free Ones" were Arnold Ruge, Bruno and Edgar Bauer, the publisher Otto Wigand, and **Friedrich Engels**. Stirner stayed aloof from their brawls but absorbed their philosophical and political arguments. After 1845 he found himself alienated from *Die Freien* and lampooned by intimates of that group such as Karl Schmidt in *Das Verstandestum und das Individuum* and *Liebesbriefe ohne Liebe* (both 1846) and **Karl Marx** and Engels in *Die deutsche Ideologie* (written 1845–1846, not published until 1932). He soon had neither supporters nor enemies and was simply forgotten.

ARCHIVES

No substantial archival sources known to exist, but some material may be located at Gosudarstvennaia Obshchestvenno-Politicheskaia Biblioteka, Moscow.

PRINTED SOURCES

Brazill, William J. *The Young Hegelians* (New Haven, Conn.: Yale University Press, 1970).

Emge, Karl August. *Max Stirner, eine geistig nicht bewältige Tendenz* (Wiesbaden: Steiner, 1964).

Helms, Hans G. *Die Ideologie der anonymen Gesellschaft* (Köln: Du Mont, 1966).

Löwith, Karl. *Von Hegel zu Nietzsche* (Zurich: Europa, 1941).

Mackay, John Henry. *Max Stirner: Sein Leben und sein Werk* (Berlin-Charlottenburg: Selbstverlag, 1898, 1910, 1914).

Mautz, Kurt Adolf. *Die Philosophie Max Stirners im Gegensatz zum hegelschen Idealismus* (Berlin: Junker & Dünnhaupt, 1936).

Paterson, Ronald William Keith. *The Nihilistic Egoist: Max Stirner* (London: Oxford University Press, 1971).

Stepelevich, Lawrence S. "The First Hegelians: An Introduction," *Philosophical Forum*, 8 (1978), 6–23.

———. "Max Stirner as Hegelian," *Journal of the History of Ideas*, 46 (1985), 597–614.

Eric v. d. Luft

STOWE, HARRIET BEECHER (1811–1896). Harriet Beecher Stowe, U.S. author, was born in Litchfield, Connecticut, in 1811 and educated at her parents' home; the home of her maternal grandmother in Guilford, Connecticut; the Litchfield Female Academy (1819–1824); and the Hartford Female Seminary (where she also served as a teacher) (1824–1827). Her father, Lyman Beecher, was among the leading Congregationalist ministers of the period, as well as a leader of the early temperance movement. Her sister, Catharine Beecher, established several female academies (including the one in Hartford) and promoted women's education and influence in American society. Questioning the Calvinist faith in which she had been raised and twice experienced conversion, Stowe by the 1850s "replaced perfectionist strivings with the imitation of Christ," a new doctrine that strongly influenced her most famous novel (Hedrick, 156). *Uncle Tom's Cabin* (1852), the best-selling American book of the nineteenth century, helped awaken Americans (as well as millions of English readers) to the horrors of Southern slavery. After the Civil War, Stowe's nostalgic novels about old New England life became early exemplars of American regionalist literature.

The books that Stowe read, or heard read aloud, as a child included religious works (the Bible as well as tracts of polemical divinity), early religious histories of New England (notably Cotton Mather's *Magnalia Christi Americana*), the didactic stories of Maria Edgeworth, Bunyan's *Pilgrim's Progress*, and the novels of **Walter Scott**. Living in Cincinnati in the 1830s and 1840s, she published, and presumably read, in a wide array of magazines: the *Western Monthly Magazine*, the *New-York Evangelist*, *Godey's Lady's Book*. From this variety Stowe honed the different rhetorics and literary devices she would employ in *Uncle Tom's Cabin*: the use of dialect, found in Scott but also in sketches of western life and customs; an ideology in which Christian and female influence were the most potent antagonists to societal sin and a market-driven culture; sentimental language designed to elicit reader's emotional response. **Charles Dickens**'s work also influenced her: In an 1843 article she praised it for addressing "the whole class of the oppressed, the neglected, and forgotten, the sinning and suffering," even though she criticized his flippancy toward religion ("Epidemics," qtd. in Hedrick, 156). Stowe also read antislavery literature, including slave narratives and Theodore Weld's *American Slavery as It Is* (1839), from which she drew numerous details for *Uncle Tom's Cabin*. In *The Key to Uncle Tom's Cabin* (1854), Stowe documented the factual basis for events and arguments in the novel; however, she likely had not read all the materials cited in *The Key* (including several antislavery newspapers and Southern legal codes) before writing *Uncle Tom's Cabin*.

ARCHIVES

Stowe-Day Library, Hartford, Connecticut.
Beecher-Stowe Collection, Schlesinger Library on the History of Women in America, Radcliffe College, Cambridge, Massachussetts.

PRINTED SOURCES

Hedrick, Joan D. *Harriet Beecher Stowe: A Life* (New York: Oxford University Press, 1994).
Kirkham, E. Bruce. *The Building of Uncle Tom's Cabin* (Knoxville: University of Tennessee Press, 1977).
Stowe, Harriet Beecher. *The Key to Uncle Tom's Cabin* (Boston: John P. Jewett and Company, 1854).
———. "Literary Epidemics—No. 2," *New York Evangelist*, 14 (July 13, 1843), 109.

Scott E. Casper

STRAUSS, DAVID FRIEDRICH (1808–1874). David Friedrich Strauss was born in Ludwigsburg, Swabia, in 1808. He studied Latin, Greek, and Hebrew at Ludwigsburg until 1821 and theology under Friedrich Kern and Ferdinand Christian Baur, first at Blaubeuren (1821–1825), then at Tübingen (1825–1830). He studied philosophy under **Georg Wilhelm Friedrich Hegel** and theology under **Friedrich Schleiermacher** and Philipp Konrad Marheineke at Berlin (1831–1832). After serving as the Lutheran curate at Klein-Ingersheim, Swabia, in 1830–1831, he became tutor at Tübingen in 1832 but was immediately fired when the first volume of *Das Leben Jesu kritisch bearbeitet* appeared in 1835. Upon this monumental antisupernaturalist attempt to separate the mythical from the historical Jesus hangs his entire reputation. By the time the other volume appeared in 1836, it had already shocked the German theological community so effectively that it gave birth to the Young Hegelian movement, which scandalized German academia throughout the *Vormärz*. After failing to gain a professorship at Zurich in 1839, Strauss drifted from career to career, eventually becoming a popular biographer and author of many works now forgotten. Despite unrelenting attacks, such as **Friedrich Nietzsche**'s in *Unzeitgemässe Betrachtungen* (1873), the status of Strauss as the fountainhead of modern biblical criticism is secure, for neither Hermann Gunkel's nor Rudolf Bultmann's work would have been possible without his.

At Tübingen, mostly under the guidance of Carl August Eschenmayer, Strauss absorbed the romanticism of Eduard Mörike, **Friedrich Wilhelm Joseph von Schelling**, Friedrich Heinrich Jacobi, Johann Uhland, and Ludwig Tieck and the mysticism of Jakob Böhme, Franz von Baader, and Andreas Justinus Kerner. Baur aimed Strauss toward Schleiermacher, but Strauss gravitated toward Hegel.

What most frightened contemporary scholars about *Das Leben Jesu* was that both its attackers and its defenders agreed that it was not the contrivance of Strauss alone but the logical consequence of centuries of philosophy, culminating in the then-dominant system of Hegel, and theology, such as the work of

Johann Gottfried Eichhorn, Heinrich Eberhard Gottlob Paulus, Wilhelm Martin Leberecht De Wette, Karl Gottlieb Bretschneider, Baur, and Schleiermacher, as well as the new scientific methods of historical exegesis pioneered by Barthold Georg Niebuhr and **Leopold von Ranke**, championed by Baur.

ARCHIVES

Schiller Museum, Marbach, Germany. Correspondence, papers.

PRINTED SOURCES

Brazill, William J. *The Young Hegelians* (New Haven, Conn.: Yale University Press, 1970).
Cromwell, Richard S. *David Friedrich Strauss and His Place in Modern Thought* (Fairlawn, N.J.: Burdick, 1974).
Gelzer, Heinrich. *Die straussischen Zerwürfnisse in Zürich von 1839* (Hamburg: Perthes, 1843).
Harris, Horton. *David Friedrich Strauss and His Theology* (Cambridge: Cambridge University Press, 1973).
Hausrath, Adolph. *David Friedrich Strauss und die Theologie seiner Zeit* (Heidelberg: Bassermann, 1876–1878).
Massey, Marilyn Chapin. *Christ Unmasked: The Meaning of "The Life of Jesus" in German Politics* (Chapel Hill: University of North Carolina Press, 1983).
Sandberger, Jörg F. *David Friedrich Strauss als theologischer Hegelianer* (Göttingen: Vandenhoeck & Ruprecht, 1972).
Toews, John Edward. *Hegelianism: The Path toward Dialectical Humanism, 1805–1841* (Cambridge: Cambridge University Press, 1980).
Zeller, Eduard. *David Friedrich Strauss in seinem Leben und seinen Schriften* (Bonn: Emil Strauss, 1874).

Eric v. d. Luft

STRINDBERG, (JOHAN) AUGUST (1849–1912). August Strindberg was born in Stockholm in 1849. From an early age, he suffered from the effects of the social inequality between his parents (his mother was a maidservant who married tardily a middle-class man). This had heavy psychological consequences (his autobiography had the cynical title *The Son of a Servant*, 1886) and was reflected in his artistic development by a burning misogyny.

He studied in Uppsala, where he attended discontinuously lectures of philology and medicine, and between 1874 and 1879 he worked as assistant librarian in the Royal Library of Stockholm. From 1883 to 1889 lived in France, Switzerland, Bavaria, and Denmark.

French naturalism and positivism influenced his first literary works: In *The Red Room* (1879), he describes realistically the intellectual circles of Stockholm, with their vices and their weaknesses. His misogyny becomes particularly evident in *A Madman's Defense*, where the idealized woman is degraded to a vampire who spiritually destroys the man. Similar ideas and feelings are to be found also in theatrical works that gave him European fame (*The Father*, 1887; *Comrades*, 1888; *Miss Julie*, 1888; *Creditos*, 1889). The core of these dramas is the elemental struggle between man and woman. To the same period belongs the novel *The Natives of Hemsö* (1888), considered as Strindberg's narrative masterpiece. In it Strindberg overcomes the objectivity derived from **Émile Zola** in favor of a naturalism brought to its tragic consequences.

A further evolution of Strindberg's poetics occurred after the correspondence with **Friedrich Nietzsche**. With the plays *Pariah* (1889) and *Simoon* (1889), and the novel *By the Open Sea* (1890), Strindberg employed the philosophy of superman. The failure of his second marriage opened a deep crisis that became evident in *Inferno* (1897) and *Legends* (1897–1898). Swedenborg's theosophy helped him regain his balance and allowed him to return to the dramaturgical activity with *To Damascus* (1898–1901) and *A Dreamplay* (1902), where he tried "to imitate the inconsequent yet transparently logical shape of a dream" where time and place do not exist and everything is possible and probable. In *Advent* (1989), *Crimes and Crimes* (1899), and *Easter* (1901) the desire to find in the Catholic religion a safe refuge is evident. But it is a particular kind of Catholicism, far from the Church's rules and characterized by a distressful need of God. At the same time, Strindberg renews the theatrical structures according to the new expressionistic and symbolistic tendencies. The last years of his tormented life saw a return to the socialism of his youth and, after the foundation of the *Intimate Theatre*, a return to the Protestant faith and to a rural socialism, where peasants are viewed as the makers of the wealth.

ARCHIVES

Royal Library of Stockholm.

PRINTED SOURCES

Lagercrantz, O. *August Strindberg* (Stockholm: Wahlstrom & Widstrand, 1983). Contains an extensive bibliography.

Morgan, M. *Strindberg: A Biography* (Basingstoke: Mcmillan, 1985).

Rapp, E. H. "Strindberg's Reception in England and America," *Scandinavian Studies*, 23 (1951).

Robinson, M. (ed.). *Strindberg and Genre* (Norwich: Norvik Press, 1991).

Steene, B. *August Strindberg: An Introduction to His Major Works* (Stockholm/Atlantic Highlands: Almqvist & Wiksell International, 1982).

———— (ed.). *Strindberg and History* (Stockholm: Almqvist & Wiksell, 1992).

Maria Tabaglio

SUTTNER, BERTHA VON (1843–1914). Bertha von Suttner was born in Prague in 1843 and educated privately. She was raised as a Roman Catholic and later declared herself a freethinker. She earned her income from journalism and novels but was best known as a pacifist and author of the antiwar novel *Die Waffen Nieder!* Her friendship with **Alfred Nobel** led to the inclusion in his will of a prize for peace alongside those of physics, chemistry, medicine, and literature. Suttner received the peace prize herself in 1905.

Die Waffen Nieder! was published in 1889 and within two years was translated into eight European languages. It was compared to **Harriet Beecher Stowe**'s *Uncle Tom's Cabin* by writers such as **Leo Tolstoy** (Suttner, *Memoirs*, 1:343) and was expected to do for war what Stowe's novel had done for slavery. Suttner's readings of **Charles Darwin**, Ernst Haeckel, and **Herbert Spencer** and, above all, her interpretation of Henry Thomas Buckle's *History of Civilization in England* were the foundation for much of her work and featured prominently in *Die Waffen Nieder!*

Suttner's connection with Nobel began in 1876, when she spent a brief period as his secretary. The pair met only twice more, although they corresponded regularly for 20 years. Nobel expressed an interest in balance of power theories, in which the mutual possession of weapons of mass destruction was expected to prevent war. Suttner's interest was in the peace movement, particularly propaganda campaigns. She tried for many years to convince Nobel to become publicly involved in the popular peace movement, but he contributed in a financial sense only. However, Suttner's preference for popular movements as against governmental agreements was recognized by Nobel in his stipulation of the terms for the peace prize, that it should be given to "the man or woman who had made the greatest contribution to the brotherhood of mankind, the reduction of armies, and the promotion of peace congresses" (Hamann, 199).

Suttner's position as an aristocratic woman in a military nation who was prepared to promote pacifist, humanitarian, and Darwinian ideas played a significant part in the transformation of Austro-Hungarian and German attitudes to the popular peace movement.

ARCHIVES

Bertha von Suttner Collection, Suttner-Fried Papers, League of Nations Archives, United Nations Library, Geneva, Switzerland. Principal pacifist correspondence.

PRINTED SOURCES

Abrams, I. "Bertha von Suttner and the Nobel Peace Prize," *Journal of Central European Affairs*, 22 (1962), 286–307. Examination of Suttner's influence on Nobel and the terms of his will.

Braker, R. "Bertha von Suttner as Author: The Harriet Beecher Stowe of the Peace Movement," *Peace and Change*, 16, 1 (1991), 74–96. Comparative discussion of *Die Waffen Nieder!* and *Uncle Tom's Cabin.*

Hamann, B. *Bertha Von Suttner: A Life for Peace*, A. Dubsky (trans.) (New York: Syracuse University Press, 1996). Comprehensive biography.

Kempf, B. *Suffragette for Peace: The Life of Bertha von Suttner*, R. W. Last (trans.) (London: Oswald Wolff, 1972). Short biography with extracts from her writings and full bibliography.

von Suttner, Bertha, *Die Waffen Nieder!* (Dresden, 1889); English trans., *Ground Arms!* (Chicago: A. C. McClurg and Co., 1892); reissued as *Lay Down Your Arms* (New York: Garland, 1971).

———. *Memoirs of Bertha von Suttner: the Records of an Eventful Life*, 2 vols. (London and Boston: Ginn and Company, 1910).

Heloise Brown

T

TAINE, HIPPOLYTE-ADOLPHE (1828–1893). Hippolyte Taine was born in Vouziers, in the Ardennes, in 1828 and educated at the Lycée Bourbon in Paris (1838—1848) and at the École Normale Supérieure (1848–1851). His life was full of contradictions. He was the best student at the École Normale, but he failed both his doctorate and the Agregation exam in 1851. Although he claimed to be a pagan, he had a Protestant funeral according to his will. He was the leading exponent of scientific approaches to art and an inescapable figure of French criticism at the end of the nineteenth century.

He was a hardworking child who learned English with his grandfather and read eagerly French and classical literature. A sensitive young man, he found comfort in the works of his "masters": Spinoza, Marcus-Aurelius, **Goethe**, Aristotle, **Hegel**, and Etienne Bonnot de Condillac were at the core of his philosophical thought, while his admiration for **Stendhal** decided the "psychological criticism" he would use in his literary essays. After his academic failures, followed by disgraceful positions at French provincial schools, he severely criticized the official philosophy prevailing in French universities—especially Victor Cousin's eclectism—in *Les Philosophes Français du Dix-Neuvième Siècle* (1857).

The question of Taine's positivism must be treated with caution. Apparently Taine did not read **Auguste Comte** until 1860, and he later criticized him as "one of the worst of all bad writers" (Chevrillon, 226). His relation to **John Stuart Mill** is also complex, as he rejected Mill's concept of cause in *Le Positivisme Anglais*, an essay forming the fifth book of his masterpiece *Histoire de la Littérature Anglaise* (1863–1864). Just as Madame **de Staël** did for Germany, he described the English character as revealed through its literary history. Taine was glad to find in English literature "the madness and genius of imagination" that was lacking in the French spirit. In the preface, he established a determinism based on the famous triad: race, milieu, moment. He explained that "behind all, we have men who arrange words and imagery according to the necessities of their organs and the original bent of their intellects." This method was reasserted in *Introduction à l'Etude de l'Histoire Expérimentale*, published a few months after Claude Bernard's *Introduction à l'Etude de la Médecine Expérimentale* (1866): "the historian will be allowed to act like a naturalist, I was in front of my subject as in front of the metamorphosis of an insect." In his *Origines de la France Contemporaine* (1875–1893), a violent critique of the French Revolution and the subsequent political state, he blended a naturalistic reconstruction of the past reminiscent of **Walter Scott**'s novels with a style borrowed from Augustin Thierry and **Jules Michelet**.

ARCHIVES

Bibliothèque Nationale de France-Richelieu.

PRINTED SOURCES

Chevrillon, A. *Taine: Essai sur la Formation de sa Pensée* (Paris: Plon, 1932).
Léger, F. *Monsieur Taine* (Paris: Critérion-Histoire, 1993).
Nordman, J. *Taine et la critique scientifique* (Paris: Presses universitaires de France, 1992).
Rosca, D.D. *L'Influence de Hegel sur Taine Philosophe de l'Art et de la Connaissance* (Paris: J. Gaumier, 1928).
Seys, P. *Hippolyte Taine et l'Avènement du Nationalisme* (Paris: L'Harmattan, 1999).

Thierry Vourdon

TAYLOR, FREDERICK WINSLOW (1856–1915). Frederick Taylor, the "father of scientific management," was born of ancestral Quaker stock in Philadelphia's suburban Germantown. After his mother was read out of meeting, she turned to Unitarianism, and his father, though remaining a Quaker, stopped attending services, while their grown son became an agnostic. Before his death, Taylor held nearly a hundred patents and had worked out a process still in use to more than double the capacity of tool steel to cut metal; but it is his management innovations designed to increase production through the rational analysis of work that continue to pervade most aspects of twentieth-century life, even after the man himself has been largely forgotten and the specifics of many of his theories have been abandoned.

Taylor's earliest education was by his mother, followed by three years in various schools during his adolescent years while the family toured Europe. Travel enabled him to perfect both French and German, and he read widely during these years in French and English fiction—a practice he repudiated later as frivolous. It was at Phillips Exeter Academy (1872–1874), where he prepared for Harvard, that he got the first germ of what later would be his famous time-motion study. There the mathematics teacher George A. Wentworth surreptitiously timed the boys as they did problems, then worked out assignments for each boy to extract from him his best effort in the time allotted.

Uncorrected astigmatism was giving Taylor such debilitating headaches while he studied to be first in his class at Exeter that he reluctantly agreed with his parents to give up Harvard and a law career. Instead, he began a series of manual labor jobs in factories owned by family friends. Once he had risen to a foreman's position at Midvale Steel Works, he wanted the authority conferred by academic achievement and—again in part through family influence—managed to graduate from Stevens Institute of Technology in 1883 without actually attending classes there, though he did cover the curriculum through rigorous self-study and he passed the required examinations.

While reading determined the course of Taylor's life—or more precisely his belief that he had to do less of it—few specific titles can be documented as crucial to his development. As far as we know, once he reached maturity, his reading was largely confined to technical materials, which he pursued in three languages. Taylor wrote that he collected "what information could be had that was written and published on what constituted a day's work" (Kanigel, 203) when he formulated such incentives as his graduated piecework scale. He was equipped to find inspiration in the writings of such theorists as Hermann von Helmholtz, who studied the conservation of energy, and such experimenters as Étienne Marey, who analyzed motion by making stop-action serial photographs against a black screen.

ARCHIVES

Frederick Winslow Taylor Collection, Stevens Institute of Technology, Hoboken, New Jersey.

PRINTED SOURCES

Copley, Frank Barkley. *Frederick W. Taylor, Father of Scientific Management*, 2 vols. (New York: Harper & Bros., 1923).

Hayward, Elizabeth Gardner. *A Classified Guide to the Frederick Winslow Taylor Collection* (Hoboken, N.J.: Stevens Institute of Technology, 1951).

Kakar, Sudhir. *Frederick Taylor: A Study in Personality and Innovation* (Cambridge, Mass.: MIT Press, 1970).

Kanigel, Robert. *The One Best Way: Frederick Winslow Taylor and the Enigma of Efficiency* (New York: Viking, 1997).

Nelson, Daniel. *Frederick W. Taylor and the Rise of Scientific Management* (Madison: University of Wisconsin Press, 1980).

Wrege, Charles D. *Frederick W. Taylor, the Father of Scientific Management: Myth and Reality* (Homewood, Ill.: Business One Irwin, 1991).

Charles Boewe

TENNYSON, ALFRED (1809–1892). Alfred Tennyson, Baron Tennyson of Aldworth and Freshwater, was born in Somersby, Lincolnshire, in 1809 and acquired his formal education at Louth Grammar School (1816–1820) and at Trinity College, Cambridge (1828–1831), though he left without taking a degree. His most important education, however, derived from the tutoring he received from his father, the Reverend George Clayton Tennyson, and from his own reading in his father's 2,500-volume library. In addition to theology, philosophy, and history, there were significant classical, oriental, and scientific volumes that profoundly influenced young Alfred (Martin, 19). His mother, Elizabeth Fytche Tennyson, was the daughter of a vicar and a deeply religious woman with strong evangelical leanings whose piety had a significant impact on her son. No other poet in English literature has become so closely identified with his age or had a more pervasive influence on it than Tennyson. Yet probably no other poet in English literature has seen his reputation vary as much as Tennyson's. Compared favorably with Shakespeare in his own day, the succeeding generation devalued him significantly until a more proper balance was restored after World War II. He is generally recognized today as the most important poet of the Victorian era and one of the greatest lyric poets in English literature.

From his earliest poems and plays as a boy, Tennyson demonstrated a remarkable facility to absorb and reflect the works of the classical and English writers he had encountered in his father's rich library. While all poets are influenced by their youthful readings, "not many recapitulate the entire history of English poetry" as did young Alfred (Culler, 9). Tennyson's mature work is rife with allusions to his favorite readings: In the scrupulously annotated Christopher Ricks edition of *The Poems of Tennyson*, there are 272 allusions to the Bible, 213 to Milton, 155 to Shakespeare, 129 to **Shelley**, 86 to **Keats**, 57 to Horace, 47 to Malory, 44 to Virgil, 38 to Lucretius, and 37 to Homer (Shaw, 27). While stylistic and idealogic influences are more problematic to trace, clearly Tennyson was strongly influenced by a variety of writers from the classical through the Romantic periods. Poems such as "Tithonus," "Lucretius," "The Hesperides," and "To Virgil" reveal important classical influences ranging from Homer, Lucretius, and Catullus to Horace, Ovid, and Virgil (Mustard). Clearly, his strongest kinship with a classical source—and one of the dominant influences on Tennyson—was with Virgil (Bush, 226–227). As a child in his father's library reading Thomas Malory, Alfred conceived the image of King Arthur that was to lead him to *The Idylls of the King* (Martin, 36). Strong Elizabethan influences predictably include Edmund Spenser and William Shakespeare, though the stronger—indeed, perhaps *the* strongest poetic—influence on his career was John Milton. Neoclassicist Alexander Pope exerted influence on Tennyson through his classical translations as well as his poetry. The strongest Romantic influence on Tennyson was John Keats, though as a youth he was strongly attracted to **Percy Bysshe Shelley**, **Walter Scott** and **Lord Byron**.

Tennyson was also influenced by minor writings such as Alexander Smith's *A Life Drama* (1853) and Sydney Dobell's *Balder* (1854). Products of the "Spasmodic School" of poetry, Smith and Dobell significantly influenced Tennyson's technique in *Maud* (Marshall, 129). Among Tennyson's more exotic interests were his readings in Eastern ideas and literature that influenced poems from "Timbuctoo" to "Akbar's Dream." He read *The Arabian Nights* in translation and consulted sources such as Alfred Lyell's *Asiatic Studies* and Abul Fazl's *Akbar-Nama*, (Marshall, 245). From childhood, Tennyson was an avid student of science, and "Locksley Hall," "Lucretius," and *In Memoriam* reflect his knowledge of scientific ideas. Among his scientific readings were **Charles Ly-ell**'s *Principles of Geology* (1830–1833), J.F.W. Herschel's *A Preliminary Discourse on the Study of Natural Philosophy* (1830), and Robert Chambers's *Vestiges of the Natural History of Creation* (1844).

Tennyson papers and other primary materials are spread among a number of major academic institutions including Trinity College, Cambridge; the Houghton Library, Harvard; the Beinecke Library, Yale; and the Perkins Library, Duke; as well as the British Library. The most important concentrations of materials, however, are in Lincoln, England, at the Tennyson Research Centre and the Lincolnshire Archives Office.

ARCHIVES

Tennyson Research Centre, Lincoln, England.

PRINTED SOURCES

Bush, Douglas. *Mythology and the Romantic Tradition in English Poetry* (Cambridge, Mass.: Harvard University Press, 1936).

Campbell, Nancie. *Tennyson in Lincoln: A Catalogue of the Collections in the Research Centre* (Lincoln, United Kingdom: Tennyson Research Centre, 1971–1973). Contains a list of books owned by Alfred, his father, and others in the Tennyson family.

Chatterjee, Kalika Ranjan. *Studies in Tennyson as a Poet of Science* (New Delhi: S. Chand, 1974).

Culler, A. Dwight. *The Poetry of Tennyson* (New Haven, Conn.: Yale University Press, 1977).

Marshall, George O., Jr. *A Tennyson Handbook* (New York: Twayne Publishers, 1963).

Martin, Robert Bernard. *Tennyson: The Unquiet Heart* (New York: Oxford University Press, 1980).

Mustard, Wilfred P. *Classical Echoes in Tennyson* (New York: Macmillan, 1904).

Shaw, W. David. *Tennyson's Style* (Ithaca, N.Y.: Cornell University Press, 1976).

Tennyson, Alfred. *The Poems of Tennyson*, Christopher B. Ricks (ed.) (London: Longman's, 1969; 2nd ed., 1987).

W. Craig Turner

THACKERAY, WILLIAM MAKEPEACE (1811–1863). William Makepeace Thackeray was born in 1811 in Calcutta, where his father was an administrator with the Board of Revenue. He was sent to England for schooling at the age of five, upon the death of his father, and was later joined there by his mother and stepfather. He was educated at Charterhouse, London (1822–1828) and matriculated at Trinity College, Cambridge, early in 1829, leaving after the spring term of 1830 without taking a degree. Apart from his formal education, he enjoyed a *lehrjahre* (year of study) in Weimar (1830–1831), where he met **Goethe**. Subsequently he entered the École des Beaux-Artes and trained at ateliers in Paris (1833–1837) with the intention of becoming an artist (recalled in *The Newcomes*), eventually settling as an illustrator, notably of many of his own books. The most cosmopolitan of novelists, his numerous travels, encompassing the Continent, the Middle East, and the United States, also contributed to his *bildung* and made his books—novels, satires, travelogues, criticism, historical lectures—a series of cross-cultural studies.

Two years before he was established among the larger reading public with *Vanity Fair* (1847), Thackeray, then a struggling journalist, presented his credentials to Thomas Longman, editor of the *Edinburgh Review*, as a potential contributor on "light matters connected with Art, humorous reviews, critiques of novels," as well as articles on "French subjects, memoirs, poetry, history from Louis XV downwards, and of an earlier period . . . German light literature and poetry . . . finally subjects relating to society in general where a writer may be allowed to display the humourous ego, or a victim to be gently immolated" (*Letters*, ed. Ray, 2:190–191). Brash as these words may sound, Thackeray was indeed one of the most versatile literary men of his age.

His dismissal of himself as having "no head above my eyes" concealed an acute, penetrating mind, but one disposed more toward concrete things than abstract ideas. As art critic, sketcher, and illustrator, he consistently promoted genre painting (the "true pathetic") as against the academic "Davido-historico-classical" school he had been trained in, which he dubbed the "sham-sublime." As a student of civilization and manners, he was drawn more to "trivial fond records"—letters, diaries, personal memoirs—than to "stately tomes" of history. Among historians, he was most influenced, notably in *Henry Esmond* and *The Four Georges*, by **Macaulay**, who stressed lively characterization and graphic pictures of social life.

The classical education that young Thackeray was subjected to (vid., his semi-autobiographical novel *Pendennis*), much as he chafed under it at the time, pervades his writings. In *Vanity Fair* he quotes from the *Eton Latin Grammar*, also in use at Charterhouse, and his fiction and nonfiction alike are replete with Latin tags, notably from Horace, Virgil, Ovid, and Cicero. Among Greek writers, Homer looms most prominently, and on record is his borrowing from the London Library of the works of Plato. Under the influence of his evangelical mother, he steeped himself in the Bible—Old Testament and New Testament—the most quoted sources in his own books (Harden). When it comes to modern writers, his ability to make the Augustan period his own—particularly in *Henry Esmond* and *The Virginians*—can be attributed to the successful course of lectures (published as *English Humorists of the Eighteenth Century*) that he delivered in England, Scotland, and America from 1853 through 1856.

Fundamentally, however, Thackeray's main affinity was with "French subjects." To an American friend he named the introspective Montaigne among his "bed books" (Wilson, 1:217), a favorite writer also of Henry Esmond and Frederick Lovel (hero of one of Thackeray's last novels, *Lovel the Widower*). The *Essais* of Montaigne inform the style and content of the meditative, retrospective Roundabout Papers that Thackeray composed for the *Cornhill Magazine* that he edited during his final years.

Among his "critiques of novels" were several by Charles de Bernard, a disciple of **Balzac**, and a personal favorite of Thackeray. In his own fiction he can be said to have wedded the French *études des moeurs* to the society novels (so-called silver-forks) of Catherine Gore and **Edward Bulwer-Lytton**. For his last work of fiction, the uncompleted adventure story *Denis Duval*, Thackeray went back to **Dumas**, a boyhood favorite.

The general tone and moral outlook of Thackeray's novels bear the impress of *Eclecticisme*, the system of thought of the philosopher–educator Victor Cousin, whose lectures inspired Thackeray as an art student in Paris (*Letters*, ed. Ray, 1:225). Cousin's *Cours d l'histoire de la philosophie* (1829), which espoused a "universal sympathy" for humankind, along with tolerance of error, and conceived of the task of the philosopher as the reconciliation of conflicting positions, goes far to account for the moral relativism and qualified skepticism of Thackeray's fiction, along with his disposition to view life through a series of sliding lenses.

ARCHIVES

"Thackeray's Manuscripts: A Preliminary Census of Library Locations," by Robert A. Colby and John Sutherland. *Costerus*, n.s., 2 (1974), 33–57; "Appendix: The Robert H. Taylor Collection [Princeton]," by Thomas V. Lange, 358–359. This census is supplemented intermittently in *The Thackeray Newsletter*, Peter L. Shillingsburg (ed.), Lamar University, Beaumont, Tex.

PRINTED SOURCES

Colby, Robert A. *Thackeray's Canvass of Humanity: An Author and His Public* (Columbus: Ohio State University Press, 1979).

Harden, Edgar F. (ed.). *Annotations for the Selected Works of William Makepeace Thackeray*, 2 vols. (New York and London: Garland Publishing, 1990).

MacKay, Carol Hanbery, and Peter L. Shillingsburg (eds.). *The Two Thackerays. Anne Thackeray Ritchie's Centenary Biographical Introductions to the Works of William Makepeace Thackeray* (New York: AMS Press, 1988).

Ray, Gordon N. *Thackeray: The Age of Wisdom (1847–1863)* (New York: McGraw-Hill, 1958).

———. *Thackeray: The Uses of Adversity (1811–1846)* (New York: McGraw-Hill, 1955).

Thackeray, William Makepeace. *Contributions to the* Morning Chronicle, Gordon N. Ray (ed.) (Urbana: University of Illinois Press, 1955).

———. *Letters and Private Papers*, Gordon N. Ray (ed.), 4 vols. (Cambridge, Mass.: Harvard University Press, 1945–1946).

———. *Letters and Private Papers. A Supplement*, Edgar F. Harden (ed.), 2 vols. (New York and London: Garland Publishing, 1994).

Wilson, James Grant. *Thackeray in the United States*, 2 vols. (New York: Dodd, Mead, 1904).

Robert A. Colby

THIERS, LOUIS-ADOLPHE (1797–1877). Louis-Adolphe Thiers, a leading politician, historian, orator, and journalist, was born into an impoverished Marseilles family and educated at the Marseilles lycée (1809–1815) and the Law Faculty at Aix. His voluminous historical and political writings popularized conservative liberal ideas. He had a gift for pithy phrases and accessible arguments. But they were works of a politician and journalist that never approached the depth of his contemporaries **de Tocqueville** and **Guizot**, even though politically he was far more successful. He advocated a British-style constitutional monarchy as a journalist and then minister in the 1820s and 1830s but recognized after 1848 that only a republic could work as "the government that divides us least." During the 1860s, he led the liberal parliamentary opposition, demanding "necessary liberties." He came to power in February 1871, presided over the bloody repression of the Paris Commune, and as first president of the Third Republic (1871–1873) rallied voters to what he dubbed "the conservative republic." The historian François Furet has called him France's most important nineteenth-century politician because he "tamed the French Revolution."

He began writing "a complete corpus of rational philosophy" in his teens— a cherished but unrealized project throughout his life—inspired by Jean-Jacques Rousseau's *Savoyard Vicar's Profession of Faith*, and aiming to include "man, the universe and God" (Bibliothèque Thiers, TMS 556). Never devoutly Christian, he maintained the deist *spiritualisme* common during his youth, denouncing materialism and atheism. His revealing *Eloge de Vauvenargues* (1820) summed up that philosopher's message as "the more active [man] is, the more he fulfils his purpose" (Bury and Tombs, 5). He was a voracious reader who amassed a library of over 5,000 works. It is difficult to classify the range of influences that he digested and that caused him to claim expertise in many fields. They included books on geography, philosophy, art, architecture, economics, military science, astronomy, physics, biology, the classics, and of course, history. He identified with philosopher–statesmen such as Cicero, Machiavelli (whose bust adorned his study), and Montesquieu and was also influenced by the writings and conversation of contemporaries including the liberal politician Royer-Collard, the philosopher Victor Cousin, and his friend the historian François Mignet, whose determinism marked his own histories, which in turn colored his political views. His pioneering *Histoire de la Révolution Française* (1823) defended the Revolution as historically inevitable and on balance positive—the enduring liberal interpretation. After the 1848 revolution, Thiers wrote the best-selling *De la Propriété* 1848), defending economic liberalism against the socialism of **Pierre-Joseph Proudhon**. His *Histoire du Consulat et de l'Empire* (1845–1862) was critical but admiring of **Napoléon**, "the greatest human being since Caesar and Charlemagne" (20:710). His last years were spent drafting fragments of his work of philosophy, still reminiscent of the writings of Cousin half a century earlier.

ARCHIVES

Bibliothèque Thiers (Place Saint-Georges, Paris): Fonds Thiers, esp. MS 2 and 22 (inventories of library) 556 and 564 (notes from reading).
Bibliothèque Nationale, Papiers Thiers. Principal correspondence.

PRINTED SOURCES

Aulard, A. "Thiers historien de la Révolution française," *La Révolution Française*, 66 (June 1914), 492–520; 67 (July 1914), 5–29.

Baschet, R. "Thiers critique d'art: les salons de 1822 et 1824," *Les Amis de Saint François*, 12, 1 (1971), 11–18.

Bury, J.P.T., and R. P. Tombs. *Thiers 1797–1877: A Political Life* (London: Allen and Unwin, 1986).

Knibiehler, Yvonne. *Naissance des sciences humaines: Mignet et l'histoire philosophique du 19e siècle* (Paris Flammarion, 1973). On historiographical influences.

Mauguin, G. "Thiers et son histoire de la république de Florence," *Annales de l'Université de Grenoble*, 30, 2 (1918), 221–294.

Michaud, H. "L'exotisme de M. Thiers," *Annuaire-Bulletin de la Société de l'Histoire de France* (1976–1977), 157–163. On his art collecting.

Robert Tombs

THOREAU, HENRY DAVID (1817–1862). Henry David Thoreau was born in Concord, Massachusetts, in 1817 and educated at Concord Academy before graduating from Harvard University in 1837. These institutions trained the young Thoreau in the classical and Unitarian Christian traditions. In the succeeding years he developed interests in nature and travel writing, as well as the humanistic spiritual ideals later generations called Transcendentalism. His famous account of a two-year experiment in simple living, *Walden* (1854), has been both hailed by twentieth-century critics as the most significant literary expression of Transcendental philosophy and adopted by modern environmentalists as a manifesto for their movement. Thoreau achieved little success in his own era despite producing 20 volumes of writings. Yet the next century's readers secured his reputation as a pioneering naturalist, perceptive social critic, and original prose stylist, establishing his dictates to "simplify, simplify" and "live deliberately" as central tenets of American individualistic thought.

The Greek and Latin works at the core of the Harvard curriculum never ceased to influence Thoreau's literary imagination (Seybold, 17). Similarly, his early interest in the English poets of the fourteenth to seventeenth centuries continued into the 1840s (Sattelmeyer, 14). In particular, Sir Walter Raleigh impressed him as an ideal heroic model (Sattelmeyer, 34). In his final years of college, however, Thoreau ventured beyond the classics. Studying German with Orestes Brownson in 1836, he discovered **Johann Wolfgang von Goethe** and **Thomas Carlyle**; the latter also struck him as a literary hero after which to model himself (Sattelmeyer, 38). Equally influential were Brownson's own ideas about humanity's innate religious understanding and French eclectic philosopher Victor Cousin's theory of the individual's ability to discover truth independently (Sattelmeyer, 19–21). Already intrigued by these concepts, Thoreau was captivated during his senior year by the complementary thoughts he encountered in **Ralph Waldo Emerson**'s *Nature* (1836).

Emerson's profound impact on his younger colleague has been well documented in many accounts of their famous friendship. It was in Emerson's company and library that Thoreau continued his education after college, reading widely, discovering an interest in Eastern scriptures that would develop further when he encountered the *Bhagavat Geeta* in 1846 and attending meetings of the "Hedge Club"—later dubbed the Transcendental Club by outsiders—along with local intellectuals such as Bronson Alcott and **Margaret Fuller** (Richardson, 175).

As an adult Thoreau read almost no fiction, but the interest in native topics seen in his adolescent preference for novels by **Lydia Maria Child** and **James Fenimore Cooper** (Sattelmeyer, 24) is also reflected in his lifelong fascination with travel narratives. Books on travel were enormously popular in nineteenth-century America, and Thoreau read hundreds of them (Christie, 313–333). Such travel accounts, as well as community sketches modeled on Mary Russell Mitford's *Our Village* (1832–1836), and nature diaries like Susan Fenimore Cooper's *Rural Hours* (1850)—a work detailing both environmental facts and local customs—all impacted the structure and style of *Walden* (Buell 26, 405–406). Yet the blending of fact and opinion that characterized most of Thoreau's works was not unlike the natural history writing of his day. Thoreau studied texts—including those by **John James Audubon** and Thomas Wentworth Higginson—that intermingled scientific observations with anecdotal asides (Buell, 415). Like these naturalists, Thoreau was influenced by seasonal imagery both from literary works—such as Virgil's *Georgics* and William Howitt's *The Book of the Seasons* (1831) (Buell, 399–404)—and from scientific accounts by, among others, botanist Thomas Nuttal, natural historian **Louis Agassiz**, geologist **Charles Lyell**, naturalist **Charles Darwin** (Sattelmeyer, 10, 83–89), and explorer **Alexander von Humboldt** (Walls).

ARCHIVES

The main collections of Thoreau papers are held at New York City's Pierpont Morgan Library, as well as six other libraries listed and described in William L. Howarth's *The Literary Manuscripts of Henry David Thoreau* (Columbus: Ohio State University Press, 1974).

PRINTED SOURCES

Buell, Lawrence. "Nature's Genres: Environmental Nonfiction at the Time of Thoreau's Emergence." In *The Environmental Imagination* (Cambridge, Mass.: Belknap Press of Harvard University Press, 1995).

Cameron, Kenneth Walter. "Thoreau Discovers Emerson: A College Reading Record," *Bulletin of the New York Public Library*, 57, 7 (June 1953), 319–334.

———. *Transcendental Apprenticeship: Notes on Young Henry Thoreau's Reading* (Hartford, Conn.: Transcendental Books, 1976).

Christie, John Aldrich. *Thoreau as World Traveler* (New York: Columbia University Press, 1965). Bibliography of travel works Thoreau read.

Christy, Arthur F. *The Orient in American Transcendentalism* (New York: Columbia University Press, 1932). Standard discussion of Thoreau's interest in Eastern philosophy and literature.

Dassow Wall, Laura. *Seeing New Worlds: Henry David Thoreau and Nineteenth-Century Science* (Madison: University of Wisconsin Press, 1995). Points to the pivotal influence of Alexander von Humboldt.

Richardson, Robert D., Jr. *Henry Thoreau: A Life of the Mind* (Berkeley: University of California Press, 1986).

Sattelmeyer, Robert. *Thoreau's Reading: A Study in Intellectual History, with Bibliographical Catalogue* (Princeton, N.J.: Princeton University Press, 1988).

Seybold, Ethel. *Thoreau: The Quest for the Classics* (New Haven, Conn.: Yale University Press, 1951). Standard work on Thoreau's classical interests.

Whaling, Anne. "Studies in Thoreau's Reading of English Poetry and Prose, 1340–1660" (Ph.D. diss., Yale University, 1946).

Wilson, Lawrence. "The Influence of Early North American History and Legend on the Writing of Henry David Thoreau" (Ph.D. diss., Yale University, 1949).

Erika M. Kreger

TOCQUEVILLE, ALEXIS DE (1805–1859). Alexis (Charles-Henri-Maurice Clérel) de Tocqueville was born in Verneuil, France, in 1805 into a family of Norman aristocrats. His father, a loyal royalist prefect, was made a peer of France by Charles X in 1827. Tocqueville studied law in Paris, finishing his studies in 1826. He was then appointed an unpaid magistrate at the Versailles court of law in 1827. In 1831 he traveled to the United States with his friend Gustave de Beaumont to study the American penal system. His observations led to his masterpiece *Democracy in America* (1835–1840). Tocqueville became a member of the Académie Française in 1841 and served as cabinet minister in 1849. He published *The Old Regime and the Revolution* in 1856. Tocqueville died in Cannes on April 16, 1859.

Studies on Tocqueville have in recent years moved away from the biographical and the historical (except for French scholars who are apt to study Tocqueville as a historian of the French Revolution) and gravitated toward the theoretical and the philosophical. In writing the first volume of *Democracy in America*, Tocqueville read such authors as Thomas Jefferson, Alexander Hamilton, James Madison, and John Jay. Tocqueville was prescient in his ability to make global generalizations on the basis of the American experiment with democracy in the 1830s, as he reflected on the greatest problem in government, the relationship between liberty and order. Tocqueville came to the United States to observe democracy in action and borrowed freely from the commentaries of Joseph Story. Tocqueville received his understanding of European history from the lectures of **François Guizot** and never wrote anything without submitting his work to Louis de Kergolay. He was influenced by **John Stuart Mill**, Baron de Montesquieu, L. P. Conseil, and his lifetime friend Gustave de Beaumont. In the second volume of *Democracy in America*, scholars refer increasingly to the influence of Pascal's *Pensées*. They also note Tocqueville's indebtedness to Rousseau's understanding of history as found in the latter's *Discourse on Inequality*.

ARCHIVES

The Yale Tocqueville Collection at the Beinecke Rare Book and Manuscript Library, Yale University, New Haven, Connecticut.

PRINTED SOURCES

Commager, H. S. *Commager on Tocqueville* (Columbia and London: University of Missouri Press, 1993).

Corral, L. D. del. *El pensamiento politico de Tocqueville* (Madrid: Alianza Universidad, 1989).

Drescher, S. *Tocqueville and England* (Cambridge, Mass.: Harvard University Press, 1964).

Dumont, L. *Homo Hierarchicus: An Essay on the Caste System* (London: Weidenfeld and Nicholson, 1970).

Jardin, A. *Tocqueville: A Biography* (New York: Farrar, Straus, and Giroux, 1988).

Lawler, P. A. *The Restless Mind* (Lanham, Md.: Rowman and Littlefield Publishers, Inc., 1993).

Mitchell, H. *Individual Choice and the Structures of History. Alexis de Tocqueville as Historian Reappraised* (Cambridge and New York: Cambridge University Press, 1996).

Nolla, E. (ed.) *Liberty, Equality, Democracy* (New York and London: New York University Press, 1992).

Pierson, G. W. *Tocqueville and Beaumont in America* (New York: Oxford University Press, 1938).

Schleifer, J. T. *The Making of Tocqueville's Democracy in America* (Chapel Hill: University of North Carolina Press, 1980).

Siedentop, L. *Tocqueville* (Oxford and New York: Oxford University Press, 1994).

Richard Penaskovic

TOLSTOY, LEV NIKOLAYEVICH (1828–1910). Tolstoy was born in 1828 in the Túla province of central Russia (about 130 miles south of Moscow) at Yásnaya Polyána, which he inherited in 1847. He was the fourth of 5 children of a retired lieutenant colonel and his wife (whose father was a Russian general in chief). He lost both parents early and was raised by aunts. He attended the University of Kazan between 1844 and 1847 but never finished a degree. Tolstoy joined an artillery regiment in the Caucasus in 1851. In 1862 he married Sofya Andreyevna Behrs, the daughter of a physician, and they had 13 children. Tolstoy is regarded as one of the great Russian novelists, and *War and Peace* (1865–1869) and *Anna Karenina* (1875–1877) are praised as two of the greatest novels ever written in any language, books of extreme complexity and detail. Later in life he went through a religious crisis, which he partly details in *A Confession* (1879–1880). *Resurrection* (1899) gave him enormous influence in the world as a guide to conscience. He created a religion that was essentially a simplified form of Christianity, and his home became a mecca for pilgrims. He was excommunicated from the Russian Orthodox Church by the Holy Synod in 1901.

Tolstoy was not a particularly voracious reader when he was young (Christian, *A Critical*, 1). But he was always tirelessly self-critical: While working toward his degree, he kept a Benjamin Franklin–inspired "Franklin Journal" that listed and evaluated his failings (Simmons, 70). During an early tour of western Europe, he read a lot of nonfiction that related to his inquisitive mind: E. About's *Germain* (which he called "a silly novel"), **Hans Christian Andersen**'s *Improvisatore*; F. Bremer's *The Neighbours* (good, he said, but "as usual with women, too sugary"); **Elizabeth Gaskell**'s *Life of Charlotte Brontë*; G. M. Sarrut's *Biographie des hommes du jour*; E. Girardin's *De la liberté de la presse et du journalisme*; **Napoléon III**'s *Idées Napoléoniennes*; de las Cases's *Le Mémorial de Sainte Hélène*; and **Alexis de Tocqueville**'s *L'Ancien Régime et la Révolution* (Simmons, 158). Evidence of religious doubt surfaced early for Tolstoy. In 1853 he wrote in his diary that he was "unable to prove to myself the existence of God . . . and [he did] not think the conception absolutely necessary" (Maude, *Private Diary*, 15).

Tolstoy established a school for children at his home in the early 1860s. During this period, while he enjoyed the works of the Russian poet **Pushkin** and read Homer, Plato, **Goethe**, **Hugo**, Aleksei Koltsov, Fëdor Tyutchev, Afanasi Fet, **Turgenev**, and **Dostoevsky**, he also liked the simple country verse poems of Russian writers like A. V. Koltsov.

As a novelist, Tolstoy was rooted in traditions of older realism. He did not like **Flaubert** or other French writers, except for **Maupassant**. However, he admired English writers, particularly **Charles Dickens**, of whom he said, "I think Charles Dickens is the greatest novel writer of the 19th century" (Simmons, 92). In the years leading up to *War and Peace*, Tolstoy read the Gospels, *Don Quixote*, Rabelais's works, Goethe's *Faust*, **Macaulay**'s *History of England*, the tales of Hans Christian Andersen, **George Eliot**'s *Scenes from Clerical Life* and *Adam Bede*, **Gogol**'s *Letters* and the second part of *Dead Souls*, Goncharov's *Oblomoy*, Kozlov's *Poems*, Saltykov-Shchedrin's *Death of Pazukhin*, and the correspondence of P. V. Annenkov and N. V. Stankevich (Simmons, 163).

After *War and Peace*, Tolstoy studied ancient Greek language and literature, particularly through Homer, Xenophon, and Herodotus. He reread Molière, Goethe, and Shakespeare as well as the Russian dramatic classics. He also read **Schopenhauer**, Kant, and Pascal (Christian, *A Critical*, 165).

In *What Is Art?* (1898), his appraisal and study of art, Tolstoy says that he liked **Stowe**'s *Uncle Tom's Cabin* (Maude, *Private Diary*, 96) not on its literary merit but because of the feeling it conveyed, one of his primary criteria of the highest art. Other examples he cited as the highest art—"flowing from love of God and man (both of the higher, positive, and of the lower, negative kind) in literature": Schiller's *The Robbers*; Hugo's *Les Misérables* and *Les Pauvres Gens*; Dickens's *Tale of Two Cities*, *A Christmas Carol*, and *The Chimes*; Dostoevsky's works, especially *The House of the Dead*; and Eliot's *Adam Bede* (Simmons, 539).

Tolstoy's religion was based upon a few simple moral commands, and it condemned modern civilization. In later years, he read established works of the past, growing disgusted with his contemporaries' ignorance of their intellectual heritage (Simmons, 654). Stirring these thoughts were Marcus Aurelius, Epictetus, Xenophon, Socrates, Seneca, Plutarch, and Cicero, as well as Montaigne, Rousseau, Voltaire, Lessing, Kant, Lichtenberg, Schopenhauer, **Emerson**, Channing, Parker, **Ruskin**, and Amiel. Late in life he also read Brahmin, Chinese, and Buddhist wisdom.

ARCHIVES

Most of Tolstoy's archival material is located at the Tolstoy Museum in Moscow. The primary work describing the Tolstoy archive is *Opisanie rukopisei khudozhestvennykh proizvedienii L. N. Tolstogo* (Moscow, 1955) by Zhdanov and Znaidenshnur.

PRINTED SOURCES

Bayley, John. *Tolstoy and the Novel* (New York: Viking Press, 1966). Includes a good discussion of *What Is Art?* and Tolstoy's reading influences.
Berlin, Isaiah, *The Hedgehog and The Fox: An Essay on Tolstoy's View of History* (New York: Simon and Schuster, 1953).
Christian, R. F. *Tolstoy: A Critical Introduction* (London: Cambridge University Press, 1969).
Jones, W. Gareth. "George Eliot's *Adam Bede* and Tolstoy's Conception of Anna Karenina," *Modern Language Review*, 61 (1966), 73–81.
Maude, Aylmer. *The Life of Tolstoy* (Oxford: Oxford University Press, 1930).
Simmons, Ernest J. *Leo Tolstoy* (Boston: Little, Brown, 1946).
Steiner, George. *Tolstoy or Dostoevsky* (New Haven, Conn.: Yale University Press, 1959, 1996).
Tolstoy, Lev. *The Private Diary of Leo Tolstoy*, Aylmer Maude (ed.) (London: William Heinemann Ltd., 1927).
———. *Tolstoy's Letters*, R. F. Christian (ed.), 2 vols. (New York: Charles Scribner's Sons, 1978).

Scott Warnock

TOULOUSE-LAUTREC, HENRI DE (1864–1901). Henri de Toulouse-Lautrec was educated at the Lycée Fontanes (Condorcet) (1872–1875). He received his baccalaureate in 1881. Toulouse-Lautrec drew upon an arts and crafts revival, Japanese print techniques, and Post-Impressionism to fashion a novel vision of fin de siècle celebrity in the service of a nascent publicity industry. His posters and illustrations helped blur the boundaries of painting and commercial art. At the same time, he created sensitive, unsentimental, and occasionally satiric portraits of the women and men in the Montmartre sex and entertainment industries.

Heir to the aristocratic lineages of Toulouse, Lautrec, and Montfa, Henri de Toulouse-Lautrec-Montfa was raised in a Catholic, monarchist home. Crippled by a debilitating genetic bone disease, he studied mainly with tutors. They gave him a solid humanistic education. Although he never entered the École des Beaux-Arts, he studied briefly in the ateliers of Léon Bonnat (1882) and Fernand Cormon (1882–1885).

In his art and in his life, Toulouse-Lautrec was fascinated by prostitutes, alcohol, and the urban underclass—subjects that played an important role in naturalist literature and theater, as well as in the canvases of **Manet, Degas**, and others. In the mid-1880s, he met the cabaret owner and performer Aristide Bruant. Bruant's bittersweet verses in *Les Refrains du Mirliton* inspired him to paint his first series of portraits of prostitutes and working-class women in 1886 and 1887. He later immortalized Bruant's scarf-clad persona in a series of posters. Scholars have seen traces of the writings of Joris Karl Huysmans (*Croquis parisiens*) and **Émile Zola** (*La Curée, L'Assommoir*) in Lautrec's images representing desire and the pursuit of sensation. Like Zola and Edmond de Goncourt, he attempted to represent the experience of prostitutes across the divide of class and gender. He proposed illustrating Goncourt's *La Fille Élisa*. In 1893, Goncourt gave him Utamaro's *Pillow Book*, which Toulouse-Lautrec's *Elles* resembles. He is said to have spoken of **Honoré de Balzac** with insight (Murray, 94, 156–157, 160, 207).

Toulouse-Lautrec was renowned as an illustrator. As a student of Cormon, he created several images to illustrate **Victor Hugo**'s *La Légende des siècles* (Murray, 51). He later illustrated the works of naturalist and symbolist authors (Jean Richepin, Tristan Bernard, Victor Joze, and Oscar Méténier) primarily on book covers, in theater programs, and on posters.

Toulouse-Lautrec also explored physicality, instinct, and sexuality in hunting, racing, and circus images—images that reveal a debt to texts his father gave him on falconry and other gentlemanly sports and to the paintings of contemporaries including Princeteau and Degas. The allegorical animals in his late drawings may owe something to the fables of Phaedrus and La Fontaine that he studied in school as well as to moral tales such as the Comtesse de Ségur's *Mémoires d'un âne*, which his mother read to him when he was a small boy (Frey, 39).

ARCHIVES

Musée Toulouse-Lautrec (Albi). Conserves his extant school texts.
Carlton Lake Collection, Harry Ransom Humanities Research Center, University of Texas (Austin).
Archives nationales de France (Paris), Musées nationaux de France (Paris), Bibliothèque nationale (Paris).

PRINTED SOURCES

Catalogue, *Musée Toulouse, Albi* (Musée Toulouse-Lautrec, [1985]).
Denvir, Bernard. *Toulouse-Lautrec* (London: Thames & Hudson, 1991).
Frey, Julia. *Toulouse-Lautrec: A Life* (New York: Viking, 1994).
Jarrassé, Dominique. *Henri de Toulouse-Lautrec-Montfa* (Marseilles: AGEP/L'Esprit des Arts, 1991).

Joyant, Maurice. *Henri de Toulouse-Lautrec, 1864–1901*, 2 vols. (Paris: Henri Fleury, 1926–1927).

Murray, Gale B. *Toulouse-Lautrec: The Formative Years* (Oxford: Clarendon, Press, 1991).

Toulouse-Lautrec, Henri de. *The Letters of Henri de Toulouse-Lautrec*, Herbert Schimmel (ed.) (Oxford: Oxford University Press, 1991).

Aaron J. Segal

TOUSSAINT-LOUVERTURE, PIERRE DOMINIQUE (1743–1803). Pierre Dominique Toussaint-Louverture, a revolutionary, was born a slave on the Breda plantation, near Cape François, Saint-Domingue (Haiti). He was the son of an educated African slave and a Jesuit missionary, Pierre Baptiste, through whom he became a Catholic and acquired his informal education, including his knowledge of French and to some extent Latin. He had humane masters who, contrary to the common practice of the time, permitted the education of their slaves and allowed them free access to books.

In 1791, Toussaint became the leader of the Haitian independence movement, thus setting the stage for Haitian independence in 1804. Toussaint's extraordinary military ability made him a darling of Spanish, British, and French generals, who courted his support in their struggle for the control of the Caribbean islands. Popularly known as the "Black Jacobin," the "Liberator of Haiti," Toussaint became the leader of the first and only successful slave revolt in the Western World and a continuing source of inspiration to revolutionaries and freedom fighters throughout the world.

Among the diverse literary influences on him was Epictetus, himself a former slave, who recommended moderation and accomodation in politics, two virtues for which Toussaint later became famous. His military tactics and diplomatic strategies showed the impact of his readings of Caesar's *War Commentaries*. A fervent Catholic, he affirmed and traced the origins of his commitment to justice and equality to his faith: "Religion, I remind you, my brother, is my Guide, it is the rule of my conduct, whatever others might say. . . . Everywhere the Holy Bible (I am pleased to mention it because it consoles me) . . . tells us of the proud being humbled and the humble being elevated" (*Proclamation of 1795*, The Schomburg Collection). In his mid-thirties, he bought his favorite book. Written by a Catholic priest and contemporary, the Abbé Raynal, it was a famous book in its time, noted especially for its biting indictment of slavery. Raynal warned the nations of Europe: "Your slaves will break the yoke that weighs upon them. A courageous chief only is wanted. Where is he? He will appear, doubt it not . . . and raise the sacred standard of liberty" (Raynal, 1780). Raynal was a most decisive influence on Toussaint, who began to see himself as the predicted black Spartacus who would avenge the outrages done to his race. He once said: "At the beginning of the troubles in St. Domingue I felt that I was destined for great things. When I received this divine message I was fifty-four years of age. . . . A necessity was laid upon me to begin my career. . . . A secret voice told me, 'Since the blacks are free, they need a leader,' and that I must be this leader predicted by Abbe Raynal . . . and the voice of God hasn't deceived me" (Lacroix, 1:409–410).

ARCHIVES

Toussaint Papers, The National Archives, Paris. Contain most of the official reports and private letters.

———. La Bibliothèque nationale, Paris. The MSS department contains three volumes of Toussaint's important correspondence with Laveaux, French general and colonial governor.

———. The Schomburg Collection, New York Public Library. Contains most of the Toussaint Proclamations.

PRINTED SOURCES

Beard, John R. *Toussaint L'Overture: A Biography and Autobiography* (Boston J. Redpath, 1863). Views Toussaint's career as an example of inspired Christianity and reproduces in its entirety his *Memoir.*

James, C.L.R. *The Black Jacobins: Toussaint Louverture and the San Domingo Revolution* (London: Allison and Busby, 1980). Extensive use of Toussaint's writings.

Lacroix, Pamphile de. *Memoires pour servir a l'histoire de la revolution de saint-Domingue,* George F. Tyson, Jr. (trans.), 2 vols. (Paris: Pilletaine, 1819). An eyewitness account. Quotes liberally from Toussaint's writings and speeches.

Parkinson, Wenda. *"This Gilded African": Toussaint L'Overture* (New York: Quartet Books, 1978).

Raynal, G. T. *Histoire Philosophique et Politique des etablissemens et du Commerce des Europeans dans les deux Indes/Philosophical and Political History of the Establishments and Commerce of the Europeans in the Two Indies* (Geneva: Jean-Leonard Pellet, 1780).

Schoelcher, Victor. *Vie de Toussaint-Louverture* (Paris: P. Oendorff, 1889). Reprints a large number of important documents.

Tyson, George F. (ed.). *Toussaint Louverture* (Eaglewood Cliffs, N.J.: Prentice-Hall, 1973). Includes about 40 pages of Toussaint's writings, made up chiefly of letters, proclamations, and speeches.

Funso Afolayan

TROELTSCH, ERNST (1865–1923). Ernst Troeltsch was born in Haunstetten, Bavaria, in 1865. The son of a physician, he received a liberal humanistic Lutheran education at St. Anna Gymnasium in Augsburg, graduating as valedictorian in 1883. He served in the army (1883–1884), matriculated at Erlangen (1884), and studied philosophy under Gustav Class. He decided to concentrate in theology but found the faculty, for example, Franz Hermann Reinhold von Frank and Theodor von Zahn, too orthodox for his tastes. Transferring first to Berlin in 1885, he studied theology under Julius Kaftan and history under Heinrich von Treitschke. Troeltsch then went to Göttingen in 1886 and studied theology under Albrecht Ritschl, Paul de LaGarde, and Bernhard Duhm. After finishing his formal studies, he was ordained a Lutheran minister in 1888 and became an Evangelical Lutheran curate in Munich in 1889–1990. He published his dissertation on Johann Gerhard and Philipp Melanchthon in 1891. He taught theology at Göttingen (1890–1892), Bonn (1892–1894), and Heidelberg (1894–1915), and philosophy at Berlin (1915–1923).

Troeltsch and his friend Wilhelm Bousett were Ritschl's last two students. Ritschl became Troeltsch's mentor. The rest of Troeltsch's career is frequently interpreted as a sustained attempt to free his thought from Ritschl's. In reaction to Ritschl, Troeltsch saw Christianity as constantly evolving with other religions in the context of world history, not as an absolute body of doctrine. His anti-supernaturalist approach to religion led him to found a "history of religions movement" (*religionsgeschichtliche Schule*) in which "historicism" (*Historismus*) primarily denotes "cultural relativity." For about 40 years, when Karl Barth's neoorthodoxy dominated Protestant theology, Troeltsch was neglected. A revival of interest in his thought began in the 1960s, encouraged by the three Niebuhrs (Reinhold, H. Richard, and Richard R.) and Paul Tillich.

In the brief intellectual autobiography published with his *Gesammelte Schriften* (Tübingen: Mohr, 1912–1925; reprint, Aalen: Scientia, 1961–1977), Troeltsch states that the study of history was his first and greatest inspiration, and only later did he appreciate theology and philosophy. Among historians he preferred **Thomas Carlyle**, Wilhelm Dilthey, and Friedrich Meinecke. Having received a thorough idealist education at Erlangen under Class, Troeltsch sought to blend **Georg Wilhelm Friedrich Hegel**'s dialectical philosophy of history, Rudolf Hermann Lotze's personalistic metaphysics, Richard Rothe's theological relativism, and **Friedrich Schleiermacher**'s religious subjectivism. Troeltsch, Heinrich Rickert, and Wilhelm Windelband were the nucleus of the Heidelberg/Southwest Baden school of neo-Kantianism, which was also neo-Hegelian in many respects, as opposed to the anti-Hegelian Marburg school of neo-Kantianism led by Hermann Cohen and Paul Natorp.

ARCHIVES

Heidelberg University. Correspondence, papers.

PRINTED SOURCES

Clayton, John Powell (ed.). *Ernst Troeltsch and the Future of Theology* (Cambridge: Cambridge University Press, 1976).

Dietrich, Wendell S. *Cohen and Troeltsch: Ethical Monotheistic Religion and Theory of Culture* (Atlanta: Scholars Press, 1986).

Mackintosh, Hugh Ross. *Types of Modern Theology: Schleiermacher to Barth* (New York: Scribner's, 1937).

Pauck, Wilhelm. *Harnack and Troeltsch: Two Historical Theologians* (New York: Oxford University Press, 1968).

Reist, Benjamin A. *Toward a Theology of Involvement: The Thought of Ernst Troeltsch* (Philadelphia: Westminster, 1966).

Rubanowice, Robert J. *Crisis in Consciousness: The Thought of Ernst Troeltsch* (Tallahassee: University Presses of Florida, 1982).

Wyman, Walter E. *The Concept of Glaubenslehre: Ernst Troeltsch and the Theological Heritage of Schleiermacher* (Chico, Calif.: Scholars Press, 1983).

Yamin, George J. *In the Absence of Fantasia: Troeltsch's Relations to Hegel* (Gainesville: University Press of Florida, 1993).

Yasukata, Toshimasa. *Ernst Troeltsch: Systematic Theologian of Radical Historicality* (Atlanta, Ga.: Scholars Press, 1986).

Eric v. d. Luft

TROLLOPE, ANTHONY (1815–1882). Anthony Trollope was born on April 24, 1815, at 24 Russell St. Keppel Sq., London. His father was a talented but quarrelsome and unsuccessful barrister, constantly in debt. His mother was a prolific novelist of minor talent whose best-known books are *Domestic Manners of the Americans* (a bitter satire) and a witty attack on Calvinism, *The Vicar of Wrexhill*. They were a "writing family." Novelist Thomas Adolphus was Anthony's elder brother. Anthony was educated, for a time, at Winchester, then as a despised day boy at Harrow. He was unhappy at both places and regarded as a dunce, though he attained a fair knowledge of Latin. When he used Winchester as the model of Barchester, the cathedral town that is the center of his most famous series, the Barsetshire novels, it was noticeable that the imagined city had no school.

He remained true all his life to the unenthusiastic Anglicanism in which he was brought up. He had a strong dislike of Evangelicals and remained untouched by the Oxford movement and the Catholic Revival. Of the many clergymen described in his pages, all are seen with a cool eye, but the old-fashioned "High and Dry" like Archdeacon Grantly are generally the most sympathetic. Although a personal friend of **George Eliot**, he was untouched by the skeptical and agnostic movements of the age.

In 1834 he obtained a clerkship in the Post Office and for seven years remained undistinguished and idle. His fortunes improved when he was given a more responsible post in Ireland in 1841 and when, in 1844, he married Rose Heseltine. His literary career began with little-read Irish novels in the late 1840s. He was a late developer, and not until 40 did he attain a modest success with *The Warden*. His industry was enormous, and until he retired from the Post Office in 1869, he regularly did three hours of writing before going to work. With 48 books, and many lesser productions, he is the most prolific of our leading novelists.

Trollope shows the slow consequences of events, choices, and character dispositions. His appearance when he writes in *propia persons* of a hearty man of the world is not exactly false but deceptive. He is infinitely subtle, especially in his dialogue. He has the keenest comprehension of the feminine of any male novelist after Richardson. He is (in strong contrast to some of the masters of his time, like **Thackeray** and **Dickens**) endlessly fair and judicious. Of all English writers he is the most sensitively aware of the strengths, vices, and foibles of the upper class.

As Dryden said of Shakespeare, he "did not need the spectacles of books to read nature." But he was widely read; he was fond of the Latin classics (actually writing a book about Cicero). He was an expert in the English Jacobean drama, though he seldom quotes from it. He learned much from **Jane Austen**, transposing many of her insights into a looser, masculine form. Of his own contemporaries, he most admired **Thackeray** and contributed one of his most popular books, *Framley Parsonage* (1860–1861), to Thackeray's new *Cornhill Magazine*. He was one of the few mid-Victorians who disliked Dickens, whom he satirized as Mr. Popular Sentiment in *The Warden*. Nevertheless, he often quotes him. His Irish experience helped to give him a detached view of English society. Though he sometimes writes of foreign countries, occasionally setting whole books in France or Switzerland, his art is always, at its best, nourished by English sources. His failure to obtain election to Parliament as a Liberal in 1868 left him time to prove himself (along with **Bagehot**) the shrewdest of all commentators on mid-Victorian politics. His six political novels (1869–1880) are perhaps his greatest achievement.

ARCHIVES

Morris L. Parrish and Robert H. Taylor Collections, University Library, Princeton University.
University of Illinois Library.

PRINTED SOURCES

Booth, Bradford Allen. *Anthony Trollope: Aspects of His Life and Art* (Bloomington: Indiana University Press, 1958).
Heinemann, Helen. *Mrs. Trollope: The Triumphant Feminine in the Nineteenth Century* (Athens: Ohio University Press, 1979).
Mullen, Richard. *Anthony Trollope: A Victorian in His World* (London: Duckworth, 1990).
Nardin, Jean. *Trollope and Victorian Moral Philosophy* (Ann Arbor: University of Michigan Press, 1996).
Super, R. H. *Trollope in the Post Office* (Ann Arbor: University of Michigan Press, 1981).
Trollope, Anthony. *An Autobiography*, Michael Sadleir and Frederick Page (eds.) (1883, Oxford: Oxford University Press, 1980).
———. *The Letters of Anthony Trollope*, 2 vols., N. John Hall (ed.) (Stanford: Stanford University Press, 1983).
Trollope, T. A.: *What I Remember* (London: Richard Bentley, 1887).

A.O.J. Cockshut

TURGENEV, IVAN SERGEYEVICH (1818–1883). Ivan Turgenev was born in 1818 in the central Russian city of Orël and educated by tutors. In 1837 Turgenev graduated from the University of St. Petersburg and then spent the next two years at the University of Berlin, studying philosophy, philology, and history. Although Turgenev wrote poetry and plays, he is best known for more than 60 short stories, a collection of sketches entitled *Notes of a Hunter* (1852), as well as six novels: *Rudin* (1856), *A Nest of the Gentry* (1859), *On the Eve* (1860), *Fathers and Children* (1862), *Smoke* (1867), and *Virgin Soil* (1877).

In childhood Turgenev read the eighteenth-century Russian classics including A. D. Kantemir, A. P. Sumarakov, G. R. Derzhavin, D. I. Fonvizin, N. M. Karamzin, and I. A. Krylov (Turgenev, 9:133; Schapiro, 7–8). However, the Romanticism of **Byron, Goethe**, and Schiller as well as the Russians A. A. Bestuzhev-Marlinsky, **A. S. Pushkin**, and M. Y. Lermontov provided the earliest literary influence (Seeley, 33). As a result, Turgenev's own early writing consisted of mostly derivative Romantic lyrical poetry, some narrative poetry, as well as translations of Shakespeare, Byron, and Goethe. Turgenev spent much of his adult life living in Europe, which exposed him to European literary and social issues and provided him with a critical perspective on issues at home in Russia. For example, in his early fiction, Turgenev focused on the peasantry, a trend that enjoyed great popularity in liberal circles in Europe at that time. Some two dozen sketches, collected together in 1852 under the title *Notes of a Hunter*, represented an attack on the institution of serfdom in Russia. Quickly translated into French, German, English, and Spanish, this work caused a great stir among writers and thinkers of the day that helped to influence Alexander II to emancipate the serfs in 1861; Turgenev considered this his greatest achievement (Turgenev, 8:55–56, 2:64; Schapiro, 66).

Among his favorite English writers, Turgenev counted Shakespeare, especially his *Hamlet* and *King Lear*, as well as **Dickens, Walter Scott**, and **George Sand**, whose literary effect on his own *Notes of a Hunter* Turgenev later acknowledged (Schapiro, 237). Turgenev also read Calderón, Lope de Vega, and Tirso de Molina in the original, but it was Cervantes among the Spaniards who most influenced his own work (Turgenev, 1:279, 8:126). Providing a key to understanding the heroes that populated his own novels, Turgenev's seminal 1860 essay "Hamlet and Don Quixote" argued that Russia needed fewer superfluous men (Hamlets) and more bold leaders, devoted to actively pursuing their ideals (Don Quixotes) (Turgenev 8:171–192). Rudin, in the novel of the same name, represented the superfluous men of the 1840s generations, whereas the nihilist Bazarov in *Fathers and Children*, Turgenev's best and most controversial novel, personified the Don Quixote ideal and made a lasting impact on Russian literature and culture.

ARCHIVES

Russian State Archive of Literature and Art (RGALI, known before 1992 as TsGALI) in Moscow.

Russian Academy of Sciences Institute of Russian Literature (Pushkin House) in St. Petersburg.

PRINTED SOURCES

Schapiro, Leonard. *Turgenev. His Life and Times* (Cambridge, Mass.: Harvard University Press, 1982).

Seeley, Frank Friedeberg. *Turgenev. A Reading of His Fiction* (Cambridge: Cambridge University Press, 1991).
Turgenev, I S. *Polnoe sobranie sochinenii i pisem* (Collected Works in 15 vols. and Correspondence in 13 vols.) (Moscow-Leningrad: Akademiia Nauk, 1961–1968).
                                                                                          Erika Haber

TWAIN, MARK (1835–1910). Mark Twain, a.k.a. Samuel Langhorne Clemens, was born in Florida, Missouri, in 1835 and moved to nearby Hannibal when he was four. A classic example of an autodidact, Mark Twain received his only formal education in primitive village schoolhouses, and even that limited education ended early. The death of his father and his family's resulting poverty pushed him into employment as he entered adolescence. Working primarily for newspapers—including several owned by his older brother–Mark Twain followed Benjamin Franklin and such contemporaries as **Joel Chandler Harris**, **William Dean Howells**, and Artemus Ward in making printing his first career. Offsetting type, reading proof, and writing occasional newspaper items fueled an interest in reading that stayed with him throughout his life.

In addition to stories that passed through the newspapers on which he worked, Mark Twain's youthful reading included the Bible, popular boys' stories, and the fiction of **James Fenimore Cooper, Alexandre Dumas, Charles Dickens**, and others. As he matured, his reading ranged more widely—into history, biography, philosophy, and science. At 18 he left Missouri to become a journeyman printer in eastern centers such as New York City, where he often spent his free time reading in printers' libraries. At 21 he began a 4-year stint as a steamboat pilot on the lower Mississippi River. Even during these years his reading interests expanded, and he developed fondness for the work of such writers as Shakespeare and Thomas Paine. As early as 1860 he expressed his admiration of Oliver Goldsmith's *Citizen of the World* (which he later satirized) and Cervantes's *Don Quixote*, on which he later modeled many attacks on Romanticism in books such as *Adventures of Huckleberry Finn* (1884) and *Life on the Mississippi* (1893).

As the outbreak of the Civil War ended the Mississippi's commercial traffic, Mark Twain went west with his older brother, hoping to get rich in the booming gold and silver mines of Nevada and California. His professional writing career began in Nevada, where he joined the Virginia City *Territorial Enterprise's* staff in 1862 and adopted his famous pen name. Although his writing mostly concerned local affairs, evidences of the growing extent of his reading pervade his early sketches and journalism. For example, his 1864 sketch "The Killing of Julius Caesar 'Localized' " is a brilliant parody recasting Shakespeare's *Julius Caesar* in the context of contemporary American ward politics. Other writing from that period reveals his increasing familiarity with history, the classics, and the Bible—which became a major source of inspiration to his satirical writing up to the last days of his life.

In Mark Twain's more mature years, his reading turned more toward historical and philosophical works. One of his favorite books was **Thomas Carlyle's** *French Revolution* (1837), which he tried to read every year. W.E.H. Lecky's *History of European Morals from Augustus to Charlemagne* (1869) had a seminal influence on his thinking. Lecky's views on determinism and the negative influence of Roman Catholicism on Western history profoundly influenced views Mark Twain expressed in *A Connecticut Yankee at King Arthur's Court* (1889) and *What Is Man?* (1906). During his extensive travels, he always read voraciously on the regions he visited.

Mark Twain's most productive years as a writer came during the late nineteenth century, a comparatively fallow period in American literature. Aside from the works of his close friend W. D. Howells, he had little interest in the books of his contemporaries and largely ignored literary trends. He read voluminously but chiefly to increase his knowledge and acquaint himself with new ideas, especially in science, history, and philosophy, and he adopted few new ideas about literary technique.

After Mark Twain settled down to become a respectable family man and literary figure in Hartford, Connecticut, during the 1870s, he participated in local literary activities and found new ways to focus his reading. For example, his admiration of **Robert Browning** moved him to conduct regular readings of Browning's poetry in his home. However, despite his growing gentility, he tried to maintain a public image as an unlettered westerner. To this image, however, he gave the lie in 1890 when he was asked to name what books he would want if he were placed in a desert island situation. In addition to the works of Shakespeare and Browning, he added Thomas Malory's *Morte d'Arthur* (his inspiration for *Connecticut Yankee*); the Arabian classic *The Thousand and One Nights*—whose influence pervades his own writings; Boswell's *Life of Samuel Johnson*; Suetonius's *Lives of the Twelve Caesars*; and *The Rubaiyat of Omar Khayyam*.

By the end of his life, Mark Twain had accumulated a personal library of several thousand volumes, many of which have proven to be invaluable documents of the literary influences on him because of the underlinings and marginal notes he recorded on their pages. Unfortunately, most of his library was scattered, so the full extent of his reading remains unknown.

ARCHIVES

Mark Twain Papers, Bancroft Library, University of California at Berkeley.

PRINTED SOURCES

Baetzhold, Howard G., and Joseph B. McCullough (eds.). *The Bible According to Mark Twain* (Athens: University of Georgia Press, 1995).
Cummings, Sherwood. *Mark Twain and Science: Adventures of a Mind* (Baton Rouge: Louisiana State University Press, 1988).
Emerson, Everett. *Mark Twain: A Literary Life* (Philadelphia: University of Pennsylvania Press, 1999).

Gribben, Alan. *Mark Twain's Library: A Reconstruction* (Boston: G. K. Hall, 1980). Unrivalled source on Mark Twain's reading.

LeMaster, J. R., and James D. Wilson (eds). *The Mark Twain Encyclopedia* (New York: Garland, 1993). Includes Gribben's updated survey of Mark Twain's reading.

Machlis, Paul (ed.). *Union Catalog of Clemens Letters* (Berkeley and Los Angeles: University of California Press, 1986).

Rasmussen, R. Kent. *Mark Twain A to Z: The Essential Guide to His Life and Writings* (New York: Facts on File, 1995).

Tenney, Thomas Asa. *Mark Twain: A Reference Guide* (Boston: G. K. Hall, 1977). Exhaustive annotated guide to books and articles about Mark Twain; Tenney has published updates in several journals.

R. Kent Rasmussen

V

VAN GOGH, VINCENT (1853–1890). Vincent Willem Van Gogh was born in the Netherlands in 1853, the son of a Dutch Protestant pastor. At the age of 16 he was apprenticed to a company of art dealers, of which his uncle was a partner, leading to periods of residence in London (1873–1874) and Paris (1874–1875). Van Gogh disliked the business but began to appreciate art through daily contact with it. Moody by temperament and longing for human connections, by the age of 27 Van Gogh had gone through a number of careers, including that of evangelical Christian preacher among Belgian miners of the Borinage. In 1880, Van Gogh in sympathy with the poverty-stricken miners gave away all of his possessions and was promptly dismissed by the church for too literal interpretation of the Bible. Penniless, he withdrew from society and began to study the technical craft of painting, determined to serve humanity through art. In only 10 years of active drawing and painting (1880–1890), he produced hundreds of paintings and drawings and became one of the most revolutionary artists of his age.

As a young man, van Gogh read Calvinistic theology. As his experience among the poor grew, he was drawn to the writings of reformers and existentialists, including **Kierkegaarde**. An instinctive painter, van Gogh often rejected European conventions and in the mid-1880s became fascinated by the work of Japanese printmakers, including Hiroshige and Hokusai. In seeking explanations for the plight of the poor, he was drawn to the literary school of French naturalism and in his developmental stage was much impressed with **Zola**'s *Germinal*. Van Gogh left his formal art training and moved to Paris in 1886 to live with his brother, Thèo, who worked as an art dealer. Through Thèo, van Gogh learned of the latest works in French Impressionism and eventually met **Toulouse-Lautrec, Gauguin**, Pissarro, **Seurat**, and others. The combination of the work of these artists and his favorite contemporary French writers—Zola,

Maupassant, Daudet, and the Goncourt brothers—led to his development as an artist.

ARCHIVES

Van Gogh archives in the Van Gogh Museum, Amsterdam. Includes letters to his brother, as well as sketches, diaries, and other memorabilia.

PRINTED SOURCES

Arnold, Matthias. *Vincent van Gogh* (Munich: Kindler, 1993).
Barr, Alfred H., Jr. (ed.). *Vincent Van Gogh: With an Introduction and Notes Selected from the Letters of the Artist* (New York: Museum of Modern Art, 1936). Includes a section on "Books van Gogh read as cited in his Letters" (44–46).
Erickson, Kathleen. *At Eternity's Gate: The Spiritual Vision of Vincent Van Gogh* (Grand Rapids, Mich.: Eerdmans, 1998).
Hulsker, Jan. *The New Complete Van Gogh: Paintings, Drawings, and Sketches. Revised and Enlarged Edition of the Catalogue Raisonné of the Works of Vincent van Gogh* (Philadelphia: John Benjamins, 1996). Thoroughly documents the context of each of van Gogh's works, making use of letters, newspaper articles, and memoirs. Essential.
———. *Vincent and Théo Van Gogh: A Dual Biography* (Ann Arbor, Michigan: Fuller Publications, 1990).
———. *Vincent Van Gogh: A Guide to His Work and Letters* (Amsterdam: Van Gogh Museum, 1993).
Masheck, Joseph D., ed. *Van Gogh 100* (Westport, Conn.: Greenwood Press, 1996). Includes an article on "Vincent as Reader: Reading in the Formation of the Artist," by Patricia E. Connors.
Sund, Judy. *True to Temperament: Van Gogh and French Naturalist Literature* (Cambridge: Cambridge University Press, 1992). Utilizes primary sources in demonstrating the intimate connection between Van Gogh's reading and the development of his visual art.
Van Gogh, Vincent. *Complete Letters, with Reproductions of all the Drawings in the Correspondence* (Greenwich, Conn.: New York Graphic Society, 1959).

Frank A. Salamone

VEBLEN, THORSTEIN (1857–1929). Thorstein Veblen was born in Manitowoc County, Wisconsin, in 1857 and earned his undergraduate degree from Carleton College (1874–1880). After studying for a semester at Johns Hopkins (1881), he transferred to Yale, where he earned a Ph.D. in philosphy and economics (1881–1884). Unable to find an academic position because of his religious agnosticism and heterodox views, Veblen eventually returned to graduate school in economics at Cornell (1891). Although he began teaching at the University of Chicago the following year, his unorthodox theories and personal idiosyncrasies continued to undermine his success in academia. Veblen's writing, however, exerted a wide influence on American intellectual life in the first half of the twentieth century.

Veblen fashioned an anthropological economics that examined the interconnections between the economy, culture, and society. Veblen was strongly influenced by **Charles Darwin**'s theory of evolution, and his social theory relied on an evolutionary framework for understanding the stages through which human society had developed. Veblen argued that the dominant neoclassical economics of his era was merely descriptive and "taxonomic," rather than explanatory. To create a truly "evolutionary science," economists needed to investigate the role of culture, habits, and instincts in economic behavior. In contrast to intellectuals such as **Herbert Spencer** and William Graham Sumner (Veblen's professor at Yale), who argued that modern social relations were based on contract rather than status, Veblen insisted that status remained an important component of modern society and that elements of "barbarian" culture still influenced human behavior. In his first book, *The Theory of the Leisure Class*, Veblen argued that conspicuous consumption, a term he coined, had its roots in the "barbarian" or "predatory" period of human society and provided the modern leisure class with a way to demonstrate their status. Extremely well read in the social sciences, Veblen drew on the anthropological investigations of Franz Boas and Edward B. Tylor. In *The Theory of the Leisure Class*, Veblen used the insights of anthropology to investigate the economic and cultural life of his own society.

The *Theory of the Leisure Class* also introduced one of the recurring themes in Veblen's work, the opposition between "industry," by which he meant the efficient and useful deployment of resources and labor, and "business," or pecuniary motivation. Veblen was a staunch critic of capitalism and emphasized its wastefulness. His reading of Edward Bellamy's utopian socialist novel *Looking Backward* strongly influenced him as a young man. Veblen was also inspired by one of Bellamy's most trenchant critics, however, the socialist **William Morris**. Indeed, much of Veblen's work manifests a tension between his admiration for the technologically advanced and efficient world of abundance portrayed by Bellamy and the anarchist utopia of free association and useful and satisfying labor portrayed by Morris. Writing from the 1890s through the 1920s, Veblen established himself as a seminal social theorist and critic.

ARCHIVES

Veblen, Thorstein. Carleton College, Northfield, Minnesota.
Veblen, Thorstein. Wisconsin State Historical Society, Madison, Wisconsin.

PRINTED SOURCES

Diggins, John P. *The Bard of Savagery: Thorstein Veblen and Modern Social Theory* (New York: Seabury Press, 1978).
Dorfman, Joseph. *Thorstein Veblen and His America* (New York: Viking Press, 1934).
Tilman, Rick. *Thorstein Veblen and His Critics, 1891–1963: Conservative, Liberal, and Radical Perspectives* (Princeton, N.J.: Princeton University Press, 1992).
Veblen, Thorstein. *The Theory of the Leisure Class* (1899; New York: Penguin Books, 1979).

John Michael Boles

VERDI, GIUSEPPE (1813–1901). Giuseppe Verdi, an Italian operatic composer, studied Italian and Latin first in private lessons, then at the village school. At the *ginnasio* of Busseto, he studied the humanities and rhetoric, graduating with honors in 1827. Verdi's early studies were marked by a profound anti-clericalism that remained with him all his life (an apocryphal story tells that after a priest kicked him down the stairs for inattention during Mass, Verdi cursed the man to be struck by lightning; and in fact the priest was killed by lightning eight years later). Competing for his attention with letters was an early love for music. Verdi began organ lessons at age six; obviously—and gloriously—music won out over literature. At the *ginnasio*, he read Virgil, Juvenal, Cicero, and Pliny in addition to anthologies of rhetoric, philosophy, and history. Verdi was a lifelong reader. In Busseto, he regularly visited the public library with over 10,000 volumes. His opera are the most obvious results of his reading. Among the most important of the writers and texts: the Bible; Dante Alighieri; William Shakespeare (*Othello, Macbeth, Hamlet, The Tempest, King Lear, Romeo and Juliet, Henry IV, Henry V, The Merry Wives of Windsor*); Johann Christoph Friedrich Schiller; **Alessandro Manzoni** (*I promessi sposi, Il cinque maggio, Il conte di Carmagnola, Adelchi*); **Giuseppe Mazzini** (*Doveri dell'uomo*); Silvio Pellico (*Le mie prigioni,* recounting his experience in Austrian prisons); **Lord Byron** (*The Bride of Abydos, Cain, The Corsair*); Count Vittorio Alfieri (*Bruto, Filippo II, Saul, Virginia* [after which Verdi and his wife named their first daughter]); **Alexandre Dumas** (*fils*) (*Le Comte Hermann, Kean, Caternia Howard, La dame aux camélias*); Carlo Goldoni (*La locandiera*); Heliodorus (*Ethiopian Things*); **Victor Hugo** (*Cromwell, Hernani, Marion Delorme, Le roi s'amuse, Ruy Blas*); **Goethe**.

ARCHIVES

American Institute of Verdi Studies, New York University, New York.
Biblioteca della Cassa di Risparmio e del Monte di Credito sul Pegno di Busseto.
Istituto di Studi Verdiani, Parma.
Library of the Museum of La Scala Opera House, Milan, Italy.
Web site: http://lascala.milano.it/ita/character/verdi.html

PRINTED SOURCES

Abbiati, Franco. *Giuseppe Verdi,* 4 vols. (Milan: Ricordi, 1959).
Cannon, Janell. *Verdi* (San Diego, Calif.: Harcourt, Brace, 1997).
Fairtile, Linda B. *The Verdi Archive at New York University* (New York: American Institute for Verdi Studies, 1989).
Harwood, Gregory (ed.). *Giuseppe Verdi: A Guide to Research* (New York: Garland, 1998).
Martin, George. *Verdi: His Music, Life, and Times* (New York: Dodd, Mead, 1983).
Petit, Pierre. *Verdi* (Paris: Seuil, 1998).
Phillips-Matz, Mary Jane. *Verdi: A Biography,* with a foreword by Andrew Porter (Oxford and New York: Oxford University Press, 1993).

Tomasini, Daniele. *La cultura umanistica e letteraria di Giuseppe Verdi* (Cremona: Turris, 1997).

Weaver, William. "The Shakespeare Verdi Knew." In Andrew Porter and David Rosen (eds.), *Verdi's Macbeth: A Sourcebook* (New York: W. W. Norton, 1984).

———. *Verdi: A Documentary Study* (London: Thames & Hudson, 1977).

Stanislao G. Pugliese

VERNE, JULES (1828–1905). Jules Verne was born in the city of Nantes in western France in 1828. He began his formal education in 1834 and remained a student in Nantes until 1847. From 1838 to 1841 he attended the College Saint-Stanislas, where he did well in geography, Greek, Latin, and singing. From 1841 to 1846 he studied at the Petit Seminaire and the Lycée Royal de Nantes, where he continued to excel in geography. During this time he began writing short prose pieces.

In 1847 Verne began studying law in Paris, earning his degree in 1849. While still a student, he began attending literary salons where he met prominent French writers, including **Victor Hugo**, **Alexandre Dumas** (*père*), and Alexandre Dumas (*fils*). In 1850, with the help of Dumas *fils*, his first play was performed. He published his first short stories in 1851. While working as a theater secretary and a stockbroker, he continued to write plays and fiction.

Verne first won fame as a writer with the publication of *Cinq Semaines en ballon* [Five weeks in a balloon] in 1863. Encouraged by this success, he went on to write many novels involving realistic descriptions of extraordinary journeys on earth and in space. These had a major influence on the development of modern science fiction and are still widely read.

As a child, Verne read French translations of the novels of **James Fenimore Cooper** and **Walter Scott**. Both authors were known for adventure novels in which exciting stories and vivid descriptions of exotic locations were more important than characterization and literary style. These same tendencies can be seen in Verne's novels. Verne was particularly influenced by Cooper's accurate and realistic sea stories. He went on to write many novels about ocean voyages, including *Vingt Mille Lieues sous les mers* [Twenty thousand leagues under the sea (1870)].

Verne later stated that the most important books he read as a youth were *Robinson Crusoe* (1719), by Daniel Defoe, and *Der Schweizerische Robinson* [The Swiss family Robinson (1812)], by Johann Rudolf Wyss. Verne wrote several novels about castaways in the tradition of these books, including *L'Ile mysterieuse* [The mysterious island (1874)].

Verne's tales of space travel were influenced by the work of earlier French writers, including Savinien Cyrano de Bergerac's accounts of voyages to the moon and sun and Voltaire's *Micromegas* (1752). His use of a realistic style to describe dramatic events was influenced by the novels of Victor Hugo, Alexandre Dumas *père*, and **Charles Dickens**.

Edgar Allan Poe was an important influence on Verne's ability to describe fantastic situations in a scientific way. Verne wrote an appreciative article on Poe in 1864. In 1897 he published *Le Sphinx des glaces* [The Sphinx of the ice fields] as a sequel to Poe's *The Narrative of Arthur Gordon Pym* (1838).

ARCHIVES

Bibliothèque Municipale, Nantes.

PRINTED SOURCES

Jules-Verne, Jean. *Jules Verne: A Biography*, Roger Greaves (trans.) (New York: Tap-
    linger Publishing, 1976).
Lottman, Herbert R. *Jules Verne* (New York: St. Martin's Press, 1996).
                                                                              Rose Secrest

VICTORIA, QUEEN (1819–1901). The restrictive Royal Marriage Act of 1772 and sheer chance determined that in 1837 the crown of Great Britain and Ireland and the British Empire should devolve not on a descendant of one of the first three sons of King George III but on the sole child of the fourth son, the duke of Kent, and his wife, Victoire, the widowed princess of the small German principality of Leiningen. Because the duke of Kent died when the infant Victoria was only eight months old, Victoria's mother—who spoke English poorly and who felt alienated from her late husband's elder brothers, King George IV (1820–1830) and King William IV (1830–1837)—raised the princess in relative isolation on the outskirts of London in Kensington Palace. By the standards of British aristocratic families of the day, the duchess of Kent's income was limited, and the young Victoria was brought up in a relatively spare and simple manner: Meals were frugal; the palace rooms were filled with secondhand furniture and threadbare carpets; and the princess lacked a room of her own.

The duchess of Kent's ladies were all German, and little Victoria did not begin to learn English until she was three years old. In due course, she became almost equally proficient in speaking and writing German, French, and English, and she learned to speak English clearly, carefully, and without an accent. Although Victoria's nurses and her governess, Baroness Louise Lehzen, had all been born in Germany, the series of private tutors who from the age of four on began to educate her were not. The most important of those tutors was a Church of England clergyman, the Reverend George Davys, who taught her the alphabet and who afterward became her prime instructor in history, geography, Latin, and religion. Queen Victoria was later to describe herself as a slow learner, but contemporary evidence contradicts that appraisal. She could be rebellious on occasion, but by age six, little Victoria could read readily and do simple arithmetic; in due course specialist tutors were engaged to teach writing, French, German, drawing, music, and dancing. In addition to five hours of lessons six days a week, Monday through Saturday, she was allotted time for walks and for play. Every Sunday her mother took her to church.

In 1830, the duchess of Kent asked two senior bishops of the Church of England to judge the appropriateness of the schooling to which the princess had been exposed. After subjecting Victoria to a lengthy oral examination, the bishops awarded high marks to both the mother and the daughter. "In answering a great variety of questions proposed to her," they reported that

the Princess displayed an accurate knowledge of the most important features of Scripture History, and of the leading truths and precepts of the Christian Religion as taught by the Church of England, as well as an acquaintance with the Chronology and principal facts of English History remarkable in so young a person. To questions in Geography, the use of the Globes, Arithmetic, and Latin Grammar, the answers which the Princess returned were equally satisfactory (Benson and Esher, 1:16–17).

The archbishop of Canterbury, Dr. William Howley, was consulted as well, and he concurred: "Her Highness's education, in regard to cultivation of intellect, improvement of talent, and religious and moral principle, is conducted with so much success as to render any alteration of the system undesirable" (Benson and Esher, 1:16–17).

In no fashion did Victoria become an intellectual, but her predominantly male tutors provided her with a more varied and comprehensive education that was received by upper-class boys at "public schools" such as Eton and Harrow. She made commendable progress in all subjects except Latin. She could also play the piano satisfactorily, and she became a well-trained dancer, singer, watercolor painter, and horseback rider. She also became a champion of the English theater at the same time that she enjoyed visits to the circus. Victoria's Kensington Palace childhood was often a lonely one, however, one that she came to feel as a form of imprisonment and one that included very few children her own age.

Her education as monarch was guided in part by letters of advice from her maternal uncle, Prince Leopold, who in 1831 became king of the Belgians. Her first years as queen also involved the dedicated tutelage of her first prime minister, the grandfatherly Lord Melbourne, who became both her private secretary and—until her marriage to **Albert** in February 1840—her prime male companion. Melbourne's approach toward the immediate past of Victoria's kingdom and her own constitutional role within it were those of a skeptical Whig who sought to steer a middle path between despotism and democracy. Albert's influence over his wife soon became dominant, however, and between 1841 and 1861 it is difficult to disentangle her opinions and actions from his. As a constitutional monarch, Victoria lacked ultimate political power, but during her long years of widowhood, not only did she serve as a symbol of domestic morality and imperial unity, but she also continued to exercise a significant influence over the appointment of diplomats, Anglican bishops, and cabinet ministers as well as occasional acts of legislation.

ARCHIVES

Royal Archives, Windsor Castle. Correspondence, Albert's memoranda, and the surviving transcripts of Queen Victoria's daily journal.

PRINTED SOURCES

Benson, A. C. and Viscount Esher. *Letters of Queen Victoria, 1837–1861*, 3 vols. (London: John Murray, 1908).

Charlot, Monica. *Victoria, the Young Queen* (Oxford: Blackwell, 1991).

Hibbert, Christopher (ed.). *Queen Victoria in Her Life and Letters* (New York: Penguin Books, 1984).

Longford, Elizabeth. *Queen Victoria: Born to Succeed* (London: Weidenfeld and Nicolson, 1964).

St. Aubyn, Giles. *Queen Victoria: A Portrait* (New York: Atheneum, 1992).

Woodham-Smith, Cecil. *Queen Victoria: From Her Birth to the Death of the Prince Consort* (New York: Alfred Knopf, 1972).

Walter L. Arnstein

W

WAGNER, RICHARD (1813–1883). Wilhelm Richard Wagner, composer, librettist, poet, and theorist, was born in Leipzig in 1813. During his life, Wagner overcame numerous tribulations and revolutionized classical music by wedding drama and music and thus creating *Gesamtkunstwerk* (total-work-of-art). Wagner's creative development can be broken into two phases. During the first period Wagner wrote the operas *Die Feen*, *Das Liebesverbot*, and *Rienzi*. The second creative phase is characterized by Wagner's focus turning toward Germanic history and an awareness of the potential that mythology offered for musical text. This led to his most popular composition, *Der Ring des Nibelungen*, among other musical compositions. These latter operas were the culmination of years of studying Germanic legends.

Wagner's father died while he was young, thus forcing the family to move in search of financial stability. Due to his mobile life, he never received a systematic education. His uncle Adolf Wagner stood as an early mentor and introduced the boy to the great German authors: **Goethe**, **Fichte**, Schiller, and Tieck. He was a voracious reader but a poor student. While attending the Kreuz School in Dresden (1827), Wagner submerged himself in Greek history and mythology. While in Leipzig in 1828, he removed himself from St. Nicholas' School, for he believed the curriculum was below his standards. As a young artist, Wagner sought inspiration from Beethoven, Shakespeare, Goethe, Greek tragedies, and Karl Friedrich Becker, author of *History of the World*.

Die Feen (1834) was based on the text of Carlo Gozzi's *La Donna Serpente* (1762), which Wagner translated as *Die Frau als Schlange*. William Shakespeare's *Measure for Measure* was the principal textual influence for Wagner's second opera *Das Liebesverbot* (1836). *Rienze, der Letzie der Tribunen* (1840) was directly influenced by Lord **Edward Bulwer-Lytton**'s novel *Rienzi* (1835).

In 1839, Wagner fled Germany to elude his many creditors. While en route to Paris, he was inspired by the Norwegian fjords that he viewed from the ship.

With an ascetically pleasing background and the hardworking sailors, Wagner was reminded of the legendary Flying Dutchman. He was familiar with **Heinrich Heine**'s version of the legend in *Memoiren des Herrn von Schnabelewopski*. The legend, due to the nature of oral stories, varied from teller to teller, thus freeing Wagner to alter the story to a grandiose level in *Der fliegende Holländer* (1841). Also influencing Wagner's work at this period was **Arthur Schopenhauer**, particularly his *The World as Will and Redemption* (1818), which Wagner read repeatedly throughout his life.

As Wagner began work on *Tannhäuser* (1845), he realized how closely legends conformed to his artistic instincts. He was captivated by literature that suggested German artistic supremacy, most notably, Friedrich Theodor Vischer's second volume of *The Pathway of Criticism* (1844). Vischer argued that German culture had developed sufficiently to produce great works of dramatic art and suggested the medieval epic the *Nibelungenlied* as a source. Vischer, in part, inspired Wagner to begin work on his largest and most grand operatic creation, *Der Ring des Nibelungen*. The work contains four separate operas, performed in four successive evenings. The unifying theme he extracted from three primary sources of inspiration: the *Edda Saemundar*, the *Volsungasaga*, and the *Nibelungen Not und die Klage*. (Wagner's personal library contained four editions of the *Nibelungen*, two written in Middle High German and two in modern German.)

The most significant secondary source of Wagner's was **Jacob Grimm**'s *Deutsche Mythologie* (Wagner owned the second edition, 1844), which contained the creeds, ideas, and values of the Teutonic order that Wagner portrayed in his work. Other works by the Grimm brothers, Jacob and Wilhelm, served as a reference for historical information on German culture.

ARCHIVES

Wagner-Archive, Bayreuth, Katalog der Bibliothek von Richard Wagner in Wahnfried [Ms., compiled 1888].

PRINTED SOURCES

Brochmeyer, Dieter. *Richard Wagner: Theory and Theatre* (Oxford: Clarendon Press, 1991). Deals with Wagner's opinion of ancient Greece as a utopian landscape.

Cord, William O. *An Introduction to Richard Wagner's Der Ring des Nibelungen* (Athens: Ohio University Press, 1995). Detailed analysis of the *Ring*'s origin, its content, production, and premier performance of the work.

Millington, Barry (ed.). *The Wagner Compendium* (New York: Schirmer Books, 1992).

Muller, Ulrich, and Peter Wapnewski (eds.). *Wagner Handbook*, John Deathridge (trans.) (Cambridge, Mass.: Harvard University Press, 1992).

Newman, Earnest. *The Life of Richard Wagner*, 4 vols. (New York: Cambridge University Press, 1976).

Olds, Mason. "Richard Wagner and the Jews," *Religious Humanism*, 28 (Fall 1994), 189. Wagner's attitude toward the Jews; how his theories evolved throughout his life; and how interpretations of his anti-Semitic views changed after the 1930s.

Osborne, Charles. *The Complete Operas of Richard Wagner* (North Pomfret, Vt.: Trafalgar Square Publishing, 1990). Analyzes the source, content, composition, and performances of Wagner's operas.

Wagner, Richard. *My Life* (New York: Cambridge University Press, 1983).

Warrack, John. *Richard Wagner: "Die Meistersinger von Nurnberg"* (New York: Cambridge University Press, 1994).

N. Michael Zampetti

WALLACE, ALFRED RUSSEL (1823–1913).

Alfred Wallace was born in Usk, Monmouthshire, and received his only formal education at Hertford Grammar School. The cooriginator with **Charles Darwin** of the theory of evolution by means of natural selection, Wallace was a naturalist and biologist, a scientific entrepreneur, an ethnologist, and a social critic. Raised in a religious family, Wallace described himself as an agnostic when he came of age (Wallace, 1: 228). From the mid-1860s, Wallace was associated with spiritualism, and he later attributed to its teaching the continuous improvement of his character (Wallace, 2:400).

Largely self-educated, Wallace was keenly aware of the books and ideas that shaped his thinking. While working as a land surveyor, Wallace read the writings of **Robert Owen**, "my first teacher in the philosophy of human nature" (Wallace, 1:104). Inexpensive books from the Society for the Diffusion of Useful Knowledge stimulated his inclinations toward physical science. During a brief stint as a schoolteacher, Wallace devoted his spare time to reading. He traced his desire to visit the tropics to Humboldt's *Personal Narrative of Travels in South America*. He called **Malthus**'s *Essay on the Principle of Population* the most valuable book he read, noting that, without it, "I should probably not have hit upon the theory of natural selection and obtained full credit for its independent discovery" (Wallace, 1:240).

As his scientific thought matured in the 1840s, Wallace read Robert Chambers's *Vestiges of the Natural History of Creation*, a book that he felt had been "undervalued" and that confirmed his belief in the evolution of species (Wallace, 1:255). He also recognized the importance of Sir **Charles Lyell**'s *Principles of Geology*, from which he drew the idea of the succession of species in time (Wallace, 1:354–355), and of Darwin's *Voyage of the Beagle*, "so full of interest and original thought" (Wallace, 1:256). Under the influence of these sources, as well as W. H. Edwards's account of *A Voyage up the River Amazon*, Wallace and the entomologist Henry Walter Bates undertook the expedition to the Amazon that was to launch Wallace on his scientific career.

Already intellectually engaged by the problem of the origin of species, Wallace gathered empirical evidence in South America from 1848 to 1852 and in the Malay Archipelago from 1854 to 1862. During a period of forced rest, he recalled his earlier reading of Malthus, which provoked the insight that the best fitted in any population would survive the various checks to their increase. Drafting a "hasty sketch" that he hoped "would supply the missing factor to explain the origin of species," he sent it to Darwin (Wallace, 1:363). The paper, along with a short extract from Darwin's substantial work in progress, was read to the Linnean Society in June 1858.

Darwin published *On the Origin of Species by Means of Natural Selection* late in 1859. Wallace wrote Bates that he could "never have approached the completeness of his book, its vast accumulation of evidence, its overwhelming argument, and its admirable tone and spirit" (Wallace, 1:374). On his return to Britain, Wallace allied with the Darwinists in defense of the theory of evolution by means of natural selection. The difficult question of human evolution, however, led to a breach between Wallace and Darwin. As he became more influenced by spiritualism, Wallace began to question the sufficiency of natural selection in explaining the development of man's moral and intellectual faculties. Despite his disappointment in Wallace's partial recantation, Darwin, in one of his last public acts, coordinated the effort to have a civil list pension awarded to Wallace for his service to natural history.

Wallace also wrote works of social commentary. His experience as a land surveyor and his reading of **Herbert Spencer**'s *Social Statics* and Henry George's *Progress and Poverty* convinced him of the value of land nationalization. Edward Bellamy's *Looking Backward* converted Wallace to the view "not only that socialism is thoroughly practicable but that it is the only form of society worthy of civilized beings" (Wallace, 2:285). Wallace's socialism distanced him from the science establishment, as did his spiritualism and his involvement in other controversial causes, such as the Anti-Vaccination campaign. Wallace nevertheless continued to publish widely on scientific and political subjects, displaying his humanitarian spirit and optimism about the chances for human progress.

ARCHIVES

British Library. Approximately 1,300 letters to or from Wallace.
The Linnean Society of London. Letters, notebooks, and journals, as well as annotated books from Wallace's library.

PRINTED SOURCES

George, Wilma. *Biologist Philosopher: A Study of the Life and Writings of Alfred Russel Wallace* (New York: Abelard-Schuman, 1964).
Kottler, Malcolm Jay. 'Alfred Russel Wallace, the Origin of Man, and Spiritualism," *Isis*, 65 (1974), 145–192.
———. "Charles Darwin and Alfred Russel Wallace: Two Decades of Debate over Natural Selection." In David Kohn (ed.), *The Darwinian Heritage* (Princeton, N.J.: Princeton University Press, 1985).
Marchant, James. *Alfred Russel Wallace: Letters and Reminiscences* (New York: Cassell, 1916).
McKinney, Henry Lewis. *Wallace and Natural Selection* (New Haven, Conn.: Yale University Press, 1972).
Raby, Peter. *Bright Paradise: Victorian Scientific Travellers* (Princeton, N.J.: Princeton University Press, 1996).

Wallace, Alfred Russel. *My Life: A Record of Events and Opinions*, 2 vols. (New York: Dodd, Mead and Company, 1906).

Susan H. Farnsworth

WASHINGTON, BOOKER TALIAFERRO (1856–1915). Booker T. Washington, educator and reformer, was born near Hale's Ford, Virginia. Washington was raised by his mother and stepfather. Traveling black tutors gave Washington his early training and later, he attended public school. His formal education included Hampton Normal and Agricultural Institute in Virginia, from 1872–1875, and Wayland Seminary in Washington, D.C., from 1878–1879. Washington credited Baptist Sunday School attendance as part of his formal education, where he learned to read using Webster's "Blue Back Speller," and the Bible (Harlan, 34).

After briefly studying both law and theology, Washington settled on a career in education, pioneering the development of higher education for African-Americans. He advocated racial compromise and stressed the need for economic opportunity for blacks. He was the first president of the Tuskegee Institute in Tuskegee, Alabama, a school formed in 1881 for educating African-Americans.

Both Washington and scholars comment that from 1865–1875, his educators put great value and emphasis on a strong work ethic. Working as a servant for General Lewis Ruffner and his wife, Viola, proved important, as Mrs. Ruffner encouraged Washington's education. This consciousness of the value of physical labor augmented his interest in learning. Future reading and teaching at the Hampton Institute added to this, and articles in the school's journal, *The Southern Workman*, repeated this theme (Harian, 74). For Washington, true learning was practical in nature. This principle became part of his educational philosophy at the Tuskegee Institute.

In *My Larger Education* (1911), Washington wrote about the influence of his reading. *Life and Times of Frederick Douglass* made a lasting impression, and he read it many times (*The Booker T. Washington Papers*): *Autobiographical Writings*, 422). He also commented that the Bible was a part of his daily reading. While declaring himself a believer, Washington also appreciated the Bible as literature, and read it daily as such (*Autobiographical Writings*, 249). Though he did not name them specifically, he wrote that writings by other prominent African-Americans of the time were a significant part of his reading diet (*Autobiographical Writings*, 423).

ARCHIVES

The Booker T. Washington Papers, Library of Congress National Archives, Washington, D.C.
———. Tuskegee Institute, Tuskegee, Alabama.

PRINTED SOURCES

The Booker T. Washington Papers. 13 Volumes. Harlan, Louis R. (ed.) (Urbana: University of Illinois Press, 1972–1984).

Harlan, Louis R. *Booker T. Washington: The Making of A Black Leader, 1856–1901* (New York: Oxford University Press, 1972).

————. *Booker T. Washington: The Wizard of Tuskegee, 1901–1915* (New York: Oxford University Press, 1983).

Matthews, Basil. *Booker T. Washington, Educator and Interracial Interpreter* (Cambridge: Harvard University Press, 1948).

Meier, August. *Negro Thought in America, 1880–1915* (Ann Arbor: University of Michigan Press, 1963).

Smock, Raymond W. (ed.) *Booker T. Washington in Perspective: Essays of Louis R. Harlan* (Jackson: University Press of Mississippi, 1986).

                                                                                    Christopher Beckham

WELLINGTON, ARTHUR WELLESLEY, 1ST DUKE OF (1769–1852).
Arthur Wellesley was born in Dublin in 1769 and educated at Eton (1781–1784) and the Royal Academy of Equitation at Angers, Anjou, France (1785–1786). Although Irish, by birth he belonged to the aristocratic Protestant ascendancy that dominated that largely Roman Catholic island and was automatically instructed in the tenets of the established British Church. As soldier, statesman, and politician, Wellington embodied a very British tradition of pragmatic and enlightened conservatism and a readiness to adapt to changing circumstances.

An indifferent student, Wellington's failure to win distinction at school persuaded his family that the army was the only possible career open to him. As a young man, however, he embarked on an extensive program of self-education, facilitated by lengthy periods of often undemanding duties as aide-de-camp to the Lord Lieutenant of Ireland (1788–1794), and he continued his studies while on military service in India (1796–1801). In Ireland a casual acquaintance encountered him reading John Locke's *Essay Concerning Human Understanding*; a biographer speculates that this work's "celebrated demonstration that all knowledge derives from *experience* was well calculated to appeal" to him (Longford, 1:28). Sailing to India in 1796, Wellington was accompanied by a trunkful of books. Besides the perhaps predictable works on Asian history, geography, and languages and on military subjects, with a strong emphasis on the British experience in Asia and Africa, these included few of the standard classics one might expect to find in a gentleman's library, which were represented only by Plutarch's *Lives* (in English) and Caesar's *Commentaries* in Latin. Instead, Wellington chose a wide selection of recent writings on philosophy, politics, government, economics, law, history, and theology, a clear indication of his preference for the practical and utilitarian. Among them were volumes by most of the prominent thinkers of the liberal European enlightenment, including Voltaire, Jean-Jacques Rousseau, Locke, Adam Smith, and David Hume. Works by the military men Frederick the Great and the Marchal de Saxe were complemented by Sir William Blackstone's *Commentaries on the Laws of England*, Lord Bolingbroke's history and political philosophy, and William Paley's theology. Wellington's personal library also included a selection of often slightly disreputable fiction and satire, Cébillon's plays, 24 volumes of Jonathan Swift, novels by Tobias Smollett, and various semipornographic literary productions (Guedalla, 54–65). It was the library of an ambitious man who deliberately prepared for a successful career as a soldier–administrator by extensive study of leading contemporary thinking on every aspect of government. Wellington's pragmatic, even cynical, ability in his post-Waterloo political years to temper his fundamental conservatism with compromise on such issues as Catholic emancipation can perhaps be traced back to this rigorous program of self-education.

ARCHIVES

Wellington Papers. The University of Southampton. Official papers.
Wellington Papers. In possession of the Duke of Wellington, Stratfield Saye. Personal papers.

PRINTED SOURCES

Guedalla, Philip. *The Duke* (London: Hodder and Stoughton, 1931).
Hibbert, Christopher. *Wellington: A Personal History* (London: HarperCollins, 1997).
Longford, Elizabeth. *Wellington*, 2 vols. (New York: Harper & Row, 1969–1972).
Maxwell, Sir Herbert. *The Life of Wellington*, 2 vols. (London: Bohn, 1899).
Petrie, Sir Charles. *Wellington: A Reassessment* (London: James Barrie, 1956).
Ward, S.P.G. *Wellington* (London: B. T. Batsford, 1963).
Wellesley, Muriel. *The Man Wellington* (London: Constable, 1937).
———. *Wellington in Civil Life* (London: Constable, 1939).

Priscilla Roberts

WELLS, HERBERT GEORGE (H. G.) (1866–1946).

H. G. Wells was born in Bromley, Kent, England, in 1866 to Sarah and Joseph Wells. His mother was a housekeeper in Uppark, a local estate, and his father was a part-time shop-keeper and a semiprofessional cricketer. After a few disastrous apprenticeships, Wells became a teacher–student at Midhurst grammar school. He received a scholarship to attend the Normal School of Science (later known as Imperial College of Science and Technology) in London to study biology. Wells provided the public with a wide range of reading material (over 80 books), which included science fiction, utopian blueprints, and social commentary novels. Besides conjuring up extraordinary visions of time travel and Martian invasions, he also anticipated future inventions and drew up plans for a world state. Often seen as a "Middle-brow" he reached millions with his *Outline of History* (1920), which became the biggest best-seller after the Bible in the 1920s. Wells met many world leaders including both Roosevelts, Lenin, and Stalin. He was a supporter of the League of Nations and involved in its formation. Wells married twice and had a number of mistresses. An interesting account of the influences in his life is provided in his two-volume work *Experiment in Autobiography* (1934).

The main themes of Well's work are clearly rooted in his early reading. He had access to the library in Uppark, and his father borrowed books for him from the local Literary Institute. In his autobiography he recalls that when he was confined to a sofa with a broken leg at the age of seven or eight, he read works of history, astronomy, natural history, geography, and fiction and also leafed through *Punch* magazine (Wells, 76–78). Among the many authors he read were Plato, Voltaire, Paine, Swift, and Dr. Johnson. Influenced particularly by **Charles Darwin**, Wells was inspired to study under his friend biologist **Thomas Huxley**. According to one of his biographers, Wells had "just enough science to imagine its potentialities" (Dickson, 34). While he was in college, he read **Blake** and **Carlyle**'s *French Revolution* instead of studying for exams (Dickson, 35). He also read **Marx**, and this influence may be seen in his joining the Fabian Society (middle-class intellectuals with socialist leanings) in 1903 and in his futuristic visions of a world state with one language and one government. It is evident from a perusal of Wellsian literature that it is the work of one who reflected, anticipated, and most of all, read widely.

ARCHIVES

H. G. Wells Papers, Library of the University of Illinois at Champagne-Urbana.
H. G. Wells Collection, Central Library at Bromley, Kent, England.

PRINTED SOURCES

Dickson, L. *H. G. Wells. His Turbulent Life and Times* (New York: Atheneum, 1969).
Foot, Michael. *The History of Mr. Wells* (Washington, D.C.: Counterpoint, 1995).
Parrinder, P. (ed.). *H. G. Wells: The Critical Heritage* (London: Routledge and Kegan Paul, 1972).
Wells, H. G. *An Experiment in Autobiography* (London: Victor Gallancz/Cresset Press, 1934).
West, A. *H. G. Wells, Aspects of a Life* (New York: Random House, 1984).

Cliona Murphy

WELLS, IDA BARNETT (1862–1931). Ida Bell (Barnett) Wells was born in Holly Springs, Mississippi, in 1862. She was the daughter of Jim Wells, the son of his master and a slave, and Lizzie Warrenton Wells, who was a slave from Virginia. In 1878, her parents and youngest brother died of yellow fever. To prevent the separation of the six remaining siblings, Wells interrupted her studies and took the examination for a country schoolteacher. She never graduated from Rust University but continued her education in Memphis, where she attended Fisk University and Lemoyne Institute. Wells is best known for her journalism, which criticized lynching and discriminatory social practices and advocated universal suffrage.

Wells states, "I had always been a voracious reader. . . . [I] read all the fiction in the Sunday school library and in Rust College" (*Autobiography*, 21). Her early teachers were white men and women who came from the North to teach after the war. Wells read **Charles Dickens**, Sir **Walter Scott**, **Louisa May**

Alcott, **Charlotte Brontë**, Shakespeare, and the Bible but nothing by a Negro (*Autobiography*, 21–22). She does not describe these readings as having a direct influence on her own prodigious output; her intellectual engagement and influences are with her contemporaries. In Memphis, Wells became involved with the lyceum, which was composed of teachers who engaged in recitations, essays, and debates ending with a reading from the journal *Evening Star* (*Autobiography*, 23). This contact ended in Wells's writing a column under the name "Iola" in *The Living Way*.

Wells also engaged in a joint venture with Mr. J. L. Fleming and Rev. F. Nightingale as editor of *Free Speech and Headlight*. An article criticizing the school system cost Wells her teaching job. "I never cared for teaching. . . . The correspondence I had built up in newspaper work gave me an outlet through which to express the real 'me' " (*Autobiography*, 31). Journalism also endangered her life; after her report on the lynching of Thomas Moss, she had to move to New York to escape threats. In Philadelphia she spoke against lynching and the pathologizing of black male sexuality. There she met William Still, who wrote *The Underground Railroad*, and Catherine Impey, editor of *Anti-Caste*, who subsequently invited her to speak in England.

Wells was acquainted with many of the foremost intellectuals of her time: **Booker T. Washington, Frederick Douglass, W.E.B. Du Bois**, the educator Green Polonius Hamilton, Mary Church Terrell, and **Susan B. Anthony**. Wells, Douglass, and Ferdinand L. Barnett, an attorney and newspaper editor who later became her husband, collaborated on a pamphlet "The Reason Why the Colored American Is Not in the World's Columbian Exposition" in 1893. In 1903, she, and her husband, defended Du Bois's criticism of Washington in *The Souls of Black Folk* (*Autobiography*, 322–323). In addition to her journalism, Wells wrote letters and essays and participated in salons and the Black Women's Club movement.

ARCHIVES

The Ida B. Wells Papers are in the Department of Special Collections of the Joseph Regenstein Library at the University of Chicago.

PRINTED SOURCES

Duster, Alfreda M. (ed.). *Crusade for Justice: The Autobiography of Ida B. Wells* (Chicago: University of Chicago Press, 1972). Wells's posthumously published autobiography was begun in 1928 and written mostly from memory.

Thompson, Mildred I. *Ida B. Wells-Barnett: An Exploratory Study of an American Black Woman, 1893–1930* (Brooklyn, N.Y.: Carlson Publishing, 1990).

Wells, Ida B. *The Memphis Diary of Ida B. Wells: An Intimate Portrait of the Activist as a Young Woman* (Boston: Beacon Press, 1995).

———. *Selected Works of Ida B. Wells-Barnett*, Trudier Harris (ed.) (New York: Oxford University Press, 1991).

Kathleen J. Wininger

WHISTLER, JAMES ABBOTT MCNEILL (1834–1903). James Whistler, American artist, was born in Lowell, Massachusetts, in 1834. When Whistler was nine years old, his family moved to St. Petersburg, Russia, where his father took up a position as a railway engineer. A brief stay in England was followed by a return to America, and Whistler's formal education was completed with three years of study at the United States Military Academy. Much of his adult life was spent in London and Paris, where his bohemian exploits and his painting rivaled the accomplishments of his European Impressionist contemporaries and helped establish an important precedent for future American artists who ventured abroad throughout the twentieth century.

It is widely claimed that Whistler did not like to read, though his decision to pursue a career as an artist was influenced by books to which he was exposed as an adolescent. His father counseled reading, as did British painter Charles Leslie, whom Whistler heard speak at the Royal Academy in London and whose lectures he surely read. Whistler was greatly moved both by Anna Brownell Jameson's *Memoirs of the Early Italian Painters*, a work that inspired him to question the nature and the substance of art, and Joshua Reynolds's *Discourses*, a work that underlined for Whistler the depth of the artistic tradition that must be assimilated by a young painter. While a student at West Point, Whistler read a number of influential novelists like Samuel Butler, Oliver Goldsmith, and **Walter Scott** (Fleming, 42), though he later acknowledged that **Charles Dickens** was his favorite writer.

Whistler is perhaps best known for his works including *Arrangement in Grey and Black*, *Portrait of the Painter's Mother*, *Old Battersea Bridge*; and *Nocturne in Black and Gold, The Falling Rocket*, the criticism of which precipitated a successful libel suit against critic **John Ruskin**. The extent to which Whistler's painting was influenced directly by his interest in the other arts is unclear; he is also noted for *The White Girl*, for example, though he claimed never to have read the contemporaneous Wilkie Collins novel *The Woman in White*, a work to which the portrait seems to owe some debt. It is more certain, however, that Whistler took little interest in American letters, though he attempted in the 1870s a painting based upon "Annabel Lee," the poem by **Edgar Allan Poe**. In his later years, Whistler claimed to enjoy the poetry of Anne Barbauld, the published sermons of Robert Blair, and the novels of Marie Louise de Ramée, who published as Ouida (Fleming, 164). More likely, these years were filled with a growing knowledge of the works of his literary friends, including Stéphane Mallarmé and **Dante Gabriel Rossetti**. Whistler was an influential figure in his own time; his work and ideas were important to the poet Algernon Swinburne, for example. The American painter even served briefly as a mentor to **Oscar Wilde**.

ARCHIVES

Pennell-Whistler Collection, Library of Congress, Washington, D.C.
Whistler Archive, University of Glasgow Library. Principal papers.

PRINTED SOURCES

Denker, Eric. *In Pursuit of the Butterfly: Portraits of James McNeill Whistler* (Washington, D.C.: National Portrait Gallery, 1995).

Dorment, Richard. *James McNeill Whistler* (New York: H. N. Abrams, 1995).

Fine, Ruth E. *James McNeill Whistler: A Reexamination* (Washington, D.C.: National Gallery of Art, 1987).

Fleming, G. H. *James Abbott McNeill Whistler: A Life* (New York: St. Martin's Press, 1991).

Fryberger, Betsy. *Whistler: Themes and Variations* (Stanford, Calif.: Stanford University Museum of Art, 1978).

Gettscher, Robert H., and Paul G. Marks. *James McNeill Whistler and John Singer Sargent* (New York: Garland, 1986).

Koval, Anne. *Whistler in His Time* (London: Tate Gallery, 1994).

Pennell, Elizabeth, and Joseph Pennell. *The Life of James McNeill Whistler* (Philadelphia: Lippincott, 1908).

Whistler, James McNeill. *Whistler on Art: Selected Letters and Writings, 1849–1903*, Nigel Thorpe (ed.) (Washington, D.C.: Smithsonian Institution Press, 1995).

Young, Andrew McLaren. *The Paintings of James McNeill Whistler* (New Haven, Conn.: Yale University Press, 1980).

Craig Monk

WHITMAN, WALT (1819–1892). Walt Whitman was born in the farming community of Huntington, New York, on Long Island, in 1819. He had only the barest formal education, having attended District School No. 1 in Brooklyn, where his family had moved, from 1825 (perhaps earlier) to 1830. He was a mediocre student and went largely unnoticed among the throng of students assigned to the lone, overworked teacher. His real education began when he became a printer's apprentice for local newspapers, beginning a long career in that business, becoming by 1836 a writer and editor, most notably for the Brooklyn *Daily Eagle* and *The Democratic Review*. Whitman also often worked as a schoolteacher during these years, sometimes concomitantly with his newspaper work.

With just 5 (possibly 6) years of schooling, then, Whitman was largely self-educated. While he received the rudiments of reading and ciphering in the Brooklyn public school, his imagination was not fired until being subscribed to a circulation library at age 11, when he began to read widely in popular literature, especially in adventure stories such as *The Arabian Nights*. Particularly influential was a collection of folk ballads by Sir **Walter Scott**, *The Border Minstrelsy*, which appeared in the United States in 1830. Later he would claim that "if you could reduce the *Leaves [of Grass]* to their elements you would see Scott unmistakably active at the roots." Not only the ballads themselves but Scott's copious notes influenced Whitman's idea of poetry being not merely the product of the romantic artist but the expression of a people.

The broader currents of Romanticism also influenced Whitman. It is uncertain whether he read John Neal's novel *Randolph*, or whether he absorbed Neal's argument for less rigid poetical structures through other Romantics such as **Ralph Waldo Emerson**. Regardless, *Leaves of Grass* epitomizes the looser meters and structures that contrast sharply with the neoclassical poetry of the eighteenth century.

Another important literary influence was Fanny Wright's *Ten Days in Athens* (1822), which Whitman described as "daily food to me." Deeply interested in the reform movements of his day (he was the author of a temperance novel), Wright's novel was an exemplar of literature as a vehicle for progressive ideas.

In addition to the aforementioned works, it should be noted that as a dreamy schoolteacher on Long Island Whitman spent time immersed in Shakespeare, the Bible, Eastern philosophy, Greek heroic poetry, and even the Niebelungen Epic. But even this inventory cannot account for all the influences on *Leaves of Grass*, for perhaps no other poet was ever more involved in the culture of his own times. The ferment of American reform movements, religious awakenings, the popular entertainments of the city, especially music and theater—Whitman culled them all for inspiration and mined them for subject material.

ARCHIVES

Library of Congress, Charles E. Feinberg and Thomas B. Harned Collections.

PRINTED SOURCES

Myerson, Joel (ed.). *The Walt Whitman Archive*, 3 vols (New York: Garland, 1993).
Reynolds, David S. *Walt Whitman's America: A Cultural Biography* (New York: Knopf, 1995).

Christopher Berkeley

WHITNEY, ELI (1765–1825). Eli Whitney was born in Westboro, Massachusetts, in 1765 and educated at Yale (1789–1792). Whitney's cotton gin (1793) was the first capable of processing the cheaper American "short-staple" cotton and created an explosion in cotton agriculture throughout the American South. In 1797, Whitney contracted with the United States government to execute the first mass production of military arms. His development of interchangeable and standardized components, and his efficient division of labor in production, presaged the future of manufacturing in early American industry.

Whitney had already established a reputation for himself in the mechanical arts well before he attended Yale in preparation for a career at the bar. At age 13, he crafted a competent violin, and during the American Revolution, he ran a nail forgery out of his father's workshop. The curriculum at Yale under Ezra Stiles's presidency reflected the intellectual currents of the Enlightenment: Newton, Locke, Voltaire, Smith, Montesquieu, and the standard Latin and Greek histories. Stiles himself lectured on, and reproduced, Joseph Priestly's experiments. Whitney's senior oration—"Does National Security Depend on Fostering Domestic Industries?"—contested Lord Sheffield's assertions about American

Atlantic economic insecurity in his *Observations on the Commerce of the American States* (Mirsky, 61). While his future was not to be found in law or natural philosophy, it is clear that Whitney's Enlightenment education added an intense enthusiasm for efficiency and systemization to his natural penchant for mechanical invention. Moving to South Carolina upon graduation, Whitney was introduced to the problem of American cotton: southern soil would yield only "short-staple" cotton, whose fibers were too short and clung too tenaciously to the seed for traditional "roller" gins. Whitney investigated mechanical operations in British textiles. James Hargreaves's spinning jenny (1767), Richard Arkwright's warp frame (1774), and Samuel Crompton's mule (1779) all sought to replicate and combine multiple human motions through mechanical operations. When Whitney observed slaves pulling the short-staple cotton fibers through their fingers to separate them from the seed, he conceived a gin with wire fingers running through a close template—the chief characteristic of Whitney's gin (later gins would employ teethed discs). In bringing his gin into production, Whitney standardized the components and individuated tasks among his workmen. When defending his patent rights nearly drove him into bankruptcy, Whitney applied his production techniques to the manufacture of guns. Applying the principles of Jean-Baptiste de Gribeauval's systematization of French munitions production to his own organizational methods, Whitney was able to turn out uniform arms by the thousands. In his two major contributions to manufacturing and agriculture, Whitney sought to impose the regularity and efficiency of the world he discovered in the French and English philosophes upon the everyday problems of the workshop: a remarkable confluence of eighteenth-century scientific sophistication and pragmatic American ingenuity.

ARCHIVES

Two fires—at his workshop in 1795 and at the United States Patent Office in 1836—destroyed the majority of Whitney's papers. The chief archival sources are: Connecticut State Library, Whitney will, codicil, and inventory; Massachusetts Historical Society, MS Letters, Whitney correspondence 1793, 1809; Historical Society of Pennsylvania, MS Letters, Whitney correspondence 1803–1824.

PRINTED SOURCES

Mirsky, Jeannette, and A. Nevins. *The World of Eli Whitney* (New York: Macmillan Company, 1952).
Whitney, Eli. *The Oration on the Death of Mr. Robert Grant, Member of the Senior Class* . . . (New Haven, Conn., 1792).

Jason M. Barrett

WHITTIER, JOHN GREENLEAF (1807–1892). John Greenleaf Whittier, poet, was born to a Quaker family in Haverhill, Massachusetts, in 1807. After several years of primary education, he received several years of religious instruction at Haverhill Academy (May 1827–November 1828). Whittier became best known for his strong abolitionist stance prior to the American Civil War (1861–1865).

The Bible, kept in the family library, was an important part of Whittier's early education. The *American Perceptor*, a book of antislavery prose and poetry, was his principal reading while attending the academy in East Haverhill. The Quaker ideals of simplicity and determination complemented the texts found in the small Whittier family library. These included biographies, autobiographies, memoirs, and Quaker journals. Whittier's love of biography provided him with a strong sense of human morality and justice.

John A. Pollard credits Whittier with the ability to imaginatively travel to far lands while keeping a strong foothold on the truth of history. To cite an instance, Cornelius Agrippa's *Occult Philosophy* and Charles Rollin's *Ancient History* informed Whittier's knowledge of the past. This schema, assimilated with his uncle's and father's (John Whittier) travel anecdotes, created a fantastic story line inherent in the poem *Snowbound*, written in 1866. Whittier was also fond of poetry by his sister Elizabeth and friend Elizabeth Lloyd.

Perhaps the first works outside of the Whittier library that had a profound effect on Whittier were those of Robert Burns. Francis H. Underwood emphasized Burns's *Banks of Doon* and *Highland Mary* as having passionately influenced the poet's heart and mind. Whittier's early attempts at poetry, such as *Barefoot Boy*, were written in a style similar to that of Robert Burns. Whittier's various jobs as an editor gave him an opportunity to review the latest in public opinion and verse. During the 1830s, the antislavery propaganda became prominent in the northern states, and Whittier absorbed much of the abolitionist literature. The works of Lucy Hooper, a poet he met and reviewed in New York in 1837, gave Whittier another source of antislavery prose, written from a youth's point of view.

ARCHIVES

John Greenleaf Whittier Archives available at the Haverhill Library located in Haverhill, Massachusetts.

PRINTED SOURCES

Bennett, Whitman. *Whittier, Bard of Freedom* (Chapel Hill: University of North Carolina Press, 1941).

Currier, Thomas F. *Elizabeth Lloyd and the Whittiers: A Budget of Letters* (Cambridge, Mass.: Harvard University Press, 1939).

Pickard, Samuel T. *Life and Letters of John Greenleaf Whittier*, 2 vols. (New York: Haskell House Publishers Ltd., 1969).

Pollard, John A. *John Greenleaf Whittier: Friend of Man* (Boston: Houghton Mifflin, 1949).

Underwood, Francis H. *John Greenleaf Whittier* (Boston: Riverside Press, Cambridge, 1980).

Brian J. Sauers

WILBERFORCE, WILLIAM (1759–1833). William Wilberforce, was born in the English port city of Hull in 1759 into a family grown wealthy from the Baltic trade. Wilberforce attended the endowed grammar school of Pocklington (1771–1776) and St. Johns College, Cambridge (1776–1779). William's aunt and uncle had been drawn to the Evangelical revival through the Methodist minister George Whitefield. William's mother, a more typical member of the Church of England, suspected this earnest religious movement and limited his contact with it when he was 12. He had a socially merry adolescence as his family brought him into the round of theater, balls, great suppers, and card parties. He early showed an interest in literature and an intense dislike of the slave trade but was much absorbed into cultivated society and entered college filled with what he would later call self-indulgent habits. Wilberforce entered Parliament in 1780, forming a fast friendship with future Prime Minister William Pitt. In 1787, two years after his own conversion to evangelical Christianity, he became parliamentary leader of the long campaign that brought the abolition of the slave trade in 1807. He continued to lead the antislavery forces until his public retirement in 1825 and died only three days after the bill abolishing slavery in the British Empire passed in 1833. Wilberforce also encouraged penal and moral reform and supported many religious, humanitarian, and philanthropic efforts.

Wilberforce was endowed with quick wit and intelligence but was physically small and weak and had poor eyesight. Despite apparently austere religious principles, he remained a lively conversationalist. After meeting him at a dinner party in 1814, the French Romantic writer **Madame de Staël** remarked that she had always heard that Wilberforce was the most religious, "but I now find that he is the wittiest man in England" (Wilberforce, 4:167). He was also among the best read. Of a popular evangelical minister, Wilberforce remarked that he had "extraordinary powers" but that "he sadly needs the chastening hand of a sound classical education" (Wilberforce, 5:189). Wilberforce's own parliamentary speeches (often extempore) were salted with quotations from Cicero, Virgil, and other classical authors but also with citations from more recent writers like Samuel Johnson, Alexander Pope, and **William Cowper**. He read many works of the Enlightenment and reviewed Adam Smith more than once in his parliamentary career (Wilberforce, 2:387; 3:349). Although he read the works of Bishop Joseph Butler and William Paley, Wilberforce's theology was more practically influenced by his personal intimacy with Evangelicals like John Newton, Charles Simeon, and Thomas Gisborne. Wilberforce's *Practical View of Christianity* (1797) suggests a lasting impact of Philip Dodderidge's *Rise and Progress of Religion*, which he had read in 1785 (Wilberforce, 1:76). Wilberforce was also attracted to the practical designs of the utilitarian philosopher **Jeremy Bentham** and spent many years promoting Bentham's plans for penal and legal reform. Wilberforce loved to read, and as his eyesight began to fail, he had both new and old books and essays read to him. The works of Maria Edgeworth, Sir

Walter Scott and **William Wordsworth** were among his favorites in later years (Wilberforce, 3:472; 4:260; 5:254).

ARCHIVES

William Wilberforce Papers. Bodleian Library, Oxford University. MS Wilberforce and MS Don e.164. Contains most of the unpublished sources used in the *Life* written by his sons.
Anti-Slavery Papers. Rhodes House Library, Oxford. MSS Brit. Emp.s. 18.

PRINTED SOURCES

Anstey, Roger. *The Atlantic Slave Trade and British Abolition, 1760–1810* (Atlantic Highlands, N.J.: Humanities Press, 1975). Remarkable discussion of the ideas influencing those involved in the antislavery movement.
Bebbington, David. "Revival and Enlightenment in Eighteenth-Century England." In *Modern Christian Revivals*, Edith Blumhofer and Robert Balmer (eds.) (Urbana: University of Illinois Press, 1993). Evidence of the literary and philosophical sources influencing the early Evangelicals and challenges the notion that the revival was merely a reaction to Enlightenment rationalism.
Pollock, John. *Wilberforce* (London: Constable, 1977). Extensive use and review of the primary sources makes this both a balanced and scholarly modern biography.
Wilberforce, Robert Isaac, and Samuel Wilberforce. *The Life of William Wilberforce*, 5 vols. (London: John Murray, 1838). The standard nineteenth-century biography, with extensive quotations from Wilberforce's letters and journals.

Richard R. Follett

WILDE, OSCAR FINGAL O'FLAHERTIE WILLS (1854–1900). Oscar Wilde, playwright and poet, was born in Dublin in 1854, the second son of the oculist Sir William Wilde and Lady Wilde (née Jane Frances[ca] Elgee, the Young Ireland poetess "Speranza"). His mother claimed descent from Dante, but her closest literary ancestor was Charles Maturin, author of *Melmoth the Wanderer*, a Gothic novel that fascinated Wilde (Ellmann, *Oscar Wilde*, 6, 25). Its influence can be seen in *The Picture of Dorian Gray* (and in the fact that Wilde adopted the name Sebastian Melmoth after his imprisonment, 1897). Wilde was educated at the Portora Royal School (1864–1871), at Trinity College, Dublin (1871–1873), and at Magdalen College, Oxford (1874–1877), where he took a double first and won the Newdigate Prize for Poetry in 1878. At Trinity, his tutor was the classicist and raconteur John Pentland Mahaffy, remembered by Wilde as "the scholar who showed me how to love things Greek" (*Letters*, 338).

Wilde's Oxford notebooks reveal his taste for Swinburne's sensual Pre-Raphaelitism and that Swinburne led him to the symbolists and Baudelaire. They also reveal his continuing philhellenism: his interest in Greek (and contemporary) philosophy and in Dante, Durer, **Keats**, and **Blake**, as "the best representatives of the Greek spirit" of his age (Smith, passim; Ellmann, *Oscar Wilde*, 40–42).

At Oxford, Wilde was exposed to the conflicting influences of **John Ruskin** and **Walter Pater**. He engaged in practical projects with Ruskin and loved his "mighty and majestic prose." Pater's *Renaissance* was his "golden book," and he reflected in *De Profundis* (1897) that it had had "a strange influence" over his life (*Letters*, 471). Ruskin appealed to Wilde's conscience as Pater did to his imagination. In his first published prose, when Wilde wrote that England, the land of "the vile deification of the machine," had yet produced artists who would foster a revival of culture and love of beauty, Ruskin and Pater were prominent in a short list of writers (Ellmann, *Oscar Wilde*, 78).

Wilde's *Poems* appeared in 1881. "Swinburne and water," jeered *Punch*, but J. A. Symonds found in them a "Keatsian openness." There was a colder reception of his work at the library of the Oxford Union, where it was attacked as immoral and lifted in large part from Shakespeare, Philip Sidney, Donne, **Byron**, **William Morris**, and of course, Swinburne (*Oscar Wilde*, Ellmann, 138–140).

Wilde turned from poetry to write short stories, particularly fairy tales. Certain tales were culled from his father's researches into Irish folklore, published by Lady Wilde as *Ancient Legends and Superstitions of Ireland* (1888), and followed the tradition of **Hans Christian Andersen** in delivering moral messages. However, the messages delivered, to parent-readers rather than child-listeners, were often from William Morris, whose influence, notably that of *News from Nowhere* (1890), is also felt in Wilde's most political work "The Soul of Man under Socialism" (1891) (Varty, 87–89).

Wilde was out of sympathy with the English novel, but the influence of French fiction was immense. **Stendhal** was "one of the few" authors he read and reread (Ellmann, *Oscar Wilde*, 235). **Flaubert**, to whose work he had been introduced by Pater, was "the sinless master" (*More Letters*, 82). **Balzac**'s *La Peau de chagrin* has been suggested as a possible source book for *The Picture of Dorian Gray* (Ellmann, *Oscar Wilde*, 293), but the clearest influences on the novel were Pater's ideas and Joris-Karl Huysmans's *À Rebours* (1884). Huysmans's Des Esseintes, scholar and debauchee, was a hero who tried to live up to Pater's ideals. Wilde's Dorian is poisoned by a book given him by the Mephistophelian Lord Henry Wotton: the book Wilde had in mind was one that synthesized Huysmans's *À Rebours* and Pater's *Renaissance* (Varty, 123–127).

The aphoristic Preface to *Dorian Gray* was a bow to Stéphane Mallarmé, whom Wilde had visited in 1891, while writing it. Mallarmé's *Herodiade* also influenced *Salomé* (1891), but Wilde also listed Theophile Gautier, Maeterlinck, Anatole France, Marcel Schwob, and Flaubert as joint authors of his "mosaic." The play was also influenced by Huysmans's reflections on Gustave Moreau's paintings of *Salomé Dancing before Herod* in *À Rebours* (Varty, 137) and by Aeschylus's *Agamemnon*, a work that had fired Wilde's imagination since childhood (*Oscar Wilde*, Ellmann, 21–22, 326).

Wilde made a false start as a dramatist. An early melodrama *Vera, or the Nihilists* (1881) was followed by the equally unsuccessful blank verse tragedy

The Duchess of Padua (1883). But while he was working on *Salome*, Wilde completed his first contemporary comedy, and with *Lady Windermere's Fan* (1892), he joined the lists of the great Anglo-Irish observers of English life, like George Farquhar and Richard Brinsley Sheridan, who were able to dress up social satires as comedies of manners. Wilde took elements of *Lady Windermere's Fan* from Sheridan's *The School for Scandal* (1777), but there were also stylistic borrowings from the well-made play formula pioneered by Victorien Sardou and, in later plays, echoes from **Henrik Ibsen** (Powell, 73–88). In his last play *The Importance of Being Earnest* (1895), Wilde subverted the other popular genre of the age, the farce as written by Arthur Wing Pinero and **William S. Gilbert** (Powell, passim).

For his last literary work, *The Ballad of Reading Gaol* (1896), Wilde took imagery from **Coleridge**'s *The Rime of the Ancient Mariner*, but the metrical form he adopted repeated that of Denis Florence McCarthy's "New Year's Song" which his mother would have recited to him from the Young Ireland anthology *The Spirit of the Nation* (1845) (Coakley, in Sandulescu, 52–53). The Irish influences on Wilde (like those that place him in the homosexual subculture of late Victorian London) are only now beginning to be researched.

In contrast with **Yeats**, who was always looking to be counted among companies of writers and thinkers, Wilde wore his learning lightly and did not feel there was any advantage in discussing his sources openly.

ARCHIVES

Widely dispersed: Major public collections are at Harvard and the University of California at Los Angeles. The major private collection is held by Merlin Holland, Wilde's grandson.

PRINTED SOURCES

Bendz, Ernst. *The Influence of Pater and Matthew Arnold in the Prose Writings of Oscar Wilde* (Gothenburg and London, 1914). On "The Critic as Artist" as an answer to Arnold's views of the superiority of creation over criticism.

Dollimore, Jonathan. *Sexual Dissidence. Augustine to Wilde, Freud to Foucault* (Oxford: Clarendon Press, 1991).

Ellmann, Richard. *Oscar Wilde* (New York: Knopf, 1987).

——— (ed.). *Oscar Wilde: A Collection of Critical Essays* (Englewood Cliffs, N.J.: Prentice-Hall, 1969). Includes Thomas Mann's "Wilde and Nietzsche" in which he acknowledges Wilde's similarity to Nietzsche in his transvaluation of values.

Gagnier, Regenia. *Idylls of the Market Place. Oscar Wilde and the Victorian Public* (Stanford, Calif.: Stanford University Press, 1986). Examines Wilde in the context of Victorian political economy and liberalism.

Pine, Richard. *The Thief of Reason: Oscar Wilde and Modern Ireland* (Dublin: Gill and Macmillan, 1995).

Powell, Kerry. *Oscar Wilde and the Theatre of the 1890s* (Cambridge: Cambridge University Press, 1990).

Raby, Peter (ed.). *The Cambridge Companion to Oscar Wilde* (Cambridge: Cambridge University Press, 1997).

Sandulescu, C. George (ed.). *Rediscovering Oscar Wilde* (Gerrards Cross: C. Smythe, 1994). Includes Davis Coakley's "The Neglected Years: Wilde in Dublin."

Smith, Philip E., II, and Michael S. Helfand (eds.). *Oscar Wilde's Oxford Notebooks: A Portrait of Mind in the Making* (New York and Oxford: Oxford University Press 1989). Considers Wilde as a philosopher with a theory of cultural evolutionism taken from Herbert Spencer.

Stanford, W. B., and R. B. McDowell. *Mahaffy* (London: Routledge and Kegan Paul, 1971).

Varty, Anne. *A Preface to Oscar Wilde* (London: Longman, 1998).

White, Terence de Vere. *The Parents of Oscar Wilde* (London: Hodder and Staughton, 1967).

Wilde, Oscar. *The Letters of Oscar Wilde*, Rupert Hart-Davis (ed.) (London: Rupert Hart-Davis Ltd., 1962).

———. *More Letters of Oscar Wilde*, Rupert Hart-Davis (ed.) (London: John Murray, 1985). Includes "Mr Oscar Wilde on Mr Oscar Wilde: An Interview," *St James' Gazette*, January 18, 1895, in which Wilde declares himself to have been influenced by no dramatists of his century (and interested only in two: Victor Hugo and Maeterlinck). Asked if any writers had influenced his nondramatic work, he replied: "Setting aside the prose and poetry of Greek and Latin authors, the only writers who have influenced me are Keats, Flaubert and Walter Pater; and before I came across them I had already gone more than half-way to meet them. Style must be in one's soul before one can recognize it in others" (189–196).

Joseph A. F. Spence

WORDSWORTH, WILLIAM (1770–1850). William Wordsworth was born in Cockermouth, Cumberland, in 1770 and educated at Hawkshead Grammar School (1778–1787) and St. John's College, Cambridge (1787–1790; B.A., 1791). Wordsworth was born and died in the Church of England, but he was influenced by the rationalist fervor of the early 1790s, particularly by Godwin's *Political Justice* (1793) and, later in the same decade, by his friend **Samuel Taylor Coleridge**, who introduced him to the associationist philosophy of David Hartley, to Spinoza, Kant, and the Platonic tradition. The religion that animates his finest poetry is his own, resting ultimately on personal mystical experience and summed up in the phrase "Love of Nature leading to Love of Man" (*The Prelude*, viii, title). Its doctrine is inseparable from its expression in his poetry. Wordsworth's achievement lies in his eloquent articulation of a comprehensive vision of human life, its greatness and its littleness, in relation to the natural world in which it is lived. However great its flights, his imagination remains grounded in very specific places; he is the most geographical of poets. Readers unmoved by formal creeds have found religious feeling in his poetry, a well-known example being **John Stuart Mill**, who was helped to recover from his early emotional breakdown by reading *The Excursion* (1814).

Wordsworth is unique among major poets in that his greatest work is an account of his own formation. *The Prelude or Growth of a Poet's Mind* (expanded from 2 books in 1799 to 13 in 1805, and later extensively revised; not published until after the poet's death in 1850) was intended as the introduction to a vast philosophical poem on man, nature, and society. The categories employed to describe his childhood ("Fostered alike by beauty and by fear" [1: 302]) come from Edmund Burke's *Philosophical Enquiry into the Origin of Our Ideas of the Sublime and the Beautiful* (1758); Burke's *Reflections on the Revolution in France* (1790) later helped to convert the enthusiast for revolutionary ideals into the conservative English patriot of Wordsworth's later years (8: 512–543). It is difficult, however, to trace specific influences, since Wordsworth generally conceals his indebtedness to books. Important influences are childhood reading in fiction and poetry, especially Edmund Spenser and the *Arabian Nights* (Moorman); John Locke and other writers who studied at Cambridge (Schneider); physical scientists (Durrant); philosophers (Rader); Enlightenment pioneers of social science (Bewell); and the English poetic tradition (Stein). In *The Prelude* Wordsworth describes a dream inspired by Cervantes's *Don Quixote* and Euclid's *Elements* (5: 50ff); this important exposition of the relation of art to science is in fact an adaptation of a dream described in a biography of Descartes. A good example of Wordsworth's lifelong manner of reading is found in a letter of January 19, 1841, where he notes parallel passages in *The Task* by **William Cowper** and a minor poem by William Shenstone, both poets adapting a thought expressed by the Roman poet Horace (*Letters*, 7:168–169).

ARCHIVES

Wordsworth Archive, Dove Cottage, Grasmere. Letters and poetical MSS.

PRINTED SOURCES

Bewell, A. *Wordsworth and the Enlightenment* (New Haven, Conn.: Yale University Press, 1989).

Durrant, G. *Wordsworth and the Great System* (Cambridge: Cambridge University Press, 1970).

Gill, S. *William Wordsworth: A Life* (Oxford: Clarendon Press, 1989).

Moorman, M. *William Wordsworth: A Biography*, 2 vols. (Oxford: Clarendon Press, 1957, 1965).

Rader, M. *Wordsworth, A Philosophical Approach* (Oxford: Clarendon Press, 1967).

Schneider, B. R. *Wordsworth's Cambridge Education* (Cambridge: Cambridge University Press, 1957).

de Selincourt, E., C. L. Shaver, M. Moorman, and A. G. Hill (eds.). *The Letters of William and Dorothy Wordsworth*, 2nd ed., rev., 8 vols. (Oxford: Clarendon Press, 1967–1993).

Shaver, C. L., and A. C. Shaver. *Wordsworth's Library: A Catalogue* (New York: Garland, 1979). Also contains information about books owned by Coleridge.

Wordsworth, William. *The Prelude, 1799, 1805, 1850*, J. Woodsworth, M. H. Abrams, S. Gill (eds.) (New York: Norton, 1979).

Worthington, J. *Wordsworth's Reading of Roman Prose* (New Haven, Conn.: Yale University Press, 1946).

John D. Baird

Y

YEATS, WILLIAM BUTLER (1865–1939). William Yeats, poet and dramatist, was born in Dublin in 1865 and educated at the Godolphin School, Hammersmith (1875–1881), the Erasmus Smith High School, Dublin (1881–1883), and the Metropolitan School of Art (1884). He was the eldest son of John Butler Yeats, the portrait painter, and his wife Susan (née Pollexfen). Yeats's poetic enthusiasm was fueled by his father, who, from an early age, read to him from Shakespeare, Homer, **Balzac**, and most influentially, **Shelley**. In 1885 Yeats began those esoteric studies through which he hoped to find a way to turn poetry into "an authoritative religion," and he reread *Prometheus Unbound*, his "sacred book," with this object in mind (*Autobiographies*, 90).

Yeats's conception of the poet owed more to Shelley than it did to any other writer. As a child he imitated Shelleyan heroes; his youthful writings, up to *The Wanderings of Oisin* (1889), blended Shelley's Romanticism with Elizabethan echoes from Edmund Spenser. In the Rose poems of the 1890s, Shelley's influence was still prevalent, albeit vying with images taken from Algernon Swinburne and ideas from **William Morris**. In 1900 Yeats published "The Philosophy of Shelley's Poetry," but thereafter a new Nietzschean aesthetic replaced the ideal of Intellectual Beauty. Yeats continued to borrow symbols from Shelley—notably the tower—but what ultimately divided them was Yeats's innate gnosticism (Bloom, 82).

Between 1889 and 1893 Yeats undertook a comprehensive reading of **William Blake**. Yeats came to Blake through his father's Pre-Raphaelite associates. However, he looked at Blake more systematically than they did. What interested him was "the Unity of Culture" Blake sought in his Circle of Destiny. This was to be paralleled in Yeats's system of gyres in *A Vision* (1925–1937) (Billigheimer, 6). Yeats's analysis of Blake was undertaken alongside his exploration of theosophy and infused by multifarious magical and Eastern sources (Bachchan, passim), alongside the voices of Celtic legend, English aestheticism, and French symbolism. Yeats's own symbolism of the 1890s was inspired by Arthur Symons, who introduced him to Paul Verlaine and Villiers de l'Isle Adam. The latter's *Axel*, which he saw in Paris in 1894, fascinated Yeats and gave him the confidence to continue working on his own poetic plays (*Collected Letters*, 1: 382n).

A second father figure for Yeats was John O'Leary, whom he met in 1885 (*Autobiographies*, 209 passim). O'Leary taught that there was no nationality without literature and no great literature that was not rooted in nationality. This led him to explore the "Irishness" of the peasant tales of William Carleton, the prose epics of Standish James O'Grady, and the poems of Samuel Ferguson and James Clarence Mangan. Yeats's publication of editions of such writers helped to invent a tradition of Irish national literature.

In 1899, Yeats launched the Irish Literary Theatre. It owed a debt to Maurice Maeterlinck, whose theater of ideals Yeats adored (*Collected Letters*, 1:459–460), but its purpose was to encourage a national drama, which bore fruit with the establishment of the Irish National Theatre Society in 1904. Yeats's search for his own dramatic form led him to explore Noh theater, to which he was introduced by Ezra Pound, in 1913 (*Essays and Introductions*, 221). He used the form most successfully in *At the Hawk's Well* (1916). Yeats's drama was also influenced by **Friedrich Nietzsche**. Yeats believed Nietzsche "completed" Blake. He found his contrasting of the Dionysian and Apollonian moods particularly useful as he developed his new aesthetic (*Collected Letters*, 3:284, 369–370). Nietzsche also influenced Yeats's ideas on Mask, as did **Oscar Wilde** (Ellmann, 73–80 and passim).

The Rhymers' Club was loosely based on a promotion of the ideas of **Walter Pater**, although Yeats thought that "a subconscious influence, and perhaps the most powerful of all" came from **Dante Gabriel Rossetti** (*Autobiographies*, 299–304). The Club was important to Yeats socially, but its members lacked the Yeatsian desire to find a coherent focus for their activities. Of more lasting value to Yeats's vision of the Renaissance than Pater, or the Rhymers, was Baldassare Castiglione. Yeats was introduced to Castiglione's *The Book of the Courtier* (1528), an idealized vision of the renaissance court of Urbino, apositely, by Lady Augusta Gregory in 1903. For Yeats, Lady Gregory's home at Coole Park, in Co. Galway, was an Irish Urbino, a haven for Irish artists, aspiring and established, and, thereby, a symbol of a unified culture. Through Castiglione, Yeats was led to the Neoplatonist Plotinus, a reading of whom in the 1920s, in Stephen Mackenna's translation, helped him resolve certain questions arising out of *A Vision* (Salvadori, 20, 68–72).

Yeats's Irish national enthusiasm took many forms, but the last and most potent was his attraction to the writers of the age of Protestant Ascendancy: Swift, Burke, Goldsmith, and Berkeley (Torchiana, passim). These authors began to impinge on Yeats's sense of Irishness from the time of the death of Synge and came to stand as a symbol of proud Protestant Ireland for Yeats as a statesman of the Irish Free State in the 1920s and 1930s. Their impact is most clearly seen in the Anglo-Irish poems of *The Tower* (1928) and *The Winding Stair* (1933).

Yeats was, successively, a late, romantic, a Pre-Raphaelite, a symbolist, a cultural nationalist, a modernist, and a poet who in old age found his own distinctive voice, which no one has yet managed to categorize or emulate. His influence on poetry in the English language is incalculable, and Yeats has been blessed by a wealth of sensible critics who have carefully weighed the influence of specific authors and systems on him—a particular difficulty given his propensity for self-mythologizing.

ARCHIVES

Yeats Papers, National Library of Ireland.

PRINTED SOURCES

Bachchan, Harbans Rai. *W. B. Yeats and Occultism* (Delhi: Motilal Banarsidass, 1965). Discusses the impact of "AE" (George Russell), of Mohini Chaterjee, Rabindranath Tagore, and Shri Purohit Swami, of Swedenborg and Boehme, of Madame Blavatsky, and of MacGregor Mathers's work on the Kabbala.

Billigheimer, Rachel. *Wheels of Eternity: A Comparative Study of William Blake and William Butler Yeats* (Dublin: Gilland Macmillan, 1990).

Bloom, Harold. *Yeats* (New York: Oxford University Press, 1970). On the influence of the Romantics.

Bohlmann, Otto. *Yeats and Nietzsche: An Exploration of Major Nietzschean Echoes in the Writings of W. B. Yeats* (London: Macmillan 1982).

Chapman, Wayne K. *Yeats and English Renaissance Literature* (Basingstoke: Macmillan, 1991). On the influence of Spenser, Donne, Milton, and Ben Jonson and of Pater and Matthew Arnold.

Coote, Stephen. *W. B. Yeats. A Life* (London: Hodder and Staughton, 1997).

Ellmann, Richard. *W. B. Yeats. The Man and the Masks* (New York: Norton, 1979).

Faulkner, Peter. *William Morris and W. B. Yeats* (Dublin: Dolmen Press, 1962). On Morris's importance to Yeats, as writer and social commentator.

Foster, R. F. *W. B. Yeats: A Life* (Oxford: Oxford University Press, 1997).

Gardner, Joann. *Yeats and the Rhymers' Club* (New York: R. Lang, 1989).

Jeffares, A. N. (ed.). *Yeats the European* (Gerrards Cross: Smythe, 1989). See Jacqueline Genet on Yeats and Villiers de l'Isle Adam; Warwick Gould on Yeats and Balzac.

Salvadori, Corinna. *Yeats and Castiglione, Poet and Courtier* (Dublin: A. Figgis, 1965).

Torchiana, Donald. *W. B. Yeats and Georgian Ireland* (Evanston: Northwestern University Press, 1966).

Wade, Allan. *Letters of W. B. Yeats* (London: Macmillan, 1954).

Worth, Katharine. *The Irish Drama of Europe from Yeats to Beckett* (London: Athlone Press, 1978). On Yeats's indebtedness to Wilde's *Salomé*, notably in *The King of the Great Clock Tower* and *A Full Moon in March*.

Yeats, W. B. *Autobiographies* (London: Macmillan, 1956).

———. *The Collected Letters of W. B. Yeats*, vols. 1–3 (1865–1904), John Kelly (general ed.) (Oxford: Clarendon Press, 1986).

———. *Essays and Introductions* (New York: Macmillan, 1961).

Joseph A. F. Spence

Z

ZOLA, ÉMILE (1840–1902). Émile Zola was born in Paris in 1840. After early schooling at the Pension Notre-Dame (1848–1862), he spent the bulk of his education at the Collège Bourbon in Aix. From 1858 Zola attended the Lycée Saint-Louis in Paris, but in 1859 he twice failed his Baccalauréat. He was, in general, fairly contemptuous of his formal education, and it is clear that the eclectic range of influences that together gel (or clash) in his literary production emerged after considerable self-education and dedicated study. Zola's status as a writer and a thinker is considerable, but the reasoning behind this eminence is deeply contested.

Many of the contradictions and ambiguities surrounding Zola result from the considerable distance between his critical writing and the practice of his literary fiction. In the former, Zola was an archpolemicist, particularly in his writing on the possibility of a scientific, naturalist literature, and as the forerunner of the modern engaged intellectual: evinced in his polemic attack on reactionary forces and injustice in *J'Accuse*.

Zola, the fictional practitioner, was a far subtler and more complex figure. His epic 20-volume work *Les Rougon-Macquart: Histoire Naturelle et Sociale d'Une Famille sous le Second Empire* charts the instantiation of modern capitalism in a variety of sites across France, using mythic and symbolist imagery alongside realist description and political critique in the creation of one of the great works of modern Western literature.

Zola's chief debts in his writing were to **Balzac**, whose realism he adapted in the generation of naturalism and whose cyclical model he borrowed in *Les Rougon-Macquart*, and the Bible, whose stories, morals, myths, and tropes Zola reworked endlessly across his vast literary output. His contemporaries **Flaubert**, Baudelaire, and **Maupassant**, each had clear influences on his work, in both stylistic terms and in the quest after modes of representation adequate to the modern world. In this context it might also be said that the work of **Monet**,

Manet, and **Cézanne** (whose work Zola championed) influenced his writing. In terms of politics, **Hegel** (or, more probably, French accounts of Hegel's work), **Marx**, and **Fourier** also influenced his thought, which, from a profound critique of utopianism and idealism in *Les Rougon-Macquart*, moved to a valorization of imagined worlds in *Les Quatre Évangiles*.

Of considerable importance in terms of Zola's scientism were the works of **Comte**, Claude Bernard's *Leçons de Physiologie*, and Prosper Lucas's *Traité philosophique et physiologique de l'hérédité naturelle*.

ARCHIVES

Bibliothèque Nationale, Paris.

PRINTED SOURCES

Baguley, David. *Bibliographie de la critique sur Émile Zola: 1864–1970* (Toronto: University of Toronto Press, 1976).
———. *Bibliographie de la critique sur Émile Zola: 1971–1980* (Toronto: University of Toronto Press, 1982).
———. *A Critical Bibliography of French Literature*, vol. 5, pt. 2 (Syracuse, N.Y.: Syracuse University Press, 1994). Contains intelligent annotated comments on Zola criticism. A particularly good introductory source for a study of influences apparent in Zola's writing.
Bell, David F. *Models of Power. Politics and Economics in Zola's Rougon-Macquart* (Lincoln: University of Nebraska Press, 1988). Excellent on the economic and political dimensions to Zola's writing and their origins.
Brown, Frederick. *Zola: A Life* (London: Macmillan, 1996).
Walker, Philip. *Germinal and Zola's Philosophical and Religious Thought* (Amsterdam: John Benjamins, 1984).
Zola, Émile. *Les Rougon-Macquart*, Henri Mitterand (ed.), 5 vols. (Paris: Bibliothèque de la Pléiade, 1960–1967). This definitive edition of Zola's principal work also includes brilliant exegetical notes and analyses of the sources of Zola's fictions. Full critical bibliographies are also included.
———. *Œuvres complètes*, Henri Mitterand (ed.) (Paris: Cercle du livre précieux, 1966–1969).

William Gallois

INDEX

Boldface page numbers indicate location of main entries.

ABOUT THE EDITORS AND CONTRIBUTORS

FUNSO AFOLAYAN has taught at Obafemi Awolowo University (Nigeria), Amherst College, and Washington University in St. Louis and presently teaches at the University of New Hampshire in Durham. His main historical research has been on slavery and states formation in precolonial West Africa. He is coauthor of *Yoruba Sacred Kingship: A Power Like That of the Gods* (1996).

JOSEF L. ALTHOLZ was educated at Cornell (B.A., 1954) and Columbia (Ph.D., 1960) Universities. He has taught history at the University of Minnesota since 1959, becoming professor in 1967. He has published several books and other works on Victorian religious history, including *The Liberal Catholic Movement in England* (1962) and *The Religious Press in Britain, 1760–1900* (1989).

WALTER L. ARNSTEIN is professor emeritus of history at the University of Illinois at Urbana-Champaign and former president of the North American Conference on British Studies. He is the author or editor of six books—including *Britain Yesterday and Today* (7th ed., 1996)—and more than 30 articles (of which 7 concern Queen Victoria).

JOHN D. BAIRD is professor of English at the University of Toronto. His main area of interest is British literature of the eighteenth and nineteenth centuries.

DEBORAH BANNER is a Ph.D. candidate in the English Department at the University of California at Los Angeles, completing her dissertation on twentieth-century British and American espionage fiction and nationalism.

JASON M. BARRETT is a graduate student at the University of Michigan at Ann Arbor. His research is primarily concerned with the adaptation of colonial parochial legal institutions and customs to political and market changes in Jeffersonian Virginia.

DAVID W. BEBBINGTON, a professor of history at the University of Stirling, has published *Patterns in History* (1980), *Evangelicalism in Modern Britain* (1992), and *William Ewart Gladstone: Faith and Politics in Victorian Britain* (1993). He is coeditor of *Gladstone Centenary Essays* (2000).

CHRISTOPHER BECKHAM, adjunct instructor of history at Morehead State University, also pastors the First Baptist Church in Flemingsburg, Kentucky. Beckham has been published in the *Southern Historian*. His research interests include Southern history and American religious history.

CHRISTOPHER BERKELEY has taught at Framingham State College and contributed essays and reviews to a number of publications including *The Oxford Companion to United States History* (2000), *The Encyclopedia of Historians and Historical Writing* (1999) and *The Encyclopedia of New England Culture* (forthcoming).

DEREK BLAKELEY received his Ph.D. in modern British history from Washington University in St. Louis in 1995. He continues to research the history of the British Conservative Party, specifically the political career of Lord Curzon, and occasionally teaches courses on British and European history, while working as an editor at Washington University.

CHARLES BOEWE's academic career included teaching at Syracuse University, the University of Wisconsin, Lehigh University, and the University of Pennsylvania. Moving to Asia, he administered Fulbright exchange programs in Iran, Pakistan, and India. Now retired, he is editor of the Papers of C. S. Rafinesque.

JOHN MICHAEL BOLES is currently a Ph.D. candidate at Washington University in St. Louis. His research interests are twentieth-century U.S. intellectual and cultural history. He has published in *Organization and Environment* (1998).

ANDREW BRADSTOCK is senior lecturer in theology at King Alfred's College, Winchester, United Kingdom. He is author of several books on political theology and coeditor of two volumes on spirtuality and sexuality in Victorian culture.

HELOISE BROWN has a Ph.D. on "Pacifist Feminism in Britain, 1870–1902," from the University of York, United Kingdom. She has published on Irish Unionism and is coeditor of *White? Women* (1999), an examination of whiteness as a raced and gendered identity. She is also a director of Raw Nerve Books.

ROBERT W. BROWN is professor and chair of the History Department at the University of North Carolina at Pembroke. His current research interests include the social history of art in France during the nineteenth century, townscape and topographical art, and German history and culture during the Nazi era.

ANTHONY BRUNDAGE is professor emeritus of history at California State Polytechnic University at Pomona. Among his four books is a biography of the historian John Richard Green. He is currently at work on a book-length study of interactions between Bristish and American historians from 1870 to 1940.

LESLIE BUTLER received a Ph.D. in history from Yale University. She teaches American cultural and intellectual history at James Madison College, Michigan State University, and is at work on a book about the genteel encounter with democracy in Victorian America.

PHILLIP A. CANTRELL II received a B.A. in history from Roanoke College and a master's degree in history from James Madison University. He is presently a Ph.D. candidate and graduate instructor at West Virginia University. His major field of interest is U.S. history with minor fields in East Africa and East Asia.

SCOTT E. CASPER is associate professor of history at the University of Nevada at Reno. He is the author of *Constructing American Lives: Biography and Culture in Nineteenth-Century America* (1999).

H. LEE CHEEK, JR. is professor of political science and philosophy at Brewton-Parker College in Mt. Vernon, Georgia. He teaches in the areas of political theory, American politics, and the history of philosophy. His work has appeared in the *International Social Science Review*, *Methodist History*, and *Journal of Politics*. Professor Cheek is the author of a forthcoming study of John C. Calhoun's political thought. He is also a United Methodist minister and a chaplain in the U.S. Army.

ROBERT CHISHOLM is an instructer of history and political science at Columbia Basin College in Pasco, Washington. His interests include Brazilian politics, the history of political thought, the development of political rights in Latin America, and revolutionary politics.

A.O.J. COCKSHUT was G. M. Young Lecturer at Oxford (1965–1994) and Fellow of Hertford College at Oxford (1966–1994). His publications include *Anthony Trollope* (1955), *The Unbelievers* (1964), *The Achievement of Walter Scott* (1969), *Truth to Life* (1974), and *The Art of Autobiography* (1984).

ANN MAUGER COLBERT, journalism coordinator at Indiana Purdue Fort Wayne, has published on journalism history and women in journalism. She is working on a book about women's editions of newspapers.

ROBERT A. COLBY, professor emeritus, Graduate School of Library and Information Studies, Queens College, City University of New York, has published widely on Victorian fiction in relation to cultural history, including *Thackeray's Canvas of Humanity* (1979). He is presently engaged in a study of Thackeray's travel writings.

BRIAN CRIM is a Ph.D. candidate at Rutgers University specializing in Weimar Germany. His dissertation concerns the political activism of different veterans groups after World War I. Crim has published an article on German Jewish veterans and several encyclopedia articles. Crim was awarded a Fulbright Fellowship for 1999–2000.

IVAN CROZIER's present interests include the history of science and medicine and the construction of medical discourses about sexuality in England in the nineteenth and twentieth centuries.

EILEEN M. CURRAN is a professor of English, emerita, Colby College, Waterville, Maine. She was an associate editor of the *Wellesley Index to Victorian Periodicals* (Vols. 1–3) and has published in *Modern Philology, Slavonic and East European Review*, and *Victorian Periodicals Review*.

RICHARD W. DAVIS is professor of history and director of the Center for the History of Freedom at Washington University in St. Louis. He has published books on religious dissenters and politics in the early nineteenth century, Buckinghamshire politics from 1760 to 1880, focusing on the question of deference, Disraeli, and the English Rothschilds.

RUUD VAN DIJK studied history at the University of Amsterdam, the University of Kansas, and Ohio University (Ph.D., 1999). He has been contributor to the op-ed page of an Amsterdam newspaper since 1991. He was adjunct professor of history at Carnegie Mellon University during 1998–1999, and assistant professor of history at Dickinson College (1999–2000). His primary research interest is Germany and the Cold War.

LAURENT DITMANN, a graduate of the École Normale Superieure of Fontenay-Saint-Cloud, France, also holds an M.A. (English) from Portland State University and a Ph.D. (French Studies) from Brown University. He teaches French at Spelman College in Atlanta.

ANDREA DIXON earned an M.F.A. from the University of Montana, and is presently studying theology at Yale University.

CAROLINE DOWSON read English at the University of Leicester (United Kingdom) for her first degree, then studied for her doctorate at the University of Bristol (United Kingdom). She is now vice principal of Mander Portman Woodward College at Bristol. Dr. Dowson's research interests include English nineteenth-century decadent poetry, turn-of-the-century art, and turn-of-the-century women's education.

PETER C. ERB is professor of religion and culture at Wilfrid Laurier University at Waterloo, Ontario. He has published on the Radical Reformation, German Pietism, German Catholicism in the Romantic era, and British Anglo-Catholics and Roman Catholics in the nineteenth century.

SUSAN H. FARNSWORTH, professor of history at Trinity College, Washington, D.C., earned her M.Litt. degree from the University of Oxford and her Ph.D. from Brandeis. She was codirector of three National Endowment for the Humanities summer seminars on "Darwin and the Victorian Milieu of Science and Religion" and has published *The Evolution of British Imperial Policy in the Mid-Nineteenth Century* (1992).

GILLIAN FENWICK is associate professor of English at the University of Toronto. She is the author of *The Contributors' Index to the Dictionary of National Biography, 1885–1901* (1989), *Leslie Stephen's Life in Letters* (1993), *Women and the DNB* (1994), and *George Orwell: A Bibliography* (1998), as well as articles and reviews on publishing history and bibliography. She is currently writing a history of the *Dictionary of National Biography* and a book about a hundred years of men of letters since Carlyle.

RICHARD R. FOLLETT earned his bachelor's degree in history at Arizona State University and his master's and doctorate from Washington University in St. Louis, where he teaches part-time. His first book (forthcoming from Macmillan Press) examines the impact of Evangelicalism on English criminal law reform in the early nineteenth century.

CHRISTOPHER E. FORTH teaches courses in European intellectual and cultural history at the Australian National University. He is the author of *Zarathustra in Paris: The Nietzsche Vogue in France, 1891–1914* (2000) and is currently preparing a book-length study of gender and the body in France during the time of the Dreyfus Affair.

PETER S. FOSL is associate professor of philosophy at Transylvania University in Lexington, Kentucky. He has studied at Bucknell University, Emory University, the London School of Economics, and the University of Edinburgh. His research interests include the history of philosophy, skepticism, David Hume, and social-political philosophy.

KATHRYN WAGNILD FULLER is a university archivist at the University of Minnesota, Duluth, and a doctoral candidate at Indiana University (A.B.D.) in U.S. intellectual history. She is writing a dissertation on women and the American Social Science Association in the late nineteenth century.

WILLIAM GALLOIS is a cultural historian of France, with interests in the politics of history, capitalism, France and Algeria, and Émile Zola. He can be contacted at the History Department, Queen Mary and Westfield College, University of London.

GEOFFREY GILBERT has taught economics at Hobart and William Smith Colleges since 1977. Besides editing Malthus's *Essay on Population* for the Oxford World's Classics (1993) and *Malthus: Critical Responses* for Routledge (1998), he has written numerous journal articles on classical political economy. His current research is on world population issues.

ERNST GRABOVSZKI studies comparative literature and German at the University of Vienna, where he is a lecturer in the Department of Comparative

Literature. He has contributed to the *Encyclopedia of Contemporary German Culture* (1998).

JOHN GREENFIELD, professor of English at McKendree College, has edited *The Dictionary of British Literary Characters* (2 vols., 1993, 1994) as well as the following volumes in *The Dictionary of Literary Biography* series: *British Romantic Poets, 1789–1832* (2 vols., 1990), *British Romantic Prose Writers, 1789–1832* (2 vols., 1991), and *British Short-Fiction Writers, 1800–1880* (1996).

ERIKA HABER teaches Russian language and literature at Syracuse University. She has written *Mastering Russian* (1994), *Russian Phrasebook and Dictionary* (2nd ed., 1994), and various articles on Russian literature. Currently she is writing a book on the creation of national identity through myth, folklore, and legend.

ROBERT F. HAGGARD earned a B.A. (1989) in history and English from the University of North Carolina at Chapel Hill and an M.A. (1991) and Ph.D. (1997) in modern European history from the University of Virginia. His dissertation has been published by Greenwood Press under the title *The Persistence of Victorian Liberalism: The Politics of Social Reform in Britain, 1870–1900* (2000).

STEPHEN G. HAGUE took degrees in history at Binghamton University and the University of Virginia. He has worked as a museum administrator and is currently director of development at Linacre College, Oxford. He has particular interest in the political, social, and architectural history of nineteenth-century Britain.

HAZEL HAHN received her Ph.D. in European history from the University of California (UC) at Berkeley in 1997. Her dissertation was entitled "Street Picturesque: Advertising in Paris, 1830–1914." She has been a lecturer at UC Berkeley. She is currently working on the history of urban planning and tourism in early twentieth-century French Indochina.

GUÐMUNDUR HÁLFDANARSON (B.A., University of Iceland and Lund University, Sweden; Cand.Mag., University of Iceland; Ph.D., Cornell University) is a professor of history at the University of Iceland. His main field of research is theories and practices of nationalism in Iceland and Europe in general. In addition to a number of articles on his field of expertise, he has published a *Historical Dictionary of Iceland* (1997).

C. MICHAEL HALL has published several journal articles and book chapters on John Muir. He works for the Advanced Business Program of the Centre for Tourism at the University of Otago, New Zealand; is visiting professor at the School of Leisure and Food Management of the Sheffield Hallam University,

United Kingdom; is editor of *Current Issues in Tourism*; and is president of the Association for Canadian Studies in Australia and New Zealand.

SUSAN HAMBURGER, manuscripts librarian at Penn State University, has published essays in *American Book and Magazine Illustrators to 1920* (1998), *Encyclopedia of Rural America* (1997), and *American National Biography* (1999) and a chapter in *Before the New Deal: Southern Social Welfare History, 1830–1930* (1999). A book on Florida horse racing is forthcoming.

SANDRA HANNAFORD is a doctoral candidate in the Department of English at Memorial University of Newfoundland, Canada. She is currently finishing her thesis entitled "Towards a History of the Book in Newfoundland: The Newspapers as a Principal Source, 1807–1949."

JENNIFER HARRISON earned a master's degree at the University of Richmond in American social history, with a concentration on the nineteenth century. Her thesis covers the subject of nineteenth-century secondary schooling for women in Virginia, 1850–1890, and the effects of that education on marriage rates. She currently serves as Coordinator of Disabilities and Pre-Major Advisor at North Carolina Wesleyan College.

RICARDO A. HERRERA received his Ph.D. from Marquette University in 1998 under Robert P. Hay. His interests are early American, military, and naval history. He has taught at Carthage College and the University of Wisconsin, Milwaukee, and is assistant professor of history at Texas Lutheran University in Seguin, Texas.

HILDA HOLLIS recently completed her Ph.D. thesis at McMaster University on dialogism and politics in George Eliot's later novels. Her work has appeared, or is forthcoming, in *ELH, ESC, Victorian Poetry, Blake Quarterly, Milton Studies*, and *Various Atwoods* (ed. Lorraine York). She is currently working on the rhetoric of female popularizers of political economy.

THOMAS ALBERT HOWARD is assistant professor of history at Gordon College in Wenham, Massachusetts. In 1996 he received his Ph.D. from the University of Virginia. He is the author of *Religion and the Rise of Historicism* (1999).

BILLIE ANDREW INMAN (Ph.D., University of Texas at Austin, 1961) is the author of two books and numerous essays on Walter Pater, was coeditor of *The Pater Newsletter* (1977–1988, 1994–1996), and is guest editor of the Pater issue of *Nineteenth-Century Prose* (Vol. 24, Fall 1997). She retired as a professor of English from the University of Arizona in 1994.

HORST KANT completed his diploma in physics in 1969 and his doctorate in the history and philosophy of science in 1973 at the Humboldt University in Berlin. Since 1995 he has been a research scholar at Max Planck Institute for the History of Science, studying the history of physics in the nineteenth and twentieth centuries, the history of quantum theory and nuclear physics, and the development of physics in Berlin.

STEPHEN KECK studied historical theology and the history of Christianity at the Yale Divinity School before completing his Ph.D. at Oxford University on John Ruskin's understanding of history. His research interests include Ruskin and British historical thought, Arthur Helps and "Victorianism," and Victorian perceptions of the American South. He has taught at the College of Charleston and is currently an assistant professor at the National University of Singapore.

CHRISTOPHER M. KEIRSTEAD, an assistant professor of English at Auburn University, has published articles on Elizabeth Barrett Browning and Arthur Hugh Clough. He is currently preparing a book on Victorian travel poetry.

DOUGLAS KING is a Ph.D. candidate in English at Duquesne University in Pittsburgh, Pennsylvania. His interests include theater history, particularly Renaissance drama, as well as contemporary American and Russian fiction and drama, acting, and performance criticism.

ERIKA M. KREGER earned a Ph.D. in English at the University of California at Davis. Her dissertation was on nineteenth-century American women writers and the periodical sketch form. She is also coediting, with James McClure and Peg Lamphier, *The Letters of Salmon P. Chase and His Daughters*, forthcoming from the Kent State University Press.

RICHARD A. LEBRUN, who retired from the Department of History, University of Manitoba in 1998, is currently a Senior Scholar at St. Paul's College of the University of Manitoba. He has published books and articles on Joseph de Maistre as well as translations of a number of Maistre's works.

STEPHEN LEVINE is currently completing a Ph.D. in history, specializing in U.S. intellectual history. He has examined Theodore Roosevelt's thought regarding the conservation of natural resources, race, art, and culture. He is a lecturer at the University of North Carolina at Wilmington.

ELIZABETH DOMINIQUE LLOYD-KIMBREL works in the administration at Mount Holyoke College, Massachusetts. She took degrees from Connecticut College and the University of Massachusetts at Amherst, with postgraduate studies at Oxford University and the University of York. She has contributed articles to *American National Biography* (1999), the *New Dictionary of National Biography* (2004), and the *St. James Guide to Biography* (1991), among others, and has published critical articles on Chaucer and Robert Frost, as well as some poetry.

BRAD LOOKINGBILL graduated from Southwestern Oklahoma State University of Toledo, where he completed the Doctor of Philosophy in History in 1995. He is currently an assistant professor of history at Columbia College, teaching courses on the American West, the American Revolution, and the American Civil War.

NANCY LOPATIN-LUMMIS, professor of history at the University of Wisconsin at Stevens Point, is the author of *Political Unions, Popular Politics and the Great Reform Act of 1832* (1999) and of several articles on parliamentary reform and popular politics in the 1830s. She is currently working on a political biography of Joseph Parkes.

WILLIAM C. LUBENOW is professor of history, Stockton College of New Jersey. He is the author of *The Politics of Government Growth: Early Victorian Attitudes toward State Intervention* (1971), *Parliamentary Politics and the Home Rule Crisis: The British House of Commons in 1886* (1988), and *The Cambridge Apostles, 1820–1914: Liberalism, Imagination, and Friendship in British Intellectual and Professional Life* (1998).

ERIC V. D. LUFT, Ph.D., M.L.S., curator of Historical Collections at the State University of New York (SUNY) Upstate Medical University, is included in the 54th edition of *Who's Who in America*, the 27th edition of *Who's Who in the East*, and the 28th edition of *Dictionary of International Biography*.

GIUSEPPE MARCHETTI earned an M.A. in philosophy from the University of Pavia and an M.A. in Literature from the University of Milan, Italy. He teaches history and philosophy at a high school in Brescia.

NANCY ANNE MARCK teaches Victorian literature and drama at Daemen College in Amherst, New York. Her articles focus on British women writers, including George Eliot, Elizabeth Siddal, and Jane Austen, and she is presently working on a book-length study of the feminist aesthetic of tragedy in George Eliot's novels.

SARAH R. MARINO recently resigned her position as associate professor of English at Ohio Northern University and has moved to Chicago to work in corporate communication. Her scholarly research and academic writing focus on British and American postal history and epistolary literature.

BEN MARSDEN is a lecturer in the Cultural History Group at the University of Aberdeen in Scotland. He has published on the history of engineering education, energy physics, technological failure, and the relationship between music and science. He is currently working on a cultural history of mechanism in Victorian Britain.

ANDREW MAUNDER teaches English at the University of Exeter. He has written articles on Trollope, on the *Cornhill Magazine*, and on nineteenth-century popular fiction, and has edited *East Lynne* by Ellen Wood (1999).

PETER MAYEUX is a College of Journalism and Mass Communications professor at the University of Nebraska at Lincoln. He has contributed articles for publications such as *American National Biography* (1999) and *History of the Mass Media in the United States* (1998). He produced a 1997 CD-ROM, *A History of Nebraska Media*, which profiles 150 years of media developments.

LAURENCE W. MAZZENO is president of Alvernia College, Reading, Pennsylvania. He is the author of four books and dozens of articles on Victorian and modern literature. His most recent book, *Matthew Arnold: The Critical Legacy*, was published in 1999.

BRIAN MCCUSKEY is an assistant professor of English at Utah State University, where he teaches nineteenth-century British literature. He is currently writing a book on the representation of domestic service in Victorian fiction.

WILLIAM R. MCKELVY (Ph.D. in English, University of Virginia) writes about eighteenth- and nineteenth-century British literature and intellectual history. His current project describes how modern political secularization was influenced by a tradition of literary criticism and new approaches to interpreting primitive, national literature.

DAVID K. MCQUILKIN is professor of history and political science at Bridgewater College of Virginia, where he teaches courses in Russian, Middle Eastern and East Asian history, and Western Civilization.

ROBIN MEADER earned degrees in English at George Washington University (Ph.D., 1998), where she teaches American literature and technical writing. She is Washington, D.C. bureau chief of the *World Tribune* newspaper. Her research interests include women's informal writing, poetry, peace studies, the American Renaissance, and Tsunesaburo Makiguchi's philosophy of education.

KITTY MILLET's publications span German intellectual history, Latin American *testimonio*, Holocaust studies, and French literature. Her newest book project explores the transformation of Aristotelian aesthetic concepts by post–1945 writers. At San Francisco State, Professor Millet teaches Classics, world and comparative literature, and the human sexuality program.

JAMES MILLHORN is Head of Acquisitions, Northern Illinois University Libraries. He is the author of *Student's Companion to the World Wide Web: Social Sciences and Humanities Resources* (Scarecrow, 1999). In addition to his library duties, Mr. Millhorn remains active in the field of modern French history.

DAVID B. MOCK teaches history at Tallahassee Community College. He earned his Ph.D. in British history from Florida State University. He has edited *Legacy of the West: Reading in the History of Western Civilization* (1996) and *History and Public Policy* (1991) and coedited *A Dictionary of Obituaries of Modern British Radicals* (1989).

CRAIG MONK is an assistant professor of English at the University of Lethbridge in Alberta, Canada. His doctorate from Oxford University traced the role of the little magazine in sharing trends in art between American and European writers. His work has appeared in *American Studies International, History of Photography*, and the *Journal of Modern Literature*.

MICHELLE C. MORGAN is a Ph.D. candidate in American history at Columbia University in New York City. She received her M.D. from the London School of Economics and Political Science in the field of international history. Her dissertation is entitled "Imperialists of 1898: Trans-Atlantic Conceptions of American Expansion."

BERT MOSSELMANS (1969) studied economics and philosophy at the Free University of Brussels (VUB). He is currently employed as a researcher at the Faculty of Economics of the VUB. His research is concerned with the history of science in general and the history of economics and logic in particular. He has published several papers in various journals, coedited a book, and published several articles in books and conference proceedings.

GENE MUELLER, Ph.D., has written two books on German military history (World War II), contributed to several other works on Germany during World War II, and has written three books on Idaho history. His research interests include twentieth century, Idaho history, and higher education. Presently, he is Distinguished Professor of Liberal Arts at Henderson State University.

ANDREW MULDOON received an M.Phil. from Cambridge University and his Ph.D. from Washington University in Saint Louis. He is an assistant professor of history at Saint Anselm College in Manchester, New Hampshire. His research focuses on British politics and India in the 1930s.

CLIONA MURPHY is professor of history at California State University at Bakersfield. She is the author of *The Women's Suffrage Movement and Irish Society* (1989) and coeditor of *Women Surviving: Studies in Irish Women's History* (1990). She has published articles on nationalism, feminism, and H. G. Wells.

DOUGLAS B. PALMER is a Ph.D. student in the Department of History at The Ohio State University. His research interests include the history of printing and print culture in seventeenth- and eighteenth-century France and the Netherlands.

SHALON PARKER is a graduate student in the History of Art Department at the University of California at Berkeley. Her areas of interest are painting, sculpture, architecture, and design of fin de siècle Europe and America. She is currently working on her dissertation, tentatively entitled "Salon Art and Its Audience in Fin-de-Siècle France."

RICHARD PENASKOVIC is program director for Religious Studies at Auburn University in Alabama. His latest book, *Critical Thinking and the Academic Study of Religion*, published by Scholans Press in Atlanta in 1997, has just been reprinted. He finds himself most at home in Augustine studies, Newman studies, and ecumenism.

CHRISTOPHER PEPUS is a teaching fellow and Ph.D. candidate in history at Washington University in St. Louis. He specializes in modern European political, cultural, religious, and intellectual history.

NICOLETTA PIREDDU teaches Italian and comparative literature at Georgetown University. Her scholarly work revolves around nineteenth- and twentieth-century European literature, culture, and literary theory. She is currently working on a book that reinterprets the aesthetic premises and the ethical goals of European decadent literature in the light of the new notion of culture promoted by late nineteenth-century anthropology.

JOHN POWELL is associate professor of history at Cumberland College. His most recent books are *The Journal of John Wodehouse, First Earl of Kimberley, for 1862–1902* (with Angus Hawkins, 1997) and a critical edition of John Morley's *On Compromise* (1997).

STANISLAO G. PUGLIESE is assistant professor of history at Hofstra University. A specialist on the Italian anti-fascist resistance and Italian Jews, he is the author of *Carlo Rosselli: Socialist Heretic and Antifascist Exile* (1999) and *Fascism/Antifascism: A Critical Anthology* (2000).

JOHN RADZILOWSKI received his Ph.D. in history from Arizona State University in 1999. He is the author or co-author of eight books, including a forthcoming work, *The Eagle and the Cross*, which deals with the history of Polish-American Catholic loyalism. He is president of the Polish American Cultural Institute of Minnesota.

R. KENT RASMUSSEN has a Ph.D. in history from the University of California at Los Angeles, where he was an associate editor at the Marcus Garvey Papers project (1986–1991). Among his publications are five books on Africa, three books on Mark Twain, and two books on African American history. He is currently working on a biography of Mark Twain built around firsthand descriptions written by people who knew him personally.

JONATHAN REES received his Ph.D. in American history at the University of Wisconsin at Madison in 1997 and has since held teaching positions at the University of Wisconsin at Oshkosh and Whitman College, Washington. He has published articles on business history in *Pennsylvania History*, *Labor's Heritage*, and the *Wisconsin Magazine of History*.

MARK REGER is chair of the English and Fine Arts Department at Johnson C. Smith University and serves also as the book review editor for H-Ideas, a Humanities and Social Sciences Network discussion list devoted to intellectual history.

SUSAN REILLY is a doctoral student at the University of New Hampshire. Her interests include the politics of Romantic patronage. She is currently helping to edit the Coleridge letters for the NEH (National Endowment for the Humanities)-funded hypertext edition, under the direction of Dr. Megan O'Neill.

CHARLES RICHMOND is coeditor of *The Self-Fashioning of Disraeli, 1818–1851* (1998). He is a member of the New York Bar and has practiced securities and banking law in New York and London. He is currently engaged in research on the life of the fifth earl of Rosebery.

PRISCILLA ROBERTS received her B.A. and Ph.D. from King's College, Cambridge. Since 1984 she has taught U.S. history at the University of Hong Kong and is also director of the University's Centre of American Studies. She has published extensively in U.S. diplomatic history.

CHARLES M. ROLL is a Ph.D. candidate at Washington University in St. Louis. His focus is in European and British intellectual history.

FRANK A. SALAMONE is professor of sociology/anthroplogy at Iona College at New Rochelle. He has conducted research on African religion and identity, popular culture, and Italian Americans. Salamone has about 200 publications and belongs to many professional organizations.

BRIAN J. SAUERS has a B.A. in history from the Pennsylvania State University. He is currently pursuing a master's degree in English as a second language at the Marymount University. He is half Cherokee Indian and plans to earn a doctorate in Native American studies.

THOMAS SAYLOR (Ph.D., University of Rochester, 1993) is assistant professor of history at Concordia University, St. Paul, Minnesota. He has written on the social welfare programs of German industry during the Imperial period and is currently working on a book that examines the German press in the Reichstag elections of 1908 and 1912.

SUEANN SCHATZ is completing her dissertation at the University of New Mexico on British women's domestic-professional fiction of the 1890s. The project investigates how female characters who are professional writers co-opt and subvert the traditional image of the ideal Victorian woman to argue for a feminist agenda.

GREGORY L. SCHNURR was born in Chepstow, Ontario, Canada, and was educated at the University of Toronto and Sheridan College, where he received numberous degrees in visual arts, art history, and history. He is currently an artist and educator at St. Mary's High School in Owen Sound, Ontario.

ANGELA SCHWARZ is assistant professor in modern history at the University of Duisburg, Germany. Her dissertation on British views of National Socialist Germany (1991) was published in 1993 as *Die Reise ins Dritte Reich*. In 1991 she received the Fraenkel Prize in Contemporary History and in 1998 wrote a postdoctoral thesis on popular science in Britain and Germany, which was published in 1999 as *Der Schluessel zur modernen Welt, ca. 1870–1914.*

MARY ANGELA SCHWER received her Ph.D in English from the University of Notre Dame in 1996, where her doctoral dissertation focused on British missionary travel narratives and nineteenth-century culture. She currently teaches at Fairmont State College in Fairmont, West Virginia.

ALBERT C. SEARS is a doctoral candidate in English at Lehigh University. His research interests include Victorian popular fiction and periodical literature. He is currently working on the reception of the sensation novel.

ROSE SECREST has an M.A. in English and is a science consulting editor for Salem Press. She is the author of a book-length literary analysis and over 200 reference book articles.

AARON J. SEGAL teaches modern European history at East Carolina University. He has published on artistic property rights, French cultural history, and the history of consumption. His current project, "Marketing the Nation," traces the relationship between advertising and national culture in fin de siècle France.

STEVE SHEPPARD is Morris Fellow at Columbia Law School. He writes on legal philosophy and history, moral philosophy, and contemporary legal issues, and he teaches a wide spectrum of courses in law. He has recently completed a two-volume edition of the works of Sir Edward Coke in honor of the 400th anniversary of Coke's Reports and is writing a book on the moral obligations of legal officials.

ANN SHILLINGLAW is a doctoral candidate in English literature at Loyola University in Chicago. Her areas of interest include nineteenth-century literature, folklore, and fairy tales.

GREG T. SMITH received his Ph.D. in history from the University of Toronto in 1999. He is currently a Social Sciences and Humanities Research Council of Canada Post Doctoral Fellow at the University of Guelph. He has published articles on eighteenth-century criminal justice history and is working on a book about violence in London.

PHYLLIS L. SOYBEL earned her Ph.D. in 1997 at the University of Illinois at Chicago, studying Anglo-American naval relations of the World War II period. Her research interests include the history of secret intelligence. She is currently adjunct faculty at Elmhurst College, Elmhurst, Illinois.

JOSEPH A. F. SPENCE is the Master in College at Eton College. He completed his doctorate on nineteenth-century Irish Tory political culture at the University of London in 1991. He has edited volumes on Swift, G. B. Shaw, and Yeats in Duckworth's *The Sayings of . . .* series.

DOUG STENBERG is a graduate of Bowdoin College. He received his Ph.D. in Russian language and literature from Bryn Mawr College in 1987. He has published articles on literature and film and currently teaches English and drama at Wilson Senior High School in West Lawn, Pennsylvania.

KEVIN STILLEY is an adjunct professor of Tyndale Theological Seminary in Fort Worth, Texas and the General Manager of the Learning Center in Germantown, Maryland, which trains store managers for Borders Books & Music. He is presently involved in two projects: a tagmemic Christology and comparisons of the anthropologies of Augustine, Jonathan Edwards, and Daniel Parker.

JAN SUSINA is an associate professor of English at Illinois State University, where he teaches courses in children's literature. His research interest is Victorian children's literature and particularly literary fairy tales.

RICHARD N. SWANSON holds master's degrees in journalism and English from Michigan State University (MSU) and has research interests in literary biography and creative nonfiction. He was a newspaper reporter and also worked in New York's book publishing industry. He is editor in chief of MSU's *The Graduate Post.*

MARIA TABAGLIO received her M.A. in German philology from the University of Verona, with a thesis on Hildegard of Bingen. She has published several articles on medieval Latin literature and is now translating works from Old French and Old German into Italian.

THOMAS J. TOBIN is a Ph.D. student in English at Duquesne University. He has published in *The Pre-Raphaelite Review* and *Nineteenth-Century Literature.* His web archive, *The Pre-Raphaelite Critic,* has received National Endowment for the Humanities funding and numerous awards.

ROBERT TOMBS is reader in French history at Cambridge University and is a fellow and tutor of St John's College. Among his books are *France, 1814–1914* (1996) and *The Paris Commune* (1999), and he is presently working on a manuscript exploring the experience of war in 1870. He is particularly interested in political culture.

W. CRAIG TURNER is professor of English and executive vice president and chief academic officer at Hardin-Simmons University. His scholarly interests include Victorian poetry and fiction, American humor, and modern American fiction.

NANCY C. UNGER teaches American history at Santa Clara University, specializing in the Progressive Era. She is the author of a number of articles on various members of the La Follete family and the biography *Fighting Bob La Follette: The Righteous Reformer* (2000).

ZSUZSANNA VARGA, a graduate of Eötvös Loraind University, Budapest, Hungary, is currently working on a Ph.D. on Margaret Oliphant at Edinburgh University. Her research interests include nineteenth-century Anglo-American nonfiction and nineteenth-century central European culture and literature.

THIERRY VOURDON has taught English at the National Academy for Non-Commissioned Officers at Saint-Maixent, France, and is now a graduate student at the University of Metz.

SCOTT WARNOCK is a doctoral candidate in the Department of English at Temple University. His areas of interest include modern American novel, composition, and science and medical rhetoric. In addition to his academic work, he is also a medical journalist and a board-certified Editor of the Life Sciences.

DEIRDRE WEAVER is assistant professor of history at West Texas A&M University in Canyon. She has recently published an article entitled "Counter-Revolutionary Discourse and Fourier's Socialist Critique of the Jacobins" in the *Selected Papers of the Consortium on Revolutionary Europe* (1998).

MARTIN WILLIS is lecturer in nineteenth-century literature at University College, Worcester, and director of the Scottish Universities International Summer School at the University of Edinburgh. His interests lie in the interdisciplinary research of literature and science and theories of science fiction and Utopian literature.

MARIANNE WILSON is presently a student in the Doctor of Letters Program at Drew University, Madison, New Jersey, majoring in twentieth-century cultural history. An accomplished cellist and pianist, Marianne received her B.A. and M.A. degrees from Jersey City State College. For the past 16 years, Marianne has been teaching orchestra and vocal music in the Woodbridge School District.

KATHLEEN J. WININGER is associate professor of philosophy at the University of Southern Maine. She is the author of *Nietzsche's Reclamation of Philosophy* (1997) and with Robert Baker is the editor of *Philosophy and Sex* (1998). Dr. Wininger has published articles on moral theory, African philosophy, and Nietzsche's thought.

ROBERT J. ZALIMAS, JR. is currently a doctoral candidate in history at The Ohio State University. His major field of study is nineteenth-century America with an emphasis on the Civil War and Reconstruction eras.

N. MICHAEL ZAMPETTI was graduated from Penn State University in 1999 with a baccalaureate degree in history. His honors thesis was entitled "The House of Morgan, the United States, the Allies, and the First World War."